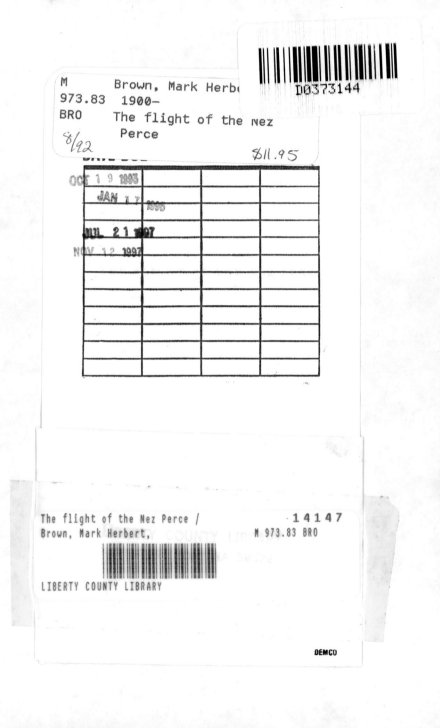

Also by

Mark H. Brown

For a complete catalogue of Bison Books write:

University of Nebraska Press
901 North 17th Street
Lincoln, Nebraska 68588-0520

The Flight
of the
Nez Perce

Mark H. Brown

University of Nebraska Press
Lincoln and London

First Bison Book Printing: September 1982

Most recent printing indicated by first digit below:
3   4   5   6   7   8   9   10

Library of Congress Cataloging in Publication Data
Brown, Mark Herbert, 1900-
   The flight of the Nez Perce.
   Reprint. Originally published: New York: Capricorn Books, 1971,
c1967.
   Bibliography: p.
   Includes index.
   1. Nez Percé Indians—Wars, 1877.   I. Title.
[E83.877.B7   1982]   973.8'3   82-2717
                                          AACR2

ISBN 0-8032-6069-5

7/92
wln
M973.8

To Paul I. Wellman
student of the Old West, in appreciation
of a helping hand on many occasions

CONTENTS

ILLUSTRATIONS

maps by Dietrich

FOREWORD

I have had the pleasure of knowing Lieutenant Colonel Mark H. Brown for many years and have watched him at work on his historical researches, which have always been to the last degree thorough. He has brought to this study of the Nez Perce war the talents of a military intelligence officer, and the zeal of an enthusiast.

Author of *The Plainsmen of the Yellowstone*, and co-author of *Before Barbed Wire* and *The Frontier Years*, he has already received wide praise for his valuable contributions to the history of the West, in which he is deeply imbued and thoroughly grounded.

In the present volume he has delved more deeply into the official government records than any other student of this war, which has been one of the most written-about of all Indian conflicts. Not only has he fully surveyed the files of the Adjutant General's office for the period covered, and the accounts of contemporary newspapers, but he has brought to his study much other important material, including letters of officers engaged in the campaign, unquoted diaries, Canadian records, civilian testimony, accounts of the Indians themselves, and the letter files of the Lapwai Agency where the Nez Perce trouble started. And to all of this has been added a detailed knowledge of the terrain, which is necessary to an understanding of military maneuvers.

The result is a work that not only more fully covers the war than any book previously published, but may create some new conceptions concerning it. Some of the author's conclusions—which he documents well—go counter to what might be called the "classic" conception of the Nez Perce war. His handling of Chief Joseph, for example, may surprise some; but he adduces considerable evidence that Joseph was not, as is popularly supposed, the real leader of the Nez Perce force. He also shows that other details of the Indian war, from its outset to the final surrender, have been garbled either through error or through outright misinterpretation.

Included are somewhat critical pictures of the Idaho settlers at the time, and numerous untold or practically untold accounts of various aspects of the campaign from both the army and the Indian side. Of especial interest is a survey of the controversy after the ending of the war between military leaders such as Howard, Sheridan, Miles, Terry and Gibbon, a sometimes acrimonious bickering which continued until General Sherman, then Commander in Chief of the Army, ordered it closed.

This book may be controversial in some aspects, for Colonel Brown has gone beyond the usual sources and has dug up some information that will at least surprise many historians. It must be regarded as an important contribution to the literature of the West, and particularly of the spectacular war it discusses.

—PAUL I. WELLMAN

CAVEAT EMPTOR

➤➤➤➤➤➤➤◄◄◄◄◄◄◄ "Military life on the frontier is a mixture of mud and romance." So wrote John F. Finerty, a reporter of the Chicago *Times*, who saw plenty of both while campaigning against the Sioux in 1876. It can also be said that many of the accounts of Indian wars which have been set down are a mixture of *fact* and *fiction*. And none of these struggles provides a better example of these two truisms than the one fought in 1877 which involved the Nez Perce Indians.

It began on Wednesday, June 13, 1877. On this day two Nez Perce warriors and a youth about sixteen years old rode along a trail that hugged the eastern side of the deep, narrow canyon of the Salmon River in what today is west central Idaho. They made no attempt to conceal their presence from the few white people who lived on the tiny bits of land beside the river, and probably none of them regarded the Indians with concern. There had been some tension for several years over a reservation boundary but the matter was now considered settled. When the trio returned the next day, four men lay dead behind them; and these murders lit the fuse to the powder keg. The ensuing campaign lasted 115 days, covered considerably over one thousand miles, and cost the Government in excess of a million dollars. What the cost was to over 800 Nez Perce, no one has ever tried to compute. And all this gave birth to a legend based on "mud and romance"—part of which happened and part of which did not.

This story has been told again and again by all sorts of authors—some apparently honest but inept, others obviously interested only in the fee for their work, and at least one who could have written a better story than he did. What follows is an attempt to sort the fact from the fiction, and to add to the story those parts which have heretofore been omitted. Lest the reader be deceived, the author states herewith that he is not a historian and that this study is not a history. Such understanding of research which he possesses, he learned in the field of science; and these techniques he adapted—by force of circumstance which lasted for two decades—to the field of military intelligence. Therefore, what follows is, in the vernacular of this "profession," an *Estimate of the Situation*.

This is not to say that an *Estimate of the Situation* and a history do not have a great deal in common. The difference lies chiefly in the nature of the evaluation made of the basic intelligence which goes into each. By and large, combat is an impartial eliminator of the incompetent for, generally speaking, wars cannot be won without sound intelligence. To this end, pieces of data are ruthlessly evaluated according to certain definite standards which are indicators of reliability. One important rule of thumb of which too many writers seem to be sadly ignorant is that the reliability of a participant's account varys inversely with the length of time which lapsed between an observation and the recording of the information—the greater the span of time, the less trustworthy the account. Knowing that even short delays in interrogation of personnel after combat can result in a noticeable lowering in the accuracy of reports, the writer has tossed many accounts quoted by others into the wastebasket. Also, the stern school of experience has taught him not to extend implicit trust to all official reports or to discard all those from individuals of questionable integrity. It is impossible to eliminate entirely a sort of sixth sense developed from many and varied experiences. Perhaps the reason the writer has found things others have overlooked is because, in the past, he has either been a part of, or has observed, situations which had their parallel in 1877. Thus he knew what to expect. Skill of this sort is not taught in an academic classroom, nor can it be explained in words.

The one rule that has governed—*wherever possible*—the selection of material has been that it must have been recorded *at the time*, and *on the spot* by someone who was both knowledgeable and reasonably reliable. Not all of this sort of data is actually reliable but, as a lot, it is far superior to reminiscences written many years later. Thus the bulk of the intelligence which was used came from a very restricted group of materials. These were orders prepared in the Departments of War and Interior, official reports, official letters and telegrams, personal diaries and, last but by no means least, private correspondence not intended for the eyes of officials. Although limited in one sense, it was voluminous in another for the aggregate of official communications which had to be sifted number in the thousands.

Another fruitful source of intelligence was those newspapers which carried appreciable amounts of material either in the form of interviews with participants, or letters and stories written by them. Particularly noteworthy were the dispatches written by Thomas A. Sutherland for the San Francisco *Chronicle*, Portland *Standard* and New York *Herald*. Twelve other papers in Idaho, Montana and North Dakota contain excellent material not available elsewhere. Some reminiscent material is worthy of note, particularly that of teamster Henry Buck, General (Lieutenant) Hugh L. Scott and Martha Sternberg, the wife of a surgeon. Their writing contains a devotion to accuracy that is generally lacking in such material.

It is unfortunate that Indian accounts merit very little trust. What purports to be Chief Joseph's story went through an interpreter and at least one magazine editor before it appeared on the pages of the *North American Review* in 1879. Such devious treatment is not desirable in intelligence materials. Lucullus V. McWhorter, who collected the bulk of the Nez Perce narratives, was apparently neither objective nor discriminating. Although some of the material is probably accurate, too much of it shows the same weaknesses that may be easily found in similar narratives written by white people, namely faulty memories, personal bias, and prejudice. In some cases these can be established beyond question by comparison with contemporary records of the highest order of reliability. This is regrettable, but it is also a hard fact.

One problem to which no satisfactory, overall solution was developed was that of casualties. Generally, the army reports list only military personnel who were killed or wounded, with no mention of casualties among civilians employed as scouts, packers and teamsters. Furthermore, numbers killed include only those who died in battle, or immediately afterward, and numbers of wounded who died later are next to impossible to determine unless mention is made of the fact in a local newspaper. The report made after one battle indicated that, in this case, if a man was a litter case he was considered wounded, but if he could still march with the troops he was not reported as injured. And as for the Indians, the only numbers which a *combat-wise* intelligence officer would accept as reasonably accurate were those reported after the final fight. In battle, it is usually expected that the enemy will try to conceal his losses and that one's own troops will—either honestly or dishonestly—over-report the amount of damage inflicted. The battle of Canyon Creek provides an excellent example of this truism. Colonel Sturgis reported sixteen Indians killed: Yellow Wolf claimed none were killed: and Surgeon FitzGerald wrote to his wife, "it is said 6 or 8 Indians were killed. I have seen only two and I made some effort to see them all." The words of the doctor are probably an approximation of the truth.

Campaigns involve many things—finances, matériel, transportation, tactics, morale, casualties, logistics and communications, to mention a few. Other less tangible factors are moments of heartbreak, anxiety, hardship, loneliness and pain. To some extent, all of these must be considered in an *Estimate of the Situation*, and they have been in this one.

One final comment. Should some be inclined to criticize the author for omitting certain reminiscent material, it is suggested that they ask themselves—soberly—if they would care to risk their life in battle on the basis of information of comparable accuracy. If the answer is "No," or even "Perhaps," the criticism is not valid. Perhaps some of those who write "history" can afford to gamble with material having a low order of dependability; those involved in the production of intelligence must not. This is why the writer, who knows something of intelligence at several echelons of command, chooses to call this study an *Estimate of the Situation*.

THE FLIGHT OF THE NEZ PERCE

1

The Nimpau—Real People

➤➤➤➤➤➤➤◄◄◄◄◄◄◄ Proper understanding of a conflict such as the Nez Perce war requires a familiarity with a number of things such as people, historical background, and the nature of the country where various events took place. And perhaps there is no better approach to a knowledge of the Nimpau, as the Nez Perce called themselves, than one which begins with the legend of their origin. As they told it, it is a revealing story.

There was once a monster which lived in the valley of the Clearwater River near Kamiah. This beast devoured all the animals that lived in the country for miles around and became such a menace that Coyote, that clever hero of many an Indian myth, decided it must be killed. Arming himself with a flint knife, he jumped down the animal's throat and stabbed it in the heart. Then he cut the body up into pieces and from them fashioned tribes of Indians which he sent to occupy the mountains and plains round about. Finally, he discovered that he did not have a tribe for the beautiful valley in which the monster had lived so he squeezed a few drops of blood from the heart and from these made the Nez Perce.[1] Thus from the lifeblood of this strange animal came a tribe having many of the most admirable qualities possessed by human beings.

Nez Perce means, of course, *pierced nose*. Although some have held that these Indians never pierced their noses, the journals of Lewis and Clark state positively that "they call themselves *Cho pun-nish* or *Pierced noses*," and that "they wear a single shell of wampum through the nose—a tooth shell of Dentalium."[2] Perhaps the practice was not universal and, apparently, it died out not long after these explorers saw them. Nevertheless, this must have been a distinguishing feature at one time for in the sign language of the Plains, this tribe was designated by an unmistakable gesture. Thus it appears that the French-Canadians of the British fur companies translated *pierced noses* into *Nez Percé*; and the Americans anglicized the name to *Nezz Purses* and similar phonetic variations.

William Clark was the first American to meet any of the tribe. While he, Meriwether Lewis and their men were crossing the Bitterroot Mountains they ran low in food, and Clark took six hunters and hurried ahead to hunt. On September 20, 1805, near the western end of the Lolo Trail, he found a small camp at the edge of a camas-digging ground that is now called Wieppe Prairie. The explorers were favorably impressed by those whom they met; and, as they made the remainder of their journey to the Pacific in boats, they entrusted the keeping of their horses to "2 brothers and one son of one of the Chiefs." One of these Indians was Twisted Hair who became the father of Timothy, a prominent member of the "Treaty" faction in 1877. The Indians were, generally, faithful to the trust; and the party recovered their horses without serious difficulty when they returned.

Clark and Lewis recorded many definite facts about this tribe. They noted that each band had a permanent campsite in the narrow valleys along the Clearwater, Snake and Salmon rivers. At these, the Indians had semipermanent dwellings which were oblong in shape, the largest one noted being 156 feet long and 15 feet wide. Near the rapids in the rivers where they had fishing camps, they had smaller, flat-topped lodges which served the dual purpose of providing shelter and a place to dry fish. And when digging camas and kouse on the prairies, small temporary shelters made of bark and brush were used.

Apparently, the Nez Perce were a loosely knit tribe composed of small bands, each of which claimed a general camping ground in one of the valleys, and this they occupied most of the time except when the salmon run was on or when the roots of the camas and kouse were ready to dig. The people were sturdy, upright, friendly, honest and had a well-developed sense of values, for one entry reads, "They are, however, by no means so much attached to baubles as the generality of Indians, but are anxious to obtain articles of utility. . . ." They proved to be sharp traders with a tendency to be selfish—a trait which probably had more than a little to do with the basic cause of the friction which brought on the war. The two staple articles of food were salmon, either fresh or dried, and the roots of camas and kouse which were prepared in several ways. These were supplemented with service berries, hawthorn, huckleberries and other small fruits, and meat. The latter was probably in limited supply except when on a buffalo-hunting trip. Large herds of horses were common and the men possessed some knowledge of breeding and herd care.[3] However, it is doubtful if spotted or Appaloosa horses were as common as popular fancy now imagines they were. And the fact should not be overlooked that the men, in addition to being "placid and gentle, rarely moved to passion," lacked neither the courage nor the energy to defend their fine herds against raiders. The next seventy years were to make but little change in these basic essentials.

There is no record of how universal the practice of crossing the Bitterroot Mountains to hunt buffalo was, or how important the jerked meat and robes were to them. When Lewis and Clark crossed the Lolo Trail it showed signs of having been used for years; and when settlers came in the 1860's, they found another trail, the Great Nez Perce Trail, farther to the south that was also deeply worn. There is evidence that these people were peddlers to some extent as they traded articles secured east of the Bitterroot barrier to tribes living near the Pacific Ocean—just as the Crows shuttled between the Mandans and the Flatheads and Shoshones.[4] This practice of hunting buffalo in what is now western Montana was to be a major factor in the war in 1877, for not only was the practice of traveling to the Plains of long standing but there were also well-cemented friendships with the Flatheads and the Absaroka, commonly known as the Crows.

Another development which was to be of major importance began to take definite form about thirty years after the visit of Lewis and Clark. Fur traders and trappers followed closely behind this initial exploration and, as the War of 1812 put a definite check to American activities, most of their contacts were with officials of the Hudson's Bay Company. It is thought the Indians may have come to the conclusion that the white men were in some way superior—or their *medicine* was stronger. And as an Indian's medicine represented his religion, it is possible that the Nez Perce decided that they should try to acquire that which gave the white man superior *power*.

Be that as it may, when hunting on the headwaters of the Missouri in 1831, a small party of Flatheads and Nez Perce, said to have totaled seven, started for St. Louis to get someone to come and instruct them in the white man's religion. Only one, Rabbit Skin Leggins, lived to return the next year.[5] This dramatic journey stirred the imagination of various church groups; and, finally, in 1836 when the Nez Perce came to the great trapper rendezvous in the valley of the Green River, they found Henry Spalding and his wife Elisa who had come to start a mission among them. That the Spaldings were of the Presbyterian faith made no difference at the time, although after Father DeSmet established St. Mary's Mission among the Flatheads in the Bitterroot Valley, some of them embraced the Catholic faith.

The Spaldings established a mission at the mouth of Lapwai Creek and began their labors in the spring of 1837. It was a Herculean task, for it involved not only transposing the Indian language to the printed page so that students could be taught, but also organizing an establishment which could supply its own needs and cope with Indian customs. And Spalding—whom some have called puritanical, arbitrary and narrow-minded—had some personal characteristics which did not endear him to those at the mission. However, the desire to learn some of the skills of the white man kept the interest in the school at a high level for several years but by 1847 this had dwindled to almost nothing.

The *coup de grâce* was administered, indirectly, by the Cayuses when they murdered Marcus Whitman, his wife, and twelve others in nearby Walla Walla Valley on November 29, 1847. Hostile Nez Perce sacked Spalding's home, Spalding—en route to Waiilatpu—had a narrow escape, and the people at Lapwai sought shelter in the cabin of William Craig, a Nez Perce squaw man who lived nearby. Shortly afterward friendly Indians escorted the Spaldings and others to the safety of Fort Nez Perces, a British trading post, and work at the Lapwai Mission came to an end. Although the Nez Perce did not take part in the Waiilatpu uprising, some of them had been friendly with those who did the bloody work. As a result, thirty years later whites pointed out in a derogatory manner that Joseph's grandfather was a Cayuse chief and that his mother probably had Cayuse blood in her veins.[6]

Some noteworthy things emerged from these mission days. Two of the first converts were Timothy, son of Twisted Hair, and Old Joseph; and the latter's two sons—Joseph and Ollokot—spent a few of their boyhood years at the Lapwai Mission. Some of the Indians, having learned how to grow wheat and vegetables, continued to till small plots and plant fruit trees; and the interest in schools did not die out completely. Unfortunately, it was the work of the missionaries that began to drive the wedge which, coupled with some other matters, was to split the Nez Perce into the two factions which became the Treaty and Non-Treaty groups. And the dominant element in the Treaty faction was made up of Indians who lived along the Clearwater River and who had been most affected by the work of the Spaldings.

To Dr. Elijah White, the missionary who became sub-agent for Oregon Territory in 1842, should go the *credit*, if this be the proper word, for creating the office of "head chief"; and he "virtually appointed" a chief named Ellis to this position. Heretofore, all tribal matters had been decided in a council composed of the chiefs of the various bands. There can be little doubt but that the creating of an office which did not exist in reality and which, outwardly at least, downgraded the authority of the traditional tribal council was one of the steps on the road which eventually led to bloodshed.

While there were certain steps which, once taken, made trouble more certain, it was the provisions of the treaty of 1855 that provided a firm foundation for very serious difficulty. This treaty was concluded in June of that year and the first three names of the fifty-eight signers were Lawyer, Looking Glass and Joseph—in the order named. Twenty years later, "Young" Looking Glass and "Young" Joseph were head chiefs of the bands their fathers had represented in 1855. The provision of paramount importance was Article 2 which delineated the boundaries of the Nez Perce Reservation. This section read:

> There is, however, reserved from the lands ceded for the use and occupation of the said tribe . . . the tract of land included within the following boundaries, to wit: Commencing where the Moh-ha-na-she or southern boundary of the Paluse River flows from the spurs of the Bitter Root Mountains; thence down said tributary to the mouth of Ti-nat-pan-up Creek; thence southerly to the crossing of the Snake River ten miles below the mouth of the Al-po-wa-wi [Alpowa] River; thence to the source of the Al-po-wa-wi River in the Blue Mountains; thence along the crest of the Blue Mountains; thence to the crossing of the Grande Ronde River, midway between the Grand Ronde River and the mouth of the Woll-low-how [Wallowa] River; thence along the divide between the Woll-low-how and Powder Rivers; thence to the crossing of the Snake River fifteen miles below the mouth of Powder River; thence to the Salmon River above the crossing; thence by the spurs of the Bitter Root Mountains to the place of beginning.

And it also specified that "nor shall any white man, excepting those in the employment of the Indian Department, be permitted to reside upon said reservation without permission of the tribe and the superintendent and agent. . . ."[7] This irregular-shaped area was about 150 miles long in a general north-south direction, and 100–125 miles at its widest east-west part, the latter dimension depending on the interpretation of the phrase, "thence by the spurs of the Bitter Root Mountains to the place of beginning."

Other articles provided for the payment of certain sums, the establishment of certain agency facilities and the payment of a salary to the "head" chief. And Article 9 stated that "the Nez Perce desire to exclude from their reservation the use of ardent spirits, and to prevent their people from drinking the same"—with a provision for punishment of those who violated this section.

This treaty with its well-intentioned provisions was not ratified by Congress until four years later, and then no financial remuneration was made until another two years had elapsed. However, settlers *immediately* moved into certain areas which the treaty would have provided. By 1861, when the Government showed some signs of recognizing its obligations, the Civil War was on the way to becoming a national problem of paramount importance, and the discovery of rich placer mines on the reservation the preceding year had created a formidable local crisis. Thus the basis for serious trouble became firmly and irrevocably established.

The area which this treaty guaranteed to the Nez Perce lay in what is now southeastern Washington, northeastern Oregon and the adjacent part of western Idaho. In the distant geological past it had been a plateau-like area lying west of the Bitterroot Range but was now carved by the deeply intrenched channels of the Snake, Salmon and Clearwater rivers, and their tributaries. The immediate valleys of the rivers ranged in width from nothing, in the case of the famous Hells Canyon of the Snake, to narrow bottomlands rarely more than half or three quarters of a mile wide. As salmon was an important item of food, the little valleys adjacent to the streams determined the location of permanent campsites and, in turn, the *domain* of the various chiefs. Away from the vicinity of the major streams, the topography was varied—low mountains, "benchlands," rolling hills and an occasional stretch of flat or gently rolling prairie. Most noteworthy of the latter were Wieppe Prairie near the western end of the Lolo Trail where Clark first found the Nez Perce, and Camas Prairie, some thirty miles to the southwest, which reaches in one flat sweep from Craig's Mountain to Grangeville.

The formidable Bitterroot Range, which lay like a wall on the east, was crossed by two trails. One was the Old Nez Perce Trail. This began in the vicinity of Harpster, near the eastern side of Camas Prairie, and went in a southeasterly direction to Nez Perce Pass and then dropped down to the head of Bitterroot Valley. From this point, the Indians could go southward to the valley of Lemhi River, northward to the country of the Flatheads, or eastward to the plains of the Missouri and Yellowstone rivers. The distance from Harpster, Idaho, to Montana was about 125 miles; and although all of it was through a mountain wilderness, it was a much-used trail. The other route across the mountains followed the divide between the North Fork of the Clearwater and the Lochsa rivers to the head of Lolo Creek and down this to the Bitterroot Valley in Montana. The Lolo Trail, as this was known, was a direct but formidable route. It twisted continually—both laterally and vertically—and the slopes on either side varied from steep to precipitous. There was but little grass, and rocks and down timber presented almost never-ending obstacles.

Few of those having contact with the Nez Perce after the time of Lewis and Clark left descriptions which have the precise quality of those written by the explorers. One such was Henry Miller of the Portland *Oregonian*, who made a trip by steamboat in the spring of 1861 to the head of navigation on the Clearwater River to report on the new gold rush. This provided him with fleeting contacts with the Upper Nez Perce—later the Treaty faction—and allowed him to observe some aspects of their life and hear stories about them. On June 2, 1861, after detailing several instances of gratuitous assistance given to the miners by the Indians, he wrote:

> The Nez Perces are not mercenary, but are shrewd in trade; asking their rights, they want no more. They are not mendicants; they do not steal, and there again they are superior to the whites!
> They look upon the American Government as the symbol of perfect justice. They look to good white men for protection. They expect to punish all crimes committed by Indians, and ask the whites to take care of white criminals. If trouble ever ensues here, the whites will be the cause.

And he made this comment about their farming:

> The Indian farms are, for the most part, fenced with rails. I noticed a good variety of garden vegetables, and some fine patches of green corn. The land is closely cultivated, and is as clear of weeds as any I ever saw. These farms are seen at almost every available point from Palouse to the forks of Clearwater.[8]

In a rather general description, he noted:

> It is only six days ride from the forks of the Clearwater to the buffalo Country; where the Nez Perces go in large numbers every year and from whence they return laden with meat and buffalo robes. * * * Besides this they have elk, deer and small game in abundance in their own country. They have the finest brook and salmon trout in

innumerable small streams at convenient distance all over the territory. The *camas* and *kow-see* roots are principally relied on for
bread. . . . With the articles of food I have mentioned and a plentiful supply of goose, black and other berries and fruits, the Nez Perce
are able to live abundantly. . . . In their gardens they raise beans,
Indian corn and a variety of vegetables.—many of them have small
bands of cattle, some of which are tame. * * *

The generality of the Nez Perces horses are much finer than any
Indian horses I have yet seen. * * * I have seen thousands of these
horses grazing on the mountain, apparently the property of a few
lodges. In one place—to be more exact—these lodging of common
Indians—calling themselves poor—have six or seven hundred of
them, running from common Cayuses to elegant chargers, fit to
mount a prince. They value their fine horses beyond all price, and
will not sell them, unless forced to. Of those which they have for
sale, the range of prices may be from $15 to $100 a piece.

The Nez Perces cattle are those which the Indian Department
have furnished them, and their increase. They value them very
highly, and are anxious to get more.[9]

Although Miller's contacts were fleeting, he was apparently a discerning
observer. He sensed that the whites were not to be trusted and the pleasant
relations which he sketched soon turned bitter as the self-centered miners
and the horde of undesirables who followed returned evil for good.
However, he made no mention of observing any of the Lower Nez Perce
who still dressed largely as they did in years past, lived in a nomadic
fashion with great herds of horses, and viewed with disfavor the manual
labor required by fields of grain and vegetables.

While the white man found it convenient, perhaps necessary from a
practical standpoint, to treat the Nez Perce as a single body, the fact
remains that there was no tribal organization that welded them into a
tight, cohesive unit. Agent White's effort to establish a head chief in 1842
did not create a *fait accompli*, and merely ignored the reality created by the
deeply incised, narrow valleys in which these people lived—namely that
the tribe was composed of bands which were isolated and practically
independent of each other. General Howard ran head-on into this hard
fact when he held a council with the Nez Perce a month before hostilities
began. He wrote later that one chief stoutly maintained, "We never made
any trade; part of the Indians gave away their lands. I never did." And
after a long and heated argument the leader still stubbornly insisted, "I
never gave the Indians authority to give away my lands."[10]

Not only was the tribe made up of a number of small bands, each of
which tended to recognize no chief except its own, but it was also split

into two factions. Just how long this division existed is not clear. An agent who began his supervision over them in February, 1859, informed General Howard shortly before the outbreak of hostilities:

> "In assuming charge of the Nez Percez I found them divided into two parties; and the upper and lower Nez Percez who resolved themselves into the treaty and anti-treaty parties, which line of division has been kept up to this time. . . ."[11]

The Upper Nez Perce, which contained most of the Christian Indians, became—in 1863—the Treaty Indians; and they lived along the Clearwater River. The Lower Nez Perce included those bands which lived along the lower Salmon, in the country between the Salmon and the Snake just south of their junction, and in the basins of the Grande Ronde and Imnaha rivers immediately to the westward. This area west of the Snake River was claimed as a home by Old Joseph—the father of "Young Joseph" and Ollokot.[12] It was the "homeland" of the Non-Treaty bands which became the bone of contention after the Upper or Treaty Nez Perce signed the Treaty of 1863. Also, it was Old Joseph's band which was most closely allied with the Cayuses, Walla Wallas and Umatillas who lived farther west. And, although Old Joseph was one of Spalding's first converts, the Treaty of 1863 alienated him, and his sons grew up believing in the Dreamer religion, the basis for which was the idea that the Earth was the mother of all life and that changes due to farming, establishment of civil boundaries, etc., constituted a desecration. It may also be noted in passing that although Old Joseph was opposed to the treaty, which drove a deep wedge between the Upper and Lower Nez Perce, he was the second chief to sign a temporary agreement in 1861 which preceded the treaty in question.[13] However, there was nothing in this agreement which set a precedent for the drastic changes of the second treaty.

The practice of hunting buffalo on the plains in Montana involved the Nez Perce in a second treaty in 1855. This one was designed to reserve to the Blackfeet certain hunting grounds; and the tribes "residing west of the main range of the Rocky Mountains agree and consent that they will not enter" certain areas. Apparently this treaty was all that was necessary to keep the Nez Perce away from the buffalo herds *reserved* for the Blackfeet.

These buffalo-hunting trips were a part of a way of life for many Nez Perce. Their visits to the plains varied in length from a few months to sometimes as long as a year or two. They often hunted with the Crows and, on occasion, helped them fight the Sioux, thus establishing friendly ties—ties which were to prove something less than binding in a time of need! Their comings and goings through the settlements of western Montana were orderly, and they often traded in the towns where their passing was noted by local editors—as in this item dated August 27, 1875, in Deer Lodge's *The New North-West:*

> The streets were filled with Nez Perces and their cayuses on Saturday and Sunday returning to their stamping ground in the vicinity of Lapwai Agency from their hunt on the Yellowstone where they have been for nearly a year past. The chiefs and headmen as usual went around by the Big Hole sending their families and meat laden cayuses by the easier trail. They say they had a good hunt and killed seven Sioux.

And as military officers were anxious to discourage lawlessness, post commanders sometimes detailed a junior officer and a small escort to conduct hunting parties past the settlements.[14]

Although one trader of Scotch-Nez Perce descent recalled two or three murders by whites, the Montana press has reported but one occasion where Nez Perce committed an act of aggression. On June 16, 1877, two young bucks robbed a rancher living between Helena and Fort Benton of a watch, saddle, rifle and ammunition.[15] They were misidentified as Sioux at the time and their real identity was revealed many years afterward by a Non-Treaty warrior.

Agent John B. Monteith was strongly opposed to this wandering as the "wild" Indians were continually urging relatives who were farming to go with them, and the tales they told of their adventures made the young men restless. He complained again and again to various authorities[16] and finally, in 1874, he managed to get the Commissioner of Indian Affairs to establish an official policy forbidding such hunts. However, when he began to intimate that he would use force to stop them, the Indians concerned became resentful and defiant. Matters reached a point where, on July 15, 1876, the Agent wrote to General Howard that "I might as well talk to the wind as talk to the Non-treaties."

While matters of this sort were a cause of friction, it remained for the patent unfairness of the Treaty of 1863 to outrage the ideas of justice held by the Non-Treaty group. Then the fundamentals of the Dreamer religion, which many of them accepted, made compromise practically impossible. This religion taught that the present ills of the Indian were the result of abandoning their native faith, and that if they should return to this faith, the time would come when they would regain their lands.[17] Actually, aside from the superficial trappings and the impossible hopes which it propounded, there was nothing vicious in the Dreamer faith. It was based on the idea that the earth was the mother of all living things and that it was a sacrilege to despoil her—a basic reverence that lies close to the surface in many Christians.

On one occasion, "Young Joseph" explained this to a Government Commission in this manner:

> "[When] the 'Creative Power' . . . made the earth, [he] made no marks, no lines of division or separation upon it, and that it should be allowed to remain as then made. The earth was his mother. He was made of the earth and grew up on its busom. The earth, as his mother and nurse, was sacred to his affections. . . . Moreover, the earth carried chieftainship . . . and therefore to part with the earth would be to part with himself or his self control."[18]

Ironically, this "new-fangled religious delusion" taught some sterling virtues. Agent Monteith, in reporting the failure of the white man's law to punish the murderer of an Indian, wrote:

> The witnesses were Non Treaties, and could not be induced to be sworn. . . . They do not believe in a God, and say that the earth made them, and that *they could tell the truth without holding up their hand.*[19] (Italics are author's.)

These, then, were the Nimpau—the Real People. They were resourceful, honest, courageous, friendly, capable of deep faith, and had an admirable affection for a country which they had occupied for unknown generations. These were the people who, when precipitated into a deadly struggle by a rash act committed by three of their number, gambled everything in a futile fight against what they regarded as injustice.

2

The Curse of Gold

➤➤➤➤➤➤◄◄◄◄◄◄◄ The chain of events which was to lead to disaster started in 1860. In this year, an Indian trader named Elias D. Pierce managed to slip onto the Nez Perce Reservation where he found traces of gold deposits. By December, he and thirty-three recruits from Walla Walla had set up a camp on Oro Fino Creek, not far from Wieppe Prairie, with the expectation of beginning operations the following spring.

Indian Agent A. J. Cain had no difficulty in forecasting what might be expected, and asked the Superintendent of Indian Affairs for Oregon and Washington for advice. When none was forthcoming, he called the Nez Perce leaders together in the spring, and all sat down to work out a solution. Just after an agreement was reached, Edward R. Geary, Superintendent of Indian Affairs in Oregon and Washington, arrived and the group then rewrote into a more final form the concessions which Cain had induced the Indians to make. This second agreement read:

Articles of agreement made this 10th day of April, 1861, between Edward R. Geary, superintendent of Indian affairs for Oregon and

Washington, and A. J. Cain, agent for the Nez-Perces, in behalf of the United States, and the chiefs and head men of the Nez-Perces in behalf of said nation, said parties acting in accordance with authority vested in them by the 2nd Article of the treaty between the United States and the Nez-Perces on the 11th of June, 1855.

1. That portion of the Nez-Perce reservation lying north of the Snake and Clearwater rivers, the south fork of the Clearwater and the trail from said south fork by the "Wiepo" root ground, across the Bitter Root Mountains, is hereby opened to the whites in common with the Indians for mining purposes, provided, however, that the root grounds and agricultural tracts in said district shall, in no case, be taken or occupied by the whites, but shall remain for the exclusive use and benefit of the Indians.

2. No white person, other than those in the service of the United States, shall be permitted to reside upon or occupy any portion of the Nez-Perces reservation south of the line above described, without the consent of the superintendent, agent and tribe, except that the right of way to the mining district north of said described line may cross Snake river at any eligible point below the mouth of the Clearwater.

3. [Area opened subject to laws of the U.S. regarding trade, etc., in Indian country.]

4. It is further agreed upon the part of the United States that a sufficient military force shall be placed on the reservation to preserve the quiet of the country and protect the Indians in the rights secured them by treaty and these articles of agreement.[1]

This was signed by Lawyer, as "Head chief of the Nez Perces Nation," and forty-seven others.

This document makes it clear that the *only* area the Indians agreed to open to mining was that lying north of the South Fork of the Clearwater—in which the towns of Oro Fino and Pierce sprang up—and a corridor which would permit travel to and from the country to the west. Now, having been given the first "inch," the whites proceeded callously to take the proverbial "mile." By the time the agreement was signed, there were some 300 miners along Oro Fino Creek and two months later, there were two towns. While the spring rise was on, steamboats delivered supplies to a point named Slaterville which was about forty miles from Pierce. However, as the level of the stream dropped, the rocks in the rapids interfered and sometime shortly after the first of June, a steamboat discharged her passengers and freight on the southern bank of the Clearwater just above its junction with the Snake. Thus, Lewiston was born in direct violation of the Treaty of 1855 and the recently signed but unofficial agreement.

Charles Hutchins, who succeeded Cain as agent, reported further developments in the landing area:

About the 15th of October last, a man by the name of Capt. A. P. Ankeny [Levi Ankeney] whose business in these parts last summer, was that of a packer and trader at "Oro Fino" visited "Lewiston" and by his instigation and council to others survey and map off at that point a town, and at sundry meetings of those having the affair in charge they established the size of blocks and lots, the condition of obtaining and holding through the whole organization and effecting the scheme the said Ankeny was the directing genius, and aided the work by personally measuring the lands and establishing the monuments of boundaries.[2]

The Agent posted signs that trespassers would not be tolerated but the whites paid but scant attention to them and proceeded to appropriate the locality without further formality.

By the early summer of 1861, there were an estimated 5,000 miners in the "opened" area, and those not fortunate enough to locate a paying claim began to prospect elsewhere. By fall, some had gone far south of the specified South Fork of the Clearwater. Here, along the Salmon River, they discovered other areas which promised great riches. Again there was a frantic rush without any regard to treaty restrictions. This time, the Lower Nez Perces under Eagle-from-the-Light made a brief but ineffectual show of resistance.

This horde of irresponsible, lawless miners alarmed Agent Hutchins, who had no difficulty in seeing that the situation was about to get out of hand. On January 4, 1862, in a letter renewing previous requests for troops, he stated:

> Without the presence of troops it is impossible to enforce the laws of the United States on this reserve—the town of "Lewiston" will be built despite the laws and proclamations of officers—the rivers and streams will be cut up with ferries—"squatters" will settle down on every patch of arable land—the fences of the Indians will be burned for fire wood by travelers—their horses and cattle will be stolen without redress—whiskey is and will be sold to them without an effort at concealment, and the Indians will be overreached, plundered and destroyed. . . . If my first requisition for troops had been furnished the moral influence of their presence here would have been sufficient to keep all the current violations in check but . . . it will take at least half a regiment to be as efficient in the spring as half a company would be now.[3]

Time was to prove that there was much truth in this grim forecast.

Lawlessness quickly became a major problem, and in the fall of 1862, General Benjamin Alvord, Commanding the District of Oregon with headquarters at Fort Vancouver, made an inspection trip to the Nez Perce Reservation. On his return, he notified the adjutant of the Headquarters of the Department of the Pacific, at San Francisco:

> I have been compelled to establish a military post on the Lapwai, three miles above its mouth, where the Nez Perce Agency is established. . . . I have left there Major J. S. Rinearson in command, with two companies—one, Captain Mathew's company (F), First Oregon Cavalry, and the other, Captain Knox's (E), of the First Washington Territory Infantry.[4]

In his report, Alvord also expressed concern about the "15,000 people, mostly gold miners, on the Nez Perce Reservation in defiance of the express provisions of the treaty" of 1855, and also the Government's tardy ratification of the treaty and its even tardier compliance with certain stipulations of that treaty. Then he echoed the tenor of comments made previously by Agent Hutchins:

> I have reason to hope that under existing circumstances no general outbreak will occur, but we may from time to time hear of more murders, as it can hardly be anticipated that even the virtues of this tribe and the establishment of the military post will prevent the natural consequence of such provocation, of whiskey and of contact with bad white men. The military post will act as a check both on the whites and to the Indians, and I trust that my course in establishing it will be approved. As the roads are now painfully infested by robbers and cutthroats, the presence of the military will materially aid the civil authority. Still I declined the entreaties of some of the citizens of Lewiston to establish martial law for the preservation of order among the whites. * * * Of the interest centering in Lewiston you can form some idea when I state that half a million dollars for freights have been paid at that place during the last year. I have called the new post Fort Lapwai. . . .[5]

Fort Lapwai was not a fort in the sense that it was a fortified strongpoint. It was a camp or post with permanent buildings. At the time of the outbreak in 1877, according to General Howard:

> The usual officers' quarters are on the West, facing inwards. The barracks opposite; office on the South; guardhouse . . . on the North, and the parade [ground] between. The post traders and laundress' houses are nearer the Lapwai; while the stables and other outbuildings are arranged a few paces outside the square and up the valley.[6]

It was about twelve miles from Lewiston, and three miles above the mouth of Lapwai Creek, at which point the Agency was located. At this location there was a little flat on the western side of the deep valley through which the creek flowed, and it was hemmed in on either side by great, grass-covered hills which rose steeply from the edges of the valley floor.

It now became evident that, in spite of the fact that the Government was deeply involved in the Civil War, official steps had to be taken to bring a measure of order to the situation. Although tentative plans were made to hold a council in November, 1862, it was not until May, 1863, that a solution—of sorts—evolved. Four companies of cavalry were sent to make a show of force, and an orderly village of tents was erected near the post for the Indian visitors. The council was well attended. Looking Glass had died a few months before, but Old Joseph, Eagle-from-the-Light and Big Thunder and their people were there, as were Lawyer and the chiefs closely associated with him. The Government was represented by Calvin H. Hale, superintendent of Indian affairs in Washington Territory, and Indian agents Charles Hutchins and S. D. Howe.

When the council opened, Old Joseph and Eagle-from-the-Light pointed out the areas which they regarded as their own domains and indicated that they would not part with them. Negotiations then settled down to some rather stiff dickering in which the Indians used the Government's poor record to put Hale at a disadvantage. Finally, Hale took the Lower Nez Perce to task for their uncooperative attitude, whereupon the chiefs again stated their views and withdrew from the council. What then happened is not known with certainty. Apparently, the Nez Perce chiefs held a tribal council at night and, not being able to reach an agreement, the Lower Nez Perce walked out of this, leaving Lawyer and his following to go their way. At the next council meeting, Lawyer—who was the *Government-designated* head chief—assumed the authority to speak for the entire tribe and quickly came to an agreement with the commissioners. On June 9th, the treaty which provided the focal point for later difficulties was signed.

The troublemaking provision in this treaty was Article 2 which states, in part:

> The United States agrees to reserve for a home, and for the sole use and occupation of said tribe, the tract of land included within the following boundaries, to wit: Commencing at the northeast corner of Lake Wa-ha, and running thence, northerly, to a point on the north bank of the Clearwater, three miles below the mouth of the Lapwai, thence down the north bank of the Clearwater to the mouth of Hatwai Creek, thence, due north to a point seven miles distant

from its mouth; thence eastwardly to a point on the north fork of the Clearwater, seven miles distant from it mouth; thence to a point on Oro Fino Creek, five miles above its mouth; thence to a point on the north fork of the south fork of the Clearwater, one mile above the bridge, on the road leading to Elk City (so as to include all the Indian farms now within the forks), thence on a straight line westerly, to the place of beginning.[7]

The area thus defined was roughly rectangular in shape. It embraced an area which might be described as beginning on the north side of the Clearwater River a few miles east of Lewiston, from which it extended a little over 30 miles in an easterly direction to a point roughly north of the diggings on Oro Fino Creek, thence southeasterly for about 45 miles, and then west-northwest about 45 miles to Lake Wa-ha, which was about 23 miles south of the point just northeast of Lewiston. This was a vast reduction from the area set aside in 1855 which has been estimated at 100,000 square miles! Included in the new area were *all* the lands claimed by Lawyer and the chiefs closely associated with him—*but none of the lands of the Lower Nez Perce.* Thus, the Upper Nez Perce, while feathering their own nest in several ways, had assumed the right to barter away all the areas which the Lower Nez Perce had regarded from time immemorial as their own homeland. Lawyer's attitude had been anything but unselfish.

In 1879, the *North American Review* printed what was purported to be "Young Joseph's" side of the story. While this cannot be accepted as a verbatim statement, there is a ring of truth in the following:

> If we ever owned the land we own it still, for we never sold it. In the treaty councils the commissioners have claimed that our country had been sold to the Government. Suppose a white man should come to me and say, "Joseph, I like your horses, and I want to buy them." I say to him, "No, my horses suit me, I will not sell them." Then he goes to my neighbor, and says to him: "Joseph has some good horses. I want to buy them, but he refuses to sell." My neighbor answers, "Pay me the money, and I will sell you Joseph's horses." The white man returns to me and says, "Joseph, I have bought your horses, and you must let me have them." If we sold our land to the Government, this is the way they were bought.[8]

Later, it was found desirable to amend the provisions of this treaty. In 1868, Lawyer and three other Treaty chiefs went to Washington where they signed what is known as the Treaty of 1868. This provided that the desirable lands on the Reservation should be surveyed and parceled out to those approved by the agent and the Indians themselves; and that those

Indians living off the reserve might be permitted to retain lands (not to exceed 20 acres) which had been occupied and improved by them. The latter provision led to numerous difficulties because the lands so occupied were invariably choice acreages which lay within areas whites wished to homestead. To get a desired homestead, the white man often had to either buy the Indian out or run him off by using questionable tactics—and the latter was usually resorted to, thus providing additional friction.

As the Treaty of 1863 was the real cause of the conflict which took place fourteen years later, its legality has been subjected to considerable questioning because of the patent disregard for the rights of the Lower Nez Perce. The Government's argument was based on the thesis that the minority of any group was bound by the decisions made by the majority—and that the forty-six signers of the treaty did represent the necessary majority.

In the absence of accurate census figures, it is not possible to arrive at a definite and positive answer. The indications are that the majority on which the legality of the treaty stood was a very thin one—*if it existed at all*. On August 31, 1872—*before this matter became a highly controversial issue*—Agent John B. Monteith stated in his annual report:

> The tribe is about equally divided between Treaty and those who term themselves Non-Treaty Indians. The Non-Treaty portion with very few exceptions reside on the outside of the Reserve along the Snake River and its Tributaries. They never ask for assistance. . . .[9]

And in his annual report for the year 1876–1877, the Commissioner of Indian Affairs admitted that of the forty-six signers only "twenty . . . were parties to the treaty of 1855" which had fifty-eight signers.[10] Whether Monteith's count made after the Non-Treaty faction had left Idaho can be trusted is problematical, as it may have been made to counter a similar census presenting a smaller figure which was made by a land-grabber clique and publicized by the Lewiston *Teller*. Thinly veiled comments were made by settlers which indicate that they did not trust either Inspector E. C. Watkins or Agent Monteith's picture of the situation. And while but little trust can be put in anything newspaper editor Alonzo Leland of Lewiston wrote about the Nez Perce at the time of the war, the letters Inspector Watkins wrote to the Commissioner of Indian Affairs at the time of the first crucial battle indicate that he and Monteith were considerably worried about the loyalty of the Treaty faction. Less than a month after the war started, the wife of the surgeon at Fort Lapwai—a very intelligent lady—wrote her mother, "You know two-thirds of the Nez Perces are Non-Treaty Indians."[11] This statement cannot be taken literally as it obviously means that at this time the Non-Treaty faction, plus their sympathizers, represented about two-thirds of all the Nez Perce.

The thinness of the ice on which the legality of this treaty rested is indicated by the fact that in recent years the Nez Perce have won two claims in U.S. Courts, one of which (Docket 180-A, the "gold claim" case) netted the tribe about $3,000,000. Another (Docket 175) for damages due to inadequate compensation based on the Treaty of 1855 remains to be tried. In the months before the start of the war, Major H. Clay Wood (General Howard's very capable adjutant at the Headquarters of the Department of the Columbia) made a scholarly study of this problem in which he stated:

> In my opinion the non-treaty Nez Perces cannot in law be regarded as bound by the treaty of 1863, and in so far as it attempts to deprive them of a right to occupancy of any land its provisions are null and void. The extinguishment of their title of occupancy contemplated by this treaty is imperfect and incomplete.[12]

In the years which followed, the Non-Treaty Indians steadfastly declined to recognize the Treaty of 1863, and refused to accept any part of the payments which the Government made as a result of its provisions. Nor did they hesitate to chide their fellow tribesmen when the Government failed to fulfill its part of this agreement.

In 1869, the Government, becoming weary of a succession of scandals involving Indian agents, transferred the administration of the reservations to the Army and then in July, 1870, to the various religious denominations. The Presbyterians, on the basis of Spalding's work, claimed and were given the Nez Perce Reservation. The Catholics had hoped to control this reserve; and they stubbornly held to a small toehold and, with what must be considered rather poor grace, added their bit to the harassment of Agent John B. Monteith when matters pertaining to the Non-Treaty Indians were reaching a climax.

Old Joseph died in 1871 and, it is said, on his deathbed, charged Young Joseph never to part with his homeland in the Grande Ronde and Wallowa valleys. The Treaty of 1863 had opened this country to homestead, and in 1872, settlers from the Walla Walla Valley began to cross the Blue Mountains and settle in the Wallowa Valley. When Joseph's band encountered these squatters, the situation became tense, and the whites, believing that they were within their rights, sent a messenger to Monteith asking him to come and quiet the Indians. The Agent went promptly to the scene of the difficulty and held a council with Joseph and the whites on August 22nd and 23rd.

This was a rather unproductive meeting. Joseph insisted that his father had bequeathed this country to him and that neither his father nor any of his band had had anything to do with the Treaty of 1863; and he demanded that Monteith make the settlers leave. Monteith tried to argue that Joseph and his people were bound by the treaty in question and finally:

> I told him that it was useless for them to talk about sending the whites away, that they were there by higher authority than I and I could not remove them. That it was to their interest to keep the friendship of the whites and the Govt. would protect them in all their rights.

All that was accomplished was that "the settlers were willing that they should hunt and fish in the area and would not disturb or molest them in any way," and "Joseph said he would not let any of his men do anything that would cause trouble, but would have the trouble settled peaceably."

Monteith concluded the report which he wrote to the Commissioner of Indian Affairs with these two statements:

> It is a great pity that the valley was ever opened for settlement. It is so high and cold that they can raise nothing but the hardiest of vegetables. One man told me that the wheat was frozen after it was in the milk. It is a fine grass country and raising stock is all that can be done to any advantage. It is the only fishery the Nez Percés have and they go there from all directions. The valley is surrounded by high mountains and it is impossible to get a wagon in the valley until a road is built.

> If there is any way in which the Wallowa Valley could be kept for the Indians I would recommend that it be done. There is not one house in the valley so far as I could ascertain but some will be built this fall. The question will have to be settled soon to those Indians living outside the Reserve. . . .[13]

Although this letter contains nothing of a derogatory nature about the settlers, the Agent made one observation of which he was highly critical. This formed the chief subject for another letter which will be noted when the character of these settlers is examined.

As the Commissioner of Indian Affairs was already involved in one thorny problem (that pertaining to the Modoc Indians in southwestern Oregon), it would appear that he wished to avoid the development of a second. To this end he directed T. B. Odneal, superintendent of Indian affairs in Oregon, and Agent Monteith to hold a council with Joseph and his people and try to find an acceptable solution to the problem of the

Wallowa Valley. He made it clear that he wished them to try to persuade the Indians to come on the existing Reservation, but if this was not possible to "ascertain whether they will require all of the valley in which they are now living, or whether they will be content with a part of it . . . in order if deemed advisable it may be set apart by executive order."[14]

The council requested by the Commissioner was held on March 27, 1873, at the Lapwai Agency; and the report which was made merely reviewed the obvious facts with the addition of a couple of pertinent statements. One was that the Indians "do not desire a separate reservation made of the Wallowa Valley. They claim the whole valley belongs to them, and are opposed to the whites settling there." The other revolved around the validity of the Treaty of 1863. Odneal and Monteith felt that it must be determined whether or not this treaty extinguished the title of the Indians. And if it did not, the Indians should be permitted to occupy the country, and the settlers reimbursed for any improvements made or inconvenience incurred.[15]

Acting on this report, the Secretary of Interior recommended to President Grant that this area be set aside for the Nez Perce; and on the 16th of June, 1873, an executive order was signed setting aside a *part* of the Grande Ronde, Wallowa and Imnaha valleys for Joseph and his band. Unfortunately, this order excluded the upper part of the Wallowa Valley which contained the grave of Old Joseph, and thus provided no complete solution to the problem.

In the fall, Monteith tried to pressure Joseph into settling down and farming but, "They said that they did not want the [Wallowa] valley for farming purposes, but for that of hunting and fishing. I replied that that was not sufficient, that the Government expected more of them. Still they refused." Monteith seems to have been both hardheaded and narrow-minded about how the Indians should make their living. He could not see them as stockmen, hunters or fishermen—only as tillers of the soil, which was against both their religion and their inclinations. In closing his report to the Commissioner about the matter, Monteith wrote:

> I am of the opinion that Joseph and his band are not entitled to the Wallowa unless they go there and settle down. . . .
> I would ask what course I shall take in case Joseph attempts to create a disturbance.[16]

The letter files of the Lapwai Agency provide evidence that Monteith was harassed by various troubles in 1874. Some of them centered about the Circular Letter dated October 21, 1873—which Monteith was instrumental in having written—that allowed him to order the Indians to "confine their movements wholly within the limits of their reserve." Shortly after the first of the year, one Non-Treaty chief camped within two hundred yards of the Agency office where, to show his contempt of the Agent's authority, he and his people "commenced operation by a regular war dance, kept up through the night accompanied by drumming and savage yells, which terrified our women and children and disturbed all our rest." After several days of outright defiance, Monteith had to ask that troops from Fort Lapwai run him out of the area.[17]

However, this was but a minor irritation compared to that provided by the post sutler at Fort Lapwai. This man, D. C. Kelley, reportedly told the local Indians that "the Govt. did not care how much they went to the Buffalo Country, if they did not molest the whites," thus placing the Agent in a difficult position.[18]

Kelley was a thorn in the side of Monteith, who felt certain that he sold liquor secretly to some of the Indians and half-breeds (one Joe Craig in particular). Furthermore, as the post commander, Captain Henry M. Smith, was, allegedly, a heavy drinker if not actually an alcoholic, the Agent got very little cooperation in his efforts to suppress the flow of liquor from the post trader's shop. Monteith's letters reveal that several other complaints were made during the next several months—squaws being given liquor for unstated but obvious reasons, Joe Craig's squaw complaining that he beat her while drunk, and the failure of civil authorities to prosecute Craig for a brutal murder. Finally, after General O. O. Howard assumed command of the Department of the Columbia in July, 1874, Monteith filed a formal complaint which resulted in the man being removed from his tradership but not from the military reservation. Kelley's attractive wife then pleaded his case with the general, who finally "passed the buck" to the post commander. One of the scandals of President Grant's administration was the traffic in post traderships which was directed by Secretary of War Belknap and the President's brother, Orvil. Getting rid of a post trader was a difficult task.

The spring, summer and fall months were busy ones for the Agent. To keep trouble from erupting in the Wallowa Valley, he requested that a detail of troops spend the summer in the valley. Four incidents resulted in violent death for five Indians—one of them the murder which eventually provided the match that lit the fuse to the powder keg. And stories reached Monteith that the Non-Treaty chiefs had held a council where a war was discussed:

> They proposed to kill as many of the Indians as possible who have adopted the Christian religion and are trying to lead a civilized life and to attack the White settlers on Camas Prairie and surrounding

country, and destroy as much as possible at Kamiah, and finally after having completed their hellish design, immediately strike for the buffalo country.

It would appear that there was more fiction than truth in stories which brought the war alarm to the Agency.[19]

However, there was one storm cloud which rose higher and higher on the horizon and dwarfed those originating from murders, bootlegging, tales of conspiracy and claim jumping. This was the trouble in the Wallowa Valley. The ink was hardly dry on the President's executive order setting aside the Wallowa Valley, before Governor Leonard F. Grover of Oregon addressed a long letter of protest to the Honorable Columbus Delano, Secretary of the Interior. After reviewing the background of the Treaties of 1855 and 1863, the Governor proceeded to add, either from ignorance or intent to confuse, some misconceptions of his own. Without a hint as to the characteristics of the country involved, or the real character of the squatters involved, he blandly claimed that:

> The region of country in Eastern Oregon not now settled, and to which the Wallowa Valley is the key, is greater in area than the state of Massachusetts. If this section of our State, which is now occupied by enterprising white families, should be remanded to its aboriginal character, and the families should be removed to make roaming ground for nomadic savages, a very serious check will be given to the growth of our frontier settlements, and to the spirit of our frontier people in their efforts to redeem the wilderness and make it fruitful of civilized life.

And he callously requested:

> I would respectfully press upon your consideration the general policy of the Government, heretofore steadily pursued, of removing as expeditiously as circumstances would permit of, all the Indians from the confines of the new States, in order to give them opportunity of early settlement and development, and to make way for civilization.[20]

General Howard, whose views were not above criticism in the months before the outbreak, at first gave this letter partial approval,[21] and then gagged on it a few years later when he wrote, part ruefully, part apologetically:

> So much for our ideas of justice. First, we acknowledge and confirm by treaty to Indians a sort of title to vast regions. Afterward,

we continue, in a strictly legal manner, to do away with both the substance and the shadow of the title. Wiser heads than Joseph's have been puzzled by this manner of balancing the scales.[22]

There are several statements in the concluding paragraphs of Grover's letter which are interesting mixtures of truth and fiction:

> I learn that young Joseph does not object to going on the reservation at this time, but that certain leading spirits of his band do object. . . . Joseph's band does not desire Wallowa Valley for a reservation and for a home. . . . The reason for this is obvious: they can have better land and a more congenial climate at a location which has been tendered them upon the Nez Perce reservation. * * * There are but seventy-two warriors of this band. The white settlers in the Wallowa Country number eighty-seven. There are also in the Wallowa Valley two incorporated companies, the Wallowa Road and Bridge Company and the Prairie Creek Ditch Company. The improvements of these settlers and companies have been assessed, as I am informed, by a commission appointed under the direction of your Department, to the amount of $67,860.37.[23]

On June 10, 1875, political pressure won out and Grant rescinded his executive order and returned the proposed reservation to the public domain. In his study of *The Status of Young Joseph and His Band* (etc.), General Howard's adjutant branded this action as "a political fault. If *not* a crime, it *was* a blunder. In intercourse with the Indian it is not wise to speak with a forked tongue."[24]

The honesty of the governor's claims become suspect when they are compared with statements made by others with no political ax to grind—Grover having senatorial aspirations. The following August, Captain Stephen G. Whipple, who was in charge of the detachment of cavalry detailed to patrol Wallowa Valley, wrote a long letter to General Howard. In this he pointed out that the settlers had made no complaint about the President's executive order and that:

> One of the most enterprising, reliable, and best citizens in the settlement, has told me, within the past week, that he thought the people of the valley were disappointed to learn that it was not to be taken for an Indian reservation; that he regretted it for one; that he would sell out at the first opportunity, and settle in a more promising locality.

And of Joseph's band, he stated:

This band of Indians are by no means a vagabond set. They are proud-spirited, self-supporting, and intelligent. . . . At the present moment there are no evidences of enmity between the whites and Indians in this valley, but the truth is each party wishes the other was away.[25]

The truth of the matter was that the settlers were not happy with their location and would have been glad if the Government would have purchased their improvements. Even General Howard, who viewed the problem rather objectively at this time, wrote:

I think it a great mistake to take from Joseph and his band of Nez Perces Indians that valley. The white people really do not want it. . . . possibly Congress can be induced to let these really peaceable Indians have this poor valley for their own.[26]

And as for the settlers being "enterprising white families," as Grover claimed, it can be said both truthfully and cynically that part of them were "enterprising" in ways that do not merit praise, as the following pages will indicate.

Thus the problem of the Non-Treaty Nez Perce reached a point where it would soon be necessary to apply force to bring matters to a conclusion. Such unpleasant tasks fell to the Army to accomplish, and some of its officers did not look kindly upon the civilian bumbling which they had to correct with hardship, pain and blood.

3

"Enterprising Settlers"

>>>>>>>><<<<<<<< The Non-Treaty Nez Perce have been referred to by many of their white contemporaries in terms which run the gamut from "outlaws" to "incarnate fiends." When it is remembered that these Indians—as far as is known—did not commit a single act of armed aggression or murder against the whites for at least fifteen years before the outbreak, and very few, if any, before that, these epithets have a suspicious ring. To put this struggle in its proper perspective, it is necessary to know something about some of those whom Governor Grover called "enterprising settlers." Such a study begins, properly, with the discovery of gold.

Included in the treasure-seeking tidal wave that engulfed the Reservation were human parasites of varying degrees of undesirability. And while Idaho's outlaw period never achieved the degree of notoriety which Montana's did a year or two later, Henry Plummer was a resident of Oro Fino before he moved on to Bannack, Montana, where he took over the dual task of being sheriff and leading the most formidable gang of cutthroats the West ever knew. It was the murder of Lloyd Magruder, a merchant-freighter plying between Lewiston and the Montana camps, that touched off a vigilante movement in Lewiston—activity which had been preceded by a similar action in 1862 at Florence on the upper Salmon River. When the Lewiston committee disbanded in April, 1864, it had hanged 3 murderers and thieves, and banished 200 gamblers and highwaymen.[1] This does not mean, of course, that those who were banished actually went very far.

In 1875–1876, General Howard's adjutant, Major H. Clay Wood, prepared a searching and scholarly study on the Nez Perce problem, the first draft of which was apparently released January, 1876—the printed version containing some material gathered after this date. After pointing out that the Indians had signed an unofficial agreement on April 10, 1861, Wood noted other gold fields were soon found and:

> . . . the reservation was overrun in every possible direction to all the mines. * * * . . . the landing and warehouse became a town, now known as Lewiston, their reservation was overrun; their enclosed lands were taken from them; stock turned into their grain fields and gardens; their fences taken and used by persons to enclose the land to which they laid claim, or torn down, burned, or otherwise destroyed.

Of Lewiston, its newspaper and stopping places along the trails, he wrote:

> Lewiston became an absolute necessity as a depot of supply to the large mining population. . . . and despite the agent calling attention to the laws forbidding it, an active village sprang up with a population approximating twelve hundred whites. . . . * * *
>
> A journal, The Golden Age, published in that vicinity, in a most incendary manner, called upon the whites to settle, occupy, plow up and cultivate the land upon the reservation without regard to the Indian title and in contempt of any treaty which might be made with them. * * *
>
> . . . along all the roads on the reservation to all the mines, at the crossing of every stream or fresh-water spring, and near the principal Indian villages, an inn or "shebang" is established, ostensibly for the entertainment of travelers, but almost universally used as a den for supplying liquor to the Indians. The class of men that pursue this infamous traffic are, as might be expected, the most abandoned wretches of society.

And he also noted: "I could fill page after page in portraying the number and nature of outrages the Indians and their families were subject to."[2]

That Wood sketched an accurate picture is borne out by a statement made by J. W. Poe, District Attorney of the 1st District of Idaho, who had lived in this area since "July 1861." In a letter dated December 22, 1877, which detailed the outrages which took place at the time of the outbreak, is this statement:

> The discovery of gold . . . attracted a large immigration of miners and traders to that place. During the following summer and subsequently, other mining camps were discovered. . . . These camps may justly be termed the key that unlocked this country to civilized men, for the first who came to any considerable number, were attracted hither by the reputed richness of the same. Many however, when here, after laboring to their satisfaction in the golden fields, turned their attention to agricultural pursuits, and built for themselves permanent and happy homes, or what would have been, had it not been for the treachery of the Indians, who laid waste some homes and made the scene, the untimely grave of the inmates.[3]

There is not a single word in this statement that even intimates that those who "*unlocked this country to civilized men*" did so by violating the rights of others!

Nor was the district attorney alone in this one-sided viewpoint. After commenting on the problem of securing fuel in Lewiston, Alonzo Leland, editor of Lewiston's *The Teller*, noted (on December 16, 1876) that it was rumored that there were deposits of coal on the Reservation but that those knowing where they were would not attempt to open them because the whites could not acquire rights there. The item closed with this comment:

> Why should nature's gifts remain locked up here by reservation lines? . . . The white man's necessities are paramount to the easy indolance of any tribe of Indians. If the Indian will not bring to use the natural products of the land, let him give way to those who will.

Alonzo Leland came to Idaho in the early days of the gold rush and, later, made a permanent record of his anti-Indian views in printer's ink. Just how twisted his thinking was is apparent in many items but in none more clearly than one dated February 17, 1877, which noted the possibility of the use of troops to force the Indians on the Reservation. He noted that not "until there was an Indian killed in the Wallowa valley, by the whites, causing fresh insolence and arrogance from these Indian outlaws . . . did the government . . . do anything. . . ."

This murder of a member of Joseph's band was brutal and unprovoked—yet Leland's statement would indicate that the Indians had *no reason* to be exasperated. Four months later when the situation was reversed, the editor screamed "bloody murder." And months after the war was over, when the problem of disposing of the prisoners was under discussion, he wrote:

> But let them send these Indians back among the friends of the murdered men and women if they think it best for them. We wont be responsible for their lives 24 hours after their arrival. . . .[4]

There is one bit of evidence which indicates these were not idle words.

Statements made in Agent Monteith's letters, and on the pages of *The Teller*, indicate that another individual of the same stripe was the "Hon." S. S. Fenn, delegate to Congress from North Idaho. In 1877, Fenn was about thirty-seven years old and lived on Camas Prairie not far from Mount Idaho. On April 28, 1877, *The Teller* carried what was claimed to be an extract of a very lengthy letter written by Fenn to the Commissioner of Indian Affairs. In this, Monteith was arraigned for a number of things— writing the Commissioner that Father Cataldo, a priest on the Reservation, had tried to stir up trouble with Joseph when an effort was being made to get him to come on the Reservation; trying to get rid of certain squatters and half-breeds; making harsh remarks about a lawyer in Lewiston who was trying to promote a swindle involving part of the Reservation; and using the head chief as a tool, pandering to religious feuds, and driving some Indians from the Reserve and preventing others from coming in and settling. That there was little if any substance in these charges is indicated by the fact that a few months later Indian Inspector E. C. Watkins reported to Washington that Fenn would not comply with his requests that he come in to the Agency and substantiate his charges.

According to *The Teller*, Fenn supported his letter with affidavits from a number of people, among them D. B. Randall, W. A. Caldwell, W. G. Langford, and J. W. Craig. Randall, prior to his ejection from the Reservation, had been the proprietor of a roadhouse on the trail between Lewiston and Mount Idaho. Little is known of him except that he had the reputation of having a strong dislike for Indians, and that such as he were suspect because many sold whiskey and encroached on the Reservation with unnecessary numbers of livestock. Caldwell was a squatter living on a desirable piece of land along Lapwai Creek and was alleged to be closely linked to the liquor interests in Lewiston. The character of Craig and Langford will be noted elsewhere in detail.

On May 24, 1878, *The Teller* devoted ten full columns to what purported to be a verbatim reprint of a speech Fenn made on the floor of the

House of Representatives which aired his views on a bill which would have transferred the administration of Indian affairs from the Department of Interior to the Army. This is an interesting example of the sort of propaganda that was peddled in high places. Not only are Fenn's sentiments suspect by reason of his being a member of a community which was outspoken against the Nez Perce, but it is also possible—as indicated by his championing such a character as Joe Craig—that he may have had some interests which could have been served by the breaking up of the Reservation for he stated that "The mass of the Indians remaining on their reservation after the late exodus of the hostiles, were anxious to greatly reduce the dimensions of or break up their reservation and homestead their lands and become citizens."

This was an idea which Editor Leland was pressing blatantly, and which the land-grabber clique were using Craig to help them prosecute.

In this speech Fenn accused Monteith of using his efforts to get Indians living off the Reserve to come on the Reservation so that he would have an excuse to eject certain white "settlers" and the half-breed descendants of two trappers, Craig and Newell, from their holdings.

> The most aggrivated case is that of Mr. Craig, just mentioned . . . who has a full Indian wife and several children, a valuable improved farm, with a good orchard, house and outbuildings, all the proceeds of his own labor, who has always possessed great influence over his Indian brothers and has the confidence and respect of the white citizens.

The campaign to get rid of Caldwell and Finney, both squatters in the Lapwai Valley, dated back to November, 1873. Acting under orders from the Commissioner of Indian Affairs, Monteith ordered them off. When they did not go, he asked the post commander at Fort Lapwai to eject them—which the military refused to use force to do. On November 25th, Monteith reported that he had been told that "they will resist the military having at their command all the roughs in Lewiston and surrounding country." In another letter dated three days later, he noted that Caldwell and Finney "have a petition with about 175 names attached, comprising all the roughs and whiskey men in this part of the country, asking for my removal."[5] And it did not help smooth matters of religious difference when the Catholic priest lined up with the squatters.

In a letter dated December 12, 1873, Monteith dwelt at some length on the problem:

> These half breeds have given me a great deal of trouble heretofore by bringing liquor to the Indians, but they have been so cunning in

giving it out that I have been unable to convict them of the crime.
. . . Joe Craig's wife (who belongs to the Umatilla Reserve but lives
here with him) has repeatedly made complaints of ill treatment from
him during his drunken spells.

They are both very bad men. Newell was confined in the Lewiston
jail for nearly five months, for being engaged with others in robbing
the Commissary at Fort Lapwai, but got clear by turning states
evidence. At Kamiah the Indians are so strongly opposed to the half
breeds that they wont allow them to learn trades in the shops or
Mills or even to attend to the Ferry. They say they are afraid of
them. . . .

* * *

Caldwell and Finney are making every conceivable effort to gain
their point and retain the lands they have so long held to their own
advantage and prejudice of the Indians.

They are both whiskey men and having considerable pecuniary
ability they draw around them the entire influence of the whiskey
dealers in Lewiston. They are of course heartily opposed to me, as I
have made some successful efforts to bring some of those who have
sold liquor to Indians to justice.[6]

Joe Craig was also accused of other things besides bootlegging and wife
beating. On July 20, 1874, Monteith reported:

About six weeks ago two Indians were coming from Lewiston both
under the influence of liquor. On the road they got into an alterca-
tion, when one of the Indians struck the other with a stone and
killed him. The murderer threw the body of the murdered Indian
into the river. About two weeks after the above it was discovered that
a murder had been committed. As soon as I was satisfied as to who
the murderer was, I placed the matter in the hands of the Depty.
U.S. Atty. who said he would attend to it, but before the murderer
could be arrested, one Joe Craig, a halfbreed, met in Lewiston the
Indian who was suspected as being the murderer and after drinking
with him persuaded the Indian to come out of Lewiston with him.
When about three miles out of Lewiston said Craig made a brutal
attack on the Indian, stabbing him in the back and breast, and
cutting him in a brutal manner. He finished his work by cutting the
Indian's throat, and left him at the roadside dead.[7]

The Agent had Craig arrested but the judge before whom he appeared
"discharged the prisoner."

With the Delegate from North Idaho using affidavits from people of questionable character to support his views, it should not be surprising to find deviations from obvious facts in his speech, such as:

"And I here proclaim upon this floor, and I speak from personal knowledge, that . . . J. B. Monteith, the United States Indian Agent for the Nez Perces, was the primary cause of every drop of blood that was shed and every dollar's destruction of property and every dollar's expense either by the government or individuals in the course of the Nez Perce war, unless it be considered he was the tool in the hands of Presbyterian Missionary Society, and, if so, he may divide with them the responsibility."

In another remark, he stated:

". . . within twenty days of the outbreak, he, J. B. Monteith, by letter, authorized the selling of ammunition to the Indians to enable them to effectively carry out their hellish designs."

Both statements are absurd to the point of being ridiculous.

It has been noted that the Catholics held doggedly to a small toehold on the Nez Perce Reservation after its supervision was awarded to the Presbyterians. The leader of the small group of converts was Father Cataldo, who was located not many miles from the Agency. Friction became open in 1873 when—permission having been granted them to build a church—the priest expected Monteith to have it built for them. When the Agent refused, the priest circulated a petition for his removal, a petition which received some support from the whiskey faction of the whites.[8] Then, in 1877, when the Government was pressuring Joseph to come on the Reservation, Father Cataldo was apparently instrumental in spreading some misinformation calculated to place the Agency at a disadvantage.[9] When this was reported to the Commissioner of Indian Affairs, Fenn entered the controversy as noted. Then, in his speech to the House of Representatives, the delegate returned to the religious feud:

"But the crowning infamy of Monteith was his base slanderous charges made to the Interior Department, in the early part of the year 1877, against the Rev. Father Cataldo, the priest at the Nez Perces Catholic Mission, for the purpose of excluding him from the reservation, that he was using his influence to keep Joseph and the non-treaty Indians from coming thereon, and that he was stirring up dissentions, all of which he, Monteith, was compelled to admit at a council with the Nez Perces in May last, in the presence of General Howard were false in every particular."

There does not appear to be any evidence which indicates that there was any truth in this statement. Apparently Fenn did not return to Idaho until after this "May" council was held and therefore did not know whereof he spoke. Furthermore, in General Howard's lengthy report of this council there is no mention of any such open apology or even any indication of one. On the other hand, Howard did report that previous to the council in question, he paid the priest a special visit, heard his side of the story, and then took him to task on general principles for " 'neutrality' [which] was, in my judgment, equivalent to positive opposition." And although Howard "deemed it best to ignore the [Monteith-Fenn] subject altogether" when he passed through Lewiston en route to the council, he wrote later:

> In my own opinion it is that the same "speculators" who want the Indians' land and property, who are at the bottom of the fearful charges against Agent Monteith have striven to promote their subjects by fanning into flame, prejudices and misstatements, that have from time immemorial existed between Protestants and Catholic Christians.[10]

Unfortunately, Fenn's inflammatory speech with its blatant inconsistencies was but a small bit in the picture of the character of the Idaho settlers. However, it does provide one concrete example of just how much truth some statements did contain. Monteith undoubtedly had his shortcomings, but he also lived in a community which, on occasion, did its best to obstruct his work.

Fenn mentioned another individual favorably who seems to have been a shabby character. This man was William G. Langford, an attorney-at-law who resided at Lewiston; and Monteith's letters provide a picture of what happened.

There was a section of the organic act of Oregon which gave a square mile of land to each mission which was operating in August, 1848. Although the Lapwai Mission was abandoned in 1847, Spalding and a man named Eells, acting for the American Bible Conference for Foreign Missions, "sold" the Lapwai claim to Langford. The attorney made no move to possess the area until January, 1874, when he "attempted to exort from congress $120,000 for the improvements made by that body."[11]

On January 24, 1875, Monteith wrote to the Commissioner of Indian Affairs:

> I respectfully transmit for your information an order from the 1st District Court of Idaho commanding the Sheriff to take possession of this Agency and land to the amount of 640 acres.
> I promptly refused to recognize the right of the Sheriff to serve any papers of the kind on me. . . . * * * After my refusal to give peaceable possession he left. . . .

The claim is what is known as the "Mission Claim" and was sold to Langford in 1862 for $500.00.

The Secretary of Interior advised Monteith to continue in possession of the disputed property—which involved all the agency buildings—but not to use force "in attempting to remain." Eight months passed quietly and then, on November 13th, the Sheriff forcibly ejected the Agent and demanded possession of all the buildings. This accomplished, Langford's Agent rented part of the buildings back to Monteith and the agency employees. Again there was a period of quiet. Then, early in February, 1876, Langford again had the Agent ejected and demanded the premises occupied by the agency employees. When these demands were refused, the lawyer came back with the sheriff and a posse of "twelve or fifteen men" and renewed his demand. This time some troops came down from Fort Lapwai and prevented the sheriff from carrying out Langford's design. The lawyer then served notice that he would commence suit for "forcible entry and detainer." However, as Langford had previously secured the keys to the school, sawmill, gristmill, church and other buildings, Monteith's work was brought to a halt.

On June 1st, the Agent informed the Commissioner of Indian Affairs that Langford's representatives had shut off the water used by the Indians for irrigation, and had placed a man in charge of the mill whom Monteith had previously discharged as being incompetent. And he complained bitterly that Langford's previous Agent, a fairly decent sort, had been replaced by

two persons [who] keep a den of prostitution in the Mill [just across the street], lodging Indian women there. The youngest of the two has a squaw in his room continually and it is not only pretty hard but shameful that we are forced to submit to having such prostitution carried on under our immediate observation.

* * * Langford's agent is Dep. Sheriff . . . and I cannot exert any authority over his action as the authorities at Lewiston are in sympathy with Langford and the military will not assist me. . . . It would not be quite so bad if there were no women here. But there are such, my brother's wife and the Miller's wife and five little girls who live about five rods below me.

However, the legal machinery of the Government had finally begun to function and in June, Langford was evicted. Hope died hard with the lawyer—and the editor of *The Teller* who noted, almost two years later, that a member of the House of Representatives from Massachusetts had introduced a bill to restore the claim to Langford. But the shabby legal farce was over.

In view of this brazen attempt by a leading citizen of Lewiston to appropriate a choice piece of property on the Reservation, it should be expected that less important citizens would attempt smaller land grabs. An almost never-ending source of trouble stemmed from the provision in the Treaty of 1868 which allowed Indians living outside the Reserve to keep their farms if they desired, or to dispose of them and move on the Reservation later. If a settler desired to homestead an area containing Indian farms, he had to satisfy the Indian claim or claims first by buying them out. Monteith's letters to the Commissioner of Indian Affairs contain many references to squabbles arising over Indian farms. On one occasion, he wrote:

> One Indian living on the Alpowa has just sold his improvements to a settler for $150, one half in cash and the balance in cattle, but where you find one man willing to pay the Indian you find twenty ready to drive him off and take all he has got. . . .[12]

The sale of liquor to Indians was a constant source of trouble. In addition to having to watch certain settlers living beside the trails, like Caldwell and Finney, the post sutler and others, bootleggers were always on the alert for Indian gatherings. A prime target were the camas diggings when the Indians gathered on the prairies to dig camas and engage in festive activities like dances and horseracing. On one occasion, Monteith took thirty-five soldiers and spent ten days guarding one digging. On his return, he reported:

> There were about twelve hundred Indians on the grounds belonging to the Nez Perce and Umatilla Reserves, together with some Coeur d'Alenes and Columbia River Indians. After having spent one week with them and saw that they had gathered an abundance of roots, I ordered the Nez Perces to get ready to start home. The Treaty Indians complied and after thanking me for taking the soldiers with me they broke camp and returned to their homes. Heretofore Whites have been in the habit of frequenting such places for the purpose of racing horses with the Indians and have always taken liquor with them and disposed of it among the Indians. . . . Since my return I learn that the Indians got liquor from Oro Fino and had a rough time.[13]

It was frequently impossible to get a conviction in the courts on a bootlegging charge. On one occasion, Monteith wrote cynically, "It is an easy matter to convict a Chinaman, but it is hard to get testimony that will satisfy the jury to convict a White man." This is borne out by a small item which appeared in *The Teller* on April 21, 1877. Samuel Newell—one of the troublesome half-breeds—was indicted "for disposing of whiskey to an Indian of the Nez Perce nation." When the case came up in District Court, "The testimony of the prosecution was clear and direct. No testimony was offered in defence." But the jury would not agree on a verdict! When the case was tried before a second jury, this body brought in a verdict of guilty in "about a half hour." Sentencing was postponed and in the meantime a petition asking mercy was "circulated among and numerously signed by our citizens." The judge sentenced him to one day in jail and fined him $150.

What proportion of Lewiston's citizens followed the pattern of conduct set by some cannot be determined. As noted, the town itself had an illegal beginning; it was the home of William G. Langford; and it had as a newspaper editor, anti-Indian Alonzo Leland, who espoused the cause of the would-be land-grabbers so vigorously that his writing drew fire from at least one Portland, Oregon, newspaper. The saloonkeepers, liquor dealers and gamblers apparently championed any member of their clan who came under fire from Monteith—as indicated by reluctance of a jury to convict Newell, and the judge to hand down an effective sentence, and the action which turned Joe Craig loose on a murder charge, for which murder there had been an eyewitness. And the town had its share of grafters as the Nez Perce war was to indicate.

On at least one occasion, Lewiston whites meddled in Indian affairs. About the first of February, 1874, two Indians of Huishuis Kute's band, which resided down the river from Lewiston, got into a quarrel and one knifed the other. A justice of the peace issued a warrant for the murderer's arrest but when a white man, alleged to have been a "constable," tried to make the arrest, the Indians insisted the matter came under the jurisdiction of Agent Monteith. The officer "called upon Whites for help"—perhaps a group of toughs—and

undertook to tie one of the headmen who was foremost in resisting arrest. An Indian came forward to assist his companion, who was being tied when one of the whites shot him with a double-barrel shotgun, the charge entering at the back between the shoulders and five large shot coming out under the chin. The Indian lingered along for five days and then expired from the effects of the gun shot. The whites also shot at the Indian who committed the murder, but did not hit him. * * * The Indians want the murderer of their companion arrested and punished.[14]

In view of the fact that the settlers who lived in this area were frequently involved in jumping Indian claims, perhaps there was more to this incident than meets the eye.

As the Wallowa Valley was a hard two days' ride from the Lapwai Agency, this area enjoyed a measure of isolation, and information about the settlers here is lacking in both quantity and detail. However, there are three incidents which stamp these people as but little, if any, different from those elsewhere in the general area.

It will be recalled that the first clash between Joseph's band and the squatters here occurred in August, 1872. While Monteith made no mention of the incident in his report to the Commissioner of Indian Affairs, he immediately notified the agent on the Umatilla Reservation:

> While there I found that two parties had been selling liquor to the Indians. Their names are John Turner and George Durner. They live on wild horse creek in Umatilla Co. Oregon and as the offence was committed in Baker Co. they would have to be tried in Portland. I send you the names of the parties who took a keg of liquor from them and destroyed it and who would be witnesses against them. I can send two Indians who saw them pour the whiskey out of a coffee-pot and deliver the same to the Indians.[15]

To bootleg to Indians who were already edgy was like playing with matches in a strawstack.

During the winter following President Grant's rescinding of the order giving the Wallowa Valley to Joseph's band, the "enterprising settlers" attempted a manipulation that amused Monteith and the Indians while arousing the ire of two troops of cavalry. Monteith stated in his report for January, 1876:

> The only excitement that has occurred during the month was created by a Party of White settlers living in the Wallowa Valley. They telegraphed the Governor of Oregon that Joseph and his band were in the valley (Wallowa) driving off and killing stock and threatening settlers. All this trouble took place about one hundred miles from here, and the Indians in question had their fun over the reports.
>
> Joseph and most of his band have been spending Christmas and New Years in the vicinity of the Agency attending feasts and having a good time generally . . . and were here at the time the trouble was said to have taken place in Wallowa Valley, in connection with them.[16]

The passing of time did not soften Lieutenant W. R. Parnell's feeling of resentment. Years later he recalled that he was ordered to take two troops

of cavalry across the Blue Mountains from Fort Walla Walla to the scene
of the alleged outbreak. They were called out on New Year's day and had
"to forego their New Year's calls, egg-nog and other attractions" to march
in temperature that was "twelve degrees below zero with from two to four
feet of snow on the ground."

> On reaching the valley we found, however, that there was no
> evidence of any trouble whatever on the part of the Indians. The
> report was a ruse of some white men in the Grande Ronde Valley to
> get cavalry into the valley, hoping, thereby, to dispose of their hay,
> grain, and provisions at prices at inverse ratio to the mercury in the
> thermometer. Imagine their chagrin when they found that the Govern-
> ment contractor had made all necessary arrangements in the premises
> before we reached the valley![17]

It should not be surprising that among such "enterprising settlers" were
some who would commit deeds of violence—such as the brutal, unprovoked murder which was committed on June 23, 1876. Monteith set down
the essence of the incident in an official report:

> Some four weeks ago while a party of four of . . . [Joseph's]
> band were hunting in the Wallowa Valley, they met two White
> men, and got into a dispute about something. The White men
> proceeded to take the fire arms from the Indians. During the scuffle
> to get possession of the same, one of the Indians proved to be too
> much for the White man, whereupon the other White man shot the
> Indian dead.

What apparently happened was that a settler named A. B. Findley and a
neighbor, Wells McNall, while hunting missing horses came across the
hunting camp of a small party of Indians. On questioning the Indians
about the stock, McNall became abusive. Then the whites edged between
the Indians and their rifles, which were lying nearby, and one of the
Indians, a man named Wilhautyah (or Wil-lot-yah), and McNall
grappled for the possession of a rifle. When McNall began to get the worst
of the wrestling match, he called to Findley to "shoot the son-of-a-bitch
before he gets me": and Findley did. None of the other Indians became
involved and the settlers left. A few days later the missing horses were
found near Findley's cabin.[18]

Howard dismissed the matter rather casually, stating that Joseph threatened to destroy the farms of the settlers if the murderers were not
delivered up, and that he sent Lieutenant Albert G. Force and "E"
Company of the First Cavalry to maintain order. Force quieted Joseph

without difficulty and—apparently—got McNall and Findley to surrender and stand trial.[19] The murderers pleaded self-defense and were—as might be expected—acquitted.

It is impossible to determine how serious the situation was. The settler version is a hair-raising story which must be doubted—on general principles if nothing else. And the version attributed to Lieutenant Force was printed 38 years after he had been killed in battle, and then in a publication of dubious merit—and is therefore suspect as being phony. However, what is undoubtedly a very trustworthy statement was made by the wife of a surgeon at Fort Lapwai in a letter to her mother. After noting that "E" Company had already been sent from Fort Walla Walla and that "Colonel [Captain David] Perry's company was ordered to be in readiness to move at short notice," she wrote:

> Then we have other news through the papers and the officers (who are already in the Wallowa Valley) that makes us all feel worried and anxious. . . . the settlers, about seventy or eighty, have joined together and are armed. The Indians are determined that they shall not settle in the Valley. . . . Everybody wants to prevent bloodshed, for this lot of settlers in the Wallowa are an awful set of men and have made all the trouble for themselves.[20]

The opening days of the Nez Perce war brought to the forefront questionable individuals from Columbia County, Washington Territory—to the north of the Grande Ronde Valley in Oregon. A group of about twenty volunteers under "Captain" J. W. Elliott, calling themselves the Pataha Rangers, came rushing to the "aid" of the Idaho settlers. They were given the task of patrolling the western side of the Snake River below Lewiston. Not long afterward some of the party returned to Lewiston, turned in their arms, and went home; and soon *The Teller* admitted that "some of the Columbia Co. volunteers are complained of as having a great affinity for stock." About the same time, the Portland *Daily Standard* noted that "Captain" Elliott fabricated a story to the effect that he had had a fight with the Nez Perce. When a party from Union, Oregon, went to his assistance, they found the story was false. This made them so angry—so the story goes—that they wanted to lynch Elliott.[21] Perhaps there were others of the same stripe, for not long afterward, Captain Birney B. Keeler reported to General McDowell, "Volunteers of the character and status of those operating with General Howard would be worse than useless. I am sure you would discourage the use of volunteers in any possible emergency."[22]

Wilhautyah's murder was the last crime of this sort before the three Nez

Perce went on a killing spree. It may be noted in passing that L. V. McWhorter has listed—just how accurately cannot be determined— twenty-seven Indian deaths at the hands of white men; and in only one case did he find that the murderer had been convicted—with no record that the sentence was ever carried out.[23] Of these, only the deaths of Wilhautyah and Eagle Robe were closely related to the outbreak of hostilities; and it was the murder of Eagle Robe that indirectly provided a fuse to the powder keg. As this killing was one of the causes for some fifteen, perhaps more, murders within a span of two days, it is necessary to take a searching look at the character of the people who lived in the relatively small area where these occurred.

There are two curious facts. One is that in this area the Indians spared some whom they could (apparently) have killed just as easily as those they did murder. The other is that the very narrow valley of the lower part of the Salmon River had very few attractions for settlers. There were no rich gold deposits in the bars of the streams; and throughout much of the area, rounded hills 2,000 to 3,000 feet high rose steeply from the channel of the river. There was very little land suitable for agricultural purposes. Why did these people—other than two or three storekeepers—want to live here?

Perhaps the answer to the second question lies in a third. Vigilante committees could impose but two sentences, namely death and banishment. Where did the thugs, some 200 according to one historian, go when they were banished from Lewiston in 1864? Certainly it would not have been healthy to have gone to the gold camps in Montana, where vigilantes ruled with an iron hand, or to the Florence or Boise City areas. And there were citizens in California who knew how to use a piece of rope and a convenient branch in a tree. It would seem that, under the circumstances, the rough breaks along the Salmon River must have had some very attractive features—features equaled, but not surpassed, by Wyoming's notorious Hole-in-the-Wall country. What went on in this area in 1877 indicates that this region contained far more than a normal proportion of tough characters.

Indications of the character of the settlers in the Salmon River breaks and surrounding area are contained in several sources. Old Nez Perce warriors provided a friendly rancher, L. V. McWhorter, with several bits. Immediately after the war ended, General Howard directed Major D. P. Hancock, then in charge of Camp Howard near Mount Idaho, to gather what he could about the initial murders and other acts of aggression. Hancock asked J. W. Poe, District Attorney for the 1st District of Idaho, to prepare a statement for him; and this the major then revised and amplified before forwarding it. Poe's statement was printed in *The Teller*, as were several other revealing bits from time to time. Other notes were made in the reports of officers commanding local volunteers; and Monteith detailed items affecting the Indians to the Commissioner of Indian Affairs.

A relative of Chief Joseph charged that an old man, who lived along the Salmon River eight miles above Slate Creek, set his vicious dogs on Indians who passed by, cursed them, and shot a crippled Indian man. Obviously, this individual was Richard Devine, the first victim. A member of Looking Glass' band said that a "mean white man who kept a saloon store" near the mouth of White Bird Creek was "always robbing Indians by keeping money coming to them when buying anything from him. He never gave back change no difference if dollars or cents." Also, that an Indian named Chipmunk was shot and killed near this man's store. Apparently, this settler was Samuel Benedict, another who was killed in the outbreak.[24]

Major Hancock supplied the following information to General Howard about Samuel Benedict, Harry Mason and Henry Elfers.

> In August, 1875, Samuel Benedict, who then resided with his family at the mouth of White Bird Creek, killed an Indian. The circumstances under which the killing took place are as follows: Late at night several intoxicated Indians came to Benedict's house and demanded admission; and upon being refused, commenced breaking the doors and windows of his residence. The wife of Benedict and her two children made their escape under the cover of darkness through a back window, waded White Bird Creek, and found shelter in a neighboring house. Benedict fired and killed one Indian and wounded one or two more. He is accused of having sold liquor to the Indians.
>
> Harry Mason whipped two Indians last spring [1877]. A council of arbitration met to decide who was at fault. Mr. Elfers (I believe chosen by the aggrieved Indians) being a member of the council. The decision of the council was unfavorable to the Indians.[25]

Mason and Elfers were also among the victims.

Poe's letter to Hancock detailing the incident at Benedict's home was printed by *The Teller* on April 13, 1878; and Benedict's widow promptly took issue with the allegation that her husband had killed an Indian. According to the long and detailed letter she wrote, five Indians came to their house on August 29, 1875. Each had a bottle of whiskey which "they said they had obtained at John Days." After loitering about for some time and begging for melons, they left at which time "they had been drinking and were drunk."

That night after all had gone to bed, a disturbance was heard outside and Sam got up to investigate. Finding a window partly raised at the "shop or store," he nailed it down and went back to bed:

> About 12 o'clock midnight, they came back shooting, throwing rocks and screaming like so many wild demons. My husband . . . got up and took his gun (which was only loaded with fine bird shot . . .) and went out and discharged it at them. We afterward learned that some of these shot hit Stick-in-the-mud in the side, and one or two struck young Mox-Mox in the head. This was all the shooting my husband did that night.

According to Mrs. Benedict, she then persuaded her husband to leave the house and they made their way up White Bird Creek, followed partway by the Indians, to a small gold claim being worked by some Chinese. With the moral support of a couple of the Celestials, the family then made their way across the Salmon River to the claim of some Frenchmen. Mrs. Benedict was now soaked by repeated falls in the creek and so terrified that "I did not recover from that night's fright for more than a year." The next day they found the door and windows of their house broken and the yard strewn with rocks. Nearby lay a dead Indian who had been "shot with a pistol ball. . . . with the pistol so close to him that it had burned his shirt. . . . The men asked the Indians the next morning which one of them owned the pistol, and they said that the one who was shot owned it."

The details in this letter indicate that the Indians were camped nearby—undoubtedly White Bird's band—and "young Mox-Mox" may well have been Sarsis Ilppilp, son of Chusulum Moxmox and one of the three culprits involved in the initial murders. Mrs. Benedict was evasive about her husband's place of business, calling it a "shop" and a "shop or store," and her account would seem to indicate that the Indians hated Sam Benedict. At the end of this letter, reference was made to a petition which was circulated in that area just before the final council with the Indians in May, 1877. Again attempting to create a favorable image of her husband, she stated:

> I now think that if that petition for the removal of the Indians had not been circulated and signed, my husband would be alive today, my husband was indifferent about signing it. . . . To me it has always seemed a great wrong in Gen. Howard causing the names of the signers of that paper to be read to the Indians when in council at Lapwai. It seemed to point out to the Indians their victims for revenge.[26]

This petition, read to Chief White Bird on May 15, 1877, contained the following statement:

To GENERAL HOWARD *Commanding*
  The Department of the Columbia

SIR:

We the undersigned residents of Salmon river Idaho Co. I.T. respectfully represent that we are sorely annoyed by the presence of a lawless band of Nez Perce Indians numbering about two hundred. They tear down our fences, burn our rails, steal our cattle and horses, ride in the vicinity of our dwellings, Yelling firing pistols, menacing and frightening our women and children and otherwise disturbing our homes. We there fore pray that measures may be speedily adopted to remove these from our midst upon the reservation where some restraint, can be imposed upon their lawless acts, and as the duty bound we will ever pray.

Salmon river, I.T. May 7th 1877

> (signed) JAMES BAKER
> and
> Fifty six others.[27]

Obviously, this paper was prepared for the purpose of influencing the general at the time an important "council" was under way. Regardless of any merit it may have had, it deserves two criticisms. The first is that if these citizens permitted some of their number to peddle whiskey to the Indians—as they obviously did—it is not at all strange that they were disturbed, for drunken Indians have always been known to be noisy and ugly. The second is that—and of this the signers must also have been aware—the complaint that the Indians "steal our horses and cattle" was stretching the truth to the breaking point. This area was full of thieves—*not red but white!*

On June 30, 1877—when the war was just getting started—the Lewiston *Teller* printed a letter from its correspondent at Mount Idaho in which it was noted that white rustlers were stealing stock:

> We cannot stand to be robbed by Indians and whites, and should anyone be caught driving away stock they will need no judge, jury or coroner to pass on their case.

And another item in the same issue stated that news had been received that settlers near this place had hung a horse thief. "No name given of the offender." On August 11th this item appeared:

> STOCK THIEVES—It is strongly suspected that several parties are playing Indian on and in the vicinity of Camas Prairie by firing upon parties and retreating and causing alarm, while they take advantage of the alarm and run off stock containing both horses and cattle.

Some men are carefully noticed in their movements even when they are in and about Lewiston. These men must remember that there is left standing many a pine tree whose projecting limbs will sustain the weight of short bits of rope with carcasses at the end thereof and the season is so hot and dry that a little elevation will prevent disagreeable smell.

At the time General Howard was preparing to follow the Nez Perce eastward into Montana, he wrote a letter of instruction to "Major" George M. Shearer of the Idaho volunteers,[28] directing that he take the 622 Indian horses receipted for by the Mount Idaho company of volunteers, select what he needed for remounts, and drive the balance to the head of Rocky Canyon and kill them. He was also instructed to watch for thieves:

> People who have followed the operations and who belong to no company, but have picked up bands of Indian ponies to enrich themselves should be deprived of them: if you with the two (2) vol. Co[s] will take their ponies from them, put to use such as your Companies need and kill the remainder you will do a good service to your people and to me.[29]

And in an undated report, probably written early in August, "Lieutenant" Wilmot of the Mount Idaho volunteers informed Governor Brayman that

> a great many persons are getting up and branding horses that have been lost by the Indians. I have gathered up one band and such as was serviceable I have turned over to the Vol. . . . I told one man that I did not want him to get horses up and brand them and he said I had no authority to take them he had or keep him from getting more. I told him I thought I had. . . .[30]

After the war was over, Shearer wrote a report to Howard stating that he believed there were seven or eight hundred head of horses and cattle in the mountainous country between the Salmon and Snake rivers, and that "parties of the character you wished me to deprive of Indian ponies have been, and are still, over there for the purpose of driving off this stock." And shortly afterward, Monteith informed the general the rustlers stealing stock believed to belong to both friendly and hostile Indians on the west side of the Snake "threaten to shoot anyone who goes there to bring them out."[31]

Although the rustlers have remained nameless, there are letters which indicate clearly that the activities of the Chapman brothers were viewed with suspicion by some. According to war correspondent Thomas Sutherland, these Mount Idaho settlers were the sons of "Colonel Chapman of Portland, a well known and courageous frontiersman." Tom and Arthur I. ("Ad") Chapman served with Howard during the war. The latter had what was referred to as a "farm" near Mount Idaho, was elected captain of a group of volunteers at the time hostilities broke out, served as Howard's chief white scout, and later went to Fort Leavenworth with the prisoners after the end of the war. L. V. McWhorter characterized him as a "low-principled scoundrel" who was married—Indian fashion—to a Umatilla squaw. One comment indicates that while he was with the Indians in Indian Territory, he took, again Indian fashion, a Modoc woman.

Shortly after Monteith assumed his duties as Agent at Lapwai, he notified A. I. Chapman that "the Indians on White Bird accuse you of killing some of their cattle and selling the same to Chinamen," and set a date for him to appear at the agency office to answer to the charge. A few months later, the Agent informed him that "Complaints is again made to me that you are taking Indian farms without giving satisfaction for the same. * * * I do not depend altogether upon Indians for proof but settlers who live near you are willing to swear you are interfering with the Indians and creating trouble."[32]

While with Howard during the war, Chapman was involved in two questionable horse deals. Early in July, he bought a horse from G. C. Crooks of Grangeville, allegedly telling the owner that the general would "stand good for the horse"; and six months later was explaining to Howard that the quartermaster had agreed to take the horse upon his property lists. While Aide-de-Camp C. E. S. Wood was trying to get at the bottom of this matter, another complaint came into the office concerning a horse secured from a Flathead Indian in Montana about a month later. Wood wrote Chapman: "You were furnished a voucher for this horse, whereas the Indian claims he was never paid. His claim is presented through a priest of good standing and the matter must be satisfactorily explained. . . ."[33]

While Department Headquarters was trying to straighten out Ad's horse deals, his brother Tom—to whom Howard had naïvely given a letter of recommendation for his services in the war—wangled a job helping gather up stock belonging to the hostiles. Immediately there was a storm of protest from the Treaty Indians, and Colonel Frank Wheaton, who had hired him, promptly discharged him.

At least one citizen in the Mount Idaho area believed that there was an easier way to make a fast dollar than chasing Indian stock. After the war was over and General Howard had returned to his headquarters, Dr. B. J. Morris wrote asking for an appointment as contract surgeon for nearby Camp Howard. To this request was added:

I also wish to ask a favor of you. . . . I . . . did all in mi power to assist the wounded [civilians at Mount Idaho]. Furnished all the medicine and dressings at mi own expence. I have put in a memorial before Congress for the amount of Fifteen Hundred dollars $1500.00. . . . * * * I now ask you to write to the Department and recommend the passage of this bill. either have your letter placed on file and notify Hon S. S. Fenn . . . or send direct to him who says and promised to do all he could and in fact is one among many of mi friends who asked me to make this request of Congress.[34]

Morris was in Portland when the outbreak occurred, and the total number he could possibly have cared for did not exceed fifteen. There is nothing to indicate that the general did more than paste the letter into his file book where it now rests as a silent testimonial about an "enterprising settler."

Of all the incidents which took place between the Idaho settlers and the Indians, the most serious occurred along the Salmon River late in March 1874. In a report of the matter, Monteith stated:

The last of March an Indian and a White settler on Salmon River (75 miles distant from the Agency) got into a dispute about a piece of land. The White man settled on the last some two years ago but had fenced only a part of it. This spring he extended his fence so as to include a small piece of land that had formerly been occupied by the Indians as a camping ground. The Indians objected, but the settler paid no attention to them and began plowing. One of the Indians went into the field and commenced stoning the man and throwing up his blanket to scare the horses. The settler drew a revolver and shot the Indian, from the effects of which he died in a few days.

The settler was examined before a justice and discharged. I shall bring the matter before the grand jury which meets in May. The Indians were Non Treaties and belong to Eagle-from-the-Light's band.

In reporting the action of the grand jury, the Agent stated further that "in my opinion the settler was not justified in committing the act" but that Indian witnesses refused to be sworn, saying that "they could tell the truth without holding up their hand." Also, that "one of the jury told me that if I could get them to swear to the statement made, he thought the man would be indicted, but not otherwise."[35]

This was the murder of Chief Tipyahlanah Siskan, otherwise known as Eagle Blanket or Eagle Robe. The killer was a squatter named Larry Ott. And the incident took place near the Horseshoe Bend of the Salmon

River, a pronounced loop midway between the mouths of Slate and White Bird creeks. Perhaps the best Indian account was set down about four years later by Duncan McDonald who lived near Missoula, Montana. McDonald was a very intelligent, well-educated half-breed who was the son of a well-known Scotch trader and a Nez Perce woman, said to have been a relative of Looking Glass.

According to this account, Ott had settled here the year before and had made an amicable agreement with Eagle Robe about part of the plot of land claimed by the latter. However, in 1874, he began moving his rail fence over onto the land the Indian regarded as his own, and when the Indian objected, Ott picked up his rifle and shot him—which is in reasonable agreement with Monteith's report. At the time of his death, the chief was alleged to have told his people:

"I know that my days are short upon this earth, and it is my desire that you do not get excited by this event, and send this message to my son Wallitze: Tell him for my sake, and for the sake of his brothers and sisters, and in fact for the whole Nez Perce nation, to hold his temper and not let his heart get the best of him. * * * When I am dead tell him all I have said and lastly of all not to wage war upon the whites."

This message was transmitted to Wahlitits, who expressed pride in his father's desire that the incident not lead to further bloodshed.[36] Three years later it was—allegedly——a taunt about Eagle Robe's death that was the match that lit the fuse.

Who was Larry Ott? The census records for 1870 show that he was (then) *thirty-six years old*, had been *born in Pennsylvania*, and had property valued at $200. His name on the muster rolls of the Slate Creek Volunteers in 1877 is written in a neat script. The murder indicates that he was of the ruffian type often found on the frontier; and his presence on this tiny bit of land beside the Salmon River gives rise to the supposition that he was a miner who failed to make a profitable strike or that he may have been one of the undesirables run out of Lewiston or Florence.

Other possible bits of the story are these. In the early 1840's, a "rough, daring, wily frontiersman" settled along the Des Moines River in Iowa. This man was Henry Lott, and although there is much disagreement in various accounts, old-timers recalled that he came from Pennsylvania with a wife and two boys. The oldest of these was a stepson. Lott peddled whiskey and trinkets to the Indians and was accused of being a horse thief—a not unlikely combination. By 1852, Mrs. Lott had died, and the father and stepson had drifted up the Des Moines River to the vicinity of Fort Dodge, Iowa. Here, in January, 1854, Lott and his stepson murdered a minor Sioux chief named Sidomindota and some seven or eight members of his family circle, the only survivors being a girl who escaped to the brush and a small boy who was left for dead. (Because Lott was never caught and punished, Inkpaduta, the brother of the murdered man, took his revenge by killing some thirty people in northwest Iowa.) The two murderers were traced as far as the Missouri River and a year or two later the stepson wrote from California that Lott had been killed in a brawl.[37]

Was Larry Ott the stepson of Henry Lott? The gold strikes in Idaho did attract many from California. And, as nearly as can be estimated, Henry Lott's stepson—an Indian murderer in 1854—would have been about *thirty-six years old* in 1870, and he was probably *born in Pennsylvania*. This coincidence is too strong to be disregarded.

It is obvious that many of the "enterprising settlers" who regarded the Non-Treaty Nez Perce as "outlaws" and "incarnate fiends" were people who openly coveted their lands and property, peddled whiskey to them, and even murdered some of them; and they ranged from the illiterate to holders of high offices. What percentage of the total population this class represented cannot be determined. One thing is certain—there were too many of their ilk, and the respectable portion did very little, if anything, to curb their schemes and activities.

Only ten days before the outbreak, General Howard wrote bitingly:

> I believe if the operations now inagurated . . . be continued with vigor for a month longer there will be no further trouble of any importance; certainly none until some ill disposed, Indian hating, avaricious settlers begin actual encroachments upon Government reservations.[38]

Three months before the outbreak, Monteith stated in a letter to Howard:

> The reports that are being published in various papers pertaining to Joseph's movements are groundless, the fact is there is a certain class here who are afraid there will not be an Indian war.[39]

Three weeks after the hostilities started, Major Edwin C. Mason—the general's Chief of Staff—wrote in a letter to his wife:

> We have no certain intelligence in regard to the Indians. I expect. . . . We will be obliged to hunt them up ourselves, for the frontiersmen are utterly worthless, a cowardly pack of whelps—what they desire is to steal horses—A more worthless set of trifling rascals from Lewiston out I have never seen. I would not give such people protection—if I was King. . . .[40]

And correspondent Thomas A. Sutherland of the Portland *Standard,* writing some two months after General Howard began his campaign, was equally caustic on one occasion:

Undoubtedly there were some intelligent and courageous men among these gangs [sic—companies of volunteers]—gangs which we sampled from 3 territories—but, taken as a body, the frontiersman of today is an undoubted fraud. . . . One band of men from Wash. Terr. who represented themselves as thirsting for Nez Perce gore turned out to be a gang of organized horse thieves.[41]

"Enterprising settlers!"

4

A Futile Agreement

>>>>>>><<<<<<< When General Howard assumed command of the Department of the Columbia in July, 1874, he was faced with several knotty Indian problems. A mere handful of Modoc Indians had fought a nasty little "war" about a year and a half before; and scattered throughout the basin of the Columbia River were groups of Indians who had either never gone on a reservation or had assorted grievances. The problem of the Non-Treaty Nez Perce was, of course, the most perplexing.

To provide a basis for evaluating the Nez Perce problem, Howard directed his adjutant, Major H. Clay Wood, to prepare a study for him. Wood, whom the general regarded as the "best adjutant I ever had," combed official records and newspaper files, corresponded with Monteith, interviewed Joseph and delved into court records and judicial implications. The result was a forty-nine-page booklet entitled *The Status of Young Joseph and His Band of Nez Perce Indians Under the Treaties Between the United States and the Nez Perce Tribe of Indians and the Indian Title to Land* which bears the date January, 1876, even though it was obviously published five or six months later.

Although this study is so concise that it practically defies summarization, a few points must be noted. Under "Conclusions of Law," the major stated:

> Tenth.—The Nez Perces, undoubtedly, were at liberty to denounce the treaty of 1855 (and probably the treaty of 1863), the Government having violated the treaty obligations.

> Fifteenth.—The non-treaty Nez Perces cannot in law be regarded as bound by the treaty of 1863; and in so far as it attempts to deprive them of a right to occupancy of any land its provisions are null and void. The extinguishment of their title of occupancy contemplated by this treaty is imperfect and incomplete.

Elsewhere, he indicated that he had no "matured sentiments" other than thinking a "just, yet speedy" solution should be formulated. Also he pointed out:

> The birthplace of Lawyer, the homes of his followers, the parties to the treaty [of 1863], were included within the limits of the established reservation; while the contracted area excluded the homes of Joseph and all the prominent non-treaty chiefs and their bands, and ceded their venerated Penates to the United States. . . . In this God-given sentiment—the love of home—is to be found the true cause of the Nez-Perce division.[1]

However, there was a hardheaded recognition of conditions in Wood's findings. He could not find that the Wallowa Valley was the *exclusive* domain of Joseph's band but rather that it belonged to the entire tribe for fishing and hunting. And while he acknowledged their legal right of "occupancy" as a part of the tribe, he felt that they would have to accept some reservation other than this area.

Sometime during this early period, the idea developed at the Headquarters of the Department that a special commission should be set up to meet with Joseph to work out a solution. The murder of Wilhautyah by Findley and McNall provided a convenient excuse to introduce this idea which, obviously, was an intrusion by military personnel into the affairs of the Indian Department.

After this killing, Monteith held a conference with Joseph and reported to Howard that "Joseph seemed to care but very little for the man killed and seemed satisfied with the state of affairs." However, the general had telegraphed to Captain David Perry at Fort Lapwai asking that he try to pacify Joseph—and this irritated the Agent. Then Major Wood, acting without prior approval or formal orders, came to Lapwai and requested

Monteith to arrange a council with the chief.[2] This took place on the 22nd of July and consisted of two sessions. The first took place in the afternoon at the Agency where Howard's headquarters was represented by Wood and three other officers. With Joseph were about forty Indians, including his brother, father-in-law, and several minor chiefs, with his nephew, James Reuben, acting as interpreter.

The murder was discussed first, with Joseph presenting a much increased idea of the importance of the worth of the deceased—according to Monteith, who had now become highly critical of all that was transpiring. Then Wood introduced the idea of having a commission try to solve the problem and asked the Indians to describe just what they claimed as their territory as compared to that set aside by the Executive Order of June 16, 1873. The second conference was held the following evening in the adjutant's office at nearby Fort Lapwai with a small number being present, and not including Monteith. This time, Joseph's brother, Ollokot, produced a well-drawn map which showed that Joseph desired considerably more territory than the 912,000 acres previously covered by the President's order; and the chief indicated he would be glad to meet with the proposed commission "if good honest men were sent." One objective of this second meeting may have been to discover if Joseph disliked Monteith, for in his formal report Wood stated, "I did not, however, learn nor do I believe the Nez Perce Indians have any just reason to complain of their present agent."[3]

Quite naturally, Monteith was irritated by the course pursued by Howard's representatives, and his injured pride made him highly critical of what had taken place. He wrote an angry letter to the Commissioner of Indian Affairs in which he pointed out that Wood's visit had given Joseph an inflated idea of his importance, and he protested pointedly that "for the military to step in without being requested by the agent to do so, simply destroys the agent's influence, and creates an impression in the minds of the Indians that there is local authority to go to with their complaints and troubles other than their agent." In this, the Agent was correct, but he was also being shortsighted in failing to recognize that if matters kept getting worse, Howard's troops would be involved in no uncertain manner.

After Monteith had vented his indignation about Wood's council, he made some critical and prophetic comments about the proposed commission. Although his name had been included in the list of five whom Howard had proposed, the Agent recommended that E. R. Geary, Joel Palmer and himself constitute the commission as they were experienced in Indian problems. Moreover, he regarded the proposal as one which would result in "great expense" and, in his opinion, was not necessary. However, Monteith's view was a narrow one and clouded by his own pique. The Nez

Perce question was but one of Howard's problems. When the Commission that was finally set up made their report, they stated that they had also been instructed to survey the problems of the "Coeur d'Alênes in northern Idaho, the Spokanes, Pend d'Orelles and Kootenays, also the Colville Indians," but that the nearness of winter made it inadvisable to try to travel to other areas after meeting with the Nez Perce. The general's basic idea may have had some merit, but its timing and execution were to prove very poor.

General Howard's proposal was given a hostile reception by J. D. Cameron, Secretary of War, who was out of Washington when it arrived on the Adjutant General's desk. He sent a curt telegram: I SEE NO NECES- SITY FOR THE NEZ PERCE COMMISSION AND CANNOT CONSENT TO IT UNLESS RECOMMENDED BY THE DIVISION COMMANDER. However, Major General Irwin McDowell, who had recently assumed command of the Division of the Pacific, approved the idea and after some jockeying between the War Department and the Secretary of Interior over personnel and expenses, a five-member commission was selected. Named were two businessmen, D. H. Jerome of Saginaw, Michigan, and A. C. Barstow of Providence, Rhode Island, William Stickney of the Board of Indian Commissioners, and General Howard and Major Wood from the Department of the Co- lumbia. Four of the members met with General McDowell on October 25th, at which time they received their instructions, and Wood joined them when they reached Portland. Here Jerome was elected chairman, and Stickney, secretary. The entire party then proceeded to Lapwai, where they arrived on the evening of November 7th.

As there were no accommodations for transient officers at Fort Lapwai, military courtesy required that married officers having quarters provide the necessary shelter and food. Thus, General Howard and Major Wood became the guests of the post commander, Captain David Perry, and the surgeon, Captain Jenkins A. ("John") FitzGerald. These two officers occupied a double set of quarters—a building divided by a hallway through the center but with a porch which extended from one end to the other. Dr. FitzGerald's wife, Emily, was an intelligent, observant woman, having the ability to write colorfully and (apparently) accurately about things which came under her observation. As she attended part of the council meetings and undoubtedly heard many matters discussed in her husband's quarters, the frank, uninhibited letters she wrote to her mother are more revealing than the official report of the Commission.

Although the party arrived on the evening of the 7th, Joseph took his time in arriving for the affair and it was not until noon on Monday the 13th that the business of the council got under way in the church at the Agency. By Wednesday morning, the members of the Commission considered the business completed and were on their way back to Portland! Editor Leland of *The Teller* wrote two weeks later that "the whole thing was a farce." He had been critical from the start, insisting that "nineteen-twentieths of all the Nez Perce . . . could not be induced to break [the existing] peace" and also that "none of the present generation of the main body of the Nez Perces possess any tactics of war, and hence have no ability to go to war."[4] And in a story written after the meetings were over, he stated:

> We understand that Gen. Howard had become a little impatient with his [Joseph's] insolence and intimated that he would compel him by force to come in on the reservation, and that one or two others of the Commission were more lenient towards the outlaw and disposed to indulge, if not justify his independent attitude.[5]

Also, he picked up the rumor that Joseph had snubbed Howard, which he corrected a month later, saying, "Commissioner Jerome was the person Joseph snubbed."

Of the three civilians, Mrs. FitzGerald wrote revealingly:

> They are all such good pleasant men. One of them, a Mr. Stickney from Washington, reminds me of Uncle Essick. Then there is a lovely old Mr. Barstow from Providence, Rhode Island, who, when he spoke to my babies, said he had seventeen grandchildren between the ages of 10 years and two weeks, who were all waiting for him to spend thanksgiving with them. Then there is a Mr. Jerome who is an exceedingly good-looking gentleman. He is president of the Commission. They are all fine looking men, and men of means.[6]

Being good, pleasant, handsome and wealthy was not an adequate substitute for experience in dealing with Indians—the Commission was weak in the very quality that Monteith had predicted it would be.

Emily FitzGerald, curious to see the Indians arrive in their best clothes, went down to the Agency on the first day—with misgivings that the Indians might turn the affair into a "sort of Canby Massacre"[7]—and was persuaded by the Agent's sister-in-law to join the rest of the whites who were going to observe. However, she was too fastidious and apprehensive to enjoy the experience although she wrote a vivid description of the "horrible, dirty things all rolled up in blankets and robes" inside the church, and the squaws "all gathered around outside in their best, brightest clothes, with lots of babies on their mothers' backs. . . . None of the squaws but us were inside. . . ."

Well the council was not very satisfactory. Doctor and I left soon. We did not stay more than an hour. The Indian smell was awful, and I wanted to get home to the children. We heard, after the gentlemen came up [to the post], that Joseph will make no terms or acknowledge any authority. I hope they can arrive at a more comforting settlement than they hope for today. This Joseph will admit no boundary to his lands but those he choses to make himself. I wish somebody would kill him before he kills any of us. The Agent leaned over in the Council room yesterday and asked me if my hair felt on tight. It dosen't feel very tightly on when I think of these horrible devils around us.[8]

It is clear that the Commissioners and the Indians clashed the first day over the fundamentals of the Dreamer religion, although the official report provides no indication of the friction. This states:

From the first it was apparent that Joseph was in no haste. Never was the policy of orderly inactivity more fully inagurated. He answered every salutation, compliment, and expression of good-will, in kind, and duplicated in quantity. An alertness and dexterity in intellectual fencing was exhibited by him that was quite remarkable.[9]

The second day was a stormy one in which the Commissioners tried to ride roughshod over the Indians, a situation also not noted in the official report. Mrs. FitzGerald wrote:

They all got indignant at him at last and threatened him. They told him of the Modocs . . . the Seminoles and the Sioux. . . . He said he was ready for them. General Howard was telling me of it in the evening after the last Council and said the Indians were just unwilling to admit the government's authority. . . . General Howard says Joseph has taken the course that will lose him all sympathy for him, and the next summer, if the trouble in the Wallowa is brought up again, he will send out two men to Joseph's one . . . and whip him into submission. Delightful prospect for us whose husbands will probably be in the fight isn't it?[10]

Early Wednesday morning, shortly after the Commissioners had left to return to Portland, a curious development took place. As Emily described it to her mother:

But there is one thing rather pleasant, I forgot to mention. Colonel [Major] Wood[11] felt all the while that Joseph would come to terms as soon as he knew they were in earnest, and the last

evening here, after the Council was all over and the gentlemen were
going to leave early in the morning, Colonel Wood said a dozen
times in the course of the evening, "I am expecting to hear from
Joseph every minute. I am certain he will come to terms, knowing
that this is his last chance and that we leave in the morning." Joseph
did not come or send word, and the party started off for town at six
in the morning. About nine o'clock in the rain, four most gorgeously
gotten up Indians rode up to our back gates and asked for General
Howard. (They seem to think he is the most important big chief.) I
wish you could have seen them. You never saw such style. I happened to be in the back of the house and went to the gate and called
John. Mrs. Perry soon came to her gate, then the Colonel [Captain
Perry], then two or three officers joined us, and we all stood in the
rain, as we hadn't seen such a gorgeous array before. One of them
who did the most talking had a headpiece for his horse that covered
his horse's whole head. It was just covered with beads. There were
holes for the eyes, and it was really very showy. His own costume was
of some kind of skin trimmed in ermine. A fringe of ermine skins
(whole skins) was around the jacket, and about the knees, and down
the seams of the sleeves from shoulder to waist, and around his cap.
Their faces were all painted, and all had bows, and quivers of arrows
slung at their backs. The quivers were all highly ornamented with
beads. A ferocious looking old medicine man was with them (an old,
old man). The other three were quite young chiefs. One was Joseph,
himself, who is a splendid looking Indian. As far as we could understand, they had come to make terms of some sort with General
Howard. They were all very smiling and pleasant and seemed very
sorry about not finding him. We don't know whether this is the
beginning of a settlement, but we hope it is.[12]

Major Wood's prediction that Joseph would come to terms was probably
based on an impression gained at previous meetings with the chief. The
question of whether he was right or wrong is an intriguing one that was
never fully answered. It seems likely that Joseph quickly arrived at an
uncomplimentary opinion of the three "men of means" and, in trying to
negotiate as favorable a settlement as possible by using a strategy of
indifference, pushed this course of action too far. Such an analysis does
have support in that when Joseph sent word to Howard the next spring
that he desired to see him, there was tied to this request the implication
that "Joseph understood that General Howard would have another council
with him."

Emily FitzGerald's record of Howard's animosity is also a matter worthy
of note for, prior to the summer of 1876, the general had been sympathetic
to the desires of the Indians. When the final series of councils was held the

next spring, he no longer showed signs of being sympathetic and understanding but acted rather like an officer who brooked no questioning of his authority, right or wrong. In considering this change of attitude, two things should be remembered. One is that other aspects of the general's private and official life were contributing considerable strain and tension at this time. The second is that this Commission was, probably, Howard's own idea and its failure involved his personal pride to a considerable extent.

On their return, the Commission broke up at Walla Walla, Washington Territory. Jerome and Howard made a side trip to the nearby Umatilla Reservation while the others proceeded to Portland—from which point, Barstow hurried home for a Thanksgiving dinner with his seventeen grandchildren. The final report, dated December 1, 1876, was written at the Headquarters of the Department of the Columbia and, apparently, represents little more than a perfunctory approval of General Howard's opinions. His dislike of the Dreamer faith is mirrored in the first recommendation of the summary of that document: "That the leaders and teachers known as dreamers belonging to the treaty and non treaty and roaming Indians . . . be required to go upon their reservations. In case of refusal, that they be removed to Indian Territory." The second, third and fourth provided that the Nez Perce be allowed to visit the Wallawa country for hunting, fishing and grazing each year, with a military guard to prevent hostilities, and if they did not come on the Reservation "within a reasonable time, that they should be placed upon the reservation by force." The sixth pointed out that the Government had been remiss in its observance of treaty stipulations and suggested that it "give speedy attention to this important matter," and the seventh proceeded, ironically, to reverse this recommendation by urging the Government to reduce the number of reservations in the Department and sell the vacated land![13]

Major Wood refused to sign this report, and the balance of the Commission would not attach his minority report and discouraged his views being given any publicity. In his own report to the Commissioner of Indian Affairs, Wood quoted the original instructions which specified that the Commission probe far deeper than it did, and then reaffirmed his previously rendered opinion that Joseph and his band "has in law an undivided, individual interest in all the lands ceded to the United States by the treaty of 1863." Then he went on to point out, in an involved but obviously carefully considered opinion:

> Joseph, unless he and his band, abandoning their tribal relations and adopting the habits and pursuits of civilized life, should accept the provisions of the act of March 3, 1875, *must* be excluded from the Wallowa valley and the state of Oregon, and permanently settled

elsewhere, with just compensation, in the shape of houses, fences, farm implements, pasturage, &c., for his legal right in the Valley. * * * But until Joseph commits some overt act of hostility force [must] not be used to put him upon any reservation.

Finally, he took issue with the basic recommendations of the Commission:

> I recognize the fact that the Indian must yield to the white man; the inferior to the superior race; barbarism to civilization; but power is not justice, force is not law. The American Republic cannot afford to consumate a wrong, even toward an Indian, especially a Nez-Perce Indian.[14]

The body of the official report contained an interesting statement in regard to the Reservation of the Umatilla Indians, which was visited by Howard and the President of the Commission. After pointing out how much good the money from the sale of part of the Reservation might do these Indians—naïvely overlooking the fact that the Indians would probably be defrauded of this money by corrupt or inefficient officials—the statement was made that a

> whole tract of valuable land [is] being suffered to lay waste, occupied by a mere handfull of Indians who are incapable of developing its rich treasures, all ready to reward the industry and skill of the farmer.

There is a striking inconsistency in Howard's coveting land in this Reservation in November, 1876, and the following May referring to settlers who had similar desires as "avaracious." Such a comment can only give rise to a cynical disbelief of the sincerity of this Commission, or its ability to reach an unbiased conclusion.

Although the Commissioner of Indian Affairs lost no time in acting on the recommendations of the Commission, the instructions sent to Monteith urged restraint instead of immediate and decisive action. The latter was directed to notify the Indians claiming the Wallowa Valley of the decision, to have other Indians urge Joseph to come on the Reservation, and to make arrangements for their accommodation when they did come. The Commissioner further cautioned the Agent, "You will give them a reasonable time to consider and determine this question," and he was advised that the General of the Army had been requested to cooperate by occupying the Wallowa Valley to prevent friction between the Indians and the whites. The final paragraph of this communication contained this restriction:

It is to be understood, however, that should violent measures become necessary for effecting the end desired, that report thereof must be submitted to this office for consideration of the department, when more definite instructions will be issued.[15]

Monteith sent a formal request to Howard asking that two troops of cavalry be sent to occupy the Wallowa Valley, and then moved promptly to apply pressure on the Indians. To this end, he sent to Joseph a delegation of four, which included Reuben (brother-in-law and head chief), James Reuben (nephew), and Whis-tas-ket (father-in-law). These returned with the report that Joseph had said, "I have been talking to the whites many years about the land in question, and it is strange they cannot understand me; the country they claim belonged to my father, and when he died, it was given to me and my people, and I will not leave it until I am compelled to."

In the letter reporting the failure of this delegation, Monteith, apparently recognizing that it might be necessary to make a forcible removal, proposed a concession—would the Department of Indian Affairs allow the Indians to visit the relatively inaccessible Imnaha Valley for a period of four to six weeks each year to fish? And he revealed that he had set a deadline for the move—

I have given Joseph until April 1, 1877, to come on the reserve peaceably. They can move one time just as well as another, having nothing to hinder them moving.[16]

This timetable reveals that Monteith was acting with undue haste—the very thing he had been instructed not to do. For one thing, it was not practical to move troops into the area at this time, and subsequent events were to indicate that the Agent did not advise Howard of this deadline. Also, the date was not realistic as far as the Indians were concerned, as their wealth consisted of herds of horses and cattle which, at this time would not be in condition to move by reason of many small calves and colts. The Snake River, a formidable barrier even in the summer, was almost impassable at this time, and it was absurd for Monteith to say that Joseph's people "can move one time just as well as another."

The Commissioner advised the Secretary of Interior that he was approving Monteith's compromise proposal, and asked that he request the Secretary of War to issue orders authorizing the use of troops "to aid the Department in the execution of some efficient plan for their peaceful removal to the Nez Perce Agency." Howard, who had been unofficially informed of the contemplated request, was already proceeding with plans for the establishment of a temporary post in the trouble area. This was to

be under the supervision and control of Colonel Cuvier Grover, commanding officer of the First Cavalry which had its Regimental Headquarters at
Fort Walla Walla.

By the time the orders from General Sherman reached McDowell's
office in San Francisco, rumors had begun to sprout that *shooting* trouble
was in the offing. In forwarding these orders, McDowell directed his
adjutant to add this emphatic endorsement for General Howard's guidance:

> The Division Commander has examined the various papers trans-
> mitted from the Headquarters of the Army hereinbefore referred to,
> and it seems to him that the Indian Bureau anticipate possible, not
> to say probable, resistance to the demand on Joseph to remove to the
> reservation. . . .
>
> It is therefore of paramount importance that none of the respon-
> sibility of any step which may lead to hostilities shall be initiated by
> the Military Authorities. You are to occupy Wallowa Valley *in the
> interest of peace.* You are to comply with the request of the Depart-
> ment of Interior as set forth in the papers sent you to the extent only
> of merely protecting and aiding them in the execution of their
> instructions. * * *
>
> As this question of the removal of Joseph's band is a very delicate
> and important one the Division Commander directs that it be done
> under your personal direction if practicable.[17]

And it was also requested that Colonel Grover see that the editor of the
newspaper in Walla Walla stop predicting serious Indian trouble.

Although it slowly became obvious that Monteith's April 1st deadline
would not be observed to the day, the Indians began to realize that the
threat to move them was something to be regarded seriously. Sometime in
February, a council was held in Joseph's camp to consider the problem;
and when Ollokot was at Lapwai about the middle of March, Monteith
questioned him about it. The former replied that a "great many lies had
been told them and their council. . . . they say I want to fight, which is
not true. . . . I have a wife and children, cattle and horses. I have eyes
and a heart, and can see and understand for myself that if we fight, we
would have to leave all and go into the mountains."

And, in reporting the interview, the Agent noted:

> Some person has told him that Gen. Howard was coming here to
> talk with him again, and in this connection he said, "When Genl.
> Howard comes, we will tell him and you what we have made up our
> minds to do." * * *
>
> I have written Genl. Howard asking him to come up, and with

myself have another talk with Joseph, and see if we cannot prevail upon him and his followers to come on the reserve without further resistance and controversy.[18]

It was now fairly obvious that Joseph's band was wavering in that they were beginning to consider whether they wished to come to the reservation of their own people or to go to that of the Umatillas, with whom they had some ties.

About the same time, another member of Joseph's band went to the Umatilla Reservation to see Agent W. A. Connoyer. Later, when Howard was at Fort Walla Walla setting up plans for the proposed occupation of the Wallowa Valley, he met the Agent who informed him that Joseph wished to have a talk with him "because the interpreters at Lapwai had not told truly what he, Joseph, wished to convey." So, Connoyer arranged a meeting which was held on April 10th. Ollokot and a few others came to represent Joseph, and Howard sent one of his aides, Lieutenant William H. Boyle. Nothing was accomplished other than Ollokot and Boyle made plans for a second meeting at Fort Walla Walla when both Howard and Joseph were to be present.

This conference was to have been held on April 20th, but Ollokot did not arrive until evening. He apologized "in the most gentlemanly manner" for being late and explained that his brother was ill. The discussion took place the next day (according to Howard) with Young Joseph "declaring over and over again the peaceful intentions of this brother and his people," and indicating that if "they were to be forced upon a reservation they would like to have the privilege of choosing between Lapwai and Umatilla agencies." In a report written some months later, Howard amplified this statement:

> The Indians seemed first to wish to join the Umatillas; then it appears there was a project (probably originating with white men) to combine the reservation Indians of Umatilla with the non-treaty Nez Perces, and ask for them just joined the Wallowa and Imnaha country, giving up the Umatilla reserve.[19]

This would indicate that there was a land-grabber faction which was interested in getting the Umatillas to trade their country—at which Jerome and Howard had looked with covetous eyes—for the rough, high, and relatively inhospitable valleys of the Imnaha and Wallowa rivers.

Howard told the Indians—Ollokot, a Umatilla chief named Young Chief, and a few others—that his instructions were positive and that he could do nothing until they showed a disposition to comply with the order to move; but, as he had planned to go to Lapwai in the near future, he would meet them there if this was desired. Thus a date was set for a third council. However, when Howard reported this meeting, he was careful to state that "I am steadily going forward to carry out the necessary preparations in accordance with my instructions from Generals Sherman and McDowell."[20]

Again, Howard prepared a report indicating that this council had proceeded smoothly—as at Lapwai the preceding November. Again, there is an apparently reliable, eyewitness account to the effect that this was not the case. Martha Sternberg, wife of the post surgeon, wrote years later that the council was held in a large room used by the band, with the Indians on benches on one side, and officers and their wives and civilians seated opposite. Ollokot used a large map drawn on a cowhide to explain why the tribe needed the Wallowa country for their stock.

> But he could see that he was not convincing his listeners, and some of the others not so diplomatic grew loud and boisterous. The ladies had to leave the court room and were not permitted to be present the next day.[21]

Thus it appears that the civilians became so rowdy—or indecent—that the ladies had to leave. Also, that the council lasted two days instead of one. Perhaps the only statement that is completely trustworthy in the official account is that plans were made for another meeting.

Thus, the stage was now set for the final council with the Non-Treaty faction. And, although this final meeting was to be called a *council*, it never had the potential of give-and-take in arriving at a solution. Its outcome had been predetermined before it ever started.

The two weeks' interval between the council at Fort Walla Walla and the opening of the one at Fort Lapwai was a busy one for General Howard.[22] First, he held a conference with some troublesome "Columbia River Renegades" near Wallula, the river port at the junction of the Columbia and Walla Walla rivers. Then, with two aides—Lieutenant Boyle and Melville C. Wilkinson—he took passage on a steamboat to Lewiston. Here, while the boat unloaded and prepared for her return trip, he met with Monteith and Captain Perry and the five worked out plans for the coming council; and Howard, probably at Monteith's prompting, drafted a telegram to General Sherman asking that steps be taken to remove squatters Caldwell and Finney from their choice acreages in the valley of Lapwai Creek.

Leaving the two aides to assist Perry, Howard returned to Fort Walla Walla where he was met by Adjutant Wood and Lieutenant Joseph A. Sladen, another aide, who had come up from Department Headquarters with other items of business. Chief among these were matters pertaining to the evacuation of the posts in Alaska, a move which had been pending for some time and which, as will be noted shortly, took place at a most opportune time. When these items had been disposed of, the general and Colonel Grover turned to the details presented by the requested occupation of the Wallowa Valley.

Snow in the Blue Mountains having melted to the extent that wagons could be taken on the trail, "E" and "L" Companies of the First Cavalry under Captains William H. Winters and Stephen G. Whipple, respectively, with the latter in command, were ordered to move out for the Wallowa Valley. With them went a Gatling gun for each company, an ambulance, two government six-mule teams, five or six citizens' teams and about a dozen pack mules. They marched on May 1st—exactly a month later than the deadline Monteith had put on the coming in of the Indians! In addition, Howard asked that Captain Joel G. Trimble and troop "H" be ordered to Lewiston for possible protection of that area.

Then, as Colonel Grover objected to his post being stripped in the face of widespread uneasiness among the Indians, Howard ordered Lieutenant James A. Haughey and "H" Company of the Twenty-first Infantry up from Fort Vancouver. This post, just across the Columbia from Portland, was both the Headquarters of the Department of the Columbia and the Regimental Headquarters of the Twenty-first Infantry whose commanding officer was Colonel Alfred Sully. These matters arranged, Howard took the stage for Lewiston, stopping overnight at Dayton where he had a visit with A. J. Cain, one of the first Nez Perce agents. Back in Lewiston, he sidestepped becoming involved in the Monteith-Fenn controversy which Leland was airing on the pages of *The Teller*, but he did visit Father Cataldo, as noted previously, whose "neutrality" was considered positive opposition. Everything was now in readiness for the first meeting of the council.

The conferences began on Friday, the third of May. The following day, Emily FitzGerald penned this description for her mother:

> There is a big tent pitched on the parade ground, about as far from our porches as from your front door across the street, and in and around it, squatted on the ground, are about a hundred Indians in the most gorgeous get-ups you can imagine. General Howard and his aides, the Indian Agent, and several officers of the post in full uniform are inside talking with Joseph. The outside line of Indians around the tent consists almost entirely of squaws and papooses. We go over every now and then, but I soon get tired, and the smell is strongly Indian.
>
> I suppose the talk will continue for two or three days. We feel just a little afraid, just enough to keep it interesting. * * * No one

really expects anything horrible, but I feel very glad of the precautions the General saw fit to take, not that he feared a surprise, but he
says that he has made it a rule all his life to be prepared for one
among hostiles of any kind. The guards were doubled this morning
and both companies are armed in their quarters. Of course, all of this
is out of sight of the Indians, and none of the officers in the Council
are armed. It is interesting, though, to see the bright picture before
me—the tent and the bright blankets out on parade.

The proceedings before this Council were weird and queer. . . .
The Indians rode out from the Canyon in single file. All were on
ponies and in their gorgeous array and instead of turning into the
post gates, they circled the post three times, cupping their mouths
with their hands, making the sound of Wah-Wah-Wah. When they
finally stopped at the gate, they stacked their arms before entering
the post.[23]

Joseph, the most prominent leader among the Non-Treaty Indians, and
his brother Ollokot represented those who claimed the Grande Ronde,
Imnaha and Wallowa valleys. White Bird spoke for those living in the
valley of the Salmon River—his own band and part of the one previously
led by Eagle-from-the-Light. Too-hool-hool-zote and his followers made
their home in the country between the Salmon and Snake rivers just south
of their junction; and Huishuis Kute's people lived on the north side
of the Snake River below Lewiston.

General Howard and others have left short descriptions of the various
principals. According to the general, Agent John B. Monteith was a "tall,
well-built, young man, apparently about thirty-five years of age. His health
has not been good, yet he had been unsparing of himself in his journeys
over his reservation. . . ." Major Wood had described Joseph the preceding summer as a man who dressed plainly but whose appearance commanded attention. "His face, manners, and general impression are calculated to impress one favorably. He wears no smile, but . . . [gives close
attention to] the business under consideration. His speech is fluent and
impressive; his action energetic, yet graceful." His Indian name was Hein-
mot Too-ya-la-kekt meaning Thunder Traveling to Loftier (Mountain)
Heights; and he was about thirty-seven years old. His younger brother,
Ollokot, "was over six feet tall, and perfectly formed. He had small hands
and feet, was very intelligent [with some ability as a topographer] . . .
was very quick and graceful in his motions." His Indian name was said to
be the Cayuse or Umatilla word for frog.

After the two Josephs, White Bird was a chief of some importance. The
Scotch trader, Angus McDonald, once described him as "a handsome man,
of about five feet nine in his moccasins, square shouldered, long waisted,

and of clear sinewy limbs. His hair when in the prime of life was dark chestnut, rather than black; his face of a longer than rounder form. . . ." His Indian name, Peo-peo Hih-hih, has been translated variously as White Goose, White Brant and White Pelican; and at this time, he was probably over sixty years of age. Howard observed that "he was a demure looking Indian, about five feet eight inches tall. His face assumed the condition of impassibility or rigid fixedness while in council; and probably for fear that some passing event, some look or emotion might surprise him into a betrayal of the slightest emotion, he kept his ceremonial hat on and placed a large eagle's wing in front of his eyes and nose." However, a few days later while riding on the Reservation, he chatted amicably and even bantered one of the general's aides into engaging in an impromptu horse race with him.

Too-hool-hool-zote, or Sound, who clashed with Howard on the second day, was described as "broad-shouldered, deep-chested, thick-necked, five feet ten in height, had a heavy gutteral voice, and betrayed in every word a strong and settled hatred of all caucasians." He was also referred to as an "ugly, obstinate savage" and as a "cross-grained growler." The fact that he was a *too-at* or priest of the Dreamer faith was sufficient to insure him of the general's dislike. However, he was a stout-hearted leader who was not afraid to stand up to Howard and demand that which he believed was his. Huishuis Kute, or Naked (bald) Head, was an "oily, wily, bright-eyed young chief who could be smooth-tongued or saucy, as the mood siezed him, or as he thought it would best subserve a present purpose."

After the usual handshaking, during which the squaws, children, and some of the Treaty Indians gathered outside the tent, Father Cataldo opened the first session with a prayer in the Nez Perce language. Howard then began negotiations by asking Joseph what he had to say. The chief replied that as White Bird's people were still en route, he thought they should wait until he arrived. Monteith then reviewed his instructions from Washington; and after a bit of sparring with some over questions of law and obedience, the general dismissed the council—having taken the opportunity to "pay my respects" to "two old medicine men, who are evidently the worst malcontents." Then, when they replied "saucily," he threatened to arrest them and send them down the river—a sample of the attitude with which he was to conduct subsequent meetings.

On Saturday, the same formalities were observed with a Nez Perce Indian, Alpowa Jim, offering the prayer. Monteith again read his instruction; and the Indians put Too-hool-hool-zote forward as their spokesman. As the discussions quickly reached an impasse, Howard recessed the council until Monday.

Howard gave as his excuse that he wished White Bird's people to be able to rest after their journey, but what he really wanted was a little time to get a show of force into position. A little more time would permit Whipple to get his men well down in the Grande Ronde Valley and close to Lapwai not far from where Joseph's people were camped. Also, Trimble's company could be moved from Lewiston to Fort Lapwai. And he ordered two more companies of infantry from Fort Vancouver to Wallula where they would be near the troublesome Columbia River renegades.

Howard's report does not reflect any particular concern, but on Sunday, Emily FitzGerald wrote:

> The Indian council has not had the result we expected. Joseph won't answer yes or no, and so he must be made to answer. On Monday the Indian chiefs . . . will again see the general and the agent and unless they say unconditionally *yes* . . . six or eight companies of troops will be on the move after them by Tuesday morning. Two-thirds of the troops from Lapwai are of the number that will be under marching orders. * * *
>
> We can all see that General Howard is very anxious, but I don't think it is only about this, for Joseph's band is the only one under consideration now . . . but the General expects to spend the summer in the field [putting other non-treaty Indians on their reservations]. * * *
>
> It would seem sort of funny to you that the people here take things so quietly. I am continually wondering why no one (but Mrs. Perry) seems excited. Yesterday an Indian (a good one) was sent off with dispatches, taking with him spare horses and is going to ride day and night so as to have certain companies of troops [Whipple's?] near here by Monday night, but we fuss over our dinners and clothes, etc, as if it was the most usual thing in the world to have trouble with Indians. * * * General Howard is promenading the porch quoting scriptures. Indeed, I think he is real good, but he is awfully queer about it.[24]

By Monday, Huishuis Kute's band had arrived and the preliminary instructions were reviewed once more. Then Howard found that he again had to deal with Too-hool-hool-zote who was "loud, harsh and impudent. . . . [with] the usual words concerning the earth being his mother," etc. Howard, whose religious tolerance seems to have been limited to fellow Christians, met the resistance head-on and neither side made any progress. Finally, the general became exasperated and probably lost his temper. In the official report written shortly afterward, he stated, "I . . . called for the Captain to take him out of the Council. He was led out accordingly and kept away until the council broke up." But in an unofficial account he wrote, "At this time I called for a messenger but he being away, Col. Perry and I led Too-hul-hul-sote out of the council. My conduct was somewhat summary, but I knew it was hopeless to get the Indians to agree to anything so long as they could keep this old dreamer in the lead. . . ."[25] Perhaps Howard's action was justified; but to the Indians, this was a *council* and throwing one of their principal chiefs in the guardhouse was a violation of the *diplomatic immunity* expected by the participants. This use of force may have produced the result Howard desired but it did so at the price of goodwill and respect. After this the Indians talked "in a different spirit" and agreed to go on the morrow to inspect possible sites where they might settle.

The remainder of the week was spent looking at sites in the valley of Lapwai Creek and the country along the Clearwater River above the sub-agency at Kamiah. By Saturday noon, all were back and things were in readiness for the final meeting. Trimble and his company had arrived and were camped near the post; and on Sunday, a dispatch arrived from Captain Whipple stating that he had reached the crossing on the Grande Ronde River, about forty miles from Lewiston. According to Mrs. Fitz-Gerald, "Ollikut, who was on his way down towards the Wallowa to see about his stock, met Colonel Whipple with a couple of companies of cavalry on their way up here. He was rather alarmed, for he sent back to Joseph to make the best terms he can with General Howard." And Howard noted that Joseph "sought Lieutenant Wilkinson immediately for protection and passes against it. Thus the desired effect was evidently gained."

The last meeting was held on Tuesday, May 15th, at which time the chiefs made a final decision as to which localities they desired. Joseph, who had first desired the place occupied by the squatter Caldwell, finally decided to move to a spot above Kamiah, and Howard breathed a sigh of relief for they had not yet been able to move Caldwell and Finney. It was at this meeting that the general read to White Bird the petition sent by the settlers living along the Salmon River—which Mrs. Sam Benedict charged was a blunder on Howard's part. White Bird

replied substantially that when the white men sold Indians whiskey, and drank it themselves, both acted with folly. He had advised his people against it, but some of it was impossible for him to control. . . .

In view of what was to come, these were prophetic words.

The limit of thirty days placed on Joseph's band to make the designated move stands as an indication of the lack of consideration and/or judgment of which both General Howard and Monteith were guilty. In speaking of the courier who carried the dispatch to him from Captain Whipple, as the council was nearing its end, Howard wrote: "Sergeant Coffey (?) 1st Cavalry with a citizen for a guide had swam the Grande Ronde with their horses. It was with much peril for the river here is wide and full and torrent like, with water very cold." This indicates that they proceeded from this point via Lewiston which allowed them to ferry over the Snake, a far more formidable stream than the one they did swim.

A few days later, Lieutenant Sevier M. Rains also came in with a dispatch from Whipple. At this time, *The Teller* reported:

> DROWNED.—Lieut Rains arrived Wednesday from the Grand Ronde river crossing. He informs us that on Tuesday morning between nine and ten o'clock as himself and Dr. G. A. Going Veterniary Surgeon with Whipple's command on the Wallowa were attempting to ford the river on horseback, Going was swept down the current and drowned. Every effort possible was made to rescue him but all to no avail. He suddenly and unobserved became separated from his horse, and within a few minutes threw up his hands and disappeared in the rapid and swolen stream. The horse came ashore in safety. Although diligent search was made but no discovery of the body of the unfortunate man after he first went down.

The corpse of the Irishman was found four months later along the Snake, six miles below Lewiston.[26]

It was the formidable Snake and not the Grande Ronde that Joseph's band had to swim to reach the southern edge of Camas Prairie where the deadline of June 15th was to find them. During this time the danger and difficulty in making a crossing did not diminish. Nevertheless, the Indians —the weak and the strong, the aged and the young—crossed, although they were not able to swim all their stock.

The council over, Howard sent a courier to the telegraph office in Walla Walla with this dispatch:

Walla Walla, W. T. May 18, 1877

To Adjt Gen U S A
Washington D C

Dispatch forwarded eleventh instant from Portland Oregon received. We have put all non treaty Indians on reservation by using force and persuasion without bloodshed. Have not exceeded my instructions.

Howard
Comdg.[27]

In that portion of his report which detailed these meetings, the general added this statement:

> Having now secured the object named [in the order dated May 3rd] by persuasion, constraint, and such a gradual encircling of the Indians by troops as to render resistance evidently futile, I thought my own instructions fulfilled.
>
> The execution of further details I leave in perfect security to the Indian Agent and Captain Perry whom I put into my place for the work by issuing Special Field Order No. 8. . . .

"*I leave in perfect security*"—this little peculiarity of making positive statements before matters became a *fait accompli* was to become an annoying shortcoming of General Howard in the weeks ahead.

5

Vital Intelligence

≫≫≫≫≫≫≪≪≪≪≪≪ No competent commanding officer willingly embarks on a campaign without gathering certain basic data. In this case much of what might be called vital intelligence was already common knowledge among army officers in 1877 and, to a more limited extent, the general public and even the Indians.

The ancient home of the Nez Perce was a plateau-like area (deeply dissected by the Snake, Salmon and Clearwater rivers) lying immediately to the west of the Bitterroot Range. Between this and the open prairies of Montana Territory, where the final scenes took place, lay the ranges forming the backbone of the Rocky Mountains. Many of the problems of the campaign involved the natural routes across this rugged area—the passes, the river valleys and the bits of open prairie (called "holes") through which travel naturally gravitated.

Most formidable of these mountain barriers was the Bitterroot Range which extended southward from Pend d'Oreille Lake in northern Idaho to the Great Snake River Plains, a distance of about 350 miles. It was then, and still is, a vast wilderness area of mountains and coniferous forests. It could be crossed by going north to the vicinity of Coeur d'Alene Lake and then following the old Mullan Road down St. Regis River to Clark Fork River, and thence up the valley of this stream to the vicinity of Missoula, Montana. Or the traveler could follow the previously noted Lolo or Old Nez Perce (sometimes called Elk City) Trails which ended at either end of the valley of the Bitterroot River. The eastern ends of these routes were only seventy miles apart and the Bitterroot Valley ran like a broad avenue straight from one to the other.

Once across the Bitterroots, there were a number of routes to the plains. However, as the "retreat" developed, the Nez Perce abandoned the ones they had used for years—by reason of proximity to the Montana settlements—and followed a trail used by the Bannocks. This crossed the Yellowstone Park area to the headwaters of Clark Fork and thence to the relatively open country between the Absaroka Range and the northern end of the Big Horn Mountains.

The Nez Perce trouble was not an isolated incident, and it was affected by other troubles which preceded it or were in being at that time. In the immediate past there had been a nasty little fight with the Modocs who lived on the California-Oregon border some 250 miles to the southwest. This was fresh in the minds of many, for some of the troops which had been involved were still stationed in the Department of the Columbia. Howard's aide, Lieutenant William H. Boyle (soon to be promoted to captain), had experienced a very narrow escape. Captain Perry had been seriously wounded in the left shoulder—which his emotionally unstable wife apparently never forgot in the days ahead. Major John Green, a Prussian soldier of the old school, had acquired something of a reputation as a fearless leader by shaming his troops into action after they had balked in a trying situation. And Major Edward C. Mason, soon to be Howard's Chief of Staff, and Colonel Frank Wheaton had also seen action in the lava beds.

Fresh in the minds of every soldier and civilian in the entire country were the incidents in the Sioux war, fought on the plains of Wyoming and Montana the year before. The flamboyant Custer had taken approximately half of the Seventh Cavalry to a spectacular death; and General Alfred Terry, who had left the Headquarters of the Department of Dakota to lead the "Dakota Column," had returned to St. Paul with nothing to show for his summer's work. Colonel Gibbon and the Seventh Infantry had toiled along with the Dakota Column on a no-fight campaign; and during the fall and winter, Colonel Miles, whom Terry had left along the Yellowstone, had been campaigning vigorously with his Fifth Infantry. Thus the troops east of the mountains had been involved in an Indian war for well over a year before the Nez Perce situation exploded.

In addition to Howard's assorted troubles involving the Coeur d'Alenes, Spokanes and "Columbia River Renegades," there were difficulties of several years' standing with the Flatheads, friends of the Nez Perce living in western Montana. Even greater concern was felt about the temper of the Bannocks in eastern Idaho. As one reporter wrote just after the Nez Perce outbreak, "It was the old story of dishonest agents, and the appropriation of their root producing prairies by the encroaching whites." The following year these Indians did fight a needless war to a tragic, inevitable conclusion; and after this was over, General Crook was to write: "It was a matter of surprise to no one acquainted with the facts that some of these Indians should so soon break out into hostility; the great wonder is that so many have remained on the reservation."[1] It is no wonder that the settlers in southern Idaho thought they were sitting on a powder keg when the Nez Perce started fighting.

This uneasiness even extended into northern Nevada where Winnemuca, Chief of the Piutes, sent a telegram to General McDowell asking to come to San Francisco for a conference—giving as a reason "danger that whites may make trouble for their own benefit." In reporting this meeting to General Sherman, McDowell commented that "there is a deep feeling of distrust and dread on the part of both whites and Indians, each of the other that is very favorable to the spreading of the present hostilities."[2] And to the east of the mountains, there was trouble on the Crow agency over an agent and failure of annuities to arrive; and to the north were uneasy Blackfeet, Assiniboins and Gros Ventre—to say nothing of the threat of invasion posed by Sitting Bull's Sioux in Canada.

It is also necessary to understand something of the *modus operandi* of the Army. This permits the understanding of how and why certain things were done, and also explains why tempers became brittle during this campaign. Before the campaign began, a certain amount of bunglesome— but necessary—protocol had to be observed. Matters involving Agent Monteith and General Howard had to be coordinated between the Secretary of the Interior and the Secretary of War in Washington. Thus, although Howard and Monteith discussed the removal of Caldwell and Finney before the May Council, Howard's formal request for action reached Monteith via General McDowell, General Sherman, Secretary of War McCrary, Secretary of Interior Schurz, and Commissioner of Indian Affairs Smith—in the order named. A proper, but far from speedy route!

Although military matters did not require—as a rule—coordination at Cabinet level, any business involving troops in *both* Idaho and Montana did have to be routed through Washington; and anything involving the approval of President Hayes went across the desk of George W. McCrary, Secretary of War. The head of the Army was, of course, General of the Army William T. Sherman, and the "work horse" in his office was the Adjutant General, General Edward D. Townsend, usually referred to as the A. G.—his counterpart in a subordinate office being an Assistant Adjutant General or A. A. G.

For the purposes of administration, the United Sates was divided into *Military Divisions*, of which three were involved in the Nez Perce war. These were the Division of the Atlantic, commanded by Major General Winfield Scott Hancock with headquarters on Governor's Island in New York Harbor; the Division of the Missouri under Lieutenant General Philip H. Sheridan with headquarters in Chicago; and the Division of the Pacific under the direction of Major General Irwin McDowell at San Francisco. All business between these Divisions was coordinated by either Sherman or Townsend, depending upon its importance.

Each Division was subdivided. The Division of the Missouri contained four Departments, among them the *Department of the Platte* and the *Department of Dakota*. The former included Nebraska, Wyoming Territory, Utah, and the extreme eastern part of Idaho Territory, and affairs within this area were administered by Brigadier General George Crook from Omaha, Nebraska. The latter consisted of Dakota Territory (later North & South Dakota), Montana Territory, and Minnesota, all under Brigadier General Alfred H. Terry at St. Paul, Minnesota.

As the heaviest concentration of troops under Terry was in Montana, the posts in this area were grouped under the *District of the Yellowstone* and the *District of Montana*. The former contained the Tongue River Cantonment (with Fort Keogh under construction nearby), which was the Regimental Headquarters of the Fifth Infantry under Colonel Nelson A. Miles, and Fort Custer, also under construction and not yet officially named. The latter was under Colonel John Gibbon, commanding officer of the Seventh Infantry, with headquarters at Fort Shaw on the Sun River. Under his direction were Fort Ellis at the head of the Gallatin Valley, what was soon to be Fort Missoula in the Bitterroot Valley, Camp Baker in the valley of Smith River to the east of Helena, and a small detachment at Fort Benton.

In the extreme west was the *Division of the Pacific* containing the Departments of Arizona, California, and the Columbia. The *Department of California*, containing Nevada Territory and all of California except the southern part, was administered by Division Headquarters. Included in the *Department of the Columbia*, with headquarters at Vancouver Barracks (near Portland, Oregon), were Alaska, Oregon, Washington Territory and all of Idaho except the eastern portion. Its commanding officer was, of course, Brigadier General Oliver Otis Howard.

As the exercise of military authority is predicated on the rule that each commanding officer is responsible for the troops directly under him, the "chain of command" was sometimes involved. Thus, for General Howard to secure the assistance of a handful of troops under Captain Charles C. Rawn at the embryonic Fort Missoula, which was slightly over 100 miles away from the scene of the outbreak, his request had to clear—successively—McDowell, Sherman, Sheridan, Terry, and Gibbon at the above-noted headquarters. Such routing made coordinated effort difficult, although any intelligence deemed urgent or important could be transmitted directly to the interested officer. General Sherman, recognizing that the Nez Perce trouble might not confine itself to the area under Howard's supervision, issued orders nine days after the start of hostilities which cut this procedure to an absolute minimum. While this was to expedite the fighting of this war, it left irritation, flaring tempers, and considerable hard feeling in its wake.

The channels of command were not the only features which were involved and devious. The telegraph office at Walla Walla was over 100 miles from Fort Lapwai and any dispatch to or from it had to be carried by a courier. The communication link with western Montana was by way of a telegraph line which left the Union Pacific Railroad at Corrine, Utah, just north of Salt Lake City. From here it ran northward beside a freighting trail across the Great Snake River Plain, over Monida Pass, and thence to several towns, among them Bozeman, Helena, and Deer Lodge. Thus, a message for Fort Shaw or Fort Missoula still had to complete its journey with the assistance of a horse. Messages for Colonel Miles at the mouth of Tongue River either went down the Yellowstone Valley from Bozeman or across the prairie from Bismarck, Dakota Territory. At one time, a message for Major Hart, in a camp near the present site of Sheridan, Wyoming, was carried up the eastern edge of the Big Horn Mountains from Fort Fetterman on the Platte River. This is why, when General Howard had an urgent message for Captain Rawn at Missoula, he entrusted it to a courier who carried it via the Old Nez Perce Trail and the Bitterroot Valley—some 200 miles, over half of it through a wilderness—to its destination. When the Indians cut the telegraph line in Idaho (north of Corrine), it took several weeks for one message to reach Howard.

Troops actually involved in the fighting came principally from seven regiments. In the Department of the Columbia, there were the Fourth Artillery (acting as infantry), Twenty-first Infantry, and First Cavalry. None of these troops had seen action since the Modoc war a few years before. The Second Infantry, under Colonel Frank Wheaton who had seen service in the Modoc affair, was shipped from Atlanta, Georgia, to Lewiston, where it acted as a sort of garrison for western Idaho while Howard was in Montana.

In the Department of Dakota were the Fifth and Seventh Infantry Regiments, the Seventh Cavalry, and a battalion of the Second Cavalry. Many of these troops had seen action against the Sioux, and Miles' Fifth Infantry had been campaigning almost constantly for about a year. Before the Seventh Cavalry entered the Nez Perce campaign, it had spent most of the summer camped along the Yellowstone near the Tongue River Cantonment. Its commanding officer, Colonel Samuel D. Sturgis, was an old officer who had served since 1842 and was past his prime. He had been away from the regiment when Custer, its second ranking officer, led it to the disaster that claimed the life of Lieutenant James G. Sturgis, the colonel's son. There were many recruits in its ranks and, although they had been toughened by the activities of the summer, they had not been "blooded." And the Fifth Cavalry from the Department of the Platte was sent to an area traversed by the Nez Perce, but arrived too late.

In addition to these routine matters, there were other facets of the military situation which centered around personal pride and ambition. One of these has been termed, quite appropriately, *glory hunting*. For the combat soldier, this was often a route which led to recognition and promotion. Opportunities for *glory hunting* had been limited since the Civil War; and, with the major Indian problems fast being settled, it was easy to see that the future might hold few possibilities in this line. The maneuvering of certain individuals was sometimes quite obvious as the campaign progressed.

This sort of ambitious effort also extended to Department and Division commanders. Howard was to represent not only his own Department but the Division of the Pacific as well. The loyalties of Gibbon, Miles, and Terry belonged to the cocky, hot-tempered, and somewhat vain lieutenant general who was not only the commanding officer of the Division of the Missouri but also the second ranking officer in the Army. As there was a certain amount of prestige involved, Terry did not care to have his counterpart—Howard—shine brightly at his expense; and Sheridan, who had both his rank and prestige to uphold, did not relish having one of McDowell's officers coming into his Division and attracting favorable attention at the expense of any of his officers. Sherman's summary cutting across all chains of command for operational expediency was to allow Howard to operate in Montana under conditions which were to promote professional jealousy in no uncertain manner.

In addition to this explosive situation, there was a smoldering feud between Terry and Howard. This involved seniority based on "date of rank," an important factor when two officers held the same rank. Howard's date of rank as a brigadier general was December 21, 1864, while Terry's commission was dated January 15, 1865—thus Howard "ranked" Terry by twenty-five days. Early in 1877, Terry claimed that, because of a technicality, he should have the preferred position—and Howard bested him in the argument.[3] Thus, Howard's presence in Montana with the *carte blanche* supplied by Sherman was to constitute a double irritation to the Department commander. Shortly after the campaign ended, Howard wrote this appraisal of his position for the President of the Historical Society of Montana:

> I am not worried with regard to the part my command bore in the campaign, in fact I was the senior officer in the Dept. of Dakota & therefore bore the responsibility of what several officers, viz:— Miller, E. Miles, Sanford, Sturgis and N. A. Miles did. The Campaign which was rendered lively by Joseph's escapade was conducted under *my direction*, & therefore *I* must submit to be loaded with the usual amount of criticism.[4]

Jealousy was present in various forms. The regular soldiers looked down on the volunteers—partly because of professional jealously, and partly because they could not be depended on when the going was tough. And Howard's foot troops regarded the First Cavalry with disdain. Some of this may have been interservice rivalry but not all of it, for the Cavalry, which fought in Idaho, gave a rather poor account of itself. Early in the war, Howard's Chief of Staff wrote to his wife that "I thank my stars that my lot was not cast with an arm of the service that *will not* fight. We hope for [Major] John Green, if he can't make these fellows fight, it is useless to try."[5]

And within the ranks of this regiment, Captain Trimble's junior officer pointed an accusing finger at Captain Perry after the Clearwater battle.[6]

Perhaps there are no pieces of vital intelligence that are more important than those which pertain to the characteristics of a commanding general, as these often make possible reasonable explanations of what has happened, as well as predictions of what may be expected. General Howard was no exception, and some of the factors which affected his decisions have heretofore gone unnoted.

Howard graduated from West Point in 1854, the fourth in his class, and went on to a distinguished career in the Civil War. At the Battle of Fair Oaks, he had two horses shot from under him, was severely wounded, and finally his right arm was so badly shattered that part of it had to be amputated; and in 1864, he was given prominent mention in a "resolution of thanks" passed by Congress for the victory at Gettysburg. In May, 1865, he was appointed head of the recently established Bureau of Refuges,

Freedmen, and Abandoned Lands. This assignment brought him a great deal of trouble, for the rank and file of the minor officials in this bureau were either unfit or unworthy, and soon the organization reeked with fraud, corruption and inefficiency. Howard refused to believe that some of his subordinates were guilty of misconduct, and in 1870, a Congressional committee made an investigation. The general was cleared by the committee, only to have Secretary of War, General William W. Belknap—who was later impeached for fraud—prefer charges for misuse of funds and keeping unsatisfactory records. Howard requested a Court of Inquiry, and, in 1874, was again exonerated.

In July, 1874, the general was placed in command of the Department of the Columbia—which removed him from the scene of his troubles but not from the entangling web of circumstances. In the winter of 1876–1877, the old trouble was revived by the Adjutant General's office, and not long afterward, Howard wrote a revealing personal letter to General Sherman, who was a very close friend—Howard having commanded the right wing of Sherman's army on his famous march "from Atlanta to the sea." This read, in part:

> Permit me to write you on public matters that affect me personally from a personal standpoint.
>
> In the middle of page 5 (Annual Report on Freedmen's Branch Adjutant General's Office, 1876) of Major Vincent's[7] report just issued you will notice the old summation which was presented to the court in one shape or another again rehashed.
>
> * * *
>
> You say, dear General, patience, patience, and I am patient and hopeful. but in spite of my philosophy, I begin to meditate on these things when I ought to be asleep.
>
> I worked last year besides my official duty by writing for the Magazines so that I cleared about $800.00. To my surprise the law firm that I had to employ . . . sent me a bill . . . of $575 additional to what I had already paid making just $800 for all such services in Oregon. I have sold my carriage and horses. I live in as cheap a . . . [state?] as I dare . . . consistent with my duty to the Government. I keep but one servant and my excellent wife is very economical. . . . I have had taken from me for a series of years more than half my pay for [legal expenses]. . . . * * *
>
> When I went to Washington in 1868 I had more than $20,000 worth of property. Now it is all heavily encumbered so that I would be glad to be made square with one fifth of that amount. Now by technicality of law . . . it is sought to recover from *me* personally money accounting to hundreds of thousands of dollars. * * * You laugh at this; every body does; & says "Wait it will come right." Yes,

but my hair is whitening, and my *heart* is very heavy. I have given loyal service to my country. I have spilt my blood on more than one field. * * * but Vincent through the Adjutant Generals office issues to the army and to the world documents that reflect upon my administration & upon my integrity & he is diligently through the Attorney General, through the U. S. Treasury & what not, to follow me with exhausting suits even into Oregon. * * * May I not rest![8]

There was to be no rest for Howard until over a year later when he again stood trial in Washington and was cleared in a civil court. Many letters in his files stand as evidence that this matter was a worry of *considerable* magnitude during the time the Nez Perce campaign was in progress—some of these even being written while in the field. It would seem that the tension from this affair had a subtle but definite effect on a number of things which the general did. However, all of Howard's financial troubles did not stem from the Freedmen's scandal. They came from a variety of sources and even a casual perusal of Howard's files, for the period preceding this campaign, is ample to indicate that poor judgment was probably to blame for much of his financial grief.

While the general public may not have been aware of Howard's lack of financial ability, he had other characteristics of which few, if any, were ignorant, One high-ranking staff officer who knew him during the Civil War noted that "he is the only religious man of high rank I know of in this army," and he was widely known at the "Christian General." He commanded professional respect from fellow officers because he was capable and had the kind of guts it took to sit on a horse and lead a charge with a bloody, shattered arm flopping at his side. But he also taught Sunday school, preached, and led temperance rallies with equal zeal—to which he once referred as "my peculiar reputation." And he was accused of not campaigning on Sunday during this war—although a day-by-day study of events indicate that this slur was without foundation. Nevertheless, he was the butt of jokes such as this one:

THE INDIAN WAR

Scene—Camp at Kamia

Aide de Camp—General, Joseph is again in full retreat, and I think he is making for the Buffalo Country. Shall we pursue?

The General—No! Telegraph the glorious news to McDowell. Go ask Keeler[9] to endorse it and then come in to prayers.[10]

Emily FitzGerald—a religious lady who also taught Sunday school on occasion—first met General Howard while her husband was stationed at Sitka, Alaska. The description she penned her mother on June 29, 1875, is revealing in several ways. Of the general, who, with his aide Lieutenant

Melville C. Wilkinson, had arrived to attend a court-martial hearing, she wrote:

> General Howard has come to command this department. * * * I have heard the officers discuss him and he is not very popular among them. It is owing to his ferocious religion. He is one of those unfortunate Christians who continually give outsiders a chance to laugh and have something to make fun of. He says himself, "You know, I am a fanatic on the subject." He. . . . preaches and leads meetings on all occasions—on street corners, steamboats, etc. General Howard is an excellent speaker, has a charming voice, and uses beautiful language, but he does all his good in such a queer way, he gives people something to smile at. About eleven o'clock the night the boat came in, Captain Hayes, the old captain of the California,[11] came in to the steps to shake hands with me. I said, "Well, Captain, you brought us a crowd this time." He said, dropping his voice, "Mrs. FitzGerald, the knees are worn out of every pair of pants I got praying."[12]

His aide, Wilkinson, was cast in the same mold. He also told Mrs. FitzGerald, "You know, I am a ranting religionist!"—a statement that was confirmed by another officer who was "a good church member." Chief of Staff Major Edward C. Mason was also a religious man, although not of the "ranting" sort. On one occasion, when the troops were plagued by rain, he wrote to his wife that his "nice Bible that mother gave me" was having a hard time of it, and on another occasion, he requested that she send him one of Moody & Sankey's hymnbooks—"The General wants me to sing 'What Shall the Harvest Be' and other hymns, to him."

In spite of Howard's religious professions, there is a curious inconsistency between what he professed and what he advocated for the Nez Perce. At first he was sympathetic with the Indians, and then, after being subjected to political pressures and contact with Barstow, Stickney, *et al.*, he espoused the popular hue and cry that if a white settler could grub more dollars from a piece of land than an Indian, the former should be allowed to take it. He hated the Dreamer faith—which contained some admirable beliefs—probably because its tenets ran counter to a policy to which he was committed. And he apparently gave wholehearted support to the shabby treatment given Joseph's people after their surrender—even to finding excuses to support the policy. It would seem that if it was necessary to give *official* approval, he might have withheld his *personal* sanction.

Thus, there were subtle forces in the background which have made some aspects of the Nez Perce war difficult to understand. Howard's military decisions were basically sound, but psychological forces undoubtedly colored many minor details.

6

"The Die Is Cast"

>>>>>>><<<<<<< Little is known of the movement of the Non-Treaty Indians from the areas claimed by them to the Reservation. Huishuis Kute, who lived along the Snake River below Lewiston, came on the Reserve about a week before the outbreak and located some ten miles north of the Agency. Immediately after coming in, the chief came down to the Agency and asked for a pass to go to the country of the Spokanes— farther to the north. This was refused. Then as soon as word of the initial murders arrived—on the evening of June 15th—a messenger was dispatched to his camp. Here only the very young and the aged were found, the others having departed—without permission—to visit the Spokanes.[1]

The bands of Joseph, White Bird, and Too-hool-hool-zote gathered at Tepahlewam, an ancient camping ground on the southern edge of Camas Prairie between Lake Tolo and the head of Rocky Canyon. Although the rivers were at flood stage from melting snow in the mountains, the hazardous crossings were apparently completed without serious mishap as far as members of the bands were concerned, but the roundup of their stock was incomplete. Perhaps a large part of the horses was gathered but certainly most of the cows and calves had been abandoned. Enough of both were left to attract white thieves in the weeks ahead.

At Tepahlewam, as in years past, the assembly took on a festive air. Indians from the Agency, from the sub-agency at Kamiah, and from the Clearwater Valley gathered to join the festivities—among them Looking Glass and his band. While the women dug camas, they visited, danced, gambled, and raced horses. But it was not a completely happy occasion, for there was an attitude of smoldering discontent, and resentment. In spite of this, it does not appear that there were any evidences of this on the surface, although settlers imagined and/or reported sinister councils were held with warlike parades and maneuvers.

It is impossible to state with certainty the actual reason for the initial murders. At the time, many people, among them General Howard, jumped to the conclusion that it was a reprisal killing for Larry Ott's wanton murder of Eagle Robe. But Ott turned up unharmed. About a month later, General McDowell's aide asked Ad Chapman why the trouble began. According to this officer,

> Mr C stated that the war had been precipitated by 13 thieving desperadoes of White Birds band who had been some time of that section; that these scoundrels believing that Joseph & the other chiefs did not intend to make war commenced it on their own account on the AM of June 14th by murdering 4 citizens & robbing their ranches; that by boasting of their prowess, exhibiting their stolen plunder etc the mass of the band were induced to join in force, that Joseph joined reluctantly.[2]

While there is probably a certain element of truth in this opinion, part of it is not in agreement with other, more logical, accounts.

There are several variations of the Indian account, of which one seems far more probable than all the others. And of this one, there are at least two, slightly different, versions. One of these was sent to the Portland *Daily Standard* by an unknown correspondent and appeared in print on the 28th of August:

> At their last meeting [Tepahlewam] everything went on as before, but, says the Indian, they had liquor there, and that caused hard words among them. One Indian, who was engaged to a young maiden from the Umatilla reservation was considerably enraged by sundry taunts from his half drunken comrades. They told him that the girl would never be his squaw because he was a coward, as he had never killed a white man. Then they bantered him, and even bet

him, that he dare not do it, because his heart was "skukum," and that he was afraid. He stood it for some time, but presently went away, and no one cared. Toward evening he returned to camp and yelled, "Now I have killed a Boston man!" And he proved it. They went back to the house and found the dead man, but all was quiet and deserted. He kept a store, and the Indians began helping themselves. They also found some liquor and all drank freely, because a strange feeling pervaded them, and they said, "liquor will drive it out." That night they killed three more white men, and with one accord shouted the war whoop. This is the way, says the Indian, the war began.

Except for one or two minor discrepancies which are not particularly important, this account checks very closely with details provided by others. And it indicates that whiskey created the necessary environment to start trouble—which various stray bits of intelligence tend to support.

A second version appeared less than a year later. This was written by Duncan McDonald, the Scotch-Nez Perce half-breed trader who lived near Missoula. There is no clue as to where he got the story—perhaps from Poker Joe (Lean Elk), a Nez Perce living in the Bitterroot Valley who visited the Hostiles just after this trouble flared:

Wallitze was a gay Lothario among his tribe, and one evening he made love to one of the red female beauties, and advancing toward her asked her to go with him to his lodge. At his request she consented and went with him. Early the next morning the mother of the girl was told her daughter had gone to live with Wallitze. She started for his lodge raving mad and seeing her daughter lying with Wallitze she took hold of the girl and threw her toward the door. Then turning to Wallitze [she upbraided him for continually seducing women]. . . . "But you did not act like a man after your father Tip-iala-natzikan was murdered. . . . Why don't you go after the whites?"

To these words Wallitze gave no notice. That evening there was a Kissing Dance among the Nez Perces, a place where any Indian would have been pleased if Wallitze had not gone. On reaching the dancing floor and while dancing around he was told by one of the young braves, a relative of the girl he took the night before: "Here you are again. You need not be so stylish when in public. We know you are a coward." Of these words he took no notice. On the second round the same language was repeated by the same Indian. Wallitze stopped and asked, "Do you mean what you say?" The brave replied, "I do. You are a coward and nothing else. There is your father's grave. He was murdered by a white man and you have not the manliness to kill him who slew your father." Wallitze being thus spoken to in the presence of so many women and men of his own people was abashed. "All right," he said, "you will be sorry for what you have spoken." He left the dance and went to his lodge to sleep. The next morning at day-break he was up. Some Indians say that Tap-sis-ill-pilp was with him already, but the third man, a young boy, was not seen. He said, "I remember the last words of my father. . . .* * * Do not go to war. You will lose your country. . . . But now I am going to satisfy the man who insulted me last night." On this very day Wallitze, Tap-sis-ill-pilp and the third began their bloody work on the Idaho settlements.[3]

The only difference of major importance between these two accounts is that the first states that there was whiskey in the camp. Either with or without the liquor, this account has a convincing ring.

For his foray, Wahlitits recruited two relatives. One was Sarpsis Ilppilp (Red Moccasin Tops) who was the son of Chusulum Moxmox (Yellow Bull), and Wetyetmas Wahyakt (Swan Necklace), a lad about sixteen years old who was taken along, perhaps to act as a horse holder.[4] Apparently, Wahlitits made no secret of his purpose, for Yellow Wolf claimed later that he rode after the trio and tried to persuade his son to turn back. It was but a short distance to the breaks along the Salmon River, and the three then descended the great hills and boldly rode up the trail along the river to search for their victim. It was Wednesday, June 13th.

There are several accounts of what happened during the first days of terror. These consist of letters written at the time or shortly afterward, and interviews with participants which were set down by J. W. Poe, L. P. Brown (the hotelkeeper in Mount Idaho), and by Thomas Sutherland, the war correspondent who accompanied General Howard throughout the campaign. All agree remarkably well as to various details; and, fortunately, Editor Leland seems to have printed verbatim the material sent to him.

"Three Indians had gone up the river the day before. . . . Squaws passed up and down about as usual [on the morning of the 14th] and the leading indications of Indian war were wanting," according to Helen J. Walsh who was at the store of her brother, Harry Mason, about two miles above the mouth of White Bird Creek. About eight miles farther on at the mouth of Slate Creek, the trio stopped at an establishment operated by Charles and Harry Cone. The latter, who could speak Nez Perce, recalled years afterward that they asked for food and "bullets" (cartridges?). They were sold food but no ammunition; and Cone thought it strange that two were riding double on a very ordinary-looking pony, when they usually had good horses.

There were amiable relations between the Indians and the settlers in the Slate Creek settlement, and these had dated from 1861 when an early settler had purchased the site from an Indian named Captain John. The next year, John Wood bought the tract and, with his wife, opened a way station called the Slate Creek House. In 1874, Charles F. Cone purchased a part of Wood's holding and opened another station, and in 1876, Wood and Joshua Fockler opened a store.[5] As Wood and the Cone brothers had treated the Indians decently—in contrast to Sam Benedict, Harry Mason and, perhaps, H. C. Brown where evidence indicates otherwise—the Indians now acted with equal consideration.

Larry Ott's part in what took place is puzzling. The oft-told story is that he became alarmed and fled to Florence where he disguised himself as a Chinaman until the danger passed. Against this stands the hard fact that the roster of the Slate Creek volunteers—made up on June 30th and forwarded to Governor Brayman on July 4th—contains the name of Larry Ott in what appears to be his own handwriting; and on the roster of the Mount Idaho volunteers, dated July 15th, his name appears as No. 39 on the list.

The main trail up the valley of the Salmon runs beside the right or eastern bank; and Ott's "farm" was on the opposite side of the stream in the vincinity of Horseshoe Bend—a horseshoe loop midway between the mouths of White Bird and Slate creeks. It lay in front of a semicircular-shaped indentation in the hills which was favorable to the creation of echoes. According to a story still told at Grangeville, the Indians, in passing up and down, would "holler at Ott" across the river, and this finally made him so nervous that he went to Florence and hid.[6] But this explanation, in view of the muster rolls, is unconvincing. Perhaps the trio did not care to swim the Salmon just to shoot a man when there were others who were also disliked.

In a summary prepared for Major Hancock after the war was over, J. W. Poe stated: "The commencement of the [outbreak] . . . as near as I can ascertain, was late in the afternoon of Wednesday, June 13th, by the killing of Richard Devine, an old man who lived alone on Salmon River, about 12 miles above Slate Creek."[7] Contemporary accounts indicate that the man was ill at the time, and that the Indians entered the house and shot him, perhaps with his own gun.

Then the trio began to retrace their steps. Early the next morning they were a few miles downstream at the John Day ranch where Henry Elfers lived. Elfers had been involved in the arbitration of a case decided against the Indians—namely, the charge that Harry Mason had whipped a couple of Nez Perce. Here, according to Poe, they killed Henry J. Elfers, Robert Bland, and Harry "Burn" Becktoge "between six and seven o'clock in the morning" as the men were working in a field. Apparently, they did not molest Mrs. Elfers and her three children, although they took a couple of "fine guns" (probably 1873 model Winchester rifles), a quantity of ammunition, two workhorses, and a "race" horse.

At the little Slate Creek settlement, the Indians made a detour and came back into the trail a mile or two below where they met Charley Cone. Cone recognized the horses they were riding as being the property of Elfers and when he made inquiry about them, Wahlitits told him frankly that they had killed their owner and indicated there would be trouble. Then, naming many of the settlers in the area, he advised that they go to Slate Creek indicating that as the people there had treated the Indians fairly, they would not harm or rob those named. Cone promptly spread the alarm.

In a letter written about two and a half months later, Mrs. Helen Walsh detailed what happened along the Salmon River just above White Bird Creek. Cone's warning reached them early in the afternoon, but her brother, Harry Mason, believed the trouble was the result of the three Indians, whom they had seen the day before, getting drunk; and that there was no uprising. Then a man known as "Koon" came up from White Bird with the information that Sam Benedict had been shot in the legs and that the settlers were to gather at James Baker's place at White Bird. After some indecision, a party consisting of three men, two women, and six small children started:

> About six o'clock the Osborne's came down and we started down the river for Mr. Bakers. We only had three horses in all. When we got to the Whitebird creek, near Mr. Bakers, we who had horses rode over, there dismounted and sent the horses back for the others; we had all crossed, and were just mounting our horses again, when we heard a whoop, and looking ahead saw a band of about 18 or 20 Indians right in front of us; we were on a flat near an enclosure which I believed to be Mr. Baker's garden. The Indians called out for the men to come and talk with them. But the men only told them to leave, when the Indians began firing. Mrs. Osborne ran to the fence and pulling off a couple of pickets pushed two of her children through and followed after. Her husband went through with the other two. I waited to see what Harry was going to do. He stood with his gun in position looking around as if considering whether to fight or run. He could not get his ammunition off his horse, and he decided it was better to save that in his gun (a Winchester) for a greater emergency. When I asked him if I could go after the others he said yes; so I started with my children and he followed. We crossed a corner of the garden through tall grass and bushes. The Indians firing every little while haphazard, as it was getting quite dark. We waded across the creek and hid in some bushes until the moon went down. Mr. George did not follow us when we ran. I will

mention here that French Frank and Shoemaker stayed at Harry's place. When it grew quite dark and we could see nothing of the Indians, we started up one of the gulches to the ridge. About half way up we met Mr. George who had been wounded in the finger. He had started for . . . [Camas] prairie. Harry gave him directions to find the way without getting in the road. Harry would not start for the prairie then because there was danger unless we could get to Mt. Idaho before daylight. His plan was to go back to his place, get some food for the children and cross the river before daylight, hide on the other side during the day and start out the next night. But it was slow traveling with six small children, the oldest I believe was 9 years old, and the sun rose before we reached Harry's house: . . .[8]

Several people lived in the little valley near the mouth of White Bird Creek. James Baker, who was seventy-four years old, lived near the river; and H. C. Brown had a store just below the mouth of White Bird Creek. Sam Benedict's "store" was a little farther up the valley and nearby lived J. J. ("Jack") Manuel and his family. It was somewhere near this area that, on their return to camp, Wahlitits and his confederates met Sam Benedict, who was out hunting cattle. They wounded him in the legs, but he managed to elude them for the time being.

About five days later, George Popham related his experiences to L. P. Brown. He began, "I was stopping at Jack Manuel's, my son-in-laws, since last fall. The first alarm we had was on Thursday about noon, when we saw three Indians go past, soon after Mr. Baker and Fruth came to Manuel's and told us that three Indians just past had shot Sam Benedict in the legs. Mr. Baker wanted to come to the prairie and inform the people, but Manuel did not deem it was safe for any of them to leave. Mr. Baker went home and in a short time returned with Pat Price and intended to come to Mt. Idaho, and they had only gone a short distance when they saw the Indians coming."[9]

It was only about ten miles, as a crow flies, from the White Bird settlement to the Indian camp on the prairie above, but much of the distance was up a great broken slope that was not conducive to speed. Probably the trio reached camp early in the afternoon, whereupon their arrival created immediate and intense excitement. According to one Indian account, one of the stolen horses and a rifle were given to Big Dawn, who rode through the camp calling attention to the spoils of the foray and sounding a rallying cry for the malcontents who had desired war. Soon a party, said to have been seventeen in number, collected and set off for the cabins nestling at the foot of the great White Bird Hill. Here, at Sam Benedict's and, probably, at the store of H. C. Brown, they found sufficient liquor to fire their passions to a high degree.

According to Popham's story:

> Baker, Manuel's wife and children started to go down to Baker's house, had got but a short ways when they were surrounded by the Indians, about 20 in number, they killed Baker and Manuel. Mrs. Manuel fell from her horse and they ravished her and afterwards killed her by a stab in the breast. The little girls arm was broken and the baby boy was killed. Mrs. Manuel got back to the house and the Indians told her that if Price and myself would give up all the arms and ammunition we had they would not kill us. We gave up a Henry rifle and a shot gun. We kept secreted through that night and Friday night. On Saturday about 11 A.M., the Indians came down the hill from the prarie, Price went to the brush and stayed all night, I also took to the timber. On Sunday morning they burnt the house and Mrs. Manuel and the child were burnt in it.[10]

This account is scanty, incomplete and confusing in that it does not state that Mrs. Manuel was killed *after* returning to her home. About two weeks later, Howard's troops "rescued citizen Manual wounded and starving"; and Sutherland, who saw him in Mount Idaho a few days later, wrote:

> The Indians attacked his house in the night [sic—evening], Manuel being shot through the fleshy part of the small of the back by a rifle and wounded between the shoulders with an arrow with a steel barb. He escaped to an outhouse and remained there for several days, living on strawberries and roots.[11]

Baker was killed along the road between his cabin and Manuel's, where Mrs. Benedict saw him a short time later with his papers scattered about him. However, the Indians dragged his body into the brush where it was not found until a month later.[12] Sam Benedict was shot as he attempted to escape across White Bird Creek, and his body was found later lodged against a rock in the stream. And, according to L. P. Brown, Mrs. Benedict "reports Geo Woodard and Peter Bertard killed at Baker's house and her husband and August [Bacon] killed at her home. About 20 Indians made the attack. They then went to H. C. Brown's house and store."[13]

Scattered bits indicate that when Wahlitits and his companions returned, the women came in from their camas-digging at once, and the attitude of the camp ranged from excitement at one extreme to alarm and consternation at the other. The men began to gather their stock, and the women to take down the tepees and pack personal effects. In the midst of this confusion—according to statements made by Indians not long after-

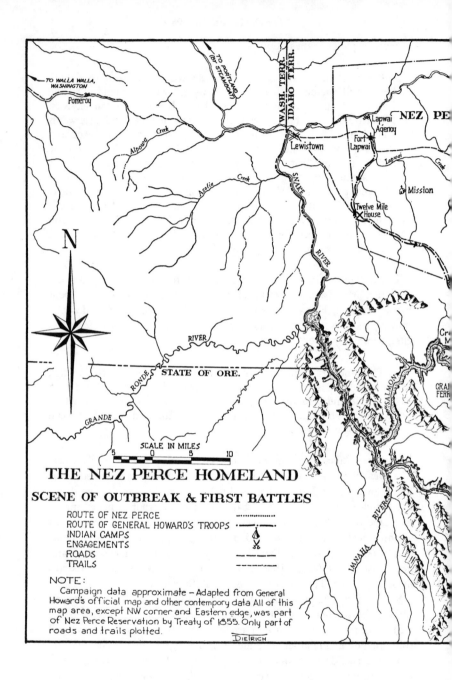

THE NEZ PERCE HOMELAND

SCENE OF OUTBREAK & FIRST BATTLES

ROUTE OF NEZ PERCE
ROUTE OF GENERAL HOWARD'S TROOPS
INDIAN CAMPS
ENGAGEMENTS
ROADS
TRAILS

NOTE:
Campaign data approximate – Adapted from General
Howard's official map and other contempory data All of this
map area, except NW corner and Eastern edge, was part
of Nez Perce Reservation by Treaty of 1855. Only part of
roads and trails plotted.

DIETRICH

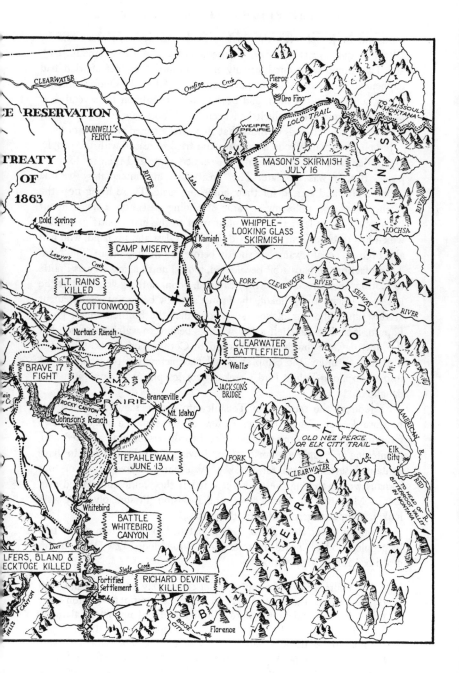

E RESERVATION

TREATY
OF
1863

CLEARWATER

DUNWELL'S FERRY

Orofino Creek

Pierce

Oro Fino

WEIPPE PRAIRIE

LOLO TRAIL

TO MISSOULA MONTANA

MASON'S SKIRMISH
JULY 16

Cold Springs

RIVER

Lolo Creek

Lawyers Creek

CAMP MISERY

Kamiah

WHIPPLE-
LOOKING GLASS
SKIRMISH

LT. RAINS
KILLED

COTTONWOOD

Norton's Ranch

M FORK CLEARWATER RIVER

SELWAY RIVER

LOCHSA

"BRAVE 17"
FIGHT

CAMAS

Grangeville

PRAIRIE

Mt. Idaho

CLEARWATER
BATTLEFIELD

Walls

JACKSON'S
BRIDGE

Nez Perce

ROCKY CANYON

Johnson's Ranch

TEPAHLEWAM
JUNE 13

FORK

OLD NEZ PERCE
OR ELK CITY TRAIL

CLEARWATER

Elk
City

R.

TO HEAD OF RED
BITTERROOT VALLEY
IN MONTANA

Whitebird

BATTLE
WHITEBIRD
CANYON

LFERS, BLAND &
ECKTOGE KILLED

Deer Cr.

Slate Creek

Fortified
Settlement

RICHARD DEVINE
KILLED

HELLS CANYON

Day Cr.

TO BOISE CITY

Florence

BITTERROOT MOUNTAINS

ward and by Joseph after the final surrender, as well as a story told by Ollokot's squaw years afterward[14]—Joseph and a small party came in sight, and Two Moon went out hurriedly and informed the chief of what had happened. This party, said to have consisted of Joseph, Ollokot and his squaw, and four other men, had been across the Salmon for several days butchering some cattle which had been left behind; and it was on their return with several loads of meat that they were greeted with this news.

Joseph immediately rode into camp and tried to reason with the people, saying that they should wait until the soldiers came and then try to make peace. But, it was too late. The Treaty Indians immediately became apprehensive and started for their homes in haste. Those living near the Agency, some 60 miles away, came streaming past Fort Lapwai about twenty-four hours later to add confirmation to the first reports of trouble which had reached General Howard. Looking Glass and his band, who had also been at Tepahlewam, left shortly before the trouble began. The Non-Treaty faction, perhaps a bit bewildered, moved north across Camas Prairie to Cottonwood Creek where they camped. Soon, nothing was left but the lodges of Joseph and Ollokot, the former's squaw being near confinement at this time. The war faction, suspicious that the brothers might go to Lapwai, is said to have left a few warriors behind to watch the chief; but the next day, the brothers also moved to Cottonwood Creek. Then the next day, Saturday, the camp streamed back across the prairie and went into camp along White Bird Creek, where Joseph's wife gave birth to a daughter.

As soon as the move from Tepahlewam began, scouts scattered out northward over Camas Prairie. A few of these met a wagon or two freighting goods to Mount Idaho. The two drivers became alarmed and, unhitching a couple of horses, fled, leaving their loads—said to have contained several barrels of whiskey. As evening neared, three or four Indians were watching the trail where it left the prairie and started over Craig's Mountain for Fort Lapwai and Lewiston. Presumably, they were looking for messengers headed for the post.

According to the story Editor Leland patched together from stories told by people who had "heard the statements of Joe Moore, Lew Day upon his death bed and of Mrs. Norton":

> On Thursday eve at about 6 o'clock Lew Day left Mt. Idaho with dispatches for Ft. Lapwai. He crossed the prairie to Norton's, 17 miles. Norton and family were still at home and not much alarmed. Day proceeded up the mountain. . . . Three or four Indians pretending to be friendly had joined him on the mountain and were riding in his company. Day told them he was getting cold and must ride faster, and spurred his horse to go ahead. He soon came to a

mudhole and his horse checked his speed a little and the Indians fired at him from behind and wounded him. He spurred his horse from the road to the timber and returned the fire, and the Indians disappeared. He took a cross cut and returned to Norton's. . . .[15]

On his return to Cottonwood House, Mrs. Norton dressed his wound as best she could. Then, believing that the Indians meant trouble, he insisted on returning to Mount Idaho to warn the settlers. Staying at Norton's that night was a settler named John Chamberlain, his wife and two children; and it was decided that all would seek protection at Mount Idaho. Chamberlain's team was hitched to a wagon, and the party set out with Chamberlain driving the wagon and Norton on Day's horse. (Howard wrote that Moore was also mounted; and, when a very old lady, Mrs. Norton stated that Day was too.) In addition to the transient family and Day, the group included Mrs. Norton and her son, Hill B. Norton, aged nine and a half, her sister, Miss Lynn Bowers, and a man named Joe Moore, who was probably a helper employed by Norton—a total of ten persons. It was about 10 o'clock when the start was made and, as it was a "starlight" night, they were able to see fairly well.

The Indians attacked them about 7 or 8 miles on the road to Mt. Idaho. They ran their horses and returned the fire, and kept the Indians at bay. * * * Norton rode Day's horse until shot under him and after a running fight of some time they arrived within six miles of Mt. Idaho. The Indians shot the horses attached to the wagon; and killed them. Norton then came to the wagon, and he and Mrs. Norton, Mrs. Chamberlain and Linn Bowers and the children got under the wagon, the Indians shooting at the bed of the wagon. Day and Moore got between the two dead horses and used them as breastworks, keeping up the fire upon the Indians and kept them at bay until daylight.[16]

Several things happened before daylight came. Day became very thirsty —as wounded often do—and Norton went to hunt for a puddle of water. During this search, he was hit in the thigh by a bullet which cut an artery. Realizing that he was doomed to bleed to death, he directed his son and sister-in-law to crawl away through the high grass and try to escape to Mount Idaho. Mrs. Norton, having been hit in the calves of both legs by a bullet, was unable to travel far. Day had been hit again—if Mrs. Norton's memory can be trusted fifty years later—and Moore lost two fingers and then was completely disabled by a shot in the hips. And Chamberlain had taken his wife and children and vanished into the night. Two weeks later, after visiting the improvised hospital at the Mount Idaho Hotel, correspondent Sutherland reported that

Mrs. Norton, wife of the Cottonwood creek settler and stage station keeper, is a very pretty brunette, with soft, large eyes, like an antelope. She was very communicative, and recited to me the entire story of her husband's and Mr. Chamberlain's deaths, and how, when she was shot through the calves of her legs, and all ammunition gone, Moore gallantly frightened off the remnant of the red devils left to guard her till daylight, by pointing at them his empty gun.[17]

Apparently, there was a little more to the story than this. Emily Fitz-Gerald, who probably got the story from Captain Perry after the White Bird fight, wrote:

At last these people used up all their ammunition. . . . but they knew that in Norton's pockets were some cartridges that fit another gun [shotgun?], and one of them crawled under the wagon where Norton's dead body was and got them. Then . . . [they] opened these cartridges and got out the powder, so that the men could, at intervals of five and ten minutes make a flash with it to make the Indians think they were still prepared for them and on the alert.[18]

Early the next morning, three settlers—Frank Fenn (not the Delegate), Charles Rice, and James Adkinson—found young Norton, who had become separated from his aunt during the night. They immediately rode in search of the survivors, finding them in the nick of time. Stripping the harness from the dead horses, and hitching two of their horses to the wagon, they put the living into the wagon and, with Rice on the spare horse and the other two on the horses hitched to the wagon, were ready to start.

just as the Indians made another charge upon them. . . . [they ran the horses] at the top of their speed pursued by the Indians to Crook's lane [Grangeville]. The Indians then abandoned the chase. They had to leave the body of Norton . . . , also their saddles which were taken by the Indians.[19]

Soon after, a searching party, numbering about forty, found Chamberlain about a hundred yards from the dead horses. The children were beside him, one dead, the other alive. Their mother was found some distance away. Sutherland, who visited them at the same time as he did Mrs. Norton, wrote:

Mrs. Chamberlain and her child . . . tried to escape in the dark, but both were captured, the mother having previously been wounded in the breast by an arrow. The fiends, in order to hasten the steps of the child, jabbed a knife diagonally through its neck, and when she cried they cut off the end of her tongue. The poor mother, already on the verge of maternity . . . was brutally outraged by the brutes. . . .[20]

And Poe, in his report, noted, "when this was accomplished, they took their hands and lacerated her womb and the poor woman was left broken and bleeding on the prairie."

[And the little boy] was killed according to the statement of the mother by having its head placed between the knees of a powerful Indian and crushed to death. . . .[21]

Lew Day, hit in the shoulder and leg, lived six days. Joe Moore lingered for about three months before the end came.

Although security and kind hands were in the offing for the two wounded women on Camas Prairie when the sun rose on June 15th—and Lynn Bowers would be found shortly—this was not true for the others who had spent the night on the hills near the mouth of White Bird Creek. Mrs. Walsh recalled:

The sun rose before we reached Harry's house; when we were near, still back of the ridge. Harry went ahead to reconnoitre. He saw the two men who had stayed there, moving around as though getting ready for breakfast and of course concluded that all was right there, so we went down the mountain. When we arrived at the house, we found that the Indians had been through and plundered the house in the night and had gone up the river. The two men had run out and hid until the Indians went on. Harry said we must get out as soon as possible. I turned out the contents of two stone crocks of bread and cake and set out a dish of cold meat and the children were each given a handful, and two of the men each filled a sack and tied them around their waists, and we started out again. It was considered best to cross the river at the french claim [gold placer mine]; and we started up there. French Frank went with us; Shoemaker stopped to let the calves out and did not catch up with us. Just as we got near Osborne's cabin the Indians came in sight, we all ran in and the Indians rode up and called on the men to come out; Mr. Osborne told them to *Clatawa*. They called out again, and Mr. Osborne told them to leave. They shouted that they would make us come out and began firing rocks at the window, a small one with three lights. As soon as the window was broken the men raised their guns to fire on the Indians and each man was shot down before he had time to shoot. In two minutes from the first shot all three were prone on the floor. Mr. Osborne was killed almost instantly, and the others were

badly wounded. The Indians continued firing for some time before
venturing to come in. They also threw a bundle of burning rags into
the house. Mrs. Osborne and myself with our children, only escaped
being shot by crawling under the bed. When the cowards found our
men were hopeless, they came in and dragged them out of doors,
giving Harry and French Frank each a final shot. They told us that
they did not want to kill us; that we could go to Slate Creek or
Lewiston without fear. They also told us who they had killed up the
river and down. They mentioned some who were afterwards found
alive. Harry did not live to know that his friend at John Days
[Elfers?] was killed. When the Indians first surrounded the cabin,
my brother sprang on to one of the beds to fire through a crevice
between the logs. He had a good chance at about 6 or 8 savages, who
seemed to be unconscious of danger, but just as he was going to
shoot, Mr. Osborne called out, "don't shoot yet!" At the same time
Mrs. Osborne called, "don't shoot, Harry." He turned and looked at
them lowering his gun without a word. I shall never forget that look.
There was a prophecy in it. He knew he was giving up his last
chance.[22]

Although Mrs. Walsh ended her letter at this point, there is more to the
story. Poe reported that "Mrs. Osborne and Mrs. Walsh fell into the
hands of the Indians and received treatment that was but little better than
death." They went to the stockade at Slate Creek afterward, where a
trooper with a guard detail later made a note in his "diary" which confirms
Poe's statement. When Howard's troops were at White Bird thereafter, a
group of volunteers went up the river to bury the dead men. The leader of
this detail recalled that "there was little left but the feet which were
encased in boots."

There were anxious moments at Slate Creek, despite the assurances
Wahlitits had given Charley Cone. Here, as at Mount Idaho, the settlers
erected rough fortifications behind which all the women and children in
the surrounding area took refuge; and the settlers prepared to resist with
every weapon available. While tension was at its greatest, John Wood
described conditions in a letter addressed to Editor Leland:

We can't get below [to bury the dead at White Bird]. . . . We
have sent above and buried the dead found on the river. We have
here with us the following families: Mrs. Walsh and her two
children, Mrs. Osborne and her 4 children, Mr. and Mrs. Titman
and two children, Wm Rhett and his family, Mr. and Mrs. Baldwin
and girl, Mrs. Elfres and her three children and Mr. Sherwin and
family. With the men who have come to our aid from Florence we
have fifty men. We are forted up, and can hold the place even if

Monteith was with the Indians. I see that about one third of the hostiles are reservation Indians. The rest are Joseph's band and the Salmon rivers. We have sent for men and arms but have not got them. If men cannot be sent, do send us guns and ammunition and we will save what we have as long as our provisions hold out, which may be 4 weeks, besides beef. They are now driving Henry Elfers horses by here on the opposite side of the river. They are driving the stock off and swimming it at Horse Shoe Bend, and ferrying all the goods and plunder that they have taken from the settlers. It would make your heart ache to see the little children walk here and sleep for 36 hours [and] never cry except when you name Indians. We can't leave here, we have to guard day and night.[23]

About ten days later—several days after General Howard had sent a troop of cavalry there—C. B. Wood reported to Governor Brayman that "our arms consist mostly of shot guns and a few revolvers and we have all the women and children on Salmon River here thirty in number."[24] And the muster roll of the volunteers, which was submitted at the same time, contains thirty names—*among them that of Larry Ott*. It is said that seventeen of the men who helped guard this little settlement were miners who had come over from the town of Florence—and that the person who went there to solicit aid was a friendly Nez Perce woman named Tolo.

Although the little settlement was apparently tense with fear, one curious recollection exists. When an old man, one of the Cone brothers recalled that on two occasions Indians came in under a white flag to settle accounts which some of them had at the little store operated by Wood and Fockler.[25] If true, the implication is obvious.

With the passing of years, an air of mystery has come to surround the fate of Mrs. Jack Manuel. A month later, *The Teller* quoted a bit of *squaw-gossip* to the effect there were white women among the Hostiles[26] and these rumors were repeated by papers in Montana. There may have been some truth to these, as a reliable source reported years afterward that when the Indians passed up the Bitterroot Valley, a young white woman was seen among them and was, presumably, killed in the Battle of the Big Hole.[27] Years later, Yellow Bull claimed, in a highly improbable story, that he took Mrs. Manuel and that *someone* dragged her into the brush along the Lolo Trail and killed her.[28]

Against these very dubious statements must be placed that of Popham, who stated that her body was burned when the cabin was burned, and also that which J. W. Poe made on July 19th—"It was currently believed that Mrs. Manuel and child were still alive until after I had examined the ruins and found positive evidence to the contrary."[29] E. C. Brown, who visited the ruins of his store about the same time, made a similar statement. And years afterward, Maggie Manuel Bowman—then a child six and a half years old with a broken arm—insisted that she saw "Joseph" stab her mother and had a piece of jewelry made from an earring recovered from the ashes.[30] The earring may have been real, but the accusation is probably without foundation.

Although there is no positive intelligence that whiskey provided the match that lit the fuse, many bits of evidence indicate this was the case. There can be but little doubt that people in the White Bird area had whiskey and that some were not above selling it to Indians. According to the previously noted story in the Portland *Daily Standard*, there was whiskey at Tepahlewam and more was secured when they looted the settlement at White Bird—which was allegedly confirmed by Nez Perce informants years later. This evidence was also supported, in an oblique manner, by Joseph after the final surrender when he told correspondent Sutherland that "captured whiskey was usually at the bottom of all murders, the Indians getting almost crazy with it and utterly beyond his influence."[31] It would have been surprising if the situation had not developed into an ugly one.

And it seems probable that whiskey contributed to the horrors to which the Norton party was subjected. The half-breed Duncan McDonald completed his series of newspaper stories, "The Inside History from Indian Sources," *after* visiting the refugees who reached Canada. In an installment dated November 29, 1878, he wrote:

> It seems that at the earliest commencement of the Nez Perces war there were two white women murdered. One of them was murdered by an Indian who was drunk. The other white woman was burned in a house with her child.[32]

Obviously, the persons referred to were Mrs. Chamberlain, whom the Indians probably believed dead when they left her, and Mrs. Manuel.

The settlers at White Bird who survived slowly found their way out to Mount Idaho. Although the distance was only sixteen or seventeen miles, it was across country that provided but very little shelter in the way of timber or brush. On the following Sunday, soldiers found Mrs. Benedict and her children hiding in a patch of brush along the trail leading down into the canyon, and they sent a couple of citizen volunteers to escort her to Mount Idaho. On Monday, Mr. George, who had separated from the Mason-Osborne party near the mouth of White Bird Creek, came in; and the next evening about 7 P.M., George Popham arrived to relate his experiences to L. P. Brown. The remainder of his story, previously quoted in part, was that:

The Indians told me that they had sent a messenger up the Snake river and that there was a lot of Indians who would join them, and that they had plenty of good guns; that they would kill and capture all the country about Weiser, Piette, and Boise valleys, with Boise City, they also said that runners had been sent to Palouse, Spokane, Columbia river and Umatilla tribes who would join them and that they would capture the whole country about the Snake and Clearwater rivers, including Lewiston; they said it would take them two months to accomplish it and then they would have a good time.[33]

No doubt the Indians were boasting in making this statement, but, apparently, they sent runners to the Bannocks, Columbia River Renegades, the tribes in the Palouse area, and—possibly—the Flatheads in Montana. Howard's fear of a coalition of various disaffected elements did have some foundation, although time was to prove it was not as real as he imagined.

H. C. Brown, proprietor of the store just below the mouth of White Bird Creek, and his wife escaped the raiders Thursday afternoon by crossing the Salmon in a boat, but not, however, before Brown was wounded. Later, they recrossed the river and made their way northward to Norton's Cottonwood House where Ad Chapman and a party of volunteers found them six days later. As noted, Jack Manuel hid near his cabin until Howard's troops arrived. And across the river, six Frenchmen kept out of sight until they saw soldiers on a distant skyline—when a party of Nez Perce finally found and robbed them.

Some of Popham's account sounds improbable but no more so than that of Pat Price, for which there is ample confirmation. L. P. Brown chronicled the Price episode as follows:

> Price left White Bird at 3 P.M. Sunday packing the little 6½ year old girl by permission of the Indians. . . . He arrived at Mt. Idaho Monday evening where they now remain.[34]

Sutherland noted after hearing a lot of "blood thirsty stories":

> I was quite refreshed with the following: At the time Jack Manuel's farm was attacked a laboring man, an Irishman named Patrick Price, picked up Manuel's little daughter in his arms, and, opening his shirt front, told the Indians they were free to shoot him if they wished, but they could only kill the child over his dead body. The pluck of the son of Erwin touched a chord in the Chief's heart, and with a waive of the hand he said, "Skookum tum-tum kintawa," which freely translated, means, "A laconic sentiment, begone!" . . .[35]

This Irishman made a sort of pack from a box, put Maggie with her broken arm in it, and packed her out on his back. Probably Price enjoyed telling the story afterward, and it was not long before the tale was embellished with the statement that Pat had a cross tattooed on his chest and that it was this that caused the Indians to spare his life.[36] It should also be noted that this trip out of the canyon took place but a few hours after the Indians had routed two companies of cavalry not far from the place where Price must have started, and he reported seing a number of dead soldiers along the route he followed.

The number reported killed varies. On June 26th, Howard wrote, "The number of murders thus far are seventeen (17), one woman, two children and fourteen men."[37]

The New York *Herald*—apparently using a dispatch sent by Sutherland on June 30th—listed nineteen names. Curiously—for this correspondent was at Mount Idaho on the 29th—the name of Jack Manuel was included; however, Chamberlain's small son was omitted.[38] To both of these lists must be added the name of Joe Moore, who lingered for three months before he succumbed, although Lew Day had already died.

Of all the questions presented by this outbreak, none is more pertinent than that concerning the role of Joseph. The residents of the area of the outbreak have found it convenient to insist that it was a premeditated act of treachery. General Howard—for reasons unknown—also espoused this view. Only the Indians knew the answer, and much of the data supplied by them years later appears to have a protective coloring.

As to Joseph's role, one of Howard's aides, who was present when the Nez Perce surrendered, wrote seven years afterward that the chief told him a few days later:

> "I intended to go on the reservation. I knew nothing of these murders. Had I been home they would not have happened; but I was away on the other side of the Salmon River, killing some beef for my wife, who was sick, and I was called back by messengers telling me what the young men had done. Then I knew I must lead them in the fight, for the whites would not believe my story."[39]

Less than two months later, Major H. Clay Wood wrote a letter to the *Army and Navy Journal* which contained this:

> An officer of sound judgment and with a good opportunity for ascertaining facts writes me as follows, viz: . . . during all this time and for some days before, it is known Joseph and his brother were over on the Salmon river, curing or jerking beef for their families, and returned on the evening of the 14th to hear *for the first time* of the Outbreak; and Joseph proposed to go at once to the Agency and give himself up, but was persuaded by his squaw and brother not to

do so. They then went over to White Bird's camp and had a talk, Joseph being urged on by the others, although none of his band had been implicated up to that time. That night, however, a few of his men, who had some grudge against Norton, living on Cottonwood Creek, started off to kill him. * * * It is said that Joseph, on learning of this, said it was too late to turn back, or words to that effect, and that he would cast his lot or take chances with the rest. * * * It is my belief that Joseph was urged into this war against his judgment and inclination, and would gladly be well out of it.[40]

It is not known who the officer "of sound judgment and with a good opportunity for ascertaining facts" was. Circumstantial evidence points straight at Captain William H. Boyle, formerly an aide to General Howard and just previously a member of the Inspector General's Department at Department Headquarters. When liquor-loving Captain Henry M. Smith died on April 23rd, Boyle had automatically been promoted from lieutenant to captain and succeeded Smith as commanding officer of "G" Company, Twenty-first Infantry, then stationed at Fort Lapwai. Evidently, Boyle was a man of "sound judgment," he was on the spot—and Wood knew him personally. As this letter of the adjutant's was written shortly after Joseph wished to surrender at Kamiah, Wood was not exactly guessing about Joseph's attitude.

Later, a grand jury at Lewiston indicted a considerable number of Indians for murder. In writing to the U. S. Attorney General of certain legal aspects involved, John W. Huston, U. S. Attorney General for Idaho, expressed this opinion:

> The massacres on Camas Prairie Salmon River and White Bird Creek in June last and which were the initatiory steps to the general outbreak by Joseph's band were committed by a few Indians belonging to the band but were not I am satisfied from all the evidence I have been able to procure either advised or sanctioned by Chief Joseph.[41]

7

Prelude to Disaster

>>>>>><<<<<<< On June 13, 1877, Fort Lapwai was a quiet, pleasant little post. Its normal complement was two companies; and at the moment these were "F" Company of the First Cavalry under the post commander, Captain David Perry, and "G" Company of the Twenty-first Infantry which had a new commanding officer, recently promoted Captain William H. Boyle. "H" Company of the First Cavalry, which General Howard had ordered here at the time of the May council with the Non-Treaty Indians, was still camped just outside the confines of the post.

At Captain Perry's quarters, his wife was preparing to leave on the morrow to go down the river to visit friends at The Dalles. Mrs. Perry was a gracious hostess, a fine cook, interested in those activities expected of the commanding officer's wife; and she "adored" her husband. But she was also "a very foolish and hysterical woman" who lacked the self-dicipline and Spartan courage expected of an officer's wife. Next door was Emily FitzGerald, wife of the post surgeon—sensitive, perceptive, but not quite fitted for the trials of the wife of an officer stationed at a frontier post. During the day, Emily began a letter to her mother, who lived in Columbia, Pennsylvania. Like many of her letters, it was written in installments. The first one read:

> *Fort Lapwai*
> *June 13, 1877*
>
> MAMMA DEAR,
>
> It seems a long time since I wrote to you, as I did not write at all last week, but I suppose you will find so many of my letters waiting for you when you get home, you will think I spent all my time writing.
>
> John is in Portland and I am awfully lonesome without him.[1] I do hope he won't make many trips of this sort away from us. I know, too, that he wants to be back as much as we want him. He left a week ago today, and I hope he will be home a week from tomorrow, but Major Boyle and Mr. Monteith[2] told me they don't think it is possible for him to come back so soon. I will be dolefully disappointed if he doesn't.
>
> I hope the check for 150 dollars has reached Uncle Owen[3] long before this and that the watch will soon be on the way. I am anxious to know what it costs and how much money there is over and how much I owe you, so I can make up my mind if I can comfortably invest in a locket or whether I had better hold on to the money. We are going to be very short of funds until after Congress meets in the fall,[4] and we won't be very rich then.
>
> Major Boyle's family arrived last week and they are nearly fixed. Mrs. Boyle is a very pretty woman and pleasant. They have children, for which I am very glad. They are much older than mine,[5] but it is pleasant to see young people about this quiet post. They have a pretty girl about twelve, a boy about ten, and a grown-up son.[6]

Two days lapsed before Emily FitzGerald resumed this letter. In the meantime—on the following day—General Howard, his aide, Lieutenant Melville C. Wilkinson, and Inspector E. C. Watkins of the Indian Department arrived in Lewiston for a brief stop, and Perry had insisted that the general come to the post and stay with him while Watkins attended to his affairs at the Agency.

At the end of the May council, the general had returned to his headquarters. Here, he was met later in the month by Inspector Watkins and the two conferred about certain Indian problems of mutual interest. Howard had a sincere liking for the man whom he described as "a large, full-built, wholesome man, backed up with genuine courage." And he had also served "acceptably" as a captain during the Civil War. On May 30th, the trio had left Portland to visit various trouble spots, but timing their travels so that they would be at the Nez Perce Agency at the expiration of the 30-day period given the Indians to move on the Reservation.

Waiting at the steamboat landing early in the morning of June 14th were several officers from Fort Lapwai, Monteith's brother Charles who acted as his clerk, and Mrs. Perry who would take passage downstream after the boat had unloaded. According to Howard, Perry—who held the brevet rank of colonel—was "A little over six feet in height and standing straight, he is so gracefully formed and young looking, that he does not seem tall. He has a clear Saxon eye and usually wears a pleasant smile— pleasant, but with a reserve in it. One can hardly command men and go into battle often and still keep altogether sunshiny."

Captain ("Major") Joel G. Trimble, commanding "H" Company, was also there. ". . . another good officer. Shorter than Colonel Perry, a slight cast in one of his eyes which have been somewhat affected by a wound received at Gettysburg, . . . a well-knit form and modest bearing."

And the third was Lieutenant Peter S. Bomus, Perry's junior officer who was also the post quartermaster. "He is one of the young men to rely on in an emergency, well-made, of West Point build, such a one as finds little sympathy in his heart for men of sanguine or nervous temperment, but believes in duty. . . ."[7]

According to General Howard's recollections:

> By seven o'clock . . . we wind into sight of the distant village, we say "village" for, however large as a mining town Lewiston may have been, after the change of the mining reserve to other centers of fortune-hunting and gambling, the city of Lewiston has relapsed into its normal condition of a frontier village. . . . Lewiston has a mill, a newspaper,[8] and several well-to-do merchants. .
>
> As we near the landing, the people of the village are seen in waiting. As soon as we strike the shore Colonel Perry, Major Trimble, Lieutenant Bomus, and the brother of the Indian agent, whom the people call Charlie Monteith, spring on board and give us welcome.
>
> * * *
>
> "How is Joseph, Colonel?" I ask.
> "All right at last accounts. The Indians are, I think, coming on the Reservation without trouble."
> . . . Young Monteith, who is the efficient clerk of his agent brother . . . has come to meet Colonel Watkins, the Inspector. He tells the same story: "All quiet at last accounts; Indians seem to be acting in good faith; guess they will make no trouble." I met Mr.

Coburn, too, of the firm of Lowenberg [Brothers], and several of the other citizens of Lewiston. All united in the same testimony, "The Indians are all right." I said at first to Colonel Watkins [that he would wait in Lewiston until the Inspector finished his business at the Agency]. . . . Then, we would proceed to the Spokane and Colville country . . . and settle the vexed questions of the up-country.

"All right!" But Perry said to me, "You had better go with me. It will be pleasanter for you to wait at the Fort." I accepted the Colonel's kind hospitality and we rodᴜ the twelve miles behind his spirited and handsome horses, leaving Lewiston early in the after-noon.[9]

When Howard reached the post, the other officers undoubtedly came to pay their respects. Foremost among these was Captain Boyle—"a sturdy officer, ready to go or stay at command, of conservative build, endorsing his General most loyally." And there were three lieutenants: Brevet "Lieu-tenant Colonel" William R. Parnell who was Trimble's junior officer, Robert R. Fletcher of the Twenty-first Infantry, and Edward R. Theller, also of the Twenty-first Infantry.

Fletcher had just been promoted into the first-lieutenant vacancy created by Boyle's promotion, and was awaiting orders to transfer him to another company located elsewhere. Curiously, he was a graduate of the U.S. Naval Academy who had requested a commission in the Army; and Howard had requested his assignment to his Department on the strength of the recommendation of a mutual friend in the Medical Department— who had stated that he was a promising officer with considerable ability as a "topographical engineer."[10] Before another month had passed he would be an aide-de-camp to the general, and have charge of the scouts—a convenient sort of assignment for an unattached junior officer. And at the end of the war, he demonstrated his engineering talents by preparing an excellent map of the campaign.

Theller, who was Boyle's junior officer, was an enigma in some ways. He was forty-two years old, had served as a Captain of Volunteers in the Civil War, and was happily married to a well-liked, energetic lady. The general characterized him as "of medium size, a bright face, a generous, brave man with a warm heart"—who was considerably interested in the "speed of his stallion." Yet, in Howard's file was a confidential letter written about a year before by Boyle—while in the Inspector General's Department—which recommended that "G" Company be relieved by some other company "if for no other purpose than to remove Lieut Theller from his present associations who are by no means fit companions for an officer holding the position he does. I will explain fully when I return."[11]

At the time this letter was written, Theller was post quartermaster—Perry having secured Bomus to replace him in the meantime. His love of fast horses suggests the undesirable "associations" were those of the gambling fraternity at Lewiston, an unsavory lot. Was there a reason why this infantryman "volunteered" to go out with the cavalry companies on the following day? Death was to close the case and leave a riddle without an answer.

Howard recalled that as the afternoon of the 14th passed "we visit and banter and chat, and all seems as peace like and happy as home." Then, at evening, a courier arrived with a letter from L. P. Brown,[12] the hotel-keeper and self-appointed spokesman for Mount Idaho. This read:

Mount Idaho, June 14, 1877

COL. PERRY.—DEAR SIR

Mr. Overman who resides at or near the head of Rocky Canyon, eight miles from here, came in to-day and brought his friends. They are very much alarmed at the actions of the Indians who are gathered here. He says there are about sixty lodges, composed of Salmon River Indians, Joseph and his band, with other non-treaties, and that they are insolent and have little to say to the whites, and that all their actions indicate trouble from them. Mr. Overman is regarded as a very truthful man and confidence can be placed in all his statements. Some of the other neighbors have also moved over this way, where there are more people.

Yesterday they had grand parade. About one hundred were mounted and well armed and went through the maneuvers of a fight—were thus engaged for some two hours. They say openly that they are going to fight the soldiers when they come up to put them on the reservation and I understand that they expect them up on Friday next. A good many were in town to-day and were trying to obtain powder and other ammunition. Mr. Scott told me to-day that they offered him two dollars and a half for a can of powder. Up to this time I think they have been buying all the arms, etc., that they could get, but do not think they can purchase any now. They have a strong position at the head of the Canyon among the rocks and should they make any resistance could give the troops much trouble.

I do not feel any alarm; but thought it well to inform you of what was going on among them. Early this morning one Indian came here and wanted to know when General Howard was coming up. As the stage came up last night perhaps they thought we might know when he would be up. They are evidently on the lookout for the soldiers. I believe it would be well for you to send up, as soon as you can, a sufficient force to handle them without gloves, should they be disposed to resist. Sharp orders and prompt action will bring them to understand that they must comply with the orders of the Government. We trust such action may be taken by you so as to remove them from the neighborhood and quiet the feelings of the people.

I write this for your own information and at the suggestion of many settlers, who are living in exposed localities.

Very Respectfully yours,
L. P. Brown[13]

Perry read the letter and handed it to the general with the comment that the writer did not seem to be greatly concerned; but if the latter approved, he would send a detachment to check on the situation. After all, unwarranted concern and excitement on the part of settlers was nothing new. And at dawn on the following morning, a detail composed of a sergeant and two men, with a half-breed named Joe Robosko as interpreter, set off briskly on the road up the valley.

Mount Idaho was about sixty-two miles from the post by the wagon road. This ran, generally, in a south-southeasterly direction up Lapwai Creek, over Craig's Mountain—a rounded, pine-covered elevation—and then, for nineteen miles, across the flat sweep called Camas Prairie to the village which was situated among the pines and hills of another semimountainous area. Norton's ranch or Cottonwood House was situated just where the road came down off Craig's Mountain; and four miles on the near side of Mount Idaho was Crook's ranch where there was a tiny settlement consisting of a community hall and a few houses known as Grangeville.

About noon, the sergeant and his companions returned, their horses showing unmistakable signs of hard riding. With them were an Indian named Pu-ton-ah-lo and a boy about fourteen years old, whom they had met on the trail at the point where it started up over Craig's Mountain. Excitedly, they told a story of trouble and, as Howard and Perry were not certain of Robosko's interpretation, all went down to the Agency, where there was a good interpreter. Here, they sifted through the story which seemed to be that three or four Indians had killed Larry Ott.

Although Howard and Perry had not been concerned over Overman's report—which could not be confirmed even years afterward—"all believed that matters were getting into serious trouble." Monteith and the interpreter now thought it wise to send someone to the Indian camp; and a subchief named Jonah and Joseph's father-in-law volunteered to go, the latter expressing the opinion that Joseph would not fight. This pair started off at "full speed" but soon returned—"about half-past four"—"running their horses" and bringing with them a brother of Looking Glass and a half-breed whose name was West, both of whom were carrying messages.

As this party rode into Fort Lapwai, they came straight to the quarters of the commanding officer. The excitement was intense, and General Howard recalled:

It was a time to be remembered. . . . A large group of us were on Colonel Perry's front porch, the officers, the ladies of the post, several principal friendly Indians, [and] the newcomers gathered around the steps at their feet. . . . The dispatch was instantly opened. One of the essential things in warlike operations is for the commanding officer to preserve his equipoise under all circumstances. . . . So . . . I made an unusual effort to be perfectly cool and self possessed, while I read to myself, the startling communication:

Mt. Idaho, 7 A.M., Friday, June 15, '77
COMMANDING OFFICER, FT. LAPWAI.

Last night we started a messenger to you, who reached Cottonwood house, where he was wounded and driven back by the Indians. The people of Cottonwood undertook to come here during the night; were interrupted; all wounded or killed. Parties this morning found some of them on the prairie.

The wounded will be here shortly, when we will get full particulars. The whites are engaged (about forty of them) in getting the wounded. One thing is certain, we are in the midst of an Indian war. Every family is here, and we will have taken all the precautions we can, but are poorly armed. We want arms and ammunition and help at once. Don't delay a moment. We have a report that some whites were killed yesterday on Salmon river. No word from them; fear that the people were all killed, as a party of Indians were seen going that way last night. Send to Lewiston, and hasten up.

You cannot imagine people in a worse condition than they are here. Mr. West has volunteered to go to Lapwai; rely on his statements.

Yours truly,
L. P. BROWN

This letter had been written immediately after Norton's young son had been found near Crook's ranch. West was hardly started with it when a wagon hastily pulled up in front of Brown's Mt. Idaho Hotel. On the seat, wounded but still able to hang on, was Joe Moore and in the box lay Lew Day and Mrs. Norton. As soon as the wounded were carried in, the hotelkeeper scribbled a second message which was given to Looking Glass' brother. This Howard opened after reading the dispatch carried by the half-breed. There was no mistaking its message:

Mt. Idaho, 8 A.M., June 15, 1877

COMMANDING OFFICER, FORT LAPWAI.

I have just sent a dispatch by Mr. West, half-breed. Since that the wounded have come in—Mr. Day mortally; Mrs. Norton with both legs broken; Moore shot through the hip; Norton killed and left in the road six miles from here. Teams were attacked on the road and abandoned. The Indians have possession of the prairie and threaten Mt. Idaho. All the people are here, and we will do the best we can. Lose no time in getting up with a force. Stop the stage and all through traveling. Give us relief and arms and ammunition. Chapman has got this Indian to go, hoping he may get through. I fear the people on the Salmon have all been killed, as a party was seen going that way last night. We had a report last night that seven whites had been killed on the Salmon. Notify the people of Lewiston. Hurry up, hurry. Rely on this Indian's statement. I have known him for a long time. He is with us.

L. P. BROWN

P.S.—Send a dispatch to town for the express not to start up unless heavily escorted. Give the bearer a fresh horse and send him back.

[Ad ?] CHAPMAN.

The moment had now come when all turned to the Commanding General for orders to start operations. He turned to Captain Perry.

"Well, Colonel, this means business!"

"Yes, Sir."

"Are your men in readiness?"

"Everything but some transportation that must come from Lewiston." Howard then turned to his aide:

"Captain Wilkinson, get ready to go to Walla Walla at once."

As the others went to their various tasks, General Howard questioned West further about the outbreak, and such information as he could supply soon had additional confirmation:

Other Indians came in to Fort Lapwai about the same time, among them several who belonged to the Catholic mission, who had been with the non-treaty Indians to participate in their sports of horse racing, etc. As soon as they found that these malcontents meant war, they broke from them and rushed with their small herds toward their homes.

Howard penned a reassuring note to L. P. Brown and gave it to West to deliver, and then sent the couriers to the Agency. In a few minutes,

Lieutenant Bomus stood ready with a team and buggy for Lieutenant Wilkinson, and soon these two officers were on their way to Lewiston. Here, Bomus hired a "team" from the stage company for the general's aide, and then went to the freighting company of Grostein & Binnard in search of a pack train. He reported six months later that,

> I obtained thirty (30) mules agreeing to compensate them at the rate of one (1) dollar coin each, per day, the United States to furnish packers and remunerate them for the loss of mules and rigging by the accidents of the service. * * * Packers were soon engaged . . . at the usual wages. . . .[14]

However, he did not get the train to Fort Lapwai until between 10 and 11 P.M., several hours after the troops had left.

After the return of the sergeant's detail, Mrs. FitzGerald sat down to continue the letter to her mother, which letter now became a colorful record of a tense day:

Friday, June 15, 1877

Well, our Indian troubles, that we thought all over, have begun again, and this time the officers here seem to think it means business. General Howard is here again, and an Indian inspector from Washington is at the Agency. The thirty days that was given to the Indians to come onto the Reservation expires today, and early this morning a party was started from the post to the upper part[15] of the Reservation to see if they were keeping their promises. The party came back an hour ago, riding like mad people, and brought with them two friendly Indians that they met on the mountains and who were bound for the post and the Agency. The Indians had been riding all night and said that other Indians, not friendly, were after them. These Indians bring word that the Indians have murdered four settlers up in the mountains, and that they are holding war dances, and that White Bird is riding around his tent on horseback and making circles on the ground,[16] which is his way of declaring that they have taken up the hatchet, etc.

General Howard sent at once for four companies more to move up here and has sent off for hard bread and all such things that troops on a scout need. Things look exciting.

The story of the Indians is corroborated by a letter sent to the General from some settler up in the region. . . . I have heard the officers discussing it, and the general impression is that if the Indians have begun, the troops are in for a summer campaign. General Howard said, "I wish the doctor was here, but I will dispatch at once for Dr. Alexander, who is at Wallula, and he can join us at once."

My first thought was that I was glad John wasn't here, but I know that he would feel that his place was with the troops from the post he belongs to. If there is trouble he will have to go anyway, as soon as he gets back. So I expect that all my delight in getting him back will be spoiled by knowing that he will have to leave me again at once. We here will feel perfectly safe. The post will not be left without a good garrison. Two companies of infantry, at least, will be left here. But how anxious we will be about the little party out after Indians. It is all horrible.

Mrs. Boyle just ran down the back way for a minute to discuss the matter for a little. She says it makes her feel sick. It is dreadful to think what might happen, but I can't think these Indians, those we have seen so often, are going to fight the troops. General Howard, the inspector, the Agent, and Colonel Perry and the aides are all just now counciling together as to the country and the best plan of action. I wish John was home, and I wish the Indians were in the bottom of the Red Sea. I don't feel as if any other matter deserved consideration this morning.

But I must tell you about the children's stockings. I wish you would get me two pairs more, not any better than those you paid 42 cents for. The children are very well and they miss their Papa very much indeed. He plays with them, or rather entertains them so much. I do wish Doctor would come home. I feel as if the bottom was knocked out of everything.[17]

As the vine-covered porch across the front of the quarters of Captains Perry and FitzGerald was the site of most of the planning activities, little that transpired was out of the sight or hearing of the Doctor's wife. Not long after completing the second installment of her letter, she began a third. By now, she was tense with excitement.

Afternoon

Mamma, dear, I have only time to write a few lines, as the mailman will be here. Oh, Mamma, we have just heard such horrible news. The Indians have begun their devilish work. An Indian and a half-breed came in this afternoon with dispatches from Mount Idaho, a little settlement up on the mountains. The Indians have murdered seven more men on the road and also attacked an emigrant train killing all. They broke one poor woman's legs, and she saw them kill her husband and brother. They say that everybody is gathered into this little town. They want help, and arms, and ammunition immediately. They say in the most piteous manner, "Hurry, hurry, hurry. We are almost helpless and the bands of Indians are all around us." They fear the settlers in the ranches around them are killed, as nothing is seen of them.

Our post is all in commotion. The two companies of cavalry will leave in a few hours. They don't dare wait even for more troops, though dispatches have already been sent everywhere to gather up the scattered troops in the Department. My dear old husband will have to follow Colonel Perry's command, as soon as he gets back here. These poor people from Mt. Idaho say, "One thing is certain. An Indian war is upon us." You know these devils always begin on helpless outlying settlements. Poor Mrs. Theller is busy getting up a mess kit for her husband. Major Boyle remains in charge of the post. The talk among the officers is that there will be a great deal of trouble.[18]

Although the post was "all in commotion," Trimble's troop—having lived with the alarms from the Wallowa Valley for several years—took matters in stride. Michael McCarthy, first sergeant of the company, wrote in what he called his "diary":

The weather . . . [had been] wet and disagreeable. . . . On the morning of the 15th of June, the first warm clear day for a long time, everyone had his blankets out to dry and some were bathing and washing the only shirt brought along &c when we were alarmed by the report that the Indians had broken out. . . .[19]

And "H" Company lost no time in putting itself in readiness to move.

Although Perry told Howard that his troops were in a state of readiness, McCarthy remembered otherwise. As a footnote to what happened two day later, he wrote:

The Command . . . was composed of troops but poorly instructed in the use of arms and in horsemanship. F Company had been stationed at Ft. Lapwai for some time and as was the case in those days, most of the enlisted men were employed on extra duty,—clerks, carpenters, blacksmiths, officers servants, etc. The men so employed rarely attended a drill and target practice was not . . . encouraged. H Company had come from Walla Walla and the march and the 5 or six weeks field service had better acquainted them with their duties as soldiers, but still they were in a measure raw. . . . We were poorly supplied with ammunition. . . . the guns [were] rusty and foul.[20]

Regardless of the state of readiness, whatever force was available had to be committed. And so ninety-nine cavalrymen, with rations and supplies on a few pack mules, assembled on the parade ground as the sun disappeared below the horizon. The families of the officers of "H" Company were miles away. Mrs. Perry—perhaps fortunately—was not present to create a scene, Emily FitzGerald watched with mixed feelings, and Mrs. Theller had to steel herself for the parting. When the moment for departure came, "Perry and I stood there in the doorway of his hospitable home and looked into each other's faces. How tall, strong and confident he appeared. One hundred [sic] cavalrymen—too few for the work ahead, but the best we could do. . . . 'Good bye, General!' 'Good bye, Colonel. You must not get whipped.' 'There is no danger of that, sir.'"

The troopers mounted. A few horses pranced and bucked. Then the column moved out into the gathering darkness for a night march. Anxious eyes and ears followed them as long as they were within sight and hearing—and then the long wait began.

Before she went to bed, Emily FitzGerald wrote one last paragraph at the end of her mother's letter.

Later

We have just watched the little party of two companies start off at dusk. General Howard remains here. If John had been here, he would have been out there tonight marching with them. I can't help but feel glad that he is not, but I know that he would feel that he ought to have been there, and General Howard was so concerned tonight about the command starting off without a medical officer.

It is ten o'clock and I am going to bed. We all feel so anxious. I will write soon again. I have only told you the news we have had that we know is true. Rumors of all sorts have been coming into the post all day. Everything centers here, and you can imagine how we all feel. I hope and pray it won't be another Modoc War. Love to all.

Your loving daughter,
EMILY F.[21]

The Nez Perce war was under way.

8

Rout at White Bird Canyon

➤➤➤➤➤➤➤◄◄◄◄◄◄◄ In the camp along Cottonwood Creek, on the night of June 15–16th, some of the Indians must have realized they were faced with a problem of some magnitude. Probably, they had fled in something akin to panic from the campground at Tepahlewam. Now, certainly the chiefs knew they faced a war for which no plans had been laid.

According to trader Duncan McDonald, Looking Glass sent word to White Bird and Joseph that

> My hands are clean of white men's blood, and I want you to know they will so remain. You have acted like fools in murdering white men. I will have no part in these things, and have nothing to do with such men. If you are determined to go and fight go and fight yourselves and do not attempt to embroil me or my people. Go back with your warriors; I do not want any of your band in my camp. I wish to live in peace.[1]

To the northwest was Fort Lapwai, and in the Wallowa country to the west were two companies of cavalry. In an opposite direction were Looking Glass and the unsympathetic Treaty Indians at the sub-agency at Kamiah. The most logical place in which to await developments was the rough breaks along the Salmon and Snake rivers. So, these Indians were acting with some logic when they streamed back across Camas Prairie the next day to a campground near the mouth of White Bird Creek.

While the Indians were—probably—spending an uneasy night, Howard's aide, Lieutenant Wilkinson, was pushing along in the darkness on the road to Walla Walla. Apparently, his conveyance was a team and buckboard hired from the stage company at Lewiston—which the post quartermaster reported later cost "fifty (50) dollars coin"—and which, by the next morning, had put about 110 miles behind it. At about 8 o'clock, Wilkinson was at Colonel Grover's headquarters with the dispatches. The telegram for Division Headquarters read:

Fort Lapwai, I. T., June 15, 1877

Assistant Adjutant General, Division of Pacific
San Francisco, Cal.

Indians began by murdering a white man in revenge for a murder of his, killing three others at the same time. Since they have begun war upon the people near Mt. Idaho. Captain Perry started with two companies for them. Other troops are being brought forward as fast as possible. Get me authority for twenty five Indian scouts. Think we shall make short work of this.

Howard
Comdg Dept.[2]

Another telegram informed Major Wood, the Adjutant at Portland, that the general wished more troops and three months' supplies sent to Lewiston at once; and a third was addressed to Mrs. Howard, assuring her that there was no occasion for alarm. Wilkinson also carried instructions directing Colonel Grover to order the two companies of cavalry under Captain Whipple, then in the Wallowa Valley, to move to Fort Lapwai by the shortest route, and to send the infantry at Wallula and Fort Walla Walla to Lewiston on a steamboat.

Meanwhile, during the night, the detachment under Captain Perry, together with ten or eleven friendly Nez Perce scouts, had been pushing steadily along the trail up the valley of Lapwai Creek and over Craig's Mountain. By midforenoon, with about forty miles behind them, they stopped at Norton's Cottonwood House to cook breakfast and allow the horses to graze. In the distance could be seen three smokes from burning haystacks or buildings, indicating that either raiders had been at work or that scouts had observed their approach. The trail had been very muddy, and considerable time had been lost waiting for the pack mules to catch up—mules being notoriously hesitant where the footing is uncertain. However, the train was small—said to have been but five animals. Howard was to write a few months later that the troops had a pack train; but Lieutenant Bomus, in his report at the end of the campaign, stated that he had difficulty in Lewiston when he tried to hire the desired thirty mules and that he did not get this train to Fort Lapwai until several hours after the column had moved out.[3]

After resting about three hours, the troopers resumed their journey, which had now become a test of endurance. When within a few miles of Grangeville, they met a party of armed settlers who brought the information that the Indians had been crossing Camas Prairie and were believed headed for one of the places where they usually crossed the Salmon River. As Perry remembered years later:

> They also insisted that unless they were pursued and attacked early the following morning they would have everything over the river and be comparatively safe from immediate pursuit. . . . While realizing that men and animals should have a night's rest, I also understood that if I allowed these Indians to escape across the river with all their plunder . . . without any effort on my part to prevent it, I should . . . be open to censure. . . .

It was almost sundown when the column reached Grangeville. While the men made preparations to camp, Perry and his officers reviewed the problem and, "after considering all the circumstances, it was decided that to make the attempt to overtake the Indians before they could effect a crossing of the Salmon River was not only the best, but the *only* thing to do."[4]

Perry then informed the citizens that he would start as soon as the horses and men had an opportunity to eat, and requested that they provide a guide and bring as many volunteers as they could muster. Although they estimated that they could provide twenty-five or thirty men, only eleven came, among them Ad Chapman to act as guide.

Sergeant McCarthy recalled that the troops expected to camp for the night:

> The men and horses were tired. Some of the horses laid down and refused their feed. We made an attempt to cook some soup but *boots* and *saddles* sounded before it was cooked. The beans were served out

half boiled, and we saddled up and [leaving a detail in charge of the baggage] were again on the march by half past 9 P.M. We marched in column of files in direction of White Bird Creek. The march was very hard on the horses, especially the rear files, the riders losing distance, and galloping to catch up. Coming on the head of the Cañon of White Bird, we halted, dismounted, and were ordered to keep on the alert. In a few minutes, half of the men were asleep and in many instances the horses lay down beside their riders, and went to sleep also. We remained in this position about two hours, or until the dawn of day, when the word was passed to mount without noise and move forward. Just then a coyote howl was heard on our left. . . .[5]

That quavering howl did not evoke particular attention at the time, although it was remembered afterward that it came almost immediately after a trooper in Perry's company disregarded the instructions for security and lit his pipe. Although no two of the Indian stories agree as to details, they do agree that their scouts were out and that a warning was received that alerted the Indian camp.

According to McCarthy's diary, as the column moved out, Lieutenant Theller and a small party were a short distance in advance, followed by Perry's company in a column of two's with Trimble's men behind in a column of files. The citizens and friendly Indians were on either side but, as the trail was narrow, they were not far enough away to be classed as flankers. When about a third of the way down into the canyon, "just as Colonel Perry was passing some bush, a voice said, 'Are you soldiers?' A woman carrying a baby dragged herself into view, with another little girl, three years old hanging to her skirts. She had been hiding there since Thursday (this was Sunday morning)."[6]

Presumably the woman, Mrs. Benedict, had been hiding since her husband was killed. McCarthy recalled that they were scantily clad and that a man in his company gave her a loaf of bread—part of which he was happy to find later; and he noted that "she was hiding when the main body of the Indians returning from their raid near Grangeville, went down the Cañon the evening before. She counted about sixty warriors, or nearly the whole force yet on the warpath. . . ."[7] A couple of volunteers were detailed to escort her to Mount Idaho, and the column proceeded on.

White Bird Canyon, into which the troops were now descending, was the drainage basin of White Bird Creek. It started near Grangeville and extended about ten miles in a southwesterly direction to the point where the creek emptied into the northward-flowing Salmon River. During this distance, the bed of the stream dropped about three-quarters of a mile in elevation. At the point where the troops began their descent, the straight-line distance to the Indian camp was about four miles with a drop in elevation of approximately 2,600 feet, of which, perhaps, two-thirds occurred within the first third of the distance traveled.

Within the basin or valley were lateral drainageways, which further dissected the surface into a succession of ridges of various heights and shapes. In cross-section, the ridge on which the initial encounter was about to take place was extremely lopsided. The slopes down to the drainageway along its western side were very steep, while to the east it dipped down in a succession of undulating, grassy slopes which presented no obstacles either to maneuvering troops, or to visibility. The southern tip, which was near the Indian camp, ended in a steep, abrupt slope surmounted by two small, rounded knolls. And upwards of a half mile away toward the north was a long, rocky outcrop which resembled the backbone protruding from the carcass of some gigantic, skinny beast. It was at the top of the western slope, between the two knolls and the "backbone" of rock, that the first shots were fired.

As the troops moved down the trail toward the creek, Theller, with the advance guard and the friendly Indians, scouted ahead. With them rode Ad Chapman, wearing, so warriors claimed later, a large, white hat which made him conspicuous. The troopers were dog-tired, having been without sleep for almost forty-eight hours, and the last twenty-four with but two scanty meals. Their mounts were leg-weary from having been ridden approximately seventy-five miles over muddy trails with but three short stops for rest. And the Indians, instead of being involved in crossing the swollen Salmon as anticipated, were comfortably camped about two miles above the mouth of the creek—some of them, it is said, still drunk to the point of inefficiency. But the camp had been alerted, and the warriors were ready with changes of ponies, tended by the squaws, picketed nearby.

Various stories have been told of how the fight opened. Perhaps the most plausible one is that Joseph, still hoping to avoid a war, sent out a little party—Yellow Wolf stated afterward that there were six—under a white flag to attempt to arrange a parley when the troops appeared on the ridge above the camp. Also, friendly Indians were alleged to have told the sub-agent at Kamiah shortly afterward that they had persuaded the Non-Treaty Indians to surrender the murderers and that a messenger was sent forward under a white flag to arrange this. Both stories agree that these emissaries were fired on by the volunteers—Yellow Wolf claiming that the first shot was fired by the man in the large white hat.[8] And McCarthy's "diary" contains this significant statement: "As the head of the column came in sight of the creek, a shot was fired and then several immediately afterward. We could see a few Indians riding back toward the creek."[9]

As soon as the initial shots were fired, the Indians assumed the offensive. The civilians promptly occupied one of the small knolls overlooking the camp, and Theller and the advance guard took up a position just to their right. Captain Perry recalled that he

> immediately formed my troop into a line on the trot, but when I reached the advanced position I saw the Indians coming out of the brush [along the creek], and realized that to charge would only drive them back into the brush and under cover while my command would be in the open. . . . [As] I was in the most defensible position in that vicinity, I accordingly dismounted my troop and deployed on the ridge, sending my horses into the valley [at the rear]. . . .[10]

One of the first long-range shots from the Indians killed John Jones, Perry's trumpeter. As a bugler was considered a necessity for handling cavalry in battle, the captain turned the line over to Theller and rode back to "H" Company to see if Trimble had a "trumpet."

Meanwhile, according to Sergeant McCarthy, Trimble's line had

> moved forward and halting about a half a mile from the Indian camp then visible on a creek to our left. In our front the ground dropped suddenly. We were on the edge of a bluff overlooking the creek on which the Indians were camped. Some wild firing was done by our people from horseback, a rather short-sighted thing to do, for we had only an average of fifty rounds in the whole command. . . .[11]

By the time Perry had gone "three-fourths of the way to Trimble's position" he was aware that something was wrong. And, as there was no cover in the form of rocks or shrubs on the southern part of the ridge, he had no difficulty in ascertaining what was the matter. The warriors had swarmed over the tip of the ridge, and the citizens had hastily evacuated their commanding elevation, thus leaving the enemy in position to enfilade "F" Company's line. While some of the warriors sniped at the soldiers, the greater part mounted their ponies and pressed the attack. Thus, as some turned the left flank, others swept up a shallow ravine and through that part of the line held by "H" Company.[12] The rout, which began when the civilians fled, now became general. With mounted warriors in their rear—the only direction possible for a retreat—"the whole right of the line, seeing the mad rush for horses on the left, also gave way and the panic became general."[13]

As Trimble's bugler had also been killed, both company commanders were left without the usual means of conveying orders when the confusion of battle was greatest. Perry recalled that

> to stem the onrush was simply impossible. I did everything in human power to halt and reform my line, but no sooner would one squad halt

and face about than that the other, just placed in position, would be gone. The panic soon extended to H troop which disintegrated and melted away. . . . From that time on there was no organized fighting, but the battle was confined to halting first one squad and then another, facing them about and holding the position until flanked out.[14]

However, not all of the men joined in this undisciplined retreat. McCarthy recalled that "several squads were detached to hold the [western] edge of the bluff." These, along with Theller and his men, were left to save themselves—if they could.

The civilians—with Ad Chapman in the lead according to one volunteer—led in the rush for Mount Idaho. By 9 A.M., a number had returned and hotelkeeper L. P. Brown was writing the first account of the disaster. When the position on the ridge disintegrated, the two companies became separated. Trimble's men worked their way back by way of the trail they had followed on their way down; Perry's men broke for the top by the most direct route. Part way up to the canyon rim, Perry's horse gave out; then, he rode double with one of his troopers for a ways and finally continued on foot until he managed to catch a stray horse near the top. So exhausting was the terrain that the captain saw one warrior's squaw bring him three changes of mounts. Warriors hovered around the remnants of both companies, sometimes pressing their attack until the troopers stopped and made a desperate stand, and then continuing their harassment when the retreat was resumed.

When Perry and the remnant of "F" Company reached the rim, they turned eastward and followed the edge of the canyon to the head of the trail where they met Lieutenant Parnell and what remained of Trimble's company. There were but twenty-two left of the original ninety-nine. Dead on the slopes behind them were Theller and thirty-three others. Fleeing elsewhere, or hiding like frightened rabbits in the little clumps of brush in the bottoms of the draws, were the remainder, among them Sergeant McCarthy who did not rejoin his company at Mount Idaho—only sixteen miles away—until three days later. The sergeant was to remember that all he had to eat during this time was a small piece of the loaf of bread that Trooper Shay had given Mrs. Benedict, and which he found beside the trail.

By now the men had steadied somewhat—or the foolish ones had been weeded out—and the remainder of the retreat was orderly, although the Indians continued to hover about until Grangeville was reached. One trooper was rescued from a marshy area at the edge of the Prairie, and Parnell was nearly left behind once just after Perry contemplated making a stand on a rocky knoll. The lieutenant recalled that Perry had commented that as it was 7 o'clock, they could hold the knoll until dark. Apparently, the captain was in a slight state of shock, for Parnell had to remind him that it was 7 A.M. and not 7 P.M.!

That evening, Perry stated in an informal letter to General Howard that

It was only by the most strenuous efforts of Colonel Parnell and myself in organizing a party of twenty-two men that a single officer or man reached camp. * * * The Indians fought us to within four miles of Mount Idaho, and only gave it up on seeing that we would not be driven any further except at our own gait.

And he closed with, "Please break the news of her husband's death to Mrs. Theller." Howard tried hard to carry the tidings gently, "but Mrs. Theller read them in my face, and words had no place. 'Oh, my husband!' "[15]

Curiously, a rumor of disaster preceded this defeat. Howard wrote in his "diary" under the date of June 16th:

Ten P.M. Jonah's wife (Jonah having gone with the Cavalry to the front) comes to garrison with woman who ran in from hostiles; believes Jonah killed and all troops.

This, he amplified a few months later:

I was awakened by loud talking in front of the porch [of Captain Perry's quarters]. . . . I went out as soon as I could. Jonah's wife, a large-sized Indian woman, sat upon her horse. She was accompanied by another woman, the one, as I understood, that had just come from the hostiles. One of the half-breeds interpreted. She spoke so emphatically and so excitedly that she wakened everybody.

"The Indians had fixed a trap—all our troops had run straight into it. They, the hostiles, had come up on every side and killed all the soldiers and all the Indian scouts, including the friendly Indian scouts. * * * The next morning . . . Colonel Perry and our soldiers were actually fighting there, as the Indian woman had predicted. . . ."[16]

Considering that Mount Idaho was about sixteen miles from the battle-field, and Lewiston was at least eighty by a trail that led over a wooded mountain, news of the defeat reached Fort Lapwai and Lewiston quickly. As *The Teller* was published on Saturday of each week, it was not until June 23rd that this paper carried accounts of the fight; and the log on the front page of this issue is interesting. Under a dateline of "June 17th, half past 6 P.M."—the date of the encounter—was printed a short but reasonably good account. This was followed by:

8 o'clock A.M., June 18

D. Monroe arrived from the garrison at ½ past two this morning and tells us that a third soldier had arrived at the garrison last evening from the fight. . . .

And among other items was a letter from L. P. Brown at Mount. Idaho dated "June 17, 1877, 9 o'clock A.M." at which time only Chapman and the volunteers had arrived, but containing the postscript: "Since writing this Col. Perry has come in safe, but we hear Theller and Trimble are missing. . . ."

On June 18th, Howard's adjutant forwarded to Division headquarters, the first message from the general:

> Rather gloomy news from the front by stragglers. Captain Perry overtook the enemy about two hundred strong there, in a deep ravine well posted, and was fighting them when last messenger left. I am expecting every minute a message from him.
>
> The Indians are very active and gradually increasing in strength drawing from other tribes. The movement indicates a combination uniting nearly all disaffected Indians, probably will reach a thousand or fifteen hundred when united. * * * 17

In a dispatch dated two days later, Howard informed his Headquarters:

> A message received from Colonel Perry makes the loss 33, meaning exclusive of Lieutenant Theller, whom Captain Trimble placed, wounded, upon his horse. Theller was afterwards killed. . . . Tell all our friends to be patient and await results. Officers Perry, Trimble and Parnell are well.[18]

General McDowell later ridiculed the idea that there were 1,000–1,500 disaffected Indians in the area. However, the idea that a coalition of various tribes might develop was to dominate Howard's perspective toward the trouble for several weeks. Probably this was a groundless fear, but it did have a positive bearing on steps taken by the Department commander as subsequent events were to indicate.

Just how humiliating this defeat actually was hinges around the number of warriors who whipped the cavalrymen so quickly. As noted, Howard's first dispatch indicated that they numbered "about two hundred" and in his interim report submitted to the Secretary of War on August 27th, he put the number at "more than double Perry's numbers." This figure would be over 200, or over 250, depending on whether the number of volunteers and scouts was added to the total number of soldiers in making the calculation. In a telegram to the Commissioner of Indian Affairs dated the day after the fight, Inspector Watkins and Agent Monteith reported that, "Hostiles about one hundred strong and are reported to have gone to Salmon River country." In a second message of the same date, the statement was made: "Joseph's band increased by renegades number one hundred and fifty are near Mount Idaho." Presumably, these two estimates were based on intelligence secured from Treaty Indians.

However, there is some very good intelligence which indicates that Howard's figures were considerably inflated. Captain Stephen P. Jocelyn, Twenty-first Infantry, who was in the field with Howard, shortly afterward wrote home that "Perry estimates that he engaged 125 Indians." Surgeon FitzGerald's wife, in a letter written to her mother two days after the fight, stated that "there were supposed to be about eighty under Joseph and White Bird." Two years later in an interview, Joseph was alleged to have said, "We numbered in that battle sixty men. . . . The fight lasted but a few minutes. . . ." And, as noted, Sergeant McCarthy recalled that Mrs. Benedict told Perry that she had counted "about sixty warriors" as they passed her hiding place the day before.[19]

Three of the Treaty Indians who were with Captain Perry as scouts were "captured" by the hostiles; but they slipped away without much difficulty and returned to the Agency. The account which they gave when they returned may have been very close to the truth:

> Three Indians held as prisoners in Joseph's camp made their escape since the fight, and report that * * * [the hostiles] had in the fight only 70 men besides the squaws who brought up fresh horses in the rear. They took 36 guns from dead soldiers and those who had thrown them away. Only 4 Indians wounded, . . . ["one shot through the body, perhaps fatally"].[20]

The Lewiston correspondent who forwarded this news to the Portland *Standard* vouched for it with this statement: "This news I get from a reliable Indian and comes direct from the camp."

It would appear that the cold facts were that approximately seventy warriors, some of them perhaps under the influence of whiskey, indifferently armed, quickly and completely routed a column consisting of four officers and ninety-nine men plus ten or eleven armed citizens. Not only did the Indians whip them soundly, but they wiped out one-third of the cavalrymen and chased the remainder for about thirteen miles. In justice to the troops, it must be said that they and their horses were very tired, and that Perry was foolhardy in committing them to battle without trustworthy intelligence about the enemy. Nevertheless, it is an inevitable conclusion that these two companies of First Cavalry were far from being dependable troops in combat, and the wounding of but "4" Indians indicates that either the men were deplorable marksmen or the rifles were in poor condition or both. The shortcomings of Perry's company which McCarthy listed in his diary were borne out in the casualty lists, "F" Company losing twenty killed to Trimble's thirteen. As the dispatches indicated that the *troops* were outnumbered, the public did not become critical at the time; but a few weeks later, after other developments were added to this defeat, editorial comments sharply criticizing Howard began to appear in the newspapers. What they might have said had they known some of the Indians went into battle with bows and arrows and old cap-and-ball revolvers, instead of first-class arms, is another matter.

Presumably, the troopers rode into battle with a false sense of superiority. Not only were these Indians wholly untested in battle against troops, but there had even been predictions that they would not fight. In one salutary demonstration, the Nez Perce showed that not only would they fight but that they could fight with the skill, courage and determination that would have been creditable to the best troops in the Army. Several officers who had served meritoriously during the Civil War were to learn the hard way that these Indians were formidable fighters and, undoubtedly, the general public never did get an adequate idea of the problem which the troops had to face.

The days immediately following the initial murders were tense ones. At Kamiah, the chief, James Lawyer, promptly informed Francis M. Redfield (the sub-agent) of what had happened. As there were some Non-Treaty Indians about, and as the Agency employees had no arms, Redfield was in a quandary, as this group totaled four men, three women, and three children. Not daring to risk a trip down the swollen Clearwater in a boat, they hid out for a day or two and ignored Monteith's letters directing them to come to Lapwai. Then, late in the afternoon of that fateful Sunday in White Bird Canyon, Agent Monteith wrote another letter directing Redfield to "Take all the women in the Wagon and mount the employees and start for Lapwai under guard of James Lawyer and the friendly Indians immediately upon receipt of this." And he added that he had already sent all his people to Fort Lapwai for protection and that he expected Joseph would strike the Agency and burn it. Redfield then promptly ferried the personnel and the wagon across the river and with James Lawyer and about forty of his men riding escort, all headed for Lapwai some sixty miles away. About ten hours later, they rattled into the post—a rather hurried journey for a "dead axle" (springless) vehicle. Later, Miss Sue McBeth, the missionary-teacher, commented appreciatively to General Howard about the thoroughness with which the escort searched the vicinity of the trail for unfriendly Indians.

Even Fort Lapwai had tense moments; and General Howard, who had seen some panics during the Civil War, recalled that "nothing there was so continuous, so intermittent and fever like as the panics at Lapwai, while waiting for the marching troops." Four days after the rout at White Bird, some white ruffians chased and fired on two friendly Indians who promptly whipped their ponies to top speed and dashed to the post. Before their excited remarks could be properly interpreted, the cry spread that the hostiles were coming; the troops took up defensive positions, and the wives of the enlisted men and their children "came running, wild with fear, to the officers' line of houses" where "a block house had been established . . . , and casks of water and provisions were kept in the cellar. Cord wood had been stacked around the house to protect it from shot and all the women and children had been instructed in case of attack to take shelter there."[21]

After this occasion, Emily FitzGerald wrote "Dear Aunt Annie" that "For a few moments, I think, we women with our helpless little children suffered as much as if the Indians had really come."

When correspondent Thomas Sutherland arrived from Portland on the 28th of June, he noted that Lewiston was patrolled at night by eighty men. And even after Howard won a decisive victory, Surgeon Sternberg's wife noted that "The settlers were in a constant state of stampede because of rumors."

9

The Chessmen of War

➤➤➤➤➤➤➤➤◄◄◄◄◄◄◄◄ Napoleon's remark that "an army marches on its stomach" leaves much unsaid. Before troops can march against an enemy, they must be assembled, equipment procured and moved where needed, and a staff selected for the commanding officer. And the latter must be supplied with proper intelligence so that he may act efficiently, either on his own or in cooperation with other commanders. These things happen only when there is proper staff planning and coordination. In this campaign, the smooth-running machinery which began to function promptly and efficiently reflected the extensive experience acquired during the years of the Civil War.

Within the Headquarters of the Department of the Columbia, Major H. Clay Wood (Assistant Adjutant General) handled the "paper work." Matters referred to the Headquarters of the Division of the Pacific for General McDowell's coordination or approval passed over the desk of Lieutenant Colonel J. C. Kelton, Wood's counterpart. Administrative details, requiring approval in Washington, were routed to General E. D.

Townsend, the Adjutant General of the Army, and thence to General Sherman, the Secretary of War, and, if necessary, the President. Routine matters involving General Sheridan's Division of the Missouri normally cleared across Townsend's desk, but when operational urgency demanded, McDowell communicated directly with Sheridan, or vice versa. As communications in the field were often slow, and as neither Sherman, McDowell, Sheridan, or even Howard had an accurate knowledge of the significant topographical features which affected operations, not all of this attempted coordination was effective or efficient but, everything considered, it was often surprisingly good. Then, to make the problem of coordination truly difficult, General Sherman left Washington on June 25th for a tour of the posts in the Northwest where for days at a time he was not readily accessible.

Thus, one aspect of this campaign was that of a gigantic game of chess in which McDowell and Howard on one side, and Sheridan on the other, tried to move their forces so as to capture the Non-Treaty Indians. Curiously, the moves of the quarry were determined not by any comprehensive plan, but rather, by various developments as they were presented, and by the nature of the terrain.

A striking example of the dispatch with which matters were handled occurred early in the campaign. On the 30th of June, when in the field and about 180 miles from the telegraph station at Walla Walla, Washington Territory, Howard handed a courier a dispatch addressed to McDowell's office. This requested that the latter request General Sherman to transfer a regiment of infantry from the East for "permanent" assignment to his Department. And he concluded, very optimistically, that if this "were sent by rail to San Francisco thence by steamer to Portland, it could get to Lewiston in fifteen days from Omaha."[1] Wood forwarded it to Keeler on July 2nd, and McDowell sent it to Sherman the next day; it reached the latter in St. Louis. By the 5th of July, Townsend notified McDowell that Sherman had approved, the President had concurred and that orders were being issued effective that date for the Second Infantry Regiment to proceed at once from Atlanta, Georgia, to Lewiston—action which, in the meantime, also had to be cleared with General Hancock of the Division of the Atlantic.

Compliance was not effected that speedily. The regimental headquarters indicated that the move would start on July 7th, but Colonel Frank Wheaton, with 416 men and families and baggage, did not leave Atlanta until 6 A.M. on July 13th. Other men were picked up en route, making the total 34 officers and 450 men. They were transferred directly from the train in San Francisco to a waiting steamer and arrived at Lewiston on

July 29th—the day before Howard was to leave Kamiah, some seventy miles away, to follow the Indians into Montana.[2]

Even more interesting was the gathering of troops from within the Division of the Pacific to operate with and in support of General Howard. It has been noted that during the last few days of the preceding April, plans were made to evacuate the posts in Alaska. Also, that Colonel Grover at Fort Walla Walla had objected to his post being stripped when "E" and "L" Companies of the First Cavalry, under Captains Henry Winters and Stephen G. Whipple, had been detailed to set up a temporary post in Wallowa Valley; and that, to meet this objection, Howard had transferred two companies of the Twenty-first Infantry from Fort Vancouver to Walla Walla. In addition, while the final council was in progress at Lapwai, the general had moved two more companies of infantry from the post at Vancouver to Wallula, the Columbia River port near which some of the Columbia River Renegades were located.

The instructions which Lieutenant Wilkinson carried to Walla Walla just after the outbreak directed Grover to send to Fort Lapwai the infantry at Wallula and the cavalry in the Wallowa Valley. This resulted in "D" and "I" Companies of the Twenty-first Infantry, under Captain Robert Pollock and Lieutenant Francis E. Eltonhead, together with twenty-five cavalrymen under Lieutenant Joseph W. Duncan, boarding the *Captain Ainsworth* the next day and arriving at Lewiston on June 18th. The two troops of cavalry, leaving their supplies in the care of a small detail, marched promptly. Apparently hesitant to try to ford the Grande Ronde River after Veterinarian Going had been drowned, they marched by way of Walla Walla where "Captain" Tom Page and twenty-one civilian volunteers joined the little column. These troops passed through Lewiston on June 21st.

At the time Howard dispatched Perry and Trimble to protect the settlers near the scene of the outbreak, he apparently considered these reinforcements would be adequate. However, when the news of Perry's defeat came, the general decided he had serious trouble on his hands and promptly sent a message to Major Wood directing him to

> Order to Lewiston every available man in the Department except [those at Camps] Harney and Boise. Start all troops at Harney and Boise except a small guard. They may receive orders en route turning them in this direction. Lewiston will be my field depot at the present. Quartermaster, Commissary and Medical Staff to act accordingly. I . . . wish these movements perfected in the shortest possible time.[3]

This telegram arrived in Portland on the 18th, and the next day Wood informed Kelton that

Companies "E" and "L," Whipple commanding, left Walla Walla overland for Lapwai this morning. Companies A D G M [4th] Artillery and C [21st] Infantry will leave here Thursday morning [June 21st]. E Artillery and B E H Infantry at Wallula en route. Have ordered Jackson B Cavalry to proceed to Lewiston via Roseburg and Portland. Have ordered one rifled gun, one howitzer and two gatlings and necessary ammunition from Vancouver Arsenal.[4]

Wood's telegram leaves much unsaid. By the morning of the 18th, the horses of Whipple's companies had already traveled over sixty miles across the Blue Mountains, and, in the next two days, they would cover an additional 110–120 miles. A normal day's march for cavalry was considered to be about twenty-five miles, not sixty or more. Captain James Jackson and "B" Company First Cavalry were at Fort Klamath which was upwards of 300 miles south of Portland—they joined Howard's command on July 12th while the Battle of Clearwater was in progress. "E" Company of the Fourth Artillery, from Fort Stevens at the mouth of the Columbia, and "E" Company of the Twenty-first Infantry from Fort Vancouver were already on their way up the Columbia as replacement troops when Howard ordered every available man sent up the river. "B" and "H" Companies of the Twenty-first Infantry, which joined the two "E" Companies on the boat at Wallula, were the temporary replacements given to Grover during the absence of Whipple and Winters. Captain Stephen P. Jocelyn, a bachelor, commanding "G" Company which had recently been transferred from Wrangel, Alaska, wrote to a sister that "I left W. W. on two hours notice—nothing packed in my house. Mrs. Whipple, who occupies half of the house will look in occasionally."[5] "B" and "H" Companies left Fort Walla Walla so hastily that Surgeon George M. Sternberg, thinking that he might be helpful in taking care of personal matters for some, rode a short distance with them as they started. The doctor returned home about 11 A.M., found orders for his immediate departure, and by 2 P.M. was on the train en route for Wallula—with his field equipment, tent, and horse.[6]

When the California left the posts in Alaska on the 16th of June, she had on board "A," "G," and "M" Companies of the Fourth Artillery. Three days laters, she stopped at Fort Townsend, near the mouth of Puget Sound, to discharge "M" Company and take on "C" Company of the Twenty-first Infantry. The boat was hardly out of sight before Captain Eugene A. Bancroft, commanding "M" Company, received his orders. Taking a boat to Tacoma, and a train thence to Kaloma on the Columbia River, "M" Company rejoined their comrades at Portland.

Thus, on June 22nd, Wood reported to Division Headquarters:

Yesterday mornings boat took Companies A D G M Artillery, Bancroft, Rodney, Morris, Throckmorton and "C" Infantry, Burton, one hundred fifty (150) men, eleven (11) officers including Surgeon Hall, General Sully; three months rations [for ?] two hundred fifty (250) men, field and gatling guns; plenty ammunition. . . .[7]

This shipment reached Lewiston on June 23rd and moved out at once to join the three hundred men who had marched two days before, under General Howard, for the scene of Perry's defeat.

While Howard's adjutant was shipping all the troops which could be moved advantageously up the Columbia and Snake rivers, he and Kelton, under General McDowell's supervision, were taking steps to move all available units stationed in eastern Oregon, California, and northern Nevada overland to join Howard in the field. The concentration point of this movement was the general vicinity of Boise City, Idaho Territory; and two officers of the First Cavalry were to be responsible for leading the troops once they were assembled. One of these was Major John Green, then at Camp Harney in east central Oregon about 130 miles due east of Boise, and the other was Major George B. Sanford at Camp Halleck in northeastern Nevada.

In addition to utilizing a reasonably direct route to the Mount Idaho area, this maneuver was planned by Howard to interpose troops between the hostile Nez Perce and the Indians in the Weiser River country. While he did not, at this time, regard the Nez Perce as a serious threat, he was fearful of a junction with the Indians in the valley of the Weiser River and/or the Columbia River Renegades, and the Spokanes and other small tribes to the north and northwest of the Nez Perce country. And, although he referred several times in his reports to this movement and its *supposed* effects, McDowell soon came to the conclusion that Howard was not being realistic. Certainly the latter's dispatches show a lack of a sound appreciation of the various problems involved in this concentration and movement, as indicated by this message written to Major Wood shortly after Perry's defeat:

Please inform General McDowell and ask him to send staff officer to me. His California troops should in my judgement be ready to move, but when, will depend on my success against Joseph, seventy five miles eastward. From the instant I have broken his back, I shall proceed against the Indians collecting and threatening on Hangman's Creek near the Spokanes. . . . shall not feed the enemy in driblets, but I had to start the two companies to stop the murder of men and women and to keep the attention of Joseph while I concentrated my troops.[8]

In this message and others, Howard showed that he had almost no conception of the time it took to get these troops into position and to move them over the mountains north of Boise City.

Most of the troops which were funneled into this area came, by way of the Central Pacific Railroad, to Winnemucca, Nevada. Then they marched northward, via Camp McDermit on the Nevada-Oregon state line and Boise City, Idaho, some 450 miles to the scene of the trouble. Mindful that these converging troops would require certain essentials, Wood suggested to Kelton on June 23rd that he supposed Division Headquarters would supply them with subsistence, medical, quartermaster, and ordnance supplies. The latter replied immediately that "supplies for the Boise troops will be sent from here, three months supplies subsistence for 350 men will be placed there at once and arrangements for foraging 450 animals."

And on July 2nd he reported that "Captain Bradley, Assistant Quartermaster who should arrive at Boise today, has been instructed to hire all guides, packers, pack train and whatever may be necessary to outfit Major Green's command for effective work. He is also ordered to purchase, contract, or make requisition for whatever may be required by the troops."[9]

The column from this area marched in two sections. Major Sanford with about 200 men, 21 packers and 75 pack animals left Boise on July 17th and joined Howard at Kamiah twelve days later, having left Captain Edwin V. Sumner and about 50 men in the vicinity of Mount Idaho. Major Green followed about two days behind, and was left to guard the Camas Prairie area when Howard, taking Sanford's detachment, left for Montana.

By the 20th of June, General McDowell was able to make this summary of actual or contemplated movements for General Sherman:

> [Howard] has at Lewiston and Lapwai, four companies of cavalry, two hundred and fifty nine (259) men and three companies of Infantry eighty eight (88) men. There are enroute to Lewiston from the two departments, six companies of cavalry, three hundred and fifty eight (358) men, five companies of Artillery, one hundred and sixty six (166) men, and three companies of Infantry eighty nine (89) men. Total force will be nine hundred and sixty (960) men. Troops from Harney, McDermitt and Halleck will probably move via Boise.[10]

Two weeks later he added this bit of information:

> In addition to the troops heretofore reported as having been sent to Howard's Command, I have given him the company of 1st Cavalry ["G" Co.] from [Colonel] Kautz's Department [of Arizona] at San Diego and sent the Light Battery of Artillery at Presidio as Mounted Infantry.

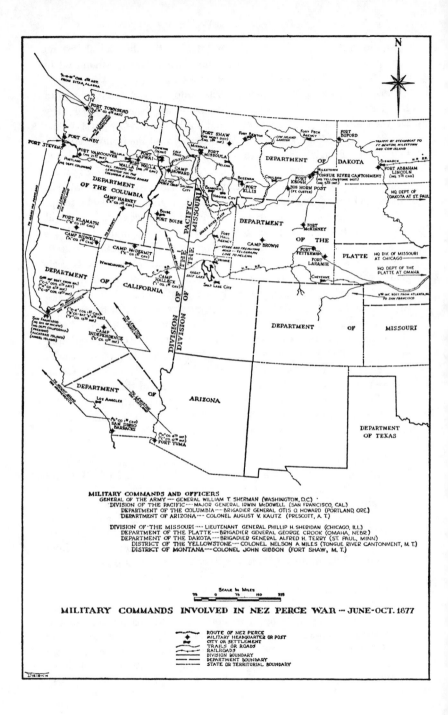

MILITARY COMMANDS AND OFFICERS
GENERAL OF THE ARMY ···· GENERAL WILLIAM T SHERMAN (WASHINGTON, D.C.) ·
DIVISION OF THE PACIFIC ···· MAJOR GENERAL IRWIN McDOWELL (SAN FRANCISCO, CAL)
DEPARTMENT OF THE COLUMBIA ···· BRIGADIER GENERAL OTIS O. HOWARD (PORTLAND, ORE.)
DEPARTMENT OF ARIZONA ···· COLONEL AUGUST V. KAUTZ (PRESCOTT, A. T.)

DIVISION OF THE MISSOURI ···· LIEUTENANT GENERAL PHILLIP H. SHERIDAN (CHICAGO, ILL)
DEPARTMENT OF THE PLATTE ···· BRIGADIER GENERAL GEORGE CROOK (OMAHA, NEBR.)
DEPARTMENT OF THE DAKOTA ···· BRIGADIER GENERAL ALFRED H. TERRY (ST. PAUL, MINN)
DISTRICT OF THE YELLOWSTONE ···· COLONEL NELSON A. MILES (TONGUE RIVER CANTONMENT, M. T.)
DISTRICT OF MONTANA ···· COLONEL JOHN GIBBON (FORT SHAW, M. T.)

SCALE IN MILES
75   0   75   150   225

MILITARY COMMANDS INVOLVED IN NEZ PERCE WAR ··· JUNE-OCT. 1877

ROUTE OF NEZ PERCE
MILITARY HEADQUARTER OR POST
CITY OR SETTLEMENT
TRAILS OR ROADS
RAILROADS
DIVISION BOUNDARY
DEPARTMENT BOUNDARY
STATE OR TERRITORIAL BOUNDARY

The latter unit, Battery B commanded by Captain Hasbrouck, was a makeshift outfit mounted on old artillery horses. It left San Francisco on July 3rd and, traveling via Winnemucca and Boise, reached Kamiah with Sanford's column. As preparations were then under way to pursue the Indians over the Lolo Trail, service for which this company's horses were totally unsuited, Howard ordered it to retrace its steps to the Presidio.

When the Second Infantry Regiment failed to arrive promptly and it was feared the crest of the spring flood on the Snake would drop so steamboat transportation to Lewiston would be difficult, McDowell scraped the bottom of the proverbial barrel. He ordered up from Fort Yuma, Arizona, "C" Company of the Twelfth Infantry and "H" Company of the Eighth Infantry. When these reached San Francisco, he added "C" and "L" Companies of the Fourth Artillery, then stationed at the Presidio and Alcatraz Head, making a total of ten officers and ninety-six men. These, with thirty-two green recruits, were put on a steamer and sent to Portland. They reached Lewiston on June 19th, making the quickest trip to the front of any troop shipment—the infantrymen from Fort Yuma spending only eleven days en route. Among the men from Arizona was Second Lieutenant Guy Howard, the junior officer of "C" Company Twelfth Infantry. Guy Howard was the general's oldest son, and his father promptly made him one of his aides.

The securing of Indian scouts was a problem because of the extreme economy made necessary by the failure of Congress to vote an appropriation for the Army for the fiscal year of 1877–1878. At first Sherman told McDowell that he would have to release scouts in Arizona if he wished to acquire others for this campaign, but shortly afterward he authorized Howard to engage twenty-five. By the 5th of July, this authorization had been raised to eighty. Some of those secured were Treaty Nez Perce, but most of them were from the Shoshone Reservation at Fort Hall. Of the latter, a number had seen service against the Sioux and Cheyennes the preceding summer.

Civilian volunteers were never a stable, dependable part of the military force. At the time of the outbreak, there was a spontaneous banding together for mutual protection. This was then followed by an attempt of the various governors to organize state militia.

At Mount Idaho, Ad Chapman first headed a group of about thirty-five, and at Lewiston, a company of about twenty-five formed under the leadership of Ed McConville. When Chapman became a guide for Howard, D. B. Randall assumed command of the Mount Idaho men, and when he was killed, James Cearley took over. Later the two groups were combined to form the 2nd Regiment of Idaho Volunteers with McConville as commanding officer. An officer of this unit, who apparently rendered noteworthy service after Howard went to Montana, was George M. Shearer who, as an officer in the Confederate Army, was said to have served on the staff of General Robert E. Lee.

Other groups in Idaho were less useful. "Captain" Tom Page and his party of twenty-one, who arrived with Whipple's detachment, stayed a short time and then pleaded "pressing business at home." As they left, William Hunter with about forty men arrived from Dayton, W.T.—a small town midway between Lewiston and Walla Walla. They stayed for two weeks, or until it was thought the war was over. Another group of twenty or twenty-five from Pomeroy, a small town twenty-five miles east of Dayton, also came dashing to the aid of the Idaho settlers. However, their leader, "Captain" J. W. Elliott, and some of the party were—according to guarded comments in *The Teller*—more interested in stealing stock than hunting Indians.

Although General Howard was courteous to these groups, others— including the correspondent Thomas Sutherland—viewed them with disdain. After spending a couple of weeks with Howard in the field, Mc-Dowell's aide, Captain Birney B. Keeler, telegraphed his commanding officer:

> Volunteers of the character and status of those operating with General Howard would be worse than useless. If you had been here during these operations I am sure you would discourage the use of volunteers in any possible emergency.[11]

This comment raised civilian hackles, but it undoubtedly had considerable truth in it.

As soon as the outbreak occurred, the governors of Idaho, Oregon, and Washington telegraphed the Secretary of War for permission to organize state militia. Governor E. P. Ferry of Washington Territory made this inflated claim:

> Indian matters look very serious in our eastern counties. Stock has been stolen driven off and other depredations committed and settlers threatened. Many have taken refuge at Walla Walla. Others are congregated and fortified. The situation in my opinion is very critical.[12]

Governor Mason Brayman of Idaho Territory did not wait for official sanction. As soon as his request was on its way to Washington, he issued General Orders No. 1, creating state militia and appointing himself commander in chief. In this order, he did insert the qualification that all organizations were to be "voluntary and without direct and special authority of any law" and that "the commander in chief has no fund for war purposes, and thus far, no authority to pledge the Territory or the United States for payment."[13] To all these requests, Secretary McCrary made the same reply—no authority would be given except at the request of General McDowell. However, obsolete but serviceable arms were made available from government stores.

On one occasion, Colonel Alfred Sully, who was at Fort Lapwai while Howard was in the field, sent a telegram to McDowell suggesting that it might be wise to call for volunteers to counter the threat posed by certain Indians whose neutrality was beginning to waver. McDowell forwarded the request to the Adjutant General, and he, in the absence of the Secretary, passed it on to the President for his consideration. Attached was this endorsement: "The Department has always objected to the employment of volunteers unless the necessity was of an immediate character and the danger imminent." The President gave verbal approval but requested that McDowell be instructed to be very cautious and careful in any steps which he took.[14] Before any action was taken, the need passed and the matter was dropped. At another time, before the Indians left Idaho, Howard accepted the offer of two hundred Washington Territory volunteers and McDowell promptly directed him to dispense with them at the earliest possible moment.

The hard truth was that such troops usually created more problems than they solved. Invariably, the men were undisciplined and lacked training and, like the volunteers at White Bird Canyon, could not be depended upon in battle—unless, as happened on one occasion, they were cornered and had to fight for their lives. And quartermasters and finance officers could look forward to little except trouble with their accounts.

As indicated in one of the early dispatches, Howard established a Quartermaster Commissary Depot at Lewiston. Some indication of the size of the supply problem is contained in a report dated July 19th which stated that by the time the Second Infantry would reach Lewiston—about a week later—there would be on hand at this point 100 days' rations for 2,000 men.[15]

Lieutenant Bomus, the post quartermaster at Fort Lapwai, engaged the first pack train on the evening of June 15th, but when Lieutenant Frederick H. E. Ebstein, regimental quartermaster of the Twenty-first Infantry, arrived, the latter assumed the duties of handling the depot. Then when Ebstein went to Montana with Howard's column, Bomus again assumed the responsibilities of the depot. His report at the end of the campaign detailed some of the more perplexing problems.

One of the most pressing involved transportation from the depot to the "three different columns." As "all available pack animals" were absorbed by Howard's column, Bomus had to turn to wagons—for which most of the country was not at all suited. Army posts and depots were drained of vehicles and when these arrived, they were "invariably" found to be of the poorest kind. Then the Oregon Steam Navigation Company often delivered the wagons with the right number of wheels, but without regard as to whether they were front or rear wheels. Harness was rotten and worthless; there were few teams to be had in the country; and, because most of the laboring class of men in Lewiston had already gone with Howard, teamsters and packers had to be drawn from neighboring towns, and these "unaccustomed generally to the ways and discipline of the Army, independent & restless" were "constantly quitting."

The lieutenant's records show that he had hired 462 "civilian pack animals" since he engaged the first thirty pack mules to carry supplies for Captain Perry's ill-fated column. Of these, 234 were covered by affidavit as "being lost"—a considerable number to the Nez Perce, of course. The going rate was "one ($1) dollar coin" per animal per day. (A four-horse team cost "$12 coin" per day.) In June, ten packers had been hired at $85 "coin" per month, and forty-eight at $65 per month. However, late in July, Bomus had to settle a dispute among the packers with Howard. At this time he took up on his payroll "one chief packer @ $150, nineteen @ $100, forty seven @ $85, & forty six @ $65 coin each month."

These wages indicate some of the financial difficulties. As greenbacks circulated at below par, prices were based on "coin" or *hard* money. Then, because of the financial straits in which Congress had placed the Army, all bills had to be paid by a voucher—a promise to pay—and this resulted in an increase of a flat ten percent in all customary charges. Bomus also noted that the depot required the services of wheelwrights, blacksmiths, saddlers, carpenters, wagon masters, one clerk, "corral & Asst. corral masters," and a Transportation Agent. The Transportation Agent and the wheelwright each drew $150 per month, the chief corral master $120, the blacksmiths $100, while an ordinary laborer was paid $2.50 per day.[16]

If Napoleon was correct that an army marches on its stomach, then some credit for the campaign which was sustained belongs to Major George H. Weeks, Chief Quartermaster of the Department of the Columbia, to Lieutenant Peter S. Bomus who handled the depot at Lewiston, and to Lieutenants F. H. E. Ebstein, John Q. Adams and Peter Leary, Jr., who searched the countryside in Montana for various necessities, and to their counterparts at Forts Ellis, Keogh, Custer, and Buford.

Not all of the picture of these days relates to commanding officers planning their tactics, adjutants working out troop movements, and quartermasters dickering for forage and hiring pack mules. These were also the times that tug at the heartstrings. Emily FitzGerald set down part of this record in a long installment letter to her mother. This read, in part:

June 24, 1877

* * *

I have not been able to write or even to think for a week. Such confusion as our quiet little Lapwai has been in. When I can, I will write the particulars. Since the battle, we have all had a great deal to occupy us. Mrs. Boyle and I have been with Mrs. Theller. The poor little laundress, who has also lost her husband, has been staying in our house ever since her husband left, as she has been afraid in her own quarters outside the garrison. Then all week there have been troops passing through and we have entertained the officers. I had eight for lunch and seven for dinner, and I think Mrs. Boyle must have had a dozen today. The parade ground is full of horses, the porches are full of trunks and blankets, everybody is rushing about, and everything is in confusion. My brain is in as much confusion as anything else. The army is so reduced, and none of the companies are full, and all the troops that can possibly be gathered from all this region only amount to three hundred. * * *

This last week is the most dreadful I have ever passed through. John came home, and I felt a little relieved of the horrors that hung over me when I heard that he was not to go out with the first detachment. I heard General Howard say . . . [that] Doctor had better be left here, as he belonged to the Post. I had Dr. Alexander (Em's brother-in-law) with me the week before John came home from Portland, and also Dr. Sternberg [from Fort Walla Walla]. You can't imagine how sad it all is here. Here are these nice fellows gathered around our table, all discussing the situation and all knowing they will never all come back. One leaves his watch and little fixings and says, "If one of those bullets gets me, send this to my wife." Another gave me his boy's photograph to keep for him, as he could not take it. He kept his wife's with him, and twice he came back to look at the boy's before he started off. One officer left a sick child, very ill; another left a wife to be confined next month. What thanks do they all get for it. No pay, and abuse from the country that they risk their lives to protect. * * * Doctor says that we are in no danger here at the post. He says to tell you he wishes he could just pick us up and set us down with you for the next month out of all this hullabaloo. But, indeed, I would not go. * * * I hope and pray that dear, old John will be spared to me and not sacrificed to those red devils for a country that isn't worth it.

Your loving daughter
EMILY F.

P.S. Can you imagine how terrible it is for us women at Lapwai with all this horrible Indian war around us, and with these two women, constantly before our eyes, and we not knowing who will be the next sufferer. They are the first, but they will not be the last. . . . If John had been there [sic—here], he would have gone with Colonel Perry and, in all probability, been killed. * * *[17]

10

A Game of Hide and Seek

>>>>>>>><<<<<<< In the two weeks following the out-
break, the pattern of movement followed by the Indians had a logical
sequence. First, the camp had moved from Tepahlewam, like a startled
deer, to Cottonwood Creek—away from the scene of the depredations.
Then, apparently realizing that they had no wish to move closer to Fort
Lapwai, or Kamiah where the Treaty Indians were concentrated, they had
retraced their steps to the shelter of the towering Salmon River hills to
await developments. Here, they had won a smashing victory, which must
have been as unexpected to them as it was to the soldiers. However, just as
at Cottonwood Creek, the chiefs must have realized that the location
offered no real security if the soldiers came again—as they probably would.
And so they moved up the Salmon a short distance and began to cross at
Horseshoe Bend to the wild, rugged country that lay between the Salmon
and the Snake rivers. At the moment, this was the best location in which
to await future developments.

When he was assured that the troops from Alaska would arrive shortly,

General Howard prepared to move with the force at hand, leaving Captain Boyle and "G" Company of the Twenty-first Infantry to garrison Fort Lapwai. At this point, he had two companies of the First Cavalry, one of the Fourth Artillery, and five of the Twenty-first Infantry—a total of 227 men.[1] Of these, about 100 were cavalrymen and to their number would soon be added 66 men and three officers left from the White Bird fight, thus bringing the total of men in the field to slightly under three hundred. And there were twenty-one civilian volunteers under "Captain" Page of Walla Walla.

Howard recalled later that the moment of starting

is always a solemn moment,—a startling moment to the apprehensive mind. The air is full of rumors. * * * Still this body of resolute men make a fine appearance. The cavalrymen set on their horses waiting the word; the infantry firmly grasping their rifles, are in line, ready to move; the artillery, who are really foot soldiers, with a bright uniform, present their perfect ranks slightly retired from the rest. The mountain howitzer, old and worn, but "fixed up" for the occasion, and the two Gatling guns flank the picture on one side with their as yet restless, spirited animals; . . . [the pack] train, now an irregular body of noisy mules, going backward and forward, unstable as water, while the last few loads of commissary supplies are being strung to their appointed *aparajos* already upon their backs, remains grouped around the storehouse door. As I move out with my three staff officers, receive the salutes and listen to the firm, unhesitating, manly orders that put the small mass in motion, a little of the old thrill of war comes back to me.

It was another noticeable occasion as the column wound its way up the foothills of the Craig Mountain. The cavalrymen led their horses, two abreast; the infantrymen followed, arms at ease, talking, smoking, and apparently light-hearted as boys on a holiday tramp. The mule column lumbered along, one and another of these indefatigable burden-carriers darting out and in, now ahead and now behind, to catch a bite of grass; while the bell-mare kept up the unending ding-dong call, occasionally relieved by the packers' oaths.[2]

It was midday, June 22nd, when the column moved out. In direct command was Captain Charles B. Throckmorton of the Fourth Artillery, but a few days later, after having impressed Howard unfavorably by "unaccountably" delaying the march, his position was given to Captain Marcus P. Miller, also of the Fourth Artillery, who had come from Fort Stevens. Miller had previously rendered gallant service and the general described him as being "of middling height, well knit for toughness, light beard and lightish hair—handsome forehead, somewhat arched, blue eye and a pleasant speaking face. [The kind of soldier who] manages to take a sincere pleasure in loyal duty."

The lighthearted atmosphere lasted until after the first camp. Then inclement weather, mud and hard work began to force a serious note—as did the sights at Norton's Cottonwood House where they camped shortly after 1:30 P.M. the following day.

> His house was deserted. The Indians has rummaged everything; what the family had left there was found in complete disorder * * * the clothing cut and torn and strewn about—the broken chairs, and open drawers, the mixing of flour, sugar, salt and rubbish—the evidences of riot run mad.

These, together with a lonely "pup . . . flowers and chickens uncared for, milk pails left on the fence" were evidence of the effects of war.

As the command did not move on the following day—Sunday—Howard was later accused of being overpious and wasting a day. This criticism the general was to answer by explaining that, as he was close to the enemy, he thought it necessary to learn what he could lest he needlessly "flush the game," and that it also provided time for the Alaskan troops, who were somewhere behind, to catch up. Here Perry visited the general and when the latter learned that the Indians were still in the White Bird area, he ordered Captain Trimble to take the remnant of his company and set out at once for the little settlement at the mouth of Slate Creek.

This movement Howard was to explain variously—as a move to protect the settlement should he drive the Indians that way, and as cover for the left flank of a proposed movement against the Indians. The march was made by way of the old miners' trail through the mountains from Mount Idaho to Florence, and then doubling back sharply toward the northwest and approaching the settlement from the rear. It was a miserable night march, as the trail was obstructed by rocks and down timber, and snow and rain fell most of the time. Trimble reached his destination about 2 A.M. Monday morning, finding the people of the settlement badly frightened.

As the movements of troops, volunteers and Indians which occurred during the next ten days are somewhat involved, they are most easily understood when placed in proper relation to each other on a day-to-day basis. These began on

MONDAY, JUNE 25TH

Trimble's men, accompanied by some volunteers from Mount Idaho, left Grangeville on Sunday and reached Slate Creek shortly after midnight. Here they were to remain on picket duty for six days. When Howard's column broke camp, the infantry was sent southeastward across the edge of Camas Prairie to Johnson's ranch, a place some four miles from the head of White Bird Canyon and not far from the site of the camp from which Wahlitits and his two companions set out on their initial foray. The general and the cavalry proceeded down the road to Grangeville where the remnant of Perry's company was camped. While the troops rested, Howard gathered all the information he could from the local citizens. Then he proceeded to nearby Mount Idaho, Grangeville's rival, where he was shown the defenses which the citizens had improvised, visited the wounded at L. P. Brown's Mt. Idaho Hotel, and made a short speech to the townspeople who quickly assembled. Howard, without promising too much, tried to assure them that he would prosecute the war with all the troops available, and asked for their cooperation in the form of whatever information and supplies might be available. As will be noted shortly, the "information" was forthcoming without much delay. Then, returning to his troops, he marched to join the infantry.

While this was taking place, Kelton forwarded to Wood a telegram which General McDowell had just received from General Sherman. This read:

> I expect to start for the Yellowstone and Montana, Wednesday. Meantime will do all that is possible to strengthen your hand, in the matter of the Nez Perce outbreak. You may instruct Howard to pay no attention to boundary lines of the Division; only in case the Indians retreat toward Montana, to send word as much in advance as possible.[3]

"*You may instruct Howard to pay no attention to boundary lines of the Division. . . .*" This was the only order of importance given Howard during these early weeks as to *how* to prosecute the war; and it provided him with a *carte blanche* for unlimited freedom of action. Later, Howard either forgot this order or placed on it a somewhat less literal interpretation than was intended. Certainly, no one instruction was to be the foundation for more controversy than this one.

TUESDAY, JUNE 26TH

At 6:30 in the morning, the troops left Johnson's ranch and went directly to the point where the trail descends into White Bird Canyon. Their purpose was to make "a reconnaissance." The general, whose writings are filled with detailed explanations of the logic of his maneuvers, wrote—in typical fashion—on this occasion:

> This reconnaissance . . . was important. It was fishing for much needed information: "Where are Joseph and White Bird? How many

warriors have they with them?" It was occupying their attention and keeping them together. It was, further, the best method of gaining time for the companies now *en route* to overtake us and for those moving northward from Boise City to get into such a position as would prevent an escape of the hostiles in that direction. This Boise movement under Colonel [sic—Major John] Green, was intended to keep the disaffected Nez Perces and the Weiser Indians apart.[4]

At the time, Howard actually believed that Major Green was moving into the stated position; but in August, when he prepared his interim report, he wrote:

> Bendire's company, ["K"] First Cavalry, was sent direct from Harney to the Weiser country and was in position on the 29th of June, in season to effect the object desired. The other troops, of which I shall hereafter speak, three companies of cavalry and three of infantry, were more slowly brought together from great distances, so that Green did not commence his northward march from Boise until the 10th of July.[5]

In this case, as with a few others during the campaign, the statement is truthful as far as it goes, but it is not a *complete* statement of all the facts. And this sort of thing taints much of what the general wrote about the campaign.

The actual reconnaissance was carried out by Page and his volunteers with Ad Chapman as a guide. They left Howard's men at the top of the trail leading into White Bird Canyon and turned westward, traveling along the rim of the canyon. Finally, when they came to the point where they could look down into the canyon of the Salmon River, they discovered Indians on the distant hills on the opposite side of the river.

The soldiers had another objective. Leaving Captain Whipple and his troop to guard the pieces of artillery and the head of the trail, the remainder, under Perry's guidance, began a search for the dead—a watchful search with a line of skirmishers under Captain Miller thrown out ahead, flankers on either side, and the whole reinforced by Captain Winters' cavalrymen. Slowly they covered the area of the rout. As the bodies had laid exposed to the sun and rain for ten days, they were in a terrible condition. A lieutenant noted in his diary that the stench was "horrible . . . , arms and cheeks gone, bellies swollen, blackened faces"— and the coyotes had been there too. One cavalryman recalled years later that "We could not handle the bodys, but had to dig a hole by the side of each, and roll the body in with the shovels and cover it with earth, and on top of it stones to keep the coyotes (prairie wolfs) from digging them out again."[6]

Graves were only deep enough to allow the bodies to be covered, and as they could not be identified, there was no designation as to identity. Correspondent Sutherland, who rode down the trail a couple of days later, wrote: "Rude graves mark the last resting place of many of the poor fellows, some having sticks driven at their heads with hats hung on them, as a species of monument."

By late afternoon, there was "a heavy rain" and the command slowly toiled back up the muddy trail, gathered at the head of the canyon, and returned to Johnson's ranch for the night.

WEDNESDAY, JUNE 27TH

The troops now moved down into the Canyon and established what was called Camp Theller a mile or two above the mouth of White Bird Creek; and Howard informed McDowell:

> Have overtaken Joseph well posted at the mouth of White Bird Creek. White Bird is in charge of entire united bands. Joseph fighting chief. Indians are bold and waiting for us to engage them. News from Green much needed. Trimble and Volunteers at Slate Creek. Headquarters tonight at mouth of White Bird Creek. Most of our dead found. Seventeen buried. Rescued citizen Manuel wounded and starving. Rains troublesome. Roads and trails bad but troops in best spirits and ready for decisive work.[7]

Companies "A," "D," "G," and "M" Fourth Artillery, "C" Company Twenty-first Infantry, and—probably—the volunteers from Dayton, Washington Territory, under William Hunter, caught up with Howard here. In "G" Company was a shavetail, Charles Erskine Scott Wood, whom the general made an aide-de-camp about a month later; and the jottings in his diary provide an intimate picture of this camp:

> [Overtook] the main column, gentlemanly officers looking like herders, rough aspect of everyone, business not holiday costumes—
>
> Camp—singing, story telling and swearing, profanity—carelessness, accepting things—horrible at other times—as a matter of course. . . . Again there is the necessary leaving of last messages for sweet hearts mothers and wives telling of jokes about being killed, about not looking for "my body" &c firing expected tomorrow. . . .
>
> Rain—eternal rain—veal & no veal—supper in camp. Visiting the different messes, youngsters with neither bedding nor shelter, roughing it jokingly—night duty, posting the pickets—rough times all night standing in the rain—no fire—no talking, no bedding—no sleeping. Up at 2 o'clock for fear of Indian habits of attack—roll call at 6—(the

alarm shot at midnight one of our own pickets shot by one of our men.)[8]

The shooting of the picket was to haunt Wood as long as he lived and he is alleged to have written years afterward, "I had nothing to do with the sorry affair, I was sound asleep in my blankets. . . ." But this denial is *far* from convincing. Hunter, leader of the Dayton volunteers, wrote some years later that "a young lieutenant mistook one of his guards for an Indian and shot him"; a cavalryman in Whipple's company remembered that "Pvt. Reed, Troop "E," 1st Cavalry shot through the shoulder by . . . Lt. Woods"; and Emily FitzGerald made this record of post gossip:

> One of the officers, a nice fellow, walks in his sleep. He was unfortunate enough to get up in the night and shoot the picket outside of his tent . . . and killed him instantly.[9]

This, as will be noted later, is not the only time Second Lieutenant Wood was involved in conflicting stories.

As the entry in Wood's diary indicates, the grisly business of burying the dead—continued this day—had its effect on the attitude of the soldiers. Theller's body had not been found the day before; Sutherland was to note later that when he saw the grave, it was one of a cluster of eight. Presumably, this put Mrs. Theller's mind at ease for she had often remarked to Mrs. FitzGerald, "If he was only buried. Oh, my poor Ned, lying there with his face blackening in the sun."

However, the body had been buried but a short time before a new worry arose. Lieutenant Sevier M. Rains, Captain Whipple's junior officer, had found the corpse and had seen it buried. As he was killed shortly afterward, Mrs. Theller feared that she would not be able to find the body and have it removed for burial elsewhere. Also, she wanted several items of jewelry that had not been found, among them a watch which was an heirloom; and, later, notices pertaining to them were run in the Montana newspapers in hopes that they would turn up in the hands of some trader. The following December, the body was exhumed and sent to Oakland, California. According to *The Teller*, December 15th:

> Mr. Pickett of Walla Walla * * * had but little difficulty in finding the rude grave of the deceased. The feet were partly projecting out of the ground. . . . The flesh was nearly all rotted from the bones, leaving the mere skeleton enveloped in the clothing he wore in the battle. . . . What is singular is the fact that in an inside pocket of the pants he wore was found the gold watch of Mr. Theller, minus the gold chain. . . . It seems to be in a good state of preservation.

THURSDAY, JUNE 28TH

It was now obvious to Howard that he would have to cross the Salmon to come to grips with the enemy. After surveying the situation, he came to the conclusion that Joseph was a "shrewd and sagacious savage" and made an analysis which borders on the amusing:

> No general could have chosen a safer position, or one that would be more likely to puzzle and trouble a pursuing foe. If we present a weak force, he can turn on it. If we take direct pursuit, he can go southward toward Boise for at least thirty miles, and then turn our left. He can go straight to his rear and cross the Snake at Pittsburgh Landing. He can go down the Salmon and cross at several places, and then turn either right or left for his old haunts in the Wallowa Valley, or turn to the right and pass our right flank threatening our line of supply; while he has, at the same time, a wonderful natural barrier between him and us in the Salmon. . . .[10]

To Howard's military mind, all these things were possible, but it is extremely improbable that "Joseph" [sic] planned them that way. Like many other things which were to occur, it is far more likely that they just happened, as one bit of intelligence which became known within the next few days was to indicate.

Howard, having decided on an aggressive policy, now moved forward to the place where the Salmon was usually crossed, and he prepared to begin a crossing. The mouth of White Bird Canyon forks about a mile and a half above the junction with the narrow valley of the Salmon River. An isolated, triangular-shaped bluff some 600 to 700 feet high sets squarely between these forks with the channel of the creek following the right, or northerly, fork to its junction with the river, while the left one leads to the point upstream where the river was usually crossed. And on the opposite side of the river, a great, grass-covered hill—or mountain—swept steeply upward to a height of some 4,000 feet.

As the troops moved toward the crossing, Howard and "Captain" Page watched from the top of the isolated bluff, while the Indians, who "speckled the hills like ants," peered down from the points of little ridges on the immense slope opposite. Howard recalled:

> We shout backwards and forth. We can hear the voices of the Indians giving their orders. While we are preparing a ferry by collecting boats and crossing a cable, the Indians start as if propelled by magic; from the hill-tops and the ravines they rush toward our position. . . . It seems for a moment that the little silvery thread down yonder, that

we call the Salmon River, can really be no obstacle. I send Lieut. Wilkinson and others for long-range rifles, and get ready with what artillery we have to fire as soon as the Indians are within range. Capt. Page [becoming excited] . . . shouts to the approaching foe in plain sight, fires his rifle rapidly [and wildly]. . . . As they draw nigh to the river . . . they turn; and down the river they run like wild cattle just let loose from the corral; and in fifteen minutes they have disappeared. Surely all was ready for them had they re-swam the swift river. It was partly a ruse and intended to make me think they had intended to turn my flank at Rocky Canyon Crossing. . . .[11]

This colorful dash by some eighty-five mounted warriors, waving their blankets and yelling derisively, did not, of course, constitute a "brisk skirmish" but rather a typical bit of Indian *grandstanding*. However, the pieces of artillery were put in position and picket lines established to command the position. Then, Camp Haughey was established nearby.

Friday, June 29th

The work of crossing the Salmon now began, and for the first time Howard began to realize just how formidable a barrier such a river could be when the spring rise was in full swing. In subsequent reports, he referred to the stream as "swift deep and difficult," etc., and a few days later, he watched with awe while friendly Indian scouts plunged into the churning river on their hardy ponies—crossing where white scouts had failed. One cannot but wonder if the general remembered that he had callously insisted some six weeks before that the people of Joseph and Too-hool-hool-zote move all their property and stock across such a raging torrent.

Three boats were secured from upstream and a "practical ferryman" attempted to rig a rope ferry. However, after the anchors had been set on either bank and the rope stretched—work that took most of a day and a half—it was found that the only pulley available would not work, and the troops were reduced to laboriously rowing the boats back and forth.

While this work was under way, Perry's company saddled up and started for Fort Lapwai with the pack train for more supplies, and with them went the volunteers from Wally Walla who felt they had *pressing business* at home. William Hunter, captain of the Dayton volunteers, and two others paddled across the river and set out to scout for the Indians who had now disappeared. They were to find nothing but trails on the mountaintop. And down the river a few miles, six Frenchmen had some anxious moments. They had hid out on the left-hand side of the river at the time of the outbreak. Seeing Howard's troops in the distance, they had started toward them when they met three Chinese who warned them that there were Indians between them and the troops. Then, they attempted to hide in an abandoned cabin, where they were found by five Indians. The warriors took three shotguns and about $100 from them and then advised that they get away as quickly as possible. They were permitted to cross the Salmon unmolested and, in due time, reached Lewiston, where they related their adventures to the editor of *The Teller*.

During the evening, Howard made plans for what was expected to be a very minor operation. However, these were to constitute what was undoubtedly the biggest blunder which he made during the entire campaign; and the general's evasiveness about one important point indicates that he never told the entire story. Fortunately, Editor Leland put some of the missing bits into *The Teller* which carried the dateline of Saturday, June 30th.

In an official report dated eight weeks later, Howard stated:

> The evening of the 29th positive information is obtained that Looking Glass, who, with his people, had stood aloof from the hostiles, had been furnishing re-inforcements to them of at least twenty warriors, that he proposed to join them in person with all his people, the first favorable opportunity.[12]

However, he made an *entirely different* statement in an official dispatch sent to General McDowell, the next day:

> Have sent the cavalry to pick up about twenty renegades doing mischief near the forks of the Clearwater. This will render the pack trains going and coming safer.[13]

And, in an article written shortly after the end of the campaign, a third version was presented:

> Looking Glass in the rear of me is beginning to give trouble. "Forty bucks have just left him to join Joseph. He is only waiting his favorable chance." Such is the information from our friendly Indians. As he is at the fork of the Clearwater and near the line of my supplies, I must take care of him.[14]

To these statements, may be added a fourth. Writing to the Commissioner of Indian Affairs from the Agency, Inspector Watkins stated that "Col. Whipple's command of Cavalry were directed to go to the forks of the Clearwater, and *ascertain the intention* of Looking Glass, who was *supposed* to be running a recruiting station for Joseph."[15] (Italics are the author's.)

On the preceding Tuesday, about 100 Indians had met in council with Watkins at the Agency, and two citizens from Lewiston had been present. The latter reported to Leland that James Lawyer, the head chief, had admitted that there were some restless bucks in Looking Glass' band but he stated that he believed that he had "allayed their anxiety to fight." Lawyer also said that Chief Huishuis Kute had recently sent two messengers to Looking Glass to learn what he intended to do, that he, Lawyer, had seen these messengers and thought that he had persuaded them that "it was not best to fight the whites." Other indications tend to confirm Lawyer's statements.

While it is possible that Howard may have gotten a distorted story from "friendly Indians," or that a few of Looking Glass' bucks were into mischief, there is no available evidence which lends support to what Howard wrote in his official report. There is, however, in *The Teller*, the outlines of a very different story that is both logical and probable.

Howard, while visiting Mount Idaho on Monday, had requested the settlers "to help me in the way of information." Apparently, there were some who lost no time in providing the requested "information," for early Wednesday morning, Ezra Baird and Robert Nugent arrived in Lewiston from Mt. Idaho "having left there at 5 P.M. yesterday." This pair told Leland that the warriors of Looking Glass' band had been plundering near the forks of the Clearwater and that the Indians told two Chinese, who in turn told the whites, that "they had declared war against the whites and would commence their raids upon the inhabitants within two days." Baird and Nugent also reported that about "30 volunteers started immediately for the Clearwater"—which, in view of what happened, probably meant that plans were *being formulated* to move against this band. Then the informants added: *"Gen. Howard was notified and said he would send a detachment of regulars to scour the country in that direction this morning."*

Thus it becomes reasonably clear that Howard's "friendly Indians" were *Mount Idaho whites* who apparently had no scruples against hatching a plot against Looking Glass' band, that the "positive information" did not reach the general on Friday evening but, probably, no later than the previous Tuesday afternoon, and that the "detachment of regulars" was not sent Wednesday but on Saturday. And Howard, who quickly realized that his participation in this scheme was a bad blunder, probably found it politic to shift the responsibility for the misleading intelligence to "friendly Indians" instead of placing it where it justly belonged. There was undoubtedly truth in the statement that there had been plundering and stealing going on, for Baird delivered a letter to Leland from L. P. Brown of Mount Idaho which stated that thieves had been active, and the hotelkeeper told the editor about some rustling which Baird had observed. *But the thieves were not Indians. They were white men!!!*

SATURDAY, JUNE 30TH

In the morning, the companies of Captains Whipple and Winters saddled up and left, taking with them the two Gatling guns. Howard's final instruction to Whipple were to "arrest . . . Looking Glass, and all other Indians who may be encamped with or near him, . . . and imprison them at Mt. Idaho, turning them over for safe keeping to the volunteer organization of that place."[16] Considering the temper and makeup of this community, these orders can be regarded only with a sort of cynical questioning. The march, thus begun, would take the troopers to Mount Idaho and then, in company with about twenty volunteers under D. B. Randall, continue for a total of approximately twenty-four hours.

That afternoon, while on the road to Mount Idaho, Whipple's men met Ed McConville and about eighteen Lewiston volunteers on their way to join Howard. With the latter were Major Edwin C. Mason, Major George H. Weeks, and a civilian whose name was Thomas A. Sutherland. Mason, an officer in the Twenty-first Infantry and Howard's Inspector General, was to be the general's Chief of Staff; Weeks, Chief Quartermaster of the Department, had assumed the duties of the chief quartermaster in the field; and Sutherland was a reporter from the Portland *Standard*, who would also act as field correspondent for the San Francisco *Chronicle* and New York *Herald*.

Thomas Sutherland was a Harvard graduate, a bit of a world traveler, and twenty-seven years old; and he was to be the only professional journalist to follow the campaign to its end. His dispatches quickly won the unqualified approval of several, among them Major Mason and Captain Jocelyn, and he was to eat with the general's mess and enjoy his confidence. Of those things which Sutherland personally observed, he wrote colorfully and, apparently, with accuracy, but on some matters he was to exhibit a lack of mature judgment and discretion. It may be noted in passing that there were two other amateur journalists with the troops. One was a Mr. Bonny who acted as a clerk to Quartermaster Lieutenant F. H. E. Ebstein. The other was Frank Parker, an Idaho miner who wrote for the Idaho *Statesman* under the *nom de plume* of Il Penseroso. Parker left his pick and shovel, made a forced ride from the Weiser River to White Bird, and joined on as a scout, courier, and general handyman. If not with the troops when Sutherland arrived, he arrived within a day or two afterward.

By evening, three companies of infantry and part of the artillery had crossed and Howard was now ready to follow the hostiles into the narrow neck of mountainous country between the Salmon and Snake rivers. As Trimble was no longer needed at Slate Creek, the general sent McConville and his detail to inform the captain that he wished them to cross the Salmon and come down the left bank to join the main column. Later, McConville reported to Governor Brayman that they marched the intervening twelve miles "through a heavy rain storm" arriving about 7 o'clock. While he went to look after his pack mules and horses, he directed his men to shelter themselves in an "unoccupied house belonging to a Mr. Rhett," and found on his return that the owner had ordered the men out into the rain. "The Mt. Idaho Volunteers Kindly shared their shelter with us for the night. I thought that this was not a very hospitable reception to be given us by one of our own citizens."[17]

SUNDAY, JULY 1ST

Whipple's men had some difficulties during the night which had not been foreseen, and the captain reported these, along with the subsequent action, to Howard:

> On account of the distance (greater by ten miles than was supposed) and the difficult approach, the village was not reached at dawn, July 1st, as contemplated, but soon after sunrise such dispositions were made as seemed most practical under the circumstances, to carry out my instructions. An opportunity was given Looking Glass to surrender, which he at first promised to accept, but afterward defiantly refused, and the result was that several Indians were killed, the camp and a large amount of supplies destroyed, and seven hundred and twenty-five ponies were captured and driven to Mt. Idaho, receipt being taken from an authorized agent. . . . About twenty citizens under the lead of Captain Randall accompanied me on this expedition.[18]

Although this report gives the gist of the matter, it warrants a closer study in view of what Sutherland wrote,[19] and what Indians stated later. Looking Glass' camp was a few miles south of Kamiah in a little valley along Clear Creek, a stream which flows into the Clearwater River from the east. The topography is typical of the region in that the streams are deeply intrenched and the country rough and broken. In approaching the camp the troops came down a hill, or "mountain," opposite the Indians and halted with the creek between them and the village.

Peopeo Tholekt, who seems to have been a rather reliable informant, recalled that he was in Looking Glass' lodge eating breakfast when the troops approached. The chief directed him to go and meet the soldiers, and to tell them, "Leave us alone. We are living here peacefully and want no trouble." Climbing on a pony, the warrior met the troops well up on the hillside where they had halted. Here he delivered the message to a civilian, said to have been squaw man Dutch Holmes. While talking to the interpreter, others—apparently civilian volunteers who had been drinking—came up, and one jabbed the Indian roughly in the ribs with the muzzle of his rifle. The interpreter restrained the unruly "soldier" and sent Peopeo Tholekt back with the demand that the chief come and talk. Meanwhile, a white flag had been raised between Looking Glass' lodge and the creek.

The Indians, who had seen the rough play, advised the chief not to go, and so Peopeo Tholekt and another Indian went back to negotiate again. This time the "commander with two or three others" rode back with them and stopped near the white flag. In a dispatch written ten days later, Sutherland identified the "commander" as Whipple's junior officer, Lieutenant Sevier M. Rains. While more parleying was in progress, someone on the other side of the creek—believed to have been one of the volunteers—fired and wounded an Indian named Red Heart who, unless there was more than one Indian by this name, had just arrived from Montana with a hunting party.

This irresponsible shot started the skirmish. Rains and his companions whirled their horses and fled to the main body of troops; and the soldiers then charged across the creek and occupied the village, apparently making no effort to corral the Indians who scattered into the brush on the hillside back of the camp. Peopeo Tholekt stated that three or four were wounded, one fatally, and a squaw and her baby drowned when the pony she was riding lost its footing in the nearby Clearwater River. After looting the lodges and burning a few, and after trampling the Indian gardens with their horses, the party gathered up the pony herd—there is no mention of finding any stolen property—and returned to Mount Idaho.[20] What became of the ponies is not clear. One news item indicates a considerable number of ponies escaped from the whites soon afterward.

Obviously, the move against Looking Glass was a failure. Major Mason, who viewed the fighting qualities of the First Cavalry with disdain, wrote caustically to his wife that "Whipple, by the way, made a perfect failure of his expedition."[21] And General Howard made a gross understatement when he wrote, "We thus stirred up a new hornet's nest."[22] At the battle of White Bird Canyon the hostiles had probably numbered about seventy warriors. This victory had attracted some recruits and, a few days after this fiasco, it was reported that 132 warriors were actually counted.[23] But this bumbling forced Looking Glass into the hostile camp and with him went Huishuis Kute and his people, plus others who had been wavering—which raised the number of fighting men in the hostile camp to *not less* than 300 warriors. Not only did this *faux pas* more than double the force of the enemy, but it gave them the one leader who was probably best suited to guide them over the long trail on which they would soon start. Howard did not stir up a *new* hornets' nest—he more than doubled the size of the one he then had! Although the general was responsible in that he ordered the action, the ultimate responsibility apparently belonged to the "enterprising settlers" who not only engineered the affair but also precipitated the resulting skirmish.

At Mount Idaho, Captain Whipple found Captain Lawrence S. Babbitt, Howard's ordnance officer, with orders for Whipple to take his men to Norton's Cottonwood House. Here he was to wait until Captain Perry arrived with the pack train from Fort Lapwai and then form a junction with him—"the object being to gain the earliest information of the movements of the enemy, should he, as is thought probable, re-cross the Salmon." The general also claimed later that this disposition was designed to block any possible movement of Joseph and White Bird should they retreat before him and recross the Salmon.

Meanwhile, troops and supplies were being laboriously ferried across the turbulent Salmon in the three small boats. Howard, becoming concerned about the whereabouts of Major John Green and the troops from Boise, decided to accompany Hunter and three or four of his men on a scout. It was a miserable day, alternately raining and snowing, and the search for Green was, of course, futile. However, the little party did discover a bunch of Indian ponies which they drove back before them. Sutherland describes the scene:

> About sunset [they] . . . returned with a band of about 500 Indian ponies. . . . Wishing to keep these ponies . . . out of Joseph's reach Gen. Howard ordered that they be swum across the river to our old camp [where Lieutenant Haughey and a detail had been stationed to guard supplies]. If there is such a thing on this earth resembling pandemonium it was on this occasion. The strong current carried them flying over rocks, with at times scarcely their ears in sight, each poor creature trying meanwhile to climb upon the other, all the while keeping up a most dismal neighing and terific splashing. Many of them were drowned, though the majority were landed safely out of the reach of the grasping Joseph.[24]

MONDAY, JULY 2ND

Trimble's cavalrymen and McConville's volunteers, having crossed the Salmon near Slate Creek, joined Howard's men on the left bank and all started the climb to the top of the Salmon River Mountains. The narrow

Indian trail which they followed went, generally, up Deer Creek and, on occasion, across the steep faces of the hills. Major Mason wrote his wife that "the country is broken beyond my power of description—a perfect sea of mountains, gullies, ravines, canyons. . . ."[25] Howard reported that "the ascent was by a blind trail, exceedingly steep and difficult, and rendering a march of not more than 10 miles equivalent to three times as much on ordinary road."[26]

Not only was the trail extremely difficult, but the weather conspired to make the climb both disagreeable and hazardous. The troops began the ascent "in the midst of a drenching rain" and this "kept up with intervals of partial clearing, all day." Then to render the night a period of torture, it "rained hard all night." As the trail was nothing but a ribbon of mud, the packers had trouble with the mules. Sutherland wrote that these individuals were "either Mexicans or Frenchmen, with a few Missourians just to give a little spice to their profanity . . . it is no wonder that they have become famous, for a more outrageous set of swearers than Idaho packers do not at this present time exist." And he added: "We climbed a mountain which is almost perpendicular, losing several of our pack animals, which fell over its side, over and over into the canyon below."

Trimble's cavalry and the mounted volunteers led the way, followed by the "foot artillery." These reached the top just at dusk and pitched camp on a beautiful, grassy piece of tableland surrounded by tall pines. But it was a cheerless camp, for practically all of the supplies were behind with the pack train, which did not get up until noon the next day. Troop "H" had their own pack mules; so, they shared their "coffee, hard bread and bacon, as far as it would go"; and Trimble's junior officer, Lieutenant William R. Parnell, noted that Surgeon Sternberg "was ill and exhausted when he reached the summit. I, therefore, made him turn in under my blankets and canvas for the night, while I joined the majority under the trees and kept the fire going all night."[27]

Howard and his staff were lucky. Major Mason wrote to his wife the following day:

> Fortunately after dark a few of our Hd. Qtr packs got up and we had the general's tent into which we all packed as I was wet through. I didn't attempt to take my clothes off but slept as I was. * * * As our mess kit did not come up we have been obliged to live on a chance cup of coffee and a bit of hard bread. . . .[28]

The pack train and the infantry had to camp along the trail and try to sleep in the rain, the mud, and the water that trickled into their beds. In his diary, Lieutenant Wood called it "Camp Misery."

About halfway up the trail, in a canyon along Deer Creek, about twenty Indian caches were found. Mason noted that "they were filled with plunder from the homes of citizens and some stores, one in particular owned by a man by the name of Brown.[29] In one cache we found 100 bags of flour, regular 50-pound sacks such as are sold by the millers."[30]

And Sutherland wrote in one of his dispatches that the scouts and packers "loaded their pack mules completely down with their bonanza. Among the different articles found were cigars, meerschaum pipes, money, store clothing, Indian clothing, camas bread and flour in large quantities."[31]

Although Howard reported that these were destroyed, they probably were not disturbed other than what the soldiers and civilians took from them. Four weeks later, Luther P. Wilmot and a party of volunteers

> was successful in finding a great many caches and distroyed such things as we could not use or carry away, which consisted in 10,000 lbs of flour 2,000 [lbs.] Roots Camas & Co [sic] 250 [lbs.] sugar 100 [lbs.] Tea 75 Camas hooks 25 Axes 3 drawing Knives 50 Grass bags 20 Brass Kettles 2 Do pans 4 Saddles 6 over coats 6 Robes buffalo and a great many articles that I did not make a memorandum of[32]

The leaders of the hostiles, having decided that Howard was determined to follow them, moved northward to the vicinity of Craig's Ferry near the mouth of Captain Billy Creek and crossed to the right bank of the Salmon River. Up to this point, circumstances of the moment had—probably—determined the moves of the hostiles. Scanty evidence and logic would seem to indicate that Joseph wished to stay here close to his traditional homeland and fight it out, if need be. However, the decision of a council, and not the wishes of an individual chief, governed the course of action followed by these Indians, and here—for what appears to be the first time—a council made a decision as to where and how to fight.

The only noteworthy reference to this council appeared in an account of an interview made about a month later. It will be recalled that Howard had requested McDowell to send him a member of his staff. The officer McDowell sent was Captain Birney B. Keeler, his own aide-de-camp. At the time this move of the Indians took place, the captain was at Fort Lapwai, waiting for an opportunity to accompany a party going out to Howard; and it can probably be assumed that he was interested in the intelligence which was filtering into the Agency via friendly Indians. It seems probable that it was at this time that

> The next information received by Major Keeler was that Joseph was going to the Snake country where he threatened to make his stand, and

sacrifice everything. There Joseph had a quarrel with the chiefs Kool Tool Hoolsit [Too-hool-hool-zote] and White Bird about their proper destination, and Joseph being in the minority they came back across the Salmon river eastward.[33]

This is the *first* bit of evidence that indicates Joseph's subordinate role in this epic struggle. The second, at a crucial turning point, would emerge two weeks later.

11

Skirmishes on Cottonwood Creek

TUESDAY, JULY 3RD

➤➤➤➤➤➤➤◄◄◄◄◄◄◄ On the divide, Howard and part of
his command idled while the infantry and the pack train finished the
climb. Fog closed in like a blanket on the mountaintop, and most of the
men spent the greater part of the day "wrapped in blankets, hugging our
immense fires," or writing letters. And the cooks, being out of fresh meat,
turned some of the Indian ponies picked up the day before into "*frican-
deau de cheval*," which Sutherland thought resembled "elastic beef."

While part of the command shivered in the dampness, Trimble's company and the volunteers were ordered to scout the Indian trail. After
following the tracks about five miles, they found that they split and then
came together farther on where a camp had been made. Here, the *sign*
appeared to be about three days old.

As Howard was preparing to follow a cold trail, Whipple discovered that
he had a hot one almost at the door of Cottonwood House. He reported to
the general that

I marched to Cottonwood July 2, and on the following morning sent out two citizen scouts, named [William] Foster and [Charles] Blewett, to examine the country in the direction of Craig's ferry for indications of the presence of Indians. Toward evening Foster returned rapidly to camp and reported that he had seen Indians about twelve miles distant coming from toward Craig's ferry. . . .[1]

According to the story told the next day to Orin Morrill, an employee of the Lewiston Stage Company, the scouts

> proceeded to Lawyer's Cañon along the road [to Lewiston] and then bore up the cañon to the south, and had not proceeded far before they came upon a large band of horses driven by one Indian in sight. They soon saw three others in another direction. They put their horses to their speed on retreat, Foster being in the advance. He soon looked back and saw that his comrade had become unhorsed and separated from him, he sung out to him to take to the brush, and he would try to catch the horse. The horse took down the cañon and he could not overtake him. He then rode in haste to Whipple's quarters.[2]

The captain prepared to move out at once with about seventy-five men and, when a few last-minute details delayed him, he

> directed Second Lieutenant S. M. Rains, of my company, with ten picked men and scout Foster, to proceed at once toward the point where the Indians had been seen, for the purpose of ascertaining the strength of the enemy and to aid young Blewett. I particularly cautioned Lieutenant Rains not to proceed the command too far, to keep on high ground, and to report at the first sign of Indians.[3]

The road from Norton's ranch went northwestward over a great, rolling ridge, then dropped through a little, open valley—curiously referred to as a "ravine"—and then climbed the not-too-steep slope on the southwestern side of Craig's Mountain. Rains, a likable junior officer anxious to distinguish himself, followed this road to the foot of the mountain where scattered pines and small thickets of willow provided cover for the Indians. A trooper in Whipple's company remembered years afterward:

> The command left about 5 minutes later; during the time the scout reported and the time of our getting ready to start out, the Indians came within 1½ miles of our camp intending to surprise us, but seeing our advance guard coming they lay'd in a ravine at the foot of Craigs Mountain, . . . and allowed our guard to ride into the ambush prepared for them, and killed them all. (Lt. Rains, Troop "L", and Pvt.

Ryan, troop "E", almost succeeded in making their escape by clearing their way through the Indians again towards us, but there were too many for these brave men.) We heard rapid firing for a few minutes, but seen nothing more of our guard. On our approach the Indians rallied on the Mountain, but they outnumbered us (three or four to one). Besides, it being after sundown, and only about 56 men in the Skirmish line, (after No. 4's were taken out to hold horses). We had two good reasons not to give battle, so we formed a square around the horses, and retreated in good order . . . to Cottonwood Rancho. . . .[4]

Morrill reported that he was told that the troopers formed a line on the eastern side of the "ravine" and the two forces faced each other at a distance of about 1,000 yards for about two hours, after which Whipple withdrew.

Apparently, Rains' men made their stand at the foot of the mountain where shells and army buttons have been found around a cluster of large boulders. Whipple was certain they had been killed, and at once sent a dispatch to Howard with the news and a request for reinforcements. Blewett was also dead, but his body was not found until the 23rd of August when Winters' troops and some of McConville's volunteers made a careful search of the area.

Wednesday, July 4th

Howard, his command together again, now moved northward about fifteen miles and camped in a pine forest about five miles southwest of the mouth of Rocky Canyon. Here Whipple's courier found the column. After the troops had been in camp for a short time, Howard sent for McConville, made him acquainted with the contents of Whipple's dispatch, and directed him to take the Lewiston and Dayton volunteers and start for Cottonwood House. This force, numbering about sixty-five, reached the vicinity of the mouth of Rocky Canyon about 8 P.M. and camped for the night.

At Cottonwood House, the atmosphere was tense. Having been advised during the night that the pack train Perry was escorting from Fort Lapwai was not far away, Whipple moved out cautiously the next morning to hunt for the captain. This detail was found about eight miles away and brought safely back to camp.

The position at Norton's ranch was a reasonably strong one. The buildings were in an open ravine at the western edge of Camas Prairie; and, to protect the area, the troops had dug four rifle pits in commanding positions and laid up a barricade of fence rails near the house. One pit was backed up by one of the two Gatling guns Whipple had taken with him from the camp at the mouth of White Bird Creek; and those pits on the lip of the ravine commanded the flat prairie which swept away for miles toward the south and east.

In a sworn statement made four weeks later, Morrill stated that he, William Baird (one of his employers) and another man arrived at Cottonwood House about 4 P.M. carrying mail and express from Mount Idaho to Lewiston.

"Here we were cautioned [by packers with Perry's train] not to proceed further toward Lewiston. . . . I went a short distance up the gulch of Cottonwood creek above the house and saw four Indians and reported the fact to Baird. Soon Indians were seen at other points and at about 5 P.M., the whole camp appeared to be surrounded by mounted hostiles. * * * As soon as the Indians showed themselves in force around us, Baird and myself took our guns and went immediately to the largest rifle pit on the hill towards the prairie, and during the attack I shot thirty cartridges from my needle gun while Baird with a Henry rifle shot several times, but Indians were too far off to be reached by his gun. After the fighting had lasted about an hour the Sergeant commanding in our pit sent to the house for the Gatling gun, which was forthwith brought and placed in our pit and forty rounds fired at the Indians . . . and dismounted several Indians at a distance of about 500 yards. The Indians soon after withdrew towards the Salmon river.[5]

However, according to Whipple's report, the Indians began to gather about midday

and but a short time elapsed before the camp was surrounded by them, and for hours they made the most frantic efforts to dislodge us. Every man of the command was kept on the lines until about sundown when the enemy withdrew for the night.[6]

As will be obvious shortly, these divergent reports are parts of what may be regarded as a propaganda battle between Editor Leland and the civilians on one side, and Howard and Monteith on the other.

What happened was that the three bands Howard was trailing, which had now recrossed the Salmon, were trying to determine the nature of the force General Howard had on or near Camas Prairie. They had merely closed in around the troops and, seeing no opportunity to make a profitable attack, had withdrawn. The troops had tipped their hand by showing that they were content to remain on the defensive. The real reason for this reconnaissance in force was to become crystal clear the following day.

When Perry and Whipple had joined, the former, being the senior officer, had assumed command of the three companies which totaled 113 men. When the Indians broke off the skirmish for the night, Perry sent a dispatch to Fort Lapwai. As noted, McDowell's aide was at Lapwai and he forwarded the message on to San Francisco:

> The following from Captain Perry dated nine P.M. July fourth at Cottonwood has just come in—"Indians around us all day in force and very demonstrative. Last evening Lieutenant Rains, ten soldiers and two citizen scouts were killed, and had not Whipple with whole command come to our rescue my little party would have all been undoubtedly taken in." The dispatch further says in brief that it is unsafe to send anything to him until the Klamath Company [Jackson and "B" Co., 1st Cav.] arrives and urges that it be sent to his aid with all dispatch. Information just up by the boat postpones the arrival of that Co. by a day or two. Still no news from Gen Howard. It is probable his couriers have been intercepted.[7] A citizen from near Colville is just in, he represents the situation on the Spokane as most threatening. General Sully who is here shares his apprehensions. It seems there is ample grounds for General Howard's application for more troops.[8]

THURSDAY, JULY 5TH

Although Howard now had reason to believe that the Indians were gone from his front, he continued to follow their trail. Sutherland wrote in a dispatch that

> At 4 A.M. we rose at bugle call and started for Craig's ferry on Salmon river, which we reached at 4 P.M. We came down a ravine from the mountain top, which was five miles in length, and so narrow that our entire force, except the flankers along the top of the mountain, were compelled to march in single file. On arriving at Craig's ferry, we found James Reuben, a Nez Perce Indian, with dispatches from Fort Lapwai detailing the fight between Whipple and the Indians. . . .[9]

Again confronted by the roaring Salmon, they decided to swim the horses and cross the men and supplies on a raft—the latter idea apparently originating with Second Lieutenant Harrison G. Otis of the Fourth Artillery. Although some of the older officers viewed it as impractical, a log cabin near the ford was torn down and a raft fashioned from its timbers.

Several miles upstream opposite the mouth of Rocky Canyon (now Johns Creek), McConville had also faced a crossing. His party swam their horses and then crossed safely in boats brought down from the camp at the mouth of White Bird Creek. Once across, they faced the problem of getting out of this narrow canyon, the walls of which rose almost precipitously to a height of considerably over 2,000 feet on either side. This problem was made even more serious by the probability that Indians might be ahead. Fearful of an ambush, McConville managed to get his men to the top; the smoke of signal fires indicated that he had moved wisely. Moving eastward to Johnson's ranch and circling the head of the canyon, they reached their destination about 6 p.m.—shortly after a fight had taken place.

Probably there is no account of the action which occurred near Cottonwood House that is accurate in a truly objective sense. Bitter feelings arose between the officers and the civilians while it was in progress, and time merely widened the gap. Certain discrepancies exist between accounts which cannot be resolved—although the differences are less marked between those statements which were set down soon afterward.

At Cottonwood, all was quiet until about 10 a.m. when two couriers were seen coming in from the direction of the head of Rocky Canyon. Soon a half dozen Indians tried to cut them off, but the men managed to elude them and reach the camp safely; and shortly afterward a group of dark objects was observed approaching along the road leading to Mount Idaho.

According to Lew Wilmot, a "lieutenant" in the Mount Idaho Volunteers, there had been rumors for two or three days that the hostiles had recrossed the Salmon and were moving toward the Clearwater, where it was suspected they would try to join with Looking Glass' people. On this morning, "Captain" Randall asked Wilmot to take a small party and scout the country west toward Lawyer's Canyon. However, they had hardly started when they met a settler who informed them that the Indians were in the vicinity of Craig's Mountain, and that they had wiped out a scouting party and skirmished with the soldiers at Cottonwood. On learning this, Randall decided to gather a party and go to the assistance of the soldiers. Although twenty-five were desired, only seventeen were able to start.

As it was sixteen miles to Cottonwood, the Brave Seventeen, as they were to be known, took care to conserve their horses, although some of the men regarded the trip as a sort of "picnic." When within four or five miles of their destination, they saw a large body of horsemen with stock ahead of them. Borrowing a field glass from one of the men, Wilmot determined that the moving mass was Indians and quickly decided that it was foolhardy to continue to advance. However, when he tried to convince Randall and the others that they should turn back, or even stop on a nearby elevation which might have provided a little advantage, they would not listen. The "Captain," who seems to have been both brave and bull-headed, said, "Lew, if you want to go back, you can go. I and the rest of the boys have started to Cottonwood and we are going." The advance continued in silence.[10]

Soon the Indians shunted their herd—together with the women and children—toward the head of Rocky Canyon, and the volunteers found themselves facing a long line of warriors strung out across the road ahead. Wilmot estimated the length of the line at about half a mile; and Editor Leland's young son began the letter he wrote that evening with: "Had a battle to-day at this place, seventeen volunteers stood off 132 Indians for an hour before the troops came to our assistance." Randall ordered a charge. The Indian line opened and then closed behind in pursuit. A horse was shot down. Then Randall's mount was killed under him and he called out, "Boys, don't run. Let's fight 'em." A few of the men reached a little elevation to make a stand and the remainder finally rallied around them.[11]

The distance from the spot where the men made their stand to the nearest rifle pit was twenty-five feet short of a mile and a half, according to a measurement made a few days afterward; and the sound of rifle fire quickly attracted the attention of those at the camp. In a sworn statement made about four weeks later, Morrill said he found

> Col. Perry about 150 yards to the east of the most easterly rifle pit watching the fight. . . . At the time of my arrival the volunteers had made their charge and broke through the Indian line and were dis-mounting and returning the fire of the Indians. Perry then made the remark something like the following: "They cannot last a minute, they are gone, men ought to know better than to travel that road as dangerous as it is."[12]

They continued to watch the fight for about "twenty-five minutes" at which time one of the volunteers rode up to the pits, was given some ammunition, and returned to the fight. According to George Shearer, later an officer in the 2nd Idaho Volunteer Regiment:

> I met Col. Perry coming down [from the edge of the ravine]: he Said to me, that those men we saw are Some of your people from Mt. Idaho, if I had my command mounted I might have saved them, but it is now too late, as they are already Sourrounded: He further Said I can no longer look at it, it makes my heart Sick * * * I remained with many others watching the bloody work for Some time (probably fifteen or twenty minutes) when the firing gradually decreased, when I remarked that the poor fellows were all killed—We Soon however, discovered Some two or three men approaching us, who proved to be . . . part of Capt. Randall's party. . . .[13]

Remarking that "it is a shame and an outrage to allow those men to remain there and perish without making an effort to save them," Shearer mounted and rode to the site of the fight. Shortly afterward a relief party started, which party consisted of Captain Whipple and about twenty-five men deployed as skirmishers, Lieutenant Shelton with seventeen mounted men, and a Gatling gun. In his report to Howard, the captain stated that

> After I reached the point where the citizens were attacked, and remained, Captain Randall having been wounded at the first onset, I took a position close at hand, so as to relieve the volunteers from all duties but the care of their wounded comrades. A few shots were fired at us, small parties still hovering around, but no damage was done except that one horse was slightly wounded.[14]

And Howard wrote that Shelton and his detachment drove the Indians in "a spirited manner" for a "considerable distance"—which he undoubtedly *did not*.

This skirmish is not difficult to understand. To move from the Salmon River breaks to the foothills of the Bitterroot Mountains, the hostiles had to cross the wide-open stretches of Camas Prairie. The events of July 3rd and 4th show that they were cautious about committing their entire camp and large herd of horses on this bare prairie until they felt they could do so with some degree of safety. Apparently, Whipple's failure to attack after they had wiped out Rains' party, and the defensive attitude of the camp at Cottonwood on the following afternoon, convinced them that they could, with impunity, make the bold move which took place on this day. The presence of the Brave Seventeen presented a small, unexpected threat that had to be neutralized. And so, while the women, children, and old men pushed the herd around and beyond this small party, the warriors proceeded to worry the volunteers much as a wolf might worry a porcupine. Once the camp and the herd were out of danger, the warriors moved on—which was about the time the relief party came out. Probably the reason the warriors did not ride the little party down—which they could have done with ease—was that many of the volunteers were armed with Henry and Winchester rifles, which might have as many as sixteen cartridges in the magazine, a far more formidable threat than a Springfield carbine with a single shell in the chamber.

The casualties were "Captain" Randall and another killed, three men wounded and five horses lost. The loss of the horses may explain why the party made no attempt to fight a rear guard action which, as the Indians did not form a complete circle around them, was certainly possible. Of the wounded, D. H. Hauser was shot through the chest and died twelve days later. There are no trustworthy figures as to Indian casualties. Yellow Wolf admitted years later that they had one man mortally wounded. In a report addressed to Governor Brayman, L. P. Brown wrote that "the volunteers estimated the number of killed and wounded at 25 to 30"—an estimate that can hardly be taken seriously.

According to the leader of the Dayton volunteers, the battle had one beneficial result. The next morning, before starting out to escort the survivors and the dead to Mount Idaho, the volunteers checked their rifles, which were not the latest model Springfields. "Not one in twenty of our cartridges would fire."

The blood on the battlefield was hardly dry before ugly accusations were leveled at Perry and, to some extent, also at Whipple. When L. P. Brown heard the accounts of the volunteers the next day, he immediately wrote a letter to Editor Leland in which he stated that

> Cols. Whipple and Perry . . . saw and knew what was going on and did not go to the field until the Indians had drawn away out of range. . . . Our officers and men say that they learned that the soldiers were anxious to go to the rescue but were ordered back by the commanding officers and time and time again they begged to go and were threatened with Court-martial for disobedience of orders.[15]

The Teller promptly printed this letter in full, together with detailed statements made by Lew Wilmot and Oril Morrill; and, as other papers copied "exchange" material from its pages, the squabble was quickly broadcast far and wide. Then, as Perry had suffered a disastrous defeat at White Bird, and Howard had not been able to corner the hostiles—in spite of his optimistic comments in official dispatches—both officers found themselves subjected to some sarcastic criticism by the public. The upshot of the whole matter was that the civilians distorted and greatly overdid their criticism—if, in fact, they were justified in making any—and certain officers then went to an equally unreasonable extreme in an attempt to counter it.

The babel of civilian criticism stemmed from the fact that civilians and sometimes—as in this case—even soldiers fail to recognize that heroics in war are not desirable, except in unusual cases. In this instance, Perry's primary mission was to protect a supply train and to try to collect certain intelligence. This was not, of course, a bar to acting in unforeseen circumstances providing it did not jeopardize things of greater importance. In this case, *sentiment* demanded that an effort be made to rescue a party in very serious difficulties—difficulties which they had gotten into by reason of their own lack of common sense. As Perry had suffered a crushing defeat at the hands of a party of only about half the size of the one that crossed the Prairie on this occasion, he can hardly be criticized for believing that death was inevitable for the volunteers, and that it was folly to risk men in what might have been a forlorn hope. Viewed in its proper light, the civilian criticism was both amateurish and unjust.

Three days after the fight, Wilmot told Howard about the Cottonwood affair and also "of the cowardice of Col. Perry"; and the general requested that the statements be put in writing so that an investigation might be made. A day or two later, Perry and Wilmot met in a camp not far from Mount Idaho and probably would have come to blows had Howard not ordered Lieutenant Wilkinson to arrest the volunteer.

Perry quickly demanded that a Court of Inquiry be set up to determine if he had been guilty of improper conduct. Due to the press of the campaign, this did not meet until the second week in September (at Fort Lapwai); and its deliberations were completed at Fort Walla Walla on November 30th. The opinion of this Court read, in part:

I. * * * After the character of the party was made evident by the attack of the Indians, there was a delay on the part of Captain Perry of about ten minutes in ordering troops to their relief, but the Court does not consider this delay in determining upon his action excessive under the circumstances. . . . * * *

II. * * * There is not a word of testimony which reflects upon the personal courage of Captain Perry, and the opinion of the Court exonerates him from the charge of having made any improper delay in the exercise of his descretion as commanding officer at Cottonwood, nearly surrounded as he evidently was, by hostile Indians, then undoubtedly outnumbering his troops.[16]

Aside from the statement regarding delay of "ten minutes"—which is probably whitewash—the findings of the Court appear to be reasonable. Certainly, it was an official rebuttal to previous criticism, although some hard-nosed editors in the area refused to be convinced, and Leland pointed out that certain would-be witnesses were ignored at Fort Lapwai.

However, there are bits of evidence which indicate that Perry may not have been considered blameless by his associates. Statements made by both Shearer and Morrill indicate the men in the ranks believed the captain was timid in not sending assistance promptly. On one occasion while the campaign in Idaho was in progress, Emily FitzGerald wrote this bit of post scuttlebutt to her mother: "Col. Perry leaves here tomorrow, he has gotten into trouble with Gen. Howard, and we feel very sorry for him, tho he has scarcely behaved exactly as he ought to."[17] And shortly before the Court closed its hearings, Colonel Frank Wheaton of the Second Infantry, then stationed at Fort Lapwai, wrote a confidential letter to General Howard in which he made these comments:

The two, David P. & his wife together are a severe load for any regiment to carry. I think if you could have understood the situation fully, you could thoroughly approved [sic] my anxiety to be rid of them. I knew when Wood left here, that he would work for Davids release, indeed [I] got the impression here that rather than be given the trouble of coming so far from Portland again, both Sully and Wood would willingly see me persecuted for life with such a field officer with such a family. . . . Have often wondered if you ever saw my letter accompanying the charges.[18]

Colonel Sully and Major Wood were President and Recorder, respectively, of the Court of Inquiry.

Thus, it would appear that Perry's fellow officers were not happy with his conduct, and all—including General Howard—regarded his emotionally unstable wife with disdain and disgust. And army personnel who knew all the details were not disposed to confide them to civilians.

12

Clearwater—the Gettysburg of the Nez Perce

>>>>>>><<<<<<< On the day following the controversial skirmish near Cottonwood House, the volunteers of McConville and Hunter escorted the living and the dead of the Brave Seventeen party back to Mount Idaho. At the same time, Whipple's men went out and buried the bodies of the ten troopers which had been lying at the foot of Craig's Mountain for the past three days. A year later Editor Leland was to complain: "The bodies were simply rolled into a hole dug 8 to 15 inches deep and covered with sod," that coyotes had dug up several and that the bones of others were protruding from the ground. "The military . . . are guilty of gross and unfeeling neglect. . . ." The corpse of Lieutenant Rains fared better. It was carried back to Norton's ranch, placed in a rough coffin, and buried with military honors the next day.

While the burial squads were at work, Howard's men faced the problem of crossing at Craig's Ferry. Lieutenant Parnell and about fifteen men, stripped naked and mounted bareback, prepared to swim the cavalry horses. Meanwhile the raft, which had been constructed the afternoon before, was made ready. Parnell recalled scornfully that

> Otis' . . . idea was to take all the cavalry lariats (light three-fifth rope), tie them together, make one end fast to a tree and the other to the raft, and then let the current carry the raft near enough to the other side to be able to throw a line from it to the shore.
>
> When it is understood that the raft was constructed of closely laid twelve inch hewn logs, thirty or forty feet long, pounded by a current of not less than seven miles an hour, in a river more than two hundred and fifty feet wide, there was not much show for a slender rope that was not strong enough to hold even a single log.[1]

Otis and a half dozen soldiers essayed the initial crossing. This proved to be a voyage instead of a crossing, for the predicted happened, and the raft—and the lariat ropes of the cavalry—all went down the river three or four miles. When the impromptu sailors returned, the shavetail was dubbed, quite appropriately, "Crusoe" Otis. As the intelligence which had just been brought by James Reuben and Levi from Fort Lapwai assured Howard that Joseph had actually headed eastward, it was imperative that he cross the river—somehow. The general turned to the Indian couriers for advice:

> James Reuben . . . told me how it was done: "Make skin rafts and load them; tie four horses abreast to the rafts with small ropes; put four Indians naked on the horses and then boldly swim across." He gave us a practical demonstration by swimming his half-breed over to us and back. Brave Scout [Frank] Parker attempted the same and failed to get many yards from shore.[2]

Convinced that his troops could not equal the Nez Perce as river-crossers, Howard promptly put his troops on the trail back up the mountain and began a grueling forced march for Camas Prairie.

Late in the afternoon of the following day, Howard's staff and the cavalry were back at the old crossing at the mouth of White Bird Creek where they at once began to cross the horses. The next day, Sunday, July 8th, the foot troops caught up. As soon as "H" and "I" Companies of the Twenty-first Infantry were across, Howard took them as part of his escort and pushed on, reaching Grangeville late that night. It took the remainder of Sunday and part of Monday to complete the crossing and for all to start to follow Howard. Night found these troops in a "wretched bivouac at the head of White Bird Canyon. No food. No anything." However, when they reached the edge of Camas Prairie they found farm wagons waiting, which Howard had engaged to provide transportation. But Howard had not tarried long at Grangeville. He had pushed on, following the miners' road which had linked Mount Idaho and the old diggings at Pierce and Oro Fino, crossed the Clearwater on Jackson's Bridge, which had been damaged but not destroyed, and had gone into camp on a height four miles beyond the bridge at a place known as Walls. Here, by the evening of Tuesday, July 10th, he united all his troops, including the three companies of cavalry which had been at Cottonwood House.

In the meantime, the volunteers had consolidated their forces into one organization and elected Ed McConville as their "colonel." This done, they rounded up a band of fresh remounts—"hostile Indian ponies," undoubtedly part of those captured from Looking Glass, which the Mount Idaho citizens had allowed to escape—and set out down the left side of the Clearwater in pursuit of the hostiles. Howard sent a courier after them, requesting that they keep him informed of the whereabouts of the Indians.

On Sunday night—when Howard was camping just outside Grangeville—the volunteers, forty-three in number, made camp not far from the forks of the Clearwater. McConville posted his pickets, checked to make certain everything was ready in case of attack, and then rolled out his bed. About ten o'clock, the officer in charge of the pickets awoke him saying that "Indians were close by having a war dance and Pow-Wow."

> I went with and ascertained that by the sound the Indians were within a half mile of our camp. I immediately returned to camp and consulted with Capt Clearly [sic—Cearley] and Lieut Wilmot to ascertain if in their judgment, it would be advisable to attack them, but those Officers knowing the nature of the country said it would not. . . . [so I] wrote a dispatch to Gen. Howard informing him of the whereabouts of the Indians and that I would keep as quiet as I could until his Troops got up unless I saw a good chance to attack them, but, asking that I be reinforced.

Cearley and Wilmot scouted the camp as soon as possible and determined that it was at the mouth of Cottonwood Creek, but any hope of remaining concealed vanished when one man accidentally discharged his rifle. This brought scouts from the village, and McConville promptly moved to the top of a nearby hill where the men built rifle pits of rocks. Here they were pinned down by snipers for the remainder of the day.

About an hour after midnight, the Indians renewed their attack and this time were successful in stampeding the horses which had been picketed within the circle of the rifle pits. Then, about 7 o'clock in the morning, they returned in force but, after looking the situation over, again withdrew. Late in the afternoon, the men saw a party of warriors ride out the canyon and soon discovered that they intended to intercept a party of volunteers whom Howard had sent, under "Major" George Shearer, to reinforce them. This move was promptly countered by twenty men under Cearley and Wilmot, and Shearer's party was brought into the fortified camp—which the men had dubbed Camp Misery.

McConville now sent Wilmot to Howard with another dispatch, informing him that McConville had been attacked and his men set afoot. Howard sent two messages in return, asking the volunteers to hold out, but neither reached the "colonel." After waiting until about noon the next day—July 11th—McConville ordered the men to retreat to the vicinity of Mount Idaho where, at Cearley's farm, the necessary horses—or Indian ponies—were sent them from the village. Then, upon receipt of orders from Howard, they returned to harass the rear of the hostiles.[3] Ironically, the retreat from Camp Misery had begun an hour or two too soon.

The composition of the hostile band had changed considerably since the start of hostilities. From about seventy warriors at the time of the White Bird fight, the number of fighting men had risen to an estimated "125 to 150" at the time of the skirmishes at or near Norton's ranch. The Indians had been able to pin down the settlers in the vicinity of Mount Idaho and, with Howard's force in the Salmon River Mountains, raiders continued to overrun Camas Prairie. This had resulted in the burning of a number of farmsteads—according to reports, some thirty or more—and it was alleged that warriors had raided to within ten or twelve miles of Fort Lapwai. Whipple's abortive attack had pushed Looking Glass into the ranks of the hostiles, and with him went Huishuis Kute and others who had been wavering. This—as definite figures obtained at the end of the war confirmed—gave the Non-Treaty faction at least 300, perhaps a few more, fighting men. Their morale was high as a result of their successes; and Monteith reported that intelligence filtering into the Agency indicated that "Joseph" [sic] was openly contemptuous of the fighting qualities of the soldiers.

There are indications—too nebulous to be regarded as fact and too definite to be disregarded—that this was not the whole story. There was a hard core in the Treaty faction that was considered to be unquestionably loyal. But there were many family ties between members of the two factions, and there was a certain amount of tribal solidarity and pride. Thus, in the face of the successes of the Non-Treaty faction, it was believed that many wavered in their loyalty to the Government. Inspector Watkins admitted, in a letter to the Commissioner of Indian Affairs, that he and Monteith were threatening any who supported the hostiles with exile to Indian Territory! If statements contained in letters from the Agency are considered, together with the gossip printed in *The Teller,* a number of fence-straddlers took part in the crucial battle now pending, after which they deserted the hostiles and returned to their farms, professing to belong to the Treaty faction.

On the eve of battle, General Howard had with him four companies of cavalry, six of infantry, and five of artillery acting as infantry—a total of about 440 men, exclusive of his staff. He wrote later: "My force engaged amounted, in effectives, to 400."[4] As the Indians fought Howard to a draw in the first day of the battle—some 300 against 440—perhaps the general wished to call as little attention as possible to his superiority in numbers and so omitted the 40 casualties from the total. Although they were not numbered on the muster rolls, Howard had more than 440 men with him. There were, probably, at least 50 packers,[5] a number of scouts and messengers, and perhaps a few friendly Indian scouts. Therefore, Howard went into battle with at least 500 men capable of serving on the firing line. Nor was this the whole story. Captain Jackson and his troop of cavalry, plus about 20 Indian scouts, escorted a pack train of 120 animals onto the battlefield during the second day, thus bringing the total of the "effectives," the wounded, and the dead to a figure which must have exceeded 600.

The weather, like the size of the hostile force, had also changed. For several weeks it had been rainy and uncomfortably cold. But when the troops arrived at "Walls," Major Mason wrote his wife that "We had the hottest march yesterday of the season—it was fearful—the sun seemed to burn like fire. The moment I got into camp I took off my flannel shirt. I shall not put it on again until the weather grows cooler." The next Wednesday and Thursday were to be hot days also—hot in more ways than one.

Howard, his movements now dictated to a certain extent by the location of the volunteers, planned to march down the right or eastern side of the Clearwater, hoping to catch the hostiles between his troops and the civilians. As the troops moved out on the morning of Wednesday, July 11th, the cavalry was in the van followed, at intervals, by the infantry, the pack train—with a few animals detached from the main body—and with the artillery companies bringing up the rear.

In this area, the Clearwater River flows almost due north in a very narrow valley which is bounded on either side, for the most part, by precipitous, pine-covered bluffs of approximately 1,000 feet in height. To the east of the valley, on the remnants of an old plateau now cut by drainageways, was a rolling prairie. The drainageways, although gentle on the prairie, became ravines as they neared the river; and as these were both steep-sided and timbered, the trail to the Oro Fino Creek settlements tended to stay well out in the open country.

About 1 o'clock in the afternoon, after marching some seven miles northward across this prairie, Captain Trimble, who was in the advance with "H" Company, noted two Indian herders driving cattle down the bluffs. About the same time, Lieutenant Fletcher and Ad Chapman, who were scouting near the edge of the breaks, discovered a small herd of cattle in the valley. Howard moved his three pieces of artillery and a company of infantry to the crest of the bluffs and, discovering that the camp was some distance behind him on a little flat at the mouth of Cottonwood Creek, directed a few futile, long-range shots at it. These only served to announce the presence of the troops to the unsuspecting Indians and to send "horsemen . . . scampering over the hills in every direction, [while] keeping up an unearthly yelling and herding their stock together, which was afterward driven by old Indians, squaws and children into the hills in the rear."[6]

Quickly realizing that he was much too far away for effective work, Howard turned back around the head of a nearby ravine to a gently rolling tableland which was directly east of the camp, hoping to get his artillery within effective range. However, a small band of warriors, said to have been about twenty under the leadership of Too-hool-hool-zote, raced their ponies to the top of the bluff where, protected by timber and the crest of the slopes, they stalled Howard's advance. Other warriors arrived soon afterward, and the battle was joined.[7]

The bit of prairie on which this engagement took place was a scant mile and a half wide—from north to south—and a couple of miles long—from east to west. Its western half was bordered on the north and south by timbered ravines, and on the west by the bluffs facing the river. As the Indians quickly occupied the fringe of timber on these three sides, the troops were forced to fight in the open where the only natural protection was tall grass.

Trimble's company was about a half mile in advance when Howard turned back. The captain and his first sergeant, Michael McCarthy, became worried as soon as they heard the sound of firing and sent a courier back for orders. He was soon seen to make signs for them to turn back, and as they moved to comply, they came up with the pack train, which was being escorted by Captain George B. Rodney's company. A few mounted warriors had just made a dash at it, killing two packers—Gillman and Pasha—and capturing a mule which, unfortunately for them, was loaded with balls for the howitzer. McCarthy recalled that they found:

> the packtrains in a sort of uncertain state. We were dismounted, in fours lea⁀ ⁀g horses and formed by the flank on one side of the train,

Captain Rodney's artillery company in the same order on the other side, and conducted the train to the plateau where the troops were forming in a sort of semicircle . . . the packtrain proceeded to a point about the center of the place enclosed. We then sent [our] horses back to the same place and took our places in this semicircle facing outwards, with the enemy everywhere fronting us or galloping by us firing from horseback . . . musketry all around our position . . . [sounded] like firecrackers on fourth of July . . . howitzers booming, Gatling guns . . . Indians yelling, soldiers cheering, and the mules of our immense packtrain braying loud enough to drown all other sounds. The sun . . . [poured] down on burnt necks, and the thermometer somewhere around the 100 mark, and no water.[8]

Howard's account of the ensuing battle lost nothing in his description of the maneuvers, and the statement that "four hundred men held a line of two miles and a half in extent"[9] is typical of the general's style. Sutherland wrote the following evening that "General Howard had the pack train driven into the center of the table land on which we were with the horses, and then dismounting the cavalry with the infantry, circled them in a single rank around [about five paces apart]."[10]

Thus, Howard's battle line of two and a half miles was in the general form of a circle, having a radius of about 700 yards; and while the perimeter may have been manned by only "400" men, he had at least 100 more who could have been placed on the line—if, in fact, part of them were not actually there.

About 3:30 P.M., the infantry under Captain Miles made a charge and cleared the ravine along the northern side of the battle area. This was followed by an unproductive attack led by Captain Miller against the Indian positions on the west. The action now settled down to a sniping duel, with the men on the line making little shelters for themselves in the grass by piling up any rocks which were handy and by digging in with their trowel bayonets—ugly weapons having blades about eight inches long and two and a half inches wide, which could be used for chopping, sawing, or digging. This activity continued until dark—about seven hours later— when it came to a halt in a sort of stalemate.

Although the first day's fighting produced no material progress, it was the sort of day that was not forgotten quickly. Second Lieutenant C. E. S. Wood made this entry in his diary of his first experience under fire:

July 11 Advance on Indians Engage them at about 11:30 A.M. [sic], we occupy a rolling broken plateau they the rocks and wooded ravines. Howitzers open fire. Skirmishing, sharpshooting, Famous Hat. The sergt & Mcanuly shot.[11] Charge by line in front of me. Firing until after dark. Indians in the ravines after horses. Caring for the wounded. No food no drink no clothing. All day without water. Night in the trenches preparing for an attack at dawn. Anxious times. Sound of Indian dancing and wailing. Williams and Bancroft wounded. I, lost on the picket line.[12]

Correspondent Sutherland, having more time for observations, wrote the following evening:

Although we outnumbered the Indians . . . , we fought to a great disadvantage. The redskins were in a fortified canyon, shooting from the brow of a hill, through the grass, and from behind trees and rocks, while our men were obliged to approach them along an open and treeless prairie. At times a redskin would show his head, or jump up and down, throwing his arms about wildly, and then pitch himself like a dead man flat upon the grass, and these were the only chances our men had to fire. . . .

During the early part of the fight an Indian with a telescope rifle was picking off our men at long range with unpleasant rapidity (evidently mistaking me for an officer the way his shots fell around me), when one of Lieutenant Humphrey's men "drew a bead" on the rascal, and Lieutenant Humphrey is now in possession of the deadly weapon. * * *

Desultory shooting kept up, with intervals of sharp firing, for seven hours. * * * Wishing to enjoy all the experiences of a soldier, I took a rifle and crept out to the front line of pickets prepared to take notes and scalps. My solicitude in the former direction was nearly nipped in the bud, for the moment I inquisitively popped up my head, a whine and thud of bullets in my proximity and a very premptory order to "lie down, you d——d fool," taught me that hugging mother earth with my teeth in the dirt was the only attitude to assume while in that vicinity.[13]

The Nez Perce marksmanship was deadly.

At one point of the line, one man, raising his head too high, was shot through the brain: another soldier, lying on his back and trying to get the last few drops of warm water from his canteen, was robbed of the water by a bullet taking off the canteen's neck while it was at his lips.[14]

One man had his hat shot off three times—probably the "Famous Hat" noted in Wood's diary—and had his cartridge belt cut as with a knife. Lieutenant C. A. Williams was wounded in the hip and, while dressing the wound, raised one arm too high, receiving a bullet in the wrist. Captain Eugene A. Bancroft, leaping to his feet for an instant to survey the situation before the charge of the artillerymen, was hit in the left side of his chest. And Surgeon Sternberg told his wife that he

> was called at night to go to the fighting line . . . and found a man who was a packer, badly wounded and bleeding profusely. He feared he could not remove him any distance without danger of great loss of blood. He instructed his assistant to light a candle and screen it with a blanket, in order to form a shield behind which he could tie the artery. No sooner had the candle been lighted than the bullets came thick and fast at this faint little mark, and it had to be quickly extinguished.[15]

On a couple of occasions, the Indians made desperate charges, at least one of which had the artillery pieces as its objective. In a report listing various individuals for commendable service, Howard noted that

> Second Private Williams S. LeMoy . . . crept through the grass and loaded from underneath a howitzer covered by a force of Indians lying intrenched about twelve yards in his front, and afterward discharging the piece with good effect, killing one Indian and rendering it impossible to remain the piece.[16]

Lieutenant Otis was commended for a similar exploit; and the couriers who carried dispatches to Fort Lapwai afterward told that the Indians

> charged to within ten feet of the soldiers, and charged up to the artillery, and tried to take the guns from the men. General Howard was heard to say that he had never seen such desperate fighting in his life.[17]

In his official dispatch written after the battle was over, Howard stated that "the Indians fought as well as any troops I ever saw and so did ours, not one man failing in duty."[18]

The night was still and clear and the voices of the Indians could be heard as they moved around nearby and occasionally sounds drifted up from the camp below. But there was no rest for anyone. Under the cover of darkness, the soldiers deepened the shallow rifle pits and piled rocks around their edges; and the Indians built shelters of rock at the edge of the tableland. Some of the latter were semicircular in shape, from six to thirty-five feet in diameter, and just high enough to protect a man lying flat on his belly.

Although no one had anything to eat during the day, the greatest privation had been the lack of water—a thing which quickly developed into a species of torture. Captain Trimble recalled that

> we were unfortunate in having no water until a small spring was discovered by one of my men, Private Fowler, who gallantly went

forward under considerable fire and filled several canteens which were sorely needed by the wounded. . . . The cavalry horses and pack animals to the number of about three hundred . . . suffered much from want of water. For thirty hours or more they were thus confined [in the circle].[19]

Although there are several springs in the ravines which bound the northern and southern sides of the battlefield, it is probable that the one which was used was near the eastern end of the northerly one. Trimble's sergeant wrote in a "diary" that

the road to the spring after dark was perfectly safe. My company, nearest the spring, watered our horses as usual after dark, without molestation. . . . This thing was easy after dark on the 11th and comparatively safe on the 12th except for some very long range sharpshooters.[20]

The battle now developed into an unusual struggle. On the preceding day, the Nez Perce had fought with unusual bravery and determination, but it was unprecedented for Indians to dig in and maintain a sustained effort. This they did, although Sutherland noted that, "the Indians were very chary and disinclined to expose themselves, so the forenoon passed off without any particular incident."[21] Howard reported: "At daylight, the 12th, every available man was on the line," and that he directed "that food should be cooked and coffee made at the center and carried to the front."

The general now pulled Captain Miller's battalion of artillery out of the line and redistributed the infantry and cavalry to fill their places. By about 2:30 P.M., this force was ready

to push out by the left flank, piercing the enemy's line just left of center, cross his barracaded ravine, then face suddenly to the right and charge, striking the Indian position in reverse, assisting [themselves] . . . by a howitzer.[22]

As usual, Howard has made his tactics appear plausible on paper—how desirable they might have been considering the terrain is another matter. However, before this plan could be implemented, a cloud of dust was noted on the road leading back toward Jackson's Bridge.

The dust cloud was stirred up by "B" Company of the First Cavalry under Captain James Jackson, now nearing the end of its long journey from Fort Klamath. With Jackson was a pack train of 120 mules, twenty Nez Perce scouts and Captain Birney B. Keeler, General McDowell's aide-de-camp, who had arrived in Lewiston about a week and a half before. Sensing trouble as he neared the battlefield, Jackson dismounted his company and put the men in a circle around the train. Howard promptly ordered Captain Miller to go to its assistance—the relief being accomplished with but little skirmishing.

As Miller's men moved to escort the newcomers to the fortified position, they were marching—in military parlance—"by the right flank" in a company-front formation. When opposite the end of the ravine along the southern side of the battlefield, Miller gave the order to move "by the left flank." Now formed in line of battle, the battalion charged the Indian positions. The warriors tried to turn Miller's left flank, but Captain Rodney's company quickly flanked the would-be flankers and the soldiers quickly "rolled up the line." As this charge started, Sutherland was

> Standing by a howitzer, which, planted on a small knoll, had been throwing shells over our lines into the timber. I watched our [infantry and cavalrymen] . . . stealthily crawling through the grass. . . . Suddenly a voice called, "Cease firing with the howitzer." Then the stillness of the advance was broken by a single cheer, which, taken up, passed all down the lines, and the men sprang to their feet and rushed on. "To the river! To the river!" came the cry, and the same moment a Gatling gun thundered past us, quickly followed by a howitzer. The gun by which I was standing rapidly limbered up and we all hurried to the bluffs.[23]

"The rout was sudden and total." The warriors fled down the bluffs to the river bank where according to Indian accounts, the chiefs tried to rally them, but the squaws would have none of it and the whole camp fled so precipitately that kettles of meat were left cooking on the fires. Sutherland, who joined the soldiers in the advance, observed:

> The hills on the opposite side of the Clearwater were swarming with flying Indians, stampeded ponies and frightened cattle. This confusion was worse confounded by the opening of the howitzers from the bluffs and the cheers and yells that assailed the fugitives . . . and scattered the terror-stricken savages far and wide. Calmly pursuing the savages the uneven tenor of my way—the full force of the expression "pursuing" will be appreciated when I say that the trail was at an angle of 45°, down to the river bank—I forded the stream and entered the village so recently occupied.[24]

Sometime during the battle, the Indians had hidden considerable property in underground caches, and the civilians with the troops immediately began to probe with the cleaning rods of their rifles to locate these. Sutherland found their search interesting:

> Such a collection as was found in those caches. . . . A handsome silk dress had, by tying together the slieves, been cleverly converted into a bag for holding bread root. An old-fashioned hoop shirt adorned with feathers and beads which I picked up had no doubt been worn in an inconceivable fashion and with much pride by a stately buck. Knives and forks, groceries, plates, clothing, in fact, the miscellaneous stocks of plundered country stores, mixed with articles of Indian dress, handsome furs, adorned with stained feathers, moccasins, immense feather head-dresses, quantities of Camas-root bread, kouse, dried berries and jerked beef, all jumbled together in a mass. . . . For my part I found a much worn pair of small moccasins and an absurd little rag doll under a tree.[25]

A few days later, civilians took several boatloads of this loot down the river to Lewiston, particularly fine beaded costumes and saddle trappings. Some of these were sold at Fort Lapwai, where Mrs. FitzGerald saw "one . . . I could not lift."

Writing four days later in a reflective mood, Sutherland commented:

> We did not at this time fully realize the extent and completeness of our victory. The abandonment of so much of their property indicated, however, a certain demoralization on the part of the Indians. It was evidently their intention to have held this place, as the trails down to the river were fortified in a way that would have done credit to a professional engineer, and their plunder was not prepared for a move. This view was confirmed by the words of an old squaw who had been captured on the rocks by some of our boys—an old hag of at least 90 years— The tears oozed out of her old bleared eyes and lost themselves in the furrows of her face as she told of some of the wounds the Indians had received. Many, many, she said had been wounded. The chiefs White Bird and Hoo-shed-skoot [Huishuis Kute?] had cried to them to stand and fight and die where they were, but the frightened women had hurried to get their horses, and the bucks following, the camp was soon in an uproar . . . and so all had fled, leaving this poor old crone alone to tell the tale.[26]

Sixteen days later, Howard sent a dispatch to McDowell stating:

> The fact of several hundred rounds of metallic ammunition being found in the hostile camp, it is rendered certain that the Indians are largely if not entirely armed with breech loading rifles of the following description Henry, Winchester, U.S. Springfield carbine Cal. .45, U.S.

Springfield Rifle, Cal. .45 and apparently some long range target rifles—
name unknown.

The .45 Cal. rifles in the enemy's possession were captured from four
Indian scouts belonging to this command. No other arms have been lost
from this column. It is also certain that the Hostiles are very short of
ammunition and will use every effort to renew their supply. . . .[27]

This dispatch is of particular interest because of the clues to the nature
of the arms of the Indians—.44 Henry, .44-40 Winchester, .45-70 Springfield, certain rifles "name unknown," and, perhaps, Sharps, Spencers, and
others. Curiously, Howard mentions the *four* rifles captured five days *after*
the Clearwater battle, but neglects to say anything about the *thirty-three or
more* taken from Perry's men. Later, those "long range rifles—name
unknown" were to puzzle certain scouts and officers, for the warriors who
had them attracted some attention because of their skill in their use.

When Howard sent the above-noted dispatch, he also advised the
Division Headquarters that he had published "General Field Order No. 4"
which stated: "The entire seat of the present Indian disturbances comes
within the above prohibition"—namely President Grant's Executive Order
of November 23, 1876, which prohibited the sale of "fixed ammunition or
metallic cartridges" to hostile Indians in certain areas of the Northwest.
This order had, of course, resulted from the bootlegging of ammunition to
the hostile Sioux. However, Howard's order probably did not have any
legal backing until August 7, 1877, when President Hayes reaffirmed Grant's
order and broadened its restrictions to include "any breech loading firearms."

Of the casualties, Howard stated in his first report: "The losses of the
Indians appeared to be thirteen (13) killed and quite a large number
wounded. We have Captain Bancroft and Lieutenant Williams wounded,
also eleven (11) men killed and twenty-four (24) wounded."[28]

However, the report of the surgeon lists 13 killed and 27 wounded, two of
them mortally.[29] Other accounts refer to at least two soldiers, whose
names are not listed, who returned to the firing line after having their
wounds dressed. Nor are the civilian casualties listed—which included at
least two packers dead and another wounded so seriously that he had to
have part of one leg amputated.

In his report to the Secretary of War, Howard altered and amplified his
numbers of Indian casualties: "I reported at the time fifteen Indians killed
and a large number wounded. After that, eight dead were found on their
trail, of those who died from mortal wounds, making for this battle 23
warriors killed."[30] After his return to San Francisco, Captain Keeler is
alleged to have told a reporter that he had "seen 17 dead bodies." At the
other end of the scale, *The Teller* stated, on August 4th:

Both [chief] Lawyer and [scout James] Reuben declare that from the best information they can get only four hostiles were killed in the fight of the 11th and the 12th, but many of them were wounded though none mortally.

Two settlers, who returned to Mount Idaho from Howard's command after the fight, told L. P. Brown that "they saw eight left on the field." And Sutherland, writing in the camp immediately after its capture, set down this:

An Indian squaw who was left behind and who fell into the hands of the soldiers, says that seven Indians were killed outright, and that the number of wounded was very great. All the Indian dead and wounded were carried away by Joseph in his precipitate retreat, and how severely he was crippled cannot be therefore ascertained. Thirteen of the band are known to have been killed.[31]

How many were actually killed? *Quien sabe?*

On the following day, the dead were buried by Captain Pollock's men in one long grave on the prairie near the spot where Howard had his "headquarters" during the fight. The twenty-eight or more wounded presented a problem, as the transportation facilities were meager. A few of the most seriously wounded were placed in a wagon or two, and Indian-style travois were constructed for the remainder. The latter proved to be the most comfortable and men riding in them declined to change to the wagons when given an opportunity.

When all was ready, Captain Winter's troop was assigned as an escort, and Surgeon Sternberg and his patients began a laborious and painful journey to Fort Lapwai. At times, the horses and mules were halted and the wounded supplied with water, food, and stimulants. When darkness came, the surgeon, exhausted from the strain and loss of sleep, found it difficult to stay awake. Winters, fearful lest he fall from his horse and get hurt, ordered his orderly to ride beside the doctor and watch him. Finally, Sternberg rode on ahead to Grangeville, aroused some people, and asked them to prepare to assist the hospital train. The wounded arrived about 2 A.M., July 14th, and were put into a building used as a community hall. Here they were allowed to recuperate for five days before proceeding on to Fort Lapwai—a journey which took from 4 P.M., July 19th, until 9 A.M., July 21st, with the surgeon having to amputate one soldier's leg at the knee while en route.

Two days after arriving at Fort Lapwai, Captain Bancroft wrote to his father in Boston:

In Hospital at Fort Lapwai
Monday Evening, July 23.

MY DEAR FATHER:

In bed at last, here I am, after sixteen years service in the army without receiving a scratch, laid up with a gun-shot wound through the left lung received on the 11th instant at a place now known as "Camp Bancroft" on the south fork of the Clearwater, about twenty-five miles from Mount Idaho, Idaho Territory, in an engagement with Joseph and his band of Indians. I was shot about 3 o'clock in the afternoon: lay on the field all that day and night and part of the next day, when I was hauled in a wagon twenty-five miles over the rough mountain trail to Grangerville. This was a very severe trip. The wagon had no springs and I was nearly dead when we reached Grangerville. Two wounded men died in the wagon on the trip.[32] Two of my best men, Sergeant Workman[33] and Corporal Marguarandt [sic—Charles Marquardt], were killed by my side. While I was being carried to the rear by one of my men, Patrick by name, he had one ear shot clean away, and I did not know it until after he laid me down. Corporal Hess was badly wounded, his left arm being broken. My company suffered a good deal in this fight. The Indians fought like devils, and were brave as lions. The Indian who shot me was not 100 yards away at the time; I think he was killed. It is now twelve days since I was wounded, and the doctor thinks I am out of danger. I shall leave this place for Fort Townsend on Thursday next. I left Wrangel [Alaska] on the 15th of June, and arrived at Townsend on the 18th. Received orders the same day, and left on the 19th for this Indian country, and, for a short campaign, have had more crowded into it that I ever experienced during the whole war of the rebellion.[34]

13

Moments of Indecision

>>>>>>><<<<<<< When last seen, the hostiles were headed westward, and for a time, Howard thought that they were doubling back toward the breaks of the Salmon and Snake rivers or their old haunts in the Wallowa Valley. However, about 4 o'clock the next morning, a messenger arrived from James Lawyer, the Treaty chief, with the information that they were at Kamiah, obviously headed for either the western end of the Lolo Trail or the Spokane region farther north where there were other disaffected Indians.

The general marched promptly in pursuit. Sutherland noted that their route took them past "a hill strongly fortified"—Camp Misery—and "over grassy, treeless hills, with very little water and no signs of life, except some young colts, which joined us, neighing for their lost mothers, and 'fool' hens . . . which our men knocked over with sticks and stones" to supplement their monotonous fare. About 3:30 P.M., they reached the top of a high "mountain" which permitted them to view "the beautiful little Kamiah Valley, rich in grain fields and vegetables." Checking the area by the aid of field glasses, Howard discovered, at a point about three miles away and a mile and a half below the sub-agency, that the quarry was just finishing a crossing of the Clearwater. The Kamiah Indians had not been cooperative—having removed the boats normally used, and making the hostiles rely on their customary methods.

Hoping to reach the Indians before they could move away, the cavalry pushed forward rapidly along the "wide roads" and soon reached the river. Lieutenant Wilkinson soon got a Gatling gun into operation and "peppered the different points taken by the Indians," making them take cover while Captain Whipple, following a road which took him well to the left, got too close to a rocky point which ran well out into the river from the opposite side. Here he was unpleasantly surprised by some hidden warriors who fired "about forty times in quick succession." The men dismounted hurriedly and dived for cover, allowing their horses to go. But no damage was done—other than one artilleryman had his scalp creased by an Indian sharpshooter. Howard now moved "a little back from the river" and went into camp.[1]

The next day was spent in reconnoitering, watching the hostiles who remained in camp on a mountainside east of the river, and developing plans. A courier was sent to "Colonel" McConville requesting that he move up with his volunteers; and this force arrived by the middle of the afternoon. Now, Howard was ready to try a bit of deception. Early the next day, Sunday, July 15th, the general took the cavalry and the Idaho volunteers and started to ascend the heights west of his camp. His plan was to create the impression that he was going to Fort Lapwai and then, when out of sight, to turn northward and cross the Clearwater about twenty miles downstream at Dunwell's ferry (on the miners' road from Lewiston to Pierce). From this point, he would proceed to the junction of the Oro Fino and Lolo trails, which would place him some fifteen or twenty miles in the rear of the hostile camp on the mountain near Kamiah. Then Captain Miller was to cross the river with the infantry and artillery and either attack the Indians or push them back against Howard's detachment.

However, after Howard's force had marched seven or eight miles, two Nez Perce, James Lawyer and scout James Reuben, overtook them with the information that Joseph wished to discuss a surrender. Instructing the troops to continue on until they found a suitable place to halt, the general turned back. These overtures had started the evening before when Reuben had brought word that Joseph had made inquiry regarding possible surrender terms, and Howard had, allegedly, replied that he would talk to him after he had called in his pickets and corralled his people and stock.

In a dispatch written that evening, Sutherland stated:

Joseph has moved over the mountains and to-day sent word by a special messenger to our camp that he desired to speak with Howard about arranging terms of peace. White Bird, Looking Glass, Tahoolhoolsute [sic] and other chiefs in command of the hostile braves are desirous of immediately making for the buffalo country in Montana Territory and . . . [therefore] do not want to talk peace or anything else. The messenger, however, under the orders of Joseph, came to our camp with a flag of truce and was met a short distance outside our lines by General Howard in person. . . . while they were conversing on the subject the disaffected Indians, led by White Bird and Looking Glass, fired on the party, but without doing them any injury. Upon this evidence of hostility, Kulkulsuitim, the messenger, explained this difference of opinion that existed in regard to a treaty of peace. . . .

Howard's reply was to the effect that Joseph might surrender "tomorrow morning," that he and his people would be treated with justice, but that their conduct would be investigated by a court of nine officers, whom he would appoint. And note was also made of the fact that "Red Heart and five Indians surrendered to James Lawyer today."[2]

While the general was involved in the parley, dust clouds rising to the east informed him that the Indians were in motion "toward the same point I had hoped to get." Convinced that it was now futile to continue the contemplated maneuver, orders were sent for Jackson to take his troop and the volunteers and investigate conditions at the ferry. (They found the boat cut loose and the buildings burned.) The remainder of the cavalry was ordered to return to camp. That afternoon, Major Mason began a letter to his wife, which closed with this note:

Evening—I was stopped by the notice that Joseph had sent in a messenger—the General and myself went to see him. The result is Joseph promises to come in tomorrow morning with all his people and surrender immediately. If he does, the bottom will drop out of this affair rapidly. Meanwhile we press our work on the ferry for crossing. I must close as the courier will soon start. . . .[3]

There was some reason for optimism, as Howard stated in the official dispatch that "Joseph has promised to break away from White Bird and give himself up tomorrow. He said he was forced to move today."[4]

Apparently, what had happened was that the Nez Perce leaders held a council on the mountainside near Kamiah. Joseph wanted to surrender, but the other chiefs outvoted him—just as it was reported they did in the Salmon River Mountains. The decision made was to go to Montana, and Joseph was either forced or pressured into going along. For the next two and a half months, it is probable that Looking Glass was the dominant figure in the councils, with White Bird next in importance.

Of course, Joseph did not surrender on the 16th, but Sutherland reported that others did:

> Thirty-five Indians surrendered to our forces to-day, making their capitulation unqualified. They consist of fourteen warriors, and the remainder are squaws and their children. They are all fine-looking people but poorly clad. As a rule they are reticent, and refuse to say anything regarding their past actions or what induced them to surrender besides the want of food. They are from different bands, and six are from Joseph's crowd ["three from Looking Glass', and five Kamiah"]. . . . * * * This surrender is looked upon by the officers of our command as the beginning of a general disintegration. . . .[5]

General McDowell's aide sent a telegram to San Francisco stating that the prisoners "report that many others will follow their example, that Joseph was forced by White Bird and other chiefs to accompany them, that want and demoralization among the late hostiles are very great. . . ."[6]

Agent Monteith who, with Inspector Watkins, was at Howard's camp the next day, reported to the Commissioner of Indian Affairs that "the report came in that White Bird had driven all the Indians who wanted to surrender before his forces in the direction of the Bitter-root mountains."[7] Other rumors indicated that, had Joseph attempted to surrender, the disagreement might have developed into an open clash.

The defeat at the battle of the Clearwater had been a crushing one. The hostiles had lost almost everything except the clothes they were wearing, the arms in their hands, and a sizable herd of horses. They had very little in the way of shelter, supplies and ammunition; their morale was low; and they were quarreling among themselves. Yet, they chose to continue the struggle. It may have been that in their naïve and simple analysis of their problem, they actually believed that if they could reach the buffalo plains of the Yellowstone and Missouri basins, they could live there as they had in the past. Whatever the reasons, there can be no question but that fear loomed very large indeed. Sutherland summed it up in a few words— "Joseph [sic] and White Bird and other chiefs were determined upon not surrendering, as they would all be hanged. . . ."[8] The precedents were very clear. Thirty Nez Perce scouts who served with Colonel George Wright during the Indian difficulties in 1858 had been witnesses of the summary hangings which marked the close of Wright's campaign. And *moccasin telegraph* had no doubt told them about the five Modocs who had been publicly hanged after the Canby affair less than four years before.

While the stragglers were surrendering, the troops were busily engaged in crossing the Clearwater, and by the evening of the 16th, all were camped on the eastern side of the river. With a decisive victory an established fact and the hostiles apparently headed for the Lolo Trail, Captain Keeler was echoing the opinion of all when he informed General McDowell: "This war is practically ended apparently." However, Howard wanted some concrete evidence to support this idea. Three days later, his Chief of Staff wrote to his wife:

> Monday evening the General directed me to take the cavalry and follow the trail to see if the Indians had gone to the buffalo country in Montana. I was up at 3 A.M., woke the cook, had him give me a cup of coffee and a bite of fried pork and was off. After getting onto the top of the mountain I found the country densely wooded. The trail led through this thicket all the way, getting worse as we went farther. I had to exercise great care to prevent the command falling into a trap—about 2 P.M. my Indian scouts ran into an ambush and one was killed, two wounded and one missing. Having accomplished all desired in making the scout, I didn't attempt to follow the Indians with the cavalry over a trail almost impossible to handle a mounted force on. I returned to the "LouLou fork" [sic. Lolo Creek][9] and camped on the hill after crossing the stream and came into camp this morning. I arrived in time for breakfast, which I needed, for I had had nothing but a bite of hard tack and a poor cup of coffee for 28 hours.[10]

This force, which moved out about 4 A.M., consisted of five companies of cavalry, McConville's volunteers, Ad Chapman—Howard's chief of scouts, and a party of Nez Perce scouts said to have been six in number, under James Reuben. They reached Wieppe Prairie, fifteen or more miles away, without incident; and here Major Mason ordered a short halt. On the other side of this camas-digging ground, the trail entered a "narrow defile, densely wooded and almost impassable with undergrowth." At this point, the scouts were in the lead, followed by Chapman and McConville, the volunteers, with the cavalry under Major Mason bringing up the rear. Shortly after entering this forbidding area, the scouts indicated that there were hostiles ahead. The volunteers now halted to allow the cavalry to close up, and Chapman rode back to report to Major Mason:

> In the meantime two scouts had run into the ambush prepared by the hostiles, but, being acquainted with the renegades, were disarmed and allowed to escape. But as soon as James Reuben, a Kamiah Indian, and our most efficient interpreter and guide, and an Indian named Levy [John Levi] came up, the hostiles exclaimed in Nez Perce, "you are the fellows we want," and immediately fired killing Levy and

wounding Reuben ["in the right arm"] and another scout ["Abraham Brooks in the shoulder"].[11]

Then, having administered this check, the hostiles disappeared. McConville reported:

> Immediately after the firing began I dismounted my men, and in a few minutes Captain Winters Co "E" 1st Cavalry came up and dismounted and gave me an order from Col Mason to advance into the woods with Capt Winters and reconnoitre. Myself and Capt Winters marched through the dense underbrush and fallen timbers, until we found one (1) of the wounded Indian Scouts. We then with our own command skirmished through the woods until we found the body of "Levy" (also one of the Scouts) We then returned to the edge of the timber. . . . I found upon coming into the prairie that, Col Mason had his command dismounted and deployed as skirmishers, it being utterly impossible for a mounted man to make his way through the timber. . . . [After the men had mounted] the Column proceeded on its way to Kamiah. Col Parnell and myself bringing up the rear, having to stop every little while to let the wounded rest. We reached the Lo Lo Creek about 11 o'clock P.M. and camped for the night.[12]

Later, Lieutenant ("Lieutenant Colonel") W. R. Parnell wrote a tall yarn about this skirmish. He stated that while they were halted at the time of the attack, the pawing of the horses uncovered fresh sawdust and this led to the discovery that "many of the trees had been sawed off here and there near the trail . . . leaving the trees standing on their stumps and easily supported by the adjacent trees," the object being to topple them across the trail in front and behind and thus trap the cavalry should an attempt be made to follow.[13] This story is absurd to the point of being ridiculous—it is *impossible* to saw a tree off and leave it standing on its stump.

While Mason was absent on this reconnaissance, the "Military Commission" headed by Captain Throckmorton convened to consider the case of the captives, and then had to adjourn for want of witnesses. Sutherland reported that the Indians "admit they have been fighting with Joseph, but deny all participation in the massacre on Salmon River, saying that the force of circumstances compelled them to join the hostiles." Witnesses who knew anything to the contrary were "necessarily scarce." Evidence would seem to indicate that some of those who surrendered were from a band which had wintered in the Bitterroot Valley and which had left that area about June 22nd to return home. Red Heart, who was wounded in the attack on Looking Glass' camp, was probably one of these. Yellow Wolf's claim that they met these people at Wieppe Prairie would appear to be only a half-truth.

Sutherland also reported that "the Indians have two white prisoners whom they captured while coming this way." The Indians did have two captives—William Silverthorne and a half-breed named Pete Matte, who were captured while en route to Lewiston where the former, so he stated later, hoped to buy some horses. Within a week, they were to escape and carry some pertinent intelligence to the Missoula area.[14]

As the Commission could not make a finding in regard to the Indian prisoners, they were taken to Fort Lapwai and placed in a stockade, where they attracted the sympathy of at least two officers' wives because some of the families were divided—some members being at liberty on the reservation. On the 4th of August, thirty-three of them were placed on board the *Tenino*, together with a guard of two officers and twenty soldiers, and taken down the river to Fort Vancouver. Here they were placed in jail, to be tried some months later.

As the intelligence brought back by Major Mason indicated that the hostiles were on the western end of the Lolo Trail and headed for Montana, Howard—either forgetting or ignoring Sherman's pointed instructions to pursue these Indians *wherever* they went—immediately turned his attention to a problem with which he and Inspector Watkins had been concerned the preceding spring. Apparently, the plans for the course of action which he hoped to pursue had been shaped up in his mind for some time for, in a dispatch written just after chasing the Nez Perce to the eastern bank of the Clearwater near Kamiah, he informed McDowell that

> I think I shall have to push [Joseph] . . . a little farther on this line, either to defeat him utterly or to secure the country against his return. I will occupy myself in this way till Sanford can join me which cannot be done before the twentieth. Green says the remainder of his troops cannot be here before the twenty-eighth. The Second Infantry should in my judgment be sent by water to Lewiston, for just as soon as Green is here to take my place I wish to move a column toward Hellgate and settle with the malcontents who have furnished aid to Joseph and secure a permanent peace.[15]

This idea, slightly amplified, was also forwarded to the Division commander by Captain Keeler:

> General Howard intends as indicated in his dispatch of the thirteenth (13) to immediately collect all his remaining forces here, proceed to Hell Gate and settle Indian matters in that section. He

apprehends that the fleeing hostiles may seek to restore their fortunes in that country.[16]

Inspector Watkins who, with Agent Monteith, was present when the Commission headed by Throckmorton attempted to hold a meeting, informed the Commissioner of Indian Affairs that the plans for this expedition were well along:

> Gen Howard recrossed the Clearwater with his command day before yesterday and started back to Lapwai enroute for the Spokane country. He and I were going with sufficient force to enforce instructions to have a talk with the Spokanes Coeur d'Alenes Colvilles and others. But while enroute last night, word came from Jimmy Lawyer that the hostiles were back again at Kamiah. This changed our plans, and the Gen at once turned about his troops and started back. I do not know how soon we can get north. Unless we go soon I fear a general uprising.[17]

Although time was to indicate that these apprehensions were not fully justified, they did loom large at the time as it was believed about three hundred Indians were under arms there who "swear they will not go on their reservation." Not only did Watkins eye these Indians with concern, but so did Peter Ronan, the agent of the Flatheads, and other officials in western Montana. However, Howard's efforts to associate the Nez Perce with this problem were farfetched. The only logical place for these Indians to go, if they left Idaho, was the buffalo plains—and Howard knew this was where they had been saying they intended to go.

As soon as Major Mason returned from his reconnaissance, General Howard detailed Throckmorton's company of artillery, Jocelyn's company of infantry, and Trimble's troop of cavalry to remain at Kamiah and guard the sub-agency. The remainder of the force was ordered to recross the Clearwater and begin a march for the Spokane area via Fort Lapwai and Lewiston for, according to Sutherland, "Our commissary department is in a deplorable condition . . . men being without salt, sugar, coffee and other camp necessaries."

What happened during the next five days is *extremely* interesting. Not only did Howard discard the above-noted plans but he saw fit not to allude to them in his annual report to the Secretary of War. In the first draft of this report, written five weeks later, he stated:

> My first plan, which I commenced the morning of July 19 to execute, was to leave a small garrison at Kamiah, proceed with my fighting force by the way of the Mullan road to Missoula, Mont., picking up twenty days supplies at Lewiston *en route*.[18]

No mention is made of what he, various officers, Inspector Watkins and Sutherland were referring to at the time as the "Spokane Expedition" which was designed to quiet the "renegades" in the north—with the movement to Hell Gate and Missoula as a secondary operation to come later.

A possible reason for this omission may be deduced from the sequence of events which occurred. General Field Order No. 3, which covered the subsequent operations, was issued on July 23rd. Six days later, several hundred miles away at "Camp on Yellowstone, 114 miles east of Fort Ellis," Sherman addressed a dispatch to McDowell which contained this order:

> From a Montana paper I see that Howard had fought and dispersed Joseph's band, and that some of them have appeared in the Bitter Root country Montana. If these Nez Perces came to Montana order the troops to follow regardless of boundary lines.[19]

The contents of this message, relayed by McDowell in San Francisco, reached Howard *twenty-seven days later*—mute evidence of the difficulties of communication on the frontier. Howard's interim report on the campaign was completed three days *after* the dispatch containing Sherman's instructions was received. If any mention had been made of the "Spokane Expedition" in a draft of his report, it would have been politic for Howard to remove it.

While this may explain why Howard made no official mention of the contemplated movement, *it does not explain why the plans were scrapped.* Howard partially concealed the reason in the official report by stating that

> I was half way to Cold Spring with the cavalry—artillery and infantry being already there—when messages came to me [that the hostiles had come back and were raiding in the Kamiah and Mt. Idaho areas; and had stolen several hundred ponies from the Indians at the sub-agency].

> I know [now] that the alarm was occasioned by a small observing band that had followed our cavalry on its return from the Lo Lo trail, and that the only mischief done by them was the stealing of some [400?] of the Kamiah Indians' horses. But at the time, the excitement was too real to admit of my leaving the vicinity, till Green or Wheaton should arrive. I moved my command to Croesdale's farm on Camas Prairie . . . [a centrally located point] here I waited gathering of my supplies.[20]

The thing which changed the plans happened between the time Howard was notified of his spite-raid and the movement to Croesdale's ranch. As noted, the artillery and infantry left the camp at Kamiah on the afternoon of July 18th, and the cavalry and staff, the following morning. By the time Howard had gone about twenty miles the courier caught up with him, bearing the message that the hostiles had returned to raid the herds of the friendly Indians. He ordered the cavalry back to Kamiah and then went on to the common resting spot between Kamiah and Lapwai—a place called Cold Springs. Here the troops stopped, worn from what Lieutenant Wood wrote was a "horrible hot stifling march across dry prairie."

Howard did not stop at Cold Springs but, in the evening, pushed on to Fort Lapwai—a driving ride of about thirty miles that exhausted the officer who accompanied him. The reason behind this urgency was that his aide, Lieutenant Wilkinson, had learned a few days before that his wife and Mrs. Howard were coming to Lewiston on the next steamboat. But when the *Almota* arrived at 10 P.M. that night, Mrs. Howard was not one of the passengers. The general wrote later: "The story proved false, and the disappointment real." However, the nervous and excitable Mrs. Perry—who had gone visiting at The Dalles just before the outbreak—was on board, and when she met her husband, she had a regular attack of hysterics, which "rather disgusted" the general.

Not only was Howard disappointed in not meeting his wife but, as he had been completely out of touch with the outside world for over two weeks, he also received a rude shock when he learned that he was being sharply criticized from coast to coast by the press. The usually conservative San Francisco *Chronicle* had carried two editorials, one after the rout at White Bird and the other after the retreat of the hostiles from Kamiah, which plugged the idea that Howard was not a successful Indian fighter and should be replaced by General George Crook or General Jeff C. Davis. On July 15th, while the controversy over the Brave Seventeen affair was at its height, this paper printed a New York and a Chicago release under the head, REMOVAL OF HOWARD TALKED OF. The latter read:

Chicago, July 14.—A *Times* Washington special says: The Cabinet yesterday secretly but seriously considered the propriety of displacing Howard and putting Crook in his place. Howard, who has made such a sad mess of the campaign, was sent to that remote country as a sort of punishment after the failure to convict him on Court-martial for his share of the Freedman's Bureau frauds. It is quite possible that he will be removed today, as Secretary McCrary who was absent at yesterday's Cabinet meeting, returned last night [and immediately went to confer with the President].[21]

Two days after the above story appeared, General McDowell had sent Howard a telegram in which he indicated that not only was Howard in a tight spot, he was also squirming in the backwash of the controversy. This read:

> Your dispatch and that of Captain Keeler of your engagement of the eleventh and twelfth gave us all great pleasure. I immediately reported them to Washington to be laid before the Secretary of War and the President. These dispatches came most opportunely, for your enemies had raised a great clamor against you, which the press reported had not been without effect in Washington.
>
> They have been silenced, but I think like Joseph's band, have been scotched not killed, and will rise again if they have a chance.[22]

Remarks which his Chief of Staff made in letters to his wife indicate clearly that this criticism cut General Howard to the quick. Although the general was guilty of not understanding some aspects of the problem which faced him and of being unduly optimistic in his dispatches to McDowell's headquarters, he had conducted a rather creditable campaign under very difficult circumstances. Perhaps his worst fault was that of criticizing the efforts of others when no just basis for that criticism existed, and particularly in holding up his own idea as *the* proper course of action. One of the infantry captains may have been close to the truth when he indicated that Howard was not a modest man.

Immediately after the disappointing trip to Fort Lapwai, Howard returned to Cold Springs, and on July 22nd, Major Mason informed his wife that

> We have made a change in our plans—as it now stands, we propose with this column to follow the hostiles on the trail they have taken to the buffalo country, to follow wherever they may go. Wheaton with the [Second] infty will—when he gets to Lewiston take the route north until he strikes the Mullan road and follow it into Montana.[23] We may there join forces if necessary. It is not possible to lay out any program very far ahead. *This plan of direct pursuit is my plan,* but it will tell in the end—if we keep after them we are bound to strike them sometime and somewhere.[24] (Italics are the author's.)

Mason may be correct in indicating that the "plan" was his idea, but, of course, General Field Order No. 3 (which was issued the next day) carried Howard's name.

It remained for Sutherland, in a news dispatch that was frank to the point of being tactless, to expose what Howard endeavored to camouflage and conceal. Writing the next day after the new field order had been issued, he stated:

> General Howard rode into Lapwai that night on special business . . . and returned the next afternoon with the face of his proposed campaign somewhat changed. He had learned at Lapwai that on account of the hounding of several influential papers, the Cabinet at Washington had been considering the feasibility of removing him from his command and appointing Crook in his stead. Hearing that the cause of dissatisfaction was want of activity—which is not only baseless but almost ironical, as we have been constantly on the go ever since the troops have been in the field—General Howard resolved to transfer the command of the Spokane expedition to Colonel Wheaton, and leaving Green at Kamiah with Throckmorton, start with the rest of his command through the impenetrable Lolo Pass, and follow Joseph to the very death.[25]

However, these new plans could not be implemented until Sanford arrived with his cavalry, and until Wheaton and Green were in position to cover the rear. And so, while he waited, Howard moved his men to Croesdale's ranch where he could watch both the Kamiah and Mount Idaho areas.

The afternoon that Howard returned from Fort Lapwai, the column made a short march southward to a point near the western end of Lawyer's Canyon[26] where Sutherland wrote that they

> went into camp on the grassy table lands, where was no wood for fires or tent poles, and the little water in the vicinity was soon worked into such a mush of mud by the pack mules and cavalry horses that it was impossible to use it. This night we slept under the blue vault of Heaven, with no covering between it and us save our blankets, and as I watched a bright star overhead, hung like a lantern from a moon cloud, I wondered [about various things of a "poetical character"] when an inquisitive cavalryman knocked all the romance out of me by calling out in the "stilly night," "Say, is that your d——d cayuse that is trying to chew up my pillow?' And sure enough it was.
>
> From this place we made a short tramp to Camp Alexander in Lawyer's Canyon, one of the best places for enjoying the dulce far niente that I have yet come across. The canyon is very precipitous, and but a hundred yards or so across, richly timbered, plenty of luxuriant grass and a trout stream that would have made Isaac Walton brave all the Indians in christendom for one day's "whipping" at it. Both Gen Howard and I tried out our luck, and . . . I shall not mention the number we had to supper that night.[27]

Here the troops who had come to Lewiston on the same boat as Mrs. Perry joined the column. As noted elsewhere, these were the two companies of infantry from Fort Yuma and the two companies of artillery from the San Francisco area which McDowell had scraped up when it was feared that the Snake River might drop so that Wheaton's regiment could not be shipped by steamboat. The senior officer was Captain Harry C. Cushing, whom Howard was to regard as a capable officer in the future, and, as noted, one of the junior officers was Second Lieutenant Guy Howard, the general's oldest son who was soon made an aide-de-camp.

Sutherland noted that as many of the officers were without horses, "a band of cayuses was driven into camp and the work of 'breaking' them began. Riding on whirlwinds with a side saddle is nothing compared with mounting a cayuse fresh from his native heath." While some of the men were trying to conquer these four-legged demons—"with five men dragging at his head and as many more beating him from behind"—others mingled with the veterans and listened to the camp scuttlebutt. One of the latter, identified only by the initials "J. F. D.," wrote to the San Francisco *Chronicle* that the opinion of the cavalry held by the foot troops was not complimentary

> and it can be summed up in those few words, uttered by Lieutenant H——, of the Fourth Artillery, and within my hearing: "Gentlemen, there is no use talking, the cavalry we have with us have been a disgrace to the service."

Apparently "Lieutenant H——" was Charles F. Humphrey, who was in charge of "E" Company while Captain Marcus P. Miller had command of the entire artillery battalion. This opinion was also held by others for, after the Indians had been chased across the Clearwater at Kamiah, Mason stated in a letter that "There is every indication from all we can learn that the Indians are very much afraid of our foot troops but hold the cavalry in profound contempt—as well they may, for the truth is they are almost worthless."[28]

Settlers came from Mount Idaho to visit the camp, to inquire about lost stock, to try to sell beef, and to gawk. Among these was Delegate Fenn to interview Howard about the Brave Seventeen affair, which he was trying to interpret unfavorably against the troops. And there were officers who came out from Fort Lapwai and Lewiston to get detailed instructions from Howard—Major George F. Weeks the Department quartermaster, Captain L. S. Babbitt an ordance officer, and the A. A. G., Major H. Clay Wood. The staff returned the next day, and the command moved to Crossdale's ranch on Cottonwood Creek, a point about ten miles from Mount Idaho and twelve miles from Kamiah.

After remaining here for three days, most of the troops marched back to Kamiah, where the final details were arranged for the impending push. Major Mason remained behind to locate and guide Major George B. Sanford, who was on the trail from Boise City. The latter arrived Friday morning, July 27th, with four companies of the First Cavalry—about two hundred men, twenty-one packers, and seventy-five pack mules—and went on to Kamiah the next day after detaching Captain Edwin V. Sumner's company to wait for Major John Green who, with his own troop and two companies of infantry, was about two days' march behind.

With Sanford were twenty Bannock scouts under Orlando "Rube" Robbins, a frontiersman from Boise City. Their leader was a fearless young chief whose name was Buffalo Horn. He, and a couple of others, had scouted for the troops in Montana the year before and, before another year had passed, he would lead his own people in a futile uprising. One officer wrote to his wife that to make certain none were mistaken for the enemy, "all wear soldier's uniforms with a kind of blue sash of stripes and stars. It looks, in fact, like a piece of old garrison flag."

One officer with Sanford's detachment was an unusual individual. Captain Charles E. Bendire, formerly from Germany and commanding "K" Company, First Cavalry, was an avid ornithologist. Later, he compiled a monumental two-volume work, *Life Histories of North American Birds.* However, it is doubtful if he found many opportunities for bird-watching on this campaign, although he did note in his description of Franklin's grouse that he saw them in the Salmon River Mountains south of Mount Idaho and along the Lolo Trail—"but had no time to observe them closely."

Sherman had directed Howard to keep the troops in western Montana informed of any significant movements which might affect that area, and particularly his own should he pursue the Indians in that direction. As his column was now about ready to move, he dispatched "Captain" James Cearley and "Sergeant" Joseph Baker of the Mount Idaho Volunteers, on July 27th, with dispatches for Captain Charles Rawn at Missoula. These couriers, who were to be joined at Elk City by Wesley Little, traveled the Old Nez Perce Trail to the head of the Bitterroot Valley, and then down that valley to the post near Missoula. The dispatch which they carried read, in part:

Camp Alfred Sully, July 25, 1877
Commanding Officer, Post of Missoula, Montana:

Sir:

All reports seem to indicate that what are left of the hostile Indians, with their stock and plunder, have escaped by the Lolo Trail, and may reach you before this dispatch. I shall start with my right column from Kamiah, in direct pursuit next Monday, the 30th. My guides say that if you could move your force this way as far as the Lolo fork, which runs into the Bitter Root river, you could prevent their escape. They have a thousand horses at least, and much stuff of one kind and another, and will not go fast after they escape from the mountains. If you simply bother them, and keep them back until I can close in, their destruction or surrender will be sure. . . . Colonel Wheaton's column will have the same objective point, viz.: Missoula. . . . Please notify all neighboring Commanders, both regular and volunteers, of my movement. We must not let these hostile Indians escape.

> *Very respectfully,*
> O. O. HOWARD
> *Brigadier General, U.S.A.*[29]

Of the force which gathered at Kamiah, Major Mason wrote that it consisted of "360 foot and 200 cavalry, 25 Indian scouts and 150 armed citizens in various capacities."[30] The infantry, under the direct command of Captain Evan Miles, consisted of Companies "B," "C," "D," "E," "H," and "I" of the Twenty-first, "H" Company of the Eighth, and "C" Company of the Twelfth regiments. Under Captain Marcus P. Miller, also acting as infantry, were Companies "A," "C," "D," "E," "G," "L," and "M" of the Fourth Artillery. The cavalry which had served previously were replaced by Companies "B," "C," "I," and "K," all of the First Cavalry, with Major Sanford in command. And there was a battery, consisting of a howitzer and a couple of Gatling guns, under Lieutenant H. G. Otis of Robinson Crusoe fame. These pieces (dismantled) were packed on mules and, legends to the contrary, none were abandoned on the Lolo Trail.

Three hundred and fifty mules and seventy-five packers made up the pack train. Up to the middle of July, the train had been haphazardly organized and some ten days before the starting date had been in danger of disintegrating. Lieutenant Peter S. Bomus, on whose shoulders rested the "housekeeping" duties of the depot at Lewiston, had to go to the field and put things in order. He reported later that

> great dissatisfaction was found to exist. . . . [the packers] complained of over work, want of adequate rest, insufficient pay & strongly of the want of proper adjustment of pay—that experienced packers were doing all the work & yet the inexperienced received the same pay. They were quitting in detachments.[31]

The lieutenant raised their pay, established a graded pay scale, and divided the train between the various battalions. There is no further mention of difficulty—which *The Teller* denied ever did take place, although this "strike" brought matters to a standstill for about three days. Later, Sutherland was to comment that most of them were Americans with a sprinkling of Mexicans—"just enough to give the proper pronunciation to *aparejos*, and swear in a musical tone." As a group, they were "a splendid class of men physically," accustomed to hardship, the happiest on long marches, and when in camp were the first to have their campfires built and their meals cooked, meals that were better cooked than any others. And when there was a fight "they were never known to falter."[32]

Captain William F. Spurgeon, Twenty-first Infantry, was given the command of a company of fifty ax men or "engineers" who were mounted and armed. These men were recruited in Lewiston and joined the column a few days after it got under way. They were used to clear trails and perform tasks normally assigned to a company of Engineers; and they were to render valuable assistance on the Lolo Trail and in the Yellowstone Park.

By Sunday, July 29th, the troops had all crossed to the right bank of the Clearwater and the last of the supplies were being taken across on a primitive ferry. While the last-minute tasks were being accomplished, Howard and a few others, together with the Bannock scouts, went to the sub-agency to hear several of Miss Sue McBeth's protégés preach, thus providing another small bit of support for the criticism that Howard refused to campaign on Sunday.

Everyone was in "good spirits and anxious for a brush with the enemy" according to Major Mason. And Captain FitzGerald put a reassuring note in a letter to his wife:

> . . . honestly, I dont think we shall see an Indian hostile. I said to Colonel [Captain M. P.] Miller, "Colonel, what are we going to do over there?" He replied, "Oh, we will have a big mountain picnic with no Indians to trouble us."[33]

The column was ready to start the next morning.

14

Fiasco at Fort Fizzle

>>>>>>><<<<<<< When the news of the outbreak reached the settlers in western Montana, there was an immediate feeling of alarm. Part of this was a deep-seated matter, for there were no military posts nearby. Many months before, they had requested protection, but the Sioux war the preceding year had delayed matters; and it was not until May that General Sheridan had requested the Secretary of War to secure an appropriation of $20,000 for the construction of a post near the town of Missoula.

On the 9th of June, Captain Charles C. Rawn left Fort Shaw with "I" Company of the Seventh Infantry to establish this post, and with him went Captain William Logan and "A" Company of the same regiment to assist in its construction. Rawn arrived in Missoula on the 19th and Logan and the troops came in a week later. Thus, the establishment of what was to become Fort Missoula became a reality just before the Nez Perce headed for the buffalo plains.

The arrival of the news of the trouble brought an almost immediate scurrying of some families to the shelter of the settlements. There was a clamor for protection, and soon Governor B. F. Potts—a sort of letter-writing, telegram-sending busybody—was engaged in correspondence with various officials. Shortly afterward, he sent his "secretary," James H. Mills—editor of the Deer Lodge *The New North-West*, to investigate and report on conditions. Then, on June 29th he telegraphed President Hayes:

> Settlements in western Montana seriously threatened by Nez Perce Indians from Idaho. Settlers are fleeing from their homes in Bitter Root Valley to Missoula for safety. More troops are needed for Missoula. We are organizing and arming the people for defense. Flathead and other Indians are seriously disaffected.[1]

This alarm, like that of the settlers, was, of course, premature. However, Mills did report that the fear was real,[2] and that there was a deep-seated feeling of vulnerability.

Everyone knew that the Nez Perce passed through the Bitterroot country regularly en route to the buffalo plains, and that these Indians and the indigenous Flatheads were close friends of long standing. Bands of Nez Perce often camped in the Bitterroot Valley for appreciable lengths of time, and only a week before (about June 22nd) a band of thirty lodges had left the valley via the Lolo Trail for the Reservation. (The probable fate of some of these has already been noted.) And the Flatheads who lived among the white settlers suddenly gathered their stock and families and disappeared.

Nor was it any secret that the Flatheads had a treaty grievance. When Governor Stevens made the first treaty with them in 1855, the location of their reservation had not been specified, although the Indians had indicated that they desired the Bitterroot Valley. Then, for seventeen years, the Government failed to take steps to settle the matter. Meanwhile, settlers came into the valley and settled in that part which had been reserved pending further negotiations. Soon, they began to clamor—as usual—that the Indians be moved so that they could take up the desirable land which was occupied.

Finally, in 1872, the Government made a shabby attempt at what was passed off as negotiation—the decision having already been made to use force if necessary to clear the disputed area. James A. Garfield got the second- and third-ranking chiefs, Arlee and Adolph, to sign an agreement to go on the Reservation proposed, but in so doing, he bypassed Charlot, the head chief. Unfortunately, Charlot was—as had been his father before him—a leader of the type that commanded respect, both by his own people and *by the whites*. Then, to add insult to injury, the idea was generated, by implication, that Charlot had signed the contract. In spite of all this, the chief swallowed his resentment to some extent and continued to live in the area which he believed belonged to his people. On the Reservation, all had not been well either; and during the preceding December, a grand jury heard charges that the Agent, Charles Medary, had not been fulfilling treaty obligations. By this time, he had been replaced by Peter Ronan, but there were still aftereffects.

Two days after Potts had dispatched his telegram to the President, Charlot's people were found near French Gulch, some 65 or 70 miles eastward. A man who talked with them reported that they gave as a reason for their sudden departure that "the Nez Perces sent them word if they would not join them and fight the whites they would come over and take them in too." As they did not wish to fight the whites, they had crossed over into the Big Hole country. Editor Mills reported to the governor that many of the families had taken shelter at old Fort Owen and others had come to Missoula. "The excitement in the valley amounted to a panic which has not yet been allayed"; and Potts promptly sent 200 stands of obsolete but serviceable military rifles for distribution. However, conditions may not have been as bad as Mills reported. Two weeks later, a settler living near Stevensville wrote to the governor that "19 or 20 families [went] to Fort Owen, while fully 50 staid at their homes somewhat uneasy but not apprehending immediate trouble"; and years later, a merchant in this town wrote dryly, "We were fairly well armed."[3]

However, the settlers did take some steps toward self-protection. Volunteer companies were organized and three strongpoints were prepared in the Bitterroot Valley. North of Corvallis a sod fort, said to have been about 100 feet square with walls upward of eight feet high, was built. On Shalkaho Creek a log stockade, with a cabin inside, was constructed. The third was the old trading post of John Owen, which was about a half mile north of Stevensville. This was 250 by 125 feet with adobe walls 15 feet high, had two bastions on the corners, heavy plank gates, a well in the center, and rooms built around the inside of the walls. All that needed to be done was to rebuild part of one wall that had crumbled. These forts the settlers named, respectively, Fort Run, Fort Skidaddle, and Fort Brave. These precautions having been taken, and the alarm subsiding, the settlers returned to their homes.

Potts' scare telegram was coolly received in Washington—as had been those from the governors of Idaho, Oregon and Washington. However, Captain Rawn went to the nearby Jocko Reservation where he and Agent Ronan interviewed the chiefs of the Flatheads and Pend d'Oreilles. Among other things, Rawn asked if they would provide ten scouts to watch the outlets of the Lolo and Nez Perce trails. To this they agreed, provided they were given uniforms and paid. The captain could furnish the clothing, but neither he nor the Agent could guarantee the pay; and there the matter rested. Rawn and Ronan then went to St. Mary's Mission where they talked with Charlot. The chief assured them that he had no desire to become involved but that he could not guarantee what some of his young men might do.

> When asked whether or not his people would side with the whites in case the hostiles came into the valley, he said: "No. We could not fight against the Nez Perces because they helped me several years ago, against my enemy the Blackfeet, but we will not fight with them against the whites." He said he would give the whites all the information he could obtain by runners, but nothing more.[4]

As the Nez Perce had not headed for Montana immediately after the outbreak of hostilities, the excitement in the Bitterroot Valley quieted down. But the lull was of short duration, for on July 13th *The Weekly Missoulian* printed a story which was headed, STARTLING NEWS FROM THE WEST. When the previously noted band, which had wintered in the valley, had gone to Idaho, a Nez Perce named Poker Joe had gone with them. Poker Joe, sometimes called Joe Hale or Lean Elk, was the leader of a small band that had lived for some time in the valley. These were "Salmon River" Indians and the chief, whom they had deposed about three years before but who still lived with them, was the formerly prominent Eagle-from-the-Light. The story which Poker Joe provided for the editor of *The Weekly Missoulian* was a rather garbled account of Whipple's attack on Looking Glass' camp, the ambush of Rains' party, and the skirmishes near Cottonwood Station—in some of which Joe said he had participated. It was also claimed that 191 whites had been killed, and that "all the Nez Perces but Jim and John Lawyer's, sons of the famous chief, bands are on the warpath, and that they are joined by Umatillas, Cayuses, Yackimas, Bannacks, Snakes, Piutes, and some of the Indians on the Columbia River."

Thus news made Eagle-from-the-Light apprehensive and, shortly after Joe's return, Agent Ronan reported to Governor Potts:

> On Saturday, July 14, Eagle of the Light . . . came to this agency accompanied by Michelle, head chief of the Pen d' Oreilles,[5] and informed me that eleven lodges of Nez Perces were encamped near St. Mary's Mission, up the Bitter Root—that they are peaceable, have never been in the hostile camp and are desirous to keep out of trouble, and to encamp somewhere out of danger. Michelle said the chiefs of the reservation would consent to let them camp here, providing I gave my permission. After reflection, I told the reservation Chiefs that as

they professed peace and friendship, it was a bad policy to throw the Reservation open as a shelter as suspicion could not be avoided. . . .[6]

He advised that Eagle-from-the-Light confer with Captain Rawn as to the proper course to pursue. This, as will soon be evident, was a *faux pas*, for it left the would-be neutrals squarely in the path followed by the hostiles.

When the news came that the Non-Treaties had left the Salmon River Mountains and were headed for the Clearwater, Potts made another request for authorization to raise volunteers. This time, the news of Howard's victory on the Clearwater provided an additonal reason for refusing—"The Department is not authorized to call out volunteers; nor will they, it is thought, be necessary." But Potts was obdurate. He answered Secretary McCrary's telegram immediately with the suggestion that it would quiet the people in western Montana if some of the troops at Fort Shaw were moved to Missoula. This McCrary agreed to do, but when this decision reached Colonel John Gibbon, he questioned the soundness of the decision:

> Your dispatch of yesterday nineteenth (19) received. Have but sixteen (16) privates for duty, a little better off at [Fort] Ellis and I will send all the men that can be spared from there. The force remaining in the District [of Montana] is so small that to scatter it any more than it is now is objectionable.[7]

This exchange was hardly completed before McDowell advised the Adjutant General that Howard had reported the Indians were headed eastward on the Lolo Trail. This injected a note of urgency, and Sheridan promptly ordered Gibbon to put his troops in the field. This time Gibbon replied:

> Dispatch of yesterday received. Have ordered one company of infantry from Fort Ellis to Missoula direct. As soon as I can assemble troops here from Camp Baker[8] and Fort Benton, I shall move [via] Cadotte Pass down the Blackfoot [River] towards Missoula. Shall probably be able to take nearly one hundred men. The troops being all infantry, these movements will necessarily be very slow and can do little but check the march of the Indians in the passes. . . .[9]

Five days later, Gibbon notified Potts that he would leave Fort Shaw on July 28th, and requested that any early intelligence about the movements of the Indians be forwarded to him by special courier.

Shortly after Rawn had arrived in Missoula, the settlers began to urge that he put scouts in the Lolo Pass and station small detachments at various places to keep watch. Rawn replied he would if they would provide him with horses—but the animals were not forthcoming, and the first scare subsided. However, when the second flurry of apprehension arose, the request was renewed; and this time, four horses "and equipments" were provided. Mounting four enlisted men, the captain turned the little party over to Lieutenant Francis Woodbridge on July 18th with instructions to proceed toward Lolo Pass and "to watch the Loo Loo trail from a point where it could be seen six or eight miles." For information about the eastern end of the Nez Perce Trail, Rawn was forced to depend upon Charlot's promises of cooperation.

When three days passed without a report from Woodbridge, Lieutenant Charles A. Coolidge was dispatched with a party consisting of one soldier and a few civilians to scout the trail as far as they thought it prudent. On the second day's march, when about thirty-five miles from the post, they met Woodbridge returning. He had been well over on the western side of the Pass, some sixty-five miles from Missoula, but had seen nothing. As the mounts of the relief party were fresh, they turned about and pushed back to Missoula, where they arrived late in the evening. Woodbridge's party, traveling more slowly, went into camp along Lolo Creek about twenty-five miles from Missoula. Here the "two white prisoners" whom Sutherland reported on July 17th as being in the hands of the hostiles came into camp. After being held for eight days, they had escaped—probably without much difficulty as they were from Stevensville—and they brought news that the Nez Perce were camped but a short distance behind.

Editor Barbour wrote in *The Weekly Missoulian:*

> A courier from his camp reached the post early Monday morning [July 23] with the news that a white man and a half-breed, who said the Indians were at Warm Springs [Lolo Hot Springs], had been in his camp the night before. The half-breed was Pete Matte and the white man Billy Silverthorne. The notorious character of Pete Matte and the suspicion that would naturally fall on anyone found in such company did not warrant implicit confidence in this report; however, the report was generally believed . . . and Captain Rawn acted upon it. . . .[10]

News, even from men suspected of being thieves, was welcome.

Immediately, there was a flurry of telegrams. Before the day was over, Potts had wired the Secretary of War:

> Large numbers of Joseph's Nez Perces arriving in Montana by Lolo trail. Profess want to pass peaceably through settlements. How should we treat them? People have fled to stockades. Less than one hundred troops in western Montana.[11]

A similar wire was sent to McDowell, who immediately informed the Adjutant General these Indians were undoubtedly hostiles and, "If possible they should not be allowed to pass but be arrested and detained and treated as hostile." The Adjutant General forwarded McDowell's telegram to General Sheridan, and his adjutant bucked it on to Gibbon with this order appended: "The Lieutenant General directs that the Nez Perces entering Montana must be disarmed and, if mounted, dismounted and held as prisoners."[12] Thus, by the time Rawn had gathered his force and was ready to block the mouth of the Lolo Canyon, Sheridan had specified the course of action to be followed.

The attitude of the Indians at this point was probably both curious and naïve. There can be but little doubt that the Scotch-Nez Perce trader, Duncan McDonald, recorded it quite accurately when he wrote:

> Looking Glass said he did not want any trouble on this side of the Lo Lo pass; that he did not want to fight either soldiers or citizens east of the Lo Lo, because they were not the ones who fought them in Idaho. The idea among the Indians, uneducated as they were, was that the people of Montana had no identity with the people in Idaho, and that they were entirely separate and distinct, having nothing to do with each other. If they had to fight it was Idaho people they should fight, not Montanians. Looking Glass therefore gave orders to his warriors that in case they should see any white men, either citizens or soldiers, on the Lo Lo, not to molest them unless, as they had compelled him in Idaho, these citizens or soldiers should compel them to fight in self defense. He said: "We are going to buffalo country. We want to go through the settlements quietly. We do not wish to harm anyone if we can help it."[13]

The Weekly Missoulian did not appear on July 27th, but the August 3rd issue appeared on schedule with "a faithful chronicle of events that have transpired during the past two weeks." As Editor Chauncey Barbour was a member of "Captain" E. A. Kenney's company of volunteers, he observed as a participant the events which he chronicled meticulously—and, probably, with greater accuracy than did Rawn, who wrote his official report about two months later. According to Barbour, on

MONDAY, JULY 23

The courier from Lieutenant Woodbridge's camp arrived in Missoula with the news that the Nez Perce were approaching; and Rawn made plans to block the Lolo Trail in the canyon of Lolo Creek.

TUESDAY, JULY 24

E. A. Kenney, captain of the volunteer company in Missoula, and four men camped on Lolo Creek "far in advance of any other force." During the night, they captured Tom Hill, a Delaware Indian who lived with the Nez Perce, "who was sent by them to ascertain if they could pass peaceably through the country. Hill was sent back asking the chiefs to come to a talk, and a courier was dispatched with the news to Missoula."

WEDNESDAY, JULY 25

Rawn, "with every available man" in his command, moved up Lolo Canyon to a point about sixteen miles from Missoula, and five miles above the mouth of the canyon. Here the floor of the canyon narrowed to approximately a quarter of a mile in width, and Rawn considered it "the most defensible and least easily flanked part of the cañon." Barbour, his description tempered by hindsight, wrote that,

> the mountains on the south side of the Lo Lo are precipitous and densely covered with standing and fallen timber, so that escape on that side was impossible; on the north side grassy ridges [steep slopes nevertheless] stretched away from the stream, allowing a passage in almost any direction.

Here, with the Indian camp two miles above according to Rawn, and "three to four" according to Barbour, Rawn's force set to work to build a barricade of logs and earthworks. This, apparently, reached from one side of the canyon to the other and was considered adequate, although it was soon to bear the ignominious title of Fort Fizzle.

As the men felled trees and dug rifle pits, Rawn wrote this dispatch to Lieutenant Levi F. Burnett, the adjutant at Fort Shaw:

> *Up the Lou-Lou Pass,*
> *July 25th, 1877, 3:00 o'clock P.M.*

> Am entrenching twenty-five regulars and about fifty volunteers in Lou-Lou canyon. Have promises of more volunteers but am not certain of them. Please send me along more troops. Will go up and see them tomorrow and inform them that unless they disarm and dismount, will give them a fight. White Bird says he will go through peaceably if he can, but will go through. This news is entirely reliable.

While Rawn's force was thus engaged,

Captain Kenney with four of the men of his company met the chiefs, and was surrounded by a formidable force of painted savages. He told them that he had no authority to treat with them, but appointed a council for the next day at three o'clock in the afternoon.

THURSDAY, JULY 26

Governor Potts arrived in Missoula about 3 A.M. and visited Rawn's barricade during the forenoon. Here, he expressed the opinion that "it would be madness . . . to attack with an inadequate force" and that "the only thing that could be done was to hold the Indians in check until such a force arrived as to compel a surrender." In the afternoon, Captain Rawn met the chiefs in the council arranged on Wednesday by "Captain" Kenney.

Looking Glass and White Bird were at this council. It appears the Indians were as anxious for delay as were the whites; and without arriving at anything definite a council was arranged [for] the next day, when the Indians were told that Gov. Potts would be present.

Rawn reported that he "told them they had to surrender arms and ammunition or fight," and that he suspected they were short of ammunition or were considering the attitude of the Flatheads, as Charlot was alleged to have sent word that if they came into the Bitterroot country, he would join the whites and fight them. As he had sent some fifteen or twenty of his men to join the troops, it appeared that the chief meant what he said.

One puzzling thing was observed at this council:

At the conclusion of the council a fine-looking Indian was seen approaching, and the Indians at the council involuntarily exclaimed among themselves "Joseph." He rode into the council, and when he was informed of its result he waved his hand in token of assent. . . . This noted Chief was either present with the Indians, or it was a ruse to surprise the people with the idea of Indian strength.

The whites, not knowing that Looking Glass and White Bird had forced Joseph into a subordinate position at Kamiah—and were probably keeping him there—now began to wonder where Joseph's followers were. While this uncertainty was short-lived, the confused thinking about the Nez Perce leadership continued to persist.

Each side distrusted the other. While the council was in progress, "about seventy-five warriors marshaled within easy range and caused some solicitude that there might be a repetition of the Canby affair [in the Modoc War]."

And, according to McDonald's version of the Indian side of the story:

> Looking Glass returned to his camp and told his warriors the conditions demanded for them to treat upon. . . . The Indians thought it was ridiculous to give up their arms to their foes. Looking Glass made a speech and said:
> "We remember a big war that took place on the Columbia River [in 1858]. * * * Colonel Wright told the Indians that if they would surrender he would treat them well and hurt no one but the murderers. . . . Then Colonel Wright hung many innocent Indians. * * * How do we know but that Joseph, Looking Glass and others will be hung immediately after we surrender?"[14]

FRIDAY, JULY 27

Governor Potts again visited the fortified camp where he remained all day; and he and Rawn debated the advisability, in view of the Indian show of force on the preceding day, of again meeting the Indians. Finally, Rawn decided to go, taking with him about one hundred mounted volunteers. With skirmishers covering both flanks, they proceeded to a knoll about a half mile below the Indian camp. Here, they halted and sent a Flathead named Pierre into the camp. He brought back word that Looking Glass would meet the captain midway between the forces "alone and unarmed." This time

> Looking Glass proffered to surrender all the ammunition of the camp as a guarantee that the Indians intended to go through the country peaceably. When told that nothing but an unconditional surrender would be accepted, he asked for another meeting at nine o'clock the next day to give him time to consult with the other chiefs. Captain Rawn told him that any further communication he desired to make must be made under a flag of truce at the fortified camp.

(Rawn's official report apparently becomes slightly confused at this point, although he may be correct in placing the next proposed council at noon on Saturday.)

"On Friday night" a count was made of all the men at Fort Fizzle and the number was found to be 216, including fifteen or twenty Flathead warriors. Rawn's report stated that he expected to be attacked after this council, but Barbour reported that "the impression in the minds of all the people was that the Indians would surrender Saturday." Perhaps both sides were stalling for time. Rawn wrote: "For the purpose of gaining time for General Howard's forces to get up, and for General Gibbon to arrive from Fort Shaw, I appointed a meeting for the 28th. . . ." If true, this is but another example of the fatuous thinking behind which various officers retreated during the campaign—Howard's column would not leave Kamiah, several days' hard marching away, until two days later, and Gibbon would not leave Fort Shaw until the following day, at which time his infantry would have to march upwards of 150 miles. And, although Rawn makes no mention of it, Barbour wrote that "it was agreed that all subsequent reinforcements that might arrive should be organized for a flank movement over the ridges into the Indian camp."

SATURDAY, JULY 28

Any complacency which Rawn and his men may have had was rudely shattered during the morning:

At half past eight o'clock Saturday morning news was brought into Captain Rawn's camp that the Indians had thrown their lodges and were packing up to move. At ten o'clock the men in the camp saw Indians filing by on the ridges above camp. At half past eleven Lt. Tom Andrews was detailed with a force of 45 mounted men to guard the trail below camp and arrest stragglers. This force was divided into two squads, one to go ahead and observe the enemy. Three of the men of the lower squad ran into the rear guard of the Indian force. As soon as Looking Glass saw them, he waved his hat, and came up and exchanged friendly greetings.

The Indians came down to within half a mile of Captain Rawn's camp before they took to the ridge, and they came off of the ridge on to the Lo Lo about a mile below camp, crossing the Lo Lo and proceeding directly up the Bitter Root. At a quarter past twelve, Capt Rawn gave orders for the entire force to move down the Lo Lo. The force moved in military order, with a skirmish line at the sides and in front.

Lieut. W. J. Stephens, of the Missoula volunteers, was detailed with a force of fifty men to skirmish along the right bank of the Lo Lo. He soon struck the trail of the Indians, and pursued them to near the spot where they camped for the night [in the valley just above the mouth of Lolo Canyon]. *The greater part of the force with Lieut. Stephens were from Bitter Root and were disposed to let Mr. Looking Glass and his people go in peace.* [Italics are the author's] Lieut. Stephens returned to town. Captain Rawn, after detailing Lieut. Stephens to skirmish along the right bank of the Lo Lo came directly to the post.

An incident that occurred after the Indians commenced moving may help to a better understanding of the disposition of these Indians. Amos, a Nez Perces who has lived about Missoula for years, came to the breastworks and proffered to surrender the eight lodges under his charge. He was taken into custody, and it has since been learned that the Nez Perces forcibly prevented his eight lodges from coming in.

Elsewhere, the editor commented that

the movement . . . was one of the most brilliant strategically of modern warfare. It was, of all others, the move that nobody expected them to make. Its audacity was stunning. It will ever stand as ⅃ monument to the bravery of that people that they moved, with their horses and women and little ones through an open country that was swarming with armed men.

McDonald's version of the story as told by the survivors in Canada is in general agreement with that written by Barbour, and by Rawn in his official report. This states that as the Indians marched past Rawn, Looking Glass said over and over, "Don't shoot, don't shoot. Let the white men shoot first." And as they came down off the ridges and on to the trail again, the best warriors were placed between the volunteers, who came down the valley, and the women, children and pack horses. This meeting may not have been as peaceful as the editor intimates, for the trader stated that when the volunteers came up, these picked guards were ready to fight; whereupon, the settlers stampeded for the camp, and Rawn had to send a half-breed named Alexander Matt and a few Flatheads to determine what was going on.[15] Barbour does not mention any shots being fired; Rawn reported, "They showed disposition to fight, they passed me on the flank. . . ."; and one reliable old-timer has stated that a few shots were fired from the ridge and a settler named Gird fired one shot in reply.

The alleged nonaggression pact between the Indians and the Bitterroot settlers is difficult to pinpoint. Some accounts have the earmarks of fabrications. Undoubtedly, the meeting of the minds took place at McLain's ranch, where the Indians camped Saturday evening. A settler named W. B. Harlan—vouched for by Editor James Mills as a "guarantee of reliability"—was with Lieutenant Stephens when his force came up with the camp. Harlan, chafing over some criticism, wrote this letter a week after the incident occurred:

Stevensville, August 4

JAMES MILLS, *Editor New North-West*

By the way, I have received letters from friends in Deer Lodge, saying that some of the returned Deer Lodge volunteers [who never reached Missoula] were branding the Bitter Rooters as cowards, &c.,

for allowing the Indians to pass through in peace. . . . When we were up Lo Lo and had equal numbers and a good position we were prevented from firing by the captain of the regulars, under whose orders we were.

When the Indians were allowed to pass into Bitter Root without a shot, and all the regulars and outside militia had gone to Missoula, does anyone think we were going to pitch into them alone, when they outnumbered us three to one, and had the advantage of position, and all our families and property were beyond them.

On that Saturday morning Fort Owen held 263 women and children, guarded by two needle guns and two Henry guns, with a dozen muskets and shot guns in the hands of as many men. When we overtook the Indians, Looking Glass met us and told us he would not harm any persons or property in the valley if allowed to pass in peace, and that we could pass through his camp to our homes.

The offer was accepted as we could do nothing else, as our place was between the Indians and our homes [sic].

We were not silly enough to uselessly incite the Indians to devastate our valley, and I do not think our critics would have done otherwise had they and their families and homes been situated as were ours.

If they want Indians for breakfast they are still within reach, and have been ever since the fiasco at Fort Fizzle on the Lo Lo trail.

W. B. HARLAN[16]

Again, Duncan McDonald's account is in complete agreement with the contents of this letter.

Immediately afterward, feeling about Rawn's course of action ran high in Missoula. Barbour wrote a fiery letter to the governor in which he stated, "Take command yourself, and don't let good men be humiliated by imbeciles or cowards. * * * Wipe out the disgrace that has been put upon us, and never let any regular officer again command Montana militia."[17]

However, he soon cooled down, and when the next issue of the paper appeared, he stated that "we are fully prepared to say that he [Rawn] pursued a course of wisdom and showed an intelligent care for the best welfare of the people of Missoula county."

But this expression of confidence did not end the matter. General Howard, holding that Rawn's force might have forced a surrender had it stood firm, criticized the captain sharply, and particularly the settlers for making a sort of peace treaty. And he heaped additional coals of fire on their heads for trading with the Indians later, a matter about which Gibbon was also highly critical. Citizens elsewhere in Montana made Rawn the focal point of their criticism and this reached such a peak that on August 23rd, shortly after his return from the battle of the Big Hole, he addressed a request to General Terry's adjutant asking for "either a Court-Martial or a Court of Inquiry as the General Commanding may direct." However, Colonel Gibbon directed his adjutant to return it with this endorsement:

> It is the opinion of the District Commander that no such vindication of Captain Rawn as asked for is required.
> If the Battle of the Big Hole does not vindicate us all from previous aspersions of irresponsible newspapers it is not thought a Court can do it. * * *

Nevertheless, the accusation was made for years that Rawn had tipped a little brown jug too many times during the night of July 27–28th—an accusation which Barbour emphatically denied at the time, and which Harlan, years later, asserted with equal firmness.

Although Secretary of War McCrary and General Sheridan had refused to take seriously Potts' request for volunteers, the situation in western Montana had mushroomed into one that Rawn and his handful of men were incapable of handling. When the arrival of the Nez Perce was imminent, Potts appealed to the local population for volunteers. Those nearby arrived quickly enough to offer assistance but others, notably two companies from Butte totaling 138 men, were still en route when the escape was effected. Now, with a formidable force moving leisurely toward the head of the Bitterroot Valley, Potts felt that he had to act. In Deer Lodge, on July 31st, he issued a proclamation calling for 300 volunteers, and naming himself Commander in Chief.[18] Then he wired the Secretary of War for the necessary permission! This time, before the Adjutant General made a positive refusal, he referred the matter to General Sheridan who, but two days before, had returned from an extensive hunting and fishing trip in Wyoming and eastern Montana.

Sheridan answered:

> I have not been able yet to realize that Joseph's band of Nez Perces is coming through from the Bitterroot valley to central Montana. There are no buffalo this year south of the Upper Missouri river, except a small herd . . . on the headwaters of Powder river. . . . I have no information from the Department of Dakota to warrant the alarm of the Governor of Montana, and do not feel justified in recommending the three hundred volunteers. General Sherman will be at Fort Ellis to night and being out there in the ground could give the most reliable opinion. . . .
> If I thought the people of Montana were in danger I would not

hesitate to recommend the three hundred volunteers. . . . I will consult with General Terry and ascertain his opinion. Should the Indians come through and go to the buffalo grounds General Miles has not less than one thousand men at reasonably convenient distance to attack them.[19]

Terry agreed with Sheridan, offering instead the battalion of Second Cavalry then in eastern Montana, and Potts' plans ground to an official halt within forty-eight hours after they were initiated.

How well Sheridan understood the problem is a matter for conjecture. On the day that the news brought by Silverthorne and Matt reached Missoula, Sherman and Sheridan—accompanied by a number of high-ranking officers, among them Generals Terry and Crook—met on board the steamboat *Rosebud* on the Big Horn River just below the new post, soon to be called Fort Custer. Apparently, no business was discussed, for all Crook's aide wrote in his diary was "We were very kindly treated and offered the luxury of iced water and iced lager beer." Sherman was to tell Potts later that had the nature of the threat been fully realized at the time, his request would probably have been approved. Considering the deadly efficiency with which these Indians could fight, perhaps it was just as well that untrained volunteers were never pitted against them.

Even though Potts' request was refused, the panic of the settlers in the Bitterroot Valley aroused feelings of apprehension in Deer Lodge, Butte, and other settlements to a fever pitch, and companies of volunteers were organized and equipped—men itching for a fight; and a few of the men did engage in scouting activities. The Deer Lodge volunteers sent two scouts to follow the Nez Perce (as will be noted later), and a squad of ten volunteers from Butte, under Mel Lowry, scouted the head of the Big Hole country. The latter returned to Deer Lodge on August 7th, a couple of days too soon to see the Indians enter that valley.

With open country before them once more, the next matter of concern to the Nez Perce was what route to take to the buffalo country. By and large, there were two main routes which began at the mouth of Lolo Canyon. One led eastward up the valley of the Blackfoot River and over Cadotte's Pass to the Sun River country. The other went up the Bitterroot Valley to its head, crossed the Continental Divide into the Big Hole, and then followed the Big Hole River and the Jefferson Fork of the Missouri to the Three Forks country, and thence—usually but not necessarily—up the valley of the Gallatin, over Bozeman Pass to the Big Bend of the Yellowstone River and into the land of the Crows. Trader McDonald was of the opinion that had there been a fight in Lolo Canyon, the Indians would have turned north through the Flathead Reservation to the Canadian line.

And he disagreed with Agent Ronan about the peaceable disposition of his Flatheads—"There were Indians on the Bitter Root and Flathead Reserve who had their guns ready."

McDonald also noted that about a week before the confrontation in Lolo Canyon, three Treaty Indians came to the Agency to visit with Eagle-from-the-Light. These had been on the plains "acting as scouts for General Miles"—probably they had been with the Crows and had gone with the Absaroka under Lieutenant G. C. Doane to scout the country north of the Yellowstone for Sioux. "On Sunday afternoon" they started for the Lolo Trail to return home but, finding the camp of the hostiles nearby, turned aside to visit. One of the trio is said to have told Looking Glass that it was folly to think of fighting the Government, and that they should turn back and head for Canada by the way of Flathead Lake.

> Looking Glass then called a council and told Joseph and others what Grizzly Bear Youth had said. White Bird and Red Owl agreed; they wanted to go by the reserve. Joseph did not say a word. Looking Glass wanted to go by Big Hole and down the Yellowstone to join the Crows, according to agreement, because the Crows had promised them that whenever the Nez Perces fought the whites they would join them. There was a disagreement, but after quarreling among themselves they concluded it was best to let Looking Glass have his way.[20]

And so the Indians began a rather leisurely march up the western side of the Bitterroot Valley. Colonel Gibbon was to note later that they traveled from twelve to fourteen miles a day—taking about nine days to travel the 95 to 100 miles which intervened between the mouth of Lolo Canyon and the fateful camp in the Big Hole Valley. As they traveled they traded with the settlers, for many essentials were in short supply as a result of their rout at the Clearwater. And while the Indians were traveling up the valley, Howard's couriers—"Captain" Cearley and "Sergeant" Baker, with Wesley Little of Elk City along for company—were coming down the valley, taking care to stay on the eastern side of the valley and travel part of the time at night.

On his return to Mount Idaho, Little told L. P. Brown that

> they have been trading at the stores in the valley and were offering one dollar apiece for cartridges, quite a number of horses taken from settlers here had been sold or traded off by the Indians for others in good condition. Mr. Little informed me that they sold Baker's large young horse for $40 and his gold watch for $50 to people of Stevensville, and stated that the title was good for they had killed the man and taken the property. He remonstrated against the traders purchasing anything

from them, and Capt. Cearley states that many of the settlers are opposed to the course pursued by the traders and went so far as to take what ammunition and whiskey they had at Stevensville on hand.[21]

Many years later, Henry Buck of Buck Brothers General Store set down a vivid picture of the visit of these Indians to Stevensville. As other items in the narrative of this pioneer are in close agreement with contemporary data, it is probable that the following is reasonably accurate:

> We had . . . moved all our goods to the Fort for safety, but that morning, July 31st, decided to move into the store again. We had one wagon load brought in and were busy arranging the goods on the shelves, when low and behold a band of squaws from the Nez Perce camp, accompanied by a few armed warriors, appeared. They soon made known their wants to us, saying that they needed supplies and had money to pay for them, but if we refused to sell, would take them anyway. Our stock comprised but a handfull of such articles as they wanted. However, we held a consultation over the matter and decided that "Prudence was the better part of valor," so decided to trade with them. Flour was their main desire and we had none; but near Fort Owen was located the flour mill to where they repaired for a supply. . . .
>
> All passed quietly that day but . . . we again returned to the Fort for the night. Peace and quiet reigned supreme [the next morning but the brothers decided to move no more stock for a day or two]. . . .
>
> Brothers Fred, Amos and myself went up town to the store that morning, August 1st, and about ten A.M. were suprised by the appearance of one hundred and fifteen warriors, well armed with Henry rifles, riding into our little village under the leadership of White Bird. . . . never shall I forget their formidable appearance, their stern looks, their aggressiveness and their actions. . . .
>
> They were all well dressed with apparently new showy blankets, well armed and rode the finest of horses. Many of these horses, I well remember, were branded "B" and sa   to have been taken from a man by the name of Baker who uved near their old home in Idaho. * * * We had always considered the Nez Perces a wealthy tribe but on this visit they seemed to have plenty of money, all in gold coin, but they . . . did not buy anything to my knowledge except some whiskey sold them by unscrupulous individuals who had no care of the well-being of our community.
>
> During their stay in town many of them came into the store, some of whom I knew personally. They told me that they held no animosity against the white people of Bitter Root, as they had always treated them kindly. They also told me of their troubles at home. . . .
>
> As a safeguard and caution against trouble, Chief White Bird took

his stand about quartering across the street from our store where he sat on his horse all the time and talked to them constantly in the Nez Perce tongue. A goodly number of our friendly Flathead Indians, armed with rifles such as they had, gathered in to protect us [at the direction of Chief Charlot?]. . . .

Finally, it was noticed that some of the Nez Perces were getting drunk and on investigation found that a white man by the name of Dave Spooner, who tended bar in the Reeves saloon was selling the whiskey. The liquor was siezed by a party of us and transported on a wagon to the Fort. Strong talk of lynching the dispenser was indulged in [but discarded lest it excite the Indians]. . . . The next move was to enter the general store of Jerry Fahy [who was treating the Indians from a barrel of whiskey kept for his customers, and to demand his barrel. When Fahy demurred and wanted to know by what authority, a South Methodist minister by the name of Reverend W. T. Flowers leveled a pistol on him and said, "By this authority." Fahy gave up the barrel]. I had a Henry rifle and plenty of ammunition lying on a shelf under a closed counter and took special care to keep close to it all the time. . . .

The older people of the Nez Perce tribe were well disposed, and tried in every way, to keep the peace and deal squarely with us; but the younger warriors knew no bounds and were hard to control, especially while under the influence of liquor. * * * One of them, going to the home of our village blacksmith, Jacob Herman, . . . was boistrous and insulting. He drew up his rifle to shoot Mrs. Herman, when a Flathead Indian standing nearby grabbed the fire arm and thus saved her life.

About two P.M., a little squad of half a dozen Nez Perces sat on the ground directly across the street in front of our store, in company with three Flathead Indians who were on guard. One of the Nez Perces drew up his gun, saying, "See me kill that man in the store." But by a quick move of one of the Flatheads, his gun was wrenched from him before he could pull the trigger. At this juncture White Bird, setting on his horse some fifty feet away and seeing the fracas, alighted from his pony and sprang to the Indian, gave him a whipping with his quirt and then sent him and his little band up the road to camp.

From this time on, the Nez Perces followed in little squads, until about three P.M., when all had left town. As soon as the Indians had gone . . . I turned the key on the store door and . . . [upon arriving at Fort Owen] my nerves gave way to the awful strain and I collapsed. . . .[22]

On the 18th of August, Sutherland wrote a dispatch in which he stated that at Stevensville

the Indians, with their plunder of gold dust, watches, money, etc. succeeded in bribing the people there to sell them goods. The whites told me there that they were compelled to open their stores through fear of their being burned, but I have since been creditably informed that the avaracious wretches followed after the hostiles for miles with their wagons loaded with all kinds of goods, selling to them to the amount of $900.[23]

And Colonel Gibbon, in his official report, stated that the Indians moved leisurely up the valley,

halting for a day or two at a time to trade off to the inhabitants their stolen stock and plunder for fresh horses, food, and supplies of all kinds, including ammunition. The pitiful spectacle was presented of these red-handed plunderers . . . being furnished by the citizens of Montana with fresh supplies, which enabled them to continue their flight and their murderous work. . . . One bright exception stands out in bold relief. . . . Mr. Young of Corvallis, refused to barter for their blood money, closed his store, and dared them to do their worst.[24]

Buck's reminiscences indicate that there were settlers who merited vigorous condemnation. But there were two sides to the coin, and McDonald wrote with sound logic:

It was very fine for officers . . . to condemn the people of Stevensville. . . . [But] These Nez Perce would never stand before a little town like Stevensville and . . . [starve] when plenty could be had there. [They] offered to buy from the first, but if they had been refused . . . they would have plundered. * * * Under the circumstances the citizens did right.[25]

And "after years of reflection," Henry Buck felt that the people of the valley were deeply indebted to Chief Charlot and members of his band for some unique protection.

Apparently, most of the Indians committed no depredations, but there were a few who did. Rev. W. A. Hall of Corvallis reported to editor Barbour that

Mr. Landrum's house was pillaged about $5.00 worth, and several houses were broken into above this place. M. M. Lockwood's house was broken open and everything demolished except the stove. Joe Blodgett's household goods and a large quantity of provisions were stolen, his harness cut all to pieces and about fifteen head of horses stolen. Alex Stewart had several head of cattle shot by the invaders.[26]

All of these took place at the upper end of the valley and the only one which attracted much attention was that for which Myron Lockwood made this claim:

Loss by stock		$ 200.00
Forage (Wheat Oats) & C		300.00
House and furniture		600.00
Miss expences		500.00
	Total	1600.00[27]

When Colonel Gibbon was asked to certify as to the correctness of this claim, he declined—because of a lack of detailed knowledge.

According to McDonald, this depredation was committed by some of Too-hool-hool-zote's band, "the worst band in the camp and a very unruly lot." When Looking Glass learned of it, he demanded seven head of horses from the guilty parties, had them branded with Lockwood's branding iron and turned loose on the premises as payment. However, Lockwood was not impressed by the quality of the stock given in exchange.

Of the body of Indians which passed up the valley, McDonald stated, no doubt correctly, that "The Nez Perces started from Idaho with 77 lodges. They got twelve more lodges in Bitter Root valley, taking them by force, making 89 lodges in all."[28]

The recruits who were shanghaied were, of course, the lodges that Eagle-from-the-Light wanted to move to the Jocko Reservation where they would have been out of harm's way; and with them went Poker Joe, perhaps fearing retribution for having participated in skirmishes in Idaho. The two Deer Lodge volunteers who followed the camp to spy on it were John Deschamps and a half-breed named Bob Irvine, who could speak Nez Perce and who knew many of the Indians. On the 5th of August, they told Editor James Mills that they had ridden with the band until they reached Skalkaho Creek beyond Corvallis. They counted 250 guns, many of which were "Winchester guns and cavalry carbines taken from dead soldiers." Ammunition belts were well filled. The horse herd was estimated at 1,500 to 2,000 head, many of which were "American horses and very valuable," but they noted that the "horses they ride are very much jaded"—a rather misleading statement, for the officers of Howard's command rendered the *considered* opinion after the war that the Indian pony was much superior to the "American" horses on this long chase.

They also noted that "the Indians make a cavalcade about five miles long"; and observed, as had others, that the Nez Perce were well supplied with "dust and greenbacks," and that they were buying what they wanted rather than trying to steal it. However, they had disarmed several whom they met, but after taking all the ammunition these men had, returned their guns to them. Also, they reported that "20 or 30 Snakes and Bannocks . . . [were] with them, giving color to their boast of alliance" with the Shoshones and Bannocks.[29]

The camp moved slowly and deliberately. Looking Glass apparently viewed the situation with complaisance; but others were worried—believing that it was dangerous to move slowly when they had met hostile soldiers in the Lolo Canyon. After crossing the Continental Divide at the head of the valley, they pitched camp at the foot of the eastern slope of the mountainous backbone formed by the Bitterroot Range. It was a pleasant campsite beside the north fork of the Big Hole River, whose banks were studded with dense willow thickets. And to the northeast, east and south stretched the Big Hole—a flat prairie about fifteen miles wide and some twenty-five to thirty miles long.

When the Nez Perce came down Lolo Canyon, the move which began as a measure to allay the fears of the settlers suddenly shifted from a matter of policy to an emergency, and Gibbon stripped the posts in his command of all the troops which could be spared. These were, of course, of the Seventh Infantry Regiment. "G" Company, which had been sent to bolster Fort Ellis early in the spring when the battalion of Second Cavalry entered the Sioux campaign again, was ordered to march direct to Missoula. At Fort Benton, Major Guido Ilges was left with six men when "F" Company was ordered to report to Fort Shaw. Some seventy miles to the south at Camp Baker (later Fort Logan), "C" Company was ordered into the field, leaving "E" Company to maintain the post. As infantry companies were small and undermanned at this time, Captain Richard Comba took six men from "E" Company to bolster his company—among them Sergeant James Bell who, as Private Bell, had earned a Medal of Honor against the Sioux the year before.

"D" and "F" Companies reported promptly to the District Headquarters and, together with "K" Company and twelve men from other companies, left for Missoula at 1 P.M. on the 28th of July. This detachment, according to Gibbon, consisted of eight officers and seventy-six enlisted men—the annual post reports indicate there were actually eighty-one enlisted men. Captain Constant Williams and Lieutenant John T. Van Orsdale, who were away from their posts at the time, managed to catch up with the column eleven days later. And in this force of "walk-a-heaps," in command of a small detachment of mounted scouts, was Lieutenant James H. Bradley, who had discovered the bodies of Custer's dead the preceding summer.

With their provisions and bedding packed on mules taken from the teams at Fort Shaw, this force marched by way of Cadotte's Pass and the valley of the Blackfoot River, reaching Missoula—an estimated 150 miles away—in seven days. "G" Company, with thirty-two men, a sergeant, and eight troopers from the Second Cavalry, made a more speedy trip. They left Bozeman in wagons on July 25th and rolled into Missoula, after traveling an estimated 240 miles, on July 30th—four days ahead of Gibbon and his men. At the time the order was received, Captain George L. Browning and a small party were escorting an officer from the Inspector General's Office on a trip through the Yellowstone Park. By making a forced march, the captain caught up with his company in Helena. Here, he was able to secure fresh transportation and, on the last part of the journey, in one day and part of a night, they rolled an estimated fifty miles.

Under the *nom de plume* of "Seventh Infantry," one of the soldiers wrote to the editor of the Bozeman *Avant Courier* of this march:

Missoula Post, July 31.

We left Ellis for this post, in the dust and terrible heat, to the music of Prof. Mounts harmonicon and "Ten Thousand Miles Away," reaching Helena on the 25th ulto. rumors of war increasing as we moved along. Capt. Browning joined us here, having secured our transportation and bringing us Capt. Rawn's dispatch. . . .

Aided by Kirkendall's teams, we made 30 miles per day over the terribly rough road, but the drivers were equal to the emergency, and no accident happened. Reaching New Chicago, wagons packed with families and effects passed us hastening to places of safety, and here parties of volunteers from Pioneer and Deer Lodge met us on the way to Missoula. Couriers were constantly arriving to hurry us along, which was unnecessary as Capt. Browning had ordered an effort to reach the scene of danger by the next night, even should the hurry result in death to every mule of the train. To our great mortification, at 11 A.M., a man reached us reporting the escape of the Indians; and the volunteers soon returning by the score, stating ceasation of danger, we slackened up a little in mercy to our animals. Such serious charges for the responsibility of the mistake were constantly heard that we almost feared that some great blunder had been made, and when we met the Governor and Secretary returning to Deer Lodge we concluded we might not be needed. * * *

Sergeant Page, 2nd Cavalry, and 8 men are with us, and the entire command is well, but disappointed over its failure to secure a fight.[30]

Probably there were two reasons for the speed of this push. One was that the Seventh Infantry was a seasoned, capable outfit. The other stemmed from the fact that they had a long campaign against the Sioux the preceding year—a campaign in which their part had been one devoid of action while others had occupied the spotlight of newspaper publicity. Now, with an Indian war in their own backyard, Gibbon and the men of the Seventh Infantry were to exhibit the eagerness of a pack of hounds in full cry on a hot trail. And probably, assuming that the Nez Perce would fight like the Sioux and Cheyennes, they—like Custer on that fateful Sunday afternoon—would soon allow their eagerness to exceed their discretion.

15

Tortuous Trail

>>>>>>><<<<<<< While General Howard was adjusting his plans to obviate further public criticism, a storm cloud welled up on the horizon. On the 18th of July, in far-off Baltimore, Maryland, workers of the Baltimore and Ohio Railroad went on strike to protest a reduction in pay. Three days later, there were fights, with the troops called out to maintain order, and these ugly disorders spread like fire in a box of tinder. The President wired General Sherman—then en route to Fort Ellis from the Tongue River Cantonment—to return to Washington (orders which were canceled a few days later). And McDowell, in San Francisco, found himself in the embarrassing predicament of having no troops to quell civil disorders.

The Division commander telegraphed Howard to return Captains Cushing and Field and their men—who had just been shipped from the San Francisco area. This telegram and the troops reached Howard about the same time, and the general, having just abandoned his plans to march to the Spokane area, was reluctant to part with half of the consignment that had just arrived. While it was not yet obvious that the Nez Perce war was *not* "practically over," McDowell now became quite critical of certain matters which probably appeared in a different light to Howard.

Howard answered McDowell on July 25th. This telegram, plus some marginal notes which McDowell made on a copy prepared for General Sherman, provides an interesting picture of the general's critical attitude which reached full bloom during the following month. Wheaton's infantry, noted herein, had passed through San Francisco on July 22nd, and Hasbrouck's Battery B, mounted on old artillery horses, was plodding up the trail from Winnemucca, Nevada.

> Column starts tomorrow morning from here, seventy miles from Lewiston on Lolo trail. If I wait for 2nd Infantry to replace Field and Cushing it would delay me two weeks and defeat the object of the move. [*It was not intended he should wait for 2nd inf. As the war was reported virtually over—he could well spare these companies and send them here where they are and have been greatly needed McD*] Again, cannot get them back to Vancouver for return transportation on the 29th. If the General deems it essential please weaken Wheaton's column by returning MacGowan's company from Lewiston and ordering back McGregor's company from Harney. Hasbrouck has been turned back as ordered. . . . [*As the others should have been! When I gave their order for their return I knew Joseph had escaped Howard and that the latter receid more than enough force for what I fear will prove a . . . Military promenade McD*] In another month I shall surely be able to make clean work of the whole field. Sanford arrives at Mount Idaho from Boise tomorrow. [*Sanford arrives at Mount Idaho tomorrow the 24' or 25' July! Yet he was expecting his immediate cooperation June 30!! a miscalculation of some three weeks!! P.S. Howard was on the 28' still waiting for Sanford to come up.—Green two days march behind McD.*][1]

It is obvious neither fully understood the problems of the other.

Leaving the disposition of these troops dangling on a thread of uncertainty, Howard gave orders for the column to march on Monday morning, July 30th. Reveille sounded at 3 A.M.—according to Sutherland, "a most unreasonable hour for those indifferent to worm gathering." Neither the reporter nor the soldiers enjoyed breaking camp in the darkness while a cold rain "poured in sheets," and continued to add to the discomfort until near evening. The column stretched out for an estimated five or six miles in length, and Sutherland likened the climb of the high hill or mountain just to the east of the Clearwater to a "monkey climbing a greased pole." Descent on the other side was no better with a trail too steep to ride down and blocked with rocks, fallen timber, and underbrush. By the time

Wieppe Prairie was reached, after a march of fifteen or sixteen miles, the men were drenched, many covered with mud from falls, and boots were like "minature wells." However, the campfires and a gleam of sunshine near evening restored everyone's spirits.

In his account of the campaign, Howard sketched a charming picture of a camp:

> The camp was generally rectangular in form. One battalion covered the front, usually, camping in line, and sending guard and picket details well out. A second covered the sides or flanks, a third the rear. The battery took its place at will. . . . For headquarters a place was sought of easy communication, and having a neat plat of ground, with wood and water convenient. . . .
>
> The "big tent" was a common square tent. Mason had a smaller one of special make. . . . His was put beside the big one, on one side; a tent-fly was pitched, with open front and back, on the other [for Dr. Alexander, Lieutenant Fletcher and Sutherland]. . . . The quartermaster, Lieutenant Ebstein, pitched still another tent-fly for himself and his clerks. A small pack train, under Louis, the Mexican, came up promptly after the night's halt was called.
>
> The kitchen was placed some twenty paces off. . . . The kitchen consisted of our mess-chest and one or two canvas bags, one or two mule-loads, according to the state of the supplies. * * * When the nights were damp or cold we always had a large fire made in front of the big tent. Our beds were common blankets or robes. . . . Our table consisted of a square of canvas, spread near the "kitchen," in fair weather, and within the big tent when it was rainy.[2]

This is a deceptive picture. The camp at Wieppe Prairie and a few others may have been like this, but few, if any, made during the next ten days resembled it. Nearer to the truth was the description Sutherland wrote of the camp made at the end of the fourth day's march:

> This camp was on the side of a mountain and so precipitous that at dinner [sic—supper?] . . . Gen. Howard had to rest his coffee cup on a stone, on one side, to keep it from going over the hill. According as the tents were pitched, or rather beds made in them, we slept almost erect or standing on our heads.[3]

And Major Mason informed his wife that "we live on hard bread, bacon and occasional potatoes, coffee."

The second day's march involved

> a perpetual vaulting over fallen timber and wallowing in mud holes until our arrival at the next camp. Here we found a most delightful

marsh, filled with mosquitoes and bog holes seemingly without depth. Our cavalry horses on being turned out fell into the holes [from which they were extricated only by means of considerable neck and tail stretching]. . . .

And the evening of the third day found them at the foot of a mountain, ready to climb to the top of the narrow divide which they were to follow for several weary days.

From this third camp to Summit Prairie, where the Lolo Trail leaves the divide and drops down to the hot springs near the head of Lolo Creek, the trail twists its monotonous way across high saddles from one pine-covered mountaintop to the next for approximately 100 miles. There was nothing but a continual turning to either the right or left while ascending or descending some slope. Steep, often precipitous, mountain slopes bordered the trail on either side; and to the north and to the south, timbered mountains stretched away in the blue haze to the horizon like the ribs of a gigantic washboard. There were but two ways to go—ahead or back.

For man there was very little that could be made to serve as food, and for horses and mules there was only starvation fare—a little coarse grass and the browse offered by bushes. Fallen trees added another difficulty that usually could not be sidestepped. In their passage, the Nez Perce had ruthlessly forced their horses over, around, or through these barricades, often leaving a trail of blood and disabled or dead animals behind. The troops dared not be so wasteful of their four-legged resources. To cope with this problem, a band of fifty men who were experienced in meeting the problems of frontier travel had been hired in Lewiston. One Jack Carleton had recruited them, and he served as a sort of foreman, although they were under the supervision of Captain William F. Spurgin. The captain reached the column early in the morning of August 2nd, after it had been on the trail for four days; and the axmen caught up soon after and were kept busy opening the trail. For a day or two, they were referred to as Captain Spurgin's skilled laborers, but this was soon shortened to "Spurgin's skillets" and "skillets" they remained until the end of the campaign.

In a letter to his wife, written the day after Spurgin's men joined, Major Mason described their daily difficulties:

This Friday morning is cold and disagreeable. It began to rain during the night and this morning it's almost cold enough to make ice—for we are up near the snow line, with the snow peaks all around us. We are making a late start this morning for our mules are almost played out on this trail. How can I describe . . . this mountain trail? It runs through the thickest of forests, and the most broken mountains I have ever seen. The fallen timber covers the trail so that every few feet there is a log to climb over or crawl around. We have to keep our pioneers at work [with] their axes all day long. We start at 6 A.M. and . . . work hard all day and make about 16 miles by 6 P.M. Our train and troops string out about 5 miles in length, as there is no danger of a flank attack in these forests, for no one can travel a foot off the trail, it makes no difference about the length of our line. The scenery is very grand from the top of some of the mountains we cross. While all day long it has been very pleasant to travel through the dense forests with the sunlight glinting through the trees. It looks a little brighter in the sky just now and I think it will clear up. We will have only a short march today—about 10 miles—but that will take until late in the afternoon. The grass is very scanty in these mountains and it's very poor feeding for the poor fellows [sic—horses and mules].[4]

On Saturday, August 4th, Howard met "Captain" James Cearley and his companions. As noted, they had followed the Old Nez Perce Trail and the Bitterroot Valley to Rawn's post at Missoula—a journey which had taken them five days. The general recalled that "Mr. Cearley's face was cheery, but he brought us bad news." The unwelcome news was in the form of a dispatch which Rawn had written three days before. In this he outlined the affair at Fort Fizzle and noted that Gibbon was "supposed to be within three days march, with 80 men," and that Captain Browning's company had arrived.

> Start tomorrow to try to delay them, as per your letter and Gen'l. Gibbon's order. Will get volunteers if I can.
> Have sent word to Gov. Potts, that it appears from information gained from men who know the country, that the Indians intend to go through Big Hole or Elk City trail. By sending his 300 Militia ordered mustered in, direct from Deer Lodge to Big Hole Prairie, can head them off.[5]

Of course, Rawn did not start "tomorrow" as he waited for Gibbon, and the projected attempt to make an interception died when the request for volunteers was disapproved.

Howard now had a reason—"the hope of forming junction with Gibbon earlier than I could with the whole"—to split his force. Taking his staff, the cavalry, the "skillets," and part of the pack train, the general left the infantry to follow at their own pace, and pushed on. Cearley and Little were given dispatches for McDowell and the troops in Idaho, and "Sergeant" Baker was retained as a guide. And Sutherland noted in a dispatch that, "Captain Robbins, with Buffalo Horn, the celebrated Indian of Crook's command, and several [10] other Bannock scouts, started directly for Missoula."

Late in the afternoon, two days later, this advance echelon went into camp beside the hot sulphur springs at the head of Lolo Canyon. With plenty of grass for the animals, hot water for bathing and washing, and fish in the nearby creek for a change of fare, the site represented real luxury. Howard recalled:

> Horses and mules were feeding on the green, as quiet and contented as if it had always been their home. . . . Blankets and clothing were spread for airing, and already the under-clothing was being wrung out by the half-naked owners, in the hot water of the pools, and waving gently on the bushes, as the sun and breeze caused speedy drying.[6]

While the men were thus engaged, a tall frontiersman named Joe Pardee rode into camp. He carried an urgent message from General Gibbon stating that he had left Missoula on August 4th and that he hoped Howard would send 100 men by forced marches to overtake him. He also brought a telegram from McDowell's adjutant containing a preemptory order to return Cushing's and Field's companies "at the earliest possible moment." In his reply to the latter, the general wrote that he expected to make a junction with Gibbon shortly, and he begged that he might be allowed to retain the two companies "till the arrival of Wheaton's column" for "this detaching imperils the whole expedition." Again—in regard to Wheaton— the general was not being realistic about the movement of troops over unknown terrain.

Howard, who believed that he could drive his troops "more miles in a day than one less spurred by the sense of responsibility," decided to keep his force intact and try to overtake Gibbon. He wrote a dispatch which stated, in substance, that he was "coming on, as fast as possible, with two hundred cavalrymen," and called for a courier to start with it at once. The soldier detailed for this assignment was Sergeant Oliver Sutherland from Captain Jackson's company. Sutherland was an Irishman whose real name was John Dennis Geoghegan. Before enlisting in the First Cavalry, he had served during the Civil War as a noncommissioned officer in the Eighteenth Infantry, and afterward as a lieutenant in the Tenth Infantry.[7]

An arduous ride lay ahead of the sergeant. He left camp as darkness was falling in company with "an Indian scout"—probably a Flathead who had accompanied Pardee. The two traveled down the canyon during the night, reaching its mouth about daybreak. Here, the Indian "deserted" to go off in the direction of Missoula, and Sutherland turned up in the valley alone. As his mount had been pushed nearly to the limit, he asked a settler for a fresh horse and was given a half-broken colt which bucked so vigorously that it broke the girth on the saddle and spilled his rider. Although "severely injured," the cavalryman managed to master the animal and proceed, reaching Gibbon (as will be noted later) about noon on August 10th —three and three-quarters days after starting.

When Howard's detachment broke camp the next morning, Pardee, Sutherland, and Lieutenant Fletcher, who was acting as quartermaster for the little column, rode on ahead, reaching Missoula late that night. The next day, while Fletcher purchased supplies and sent telegrams, Sutherland filed his latest dispatch and visited with Editor Barbour. Then, taking some necessary supplies with them, the two returned to the mouth of the canyon where they rejoined Howard about noon, and the little column resumed its forced march to catch Gibbon.

The following day—now certain that it was useless for the Spokane column to continue to Missoula—Howard sent orders for Wheaton to return to Lewiston. To make doubly certain that they arrived, the general sent a telegram to Walla Walla with instructions that it be forwarded, and he also ordered that duplicate orders be carried by a courier from his infantry—a task which Lieutenant Harry L. Bailey of Captain Jocelyn's company completed on August 17th. And, as he could no longer justify keeping Cushing and Field in direct opposition to McDowell's wishes, Howard also left orders for these two companies to proceed to Deer Lodge, and then march down the stage and freighting road to Corrine, Utah, at which point they were to take a train for San Francisco.

As Howard prepared to march up the Bitterroot Valley, he took steps to recover property which the Nez Perce had stolen in Idaho. At Stevensville, on August 9th, "F. J. P."—who undoubtedly was the free-lance correspondent, Frank Parker—wrote the editor of *The Teller* that "Captain Robbins has orders to capture all the good horses he wants and scout with his braves for Gibbon until our general catches up." Then he added:

> [Jack Carleton] is now under acting special orders to take and capture all the horses belonging to settlers on your side, and keeping a special weather eye for those the hostiles traded off when wending their virtuous way through here. He found Capt. Baker's watch which was traded off at a store here and of course took possession of the same.[8]

As Parker was writing his letter in Stevensville, Adjutant Kelton in San Francisco dispatched a telegram to Howard. This read:

> YOUR TELEGRAM OF THE 6TH, FROM THIRTY EIGHT MILES WEST OF MISSOULA RECEIVED. AS YOU SAY YOU KNOW YOUR COMPLIANCE WITH THE ORDERS GIVEN YOU TO SEND BACK CUSHING'S AND FIELD'S COMPANIES WILL EMPERIL THE WHOLE EXPEDITION, YOU ARE AUTHORIZED BY THE DIVISION

COMMANDER TO RETAIN THEM AS YOU DESIRE, BUT HE WILL REQUIRE THAT YOU HEREAFTER SATISFY HIM THAT THE EXPEDITION WOULD BE INCURRING SUCH DANGER AS YOU REPRESENT.[9]

At the moment, these two companies were at least two days' march behind the general and the cavalry—and orders had been issued for them to return. It would be another week and a half before this matter would finally be closed, and then it would be Colonel Gibbon's orders that would put an end to the matter. By that time, the labor riots would be over.

16

Death at Dawn

>>>>>>>>>><<<<<<< Captain Browning and his company arrived at Missoula on July 30th. Colonel Gibbon, with Bradley's mounted detachment as escort, came in on August 2nd and the balance of his troops, the following day. There was little to delay the colonel here—perhaps pick up some supplies, send a courier to Howard requesting reinforcements, hire additional wagons to haul troops—to hide the number of soldiers and to minimize fatigue—and ask Charlot for assistance in the form of scouts, a request which the old chief flatly refused.

At 1 P.M., Saturday, August 4th, the order was given to begin the pursuit of the Nez Perce. The force, which now included the companies of Rawn and Logan, numbered 15 officers and 146 men. H. S. Bostwick, the post guide at Fort Shaw, was guide, and Hugh Kirkendall, who had come from Helena with "G" Company, had charge of the wagon train.[1] At dark they went into camp near Stevenville, with an estimated twenty-five miles behind them.

Evening of the next day found them beside Weeping Child Creek, thirty miles farther up the valley. Here, a party of about forty-five volunteers came into camp and offered their services. There are two conflicting stories of what happened. According to that written years later by their "captain," John B. Catlin, the Stevensville company—disregarding their nonaggression pact with the Indians—wanted to go with Gibbon. After first refusing, Catlin agreed to go, and when they offered their services, "we were informed that General did not care to be encumbered with citizens. But we stuck."[2] However, one of the men in the company wrote shortly afterward that they acted as guides until the column reached the head of the valley where, being short of provisions, they considered turning back. Here, Gibbon assured them that "his men would divide their last ration with them, and would give them a fight with the Indians" and "there was great enthusiasm among soldiers and volunteers at this announcement." It has also been said that the colonel promised them all the horses they could capture. Perhaps, the whole truth never was set down. Although Gibbon seems to have been reluctant to acknowledge that these civilians may have meant the difference between life and death for him and his men, he did praise highly the services of Joe Blodgett. Not long before, Blodgett had brought lightly loaded wagons over the difficult mountain trail which lay just ahead, and his knowledge was to be invaluable.

The third day's march brought the troops to the mountainous spur which separated the major part of the valley from an isolated area known as Ross Hole—the canyon which formed the connecting link being impassable to wagons. Gibbon recalled that:

> At the foot of this spur stands Lockwood's ranch, where we found the first and only evidence of depredations seen in the valley. The house was thoroughly gutted. . . . Broken crockery and furniture, ripped-up bedding and clothing, were strewn all over the place, and the owner (a veteran volunteer of the Civil War), who joined our party looked with sad and revengeful eyes upon his wrecked home. We reached this point at one o'clock, and whilst we nooned there the scouts reported that the Indians had been in Ross Hole at nine o'clock that morning. All that afternoon was occupied in climbing the steep mountain and dragging up our wagons behind us. The trail was almost obliterated in places, and but for Joe's knowledge of the features of the country, we must have been lost in the mountains, and all our labor would have gone for naught.

Up to this point, the troops had been covering in a single day what the Indians had taken two to travel. There were no signs of travois, or of wounded. And as the camps had consisted of simple or brush shelters, estimation of numbers was difficult.

It took four hours the next morning to complete the climb to the summit of the spur, from which point the trail descended to the floor of Ross Hole. After about thirteen miles of travel, the troops reached the opposite side of the Hole and went into camp at the foot of the mountainous ridge which formed the Continental Divide. During the day, Captain Williams and Lieutenant Van Orsdale ended their chase, which had started at Fort Benton, to catch up with their men—and whatever *glory* the future might hold. Also, a courier arrived from "Secretary" James Mills with the unwelcome news that Potts' request for 300 volunteers had been refused—and with it went Gibbon's hope that there would be a force of militia in the path of the Indians to delay them.

Lieutenant Bradley now proposed that he be allowed to take his mounted detachment and push on ahead, find the Indian camp and, if possible, stampede the horse herd. To this, Gibbon agreed. With Bradley and his men, said to have been about twenty in number, went Lieutenant Joshua W. Jacobs and his nephew, G. J. Herendon from Kentucky, Sergeant Mildon H. Wilson of "I" Company, post guide H. S. Bostwick, and most, if not all, of the volunteers under "Captain" Catlin. This detail, numbering "about 60 mounted men," moved out just as darkness was beginning to gather. According to Catlin, "It soon got dark on us and the trail was [so] obstructed with lodge pole pine that in places it was impossible to lead our horses through, and owing to delay, we did not get down [the opposite side of the Divide] until daylight."

Once over the Divide, the route lay down Trail Creek, a crooked little stream with occasional boggy spots. Down this, Bradley's men picked their way, and when morning came, they were near the great open basin of the Big Hole River. Believing the Indian camp was near, the lieutenant concealed his men in the timber and sent Corporal Drummond and another soldier in advance to scout. They soon returned to report that about two miles ahead they had heard voices and the sound of chopping.

Leaving Sergeant Wilson in charge of the troops, the two lieutenants took Drummond and set out to reconnoiter the position of the Nez Perce. The three cautiously climbed a high hill which was believed to be near the camp, and, when this did not provide the desired view, Jacobs proposed that they climb a tall pine. From this vantage point, the two officers were able to see over the intervening trees, and before them was the camp with the horse herds grazing nearby. The camp was quiet—Looking Glass having given permission to stop and secure tepee poles from the thickets of lodgepole pine on the mountainside. After a quick survey of the scene, the two descended hastily and rejoined their men. A messenger—the second since leaving Gibbon—was dispatched at once to carry the news to the colonel, together with the information that they would hide and await his coming.

Bradley may not have been successful in trying to stay concealed. The following summer some of the Indians told McDonald that

> they had seen white men moving down the distant hills. . . . They gave the matter little attention. They thought they were merely scouts watching their movements, a surveillance to which they had become accustomed, and they knew that the little band of soldiers that had tried to bar their passage of the Lo Lo was following them. *They did not know* this little band had been reinforced by Gibbon's command from Fort Shaw.[3]

It is possible those whom the Indians saw were certain would-be horse thieves, as one source of questionable reliability stated that Alexander Matt and Joe Gird slipped away from the column to steal horses but were deterred by the arrival of the troops.

Gibbon's men began the ascent of the mountain ahead of them at 5 A.M. the next morning; and, although it was only about two miles to the top, it took six hours of arduous toil to reach the crest of the divide. Even though the wagons were lightly loaded, it was necessary to double the teams and attach draglines so that men could assist the animals. Bradley's first courier, with the news that the camp had not been located, reached Gibbon just before the wagons reached the top, and the second arrived after the column had started down Trail Creek. When the colonel learned that Bradley had found the camp, he left the wagon train to proceed at its own pace and pushed on with the troops to join the scouts. This junction was effected about sundown, and the wagon train came up shortly afterward.

Gibbon decided to leave the wagon train where it was and try to make a surprise attack at dawn. The wagons were moved off the trail and corralled beside the creek; orders were given for the twelve-pound howitzer with fifteen rounds of ammunition and a pack mule loaded with 2,000 rifle cartridges to follow the troops at daylight. Each man was issued two days' rations and 100 rounds of ammunition to take into battle; and supper was made of hard bread and raw bacon—fires being forbidden. As the men settled back to await the time for the advance to begin, the colonel lay down under a pine tree and quickly went to sleep.

Shortly before 11 P.M., everyone was awakened and the advance began with a civilian who knew the trail in the lead, followed by Bradley and his men, then the volunteers and, lastly, the regulars. Left behind were seventeen enlisted men and three volunteers as a guard for the train. "We had," wrote Adjutant Woodruff twenty-four hours later, "17 officers, 133 soldiers, and 32 citizens."[4] With no light except that from the stars, the troops moved down the trail "stumbling along over rocks and fallen timber and through streams and mud."

The camp was located at the extreme western edge of the flat prairie known as the Big Hole, and about four or five miles—by way of the trail—from where the wagon train was corralled. Here, the North Fork of the Big Hole River, a small stream formed just to the southwest by the junction of Ruby and Trail creeks, ran in a northeasterly direction at the foot of the mountains which the troops had just crossed. Its immediate valley, cut along the very edge of the flat plain of the Hole proper, was approximately a half mile wide and grass-covered, except along the meandering channel where there were many small, dense thickets of willow. It was on the grassed portion, adjacent to the willow-fringed stream, that the eighty-nine tepees were pitched "in the form of an open V." To the southeast, bare bluffs of moderate height bordered the valley, and beyond them open prairie stretched away for miles to the mountains on the other side of the Hole. The steep mountain slopes immediately to the northwest were covered with pine—except the one adjacent to the camp. This one was covered with grass and sagebrush and was dominated by two large fir trees growing side by side: along its lower edge, just above the valley floor, ran a branch of the trail which the troops had followed over the mountains. It was from this narrow path that Gibbon launched his attack.

Between a quarter and a half mile upstream from the camp, there was "a point of timber projecting into the valley." This "point of timber" was a moderately thick stand of pine, which covered an ancient alluvial fan built up of sediments dumped onto the floor of the Hole by a minor drainageway that came down the adjacent mountainside.

Its widest extent, measured along the foot of the mountain, was upwards of a half mile; its slopes were far more gentle than those of the mountain just behind it; and the Big Hole River had cut away part of the outer edge, leaving a sort of precipitous "bluff" standing thirty feet or more above its channel. This bit of topography was destined to play an important part in the impending battle.

Eighteen years later, Gibbon wrote a vivid description of the moments just before daylight:

> The trail led us along the bluffs overlooking the brush-covered valley of Ruby Creek [sic], and as we moved steathily forward I could hear a cautious whisper, "there they are—look!" On the opposite side of the little valley lying at our feet a single light appeared, glimmering in the darkness, and then another, and Bostwick whispered, "A couple of straggling tepees." Soon getting ahead of these, we caught sight of

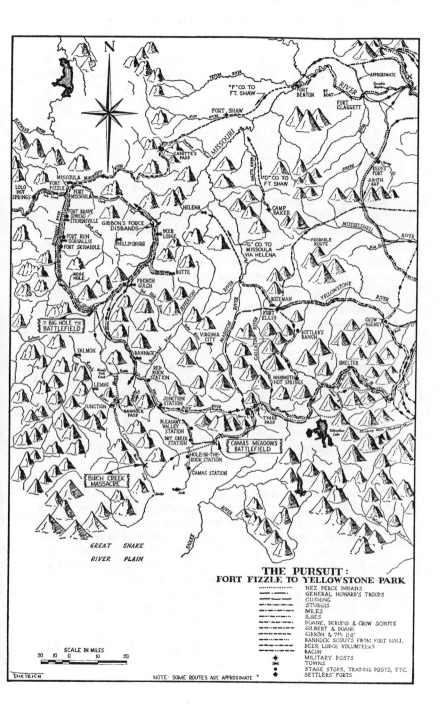

THE PURSUIT:
FORT FIZZLE TO YELLOWSTONE PARK

NEZ PERCE INDIANS
GENERAL HOWARD'S TROOPS
CUSHING
STURGIS
MILES
ILGES
DOANE, DERUDIO & CROW SCOUTS
GILBERT & DOANE
GIBBON & 7TH INF
BANNOCK SCOUTS FROM FORT HALL
DEER LODGE VOLUNTEERS
BACON

MILITARY POSTS
TOWNS
STAGE STOPS, TRADING POSTS, ETC.
SETTLERS' FORTS

SCALE IN MILES
20   10   0   10   20

DIETRICH

NOTE: SOME ROUTES ARE APPROXIMATE

numerous lights lower down in the valley, and the main camp of our
enemies was as plainly in sight as the dim starlight permitted. Our trail
now led us through a point of timber, composed of small pines jutting
down from the hills, and emerging from that we were startled by
moving bodies directly in our path on the sidehill, and realized the fact
that we were almost amongst a herd of several hundred horses,[5] many
of which as they moved away commenced to neigh and whinney. The
startled dogs in the camp took the alarm and commenced to bark, and
for a few anxious moments it seemed as if discovery was inevitable; but
the startled horses moved away up the hill, and we glided along
between them and the camp, and halting directly opposite the lights,
sat down on the trail to observe and await events.

It was about 2 A.M. when the command halted, with Bradley and his
detail and the volunteers still in the advance. As daybreak would not come
for another two hours, there was nothing to do but wait—and shiver, for it
was cold and some of the men had even left their blouses at the wagon
train. Only one thing caused momentary alarm. A soldier struck a match to
light his pipe, but an officer told him to empty it at once and the incident
passed unnoticed.

Colonel Gibbon noted later:

> we were in precisely the position I desired the mounted advance to
> take twenty-four hours previous. We were between the Indians and a
> large part of their herd, and it would be an important matter to run the
> latter off, and thus partially, at least, set the camp afoot. I therefore
> told Bostwick to get three or four of the citizens and drive this herd
> quietly back on our trail. But Bostwick, who had spent all his life
> amongst the Indians, objected that this course would certainly create
> alarm, and render a surprise impossible.
> . . . his assertion that the Indians would never allow the herd to
> remain unguarded settled the question. I have often regretted since
> that I did not insist on my order being carried out; for the herd had no
> guard, and Bostwick's life would have been saved.
> Everything now died down to a perfect quietness in the camp, and
> even the dogs seemed to have been lulled into silence, and Bostwick
> said, "If we are not discovered, you will see the fires in the tepees start
> up just before daylight, as the squaws pile on the wood."
> As the sky in the east began to brighten, the fires began to blaze all
> through the camp, and the troops were sent down into the creek
> bottom. . . .

Lieutenant Charles A. Woodruff, Gibbon's adjutant, now took orders to
Captains Comba and Sanno to take their companies, "D" and "K"—
deployed as skirmishers—and advance through the thickets toward the

upper end of the camp, which was "several hundred yards from the bluffs"; and companies "A," "F," "G," and "I" were ordered to follow in support. Bradley's detachment and the volunteers covered the lower end—Catlin having previously been instructed to detail ten men as pickets to cover their position. The orders were—"When the first gun is fired charge the camp with the whole line."

Catlin, who went on picket duty with his men, recalled:

> Our skirmishers were advanced a short distance where we remained for the signs of the coming daylight, when a solitary Indian came out from the lodges, riding directly toward us, evidently going to their herd of horses. . . . we had come between them and their stock. In order for the Indian to reach the horses, he would have to come through our line, and we could not remain long without being discovered. My men had been instructed ["Shoot the first Indian you see."], and the poor devil paid the penalty. Some four or five of the boys [firing almost simultaneously] helped him on his way.[6]

At this moment, Gibbon was:

> Seated on my horse on the bluff and overlooking this movement as well as the dim light permitted, with every sense on the strain for the first sign of alarm, I was startled by a single shot on the extreme left of the line; and as if answering the shot as a signal, the whole line opened, and the men, rushing forward with a shout, plunged into the stream and climbed up the opposite bank, shooting down the startled Indians as they rushed from their tents pell-mell, men women and children together. Like a flock of startled quail, the first impulse was to seek shelter in the brush behind the abrupt creek bank; but finding themselves rushing directly into the arms of our men, many broke for the bluffs on the opposite side of the valley, some of them dropping into any hole offering protection. * * * Within twenty minutes we had complete possession of the camp and orders were given to commence destroying it.

Tired from a dance the preceding evening, the Indians had been sleeping soundly and the surprise was complete.

When the troops entered the village, the fight quickly became a free-for-all. Apparently, Gibbon had let it be known that he did not want any prisoners taken during the attack, although there is no indication that he advocated indiscriminate killing regardless of sex or age. Dr. "John" Fitz-Gerald, who helped dress the wounds, a couple of days later stated in a letter to his wife: "I was told by one of General Gibbon's officers that the squaws were not shot at until two officers were wounded by them, and a soldier or two killed. Then the men shot every Indian they caught sight of—men, women, and children."[7]

However, each tepee or shelter, until torn open or upset, was a potential hiding place for an armed adversary. There is every reason to believe—as the first stories from participants state—that the excited soldiers "blazed away at every Indian seen," and that "many of the squaws used rifles and revolvers with considerable success in the fight, also young bucks of 12 and 13 years did nearly as well as their elders."

This stage of the fight involved a succession of individual incidents, of which the following stories were told:

> Private Lehr was struck in the head by a ball, which knocked him senseless. When he recovered he found himself being dragged by the heel into a tepee by a squaw. He kicked her from him, secured a rifle, and dispatched her.

> Private Alberts, Company A, when the charge was made, got into one of the tepees, where he was immediately surrounded by a number of young bucks and squaws with knives and hatchets. He dealt blows fast and vigorous, right and left, with the butt of his musket, thus making a pathway for himself and regained his comrades.

McDonald was told of an incident which may have involved Captain Logan:

> In a fight between an officer and a warrior, the warrior was shot down dead. The warrior's sister was standing beside him as he fell, and as he lay there his six-shooter lay by his side. The woman seeing her brother dying, siezed the six-shooter, leveled it at the officer, fired, shot him through the head and killed him.[8]

Wahlitits, one of the three original culprits, was said to have been killed as he fired at a soldier. His squaw picked up his rifle, returned the fire, and was, in turn, killed. Later in the day, Sarpsis Ilppilp, another of the trio, was killed by a shot through the neck.

However, trader McDonald, who got his information from both the Nez Perce and the whites, bitterly condemned the soldiers for killing women and children. "Many women and children were killed before getting out of their beds. In one lodge there were five children. One soldier went into it and killed every one of them." One Indian story stated that in a "maternity" lodge they found the bodies of two squaws—and a newly born infant with its head mashed. And both Indians and whites told of seeing a squaw lying dead in the open with a baby crying on her breast—one arm shattered by a bullet and the little bloody hand swinging by a bit of skin as the arm moved back and forth.

There was at least one story that was not so grim. When Gibbon took Howard over the battlefield later, he

> pointed to where women, during the battle, had waded into the deep water to avoid the firing; and told me how it touched his heart when two or three extended their babies toward him, and looked as pleasant and wistful as they could for his protection; this was while the balls were whistling through the willows near by.[9]

The initial phase of the attack had been highly successful; and that part of the camp occupied by the people of White Bird and Looking Glass had been occupied. Captain Browning and his men now started to follow a considerable number of Indians who had been pushed out on the southeastern side of the camp, but Gibbon, not wishing his force to become scattered, ordered him back and directed that the camp be burned. However, the lodge covers were damp and only four or five were destroyed. As the men started moving toward the lower part of the camp, they did not find Bradley and his men advancing as they expected. The lieutenant, eager and brave to the point of being rash, had led his men on a run for the camp when the initial shots were fired. In the willows, he met a warrior who shot him through the heart, and, although a soldier named Philo O. Hurlburt killed the Indian an instant later, the mischief was done—this portion of the force had lost its leader. His men and the volunteers drifted up and joined the rest of the force without attempting to clean out the lower end of the camp.

Now the tide of battle began to turn. When the startled Indians had fled from their lodges, many—escaping around the flanks of the infantry— took shelter in the nearby willow thickets, and behind the banks of the stream. Soon, at one end of the camp could be heard the voice of White Bird, and at the other, that of Looking Glass. In tones that stood out above the sounds of the fight like the notes of a bugle call, these two chiefs rallied their warriors and turned what had started as a rout into a desperate fight. From vantage points such as the twin firs on the hillside overlooking the camp, the bluffs to the southeast and the clumps of willows, snipers began to pour in a telling fire from all sides. Gibbon, who—with his adjutant—had ridden onto the battlefield, noted that "almost every time one of their rifles went off one of our party was sure to fall." And the colonel soon discovered that "horseback was not the healthiest position to be maintained." When he dismounted, an officer nearby pointed out that his horse's foreleg had been broken by a bullet, and Gibbon quickly discovered that the same bullet had gone through the calf of his right leg.

The adjutant offered his mount which, although wounded, was still serviceable, but Gibbon declined "kindly but firmly."

The attack had been launched about 4 A.M., and an hour and a half or two hours had now passed. To Gibbon:

> One thing had now become very apparent. We were occupying an untenable position, and longer continuance in it could result only in increased losses and inability on our part to retaliate. The men were therefore collected, and orders given to move back [toward the point of timber]. . . .

All the wounded who could be found readily were carried along, and some of the men picked up the rifles of the dead and carried them as far as the stream where they were thrown into deep water. Meanwhile, the Indian snipers continued their deadly fire.

Grizzly Bear Youth—one of the trio who had tried to tell Looking Glass that the safest route to Canada was by Flathead Lake—told McDonald that during the retreat, he was following closely and shooting at the soldiers, when a burly volunteer turned on him. Both tried to club the other over the head with their rifles, the Indian getting a cut on the forehead and the white man being knocked down.

> I jumped on him and tried to hold him down. The volunteer was a powerful man. He turned me over and got on top. He got his hand on my throat and commenced choking me. I was almost gone and had just strength enough left to make signs to a warrior, who was coming up, to shoot him. This was Red Owl's son who ran up, put his needle gun to the volunteer's side and fired. The ball passed through him and killed him. But I had my arm around the waist of the man when the shot was fired, and the ball after going through the volunteer broke my arm.[10]

Another story pertains to a curious incident that happened as the troops recrossed the little stream. As he was crossing, one of the volunteers heard a splash and saw, much to his amazement, a white girl beside him. She was not seen again nor was her body found. Years later, one of the volunteers, then the custodian of the battlefield, showed Henry Buck—the Stevensville storekeeper—a hank of yellow hair which he claimed came from a grave on the battlefield; and Buck recalled that when the Indians camped near Stevensville, a blond girl of about sixteen was seen with the Indians. But her identity is a mystery.

It is difficult to conduct an orderly retreat in the face of a strong enemy attack, and this one began to get out of hand after the stream was crossed. As the story was told in Deer Lodge a few days later, Gibbon "told them that unless they moved as ordered he would make them fight it out right there. The line moved thereafter as on parade."

The version told by the *Helena Daily Herald* was that when "several of the men commenced to run the old veteran cried out, 'Don't run, men, or I will stay right here alone.' The men halted at once . . . and fell back in an orderly manner."

And Gibbon's version, set down eighteen years later, was that a corporal became panicky and cried out "To the top of the hill—to the top of the hill, or we are lost!" "And I called out to the corporal to remind him that he was not in command of the party. The men about him burst into laughter. . . ."

As the point of timber was lightly held by the Indians, the soldiers had no difficulty in taking the area; and they immediately began to strengthen their position. Sizable stumps and fallen logs were quickly appropriated by a fortunate few, and the remainder promptly set about constructing shelters of rocks or digging shallow rifle pits. The digging was accomplished, as far as the soldiers were concerned, with trowel bayonets—ungainly-looking, multiple-purpose implements designed not only for fighting but also for chopping, sawing, and digging. However, these had been issued to but two companies; so, while one man dug, another kept watch with his rifle. Officers were to state later that probably this tool was the one thing which saved the command from annihilation.

While the troops were digging in, two shots from the howitzer were heard on the trail above, and Gibbon soon deduced that the gun, together with the pack mule and the additional ammunition, had been intercepted and captured—perhaps the wagon train also. Part of these apprehensions were well founded. The gun crew with the howitzer and the pack mule had started as Gibbon has directed. The party numbered eight—Joe Blodgett acting as guide, Lieutenant Jacob's Negro servant, William, leading the pack mule, and the gun crew consisting of Sergeants Daley and Fredericks, Corporal Sale, Privates Gould and McGregory, with an old veteran, John Bennett, riding the horse of the team that pulled the gun. When part way to the battlefield, they ran into a party of Indians. The gun crew went into action and managed to get two—possibly three—shots off. By this time, the corporal had been killed, both sergeants wounded, and the two privates, one exclaiming "This is another Custer massacre," promptly headed for Fort Ellis, which they probably reached in due time as they were later seen en route. The animals hitched to the gun were shot down, Bennett having a leg pinned under the horse he was riding. However, by prodding the dying beast with a knife, he managed to get free.

Leaving the gun dismantled, the survivors took to the brush, and Blodgett guided them back to the wagon train—except, of course, the two who had deserted. Kirkendall promptly secured his animals, and the men threw up some rough fortifications but, for some unknown reason, the Indians did not find them. However, they did carry off the wheels of the gun, and hid the piece in the brush; but not too effectively, as it was reassembled after the battle. Perhaps it was fortunate that the piece was dismantled for there was present a warrior who had been with Colonel Wright about twenty years before who might have been able to handle it. As Gibbon commented later, "It would have been a disagreeable ['novelty'] . . . to have been shelled in our wooded retreat with our own gun."

For a short time, the Indians made no effort to press the fight. The colonel recalled that:

> Few of us will soon forget the wail of mingled grief, rage, and horror which came from the camp four or five hundred yards from us when the Indians returned to it and recognized their slaughtered warriors, women, and children. Above this wail of horror we could hear the passionate appeal of the leaders urging their followers to fight, and the war whoops in answer which boded us no good.

Recognizing that the tide of battle had definitely turned, the chiefs began to press their attack; and warriors, creeping through the grass and bushes, resumed their deadly fire. One of the first hit was Lieutenant William L. English, who was knocked down by a bullet through the abdomen. Soon, the men began to fire recklessly, and Gibbon quickly issued orders that no one was to fire unless he could make a well-aimed shot.

The battle now settled down into a deadly sniping duel that resulted in a constantly increasing number of casualties among the troops. Long remembered was one warrior who hid behind a log less than fifty yards from the soldiers and kept up a murderous fire until one man aimed just below the log. It was believed that he was killed, but the Indians claimed later that he merely moved to another spot. Afterwards, a considerable number of shells were found in some of the best Indian positions, together with bits of rags which showed that the marksmen had been careful to swab the bore from time to time—an essential procedure in the days of black powder. Another casualty early in this part of the fight was Lieutenant Woodruff's horse, which had been tied to a tree within the siege area. When it was badly hit and began to pitch, someone dropped the animal with the remark that they might need him to eat.

Realizing that he was outnumbered, Gibbon expected the Indians would charge and try to overrun his position but, although a great deal of suspicious shouting went on among the Indians from time to time, no such attempt was made. However, there were some anxious moments at one time during the middle of the day. During each lull in the firing, the besieged had worked stealthily to strengthen their position and just "commenced to congratulate ourselves" on the strength of the position "when the gentle breeze blowing from the west brought us the smell of *fire*, and a little later, a line of burning grass made its appearance . . . close by, sending its stifling smoke ahead of it." The Indians had started a grass fire upwind at the foot of the mountain. In an instant, the colonel recalled a sham battle that had been staged by some of these Indians only the preceding summer for the amusement of the ladies of Fort Shaw, in which battle one side simulated the use of fire to win the encounter. As the grass was thin, the fire moved slowly and, before it reached some piles of brush where it would have been dangerous, the wind shifted and the threat was dissipated. With this, the peak of the battle passed. The Indians spent the remainder of the day sniping and, during the following night, shooting enough to keep everyone on the alert.

After the warriors left the campground to continue the fight, the women packed their belongings and the wounded on ponies. Then, with the horse herd, all moved out of the valley and onto the prairie, where they stopped for a time to observe the battle. Finally, they went to Lake Creek, some eighteen miles away toward the south, where they made camp. This time, they took the precaution to build a series of rock rifle "pits" along the side which faced the location of the soldiers. And from this point on, many of their camps can be precisely located today by the remains of rifle pits thrown up to fortify the camp.

As darkness fell, Gibbon was beset by several problems. There were over forty wounded men—two of them mortally and several with more than one wound—to whom all that could be offered was the crudest sort of assistance, and but little of that. The hard bread issued the evening before had been lost in crossing the stream, and the carcass of the adjutant's horse was the only food available—Gibbon told Editor Mills a few days later that "I ate a piece of it and it tasted very well."

Water was only a short distance away but access to it was not safe. A soldier who volunteered to go fill canteens wrote later that he was so apprehensive that he even forgot to drink at the time, even though desperately thirsty. At least five, perhaps seven, of the volunteers—fearful of the prospects of the morrow—crept away and headed for home. And it was imperative that couriers be sent for reinforcements and assistance.

In his official report, Gibbon stated that, "during the night I sent a runner to the train, and two others to Deer Lodge, via French's Gulch, for medical assistance and supplies. . . ." Apparently, the courier sent to the train was instructed to continue on and try to find Howard, for he carried a message "written in pensil, on a square piece of paper, the size of a visiting card," which read:

> GENERAL: We surprised the Nez Perce camp at daylight this morning, whipped them out of it, killing a considerable number. But they turned on us, forced us out of it, and compelled us to take the defensive. We are here near the mouth of Big Hole pass, with a number of wounded, and need medical assistance and assistance of all kinds, and hope you will hurry to our relief.
>
> GIBBON, COMM'DG
> Aug. 9, '77

This man narrowly missed meeting Howard the following morning—by reason of a fork in the trail—and continued on, as will be noted later, until he met Major Mason and the balance of the cavalry detachment.[11]

Gibbon's report would seem to indicate that two couriers were dispatched to Deer Lodge, as would Editor Mills' excellent account, in which it is stated that "during the night Edwards and another man started for Deer Lodge." However, the account Mills wrote *immediately* after the arrival of the messenger in Deer Lodge mentions only *one* man, and reminiscences of old-timers indicate that W. H. "Billy" Edwards made the trip alone. At least, Edwards was the first one to arrive. Lieutenant Woodruff remembered that he traded boots with the settler before he left, as the distance to French Gulch—both a topographical feature and a mining settlement—was reported to be sixty miles (maps indicate 40–50 miles). Presumably, Edwards secured a horse at this point and finished the remainder of the trip on horseback, arriving about 9 A.M., Saturday, August 11th.

By what must have been no mean feat in those days of human telegraphers and typesetters, the Helena *Daily Herald* went to press that afternoon with a reasonably complete and accurate story—obviously written by Mills—and the text of what appeared to be three dispatches sent to Governor Potts—all more or less repetitious—which stated that "We need a doctor and everything [food, clothing, medicines and medical attendance]. Send us such relief as you can." To these, Edwards added that as he left, the general had said: "I want an escort sufficient to protect the wagons which are going in to relieve us. Load the wagons as light as possible. The Indians cut me off from my supplies."

The dispatch sent to General Terry's headquarters was extremely terse:

> Big Hole Pass, August ninth.
> Surprised the Nez Perces camp here this morning, got possession of it after a hard fight in which both myself, Captain Williams and Lieuts Coolidge, Woodruff and English wounded, the last severely.[12]

Terry forwarded it to Sheridan, and he to Washington, where it arrived about twelve hours after it left Edwards' hands. This left the Department and Division Headquarters in a quandary after reading in the newspapers the account which Mills had written. On Monday morning, Sheridan wired Townsend that he had no further official news and that Terry was of the opinion that the published dispatches of Gibbon to Potts were not genuine. However, this uncertainty was soon to be dispelled, for about 4 P.M. the preceding day, Sergeant Wilson had arrived in Deer Lodge with a further report from Gibbon.

On the second day of the battle, small parties of Indians—estimated at 20 or 30—hovered about all day, occasionally firing on Gibbon's position and creating an atmosphere of tension. This was further compounded by the arrival early in the morning of a civilian courier, Nelse McGillian, who had come from General Howard. The settler had passed down the trail without seeing anything of the wagon train. For some unknown reason, Sergeant Sutherland—who wrote a note to Howard that he was leaving the wagon train about midnight "to endeavor to reach General Gibbon"—did not reach his destination until several hours later. In the afternoon, Captain Browning and about twenty-five volunteers were sent for the train and escorted it safely to the siege area. It had experienced a few tense moments, and one which provided a joke that was told for years afterward. During the preceding night, Lieutenant Jacobs' Negro servant was put on camp guard and armed with the lieutenant's shotgun which was loaded with "No. 6" (bird) shot. During the night, he saw some men a short distance away and hailed them, "Who dar? Who dar?" Then, without waiting for a reply, he immediately blazed away with both barrels, wounding two men.

The Indians remained around Gibbon until about 11 P.M. and then left after a parting volley. Their reason for leaving is not clear. In a letter dated a few days later, Captain FitzGerald wrote his wife that

[The Indians] actually corralled General Gibbon's command, and if General Howard's forces had not been following after him (of which fact the savages were informed), I think it probable they would have finally annihilated them.[13]

The basis for this comment may have been a statement in a dispatch Sutherland wrote about the same time:

On General Howard's arrival at Stevensville, he was informed that a Nez Perce Indian had been setting on a shed which commanded a long view down the river toward Lolo Pass, the entire morning, and as quickly as he saw the band of the column approaching, he jumped upon his horse and shot off post haste for the Big Hole. . . .[14]

This alleged happening, Howard spun out into an implausible yarn a few years later. What Sutherland reported may have been an incident that was reported to Editor Barbour about this time: "It is reported that a Nez Perce runner, who was left on the Lo Lo trail to see what he could see, arrived in Joseph's camp near Stevensville Wednesday with the intelligence that Howard is coming."[15]

When he visited Canada, McDonald was told this story:

> . . . the Indians were informed Howard's command was close upon their trail, and that volunteers were coming from the eastern part of the Territory. They continued to harras Gibbon, and would have stayed with him until they wiped him out had they not been apprehensive of his receiving reinforcements. They got their news in this way: [When they reoccupied the camp they captured a civilian who was trying to escape by pretending to be dead.] * * * Looking Glass ordered the warriors not to kill him, saying that he was a citizen, and that they might obtain information from him concerning Howard, etc. They then questioned him, and in reply he said that Howard would be there in a short time, and that plenty of volunteers were coming from Virginia [City] to head them off. While he was telling the news a woman who had lost her brother and some of her children in the fight came up. She was crying at the time, and on seeing the citizen slapped him in the face. On receiving the blow he instantly gave her a vigorous kick with his boot. He had no more than kicked her when some of the warriors killed him. . . . His statement decided them to raise camp and move on to a more secure place.[16]

Not only is this a plausible story, but the information provided—namely that Howard was expected soon and that it was hoped that civilian volunteers would block the path of the Indians—was about that which Gibbon's men had when they left Missoula.

On the first day of the battle, Howard's cavalry were nearing the head of the Bitterroot Valley where they learned from settlers that, when last seen, Gibbon's men were not far behind the Indians. Believing that it was necessary to make an unusual effort to overtake the colonel, Howard selected Lieutenant George R. Bacon and twenty-five cavalrymen with good horses, and Rube Robbins and the seventeen Bannock scouts to make a hard drive to close the gap. With the general went Aide-de-Camp C. E. S. Wood, Mr. Bonny, the quartermaster's clerk, and reporter Thomas Sutherland. Major Mason was given command of the remainder, with instructions to follow as fast as the condition of their animals would permit.

The following day, in what Sutherland called a "tremendous ride," the general's party put an estimated fifty-three miles behind them, missing—by reason of a split in the trail near Ross Hole—Gibbon's courier with the message asking for help. Night found them on the head of Trail Creek; and somewhere along the way, they met "seven" civilian "deserters," from whom Howard got his first news of the fight. That night "we barracaded a little with logs, and built fires, to make it appear that we had many troops." To Mr. Bonny and his weary horse fell the unenviable task of returning to Mason, some thirty miles behind, with a message that (must) have directed that the surgeons be sent forward with all possible dispatch.

About 10 o'clock the next morning, the little party—with the Bannock scouts in advance—noted signs of a camp ahead. Howard recalled:

> We passed rapidly along the trail, around another bluff, then the little camp came into full view. * * *
>
> It did not look like a hospital at first, though there were lines of rifle pits, and well soldiers enough to give one the impression of a heavy hospital guard. So many wounded; nearly half lying cheerful, though not able to move; . . . there were roughly constructed shelters from the heat of the unrelenting August sun. Quite on the other side, in the northeast corner of the camp, reclined the wounded commander. His face was very bright, and his voice had a cheery ring as he called out, "Hallo, Howard! Glad to see you."[17]

Gibbon's courier, who had missed Howard en route, reached Major Mason and his detail after they had camped on the evening of the 10th. After some discussion,

> it was thought best to make an early start with the cavalry and push on. So we lay down at 11 P.M., and got up at 3 and started. We marched about 20 miles by 12 o'clock, had lunch, and then Dr. Alexander and myself [Dr. FitzGerald] were sent forward with 30 soldiers and 6 citizen scouts, with our supplies on one pack mule.[18]

The surgeons and their party reached the wounded about 9 A.M. the next morning, having marched all night—with the exception of about two hours and a half they spent shivering near the head of Trail Creek, trying to get a bit of rest.

Although Howard wrote later that "the wounded were doing very well," Dr. FitzGerald told his wife: "We found a horrible state of affairs. There were 39 wounded men [sic—40] without Surgeons or dressings, and many of them suffering intensely."[19]

Lieutenant William L. English, hit in the abdomen, was to die eleven days later in St. Joseph's Hospital in Deer Lodge; Sergeant William W. Watson, whose left hip was shattered, lingered for twenty days after he was hit; and a civilian, Myron M. Lockwood, who was shot through both thighs, and one or two others lay in the hospital for a long time before they recovered. Curiously, all the casualties among the officers—both killed and wounded—were married men.

The day after the Indians left, Captain Comba was placed in charge of the burial detail, with Captain Browning as an assistant. Except for a couple of civilians reported buried on the campground, the dead were buried on the wooded point. There were twenty-nine—Captain William Logan, Lieutenant James H. Bradley, twenty-one enlisted men, five civilian volunteers, and H. S. Bostwick, the post guide from Fort Shaw. It must have been a poignant moment for Comba, for Captain Logan was his father-in-law, and not long before, they had buried one of the latter's daughters and a granddaughter.

There are no fully trustworthy data about the Indian dead. The Indians buried part of them—some in graves and some by laying them along the bank of the stream and caving dirt down on them. Part of those who were buried were dug up by the Bannocks for scalps and loot—much to General Howard's disgust. And while it was reported that he sent a detail to re-inter these, it must have been a most superficial effort. The New North-West reported that an Indian scout with Howard—apparently either Captain John or Old George—identified two of Joseph's wives, a daughter of Looking Glass, Too-hool-hool-zote, and the wealthy Black Tail among the dead. However, neither Too-hool-hool-zote nor Black Tail was dead.

In an official dispatch dated August 11th, Gibbon stated that "Forty dead Indians were counted on about half of the battlefield";[20] and this was probably the basis for Sutherland's statement that, "The bodies of 41 Indian bucks, children and squaws were found, 15 of whom were bucks."[21] The figure of fifteen dead warriors was also given to Editor Mills shortly afterward. However, in his official report, Gibbon stated that "83 dead Indians found on the field, and six more dead warriors were found in a ravine some distance from the battlefield after the command left there."

And Lieutenant Van Orsdale, writing late in September, reported:

I examined the field thoroughly . . . and determined the presence of more than 80 scattered from a point one mile below where the lower end of their camp rested at the time of battle, to a point opposite the rifle-pits constructed by the troops, a distance of nearly one and a half miles. Said number includes those visible or partially so.[22]

There are two reports of casualties from Indian sources that are of some interest. Ten days later, Sutherland wrote that the rear guard of the hostiles told one of the Nez Perce herders with Howard that "they lost 50 in all in the Gibbon fight and had thirty [bucks] wounded."[23] And according to information secured by McDonald the next summer, "There were seventy-eight Indians, all told, killed in the Big Hole battle. Of these only thirty were warriors."[24]

Amos Buck, who was in the fight and who returned to the battlefield shortly afterward when he met his brother, Henry, hauling some of Howard's infantry, told Editor Barbour that on the 15th of August

> he counted sixty-two dead Indians, many of whom had become exposed through insufficient burial, and that he saw five more about the rifle pits (ten were reported to be in that vicinity but he saw only five) and another *cache* of Indian stiffs were reported to be a quarter of a mile below the field, which he did not see. The men who were mining on the Big Hole told him that they had counted 116 Indian corpses and there is no doubt several have floated away in the river, or been carried away.[25]

And on August 24th, *The New North-West* carried this:

> Dr. Mitchell and Rev. Gilbert who went up to the Big Hole battlefield [with the relief party] mention the discovery of other *caches* of dead Indians than those found by Gibbon and Howard. One party from the upper Deer Lodge Valley finding fresh dirt and a buffalo robe protruding therefrom, supposed it to be a *cache* of property, attached a lariat, took a turn around a saddle horn and discovered there were several Indians buried there.[26]

However, even these counts leave to conjecture the number of wounded who were carried from the battlefield but who were too seriously injured to continue the flight. There are reports that ranchers and travelers later found the remains of bodies which had been cached away in the nearby mountainsides, and that sightseers who visited the area during the following weeks became suspicious that there were Indians hiding in the vicinity.

There can be no doubt but that the field was a ghastly sight. Frank Parker, who was with the "skillets," wrote Alonzo Leland: "I went over the field and the sight was the most horrible and sickening I ever beheld. The banks of the creek . . . was literally lined with festering, half putrid corpses. . . ."[27] Major Mason told his wife: "I was on the field a short time yesterday afternoon—it was a dreadful sight—dead men, women and children. More squaws were killed than men. I have never been in a fight where women were killed and I hope never to be."[28] Captain FitzGerald was curious as to the identities of the dead:

> We found over 30 bodies (mostly women and children). I saw them myself, and among them I think I recognized those two large squaws who sat in the Council tent last April at Lapwai, one of whom you questioned about her bead work leggins and who refused to answer you. Also saw the body of the large Indian who wore that robe trimmed with ermine skins. At all events it was the same robe or one just like it.[29]

In mid-September, the Rev. W. W. Van Orsdel—Montana's beloved "Brother Van"—and a Mr. Ness, while en route from Bannack to the Bitterroot Valley, found "the bodies of dead soldiers and citizens . . . dug up and dragged, some almost limbless, over the field. . . . It is supposed bears have dug them up as tracks are plentiful in the vicinity."[30]

The citizens took steps to send a party to rebury their dead in caskets until they could be moved, and Rawn sent Lieutenant Van Orsdale and a detail to care for the soldiers. The lieutenant reported that he found "some 14 including Captain Logan and Lieutenant Bradley" had been disinterred. These he reburied, with the exception of the body of Captain Logan which he brought back to the post for reburial.

There are an assortment of interesting stories associated with the battle. One pertains to old Black Tail, the Croesus of the Nez Perce, who—according to what Ad Chapman told Sutherland after the final surrender—had a buckskin bag containing $6,000 in twenty-dollar gold pieces. An officer present at the Bear Paw fight wrote:

> Many of the Indians have money, one old aristocrat having $6,000 in gold. The old chap says that he lost it in the battle of the Big Hole, and being near-sighted could not find it. Its loss so worried him that Joseph after a few days sent the old man with two young men back, and, after a few day's search, found it.[31]

And there was a story told among the settlers in the Bitterroot Valley that when the soldiers were driven out of the camp, one picked up a buckskin sack filled with gold coin. After he crossed the stream and was partway to the timber, he sat down, apparently to count the money, and was shot. Another soldier picked up the sack but dropped it when several bullets whizzed past his head—and it was never seen again.[32]

Another pertains to the widow of Lieutenant Bradley who left Fort Shaw soon afterward for her home in Atlanta, Georgia. The Helena *Daily*

Herald printed a story stating that when the courier from Helena carrying the first dispatch about the battle arrived at Fort Shaw, he met Mrs. Bradley, who was carrying a baby in her arms. On being told that her husband was dead, she fainted and fell. Shortly afterward, the Helena *Daily Independent* printed a statement from the courier saying that the story was false. However, the wife of Adjutant Woodruff recalled many years later that the letter her husband wrote, and which was carried out by Billy Edwards, was telegraphed to her. When she saw one of the officers approaching with it, she almost dropped her baby.

Several interesting comments were made by Captain Charles A. Coolidge to a reporter of the Chicago *Times*—Coolidge having been recently promoted by reason of Captain Logan's death. The captain, recuperating from three wounds and still hobbling with the aid of a crutch, commented that

> "the Nez Perce are good marksmen. One Indian sharp-shooter, when the battle opened took a position in the top of a cedar tree, eight hundred yards from the soldiers. . . . many a poor soldier bit the dust at the crack of his rifle. He was not discovered until near the close of the fight, when, seeing that the enemy's rifles were being brought to bear upon him, he descended from his perch. . . .[33]

Apparently, reference is made to the marksman who occupied one of the twin fir trees; and while this newspaper story may not be exact, there are other stories of rather exceptional shooting by some of the Nez Perce. Coolidge also stated that, "some of the Nez Perce fired percussion bullets, which, striking trees or rocks, exploded with a loud report."

This is the first reference to the use of explosive bullets in this war, and as the observer was a seasoned soldier and a Civil War veteran, this comment must be accorded proper respect. Years later, another soldier who was in this battle made a similar, although less accurate, statement.[34] The Nez Perce had some unusual arms and ammunition but it was not until after the final battle that a part of the mystery was finally solved.

In the weeks to come, there were some, including Colonel Gibbon, who tried to stretch the results into a victory—or, at least, a victory of sorts. But among the members of the "cloth," it was recognized as "a very bad defeat." Even General Sherman, who had just returned to Fort Ellis from the Yellowstone Park at the time, wired General Townsend that "Gibbon's force was too small."[35]

17

Horse Prairie and Birch Creek

>>>>>>><<<<<<< Major Mason and the balance of the cavalry battalion reached the battlefield Sunday afternoon, about five hours after Doctors Alexander and FitzGerald and their escort. Perhaps, hoping that the battered Nez Perce might still be brought to bay, Gibbon bolstered Howard's force with a detail of three officers and fifty men—who were to accompany him as far as Bannack. Captain Browning and "G" Company provided the nucleus, and to this was added Lieutenant Van Orsdale and ten men from Comba's company, all of whom volunteered for the assignment.

The general's detachment, now numbering 310 men, renewed the pursuit the next morning. That evening, after they had gone into camp, fifty of the foot soldiers who had been left trudging along the Lolo Trail rattled up in wagons which Quartermaster Ebstein had hired in the Bitterroot Valley. This addition was a mixed lot, consisting of Captain Wells and "H" Company of the Eighth Infantry and Lieutenant Humphrey with "E" Company of the Fourth Artillery.

Shortly after Howard's men marched away, the remainder of Gibbon's force began their trek down the valley of the Big Hole River—most of the civilians having already started for home. The most seriously wounded had been put into Kirkendall's wagons or on travois improvised from lodge-poles and the hides of dead ponies. As the vegetation in the Big Hole was predominantly bunch grass and sagebrush, neither type of transportation offered much in the way of comfort.

When Billy Edwards had reached Deer Lodge about forty-eight hours before, Editor-Secretary James Mills lost no time in taking steps to procure the assistance Gibbon had urgently requested. By midday, "several ambu-lances and light wagons," together with volunteers, were ready to start—the volunteers having disbanded but a short time before, after starting too late to reach Fort Fizzle before the Indians passed. Years later, Father L. B. Palladino recalled that the news reached Helena about 11 A.M. and that within an hour, the "Helena ambulance corps" consisting of himself, Dr. Mitchell, two Sisters of Charity, and a small escort was on its way. They reached Deer Lodge late that evening and by noon the next day were at French Gulch, where the nuns left the party to make arrangements to take care of the wounded. The remainder continued up the Big Hole Valley, where they joined the Deer Lodge-Butte portion of the relief column. Here, the priest was to note that the volunteers included "a couple of Protestant clergymen, who . . . were not without their rifles as a side help to their mission."[1]

William A. Clark, the banker in Deer Lodge and an owner of mining interests in nearby Butte, reassembled the volunteers in Butte and directed the collection of wagons and supplies. When the Deer Lodge, Butte, and Helena contingents all joined in the Big Hole, there were five surgeons, twenty-eight light wagons and ambulances, and two companies of volun-teers—one from Butte under "Major" Clark, and another from Butte and Deer Lodge under "Captain" Thomas Stuart. The Butte *Miner* printed this record of that town's contribution:

> The vehicles for the transportation of supplies were five in number, and furnished gratis. . . . These wagons were loaded with a full supply of commissary stores for twenty days and the following hospital stores: four gals. brandy, 2 gal. whiskey, 50 yds. bleached muslin for bandages and some lint, 2 cases of surgical instruments, $75 worth of medicine, 1 case each of strawberries, peaches, oysters and sardines.
>
> The amount collected by the committee to raise funds was $412.[2]

To swell the supply of luxuries, the Deer Lodge people later sent a wagon load of "fruit and all the delicacies" and another of "mutton, chickens &c &c."

When the relief *column* was within twelve or fourteen miles of the battlefield, a messenger from Gibbon met them with the request that they wait for his arrival, and all turned back a few miles to a good camping spot. Here the surgeons redressed the wounds and everything possible was done to put the men in shape for the journey ahead. The next day, Gibbon, leaving Rawn in command, took a buggy and set out for Deer Lodge in company with Lieutenant Jacobs. They reached the town on Wednesday (15th); and the wounded arrived about noon the next day where they received all the attention the people could extend. The wife of Lieutenant English—a bride but a few weeks before—came over from Missoula and went out to meet the train. The driver of one of the vehicles recalled, "Her's must have been a stout heart, or she had been told to be very cheerful on her husband's account. She climbed into the wagon, saying, in a cheerful voice: 'How are you, Willie?' " But "her's" was a lost cause.

The seriously wounded were left in the newly constructed St. Joseph's Hospital, while those who could travel left for their respective posts as Gibbon disbanded his force. Lieutenant Woodruff, himself among the wounded, wrote: "Twelve days after the fight, at the end of a 240 mile ride we reached our post [Fort Shaw] and home."

While the relief operation was under way, several things of note transpired. During the night following the junction of Gibbon with the citizens, signal fires were observed on the mountains "within three miles of the camp." The volunteers decided to split their force; and the next morning, sixty-two men, under "Major" Clark and "Captain" Stuart, set out on a forced march to join Howard. Meanwhile, still other groups of volunteers from various settlements began to converge on the area.

Three other matters were covered in a telegram which Gibbon sent to Terry:

> I met Norwood's company of Second Cavalry on the Big Hole, and he is probably with Howard by this time. Cushing's two companies of artillery passed here this morning, and I have ordered them to push down the stage road at forty miles a day, if their stock will stand it. Have also telegraphed the commanding officer at Fort Hall [Idaho] to start some of his Bannocks up toward Lemhi and the mountain passes to get information as to which way the Nez Perces are heading.[3]

Cushing and Field had left Howard's troops at the mouth of Lolo Canyon, in accord with the general's orders, and were proceeding, via Deer Lodge, to the freighting and stage route that ran southward to Corrine, Utah—the station where they would have taken a train for San Francisco. As soon as Gibbon saw them, he countermanded Howard's orders and sent them hurrying down the road to catch the cavalry—and advised McDowell of his action.

The preceding spring, Captain Randolph Norwood and "L" Company of the Second Cavalry—together with the other companies of this "orphan" battalion—had been sent down the Yellowstone to assist Colonel Miles in rounding up the Sioux and Cheyenne stragglers. Then, when General Sherman decided to make a trip into the Northwest, this company had been assigned to escort him from the vicinity of the mouth of the Big Horn River to points in western Montana. Sherman reached Fort Ellis on August 1st, and his escort came in the following day. Recognizing that all available troops were needed, Sherman released Norwood and, as Gibbon was at the moment beyond reach for instructions, the captain began a reconnaissance of his own. This took him to Virginia City and thence to the Big Hole, where he found Gibbon and was ordered to join Howard.

Gibbon's wire to Captain Augustus H. Bainbridge at Fort Hall on the Bannock Reservation indicates the degree of cooperation being tendered to General Howard, for this post was in General Crook's Department, whereas Gibbon, as has been noted, was in General Terry's Department. General Sheridan moved promptly to cover the colonel's request by securing the Adjutant General's approval to enlist fifty Bannock scouts for a period of thirty days.[4] And, in view of the jangle which developed after Joseph's surrender, a message Sheridan sent to Terry on August 13th is of particular interest:

> Cooperate with General Howard even to temporarily placing such troops as you may have to spare under his command and notify him that there are no hostile Sioux for the Nez Perce to join south of the line of Manatoba and such a junction is preposterous.[5]

Sheridan may have thought the Sioux threat was "preposterous"—but it wasn't.

Not only did Sheridan take steps to support Howard but he also began to plan. A few days later, he sent another telegram to Terry:

> If the hostile Nez Perces go through the Yellowstone Park, they will cross the passes on Stinking Water [now Shoshone River] and down that stream to the Big Horn and I think it would be well to send an express across the country from Bismarck to Col. Miles to keep his scouts out and as soon as he finds they cross in the Big Horn country, to go for these with such a force as he may deem necessary to clean them out completely. I have my doubts now if Gen. Howard can overtake them. I will also send scouts out from Camp Brown [in Wyoming] to watch movements.[6]

Mixed with these matters of importance were the activities of two individuals. J. W. Redington, a "traveling printer" from Salem, Oregon, was in Boise, Idaho, shortly before the outbreak. When the war got under way, Redington—then in Salt Lake City and short of funds—badgered Governor Brayman for some sort of assignment which would take him to the front. This was refused, but he turned up in Deer Lodge where he claimed to be a "special correspondent" of the *Salt Lake Tribune*. Acquiring a cayuse, he left town with the volunteers going to relieve Gibbon. When these stopped to await the arrival of Gibbon, he pressed on to find Howard—alone and without a gun. Obviously inept, he successively got lost, exhausted his cayuse and had to catch a worn-out Indian pony to continue, lived on a bit of flour found on the floor of an abandoned cabin, was set afoot by the Nez Perce but—somehow—got out of his predicaments and joined Howard's troops where he served as a scout. There is no evidence that he ever submitted a line of dependable copy to the *Salt Lake Tribune*, and the reminiscences[7] he wrote years later read like a "windy."

The other person, Lieutenant Henry McKinley Benson of the Seventh Infantry, was a most determined *glory hunter*. As he had been in poor health for a couple of years, he was given a recruiting assignment in Baltimore, Maryland. In July, learning that the Nez Perce were approaching Montana, he threw up his "leave" and started for Montana to rejoin his regiment. Traveling by train to Bismarck, by steamboat to Fort Benton, and by wagon to Fort Shaw, he arrived two days after Gibbon and his men had left. Picking the best horse from among the scrubs left at the post, he struck out on the trail of the troops. After being lost for a couple of days when storms obliterated the trail, he returned to Fort Shaw and took the stage to Missoula—where he arrived four days late.

When Gibbon arrived in Deer Lodge, Benson was there to meet him and beg for a combat assignment. As other volunteer goups were reported taking the field, the colonel sent him down the trail "to take charge of such militia organizations as he found there and to report to General Howard." The next day, he and Editor Mills "left for the front . . . [with] a supply of ammunition and a fast team and expect to make lighting time on the road." However, before they reached Howard, the volunteers turned back, and the tentative assignment vanished. But the lieutenant had not come so far to be denied the opportunity to burn powder, and the assignment Howard gave him was a rather unique one.

In the country some fifty miles to the south of the Big Hole battlefield—the town of Bannack, small mining settlements to the northward, and on ranches in the adjacent *hole* known as Horse Prairie—a state of jitters had existed for well over two weeks. When the Nez Perce started their move up the Bitterroot Valley, ranchers on Horse Prairie sent their families into Bannack, and many stopped haying; women and children from Maryville and Argenta took refuge in a mining tunnel, and the people in Beaverhead Valley took refuge at a ranch having numerous log corrals and buildings. According to one local correspondent of the Helena *Daily Herald*, it was "generally believed that the Nez Perce will take the Salmon River route, in hopes that the Bannocks will join them," and he noted that those Bannocks whom they saw no longer came into town and were friendly, although their chief, Tendoy, claimed he would stand by the settlers.

These people had good reason to be concerned about the attitude of the Bannocks, for the Lemhi Reservation where Tendoy was the principal chief was only about forty miles southwest of Bannack on the opposite side of a narrow spur of the Bitterroot Range. For some time their Agent had swindled them out of their rations and annuities. This brought them to the brink of starvation and had forced them to exist by hunting, fishing, and trading for what probably were their rightful goods. Even their fishing rights in the Lemhi River were "claimed and monopolized by white speculators . . . with dams and fish traps."

This flurry of apprehensions subsided for a few days and then, on the eve of the Big Hole battle, they welled up anew. According to the recollections of the wife of one settler:

> All the women on Horse Prairie and at Red Rock [stage station] were taken into Bannack and remained there for two weeks. The men had the courthouse barricaded; two barrels of water were taken into the building and the windows had feather beds piled against them so that the shot and bullets could not reach us. The men also had a small fort in the street near the well. * * * We had several scares. In one a woman fainted in the street because she could not find her little girl. Another woman carried a satchel which flew open in her flight and its contents spilled: they were not pearls, but silver spoons, which were quite scarce at that time.[8]

At the beginning of the war, the settlers in the valley of the Lemhi River were even more jittery than those in Montana—a condition which resulted from concern over the attitude of the Bannocks and the suspicion that the Nez Perce had sent runners asking these Indians to join them. On the 9th of July—before the battle of the Clearwater had been fought—Edd Swan, "Captain Comdg Lemhi Rifles," wrote a letter to Governor Brayman pertaining to a request for some ammunition:

> We send you this requisition on account of anticipated trouble with Indians in Idaho. Please forward to Geo. L. Shoup and Co., Salmon

City Idaho care of Fred J. Keisel, Corrine Utah who will pay all charges to Corrine.

Upon receipt of reports of trouble with Indians in Salmon River Idaho a great excitement prevailed and at a public meeting held in Salmon City [a volunteer company of 30 men was organized]. . . .

We also called together most of the Lemhi rifles at Junction, Idaho and erected some defences such as corrals and rifle pits. The rifles number 40 men, armed and equipped, but could easily swell the ranks to 60 or more, but the want of arms and ammunition prevent.[9]

On the day after the Big Hole battle ended, a correspondent in Lemhi informed the editor of the Helena *Daily Independent:*

There is considerable excitement here about the Indians, as it is feared by many that if they are pressed by the troops they will come this way. There have been scouts kept out most of the time on the trail leading to the Big Hole and surrounding country.

At the end of this letter was added, "Ten Doy is feeling much happier since the fish trap [at the mouth of the Lemhi River has been removed, giving the salmon liberty to run up the streams."

This was the state of affairs in the area toward which the Nez Perce headed after the fight with Gibbon. The women and children of Horse Prairie, Bannack and vicinity were already barricaded in the two-story courthouse in Bannack—while some of the ranchers were still carrying on their work. In the adjacent area in Idaho, two volunteer companies had been in being for some time, and one point, soon to become critical, had been fortified.

At the extreme head of Horse Prairie, a road from Bannack followed a moderate slope to the top of Bannock Pass, crossed the narrow spur of the Bitterroot Mountains which forms the Continental Divide at this point, and then descended by what was then known as Stephenson's Canyon (now Canyon Creek) to the open valley of the Lemhi River. Here, at what was known as Junction, this road joined the freighting trail which ran from Salmon City, about fifty miles to the northward, down to Corrine, Utah, the important transshipment point of the Union and Central Pacific Railroads. Although Junction was little more than a sort of landmark, the Lemhi Rifles had seen fit to fortify it as a strongpoint which settlers in the immediate area could use in case of need. In the valley about twenty miles to the north was the village of Lemhi and the Bannock Reservation where Tendoy's people lived, and some thirty miles farther on, at the junction of the Lemhi and Salmon rivers, was Salmon City, the most important settlement in the valley.

The routes followed by the pursued and their pursuers for the next several hundred miles—until they emerged from the eastern edge of the Rocky Mountains—were determined almost entirely by the nature and location of mountain ranges, passes, valleys, and their forests and prairies. To anyone who has seen this country, what happened is easy to understand; others will find the best of maps but a feeble substitute. When the Nez Perce left the battlefield, they were at the western edge of a large prairie ringed by timbered mountains. From their camp on Lake Creek, they moved southward along the western edge of this valley where they were protected on the east by a relatively unobstructed view of five to ten miles, and on the western side by ridges at the foot of the mountains which were covered by a heavy, but not dense, pine forest. At the upper end of the Big Hole, they passed over onto the head of Bloody Dick Creek and followed its narrow, forested valley, and then that of Trail Creek to the valley—or *hole*—of Horse Prairie Creek which, at this point, was an open prairie four to five miles in width and occupied by ranchers. Late in the afternoon of the third day after that fateful Friday beside the Big Hole River, bands of warriors who were in advance of the main camp rode into Horse Prairie close to where W. L. Montague and Daniel H. Winters had a ranch. The women were in Bannack, but a haying crew was at work about a half mile from the ranch buildings.

In Bannack, Sunday had been quiet but tense. Then, during the night, men began to arrive with alarming news, one of the first being T. H. Hamilton who came in about 3 A.M., after having been chased by Indians. What made the news even more frightening was that those who came in first believed some lost, who arrived later. In the morning, a party of about twenty-four men headed by a man named Trask started for the upper end of the Prairie. In the party was the Rev. W. W. Van Orsdel, the Methodist minister known throughout Montana as Brother Van; another member stated later that "with us went two brave Christian women." Years later, Brother Van recalled only one woman—Mrs. Winters. They had tried to persuade her not to go, but after they were on their way, she caught up "mounted on a very fine horse, and with a revolver buckled on, . . . [which] she knew how and was not afraid to use." Apparently, the other was Mrs. Smith.

When they reached the ranch, Brother Van saw

one of their fine cows was shot in front of the house, feather ticks and straw ticks cut open and their contents emptied in the front yard. I was selected to go with Mrs. Winters into the house. Just as we went into the kitchen there lay a man [Thomas Flynn] who had been shot four times. On first sight he had the appearance of her husband. Some thought at this juncture she would faint, but she said she could stand it as well as any of us . . . and the sooner she knew the facts [the better]. . . . From there we passed into another room where we found the dead form of Mr. [W. L.] Montague, the partner of Mr. Winters [his feet protruding from beneath a matress and with six bullet holes in his body]. Everything in the house was upset and broken. * * * A short distance from the house we found the body of Mr. [James] Smith, pierced with five bullets. He left a widow and eight children. * * * We patched up some harness with leather and ropes and hitched to a light wagon that had been left near the ranch, and started to Bannack with the four [sic] bodies.[10]

Another account, written at the time, states that the body of the fourth victim, James Farnsworth, was discovered near the ranch house by another party and brought in later. When found, "His body was covered by a quilt" and there was "about $200 in his pockets."

Mrs. Winters' anxiety in regard to her husband was short-lived. He had escaped and reached Bannack before the party returned with the bodies. When the attack was made, Winters, together with four or five others— his brother, Michael Hern, Farnsworth, Smith, and perhaps a man named Norris—were loading hay about a half mile from the house. On seeing two parties numbering fifty or sixty warriors, they drove on a run to the house, which they found surrounded. As none of the other men were in sight, they headed for the willows along a creek some 200 yards away. The Indians opened fire, killing Farnsworth and Smith, and the others made a dive for the brush. After hiding all night, the survivors walked into Bannack.

Another report stated:

They attacked the Pierce Brothers ranch, and nine men about two miles above my ranch, at 6 or 7 o'clock, but singular to say, every one of them escaped unhurt, save one hired hand, with a slight flesh wound in the arm. I believe the attack was simultaneous all along the gulch. * * * These Indians have not burned any buildings, but literally destroy and demolish all furniture, dishes, carpets, clothing and food, if the latter is not needed. * * * They take no guns except breech-loaders, the muzzle-loaders they either destroy or leave. * * * I now have left but two or three horses; all my best mares and colts are gone. John and Tom Pierce have but two or three head left, and so of all other ranchmen.[11]

The next morning, the warriors gathered up all the readily available horses—estimated by the settlers at 100 to 150 head—and drove them off.

There was one other murder, and "T. W." chronicled this death for the Helena *Daily Independent*:

Andrew Meyers has just arrived in Bannack from Horse Prairie gulch bringing the sad intelligence that his partner, Alexander Cooper, was killed by the Indians within 500 yards of Thomas H. Hamilton's ranch. The Indians called Cooper to come to them, [saying] that they were friendly. He gave his gun to one of the party, threw down his cartridges and went to them. They tried to get Andrew Meyers and Mr. Howard to come to them, but failing in this they shot Cooper. Meyers, Howard and John Wagoner made for the willows and remained there until the Indians left, when they came out and buried Cooper.[12]

By Tuesday, a band of volunteers had arrived and the tension ceased somewhat, although the people were still jittery. The first task was to bury the dead—the Masonic Lodge presided at the ceremonies for Montague, and Brother Van officiated at the services for the others.

All four corpses were taken to the . . .[cemetery] at the same time, followed by a large concourse of citizens. The procession had proceeded but a little ways when an alarm was given by a Chinaman, just getting in from the scene of bloodshed, that there was a band of Indians—or maybe soldiers just above town. The procession halted, and a dozen men were in their saddles in an instant, galloping up the road to ascertain the cause of alarm. Every man to his gun, and women and children hurrying back to the Court House citadel. It was but a moment of suspence but that moment was one of intense excitement and suffering.[13]

The approaching horsemen were but three—Mr. Osgood, a citizen scout, "Rube" Robbins, and Lieutenant John Q. Adams. Howard had arrived within about ten miles of the town, and the lieutenant had been sent ahead to secure some necessary supplies and to look for fresh horses.

At this camp just northwest of Bannack, Howard received McDowell's tentative approval—dispatched six days before—to retain Cushing and Field; but he did not know that Gibbon would shortly notify McDowell that he was ordering these men to rejoin the column. In a reply written that evening, the general reviewed the situation as he thought it existed and informed McDowell that the Indians

seem to have delayed in [Horse Prairie] . . . one day, and to day passed into Lemhi Valley. Another days delay will enable me to intercept them in the vicinity of Henry Lake near Corrine Stage Road [sic]. If I intercept them and force them back into the Salmon River Country I can gradually push them towards Green and sure destroy or capture the greater portion but if they escape into the Buffalo country beyond me is it worth while for me to pursue them further from my Department unless General Terry or General Crook will head them off and check their advance.

Then, he went on to state:

We have made extraordinary marches and with prompt and energetic cooperation from these Eastern Departments may yet stop and destroy this most enterprising band of Indians. Without cooperation, the result will be as it has been, doubtful. If Gibbon had 100 more men the work would have been complete. Surely he might have had more from all this Territory, three times as many.[14]

This dispatch was to be particularly irritating to McDowell. For one thing, Howard was either extremely ignorant or childishly naïve about troop dispositions in both Terry's and Crook's departments. Everything that could be done was being done. And, a second reason was that General Sherman had, at the beginning of the campaign, directed that Howard follow these Indians *wherever they went*. Now, irritated because he had been caught short of troops in an emergency, and probably squirming under the side effects of public criticism directed at Howard's failure to win a quick victory, McDowell—in the very near future—was inclined to be almost unreasonable in his demand that Howard follow Sherman's instructions regardless of the situation or cost.

To achieve the tactical position indicated in this dispatch, Howard had moved well to the left of the route being followed by the Indians. One result was to place his troops between the Nez Perce and the settlements in western Montana, as well as the freighting and stage route which ran southward to Corrine, Utah. However, the major objective was to try to wrest the position of initiative from the Indians, and then, either to defeat them or force them back over the Old Nez Perce Trail against Major Green's troops near Mount Idaho.

The next day's march placed the column on Horse Prairie Creek about twelve miles southwest of Bannack. As the troops passed the edge of town, the people flocked out and gave General Howard and the troops a heartwarming ovation. Here, the composite force of Butte and Deer Lodge volunteers under "Major" Clark and "Captain" Stuart caught up with the column. Part of the afternoon was unpleasant to both the general and his chief of staff. Mason wrote his wife that "the people filled our camp all afternoon, all full of advice as to what should be done and giving their opinions in an offensive manner." And Howard recalled that "here I had two annoyances. First, from some volunteers who thronged my tent, and

severely called me to account for the way I did things in the military line.
Second, from citizens, and volunteer messengers who came from [Lemhi
Valley bearing conflicting reports and making impractical requests].
. . ."[15] Various bits and pieces seem to indicate that "Major" Clark
headed this offensive element.

The Indians had gone out of Horse Prairie by way of Bannock Pass; and
the Montana and Idaho settlers wanted Howard to cross over into the
valley of the Lemhi River by way of Lemhi Pass—which was north of the
one used by the Indians—and there to join with "Colonel" George L.
Shoup and the Salmon City volunteers and Tendoy and his warriors.
Then, all should move up the valley to Junction, where it was reported
that the settlers were forted up and in danger. Howard reluctantly agreed,
but about 3 o'clock the next morning, another courier arrived with the
intelligence that the Indians had moved on and the general was free to do
as he really thought best.

The next day, the troops moved down Horse Prairie Creek and camped
at the Red Rock stage station on the Corrine Road. Shortly after the
troops moved out of camp, a courier informed Howard that Clark's
volunteers had headed well off toward the right, up Medicine Lodge
Valley, and toward the probable location of the Hostiles. Howard wrote
later:

> I immediately send an aid, Lieut. C. E. S. Wood, to explain my
> movement and show them that theirs will be likely to result as a
> diversion in favor of the enemy, and request that they move near my
> right flank, watching all approaches from the right. They consider the
> matter, and for some reason return home.[16]

Correspondent Sutherland reported bluntly and to the point:

> Sixty volunteers from Deer Lodge, who joined us last night, left this
> morning because they were unwilling to submit themselves to military
> dicipline.

On their return, Clark gave the Butte *Miner* an account calculated to
place him in a favorable light. Stuart's comments to Editor Mills at Deer
Lodge were more conservative, and he made one remark which indicated
that Clark was trying to pose as a military expert—"Maj. Clark . . . ventured to suggest to . . . [General Howard] that if he would drop his
wagons and push some cavalry out to support them [the volunteers] they
could soon get a fight out of the hostiles." In commenting on the matter,

Mills, who had been an officer during the Civil War, put Clark in particular, and the volunteers in general, in proper perspective:

> No force, regulars or volunteers, in numbers of less than 300 well-armed fighting men had any business with that Nez Perce band in an open fight. Enthusiasm and courage would doubtless have carried 100 or 150 volunteers into the Nez Perces camp. The result would have been discomfiture and a country full of stricken homes. . . .[17]

The attack which they sustained in the Big Hole must have made it painfully clear to Looking Glass and all the rest that the routes they had used in the past were now dangerous to travel. When they turned southward from the battlefield, they entered an area with which they were less familiar, although there probably were old men and women with the camp who had roamed over this country with bands in the days of the fur trade. There were several ways they could have gone from the Big Hole to Henry Lake and, for reasons unknown, they selected the most circuitous. This brought them near the Bannock Reservation, and it has been suspected that they had hopes of enlisting the help of these Indians—although no concrete information is known which supports this conjecture. As noted, this route took them along the western edge of the Big Hole, into the head of Horse Prairie, and then over Bannock Pass to the Lemhi Valley. From Junction, they followed the freighting road southward—to the head of Lemhi Valley some twenty miles away, over an easy divide, and down the valley of Birch Creek for about forty miles to the Great Snake River Plain where they turned east toward Henry Lake. Here, the two valleys constitute a sort of corridor, walled in by the rugged Lemhi Range on the west, and on the east by an equally massive spur of the Bitterroot Range. Throughout most of its extent, this area is a gently sloping prairie from eight to ten miles wide, with no obstacles to a hurried flight.

Stories that the Nez Perce made threatening maneuvers when they passed Junction have no foundation of fact. The settlers in the area, alerted by a courier from the Montana settlements, gathered inside the stockade which they had built about a month before. One of them, in reporting their condition, wrote: "The Nez Perce Indians came in here at 10 A.M., about 60 in number with Looking Glass and White Bird. We have had a talk with them. They seem to be friendly disposed toward the citizens. They say for us to go home and attend to our business." Again, as at Fort Fizzle, it is clear that Looking Glass and White Bird were the dominant figures, with Joseph somewhere in the background.

Another settler, writing two days later, set down a valuable record, not only of the passing of the Indians, but also of a number of things about them:

Junction, Lemhi Valley, Aug. 15

To THE EDITOR OF THE INDEPENDENT:

The hostile Indians struck our valley about 8 o'clock on the morning of the 13th, and continued coming all day. Mr. Swan had a short talk with one of the Nez Perces, and they promised not to molest the settlers, but said they would remain in the valley perhaps two or three days. At the same time that the hostiles arrived at my ranch, some four lodges of Bannocks came down the main Lemhi river, just below my house, and within a short distance of Mr. Swan's. On seeing the Nez Perces the Bannocks ran their extra horses into Mr. Swan's corral, mounted their other horses and met the hostiles, when a parley ensued. What the result of their talk was we had no means of knowing, but they all camped together until late in the afternoon. The Bannocks were at our stockade several times during the day, and tried to prevail on us, as friends, to go to Salmon City. In reply I told them that we would have reinforcements during the night . . . and I think the Bannocks impressed the Nez Perces with the idea that this was a fact; at any rate they moved their camp about eight miles up, under the foot of the mountains. Early yesterday morning they again broke camp and moved . . . and we have not seen an Indian since.

The Bannocks have moved down to their agency. * * * The Bannocks told me that [the Nez Perce] . . . had lost seventy men. They also say that they have a large number of needle guns [e.g. Springfield rifles and carbines] and plenty of ammunition.

"We kept out pickets all day, but could not learn the number of the hostiles. They must have had 2,000 head of horses, but they are getting worn down and look very thin. The Bannocks say that they have quite a number of wounded with them.

I am under the impression that our stockade saved us. Had it not been for that fence they would have made it exceedingly lively for us. Up to the present we do not know what our damage has been. Mr. Ed. Swan has lost a number of horses, but I am not certain of any others. All of our families were in the stockade. None of our houses were robbed. * * * We have about 20 men and 400 rounds of ammunition at our stockade.

The Bannocks say that the Nez Perces are going to the buffalo country by the head of Snake River [e.g. Henry Lake].[18]

On August 22nd, C. H. Jeanjaquet [E. H. Jeaujaquet?], a businessman in Salmon City who served as first sergeant of the Lemhi Rifles, wrote an apologetic sort of letter to Editor Mills that makes it clear that while the Nez Perce were at Junction, "Colonel" Shoup and his Salmon City Volunteers were in a more or less stampeded condition. They were out scouting at the time and rushed back to the fortifications at Salmon City on receipt of intelligence—alleged to have been much exaggerated—sent from Ten-doy. Finally, a day after the Indians had left Junction, Shoup took twenty-six men and set out to investigate. At Junction, he found all "safe and sound," and the only damages were some cattle "killed for subsistence and some horses taken." Then, he pushed on down the trail to ascertain what had happened to a freighting train believed to be on the road. Soon, he met a Chinaman who supplied a story that the wagons had been burned but he did not know what had happened to the others. Advising his men to go back home, Shoup and J. D. Woods of Leesburg continued down the trail.[19]

What happened near the middle crossing on Birch Creek was not particularly important but, because it was shrouded with an element of mystery, it is intriguing. The ill-fated outfit consisted of eight covered wagons, about thirty mules, three drivers, four passengers, a visitor, and two dogs. It was en route from Corrine to Salmon City with groceries and other merchandise for George L. Shoup & Fred Phillips of Salmon City, and J. D. Woods of Leesburg, together with "3,000" or "ten thousand" rounds of ammunition for the Salmon City volunteers. Also in the consignment were "ten barrels" of whiskey. It was a jerk-line outfit with two units of three wagons each coupled together in trail, and one unit of a wagon and one trailer. Its value is not known, other than that Shoup estimated his loss at about $1,000. A Salt Lake City paper reported that the outfit belonged to Shoup and Haydon, but Alexander Topance, a pioneer who dabbled in many enterprises, claimed that it was one he had "leased to Jim Hayden."

Two of the passengers were Chinamen who were known in the Lemhi Valley, and Shoup and his party met one or both beyond Junction. From one of them, the merchant got a semicoherent account of what happened; and when he and Woods found the train, the wagons and their contents had been burned and the mules stolen. The bodies of the drivers and the other two passengers were found in the vicinity, but there was no sign of Albert E. Lyons, the visitor. Shoup and Wood, with the assistance of one or two of Howard's scouts and a few Bannock Indians, who were shadowing the Nez Perce, buried the bodies where they were found.

After his return to Salmon City, Shoup sent a description of the two strangers to Corrine in an attempt to establish their identity.

Salmon City, I. T., August 27, '77

[Fred J. Kiesel & Co.
Corrine, Utah]

I have just returned from Birch Creek and have sad news to record. At a point on Birch Creek, 105 miles from here, I found the wagons of

Green, Haydon and Coombs (together with all goods that would burn) burned to ashes, excepting a few pairs of boots that were scattered on the prairie. After making diligent search we found Albert Green, James Haydon, Daniel Coombs and two strangers, all dead. Green was in the creek, Coombs and Haydon were laying side by side on the creek bank. There were no papers on the strangers. Each had a handkerchief; on the corner of one was the letter "W," on the other "Miegon." I learn from a Chinaman that was with the teams and permitted to escape, that the Indians stopped the boys about the middle of the afternoon. Green was required to deal out all his flour to them, and after detaining the men some time, the Indians told them to get on their horses and leave. Green, Haydon, Coombs, a passenger who had been with the teams from Corrine, and a man who fell in with the teams at Snake River (riding a brown horse with a bald face and leading a sorrel pack mule), and a white man [half-breed?] who came with the Indians, all left on horse or mule back together. What happened to them after that the Chinaman could not tell, as they soon disappeared from sight. On investigation we found that the boys had tried to escape in the hills, but had been driven back by the Indians after getting about four miles from the wagons, and were finally killed within half a mile of their burning wagons.

Can you give me any information. . . . * * * [The stranger from Snake River] had $50 in greenbacks sewed in his pants. The other stranger had $50 in his watch pocket.[20]

During the next couple of weeks, Lyons turned up, the Chinamen were carefully questioned, additional details secured from Shoup, and a reasonable story was patched together by a correspondent who signed himself "S." When a few obvious absurdities are discarded and other details are cross-checked, this story emerges:[21]

Lyons, who was herding stock in Round Valley, came over to Birch Creek to hunt for strayed stock. He met the train a little before noon and went along with it until the drivers pulled off the trail and made noon camp in a bend of the creek. At this point, the channel of Birch Creek, a small stream, was probably not over fifteen feet wide and thickly fringed with dense clumps of willow—a thread of green twisting down the middle of an open valley carpeted with sagebrush and a sparse growth of dry grass. While the men were resting in the shade of their wagons, they were startled by the sound of approaching horses; but before they could scramble into the wagons and secure their arms, a band of fifty or sixty warriors rode around the bend of the creek, halted, and leveled their rifles at them. A half-breed—who could have been Poker Joe—lifted his hand and said, "Don't shoot. We fight soldiers, not citizens."

After being fed, the Indians demanded that the freighters hitch up and proceed to the main camp, a distance of about two and a half miles up the valley. Here, after the teams were unhitched and turned out with the Indian herd, the teamsters were introduced to "Joseph, Whitebird and Looking Glass." The Indians now demanded flour from Green, paying at the rate of $2 per sack, and this raised the hopes of the little party. Soon, an Indian came up who offered $1.50 per sack in lots of ten. After a bit of parleying, Green agreed, much to the displeasure of the $2 customers, one of whom grabbed him by his whiskers and jerked him about "somewhat roughly." Then, someone asked for whiskey—or it was discovered by some warrior who was prying around in the cargo. Haydon objected, but there was no denying the demand and a barrel was rolled out—"The half-breed and the majority of the Indians drank to excess. Whitebird and Looking Glass did not drink anything." The situation quickly assumed an ugly aspect.

Lyons, convinced that safety lay only in flight, now began to walk about, edging away a bit farther each time he reached the edge of the throng about the wagons. Finally, near sundown, he made a dash for the brush along the creek and managed to hide, either in the brush or in a hole in the creek. When it became dark, he struck out for the mountains, where he became lost and had neither food nor water for four days. A week later and practically starved, he wandered into a cabin on Lost River "a wreck of his former self [and] completely unnerved."

According to the Chinese, when it was about dark, the white men were mounted on horses, without saddles, and told to leave, several Indians accompanying them out of camp. Shortly after, when a warrior knocked one Chinaman down and prepared to cut his throat, another interfered and took both the Orientals out of camp and told them to leave "quickly." Having heard gunshots and seen the Indians return with the horses the whites had ridden, the Chinese concluded the others had been murdered and struck out at once for Junction, where they arrived "unhurt but badly scared."

The Indian accounts vary, but they are in general agreement that the drinking, as would be expected, got out of hand. When the chiefs could no longer tolerate it, they appointed a detail to dump the liquor. If they were not already brawling among themselves by this time, this step brought violence and before it was over, there were stabbings and, probably, at least one fatal shooting. Then, after taking what they wanted from the wagons, the torch was applied.

Later, telltale *sign* told something of the unrecorded part of the story:

On searching for the bodies of the men they were found as below described:

Albert Green, found in the creek, stabbed in the right side, his pockets emptied. Hayden and Combs, found six rods above, on the opposite side of the creek from the wagons, close together. Hayden was shot in several places; the stock of a gun was found under him, the barrel by his side, and his face all battered to pieces. Combs was shot in several places, stabbed in the neck, his arm badly cut, and a blacksnake [whip] in his hand cut square off. The stranger, White, was found five rods above in the brush, shot in three places. White was a passenger from Corrine, late of California. * * * [The other stranger] was found about a mile above the others, shot through the back ranging upwards, as though he had been riding leaning forward [when hit].

The fore wheels and axle of one wagon has escaped the general conflagration and underneath was lying Green's dog.

Combs' dog had carried a bone up from the wreck[age] and was keeping watch over his dead master.

About ten miles beyond this point, the valley of Birch Creek merged with the edge of the Snake River Plain—a vast sweep of barren country stretching some fifty to eighty miles southward to the Snake River. The Continental Divide, which had been running southward along the crest of a spur of the Bitterroot Range, turned abruptly eastward at this point and followed the Centennial Mountains, a low range which extended to Henry Lake. This northern edge of the Snake River Plain presented a varied aspect. For the most part, it was a gently rolling country interspersed with occasional flat areas and very low ridges. Much of it was prairie, sparsely covered with grass and sagebrush, often with patches of pine near the foot of the mountains and occasional thickets of aspen out on the plain. Sometimes, along creeks which had their heads in the adjacent mountains, there were stretches of luxuriant grass that stood in strange contrast to adjacent areas dominated by the rock of old lava flows and sagebrush.

This was the country which now lay ahead of the Nez Perce. About thirty miles east of the mouth of the valley of Birch Creek was the stage and freighting road which, after crossing Monida Pass, ran southward to Corrine, Utah. It was down this road that Howard was hastening with the hope of placing his troops squarely in front of the fleeing Indians.

18

Skirmish at Camas Meadows

➤➤➤➤➤➤◄◄◄◄◄◄◄ From Red Rock Station, where Howard's detachment camped Thursday afternoon, the road ran southward up the narrow valley of Red Rock River for twenty-three miles to William's Junction, usually called Junction. Here, it left the valley of the river and turned up Junction Creek to Monida Pass, twelve miles farther on, and then down Beaver Creek on the southern slope of the Centennial Mountains to the Snake River Plain. Eighteen miles south of Junction was Pleasant Valley Station, and eight miles beyond, at the foot of the mountains, was another called Dry Creek. Out on the plain, twenty-six miles from Pleasant Valley, was Hole-in-the-Rock Station; and ten miles still farther on was a stop called Camas. And paralleling this trail was the telegraph line from western Montana to "the States."

As Howard was marching toward Red Rock Station, E. M. "Gov." Pollinger, the stage line representative at Pleasant Valley, reported that there was trouble on the road below him:

Pleasant Valley, Idaho, Aug. 16

A large party of Indians crossed the stage road going east toward Henry's Lake this afternoon about twenty-six miles south of this place. They are supposed to be the hostiles. They did not harm anyone. The stage cannot pass to-night, but it is thought it will go through tomorrow. They had to desert Hole in the Rock station, but got the horses away. We have sent a messenger to General Howard, who is camped at Red Rock station, forty miles north of here.[1]

After the Indians had moved on, a newspaper story datelined *Salt Lake August 23* stated:

The hostile Indians . . . arrived upon the stage road on the 16th taking possession of the Hole-in-the-Rock Station, twenty-six miles south of Pleasant Valley. The Indians destroyed the telegraph line in the vicinity and stopped the stages and all travel upon the road, and were in the neighborhood of this station for three days. * * * They stopped to gather all the loose stock and feed their animals, using or destroying all grain at the station and destroying all the property there, including some twenty sets of harness.[2]

The presence of the Indians also stampeded freighters farther to the south. When Captain Bainbridge came along a few days later, he found

freighters and ranchmen along the Montana stage road in the [Snake] valley in a demoralized condition. Freighters who were on the road between Sand Holes and Pleasant Valley, at the time the hostiles struck there, had left their wagons where they happened to be, in most instances loaded with valuable freight, and had taken their stock to places of safety. In one instance I found two wagons, one loaded with metallic cartridges, and the other with powder; but the hostiles had not disturbed them. As soon as I passed over the road, the freighters commenced moving again.[3]

At the camp at Red Rock Station, Howard released Captain Browning and the soldiers of the Seventh Infantry. The following day at Junction, he was joined by a party of fifty-three well-armed and well-mounted volunteers under "Captain" James E. Callaway. Most of these men were from Virginia City, which place they had left two days before. Now, the news that the Indians had already reached a point immediately to the south created a problem of which way it was best to move. Howard sent several citizen scouts to Pleasant Valley and beyond to watch the enemy and, while no mention is made of it, probably Buffalo Horn and at least two other Bannocks from Robbins' detachment accompanied them.

In addition, another party was dispatched which was to have a dual function. The general reported to McDowell later that this operation was undertaken "with a view of intercepting and hindering the Indians should they come in that direction, or of procuring and transmitting to me early information of value." Or, as correspondent Sutherland put it—"in order to interfere with the Indians advance till we get up." One of the civilian scouts with this detachment—probably Frank Parker—told the editor of the Virginia City *Madisonian* a few days later that "Bacon's command . . . [was] under strict orders to return within 48 hours if no enemy was visible." To accomplish this mission, forty picked men under Lieutenant George R. Bacon and Second Lieutenant George S. Hoyle set out eastward up Centennial Valley—the valley of the Red River which paralleled the northern side of the Centennial Mountains—to the pass at the head of that valley. This is now called Red Rock Pass, although Howard referred to it as "Mynhold's." From this point, they were to cross over to Henry Lake at the head of the Snake River and examine "Tachee Pass"—now Tarhgee or Tygee Pass—the usual route used in going from the lake to the Yellowstone Park area.

This party, with two men—Kohls and Scully—from Callaway's company, Frank Parker, and "Rube" Robbins and a few Bannocks acting as scouts, left Junction about 1 A.M. the next morning. By 4 P.M., after a march of upwards of fifty miles, they reached Red Rock Lake at the head of the valley. In the morning, Robbins discovered stock grazing on the prairie near Henry Lake, which—after a cautious approach—was found to be a herd of horses and cattle which a Montana rancher and two helpers were driving into the Snake River country. The owner, after being acquainted with the situation, left "with all possible speed."

Henry Lake sits in a flat prairie some six miles in diameter and this, in turn, is almost surrounded by mountains. After making a reconnaissance of the area and finding nothing, Bacon set out to retrace his steps.[4] Howard's logic in ordering Bacon's force to "intercept and hinder" any Indians they might find is far from clear, for there was no narrow pass which such a small party could have held against an attack by the Nez Perce. Later, Howard was to make the explanation of his tactics appear plausible—*on paper*. Actual conditions were something else.

During the night the troops camped at Junction, Pollinger rode in with an urgent dispatch from O. J. Salisbury, the superintendent of the Gilmer & Salisbury stage line, and reported that he had seen Indians about sixteen miles below Pleasant Valley. Howard wrote that "I had not quite determined at this time whether to push my main column down the road with the risk of the Indians getting past me, they having the shorter line, or to send it to Henry Lake by the trail north of the divide." He decided to let the cavalry remain in camp so that the horses could get some much-needed feed and rest, and to make an investigation by himself.

To this end, he asked "Captain" Callaway to provide an escort. The result was a sort of town hall meeting with the volunteers finally deciding to comply. However, Howard had to leave virtually unescorted—with Lieutenant Fletcher on the wagon seat beside him and one well-armed civilian riding beside the wagon. The volunteers never did come up, camping for the night at Pleasant Valley eight miles behind the general. Howard was both amused and exasperated by this display of unreliability and ineffectiveness. Five days later, Sutherland sent an unflattering comment to the New York *Herald:*

> Undoubtedly there were some intelligent and courageous men among these gangs—gangs which we sampled from three territories—but, taken as a body, the frontier volunteer of today is an undoubted fraud, having almost as little pluck as principle and as meagre a conception of dicipline as a backwoods schoolmaster. * * * In Montana the volunteers join us merely to say that they would like to fight, but their horses are worn out, that they can spare only one day, and that they are subject to no commander and similar absurdities.[5]

At Dry Creek, Buffalo Horn told the general that he and two others had been well out on a ridge at the foot of the mountains, and from this vantage point had been able to determine that the Nez Perce were in camp at Camas Meadows, about fifteen miles to the east. Howard, now confident that he was near enough to strike, ordered his cavalry forward. They left Junction in the middle of the afternoon, and by 10 o'clock that night, the end of the column reached Dry Creek. With them came Captain Norwood and "L" Company of the Second Cavalry, and Lieutenant Benson, his long trek from Baltimore at an end. Howard assigned him to Norwood's company and thus the glory-hunting infantryman ended up with an assignment as a cavalryman.

The next day, the troops marched about fifteen miles eastward and went into camp on Camas Meadows near the place where Buffalo Horn had observed the Nez Perce camp on the preceding day. Thirty-nine of the volunteers again joined Howard, the remainder having turned back.

This campsite was about seven miles south of the foot of the mountains, and beside Spring and Camas creeks. These two streams enter the northern edge of the Snake River Plain about five miles apart and flow southward in a shallow, fan-shaped depression, gradually converging toward each other. At the campsite, they occupy channels which are almost parallel and only about 500 yards apart. They are clear mountain streams, about eighteen feet wide, and twist along between banks fringed with thick clumps of willow. The shallow valley, now narrowed to approximately a mile in width, was carpeted here with luxuriant grass—thus giving the locality the name of Camas Meadows.

Spring Creek lies on the eastern side of this depression and, at the point where the camp was pitched, a strip of meadow 300 yards wide intervenes between the channel and the remains of an ancient lava flow—a broad, rather flat-topped elevation lying some forty feet above the meadow. As Howard described the camp, his tent, which was pitched on this elevated area, was the "central position." Callaway's volunteers and Norwood's cavalry camped on the meadow between the two creeks, with the soldiers covering the western edge of the camp. Sanford's battalion was "posted in line of battle" covering all the "approaches" to the location of the head-quarters tent. "Great pains" were taken by Major Mason "to cover the camp with pickets in every direction"; and before night, every animal was brought within the confines of the camp. Cavalry horses were tied to picket lines, draft horses were tied to the wagons, and the bell mares of the pack trains were hobbled. Apparently, many of the horses of the volunteers were picketed or hobbled. And all of the hobbled horses and the pack mules—which would stay close to the bell mares—were left free to graze at will on the meadow between the two creeks.

In Howard's tent, a feeling of security prevailed. Lieutenant Wood decided to remove his trousers "for the first time in weeks" and finally the general, his son, and Sutherland followed suit—all "determined to have a good rest." And down on the meadow, the volunteers rolled up in their blankets and went soundly to sleep.[6]

When the Nez Perce left the Big Hole battlefield, they lost contact with the troops and probably this was not reestablished until the day they moved from Camas Meadows. Three warriors, said to have been Peopeo Tholekt, Bull Bait, and Rattle Blanket, while idling along in the rear of the moving camp, noted the dust stirred up by Howard's troops as they marched from Dry Creek to Camas Meadows. These three carried the news to the chiefs and—apparently at a council—it was decided that something must be done to effectively discourage pursuit. What was finally planned, other than a surprise attack at dawn, is not clear. Estimates made by the officers and civilians placed the size of the attacking force at 150 warriors. However, a year later, White Bird told trader McDonald that he and about 25 men were left to guard the camp and all the rest—perhaps 200 or more—set out for Howard's camp.[7] If this is correct, then it is probably true—as the Indians claimed—that they planned to first run off the stock and then engage the entire camp. This is supported by the

Indian statement that one, irresponsible rifle shot touched off the engagement prematurely.

Looking Glass and Joseph were said to have led this foray. Someone recognized the voice of the former giving orders during the attack on the camp; and Sutherland stated in a dispatch written that night, "The hostiles told [the friendly Nez Perce herders] . . . today . . . [about their losses at the Big Hole and that] Joseph led the band that stole the horses this morning." At least two of the three Nez Perce herders had relatives in the hostile camp, and this bit of fraternizing with the enemy was observed with distrust by some of the Bannock scouts.

The war party left their camp, located some eighteen or twenty miles east of Camas Meadows in the valley of Shotgun Creek, during the night and rode to the vicinity of Howard's camp. Here, according to the Indians, the chiefs arranged the final details and sent a picked group into the camp to spy out the details and to cut picket ropes and hobbles so that when the moment came for the attack the animals could be stampeded. And Looking Glass ruled that the attack was to be made on horseback and not on foot. "The night was moonlit but cloudy, with occasional showers, until about two hours before daylight, when the moon went down and intense darkness prevailed."

After the spies slipped away into the darkness, the chiefs moved forward with part of their men on either side of Spring Creek to await the first suggestion of daylight.

The advance party infiltrated the camp without difficulty—or rather that part lying between the two creeks where Norwood and the volunteers were. Here, the Indian plans began to go wrong. They particularly wanted the cavalry horses, but these—because of the opportunity to graze on abundant feed before dark—had been brought in and tied to picket lines. Furthermore, the spies entered only that part of the camp on the meadow —although they did their work quite thoroughly in that area. While these warriors were still at work, the main body approached close enough to a picket to be detected and challenged, whereupon a rather stupid individual who was in the midst of the main band fired his rifle and precipitated the engagement. Howard put forward the explanation—termed ridiculous by the Indians—that the Indians approached in a column of fours to conceal their identity until the last moment. This he modified later by stating that it was the intent of the Indians "to make the picket think it was Bacon's party coming back," an explanation which stretches credulity well past the breaking point, considering that this officer was somewhere on the opposite side of the Centennial Mountains.

It was about 4 A.M. when pandemonium broke loose. As the editor of *The Madisonian* reported it:

About half an hour before daylight the slumbers of the men were broken by three or four shots fired in rapid succession, and immediately followed by a steady fire upon the citizens camp, which was kept up with remarkable rapidity for the space of five or six minutes, and accompanied by the most frightful yelling and shouting conceivable, while above the din and uproar of the yelling and firing could be distinctly heard the stenorian voice of Looking Glass as he issued commands and directed movements of the raiding party. Fortunately for the citizens the camp was pitched on low ground and the Indians overshot them [doing no serious damage other than killing one horse]. . . . The Indians gathered up stock from all parts of both [sic] camps, and posted a line of about twenty-five men in front of the citizens camp, within fifty yards of the wagons, and kept up their terrific fire at that distance, while the remainder of the raiders . . . were driving the animals across the creek and into the open country beyond. The surprise was sudden and complete.[8]

Sutherland wrote that to him this

uninceremonious reveille, although efficacious, was most aggravating. Of course my boots, large as they are could not be found, and the Gatling gun pistol, which I have, faithfully transported all the way from Portland with the hope of some day using on Mr. Joseph was, hidden under my saddle so completely that by the time I had ventured out with it, lashed to my waist, nothing was to be seen but a herd of mules and horses—about 150 in number—under full speed, with about 70 Indians "whooping 'em up" from behind.[9]

Callaway's volunteers were in an equally stampeded condition. Some rushed across the creek toward the elevation where Howard's tent was pitched, while others jumped in the stream in their search for cover. Viewed in perspective, the humor of these incidents became apparent later, and the men ribbed each other about the foolish things they had done. One Irishman commented, "Begorra, I didn't think the Captain was frightened at all, till I seed him come across the creek, and take hould o' me hat and thry to put it on for a boot, be jabers."

The cavalry saddled up at once, and as soon as daylight came, Howard ordered Major Sanford to take the companies of Captains Carr, Jackson, and Norwood and try to overtake the Indians who had now discovered, much to their disappointment, that the major part of their loot was pack mules and not cavalry horses. As they galloped away, the general organized the remaining cavalry, infantry, and two pieces of artillery into a defense for the camp, and then sat down to breakfast. Soon a soldier rode up and reported that the cavalry had cut off part of the captured herd, and before the meal was finished, another courier rode up and reported, "The major says, sir, the Indians have come back to attack in a large force, and are turning his left."

Taking the infantry, one company of cavalry, the few volunteers who still had horses, and a howitzer, Howard set out to try to find Sanford's men. When last seen, the Indians, stolen stock, and the cavalry were moving toward the northeast across a difficult and confusing area dominated by old lava flows. Slowly, the reinforcements picked their way over the little rocky ridges where the next sagebrush-covered rise looked like the one that lay just behind, until, finally, they met Sanford returning with Carr and Jackson's companies. Norwood was nowhere in sight; and the major explained that he did not know where he was, but that he was trying to find him—a rather lame excuse in view of the fact that when last seen, "L" Company was in the center of a skirmish line.

In a short, crisp account written a few days afterward, "Participant"— who probably was Lieutenant Benson—related what happened:

> After a sharp ride of about seven miles, the two companies of the First cavalry struck the rear of the herd, crossed its line of flight and commenced skirmishing with the Indians.
>
> Norwood followed immediately in the rear, his company well in hand. He ordered a citizen and a soldier to get ahead of and drive back about 40 or 50 animals that had been cut off from the herd. About a mile beyond the point where the skirmishing began, the Indians commenced to make a decided resistance from strong positions among ridges of lava and clumps of timber.
>
> Norwood took his position behind a low rocky ridge, dismounted his men and opened fire.
>
> After a short time it was discovered that the two companies of 1st cavalry had retired, and the Indians were surrounding Norwood's company. About this time he received an order from Lieut. [Charles C.] Cresson, battalion adjutant cavalry, to retreat. It was understood that this order came from the commanding officer of the cavalry battalion. Captain Norwood declined to obey the order until he could make proper dispositions to cover his rear. After a short time he slowly fell back, about 1,000 yards, to a strong position, where he tied his horses, placed his men, and determined to fight it out, all this time under a sharp fire and demonstrations by the Indians. By this time the Indians had entirely surrounded his company and kept up a continuous sharp fire. Some of their sharp-shooters crept up to within forty yards of our position. The fight lasted about four hours.[10]

The "low rocky ridge" which marked Norwood's first position was a narrow, rocky strip about eighteen feet high and five or six hundred feet long. In *front* of it, toward the northeast, was an open, grassy meadow that was half to three-quarters of a mile wide, and on the opposite side of this open area were lava hillocks that probably were covered with sagebrush and aspen. To the right and left of the "low rocky ridge" were more low, rocky hillocks and broken terrain which, if held by the enemy, would provide excellent p .:tions from which to enfilade Norwood's position. Presumably, the Nez Perce crossed the meadow with their loot, which they hid among the rocky knobs on the other side; and then, they turned on their pursuers. Major Sanford, deeming discretion more desirable than valor, chose to keep the meadow between his troops and the Indians and put his men on a skirmish line, with Jackson's men on the right, Norwood's in the center, and Carr's on the left.

When some of the warriors turned the major's flanks, he decided the position was a poor one and ordered a retreat. This order, which Carr and Jackson promptly obeyed, Norwood admittedly "declined to obey" and gave as his reason his wish to prevent his men from being "slaughtered." Considering the topography of the battlefield, this explanation is lacking in logic. It is far more likely that something happened here which needed concealing in double-talk or official silence. Although neither Howard nor Norwood hinted of any friction, the volunteers carried the story back to Virginia City that, "On the return of the command to camp, much bitterness was expressed concerning the action of the other companies in not going to Norwood's assistance, and the belief was general that had he been vigorously supported a decisive victory would have been obtained." (!!) And there is oblique support for this view in a statement Sutherland made four days later:

> I candidly think Joseph could whip our cavalry, and cannot blame Howard for not giving him battle with that battalion at Camas Meadows. A man who thoroughly understands the Nez Perce tongue told me that on the morning of the stampede in our camp, Joseph encouraged his men by crying out "Go ahead; you have only cavalrymen against you!" showing, as it were, a species of contempt for our horsemen.[11]

It would appear that Norwood and his men—perhaps more resolute, perhaps glory-hunting—may have regarded odds of less than two to one, for Sanford had approximately 150 men, not too great for a successful fight, and were not—at first—disposed to turn and run. However, after Carr and Jackson retreated, the Nez Perce probably enveloped Norwood's flanks, and the captain soon found his position untenable. Retreat now became a necessity and "I . . . withdrew my horses and men, dismounted, to the left and rear about 1,200 yards."

With warriors swarming all around them, the troopers retreated toward the southwest—about a mile—until they came to a bit of terrain which offered possibilities for defense. This was two, low knolls or ridges, the tops and sides of which were covered with sagebrush and studded with small blocks of lava. In length, they extended approximately 250 yards and were separated by a troughlike depression about thirty-feet deep and seventy-five to one hundred yards wide. Norwood ordered his men to tie their horses in a clump of aspen in the low area; then, he and Benson posted them on the elevations on either side. Here, protected by twenty-three circular rifle pits made of chunks of rock piled high enough to cover a man lying flat on his belly—some large enough for one man, others large enough to shield three or four—the men of "L" Company engaged in a sniping duel for a period of time estimated at two and a half to four hours. Finally, Howard and the relief detachment, accompanied by Sanford's two companies, found them, at which time the Indians retired.

Long afterward, Sergeant H. J. Davis wrote an account of the fight that is a mixture of fact and questionable material. In this, he claimed that Sergeant Hugh McCafferty was the real hero of the fight as he climbed a scrubby cottonwood growing in the depression and, hiding in the foliage, acted as a spotter for those in the rock shelters. Although this may or may not have occurred, his description of the wounds is apparently reasonably accurate: Benson, standing up for an instant at the first ridge, received a bullet that "entered at the hip pocket and went out at the other . . . [passing] through both buttocks"; at the siege area, Private Harry Trevor was shot through the left breast and lungs at a distance of about fifteen feet; blacksmith Samuel Glass was shot through the stomach; a bullet hit Corporal Henry Garland's cartridge belt (according to Davis) and drove two cartridges from it through his body, making a wound that never healed "and he blew out his brains a few years later"; Private Wilford Clark had a flesh wound in his chin and shoulder "by an explosive ball"; Sergeant Henry Wilkins suffered a slight but painful head wound; Private William Jones received a slight but painful wound in the knee; and—not listed elsewhere—"a citizen attaché, a bullet through the foot."[12]

Norwood noted in his official report that Benson rendered "valuable assistance" in spite of the fact that he was wounded early in the engagement. This Civil War veteran may have been a glory-hunter, but he was also a *soldier*.

After relieving Norwood, Howard turned back to the camp, a move which did not meet with the approval of Buffalo Horn. This energetic young chief, who had courage to spare, wanted to press on after the Nez Perce. When the volunteers returned to Virginia City, someone reported that this conversation took place after the return to Camas Meadows:

Citizen—"What do you think of Howard?"

Buffalo Horn (making a slow forward motion of the hand)—"Howard he no good; he walk-walk-walk (suddenly making a rapid grasping movement) no catchem Indian walk!"

Bernard A. Brooks, Captain Jackson's orderly and trumpeter, was the only soldier killed outright, being shot out of his saddle in the skirmish eight miles from camp. The story—apparently true—was told that when he fell, his mount came back to him, whinnied and edged up beside him. Brooks tried to pull himself up by a stirrup strap and then fell dead. Jackson, with the assistance of one or two of his men, managed to retrieve the body and take it back to camp—for which action he was awarded a Medal of Honor. That afternoon, with Major Mason reading the Episcopal service beside the grave, Brooks was buried on the knoll near where Howard's tent was pitched. Today, a solitary white tombstone and the twenty-three rock shelters eight miles away constitute the last bit of evidence of the skirmish.

Two weeks later, Major Mason informed his wife:

> I have at last gotten you a beautiful riding horse. I have had my eye on him ever since we started [over the Lolo Trail]. He was ridden by Major Jackson's bugler—I had asked the Major to sell him to me before but he had declined. At the last skirmish the bugler was killed . . . , I then found the major was willing to part with him. I shall buy him, after having him appraised by a board of officers. I trust I shall be able to get him home safely, for he is just the horse I have been looking for—perfectly gentle, and as easy as a cradle.[18]

On the following day, he wrote that the board placed a value of $73 on "George," which he was happy to pay, the horse being "as handsome as a picture and gentle as a kitten . . .[and] perfectly broken." Presumably, the story had a pleasant ending, for when the campaign was practically over he wrote in a letter that the horse was "looking very well considering that he has had no grain" and that he would ship him down the Missouri on a steamboat with the foot troops.

After the first flurry of estimates was over, the common statement of loss was "some 150 pack animals and horses." The volunteers lost 20 horses and had one killed. In one dispatch, Sutherland put the loss of pack animals at 110; Captain FitzGerald wrote his wife that they lost 115 head. Howard's comment that they recaptured "at least half" is probably overoptimistic. "Participant" put the number cut off at 40 or 50, and of these, only about 25 were finally driven back to camp. This was due to the fact that one or more bell mares were in the band retained by the Indians, and some of the mules broke away and followed their leader in what the general called a "most senseless manner." About a week later, the editor of *The Teller* speculated that the animals had been the property of Benson and Grostein & Binnard, freighting contractors in Lewiston. Sutherland, perhaps repeating camp gossip, put their value at $10,000.

Like the mules, the number of wounded was variously reported. On the day of the fight, Howard sent a dispatch to McDowell stating that one officer and six enlisted men had been wounded; but, at the same time, he informed Gibbon that Benson, six men òf the Second, and two men of the First Cavalry had been hit.[14] Perhaps the general was under-reporting to Division Headquarters for a couple of reasons. Be that as it may, the casualty list printed shortly afterward in Virginia City's *The Madisonian*, and vouched for by "Participant" in the Helena *Daily Herald*, names Benson, ten enlisted men, and one civilian—a total of twelve.

When Callaway's volunteers left the following morning, the seriously wounded—including Garland, Glass, and Trevor—were entrusted to their care, as they had "wagons" and a doctor. Glass was so bad that he had to be left at Pleasant Valley, where he died two days later. Garland and Trevor were placed in St. Mary's Hospital in Virginia City, where the latter lingered for six weeks. Curiously, this soldier had enlisted under a fictitious name, his true name being Pancoast Loose. He had been discharged the preceding June but, because he had been constantly in the field since the preceding spring, his discharge papers did not reach him until after he was mortally wounded.

19

A Pause to Refit

➤➤➤➤➤➤➤◄◄◄◄◄◄◄ When Howard's detachment reached Camas Meadows, the infantry and artillery, who were plodding along two days' march in the rear, camped between Junction and Pleasant Valley. They had been joined en route from the Big Hole battlefield by Captains Cushing and Field; and with them, to transport supplies and assist the footsore, was a makeshift wagon train. Except for three four-horse outfits, this was composed of two-horse vehicles which Lieutenant F. E. Eltonhead had been able to hire in the Bitterroot Valley. One of the teamsters with a good four-horse outfit was Henry Buck, the merchant at Stevensville, who had set out to see what happened to his brother in the battle of the Big Hole. When he overtook the troops, Eltonhead had politely but firmly pressed Buck into service.

Buck recalled that on the morning of the 20th, a courier arrived with news of the raid and orders to hurry. "On receipt of this order we piled all the men we could into all of the wagons and quickening our pace, marched as rapidly as possible, changing off footmen for riders and vice versa."[1] By late afternoon, the column reached Howard's camp, having traveled a very respectable forty-six miles.

With the addition of this transportation, Howard was able to move. The now-united column again set out on the trail of the Nez Perce, who had parlayed their advantage from one day's march to two. This time the general took no chances. He put the wagons and the pack mules in the center of the column with a company of cavalry ahead and another in the rear; the infantry marched on either side close by, and outside of these troops was the balance of the cavalry. The first day's march was across a very difficult country filled with old lava flows. By night they had made only eighteen miles, camping beside Shotgun Creek not far from the place from which the Indians had launched their raiding party.

After the column had stopped for the day, a small party of Bannocks, decked out in feathers and brightly colored decorations, rode "grandly" into camp. These proved to be the advance guard of the band of fifty who, at Gibbon's suggestion and Sheridan's approval, had been enlisted at the Fort Hall Agency. Captain Augustus H. Bainbridge arrived with the balance at 3 A.M. the next morning. One of their chiefs, Buffalo Horn, was serving under "Rube" Robbins as one of the seventeen Indian scouts.

The response to Gibbon's request had been very prompt. The telegram had been sent on the 15th. By the evening of the 19th, G. S. Fisher had been hired to take charge of the party, supplies had been issued, the enlistments had been lined up, and thirty-one, with Captain Bainbridge and ten soldiers acting as escort, were headed up the trail. The remaining nineteen caught up that night, and all joined Howard—after having marched 150 miles—before sunrise on the 22nd. By the time this detachment reached the troops, there were more than the fifty authorized—perhaps as many as eighty. The balance had come along on their own initiative, apparently hoping to acquire some stray horses.

Sutherland wrote that

a more gorgeous set of warriors I never saw. Some carried long poles, on which were single eagle feathers tied loosely with sinew, which whirled about in the breeze like toy windmills, which, with other poles having dangling scalps, meant war. They were in full paint—some all red, others red, green and yellow. Many had dyed their horses' manes and tails [green] and decorated with bunches of different colored feathers and jingling sleigh bells. They all wore dresses of buckskin, beautifully ornamented with bead work, and their brightest blankets. They were promised as a reward all of Joseph's horses excepting those belonging to the United States or citizens that they might capture. This created much excitement among them, and under their dashing young chief, Buffalo Horn, they began almost immediately to plan some way of cutting off the hostiles immense herd of nearly three thousand head. Along the route of the pursuit the Bannock scouts had picked up a few horses that had been abandoned by Joseph; and were almost as happy as if the whole herd had fallen into their hands.[2]

G. S. Fisher, a picturesque individual who was dressed in buckskin, was "the envy of several of our very young officers." Howard described him later as "a tall, pale man, of fair proportions, being slightly deaf. A stranger would see little that was remarkable about him. Yet . . . night and day, with guides and without, with force and without, Fisher hung fearlessly upon the skirts of the enemy. The accuracy, carefulness, and fullness of his reports . . . were a delight."[3] Bainbridge and his escort accompanied Howard for a day and then turned back. Two days later he was back at Fort Hall accompanied by the freebooters who had picked up a few worn-out horses.

That night, while camped beside Henry's Fork of the Snake River, Buffalo Horn requested permission to stage a war dance. This ended at midnight and the general recalled that the "wild singing, the weird shapes passing the fire during the dance" created a feeling of apprehension among the troops that was akin to panic; but Henry Buck remembered that "we all enjoyed it very much." At its conclusion, Buffalo Horn and a half-breed named "Rainé" (or Rainey) asked Howard for permission to kill Captain John, George and another Nez Perce, who were serving as herders for the horse herd.

George was called in and questioned, but the general found no evidence that the three were traitors and had "rejoiced openly" about the Nez Perce success at Camas Meadows. The chief "was very angry in consequence, and never quite forgave me for this refusal. The third Indian may have been guilty . . . for he escaped into the forest that night, and went back to Kamiah."

However, Buffalo Horn's suspicions were not without grounds, for Captain John and George had daughters in the hostile camp; and Sutherland reported certain information obtained by the trio from the rear guard of the hostiles at Camas Meadows. Be that as it may, these two herded faithfully to the end of the campaign, when they rendered very valuable services in negotiating the final surrender.

After what must have been an exceedingly short night, the men were awakened at 2 o'clock the next morning, and a determined effort was made to overhaul the Indians. Seven hours later the troops were at the Indian campsite near the southeastern corner of Henry Lake. Here scouts arrived with the information that the Nez Perce had passed over nearby Tygee Pass and were gone. Howard now stopped, at the insistence of his battalion commanders and their surgeons, to evaluate the situation.

In spite of the criticism of the press and others that Howard was dallying along, the truth was that he had driven both his troops and their horses to nearly the limit of endurance. The men had started in summer uniforms and now, with ice forming in water pails at night, many were undergoing considerable hardship. The Chief of Staff summed up the situation in a letter to his wife:

> Our men are very short of clothing, many are without overcoats and blankets, some having neither—all are ragged, dirty and *lousy*, not having had an opportunity for 23 days to wash or even take off their clothes. Since we came into this camp, men have washed their rags, going naked while doing so. I have never known a command to be as hard pushed as this has been during the past month. * * * Our cavalry has marched without ceasing, over 1500 miles, while the foot troops have marched 900 miles, without rest, making some days 30 miles, on flour, bacon and coffee.[4]

In his official report, Howard noted that the surgeons with both the infantry and cavalry reported the men in no condition to continue; and his staff surgeon, Major Charles T. Alexander, had endorsed their statements, adding:

> The command is very deficient in overcoats, blankets, socks, and shoes. * * * Without an issue of suitable clothing, the command is not in a fit condition to continue field service in this region, and must rapidly, from rheumatism and other diseases, become worthless.[5]

However, lack of supplies and fatigue were not the entire picture. When near Bannack, Captain FitzGerald had written to his wife:

> General Howard said last evening he would pursue . . . as far as [Pleasant Valley]. . . . Then if he did not succeed in overtaking them, he would notify General McDowell and terminate the campaign. . . . How glad one Doctor will be on the consummation of that event you, darling wife, may imagine.[6]

And here at Henry Lake he wrote, "Everyone, believe me, is sick and tired of a fruitless pursuit of these Indians." While at Camas Meadows, Major Mason had written home that

> I have prepared two dispatches, one to Sherman, the other to Mc-Dowell, asking for orders, either to return home or refit and mount our infantry and continue the pursuit indefinitely. We send these dispatches back to the telegraph station tonight—need I say what we all hope the answer will be.[7]

Packers who returned to Lewiston from this point told Editor Leland that there was "much dissatisfaction in the Command with Howard's method of pursuing Indians."[8] And after their return that fall, one officer noted that the troops "went with reluctance and returned with eagerness." Morale was never *really* good.

Although Howard does not seem to have made a record of his personal attitude, judging by what some of his officers wrote home and what Sutherland, who was a member of his mess, put in dispatches, he too would gladly have gone back to his headquarters. But the choice was not his to make—particularly with his reputation as a professional soldier and as an honest administrator being criticized by the press and others. Furthermore, it is probable that the general knew what was expected of him for he had received a telegram from General Sherman while the troops were camped on Shotgun Creek. Sherman had, fortunately, completed his tour of the Yellowstone National Park a few days before the arrival of the Nez Perce; and, on his arrival in Helena, sent this message:

Helena, August 21, 1877

To GENERAL HOWARD:

Just arrived at Helena. Will remain till I know you are all right and have everything. Telegraph me some account of affairs that I can understand. What is your force? What your plans? Spare nothing to insure success.

W. T. SHERMAN, *General*[9]

And so, as the troops went into camp beside Henry Lake on August 23rd, Howard tried to figure out a proper course of action. His Chief of Staff made this note of the state of affairs:

We went into camp and I have been busy all day, doing nothing in reality, for the General has changed his plans three or four times—making work for me each time. He has finally gone to Virginia City about 60 miles away to telegraph to McDowell and make arrangements for a new campaign in case he cannot get permission to return. This command is completely worn out and the chase should end here, but the General is disappointed at not reaching a brilliant end before this and is disposed to press on into the Yellowstone country.[10]

It was about 5 P.M. when the general left for Virginia City. With him as an aide went his son Guy, and Lieutenant John Q. Adams, the acting quartermaster for the cavalry battalion. The vehicle was probably a light wagon owned and driven by "Doc" Van R. Woodmancy of Stevensville. After an all-night drive, during which the passengers spent hours in a "make-believe" sleep on the floor of the wagon box, the vehicle rattled into Virginia City about 10 o'clock the following morning.

While the general sent telegrams to McDowell and Sherman, the lieutenants searched the stores for clothing, shoes and blankets. In this search they were probably joined by Lieutenant Peter Leary, the purchasing agent for commissary supplies, who was already in town. No doubt it was a profitable day for the merchants for Howard noted later that "We nearly bought them out." Then, leaving the goods to be freighted to the camp, the general and his son left early in the evening to rejoin the command. Adams was left behind to secure horses and mules. Here, and at Bozeman shortly afterward, he contracted for a total of 101 cavalry horses, 56 "Q.M. horses," and 56 mules. As the average cost of each was about $120, $70 and $112, respectively, the ranchers realized some handsome returns for their half-broken stock—a few animals being close to outright outlaws.[11]

Howard's telegrams brought interesting replies. The one sent to Division Headquarters contained a brief statement of the current situation and the request, "Wish to hear from you in answer to telegrams sent." Adjutant Kelton answered by repeating messages dated August 17th, 18th and 22nd which had failed to reach the general because the Nez Perce had torn down the telegraph line in the vicinity of the Dry Creek stage station. Of these, the one of basic importance was the one dated August 17th. This was in reply to the dispatch Howard had written while in camp near Bannack which requested additional instructions.

This message, after pointing out that Howard had already been ordered to pay no attention to Department and Division boundaries, and to follow the Indians until they were either defeated or driven from the United States, contained these emphatic statements:

> The Division Commander thinks you need no further instructions on this subject, and advises you that the United States have no body of troops so near these hostile Indians as those immediately with you and you, it seems to him, will certainly be expected by the General of the Army, the War Department and the country, to use them in carrying on the most active and persistent operations practicable, to the very end.
>
> You say that with prompt and energetic cooperation from the Eastern Departments, you may yet destroy these Indians, and without cooperation, the present result will be, as it has been, doubtful. It is not understood by the Division Commander nor is it believed in the country, that you have not had prompt and energetic cooperation. It is on the contrary held that Gibbon's aid from Terry's Department whence only effectual aid could come, was prompt, energetic and

effectual, and as abundant as the state of the Army in the Department permitted. The General in all kindness asks me to suggest to you to be less dependent on what others at a distance may or may not do, and rely more on your own forces and your own plans.[12]

And it closed with the assurance that whatever could be done to bring other forces into the field was being done.

No doubt Howard merited much of this politely worded but stinging rebuke. His dispatches were usually over-optimistic; and there had been considerable carping at Rawn for not holding at Fort Fizzle, at Gibbon for attacking before Howard's men arrived, and of Terry and Crook for not putting troops in the path of the Nez Perce. Part of this had been in Howard's official dispatches, and part of it had been in Sutherland's dispatches to the Portland *Standard*, San Francisco *Chronicle*, and New York *Herald*. This senseless faultfinding got completely out of hand in a dispatch which Sutherland wrote—apparently—before Howard returned from Virginia City, the indications being that the above-quoted dispatch— probably the original—arrived in camp before the general returned, and Sutherland learned of its contents—probably from the Chief of Staff.

The reporter took exception to various statements and then penned some vitriolic comments about McDowell:

> The hero of Bull Run may possibly know how to waddle around a parlor and toady with San Francisco capitalists, but if he can see a single instance of genuine cooperation that General Howard has received from his brother department commanders, and solace himself with the belief that the country shares his baseless impressions then he is even a more wonderful person than he is in his own estimation. * * * We have been disappointed in Rawn. . . . Gibbon . . . got whipped by not cooperating, and now 80 Bannock Indians have joined us . . . with Joseph away off in the Yellowstone country. . . . if I were a general and should receive only such assistance as this, I would make it a point to tell McDowell, "in all kindness," that he is an ass, should he unjustly taunt me as he has Howard. Another brilliant remark of this fire-eater is, that where Indians can live, of course we can. This coming from a man whose waistcoat covers the most delicate and expensive viands of the San Francisco market every blessed day, is exceedingly ironical.[13]

Not long after this appeared in print, Major George W. Weeks, the Department quartermaster, passed through San Francisco en route to Montana. He found McDowell in "exceedingly bad humor generally and particularly so at . . . Louis Scribbler * * * who should be shut up, or kicked out of camp."[14] After the war was over, Howard wrote a letter of apology explaining that when Sutherland was told that the comment about "living on the country" had been made not by McDowell but by Sherman, "he was sorry for what he had written. But I did not dream that anything vituperative had been sent."[15]

Later, Sherman, who went directly overland from western Montana to Portland, became appreciative of the difficulties Howard had faced, and wrote in his annual report: "I recognize the full measure of the labors, exposure, fatigue, and fighting of General Howard and his command, having personally seen much of the route over which he passed, and knowing the great difficulty in procuring food for men and horses in that mountain region."[16]

Yet it was his ill-considered remark, "If the Indians can find food the troops can also," that stirred up a small hornets' nest of sharp words. However, considering the foraging Sherman's army did on their march "from Atlanta to the sea," it is not surprising that the general made this remark. Nor is it surprising that Howard should have been keenly aware of just how inappropriate this opinion was, for the general who commanded the right wing of Sherman's army on that memorable march across Georgia was none other than Howard himself!

No less interesting were the telegrams which Howard and Sherman exchanged. Howard explained in his first message that he had heard rumors of activity on the part of Colonels Nelson A. Miles and Samuel D. Sturgis "not far from my front"; that "my command is so much worn by over-fatigue that I cannot push it much further"; and that "I think I may stop near where I am, and in a few days work my way back to Fort Boise slowly." To this Sherman replied kindly but emphatically:

> I don't want to give orders, as this may confuse Sheridan and Terry; but that force of yours should pursue the Nez Perces to the death, lead where they may. Miles is too far off, and I fear Sturgis is too slow. If you are tired, give the command to some young energetic officer, and let him follow them, go where they may, holding his men well in hand, subsisting them on beef gathered in the country, with coffee, sugar and salt in packs. For such a stern chase infantry are as good as cavalry. Leave Sturgis to head them off if he can. * * * No time should be lost. I don't know your officers, but you can select the commander and order accordingly. When the Indians are caught, your men can march to the Pacific Railroad and reach their posts by rail and steamboat. They are not needed back in California and Oregon now, but they are needed just where they are.[17]

Howard had too much pride to admit that he was not able to cope with the situation. When his troops were ready to resume pursuit, he advised Sherman:

Yours of the 24th received. You misunderstood me. I never flag. It was the command, including the most energetic young officers, that were worn out and weary by a most extraordinary march. You need not fear for the campaign. Neither you nor General McDowell can doubt my pluck and energy. My Indian scouts are on the heels of the enemy. My supplies have just come in and we will move in the morning and will continue to the end. I sent Cushing and Norwood, now *en route*, two days ago to operate from [Fort] Ellis and the Crow Agency.[18]

After the campaign was over, Howard referred to Sherman's and Mc-Dowell's messages as being helpful "in regaining the *morale* of my officers & soldiers."[19] Be that as it may, there was no question but that all recognized that the ultimate authority had spoken, and that an order was an *order*. Curiously, Sherman did try to replace Howard later, probably so that the latter would be present when he inspected the Department of the Columbia; but this attempt ended in a comic failure.

Of several other incidents which took place during the few days the troops delayed at Henry Lake, the most curious concerned Captains Cushing and Field and their men. Here, just as with the contemplated Spokane Expedition, Howard's report omits something. When he left camp for Virginia City on the 24th, these troops—which he had argued with McDowell about—were ready to march for Corrine and take a train back to San Francisco. Major Mason even wrote a letter to his wife which Cushing was to carry with him.[20] Yet when the general and his son were returning to camp the next day, they met Cushing *coming down the road to Virginia City!* It appears that when Howard learned that he must pursue to the end, he sent a courier riding posthaste with orders to turn these men back.

As they met on the trail, the general dictated his order:

On the road, Madison Valley, September 25, 1877

Sir:

In compliance with telegraphic instructions from Division Head-quarters you will act in connection with this command until further orders. You will proceed with your company (C, Fourth Artillery), Field's (L, Fourth Artillery), and Norwood's (L, Second Cavalry) immediately to Fort Ellis, Mont.

Thence beside the above, you will take what troops can be spared from the post (Ellis), and proceed towards, or in the neighborhood of, Crow Agency, and endeavor to head off the hostile Nez Perces. Communicate with Colonel Sturgis and with these headquarters. Procure at Fort Ellis 8,000 rations of bacon, hard bread or flour, beans, sugar, coffee, soap, salt and pepper, and 4,000 rations of vinegar, to accompany your column, and await this command at or near Crow Agency.

By order of Brig. Gen. O. O. Howard:

GUY HOWARD
Second Lieutenant Twelfth Infantry, Acting Aide-de-Camp.
CAPTAIN H. C. CUSHING,
Fourth Artillery[21]

With this detachment were about thirty soldiers whom the surgeons had pronounced unfit to continue in the field. And they may have been joined in Virginia City by Lieutenant Adams and at least part of the horses and mules which he contracted for at that place. Although no mention is made of additional instructions, clothing supplies were sent to Howard from Fort Ellis which reached him a few days later along the Yellowstone River, ten miles below Yellowstone Lake.

Orders were also sent to Major Weeks, Department quartermaster, instructing him to come to Montana and attend to certain matters which Howard felt should not devolve on Lieutenant Ebstein, regardless of how capable and energetic this junior officer was. As Weeks was then at the depot in Lewiston, Idaho, this involved a roundabout journey via Portland, San Francisco and Corrine, Utah; and he reached Fort Ellis a month after Howard left Henry Lake. Also, it was reported that on the 24th a party of Nez Perce raided in the Madison Valley about 40 miles north of Henry Lake. Although between 100 and 300 head of horses were said to have been stolen and settlers considerably frightened, neither Howard nor the Virginia City *Madisonian* made any mention of this matter.

There was one feature of the four-day halt at Henry Lake that was enjoyed by all—a change from the monotonous fare of coffee, bacon, and "bread" made of a mixture of flour and water that had been baked over a campfire. Camp was made at the northern end of the lake near the establishment of Gilman Sawtelle, a market hunter and the proprietor of a sort of hunting and fishing camp for "tourists." The Indians had ransacked the establishment and stolen "everything of value" but had not burned any of the buildings. Sutherland reported that

Our men dragged a seine through the lake today, loading their boat with immense quantities of immense trout. Swans, geese, ducks and snipe are very abundant, while on the prairies nearby antelope and deer are plentiful. [Our mess table is well supplied with these delicacies.][22]

On the morning of the 28th, the column resumed its pursuit. The wagons which had been engaged in Missoula and the packers from Lewiston who had lost their mules at Camas Meadows were released, and a new wagon train put together of vehicles from Stevensville and Virginia City. This consisted of three four-horse wagons, five two-horse wagons and another team with a light spring wagon. The soldiers were refreshed by the stop, and the cavalry horses had, in Howard's opinion, "picked up a little."

Although Sherman had indicated to Howard that "Miles is too far off [to assist]," this aggressive officer had been noting the progress of the campaign with more than casual interest after the Indians had eluded Rawn at Fort Fizzle. In Chicago, Sheridan was also watching developments closely. The struggle now began to asssume the aspects of a gigantic game of chess, with various forces being moved and positioned with the objective of checkmating the Nez Perce.

As has been noted, the preceding year saw much activity in eastern Montana and northeastern Wyoming in connection with operations against the Sioux and Northern Cheyennes, with Colonel Miles being left at the mouth of the Tongue River in the fall to establish a permanent base of operations known as the Tongue River Contonment. This post became the hub of continuing operations in the spring of 1877. The battalion of Second Cavalry stationed at Fort Ellis was sent down the Yellowstone to operate with Miles' Fifth Infantry and, on the 7th of May, a mixed force— which included Norwood's company—scattered the last hostile camp of Sioux and Cheyennes at a fight on Lame Deer Creek. Summer brought a far-flung mopping-up operation with troops ranging as far east as the Little Missouri badlands and south into Wyoming, where a battalion of the Fifth Cavalry under Major Verling K. Hart was stationed on the head-waters of Tongue River on picket duty. Sitting Bull and his immediate followers retreated north of the Canadian border where they constituted a threat to northeastern Montana. To counter this, Terry ordered eleven companies of the Seventh Cavalry, under the command of Colonel Samuel D. Sturgis, from Fort Abraham Lincoln, to the vicinity of Miles' post. Late in May this force, filled with raw recruits as a result of Custer's disastrous fight, camped on Sunday Creek and began to scout in the "Big Open," the vast stretch of prairie and badlands that lay between the Yellowstone and Missouri Rivers. To provide a screen farther to the west, Lieutenant Gustavus C. Doane of the Second Cavalry, together with a sergeant and three or four enlisted men, bartered some rations and ammunition for the services of about 500 Crow warriors. This force—involving 354 lodges and a herd of about 10,000 horses and mules—took up a position in the lower part of the valley of the Musselshell River. As noted, the three Nez Perce warriors from the Treaty faction who came to the Flathead Reserve just before the Fort Fizzle affair, and who tried to persuade Looking Glass to turn north to Canada instead of going up the Bitterroot Valley, were undoubtedly with this Crow screen.

Just before the Fort Fizzle affair, Doane had come into the Tongue River Cantonment with about 160 Absaroka scouts. One hundred of these were selected to go down the Yellowstone and join a force then combing the Little Missouri country. Presumably, the news of Rawn's failure reached Miles shortly afterward for on the 3rd of August he issued to Doane, who was about to return to the Musselshell country with the balance of the scouts, this terse but explicit order:

> You will use every effort to intercept capture or destroy the Nez Perces band of hostile Indians that have recently been engaging the U.S. troops in Idaho, who will doubtless, if defeated, endeavor to retreat and take refuge in the Judith Basin, or vicinity.[23]

Lieutenant Doane was admirably suited for this assignment for he was a very able plainsman and capable of handling Indian scouts. To provide substantial support, the colonel detailed Lieutenant Charles C. De Rudio and "E" Company of the Seventh Cavalry to accompany him. Doane immediately placed a requisition for supplies and rations to be sent by water to Carroll, a small trading post and freight depot on the Missouri near the mouth of the Musselshell. And he informed Miles that he would try to keep his force of Crows together, but that it was impossible "to state exactly what *minor* movements can be carried into effect."[24]

This done, he took the remaining sixty warriors and started back up the Yellowstone Valley. Somewhere below the mouth of the Big Horn River, he met a wagon train returning to the cantonment from Post No. 2—later named Fort Custer—which was being escorted by a shavetail fresh out of West Point, Second Lieutenant Hugh L. Scott. Much to his delight, Scott managed to swap his assignment for that of a junior officer in De Rudio's company and joined Doane's party. This lieutenant later became something of a plainsman in his own right. One of Doane's scouts was a Scotsman whose name was C. J. "Yellowstone Jack" Baronett, the builder of Baronett's Bridge across the Yellowstone in 1871. He was a fascinating figure—a prospector for gold in Africa, Australia, California and Montana, sailor on a trading vessel to China and second mate on a whaler in the Arctic seas, a soldier of fortune with the rank of captain under Maximilian in Mexico, and a scout for several military expeditions in the west.[25]

At first the Absaroka in the Musselshell Valley were cool to Doane's proposal that they scout against their old friends, and he and De Rudio left the Crow camp without the desired recruits. However, as the detail moved up the Musselshell, warriors began to come into their camps until they totaled about one hundred.[26] There was no uncertainty in Doane's mind as to where he should go. He headed straight for the Judith Gap—a flat stretch ten miles in width lying between the Little Belt and the Big Snowy Mountains. Through this natural gateway flowed most of the travel into and out of the upper part of the Judith Basin.

With the nearest telegraph stations at Bismarck, D.T., and Bozeman, at the head of the Gallatin Valley, Miles was more or less isolated. As the days passed without news of the Nez Perce—it was a week after Billy Edwards arrived at Deer Lodge before he heard of the Big Hole battle—the colonel became more and more concerned. On August 11th (the date of the first news in Deer Lodge and Helena of Gibbon's fight) Miles ordered Sturgis to take six companies of the Seventh Cavalry and march for the Judith Gap, meanwhile sending to Fort Ellis for the latest information. At the Judith Gap he was to try to communicate with Doane and to rely on that officer's advice in matters of policy involving the Crows—"The intention of the Nez Perces is doubtless to enter the Judith Basin either by the head of the Musselshell, and either Judith Gap or Copperopolis and Arrow Creek, or by crossing the Mt and it is the object of your movement to intercept or pursue and capture or destroy them."[27]

Lieutenant Ezra B. Fuller and a small detail were started to Fort Ellis for the latest intelligence. Sturgis and about 360 men marched promptly the next day. However, a complication soon reared its head—Miles received reports that Sitting Bull was about to leave Canada and come into Montana. This information was forwarded at once to Sturgis, but the colonel decided, correctly, that it was a false report and kept his attention centered on the Nez Perce. When he reached Pompey's Pillar, six days' march up the Yellowstone Valley, a courier from Doane found him. The colonel scribbled a reply on six sheets torn from a small notebook and sent the courier back. In this message he stated, "I enclose a copy of a printed slip . . . forwarded by Lieut. Fuller. . . ." This was an "Extra" of the Bozeman *Avant Courier*—a small broadside carrying the news of Gibbon's fight, on the back of which Fuller had written:

> Gen'l Howard is coming down LoLo Fork with 950 men. The Indians will go into Salmon river mountains or go up Snake river and come down Wind river. That is the only route for them unless they cut their way through the [Montana] settlements.[28]

Meager intelligence indeed on which to plan a movement involving upwards of 500 soldiers and scouts!

Two days after Gibbon reached Deer Lodge from the Big Hole, he sent a dispatch to Sturgis—who was now within the confines of "his" District of Montana—informing him of the battle he had fought and directing the colonel to proceed "with all speed" to Fort Ellis. From this point he was to go up the valley of the Yellowstone and try to intercept the hostiles. Meanwhile, the Seventh Cavalry had marched up an old trail laid out by the surveyors of the Northern Pacific Railroad which led from Pompey's Pillar to the Musselshell. Somewhere along this road a courier from Lieutenant Foster overtook them bearing fresh intelligence, and Sturgis, realizing that the quarry was somewhere in the opposite direction, turned about and headed for the Crow Agency on the southern side of the Yellowstone River. At this point—on the basis of what was probably rather poor geographical intelligence—he hoped to be in position to engage the Nez Perce when they emerged from the rugged Absaroka Mountains.

Although Gibbon's instructions did not reach Sturgis promptly, the commanding officer at Camp Baker forwarded a copy of this dispatch which did reach Doane at the Judith Gap on August 21st. This officer, taking De Rudio's company and about seventy-five Crow scouts, lost no time in striking out for Fort Ellis which he reached on the 25th.[29] Sturgis complained later that although he had informed Doane of his whereabouts and sent certain instructions to him, Doane did not comply. The reasons are not clear. For one thing, the lieutenant knew the topography of the country far better than Sturgis and he probably recognized that there were other courses of action that were more feasible than the ones proposed by the colonel. And he undoubtedly realized that if he was drawn close to Sturgis, the latter would probably repossess De Rudio's company and he would find himself with the task of handling Sturgis' scouts. Perhaps this officer of the *Second* Cavalry was reluctant to be maneuvered into a position of working for the glory of the *Seventh* Cavalry.

This, then, was the situation which existed ahead of the pursued and their pursuers on the 28th of August. However, Sheridan had more chessmen on the playing board than Sturgis and Doane. He described these pieces and their positions in a telegram which he dispatched to the Adjutant General as Howard's troops were marching away from the vicinity of Henry Lake:

> Col Gibbon telegraphs on the twenty seventh (27) that the Nez Perces crossed the Yellowstone River in the National Park just south of Cañon. Col. Sturgis with Seventh (7) Cavalry, is at Crow Agency and will cross to Clarks Fork and go up that stream to intercept them. Lieut. Doane with one company of cavalry and one hundred (100) Crows left Fort Ellis for [Baronett's] Bridge on the Yellowstone north of Cañon and on trail across Clarks Fork [between Bozeman and the eastern side of the Absaroka Range]. Gen Howard is not mentioned but I presume is following up. [According to released captives] The

Indians say they are going to Wind River and it looks a little as though this might be so. To meet it, I have sent Col. [Wesley] Merritt to Camp Brown [later Fort Washakie] where he will have four (4) companies of cavalry, and have ordered five (5) companies more to be in readiness at a moment's warning to go by rail to Green River [Wyoming] and from there to Camp Brown. This will give Merritt at Brown nine (9) companies of cavalry. Major [Verling K.] Hart is on the head of Tongue River, forty (40) miles east of Fort C. F. Smith [an abandoned post at the northern tip of the Big Horn Mountain], with five (5) companies of the Fifth (5) Cavalry. In case the Nez Perces come down the Stinking Water [Shoshone River], Major Hart will be there. If they go to Wind River, I will cross him over the Big Horn Mountains to Wind River. I have asked Gen. Crook to come back to his department, and request the Secretary of War to let Gen. Terry come back [from New York] without delay. He ought to be at his headquarters.[30]

As noted, Hart had been on picket duty in this location for some time. Crook and Terry had been detailed to duty in Chicago and New York in connection with the labor riots which had now subsided. Crook went directly to Camp Brown where Merritt was readying his column of Fifth Cavalry, and Terry was released immediately to return to St. Paul.

On the following day, Sheridan reported additional developments to Sherman who was still in Helena:

I have ordered Col. Merritt and eight (8) companies of Cavalry to Camp Brown. That will make with companies at Brown and [nearby Camp] Stambaugh, ten (10) companies—a sufficient force to meet the Nez Perces should they try to go to Wind River. I will order Major Hart . . . to cross the Big Horn [River] at Fort C. F. Smith or further south and make for the trail down Stinking Water, where the Indians would probably come if making for the Big Horn Mountains. Major Hart will have with him 100 good Sioux scouts. If the Nez Perces come through I think we will get them.

Please tell Colonel Gibbon to keep Sturgis pushed up. The Indians will come down Clark's Fork if they can.[31]

Sheridan's contemplated movements appeared to be well planned but, as sometimes happens:

The best laid plans o' mice and men
Gang aft aglee.

20

The Yellowstone Park Tourists

>>>>>>><<<<<< As Howard's troops were making their first camp beside Henry Lake, the Nez Perce were approaching the Lower Geyser Basin of the Yellowstone National Park. Ahead of them were eight or nine parties of tourists totaling at least thirty-five individuals. These were a motley lot—two women, "a boy," a fifty-five-year-old prospector, a discharged soldier, an English earl and his companion, two photographers, a music teacher, a lawyer, a brewer, at least one very capable frontiersman, and a flamboyant character known as a "blowhard," actor and scout. One noteworthy party had departed but four or five days before—General W. T. Sherman, his son, Colonels Bacon and Poe, "three drivers, one packer, and four soldiers." In addition to the tourists, there probably were several small parties of prospectors along the eastern boundary of the Park. Of these nothing is known except that the remains of unidentified persons were found in this area years afterward.

As the Indians approached the campsite selected at the mouth of what is now Nez Perce Creek, some of the warriors scouted ahead. Among them were Yellow Wolf and a tough half-breed, Henry Tabour, who could speak English. Hearing the sound of chopping, they investigated and found a solitary man preparing his evening meal. This individual, who had not heard of the Nez Perce war, was a fifty-five-year-old prospector named John Shivley. He had recently come into the area with a party of prospectors on what had proved to be a wild-goose chase, and was now waiting to travel out of the Park with a party of tourists who were camped nearby. About three weeks later, he related his strange experiences to three editors, one of whom was James Mills of Deer Lodge. Mills not only put his story into print but vouched for Shivley as being "a gentleman of strict veracity and high character," and the prospector certified that Mills' version was "faithful and strictly accurate."[1]

> It was in the dusk of the evening on the . . . [23rd] of August, nearly dark, his camp fire crackling cheerily, his horses grazing quietly off on the prairie, and his gun leaning against a tree a few feet behind him, and he peacefully eating his supper, when three buck Indians with guns cocked sprang up in the tall grass in front of him. He jumped to his feet and for his gun but found that another squad had captured that and on looking around found himself surrounded by thirty or forty of them, a number of those farther off being mounted. They told him to surrender.

At first the Indians claimed they were Sioux, but when Shivley said, "No, you are not Sioux," they admitted they were Nez Perce and began to flourish their pistols close to his head.

Thinking his time had come, the captive folded his arms and told them to shoot; but after a brief consultation among themselves, Looking Glass' brother came up, placed his hand over the prospector's heart, and then said, "*Hyas skukum tum tum*"—which, in the Chinook jargon of the Northwest, meant he had a strong heart. Shivley was then taken to the camp where a council was held. The chiefs ordered him to be seated in the center of the circle while they questioned him, Poker Joe—otherwise known as Nez Perces Joe, Joe Hale and Lean Elk—serving as interpreter.

> They asked him who he was, where he came from, what he was doing, if he knew the country, if he could guide them to the Crow country . . . , which was the best route to go, and whether he was willing to go and guide them.

As being a guide was preferable to taking a chance of being shot, Shivley had no difficulty in deciding what to do; and he was placed in the protective custody of Poker Joe, who was a sort of "straw boss" in charge of the movement of the camp—a position which was to be confusing to other captives who assumed he was head chief at this time. The half-breed accompanied Shivley most of the time, slept beside him at night, and warned him that "he must not try to escape or the Nez Perces would be heap mad." And for the next thirteen days this white man was the chief guide for the hostiles. Not only were the Indians friendly toward him but, considering the circumstances, they even pampered him to some extent.

Shivley had a unique opportunity to study this force, to estimate its number, and to observe its *modus operandi;* and the information which he supplied to Editor Mills indicates clearly that he was "a gentleman of strict veracity." His figure of 600 to 800 people was very conservative. In the end, 431 surrendered, 25 were killed in the final battle, and the Canadian authorities estimated that about 330 escaped to Canada—a total of almost 800. His tally on the horse herd was probably equally accurate. This is Shivley's picture of the hostile camp, its numbers and equipment, how it moved, *and the council which governed it:*

There are from 600 to 800 Nez Perces in the band. Of these 250 are warriors but all will fight that can carry a gun. They have almost 2,000 head of good average horses. Every lodge drives its own horses in front of it when traveling, each lodge keeping its band separate. The line is thus strung out so that they are three hours getting into camp. They are nearly all armed with repeating rifles, only half a dozen or so having muzzle loaders. They say they have more ammunition than they want. About one-sixth of the horses are disabled, lame or sore-backed, but they keep changing and hold all the good horses in reserve. The horses are all in fair condition. They seemed at first anxious about the soldiers overtaking them but soon got over that, and had no intimation any troops were trying to intercept them in front. They kept no scouts ahead and after crossing the Yellowstone had no rear guard, only a few parties striking out occasionally on their own account.

So far as he could notice *no particular chief seemed to be in command. All matters were decided in a council of several chiefs.* [Italics are author's] White Bird was not known to him at all, as such, but thinks he was present in the councils in about a dozen of which Shivley participated. Joseph is about 35 years of age, six feet high, and always in a pleasant mood, greeting him each time with a nod and smile. Looking Glass is 50 or 60 years old. He wears a white feather. Joseph wears one eagle feather, and Joe Hale two, putting a new feather in his cap after Mr. Shivley joined them. They say they have lost 43 warriors altogether, of these 6 or 7 were killed in Norwood's fight near Camas Meadows, the remainder at Big Hole, where they lost many women and children. Joe Hale says he killed two soldiers there. They had but 10 or 12 wounded with them and one was dying when Shivley escaped. They said they would fight soldiers but did not want to fight citizens—but Mr. S. says they will kill anybody.

Not only is this picture of the Nez Perce camp an excellent one, but it is also the *only* one—except for a more fleeting one made in northern Montana at Cow Creek—that was ever made. And the observation that *there was no head chief* is supported by other evidence—the Joseph legend to the contrary. A tribal council was the governing body.

After capturing Shivley, a small scouting party including Yellow Wolf, his brother and Henry Tabour rode a couple of miles farther and camped. As they were picketing their horses, Yellow Wolf saw a flicker of light some distance ahead but, as the area was swampy and contained hot springs and small geysers, they waited until morning to investigate.[2]

About the campfire Yellow Wolf spotted was the group Shivley expected to accompany the next day. The party numbered nine and was soon to be known as the "Radersburg party" as most of them were from this town and nearby Helena. They were: George F. Cowan and his wife, Emma (age 23), her brother and sister—Frank and Ida Carpenter (the latter a girl of 13)—J. Albert "Al" Oldham, William A. Dingee, Charles Mann, A. J. Arnold and D. L. Meyers.[3] Camped close by was William H. Harmon, a Colorado prospector, whom the party had met a day or two before. Meyers was slightly crippled having stepped in a boiling spring a few days before. They were "nicely outfitted with an easy double-seated carrage, baggage wagon and four saddle horses," together with ample firearms, a violin, and a guitar. The party had left home on the 6th of August and traveled south up the valley of the Madison River to Henry Lake where they had stopped for a few days at Sawtelle's resort to hunt, boat and fish.

During their visit to the Park they had seen the Upper and Lower Geyser Basins and had visited the valley of the Yellowstone farther to the east. In the latter area, an interesting meeting had taken place. While on a trail not far from Yellowstone Lake, they met a rather unusual party. First came a frontiersman driving a number of loose horses. Then another rider came into sight. As Frank Carpenter described him later: "He was a tall powerfully built man, and as he rode carelessly along, with his rifle crossed in front of him, he is a picture. He was dressed in a complete suit of buckskin, and wore a flaming red neckerchief, a broad *sombrero*, fastened up on one side with a large eagle feather, and a pair of beautifully beaded moccasins." And a little farther on they met two more men "both of whom were dressed in buckskins and wore large *sombreroes*."

The two tourists were the Earl of Dunraven and his friend, Dr. George Kingsley. The flashily dressed guide was Jack Omohondro—better known as Texas Jack—who was a scout of the swaggering type with theatrical aspirations (with William F. Cody). Some regarded him as a phony and Mrs. Cowan recalled later with withering scorn that a few days afterward he was caught red-handed with bullet holes in his saddle—holes he claimed were put there by Nez Perce but which others were dead certain he had shot there to attract attention to himself. And the horse wrangler was Earnest Boney who, forty-three years later, had not forgotten an incident which grew out of a shortage in their food supplies—a shortage of which Carpenter wrote, "[Texas Jack] inquired for 'spare grub'; we had none to give or sell. . . ."

The next morning Dingee and Arnold were up at the coming of daylight to build a fire and start breakfast. As Dingee took the coffeepot and pail and started for a nearby stream to bring water, he discovered three Indians quietly sitting on their ponies about fifty yards away. They exchanged "hows" and the trio followed Dingee back to camp where Arnold quickly awakened the others. Soon all were dressed and gathered around the campfire, except the women, who peeped out through the flap of the tent in which they had been sleeping. By this time, Arnold had created a good impression by climbing into the wagon and handing the Indians "sugar, flour and two good pieces of bacon." However, Cowan quickly dispelled this by ordering Arnold to stop handing out food, and ordering the Indians away in an overbearing manner. The Indians resented this treatment and, as his wife observed long afterward, "I think this materially lessened his chances of escape."

After first insisting that they were "Snakes," the trio admitted they were Nez Perce—of whom the party had last heard at the time they were passing up the Bitterroot Valley. Tabour explained that while they fought soldiers they would not hurt civilians, and assured them that Looking Glass would see that they were escorted safely past the bulk of the Indians and started on their way home. And so, as there was really nothing else they could do, the tourists hitched up and, guided by the three warriors, started toward the main camp which was strung out and moving up the East Fork of the Firehole River, now called Nez Perce Creek. They had not gone far when small squads of men left the moving camp and gathered around them to the number of fifty or sixty. These soon began to debate the idea of allowing the tourists to follow their back trail as "40 or 50 warriors were coming up from Henry's Lake and they would kill us if we went on." In the end, the party was taken to see Looking Glass, who was ahead.

After traveling about five miles, fallen timber forced them to abandon the vehicles and mount the horses. Mrs. Cowan remembered that they took "from the wagon the few things in the way of wraps that we could carry conveniently" and that the Indians promptly appropriated the rest of their property. Frank Carpenter now hired an Indian, at a cost of "six needle gun cartridges," to guide him on ahead to see Looking Glass—reaching the chief a few miles farther on as the head of the column stopped to make a noon camp. Looking Glass shook hands with Frank and then turned him over to Poker Joe, who took him to his campfire. Here Carpenter explained where they were from, what they had been doing, and requested that they be released to go home. As soon as the rest of the party arrived, the half-breed greeted them in a friendly manner.

A week later, Dingee—*who mistook Poker Joe for Joseph*—related that,

> [Joe] began at once, in a business-like manner, to take an inventory of our personal property. Then he "traded" poor Indian ponies and worn out saddles for our good horses and new saddles. Gradually the Indians gathered around us, became more insolent, and took away from us our arms, grub, and the horses that [Joe] had traded us. [Joe] then went around to each one of our party and said, substantially, as he said to me, "Get into the timber and don't go near the wagons. I wish you well . . . [but cannot control some of the warriors] and they are determined to kill you." As a blind, I led a horse slowly out to a spot near the timber. There I was joined by Arnold and we ran for our lives.

The Indians fired three or four shots at them but, apparently, made no effort to try to recapture the pair, although some accounts indicate that this action did make the Indians suspicious of the entire party.

Shortly after Dingee and Arnold made their dash for the shelter of the timber, the remainder of the party turned back. According to Carpenter, Poker Joe told them to "go quick" and

> We started off through the woods. The camp had all got on the move by this time, and . . . [Poker Joe] went on ahead to join them. We kept on for a distance through the woods, and the Indians kept coming back and following us, until they numbered 15 or 20. They told us to come out of the woods and go down the trail to the wagons; and, as it was almost impossible to travel in the timber, we did so. We then missed Dingee and Arnold. The Indians began to take our blankets and other property, and traded guns several times with Oldham [sic] and Cowan—the only ones in the party who retained their arms. Again we started, but after going a few yards were told that Joseph [sic] wanted to see us.

With the unruly young bucks encircling them, the party now turned around and started back toward the foot of the mountain where they had separated from Poker Joe. According to the Bozeman *Times*, this is the way George Cowan and his wife remembered the next terrifying moments:

While ascending a small sharp knoll in this timber, Mr. Cowan and his wife being in advance of the other members of the party . . . , two Indians came dashing down the trail from the front, and, stopping their horses within about fifteen feet of Mr. Cowan, one of them raised his rifle and fired, the ball passing directly through Mr. Cowan's right thigh. Another Indian who had been riding close to Mr. C. then leveled his gun on Mr. Cowan's head, but to avoid this shot he slipped from his horse, and being unable to use the wounded leg, fell to the ground. Mrs. Cowan was the first person to reach her husband after his fall and was bending over him, when two Indians who had jumped from their horses came running up, one of whom asked Mr. Cowan, who had raised up on his elbow, if he was shot *here* pointing to his own breast, and upon being told no, that he was wounded through the leg, he immediately drew a large revolver and presented it at Mr. Cowan's head. Mrs. C., observing the movement threw her arms around her husband's head and her body in front of his face, shielding him from the shot. The Indian then caught Mrs. C. by the right hand and attempted to drag her away from her husband, but she still clung to his neck with her left hand. This movement gave the second Indian a full view of Mr. Cowan's head, when, with a quick movement he drew a revolver from beneath his blanket and fired a shot therefrom which took effect in the upper part of Mr. Cowan's forehead rendering him perfectly insensible and oblivious to everything else that then transpired.

Years later, Mrs. Cowan recalled that the last thing she remembered as she was being dragged away was seeing blood running down her husband's face and Indians throwing rocks at his head. Then she fainted.

Frank Carpenter was about thirty yards behind when the first shot was fired. He recalled seeing his sister running to her husband while another Indian about thirty feet away was covering him with a rifle. Thinking his time had come, he instinctively crossed himself whereupon the buck lowered his rifle and said, "Come quick—no kill—me save you." Carpenter rode to his brother-in-law who begged for water, but "my chief grabbed me and says—come quick—Indian kill," and led him behind some brush a short distance away. After what seemed an age to Frank, the Indians commenced to drive the loose horses up the hill and shortly afterward he saw Emma riding double with an Indian to whom she had been tied while still unconscious. She told him that she had seen her sister on a horse behind another Indian. Ida had cowered beside her sister at the time of the shooting but when the latter fainted "I jumped and screamed, and ran in and out among the Indians and horses. . . . one caught me by the throat and choked me. . . . As he loosened his hold I . . . [bit] his fingers."

None had observed what happened to the other four members of the party.

The next summer when Trader McDonald interviewed White Bird and others in Canada, Red Scout told him that he was the one who saved Frank Carpenter; and that he saved him not because of Frank's making the sign of the cross—a detail about which Carpenter and McDonald had already pointedly disagreed—but because he knew Looking Glass did not want the tourists killed. Also, he named the one surviving member of the original murder trio as the warrior who fired the first shot at Cowan. McDonald was also informed that when the Cowan party was released, White Bird and Looking Glass started ahead of the Indian camp, not knowing that the tourists were being followed by the unruly young men. When the chiefs learned of the situation, they sent Poker Joe to protect the whites, but he arrived after Cowan was shot.

Ida was kept in Poker Joe's camp during the coming night, but Emma was promised she could see her the next morning. Frank and Emma were held in Joseph's camp not far from the campfire where the chief, "grave and dignified," sat "sombre and silent." All three were offered food, but both women recalled they were too distraught to even try to eat. Years later, Mrs. Cowan wrote:

> The Indians were without tepees . . . but pieces of canvas were stretched over a pole or bush, thus affording some protection from the cold night air. My brother and I sat out a weary vigil by the dying embers of the campfire, sadly wondering what the coming day would bring forth. * * * Near morning, rain began falling. A squaw arose, replenished the fire, and then came and spread a piece of canvas over my shoulders to keep off the dampness.

The next day the camp continued on eastward and, about noon, crossed the Yellowstone River about four miles below the lake. Here they went into camp. In the afternoon there was an alarm of some sort and most of the men recrossed the river and went back, leaving Poker Joe and a few minor chiefs in charge of the camp. Joe and six others held a council and voted—four to three, according to Frank—to release the captives. As Mrs. Cowan told the story, they wished to keep Frank to help Shivley and send them with James C. Irwin, a recently discharged cavalryman whom they had captured that morning. But she protested, believing him to be a deserter and not to be trusted, and they finally allowed Frank to go. Mrs. Cowan's riding habit was brought to her, and the two women were given a couple of worn-out ponies. Taking Frank up behind him, Poker Joe led the little party back across the Yellowstone and about a mile down the valley. Here he gave them a little food and some matches, and released them with the admonition, "Go home—go quick. You no meet Indians on trail. * * * You get to Bozeman in three days. Good-by."

With part of their clothing soaked from crossing the river, the three spent a chilly night huddled in a patch of brush. Late afternoon of the next day found them a few miles below the junction of the Lamar River, then called the East Fork of the Yellowstone, and the Yellowstone, and on the trail leading from Bozeman to the little settlement established, surreptitiously, by miners at the head of Soda Butte Creek on the Crow Indian Reservation. Here, about twelve miles from Mammoth Hot Springs, they came to a small detachment under Lieutenant Charles B. Schofield which had just made camp. The lieutenant had been sent out from Fort Ellis to scout for the Nez Perce and, having found no signs, was returning. He quickly decided to break camp and march on to "the Springs" where there was a small hotel. The soundness of this decision soon became apparent when, just as they were ready to move, Frederic Pfister, another tourist, joined them and told of more serious trouble. All reached James McCartney's rough hostel about 10 P.M., where they were destined to spend a rather hectic night marked by the arrival of other fugitives. The next day two photographers, Messrs. Calfee and Catlin, proffered a ride in their wagon and the three went down the Yellowstone Valley to the road ranch of the Boteler (Bottler or Botteller) brothers, and thence to Bozeman—safe but wondering what had happened to their late companions.

After their successful dash for the brush, Dingee and Arnold headed back over the route they had followed coming into the Park. After spending four days and nights in the mountains, "without arms, food, blankets, or coats" and with only "four little fish" to eat, this pair reached Henry Lake, "weak and almost despairing." Here "our ears were greeted with a cavalry bugle from across the lake." Howard's men were breaking camp and preparing to move out; and here they were to learn that one party of Indians from whom they had hidden was the general's Bannock scouts. Shortly after their arrival, Meyers came into camp and reported that Cowan had been killed and that as he and Oldham were escaping on horses, an Indian had ridden up and shot Oldham through the head with a revolver. The latter had fallen from his horse, while the Indians had chased him "on a dead run for eight miles" before turning back. About a mile farther on, he had met Fisher and his scouts.

Arnold elected to stay with Howard's troops and search for the rest of the party or their bodies. Dingee and Meyers headed homeward via Virginia City where the latter stopped to have his scalded foot cared for. Dingee's estimate of the number of warriors was in close agreement with the one made by Shivley: "As near as I am able to determine, there were

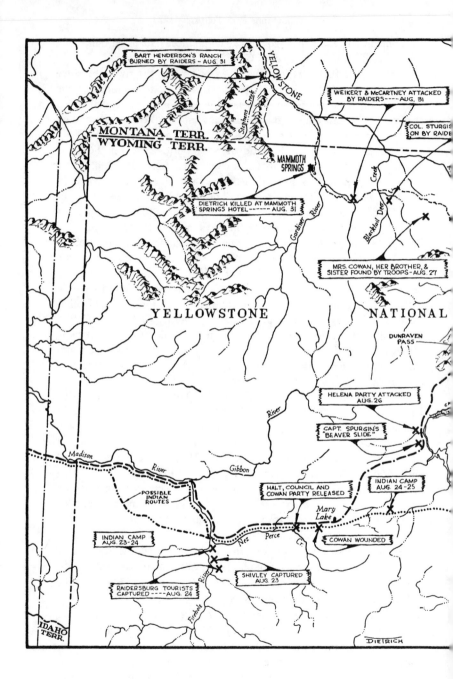

BART HENDERSON'S RANCH
BURNED BY RAIDERS - AUG. 31

WEIKERT & McCARTNEY ATTACKED
BY RAIDERS ---- AUG. 31

COL. STURGIS
ON BY RAIDE

MONTANA   TERR.
WYOMING   TERR.

MAMMOTH
SPRINGS

DIETRICH KILLED AT MAMMOTH
SPRINGS HOTEL ----- AUG. 31

MRS. COWAN, HER BROTHER, &
SISTER FOUND BY TROOPS - AUG. 27

YELLOWSTONE   NATIONAL

DUNRAVEN
PASS

HELENA PARTY ATTACKED
AUG. 26

CAPT. SPURGIN'S
"BEAVER SLIDE"

Madison

INDIAN CAMP
AUG. 24-25

POSSIBLE
INDIAN
ROUTES

HALT, COUNCIL AND
COWAN PARTY RELEASED

Mary
Lake

COWAN WOUNDED

INDIAN CAMP
AUG. 23-24

Nez   Perce

SHIVLEY CAPTURED
AUG. 23

RAIDERSBURG TOURISTS
CAPTURED ---- AUG. 24

IDAHO
TERR.

DIETRICH

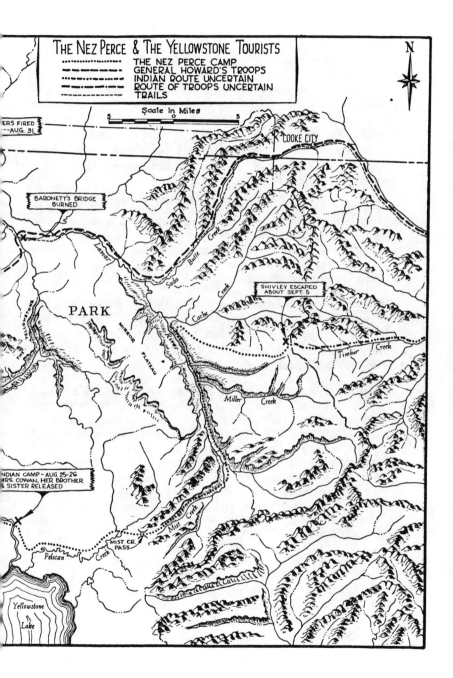

THE NEZ PERCE & THE YELLOWSTONE TOURISTS

```
•••••••••••  THE NEZ PERCE CAMP
━━━━━━━━━━  GENERAL HOWARD'S TROOPS
▪▬▪▬▪▬▪▬  INDIAN ROUTE UNCERTAIN
━ ━ ━ ━ ━  ROUTE OF TROOPS UNCERTAIN
─ ─ ─ ─ ─  TRAILS
```

N

Scale In Miles

5   0   5

...ERS FIRED
...—AUG. 31

COOKE CITY

BARONETT'S BRIDGE
BURNED

SHIVLEY ESCAPED
ABOUT SEPT. 5

PARK

THE YELLOWSTONE

MIRROR PLATEAU

Lamar

Soda

Butte

Creek

Cache

Creek

River

Creek

Timber   Creek

Miller   Creek

...NDIAN CAMP – AUG. 25-26
...RS. COWAN, HER BROTHER
...& SISTER RELEASED

Mist   Creek

MIST CR.
PASS

Pelican   Creek

Yellowstone
Lake

250 warriors, and about 3,000 horses and a good many mules. We did not see any wounded Indians, but they did not tell us of their battle with Gibbon."

Apparently, Mann and Harmon made no record of how they escaped from the melee. Fisher noted in his journal that after he had made camp on "Saturday, 25" an Indian told him of seeing a man who proved to be Harmon. "He cried for joy when I found him and was almost exhausted from hunger and fatigue." Shortly afterward, two other scouts brought in Mann who "was not hurt, but . . . had a ball hole through his hat." The next entry in the journal reads:

> Sunday, August 26. Baptiste let the man Harmon have his mare to go back to the command, as we are out of rations. Charles Mann goes on with us. I furnished him a horse to ride. . . . * * * Leaving this place [the location of the buggy and wagon] we followed the trail to where the enemy camped night before last. Here we made a careful search for dead and wounded, but found none.

However, Cowan and Oldham were alive. Part of Oldham's story was written for Frank Carpenter's exaggeration-cursed book. According to this, when the trading took place, Oldham was allowed to retain his rifle, a single-shot Ballard—probably of an odd caliber—for which he had three cartridges. When Cowan was shot, the warrior

> that was riding on the upper side of me, turned loose at me. I felt a twinge in the side of my face [apparently his mouth was open], and tumbled from my horse. I fell in a ravine, but immediately jumped to my feet, and saw that the Indian that had shot me was following me. I grasped my gun and raised it to fire, and he started back up the hill. I snapped the gun but it was not discharged. . . . I was bleeding freely from the wound in my face, the blood running down my throat and over my vest. I found that the ball had penetrated the left cheek [knocking out two teeth], and, passing downwards, had cut the tongue and come out beneath the jaw on the right side. The wound was very painful.

What probably happened afterward was that he escaped into the brush where he fell and lost consciousness for a time. A day or two later he shot a grouse which his swollen tongue prevented him from eating, and was finally discovered by two white scouts. They managed to feed him a little food and took him to the command, not "Monday" as Carpenter states but two days later. Major Mason wrote to his wife:

> Wednesday August 29 * * * The chief incident of the day was finding by the roadside the poor fellow who was shot through the face

by the Indians and afterwards escaped—he was almost dead from hunger and cold.[4]

And Henry Buck, the Stevensville merchant-teamster, recalled years later that

> Soon after leaving camp . . . we picked up a poor unfortunate young man by the name of Al Oldham. He had been shot through both cheeks and was all covered with blood and withal was a sad looking spectacle. I took him in my wagon. . . .
>
> * * *
>
> . . . [When] we made camp. . . . Mr. Bass and I took it upon ourselves to look after Mr. Oldham. [We gave him a shirt and pair of pants.] The Command gave him surgical attention, and in all we made him quite comfortable and he looked very respectable.[5]

Unfortunately, the narratives of Carpenter, Cowan and Arnold deserve to be read, in places, with a discerning eye and a critical attitude. Cowan was apparently an arrogant individual; Carpenter's various accounts indicate that he was verbose, inaccurate and conceited; and when the stories of this trio are compared to other data the resulting analysis indicates that all three were self-centered, inconsiderate, selfish, and—certainly—ungrateful. When various details pertaining to Cowan are evaluated and patched together, this is the story which emerges.

The bullet which knocked Cowan senseless hit him squarely in the forehead about two inches above the bridge of his nose and flattened against his skull. Here it stuck until removed by Captain FitzGerald. Although this may have come from a defective cartridge, it is probable that it came from an old cap-and-ball revolver which either had been loaded with a skimpy charge in this chamber of the cylinder or—still more likely— had been exposed to dampness and the powder was no longer absolutely dry. And, in addition to the two bullet wounds, "he was also wounded in the back of the head, from a blow from a rock or something else."

Cowan lay where he fell until late in the afternoon when he regained consciousness. Finding that his right leg was not broken, he managed to stand up by using a stick for a crutch—only to see an Indian riding toward him about twenty-five yards away. He scrambled for a nearby thicket but the warrior fired at him, the bullet hitting the point of his left hip and coming out in front of his abdomen. This knocked him to the ground and he played "possum," lying in some tall grass with his face on the ground. Fortunately, the Indian rode on without investigating. About twenty minutes later, twenty or thirty Indians came up the trail driving loose horses but again Cowan escaped detection.

As it was now impossible to stand, Cowan began to crawl back down the trail. In four days and nights—for exercise at night to offset the cold was imperative—he managed to crawl ten or twleve miles back to the last camp in the Geyser Basin. At the abandoned wagon and buggy, he found nothing of value except a dog, a stray the party had acquired while en route to the Park. Among the pine needles at the campsite, he found twelve matches and a small handful of coffee beans, enough to brew a little coffee. Then he crawled back to the mouth of Nez Perce Creek where his strength gave out completely. As he lay beside the trail, two men carrying rations to Fisher and his scouts found him. They made some coffee for him and then, after leaving him some food and two of Fisher's blankets, continued on after the scouts trusting that the command would find him shortly. On the following day, Messrs Taft and Carmin, two Montana settlers who were acting as temporary guides, found him "leaning up against a log with two blankets around him." Not long afterward the command arrived, and with it Arnold who took over the care of his friend.

Camp was made shortly afterward, and many officers and men went to see the nearby curiosities of the Geyser Basin. Cowan expected "attention immediately" but Arnold was not able to secure a doctor until near evening—apparently they gave excuses and one referred him to another as they pursued their sightseeing. Finally, Dr. FitzGerald came—"He grumbled about it"—and probed the wounds and removed the imbedded bullet. Then Arnold, "with the assistance of the boys," was left to care for the man.

Several days later in Bozeman, Cowan stated that he "is not under any particular obligation to Howard's Surgeon . . . for medical, surgical or other favor. . . . Mr. Arnold has waited on him like a brother . . . and did everything he could. They had a very rough time of it to Boettlers', where they received all attention the people there could afford."

Arnold was equally critical in his statements, stating that the command "offered us nothing," that Captain Spurgeon refused to sell Cowan some underclothing from the supply train, and that Cowan "wanted to be forwarded home by way of Henry's Lake" but Howard said he would send him to Fort Ellis, placing him in "an old wagon [to be] jolted over the worst road that was ever passed over by a wagon."

The worst that can be said about the treatment Cowan received is that at the time he was found the surgeons were, apparently, more interested in seeing the geysers than dressing wounds of a stray tourist. Undoubtedly the troops themselves were short of underwear, and furthermore, Spurgeon was the engineer officer and not the quartermaster who was in charge of supplies. The request to be sent in the opposite direction by troops in pursuit of an enemy was ridiculous and it is doubtful if Howard even promised to send the man to Fort Ellis, for the wagon train was sent to that post *only* after it was found that it was practically impossible for it to follow the troops. And as for the "old wagon," Henry Buck recalled that, "Before starting the next morning. . ., a comfortable bed was made with plenty of blankets in the bottom of Doc. Van R. Woodmancy's light spring wagon, thus forming a sort of ambulance for Mr. Cowan, as he was not able to set up." Cowan was provided with the *very best* transportation available. Viewed in proper perspective, it would appear that Cowan and Arnold received much better treatment than they deserved.

Some measure of the reliability contained in statements made by some members of the Cowan party (the ladies excepted) is indicated in the fact that both Cowan and Arnold stated *explicitly* that the news of the three captives did not reach them until the day *after* Cowan was found. Yet Major Mason wrote his wife:

> *Thursday August 30th, 1877.* * * * We have received intelligence (it came last night) that Mrs. Cowan and her sister have been released and are now in the hands of Lt. Schofield. . . . There was a great rejoicing in the camp last night when the news was rec'd. Today the chapter was completed by finding Mr. Cowan, her husband, alive! * * * His joy when told of the safety of his wife was most touching.[6]

It is no wonder that the soldiers—and sometimes Sutherland—wrote caustically of settlers of this sort.

This bit of news was sent to Fort Ellis by a courier whom Lieutenant Schofield dispatched shortly after his arrival at Mammoth Hot Springs. The next day Captain Benham at Fort Ellis wired it to Gibbon, and thus broadcast the information to all the telegraph operators. Presumably, one of Howard's couriers—probably Frank Parker—picked it up in Virginia City and carried it back to the command. Sometimes news traveled quickly on the frontier—even to remote places.

When the Nez Perce forded the Yellowstone, two parties of tourists were not far away. And somewhere in this area, as has been noted, the Indians captured James C. Irwin, who had recently been discharged from the Second Cavalry. As he was traveling alone and still wore a uniform, the Indians suspected that he was a spy. Fearing that he would be killed, Irwin passed himself off as a guide for a party of tourists and this drew the attention of the hostiles to others—if they did not already know about them. Later, because of what happened, the ex-soldier was criticized for using this excuse; and the editor of the Bozeman *Times* had to point out that, under the circumstances, the man should not be blamed for trying to save his own life.

One party, consisting of four men, was that of the Earl of Dunraven.

The other group, afterward designated the "Helena party," was composed of ten persons—Charles Kenck, Andrew J. "Andy" Weikert, John Stewart (also called Jack Stuart or Stewart), Frederic J. Pfister, Richard Deitrich, Joseph H. Roberts (age 20), August Foller (age 17), Leonard Duncan, Leslie Wilkie and a Negro cook—or "caterer"—named Ben Stone.[7] Texas Jack discovered the Indians and his tourists lost no time in leaving the locality. The second group was not so prudent.

The Helena party saw the Indians at a distance but mistook them for a herd of elk or a party of mounted tourists. Two of the men went ahead to scout and soon returned with the news that they had found moccasin tracks and the hoofprints of unshod horses. It was immediately decided to "advance to the rear" but the fright soon wore off and when they reached a point about three miles above the falls on the Yellowstone, they turned up Otter Creek. Here, about a mile and a half above its mouth, they made camp in a secluded area that was well timbered. Although they thought they were well hidden, no one slept soundly and, consequently, most of them were drowsy the next day. Carpenter noted later that he could have warned them had he known of their whereabouts; and the earl's horse wrangler, Ernest Boney, recalled that Texas Jack refused to make an effort to warn them.

As Boney told the story long afterward, Texas Jack had tried a few days before—just as he had tried with the Cowan party—to buy some food from the Helena party. But they had refused to sell. Perhaps they too were short, perhaps this flamboyant extrovert irritated some of the Germans in this party and they refused to accommodate him; and this angered Texas Jack. When the Indians were discovered Boney suggested that they warn the Helena party but Jack refused, saying, "To Hell with them. We aren't going to help anyone who was so selfish with us."[8]

On Sunday, August 26th, all kept close to camp except Weikert and Wilkie, who returned to the vicinity of Mud Springs to reconnoiter. The others lounged about, some catching up on lost sleep. About noon, Ben Stone, the Negro cook, started to prepare dinner and Pfister went to gather firewood. While they were thus engaged, the Indians sent a volley into camp from close range. Pfister ran for heavy timber and escaped—arriving, as noted, at Lieutenant Schofield's camp just as he was ready to leave for Mammoth Hot Springs with Carpenter and his sisters.

Roberts was resting among the packs, sound asleep. On being awakened, he lost no time in dashing for the adjacent mountainside, closely followed by young Foller. Once away from the Indians, these two young men struck out in a westward direction across the mountains for the valley of the Madison, some thirty-five or forty miles away. This they reached three days later, having had nothing to eat but three fishes and a few berries. Here they met teamsters freighting supplies to Howard's troops, and these assisted them on their way. Near evening the next day, they reached Virginia City—in reasonably good condition except for blistered feet. Unfortunately, young Roberts' escape was not observed, and this was to be the cause of the death of another member of the party.

Ben Stone fled in such haste that he "turned three somersaults" going down a little slope. "I looked up and saw an Indian 15 or 20 yards away. I said to myself—'I'm a goner!' He fired, the ball striking near me, and I rolled over into the creek. I lay there three hours while the Indians plundered the camp. The creek was very cold and I was soon chilled through." Noting that his shaking was making the water muddy and fearing that the Indians below might see the telltale *sign*, he crawled out—so chilled and exhausted that he could hardly stand. But he soon recovered and struck out for Mammoth Hot Springs.

Stewart was asleep, and when he raised up he

saw Indians within 15 or 20 feet of me. * * * I . . . broke for the brush, . . . crossed the small creek, where I again came into a small open park, saw Charles Kenck ahead of me about 75 or 100 feet. I had not passed the creek more than 25 or 30 feet when I received the wound in my leg; about the same time I heard Charles Kenck exclaim, "Oh, My God!" I ran about 50 feet farther when I received the wound in my hip that dropped me. In a very few minutes two Indians ran past me after Kenck; soon after, I heard two shots fired and Kenck exclaim, "I'm murdered." One of the Indians then came back to me, keeping his gun pointed in my face until he got within a few feet of me. I instinctively threw up my hands and begged for my life. Setting his gun down on its butt, he asked me if I had any money. I said, "I have a little."

He then put his hand in my left hand pocket, but found nothing there, rolled me over, put his hand in my right hand pocket, where he found $263 and a silver watch. By this time the other Indian had come down, (he having remained behind to plunder the body of Kenck I suppose) and they opened my roll of money and had a great laugh over it, seeming very much elated at getting so much. They then examined my wound which, at that time, was bleeding profusely, told me they would not kill me, and walked off, leaving me lying in full view of our camp, which I saw the Indians plunder. . . . ["We lost 12 horses, 4 shot guns, 1 Henry rifle, 2 revolvers and 7 saddles; clothing, provisions and camp accoutrements."] I laid there two and a half or three hours. After they had plundered and left camp, I tried to make my way up the hill to see whether Kenck was dead or alive. I was too weak and had to abandon the trip. I then called to him at the top of my voice but could receive no answer.

With the aid of a stick, Stewart managed to hobble back to the camp where he found his overcoat, some matches and food; and, after filling his pockets, he struck out for the trail down the valley. Not far from camp, his mare, which had evidently broken away from the Indians, came up to him and permitted him to climb laboriously on her back. A few miles farther on, he came up with Ben Stone. Then, as they stopped to eat, Weikert and Wilkie rode up.

This pair had been up the valley as far as Mud Springs, and had found that the Indian camp had moved on. On their return, while in some timber, they almost rode up to some Indians who were hiding behind a fallen tree. Wheeling their horses, they fled with the bullets from the first volley whistling past their heads. Weikert commented in his journal that on the second round of shots the Indians

> were a little more successful, for they cut a crease in my shoulder blade about four inches long; did not break the bone, but splintered my shoulder blade a little. Another ball took a piece out of my gun stock. I then began hugging my horse a little closer. . . . by this time we were out of range, but . . . we could hear the balls strike the trees. * * * Just at this time my horse tripped his foot and fell. . . . I went sprawling on the ground directly in front of him of course.

Taking a quick shot at the Indians while his horse regained his feet, Weikert grabbed the horn of the saddle and vaulted into it and was off again. And the Indians, their ambush having failed, abandoned the chase.

Not finding anyone at the camp, Weikert and Wilkie also headed for the trail to Mammoth Hot Springs. As Stewart was having considerable difficulty riding bareback, and Stone was inept, Weikert and Wilkie mounted double on Stewart's mare and turned their horses over to the others. Although riding taxed the strength of the wounded man, the party pushed on all night and reached Mammoth Hot Springs about six o'clock in the morning. Here they found Lieutenant Schofield, Carpenter and his sisters, Pfister, and the Earl of Dunraven's party. Dr. Kingsley dressed Stewart's and Weikert's wounds; and Duncan and Deitrich arrived shortly afterward.

For the next three days there were no alarms—other than the phony one Texas Jack tried to promote by shooting a hole through his stirrup and then claiming he had been attacked by Nez Perce.[9] Schofield's detail and all the tourists except three of the Helena party left for Fort Ellis and Bozeman. Thus there were left at Mammoth Hot Springs, James McCartney, the frontiersman who was the proprietor of the "hotel," a man named Jake Stoner, Stone, Weikert and Deitrich. Deitrich's friends begged him to accompany them but the music teacher refused, saying that he had persuaded Roberts' parents to allow Joe to go on the trip and he could not face them until he knew what had happened to their son. Determined to find out what had happened to the three missing persons, Weikert and McCartney saddled up and headed for Otter Creek.

Meanwhile, Colonel Gibbon had ordered Doane—who had reached Fort Ellis—to take Crow scouts and De Rudio's company and scout the Park. And Colonel Sturgis, who was impatiently watching near the Crow Agency east of the Absaroka Mountains, sent three scouts to probe the headwaters of Clark Fork for signs of the Indians. The three were John J. Groff, J. S. Leonard and a Warm Springs Indian boy whom Groff had raised. As for the Nez Perce, they were half lost in the wilderness at the headwaters of the East Fork of the Yellowstone (Lamar River).

Thus, on August 31st, several things were about to happen. Deitrich, Stone and Stoner were at the "hotel"; Weikert and McCartney were on a scouting trip; and Sturgis' three scouts were coming down the Yellowstone Valley en route to Fort Ellis. And sweeping down the valley was a party of about eighteen Nez Perce bucks. Although it has been assumed that this was a raiding party, then-Lieutenant Hugh L. Scott—who was with De Rudio—has stated positively that "Chief Joseph has repeatedly told me that they intended to go out to the buffalo country . . . [via the Big Bend of the Yellowstone]. But they were diverted by seeing us in front."[10] However, there is *nothing* in the accounts of Shivley and Irwin to support this statement.

The Nez Perce got as far as Bart Henderson's ranch (about two miles north of the present town of Gardnier) before their presence was discovered. Henderson and two others had gone to the Yellowstone, about three quarters of a mile away, to fish, leaving his son and another man at the house. When the latter saw the Indians coming, they took their guns and ammunition belts and went to the river. Then all returned partway to an area of about ten acres which was liberally sprinkled with large boulders. They reached this cover just as the Indians were dismounting in front of the house—which was located on a flat, open tableland.

> Without hesitation the whites commenced shooting, and the Indian horses broke away and ran about half way to the whites. The Indians went behind the house, and for two hours the opposing parties were in this position, each firing an occasional shot. Neither could get the horses. . . . The whites at last crawled away and crossed the river in a small boat.
>
> The Indians took what they desired from the house and then set it on fire, and, taking a little band of about fifteen head of horses, went back by way of Mammoth Hot Springs.[11]

While this was going on, Doane's detachment—the number of Crow scouts having dwindled to forty-two by reason of desertions—were approaching a few miles away. Scout Jack Baronett noted the smoke and identified its location; and soon a small detail consisting of Lieutenant Scott and ten cavalrymen, with a few Crows and Baronett as a guide, rode forward to investigate. Picking up the trail of the raiders, the little force pushed on in pursuit.

At McCartney's hotel, the three men were idling away the afternoon. Finally, Deitrich went to picket a horse and Stoner to look for grouse, but the latter soon returned and warned Stone that he had seen two parties of ten men approaching slowly. Both decided to hide. Stone went up a gulch back of the hotel and after a time noted Indians both ahead and behind him. In trying to elude them, he stepped on a dry stick and an Indian immediately gave chase.

> In a very few moments I found that the Indian would cut me off as from the crash and breaking of twigs I knew he was close to me. I thought I was a dead man. * * * Just then I chanced to run under a tree with low branches. I took hold of the branches and hoisted myself in, without any supposition of saving my life. I had no more than got into the tree, before an Indian on horseback dashed under it, gazing in every direction for me. . . .

It was a narrow escape, and the Negro stayed in the tree for a couple of hours before attempting to move. The next summer, the Indian who chased Stone told McDonald, "I just wanted his scalp: colored men's hair is good medicine for sore ears."

Stone worked his way along in the timber until night came, and then he came out and headed for Henderson's ranch where he unwittingly walked into Doane's camp and was momentarily terrified when he was apprehended by a Crow scout. Here he learned that when Scott's little detail rode up to the door of the hotel about 4 P.M. they found Deitrich's body near the doorway, still warm, with a bullet hole through his heart. Not long after the picket *captured* Stone, Weikert and McCartney came into camp—afoot.

They had found Kenck's body about 300 yards from the camp, bullet holes through his head and abdomen, and his pockets empty except for a watch that had been overlooked. The remains were buried on the spot and, finding no sign of the two missing boys, the men packed up what was left at the pilfered camp and prepared to return the next morning. As they started to make camp, McCartney became uneasy so they saddled up and started on. Soon Weikert saw an Indian cross an open glade. This added a note of urgency, and the two rode until long after midnight.

In the morning, when within about eighteen miles of the hotel, they suddenly discovered a party of eighteen Indians not over two hundred yards away. The only cover near was a patch of brush about a mile away. According to Weikert's journal:

> We had a lively race for a mile, for the Indians were firing at us all the time and trying to head us off from the brush. * * * We rode together for some time, then Mack started straight up the hill for the brush. I kept out on the hillside so as to give my horse a better chance. The Indians got off their horses and kept right behind a reef of rocks, so we had a rather poor chance to return fire. . . . They soon put a ball into my horse and he stopped. . . . I knew that something was wrong, so got off quick . . . [and] made all possible speed for the brush. . . . About this time Mack's horse commenced bucking (the saddle had got back on his rump), and bucked him off, and then ran out to where I was . . . with the saddle under [his belly]. . . .

As Weikert was unable to catch the horse, both men dove into the brush, and the Indians, unwilling to attack under unfavorable conditions, withdrew.

There was nothing to do but walk back, and they reached the hotel after dark. Seeing no signs of life, they called out.

> We received no answer so we went into the house, struck a match and lit a piece of candle we found lying on the table. We both turned around about the same time and discovered Dietrich lying on the floor dead. . . . we searched for the others but discovered none. . . . * * * Mack hunted around for something to eat, but found nothing, so we concluded to go down the river to the next ranch which was seven miles away.

The next day they buried Deitrich in "an old bath tub" and six weeks later Weikert made a trip from Helena in a wagon and brought back the two bodies—"This was about as lonely a ride as I ever took. Two dead men in a wagon . . . for over two hundred miles."

Sometime during this foray, the raiders met Sturgis' three scouts coming down the trail near the head of Little Blacktail Creek. This time their ambush was more successful. At the first volley, the Indian boy fell and Groff was hit in the neck. The white men ran to an outcrop of rock nearby—that was out of sight of the boy—and exchanged a few shots with the Indians. Again, the raiders abandoned the attack and rode on. Apparently, they crossed the Yellowstone River on Baronett's Bridge and then set it afire.

Night soon came and the scouts went on without searching for the Indian boy. The next day they met Doane's detachment, to whom they told their story and then continued on to Fort Ellis. Jack Baronett and another man went to the site of the attack and hunted for the missing boy. They found that he had recovered consciousness and crawled for about half a mile. Then they lost the trail near the creek and no further trace of him was ever found. At Fort Ellis, Groff and Leonard were given dispatches for Sturgis, and the two set out to retrace their steps.[12] This time they never reached their destination. Presumably, the Nez Perce killed them somewhere in the Clark Fork wilderness; and their loss was keenly felt by Colonel Sturgis who was sorely in need of the information they were carrying.

21

An Unguarded Gateway

⪼⪼⪼⪼⪼⪼⪻⪻⪻⪻⪻⪻ When Howard's troops stopped be-
side Henry Lake, Fisher, with his Bannocks and a few white scouts, set out
on the fresh trail of the hostiles. Apparently believing that the general
would bring his men up and engage the Indians when he located them, the
scout drove hard until he overtook them. Then he dogged their heels, reporting their whereabouts.[1]

Charles Mann stayed with him until he began to scout on the eastern
side of the Yellowstone River. Then, on August 28th, having spent four
days in a fruitless search for members of the Cowan party, he went back
with a courier to the command. The day after the Nez Perce raid down the
Yellowstone, Fisher picked up Irwin. Having become tired of clearing trail
for the Indians, the ex-soldier asked Shivley to identify a nearby creek.
Then he requested permission to get a drink—and never returned. Although the Indians had not minded his escaping, Poker Joe told Shivley
that "he would get heap mad" if he tried the same trick. Irwin stayed
overnight with Fisher and then he, too, left for the troops. Here he met

Sutherland whom he told that Joseph had been "reduced to the ranks" and now performed "squaw labor" about the camp. This misconception the reporter interpreted to mean that Poker Joe was now the leader in command which, of course, he was not.[2]

Fisher had hardly left the column before he began to have trouble with the Bannocks. They had apparently entered the campaign expecting to scoop up considerable plunder in a short time but when face to face with the realities they had little stomach for the chase. On the evening of the day they left Henry Lake, Fisher noted that "we number eighty-two all told"—including a few white scouts. Two days later "we number just forty now all told," and he tried to persuade these to "stand by" him. Subsequent entries in his journal show that the failure to find many ponies, coupled with scanty fare, was not conductive to high morale.

On the day the scouts crossed the Yellowstone to the campsite at which Carpenter and his sisters had been released, Howard's men resumed their march. As noted, they soon picked up Oldham and Cowan and, on the evening of the day Fisher released most of his Bannocks, they camped at the foot of a steep mountain slope at the head of (now) Nez Perce Creek. As it was impossible to take the wagons up the Indian trail, the soldiers moved to the top of the plateau the next day while Spurgeon's "skillets" took up the task of building a passable road.

On the morning this construction work started, it was discovered that about forty horses belonging to the civilians were missing. Howard recalled:

> The quartermaster's clerk [a civilian named Bonny], encountering some Bannock scouts, who had suspiciously lingered in the rear, was treated to some very rough language by them. I sent at once a small detachment of mounted soldiers, who soon returned to camp with ten of the Indian scouts as prisoners.
>
> Their leader, a half-breed [Jo. Rainey], and brother to the Rainé who had desired to murder old George and Captain John, was cross and mutinous in his manner and language. I had them all disarmed, and their handsome horses and rifles taken from them. I found also, on inquiry, that all the Bannock scouts, except one or two had deserted the brave Fisher [sic—he had released 22], and had come back to the troops, and were planning to return to Fort Hall.[3]

Not having been able to make a rich haul of Nez Perce ponies, the Bannocks had not been particular whose horses they acquired. But the theft backfired. Soon an old chief came to the general, protested their innocence, and begged that the prisoners be freed. Howard countered by saying that Indians were good at hunting strayed animals and that he would release his captives as soon as the missing horses were brought in. In a few hours about half of the missing animals galloped into camp and—after the chief found that Howard was obdurate—the remainder came into camp that night. Howard then released all the hostages except Rainé.

It took the "skillets" a day and a half to construct a passable trail up the mountain. Henry Buck remembered that the teams had to be doubled and even then it was a slow, laborious climb, "only a few feet . . . at a hitch," with men walking alongside with guy ropes attached to the tops of the wagons to keep them from upsetting in the sideling places. By the time all were at the top, two and three-quarter days had been expended in going about three miles. From this point on, the train did not encounter serious difficulties until it reached the edge of the elevation overlooking the valley of the Yellowstone at a point a few miles above the falls. Here they came to a very steep slope some five hundred feet high that was moderately timbered with lodgepole pine. Someone suggested that they prepare a slide—the slope being "as steep as the roof of an ordinary house"—and go down like a beaver.

Buck recalled that it did not take long to clear a roadway, but negotiating the "slide" was another matter.

> We had with us a very large rope—one hundred feet long—for emergency cases. . . . * * * One end of the rope was fastened to the hind axle of my wagon [and] then two turns were made around a substantial tree, with several men holding on to the end of the rope so that the wagon could not get away, they payed it out as fast as the descent was made and, with the aid of a short rope made fast to the hind axle and securely tied to another tree, we then loosened the long rope and came down and made another two turns around a nearby tree and was ready for the second drive; thence a third and so on until the bottom was reached in safety.[4]

This procedure was repeated with each wagon until the entire train reached the valley. In the snubbing process, the rope damaged the bark of the trees and these rope burns were plainly visible as long as the trees remained intact; and the spot was dubbed Spurgeon's Beaver Slide.

Here the troops, having marched by the way of the Indian trail to the ford of the Yellowstone, joined the train. As it was now obvious that it was out of the question to try to move the train with the column, the necessary goods were transferred to the pack train and Captain Spurgeon was directed to conduct the wagons to Fort Ellis and pay off the teamsters. This was accomplished—with more difficulty—during the first two weeks of September.

Meanwhile, the Nez Perce—with Fisher and a few scouts close behind—

had been in difficulty. From the ford below Yellowstone Lake they had gone eastward up Pelican Creek, over Mist Creek Pass, and then down Mist Creek to the head of the Lamar River. Of the Mist Creek area, Fisher wrote:

> *Monday,* [September] 3. We broke camp at daylight and were off on the trail, following it through the roughest canyon I ever undertook to pass through. About every foot of it was obstructed with dead and fallen timber and huge blocks of granite that had fallen from its sides. We found plenty of dead and crippled horses that had been left by the enemy. They evidently had a hard time getting through this place for the trees and logs were smeared with blood from their horses.[5]

When they were camped beside the Yellowstone River, Shivley had pointed out the general route to the head of the "Stinking river" (Shoshone River). However, "there was a Snake chief . . . with a few men along, who said that he had now found the old Snake trail and they would follow that." So the old prospector was sent back to help clear trail and the Indians, relying on the "Snake chief," proceeded to get lost. Shivley saw that, instead of crossing the divide to the headwaters of the Shoshone River, they were merely circling around to the headwaters of the east fork of the Yellowstone—but he said nothing. Two days later, when they discovered they were lost, the council convened, there was "heap talk," and Shivley was reinstated as guide.

Fisher's journal indicates clearly that the Nez Perce went down Lamar River almost to the mouth of Soda Butte Creek and then turned southeastward up the divide between Cache and Calfee creeks. An old buffalo and Bannock trail follows an easy route up this ridge to the vicinity of Canoe Lake, a small body of water near the divide between Lamar River and Clark Fork. From this vantage point the Indians were able to look eastward toward the plains of the Crow country; and somewhere in this area Shivley made his escape. It had rained during that afternoon, and the prospector erected a good shelter for the night under some trees—away from Poker Joe. Then he turned in "with his boots on." When it became dark, he took a bearing from the "Soda Buttes and the North Star" and headed for Baronett's Bridge which he reached the next evening. Subsisting on scraps found at the bridge, Mammoth Hot Springs and the ruins of Henderson's ranch, he made his way down the valley of the Yellowstone and, finally, to Fort Ellis where he told his strange story to Captain Benham.

Where the Nez Perce went after Shivley left them is a matter of conjecture. Howard and the troops picked up the trail again at the mouth of Crandall Creek; and it is highly probable that the Indians continued to follow the old Bannock Trail. This went over the divide near Canoe Lake and down an almost-precipitous slope to the head of Timber Creek, a tributary of Crandall Creek. The trail down this valley was difficult but not excessively so, and it was the most direct of the three available to them from the point where their guide escaped.

Up to this point, the campaign had been a relatively simple affair. But now the threads begin to tangle and the records do not provide a satisfactory answer to the riddle. In his original instructions, General Sherman had directed Howard to follow the Nez Perce *regardless* of where they went—directions that were repeated on two other occasions. And it has been noted that when Howard entered the Department of Dakota, he was the ranking officer within the Department—a factor which had the potential of creating an explosive situation. This did not give Howard the authority to issue orders to units under General Terry's command but—*once they became involved in the campaign in his proximity*—he assumed the responsibility for directing their use in the common cause.

When he ordered Captain Cushing's detachment to Fort Ellis and thence to Crow Agency, Howard directed the captain to retain Norwood's company so that he might have sufficient strength to deal with any stray Indians he might meet. At the end of the second day's march from Henry Lake, the general dispatched a courier with this message:

To Commanding Officer, *Fort Ellis, Mont.*

Please communicate with officer in Command Seventh Cavalry, probably Colonel Sturgis. News of the Indians crossing the Yellowstone, near Mud Springs, below Sulphur Hills, came from two of the party of nine from Helena thought to be killed there Sunday last. It is probable that the Indians will go by Clark's Fork, or make a wider detour, if bothered by troops, in order to reach the Yellowstone again below. I do not think they will go to Wind River country unless forced in that direction. I shall pursue their trail, and wish Cushing, with his command, to press out beyond Crow Agency, communicating with Colonel Sturgis, or joining him if he deems best. Sorry to have Norwood detached [from me], for Cushing's command must be kept large enough to take care of itself, protect my supplies, and hinder Indians from going northward if he meets them. So inform Colonel Gibbon. * * * [6]

Cushing reached Fort Ellis on the day this dispatch was written (August 29th), turned the sick and disabled men over to the post hospital, and prepared to leave for the Crow Agency two days later.

Meanwhile another move was taking form. Lieutenant Colonel Charles C. Gilbert, the commanding officer at Camp Baker (later Fort Logan), went to Helena on August 27th to check a contract for flour—*at the time* General Sherman visited this city and Fort Shaw. Within forty-eight hours after reaching the capital—*ostensibly to verify a contract*—he had in his possession a letter which read:

Headquarters Army of the United States
Helena, Montana, August 29, 1877

GENERAL O. O. HOWARD
Commanding Department of the Columbia in the Field
Head of Yellowstone

GENERAL:

I have received from General Sheridan the dispatch of which the enclosed is a copy. You will perceive that he has three small forces east of the mountains to receive the Nez Perces when they issue from the mountains.

1st. General Sturgis, with six companies Clark's Fork,

2nd. Major Hart, with five companies and a hundred scouts, on Stinking Water, and,

3rd. General Merritt, with ten companies at Camp Brown

Your's, as the pursuing force requires great patience, but not much chance of a fight. Tomorrow I start for Missoula and Walla Walla. There are many things in your department about which I would like to consult you, and I will feel your absence much. Really I see not much reason for your commanding a department after having driven the hostile Indians out of your department across Montana, and into General Sheridan's command. I find (General) Lieutenant Colonel C. C. Gilbert here who has served long in this Territory, and is familiar with the Indians and the country in which they have taken refuge. I don't want to order you back to Oregon, but I do say that you can, with perfect propriety, return to your command, leaving the troops to continue till the Nez Perces have been destroyed or captured, and I authorize you to transfer to him, Lieutenant Colonel Gilbert, your command, in the field, and to overtake me en route, or in your department. * * *

I am, with great respect,
Your friend
W. T. SHERMAN
General[7]

The general's wish to have Howard present when he inspected the latter's department is understandable. But, in view of the chiding Sherman had given Howard shortly before about turning his command over to a younger, more vigorous officer, these instructions directing an *older* officer to take over are most interesting. Did the idea really originate with

Sherman—or did Gilbert connive for an assignment which would permit him to go "glory-hunting"? The latter may be the correct answer.

Lieutenant Doane—obviously to avoid being absorbed by Sturgis—had gone to Fort Ellis and, while there, had been directed by Colonel Gibbon to scout up the Yellowstone Valley and try to locate the Indians. It was this operation which was in progress when the raiders swept down the valley as far as Henderson's ranch. Apparently, the lieutenant was quickly notified of Gilbert's assignment; and on September 1st he sent a message to Howard which provided the general with a tip as to what was afoot:

> The enclosed letter received by me last evening will need no explana-
> tion. I am here with one Co 7th Cavalry about 30 citizens, and 42
> Crow scouts. Camped at a burning ranch, fired by the Nez-Percés
> yesterday Will await Col. Gilbert here but to day am sending you this
> to anticipate him. Please return a courier with the bearer of this (who
> may be able to find you to-night) I will look for an answer to morrow
> night. * * *
> Gen Sturgis on Aug 29th was at Crow Agency. his command of 450
> [sic—about 360] men, and Crow scouts besides, should be on Clarks
> Fork about Heart Mt. but I fear he is *not* there. * * * 8

Howard, utilizing the intelligence brought by Irwin, had the ex-cavalry-man guide him directly to Baronett's Bridge thus saving, according to his estimate, two days' marching. Here there was a delay of about three hours while the damage to the eastern end of the structure, caused by a fire set by the raiding party, was repaired. Jack Baronett's cabin, which was nearby, was appraised at $300 and then sacrificed to secure the necessary timbers. Now the troops were on the trail which connected Clark Fork Mines with Bozeman. Although the general referred to the tiny settlement by this name, it was soon after known as Cooke City; and its principal activities centered around the New Galena Smelting Works and the nearby mines. Legend has it that the Works were partly burned by raiders but the Bozeman papers make no mention of any damage, nor did Howard, Sutherland or three officers with the command in writing home. It was in this locality that Howard engaged a prospector named George Houston for a guide, and enlisted about twenty others as scouts in a body called the "Yellowstone Scouts," perhaps to distinguish them from the Idaho men led by "Rube" Robbins. Houston was an intelligent, genial gentleman and his extensive knowledge of the country was to prove most helpful.

As the troops passed up the valley of the East Fork of the Yellowstone (Lamar River), Fisher and the remnant of his force—now "an even dozen" in number—left the Nez Perce Trail when the Indians headed toward the Yellowstone-Clark Fork divide. The scout had become "tired of trying to get the soldiers and the hostiles together" and had concluded that "'Uncle Sam's' boys are too slow for this business." Following down the Lamar a few miles, he picked up the trail of the troops at the mouth of Soda Butte Creek and overtook them the next morning near the Clark Fork Mines. The Indians and the troops were now following routes which would soon converge—but the former still held the lead in the race.

At Fort Ellis, Norwood's company was at first ordered to delay and refit, and then was "completely detached" from the detachment of Fourth Artillery. When Gilbert arrived, he informed Captain Cushing that he "was to constitute a part of the *garrison* at Fort Ellis, to be used for escort duty." Although Cushing was irked, he accepted the situation without quibbling. However, five days after Gilbert's departure—when it became apparent "no one knew anything as to what was going on"—he disregarded the lieutenant colonel's instructions and headed for Crow Agency with supplies as Howard had originally ordered him to do.[9] En route, he picked up a train of five wagons with supplies for Sturgis; and Lieutenant Adams trailed along a day's march behind with the replacement animals. As it turned out, it was indeed fortunate that Cushing disregarded Gilbert's orders, for the essential supplies arrived barely in time for Howard's troops.

As for Gilbert, if he was really glory-hunting, he made a dismal failure of his opportunity. Taking Norwood's company, the lieutenant colonel reached Doane and De Rudio the day after Doane had alerted Howard of his coming. According to Lieutenant Scott, "Doane begged him with tears in his eyes" to proceed up the Yellowstone and make a junction with Howard. But Gilbert, fearing that Indians might be in front of him, backtracked down the Yellowstone to Tom Miner's Creek which he then followed westward to the headwaters of the Gallatin and thence to the Lower Geyser Basin—where he landed on Howard's trail. Now hopelessly in the rear, this infantry officer forced his two companies of cavalry at twice the speed Howard was traveling—Scott later accused him of having "no idea of marching cavalry." By the time he reached Baronett's Bridge, many of the horses were almost exhausted. Taking Jack Baronett as a guide and the best of the animals, Gilbert continued his futile chase. When he reached Crow Agency on September 15th and found that Howard had been provided with supplies and fresh animals, he gave up and turned westward toward Fort Ellis. By this time all that remained of two companies numbering approximately 100 men were "about 20 officers and enlisted men." Furthermore, Howard—whom Cushing had informed about Sherman's letter—was apparently in no mood to give Gilbert an opportunity to take over his command.

While this farce was being enacted in his rear, Howard was trailing the

Nez Perce in the Absaroka Mountains. From the vicinity of the Clark Fork Mines, Howard sent Robbins and most of the scouts to follow directly on the trail of the Indians while he had Houston guide the column over the divide at the head of Soda Butte Creek and into the head of Clark Fork Valley by way of an old Indian trail. This route, known as Lodge Pole Trail, followed down the Clark Fork and, eventually, reached the plains east of the Absaroka Mountains. At the mouth of Crandall Creek, Houston and Fisher picked up the trail of the Nez Perce, and the latter estimated that the Indians were about two days ahead. Although Howard was to state later that he sent dispatches to Sturgis on various occasions, these references are vague and indefinite. However, of September 7th at the mouth of Crandall Creek, Sutherland wrote:

> We are here met by three scouts from General Sturgis [probably the French half-breed named Roque, a prospector and Civil War veteran named Siebert, and a Crow Indian] conveying news to the miners at the smelting furnace of the proximity of the Nez Perces, who informed us that Custer's old regiment, the Seventh Cavalry, was in the vicinity of Heart Mountain, on the east side of the great divide, waiting for the exit of the Indians from the mountains. This was very encouraging and two of the men were sent back that very night to General Sturgis to inform him of our position and the probability of our being able to drive the Indians upon him the next day or two after. Unfortunately the couriers did not reach Sturgis. . . .[10]

The campaign was now rapidly approaching the stage in which Sheridan felt success could be achieved. There were two exits from the Absaroka Mountains to the plains—the narrow valleys of Clark Fork and the North Fork of the Stinking Water (Shoshone) River—and troops could block these openings quite effectively. To this end, Sturgis and his six companies had been moved from Crow Agency to the narrow opening of Clark Fork Canyon where he occupied a position not unlike that of a cork in the mouth of a bottle. The task of sealing off the outlet of the Stinking Water was assigned to Colonel Wesley Merritt and the Fifth Cavalry.

Merritt's regiment had been somewhat scattered during the summer. Three companies under Major Verling K. Hart had been on picket duty on the northeastern slope of the Big Horn Mountains most of the summer, and these had been joined in June by "L" Company—a detachment detailed to escort Sheridan and other officers on a hunting trip into this area. Not only was the Fifth scattered at various posts, but some had been on guard duty in the Midwest during the labor troubles—which difficulties had taken Terry to New York, Crook to Chicago and Merritt to Omaha.

When the time came to order the troops out, Merritt and his staff had already gone to Camp Brown, which was slightly over 100 miles south of the point where the force was now desired. However, Crook was still in Chicago instead of at his headquarters in Omaha, and Terry had not been released from his duties in New York.

On August 27th, Colonel Gibbon forwarded Lieutenant Schofield's report that the Nez Perce had crossed the Yellowstone, and Sheridan began to move his chessmen. Two days later, the Division commander directed Crook's adjutant to "send the five companies of the Fifth (5) Cavalry, and Company "K" Third Cavalry to Camp Brown to report to Colonel Merritt. This move should be made as speedily as possible. * * *"11 And on the following day he advised that Crook was on his way from Chicago, and that the latter wished his aide, Lieutenant John G. Bourke, to meet him in Green River, Wyoming. Also: "If Clark can go with the scouts I would be delighted"—Ben Clark being a plainsman whom Sheridan trusted.

In another telegram, Sheridan directed that the adjutant order Major Hart's battalion to circle the northern end of the Big Horn Mountains "and make for the Stinking Water in the direction of Cedar Mountain, or some point nearer the Big Horn [River] if you deem it best. * * * You will be expected to make the greatest possible exertion to accomplish the above named purpose, and if you should get on the . . . [Nez Perce] trail do not give it up until you overtake them. . . . At this great distance I cannot give you any particular instructions. . . ."12

This order would go by telegraph to Fort Fetterman on the Platte River and then, by courier, at least 170 miles up the Bozeman Trail to Hart's camp. Still another message was sent to Terry's headquarters directing that Colonel Nelson A. Miles be given a summary of the situation and orders to issue supplies to Hart should the latter come by Post No. 2, then under construction at the junction of the Big Horn and Little Big Horn rivers. This message would be telegraphed to Bismarck and then carried by a messenger upwards of 300 miles to the Tongue River Cantonment. Communication with troops in the field was not a simple matter.

When part of Merritt's troops were unloaded from a troop train in Green River, Wyoming, a hawk-eyed reporter saw them. Although now nameless, he obviously had been a soldier and, sensing that something of interest was under way, he secured a horse and trailed along. The single dispatch from his pencil which the New York *Herald* printed was colorful and—probably—highly accurate.

Camp Brown, located on the Little Wind River, was a small post intended as a sort of police station on the Wind River Reservation. Washakie's band of Shoshones was camped in the valley close by.

General Crook arrived at the post by stage on the evening of the 7th inst., and remained over until the morning of Sunday, the 9th, during which time, no doubt, the plan of General Merritt's campaign was finally determined upon. About one hundred of the warriors of Washakie's village assembled on the parade ground on Saturday afternoon, where they squatted in a large circle. They were mostly attired in red and green blankets, worn with the dignified air of a Roman Senator. Most had feathers in their hats or hair, and some of the dandies of the tribe were gorgeous, with bead embroidery on buckskins. Washakie himself was an exception to this. He was plainly clad in a grey blouse, and looked fat, homely, and good natured. He addressed the assembled circle in a war speech, which seemed to make little impression on the stolid-looking faces around, but nevertheless all enrolled themselves for the expedition.[13] Washakie was presented by General Crook with a silken guidon or battle flag, which gratified the old gentleman very much. He held it unfurled while Lieutenant [Hoel S.] Bishop, Fifth Cavalry took down the names of the warriors who were to follow it [under his command]. . . .

The next morning, (Sunday, the 9th instant) the command moved out on the trail northward from Camp Brown, carrying thirty days rations in army wagons.[14]

The force consisted of Colonel Merritt, three staff officers, five companies of the Fifth and one company of the Third Cavalry Regiment.

The companies average fifty-five men, making a total of officers and men of about four hundred. The Shoshone company numbers eighty-four, while, if the teamsters are included, the total strength of the Wind River column will amount to five hundred men.

Although Merritt and his officers were tight-lipped about their destination, the correspondent suspected that "Joseph therefore must be the objective of the expedition."

Obviously, this reporter enjoyed being back with troops again for he wrote:

Five hundred men made a large war party . . ., and quite an imposing sight . . . as they seek their way, now over sagebrush desert, now along the valley bottoms through turbid streams swollen by recent rains, and again leading their horses up hill and down in the broken country bordering the mountains; the Indian company swarming along in an elongated tumultuous mass with the battle flag fluttering in advance, the cavalry gliding along snakelike and showing the glitter of its scales as a sun glimpse is reflected from the barrel of a carbine or the polished surface of a trumpet.

Like an old campaigner, he endured the miseries of rain and mud with an even temper when, on the evening of the third day after leaving Camp Brown, a rainstorm broke over the camp and then continued most of the following day while the column struggled to climb the southern slope of the Owl Creek Range. And he noted that scarcely had the evening campfires been lighted

> when the rain increased to a torrent and a cloud settled around them thick and white—a highland mist which obliterated every object from sight except one's own camp fire.
>
> Under such circumstances your correspondent writes, and as he does not care to dwell on the miseries of life on paper while enduring them de facto he will snuggle under his damp blankets and pray that the clouds may lift soon. . . .

Thus, on September 12th, Merritt's column camped in the mud when about halfway to their destination. About 120 miles north of them, some of Howard's men also camped in mud and rain—but without a correspondent to describe the tired horses and the cavalrymen with their boots full of water.

Hart, with his battalion and a band of Sioux and Arapahoe scouts, joined Merritt in the valley of the Stinking Water on the 18th of September. Not finding any indications of the Nez Perce, they scouted northward to the mouth of Clark Fork Canyon where *sign*—plain and disheartening—told them that the quarry was gone. This movement had started too late, for on the day Merritt's troops had marched from Camp Brown, the Nez Perce were nearly to the mouth of Clark Fork Canyon. On September 25th, Sheridan telegraphed Crook's adjutant that a courier should be sent with orders for Merritt to return unless the colonel saw some good reason for doing otherwise.

During the ten days Sturgis spent near the Crow Agency, he had considerable difficulty in securing competent scouts. The Crows were not anxious to be drawn into the struggle on either side; and shortly after the Nez Perce camp crossed the Yellowstone River, Poker Joe told Shivley and Irwin that four emissaries had been sent to try to persuade the Absaroka to assist them in fighting the troops. From the standpoint of the hostiles, this was a reasonable request, for in times past they had helped the Crows fight the Sioux. Thomas Leforge, a trustworthy Crow squaw man, told his biographer:

> I met Looking Glass . . . and talked with him. * * * . . . he was assured of my sadness of heart because of their distress and was promised whatever influence I might have among the Crows would be

used toward dissuading them from giving their aid in intercepting him and his people. . . . Most of the Crows felt the same way. Many of them, though, affected to array themselves against the Nez Perces, but in reality their warlike operations were restricted to the capture of ponies.[15]

However, George W. Frost, their newly appointed agent who probably did not know their temper as well as Leforge, reported that they were "thoroughly loyal"; and that, as they feared the Nez Perce might raid the agency for their annuities, "the prospect of capturing their fine ponies makes them willing to fight their former friends."

This made the problem of securing scouts difficult. Sturgis was able to hire J. J. Groff, J. S. Leonard and their Indian companion to scout the headwaters of Clark Fork. As noted, this trio ran into trouble in the Yellowstone Park and, apparently, neither of the survivors got back to the colonel. He also secured the services of six Crows and a "Frenchman" named Rook or Roque, the latter probably being one of the trio who met Howard at the mouth of Crandall Creek. These seven were dispatched to scout the country in the vicinity of the mouth of Clark Fork Canyon and the Stinking Water.

When Sturgis left the Agency, Frost promised to send additional Crows if possible. Eventually about thirty arrived, a few at a time, but these were considered "altogether worthless" as they did not have a leader. On reaching Clark Fork Canyon and "finding that no trail could possibly lead through it," the colonel decided to march on to the Stinking Water. When he was ready to start, the Frenchman and his little party came in (having left the Agency ten days before) and reported that they had been as far south as the Stinking Water and had seen no *sign*. Most of the Absaroka now left for the Agency and Sturgis sent Roque, a miner named Siebert ("whom we had found prospecting in the mountains and who had been an officer . . . under me" during the Civil War) and a Crow to take a message to the miners in the mountains. Somehow this trio escaped being picked up by the Nez Perce and, as noted, met Howard's column at the mouth of Crandall Creek—but never got back. On the 6th of September, Sturgis moved from his camp at the mouth of Clark Fork Canyon "in the direction of Hart Mountain" for the valley of the Stinking Water.

In his official report, the colonel apparently tried to present an explanation that would not reflect too much discredit upon himself and, in so doing, stretched the truth almost to the breaking point. He stated that he had been told that the distance from Clark Fork to Stinking Water was about twenty miles whereas it was *forty-eight* miles, and that the terrain encountered on the first day's march (September 6th) was "totally impracticable for wagons and artillery." Also, he noted that the Crows were not familiar with the country. The facts were that the actual distance between the two points is *twenty-six* miles; the terrain was difficult but not impassable; and the Crows undoubtedly were familiar with the country except, possibly, the *headwaters* of Clark Fork. Obviously, Roque, Siebert and their Crow companion knew of Lodge Pole Trail up Clark Fork even though the canyon—as Sturgis noted—is blocked a few miles above its mouth. However, this is an area which must be seen to be understood and fully appreciated.

Clark Fork issues from the Absaroka Mountains in a V-shaped opening having a valley floor of something less than a half mile in width. This narrow valley is flanked on either side by practically impassable rocky slopes which rise very steeply to elevations of 6,000 feet above the river. About six miles above the mouth of the canyon, this narrow valley gives way to a very narrow gorge and the stream becomes impassable to both man and beast. This box canyon, with almost vertical walls of rock which rise to heights of 800 feet, extends up the valley for approximately twelve miles—or to within a mile or two of the mouth of Crandall Creek. Below this creek, the trail followed the bench between the foot of the mountains and the southern side of the gorge. Farther down, it circled the mouths of both Sunlight and Dead Indian creeks—also impassable—and climbed to the southern rim of the canyon by way of an old game trail that went up the steep side of an elevation now called Dead Indian Hill. Although the Absaroka Range ends abruptly about six miles to the eastward, the trail angled southeastward across the edge of the range, reaching the Stinking Water and the Big Horn Basin just west of where the city of Cody now stands.

In attempting to go to the Stinking Water, Sturgis first marched about ten miles south of the mouth of the canyon and went into camp at the northern edge of the base of Heart Mountain. From this point, he sent two scouts—probably prospectors with whom the area was swarming—to probe the country to the south. On the morning of the second day (September 8th), two small parties under Lieutenants Luther R. Hare and Alfred M. Fuller were detailed to make a reconnaissance.[16] Apparently, Hare went southward up the saddle between Heart Mountain and the edge of the Absarokas. "About sixteen miles out"—according to Sturgis— this party found the scouts sent out the previous day. One was dead and the other was seriously wounded and *sign* indicated that they had been jumped by about thirty Indians. Leaving the wounded man beside water, to be picked up the next day, this detail returned to camp about midafternoon. Fuller returned shortly afterward. "When about 18 miles out he had seen from the top of a high mountain what appeared to be the hostiles, moving on the Stinking River Trail. . . ." Again the colonel's report is confusing. Fuller may have seen these Indians from either Pat O'Hara Creek or Rattlesnake Mountain—not over nine or twelve miles from camp.

Sturgis ordered his wagons and artillery to return to Crow Agency, and set out at once to hunt for the Indians. "We marched 16 miles that night, and reached the point at which the trail debouches on the Stinking River, the next morning, the distance being about 48 miles." Apparently, the Seventh Cavalry did reach the junction of the trail and the Stinking Water—but where and how far the troops traveled appears to be something of a mystery.

That night, as Howard's troops went into camp at the foot of Dead Indian Hill, Fisher wrote in his journal:

> General Howard told me that General Sturgis, with about six hundred cavalry, is supposed to be within twenty miles of us and on the other side of the enemy; so we expect a fight to-morrow. Wilbur's scouts said that they saw the Indians leave the mountain where the trail crosses over it, about a mile from here. A strong guard was put out to-night. We have a steep hill to go up in the morning and must pass through a narrow cut at its summit. The boys are apprehensive that we will get a game there.[17]

There were signs that the Nez Perce were not far ahead, for as the men were going into camp a scout discovered a wounded Nez Perce nearby and killed him.

What the hostiles did about eight miles from the mouth of Clark Fork Canyon constituted a brilliant maneuver, and it is particularly noteworthy because it was probably improvised on the spot without the benefit of prior knowledge of the terrain. When the Nez Perce scouts reached the top of the southern rim of Clark Fork Canyon, they undoubtedly stopped to study the country before them. It is likely that some climbed to the nearby top of Dead Indian Hill, a point some 800 feet higher than the "cut" where the trail topped out. From this point they saw the prairies they had come so far to find—a scant six miles distant at the foot of the Absaroka Range. To the east, sixty miles away across the brown prairie, was the dark line of the Big Horn Mountains. Far to the northeast were the Prior Mountains and on the western side of them was the broad valley of Clark Fork leading straight to the Yellowstone River—all landmarks some of them had seen on previous occasions.

To reach the prairies just ahead, the camp must come down large expanses of smooth, grass-covered mountainside where it, and its large herd of horses, could be seen for miles by anyone in the country ahead. Almost at their feet lay the head of the valley of Pat O'Hara Creek and the northern slopes of Heart Mountain where Sturgis was camped—probably *not over ten miles away!* There can be but little doubt that they saw this camp; and if they did not the scouting party that jumped the two scouts and probed at the bivouac of the troops that night discovered the presence of the soldiers not long afterward. Now it was necessary to conceal their presence and dodge the troopers just in front of them, and also, if possible, do something to delay the force that was dogging their heels.

It was Fisher who unraveled the *sign* which they left—*sign* that not only told what they did but revealed *why* they did it. He noted that

> from the top of the divide, the enemy's trail bore off towards the southeast, which direction . . . would take them onto the Stinkingwater. . . . After leaving the summit the enemy followed the trail towards the Stinkingwater about two miles [sic—about a mile?], and then attempted to elude pursuit by concealing their trail. To do this, the hostiles "milled," drove their ponies around in every direction, when, instead of going out of the basin in the direction they had been traveling and across an open plain [sic—mountainside] they turned short off to the north, passing along the steep side of the mountain through timber for several miles * * * [when they went] through a very narrow and rocky canon down to Clark's Fork. . . .[18]

Like Clark Fork Canyon, this area must also be seen to be fully appreciated.

Within a half mile of the point where the trail crossed the rim of the canyon, a four-mile-long drainageway—now called Dead Indian Gulch—starts which circles the southern and eastern sides of Dead Indian Hill, and then empties into Clark Fork just below the end of the previously noted impassable gorge. This is a deeply incised drainageway and the slopes which come down to it on the southern and eastern sides are of ample height to completely hide from view—from anyone to the east or south—all activity within its basin. Here, in a meadow beside the trail, Fisher has stated that they "milled" their herd, and then drove it into the pines on the "mountainside" which faces the south side of Dead Indian Hill—areas which are probably unchanged today. Now, completely screened by a friendly slope and hidden in a moderately thick stand of pine, the Nez Perce worked their way down to the river.

Sturgis' camp—only ten or twelve miles from the point where Clark Fork issued from the mountains—must have been uncomfortably close. According to one of Howard's aides—who probably told the unflattering truth on this occasion—the Indians sent a decoy party to mislead the colonel and make him think they were headed for the Stinking Water.[19] This was probably the party reported by Lieutenant Fuller. Be that as it may, the maneuver was highly successful and the troops ended up twenty-six miles from where they should have been.

In the six miles between Dead Indian Hill and the mouth of the canyon, there is but one place where a herd of horses could be taken down the precipitous slopes to the river. That place is Dead Indian Gulch. Its gradient is steep throughout its entire extent and, in some geologic age long past, it ended in a waterfall on the canyon wall. With the passing of time, erosion cut a *narrow*, vertical-sided slit in the solid rock so that the bed of the gulch now reached the valley floor; but in so doing it drops approximately 1,000 feet in a horizontal distance of about a quarter of a mile!

Lieutenant C. E. S. Wood likened this passage to the "spout of a funnel." Sutherland wrote that "on the day that Sturgis made a little scout toward the Stinking Water . . . [the Indians and] an immense herd of horses, came over the mountain and down through a precipitous canyon, so narrow that it was almost met in places at the top, resembling an irregular tunnel, and escaped to the plains."[20]

Howard recalled:

> My command, discovering Joseph's ruse, kept the trail which Sturgis had been so near . . . and, finally, slid down the canyon, many a horse, in his weakness, falling and blocking the way. The mouth of this canyon, which debouches into Clark's Valley, was not more than twenty feet across from high wall to high wall. And one may imagine the scene of cavalry, infantry, and pack mules crowding through it, and admire the quick wit of an Indian who had the hardihood to try the experiment, and break the almost impassable roadway.[21]

And one of Sturgis' troopers, who passed through it later, dubbed it "the devil's doorway."

In a cleanly executed maneuver the Nez Perce had countered an extremely serious threat and won a brilliant, though temporary respite. However, it was not a bloodless affair for in order to conceal their whereabouts for as long as possible they tried to kill all the whites who were in their path. Near the mouth of the canyon, Howard's soldiers found the bodies of eight Scandinavian prospectors. The men had been neither stripped nor scalped, and letters scattered nearby provided the names of four. Farther to the north, a band of Nez Perce found a little party en route to the Crow Agency with a wounded man—probably the prospector-scout discovered by Lieutenant Hare's party, and said to have been turned over to his "friends." Agent Frost reported to Fort Ellis that

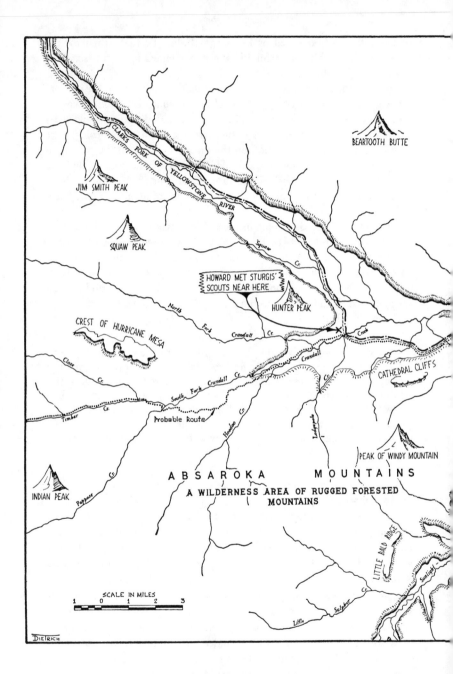

BEARTOOTH BUTTE

JIM SMITH PEAK

CLARKS FORK OF YELLOWSTONE RIVER

SQUAW PEAK

Squaw Cr.

HOWARD MET STURGIS' SCOUTS NEAR HERE

HUNTER PEAK

CREST OF HURRICANE MESA

North Fork

Crandall Cr.

Crandall Cr.

Close Cr.

CATHEDRAL CLIFFS

South Fork Crandall Cr.

Cr.

Timber Cr.

Probable Route

Hoodoo Cr.

Ledgepole Cr.

PEAK OF WINDY MOUNTAIN

Papoose Cr.

INDIAN PEAK

A B S A R O K A   M O U N T A I N S

A WILDERNESS AREA OF RUGGED FORESTED
MOUNTAINS

LITTLE BALD RIDGE

Sunlight Cr.

SCALE IN MILES

1   0   1   2   3

Sulphur Cr.

Little Cr.

DIETRICH

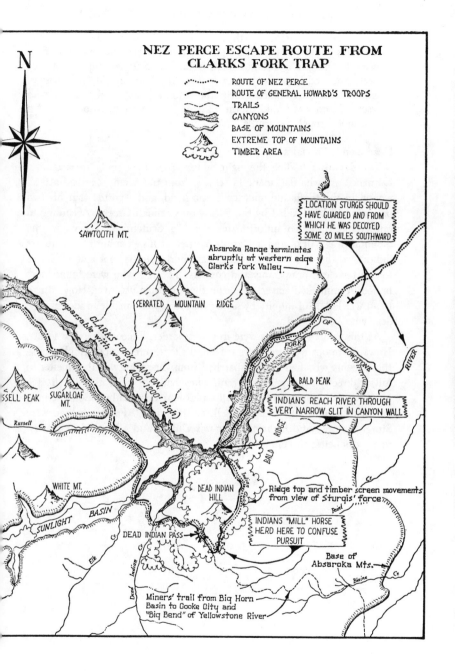

NEZ PERCE ESCAPE ROUTE FROM CLARKS FORK TRAP

.... ROUTE OF NEZ PERCE
────── ROUTE OF GENERAL HOWARD'S TROOPS
TRAILS
CANYONS
BASE OF MOUNTAINS
EXTREME TOP OF MOUNTAINS
TIMBER AREA

N

SAWTOOTH MT.

LOCATION STURGIS SHOULD
HAVE GUARDED AND FROM
WHICH HE WAS DECOYED
SOME 20 MILES SOUTHWARD

Absaroka Range terminates
abruptly at western edge
Clarks Fork Valley

SERRATED MOUNTAIN RIDGE

CLARKS FORK CANYON (Impassable with walls 400-1200' high)

CLARKS FORK OF YELLOWSTONE RIVER

BALD PEAK

SSELL PEAK   SUGARLOAF MT.

Russell Cr.

INDIANS REACH RIVER THROUGH
VERY NARROW SLIT IN CANYON WALL

BALD RIDGE

WHITE MT.

DEAD INDIAN
HILL

Ridge top and timber screen movements
from view of Sturgis' force

SUNLIGHT BASIN

Elk

DEAD INDIAN PASS

Dead Indian

INDIANS "MILL" HORSE
HERD HERE TO CONFUSE
PURSUIT

Point

Cr.

Base of
Absaroka Mts.

Cr.

Blaine

Miners' trail from Big Horn
Basin to Cooke City and
"Big Bend" of Yellowstone River

on Tuesday [September 11th] the Crows found a wounded man in the foothills about twenty miles from the Agency. He and four other men were bringing in a wounded man from Gen. Sturgis camp, when they were attacked by some 75 Nez Perces, who had flanked Gen. Sturgis, and all the party killed except the wounded man and the one who escaped and was found by the Indians. The latter was wounded by a gunshot through the arm.[22]

Dead men tell no tales.

The day after finding the eight bodies, Howard's scouts "picked up a German . . . who had made his escape from the enemy. He had a flesh wound in the thigh and another in the hand, and reported that his two partners had been killed by the enemy on Crandall Creek." According to Sutherland, the two unfortunates were "a Scotchman, known in the mountains as 'Alex,' and a Danish partner of his in mining." There are indications that this passage of the Clark Fork country took a considerable toll in travelers, prospectors and couriers. The few who were found were buried in unmarked graves and, after the campaign was over, Howard had to answer letters of inquiry by saying that they were unable to identify the dead who were buried.

At this point the troops were in reverse order. Except for a few scouts, Howard's troops were in the van. Behind them were "Rube" Robbins and those scouts who had been dispatched from the vicinity of the smelter to follow directly on the Indian trail. They had not been able to effect a junction at the mouth of Crandall Creek and were trailing along behind, out of provisions and living on "elk meat straight." Farther behind were Sturgis' troops. And far in the rear was Gilbert and a handful of cavalrymen—a hopeless also-ran in the race.

22

Canyon Creek and the Prairies Beyond

>>>>>>><<<<<<< On September 10th Howard's troops, having climbed out of and back into Clark Fork Canyon, camped near its mouth. The following day, when about ten miles down the broad valley, Sturgis' approach was noted. On the previous morning he had scouted vainly in the vicinity of the mouth of the canyon of the Stinking Water and then, probably realizing that he had been duped, had marched for Clark Fork by way of the miners' trail up Trail Creek. At the top of Dead Indian Hill, the troopers had found the trail; and then they, too, went down Dead Indian Gulch and through the "Devil's doorway."

Pushing hard, Sturgis soon caught up with Howard, and the two forces halted while their commanders assessed the situation. The colonel, disappointed and "deeply chagrined," remarked, "Poor as I am I would give $1,000 if I had not left this place." Howard immediately assumed command and incorporated the Seventh Cavalry into his own force, being "delighted to observe the elastic tread of his horses, which could in a very few minutes walk away from ours." Believing that the lesson administered by the Indians would not only make Sturgis more cautious but would also act as a goad, Howard offered the colonel an opportunity to redeem himself. It was decided that Sturgis should make a forced march and try to catch the Indians. To this end he was reinforced by Captain Bendire and fifty cavalrymen on picked horses, Lieutenant Otis and two mountain howitzers on pack mules, and twenty-five scouts under Lieutenants Fletcher, Fisher and Houston. The general's two aides protested his relinquishing command but, as Cushing and the much-needed supplies were expected, Howard deemed it best to remain with the balance of the command.

Recognizing that the proposed drive might not bring a substantial victory, Howard decided to inform Colonel Nelson A. Miles of the situation, and to suggest that he take a picked force and, by approaching along a diagonal route, try to position himself in the path of the Indians. On the following day, the general sent this dispatch, in duplicate, to Sturgis:

> *Headquarters Department of the Columbia, In the Field*
> *Bridger Crossing, Clarke's Fork, Wyoming, September 12, 1877*
>
> COLONEL:
>
> While Colonel Sturgis was scouting toward Stinkingwater, the Indians, and my force in close pursuit, passed by his right, and then after a short detour turned to Clarke's Fork, and by forced marches avoided Sturgis completely.
>
> I have sent Sturgis with Major Sanford, First Cavalry, and Lieutenant Otis, Fourth Artillery, with howitzer battery, in fastest pursuit, and am myself following as rapidly as possible with the remainder of my own immediate command. The Indians are reportedly going down Clarke's Fork and straight toward the Musselshell. They will in all probability, cross the Yellowstone near the mouth of Clarke's Fork, and make all haste to join a band of hostile Sioux. They will use every exertion to reach the Musselshell country, and form this junction, and as they make exceedingly long marches, it will require unusual activity to intercept or overtake them. Earnestly request you to make every effort in your power to prevent the escape of this hostile band, and at least hold them in check until I can overtake them. Please send me return courier with information of your and the hostiles' whereabouts, your intended movements, and any other information I ought to know.
>
> Very respectfully,
> O. O. HOWARD
> *Brigadier-General Commanding Expedition*
> *against Hostile Nez Perces*

Col. Nelson A. Miles,
Fifth Infantry[1]

As soon as Sturgis reached the Yellowstone he sent Private Sullivan, a trusted cavalryman, to carry one copy of this message, plus another which he wrote, to the Tongue River Cantonment. To insure that the message went through, the second copy was given to a rancher living near Coulson to carry downriver in a mackinaw boat.

By the evening of the 11th, Sturgis' force was ready to march. However, he requested the addition of one more man. No doubt remembering that both surgeons with the regiment had been killed in the disaster of the preceding year, he asked for a second surgeon. Captain FitzGerald, who was assigned to Sanford's battalion, was the logical choice. Although the captain pointed out that his horse was worn out, his cousin—Major Lewis Merrill of the Seventh—lent him a fresh mount and his plea was unavailing. The men of this detachment were awakened very early the next morning and when they stopped for the night, near the mouth of Rock Creek, they had marched approximately fifty miles. In a letter to his wife, FitzGerald described the dismal day in three terse sentences:

> Marched from 6:30 A.M. until 9 P.M.—a long dreary ride. It rained all afternoon and my boots and everybody else's got full of water. Made a wet and disagreeable camp with but little to eat.[2]

About 10 o'clock the next morning the command crossed the Yellowstone River and, as *sign* indicated that the Nez Perce were too far ahead to be overtaken with jaded horses, Sturgis ordered a halt. However, the Indians were not far away and at the time a party of warriors was engaged in raiding down the valley.[3] There were a number of settlers scattered along the Yellowstone in this area and about sixteen miles below the mouth of Clark Fork, on the left-hand bank of the river, was the town of Coulson—if the aggregate of a saloon, sawmill and a few tents can be called a town.

A few miles below the mouth of Clark Fork was a ranch and stage station operated by H. H. Stone and Elliott Rouse. When these two men observed the approach of the Indians, they rode down the valley to the mouth of Canyon Creek where Edwin Forrest and Bella "Bill" Brockway had a cabin. Shortly after they arrived here, the westbound "stage"—a light, two-seated vehicle commonly called a jerky—arrived carrying mail and a single passenger. On being advised of the danger, the driver unhitched the horses and put them in the corral. However, when columns of smoke began to roll up from the burning buildings and haystacks at Stone & Rouse's station, all fled for some brush which was nearby.

Years later an old-timer, who probably heard the story from some member of this little group, wrote:

The young bucks at once set fire to the hay-stacks, some starting to drive off the horses, having taken two and hitched them to the stage. Before starting they gleefully distributed the mail, throwing one sack in the well, cutting others open, leaving letters and papers blowing over the prairie, these were collected for months afterward in a very weather-beaten state. After the horses were attached to the old jerky, an Indian mounted each horse and with one on the box [sic—driver's seat], off they went tearing and whooping like lunatics. . . . * * * Their object then was to overtake the main party which was making for Canyon Creek; but in their frolic they had not observed the approach of General Sturgis until he was almost upon them. Then cutting loose from the stage, they wildly followed their comrades.

Probably the jerky was driven for several miles, for one of Howard's scouts recalled that it was abandoned near where the skirmish took place later in the day.

According to Sutherland, "the solitary passenger [was] one Fanny Clark, a well known public character in Portland in other days. When the fascinating Fanny was discovered by us she was dressed in a pair of man's breeches, and a gray wollen shirt ['having changed her dress to better facilitate her flight'], looking very much like a native to the manner born." As to what Fanny was doing out there in the wilderness, the reporter did not say. Perhaps in 1877 that was not necessary.

Most of the warriors may have returned to the main body after this bit of high jinks. Although they burned haystacks and buildings, only one shot is said to have been fired at the people who hid in the brush. A few warriors continued on down the valley to the outskirts of Coulson. A short distance below Forrest & Brockway's cabin, "five young bucks and one old wrinkled warrior" crossed the Yellowstone and approached a logging camp that was partly hidden in the timber. The workmen, having previously been alerted that the hostiles had turned north after leaving Clark Fork Canyon, were ready for trouble. Joseph Cochran, the boss of the camp, walked out and intercepted the little party—hoping to steer them away from his horses. The old warrior, watching Cochran's rifle apprehensively, finally came up and talked with him but refused to visit the camp. Then the group started on warily but soon became alarmed and ran their ponies toward the river, sweeping up the teams in their flight.

Cochran, who had some property on the north side of the river, then took a man with him and set out to see if this had been molested. During his absence, two trappers, Clinton Dills and W. Milton Sumner, had been living in his tent. The two found the trappers dead. *Sign* indicated that they had allowed the Indians to approach, perhaps thinking them friendly. One body was found near the tent and the other some distance away as though shot down while trying to flee. Cochran and his companion then went on toward Coulson, coming in sight of the Indians while they were burning a saloon. After hiding in a buffalo wallow until the Indians left, they continued on to the main logging camp where they discovered that the other men had been fishing when the raid occurred and were not aware of what had happened.

While this party of marauders was sweeping down the valley, some of the scouts and soldiers had started fires for the purpose of drying their clothing, and all eyed the columns of smoke rolling up to the east of them. Soon a Crow Indian and then a white scout came in and reported that the Nez Perce were not far away. The Indians had gone down the valley for a few miles after fording the river and then, turning back toward the northwest, were now going up Canyon Creek.

The north side of the valley of the Yellowstone, for some distance above and below the mouth of Clark Fork, is bordered by an impassable wall of rimrock. Often this is 400 feet or more in height; and in places the rimrock itself—a sheer wall of yellowish-gray sandstone—is upwards of 200 feet in elevation. In this particular area, the barrier runs in a northerly direction for about eight miles and then turns abruptly eastward. In this *corner* of the wall there is an opening about a mile and a quarter wide through which Canyon Creek enters the immediate valley of the Yellowstone. However, the rimrock parallels each side of the creek for some distance so this opening does not constitute a real gateway in the wall.

About a mile and a half west of this breech in the main wall, Canyon Creek divides into three branches; and the North Fork reaches the adjacent prairie after passing through a narrow, difficult canyon for four and a half miles. The buffalo trail up the North Fork was the *only* route near the mouth of Clark Fork which led from the floor of the Yellowstone Valley to the flat prairie that stretched away to the northward for miles. Thus the impending skirmish was fought to control this gateway to the broad prairies between the Musselshell and Yellowstone rivers. The first contact was made about five miles north of the Yellowstone where a high, flat-topped ridge lay between the Yellowstone and Canyon Creek, and in the vicinity of a minor drainageway called Dry Creek. Neither creek was more than a dry wash with a gullylike channel.

As soon as Sturgis learned of the proximity of the enemy, he ordered "to horse" sounded and all set off with the scouts in the advance. Fisher noted that

> we rode at a good gait across an open country. Upon reaching the rise of the table-land, bordering the valley, about 2 P.M., the Indians opened fire on us from the tops of the hills. We kept on, however, and

got well onto the bench, across which the Indians had retreated and where they were now strung along for about a mile and keeping well under the cover of the banks of the creek . . . [Dry Creek], giving us a sight of their heads only when they raised up to shoot. Just at this time . . . [Major Merrill's battalion] came up and, instead of charging which should have been done, dismounted about five hundred yards from the enemy's lines, deploying to the right and left, and opened a very rapid fire.[4]

This put the scouts between the two lines of fire, and they hastily moved to the flanks of Merrill's line.

Within about a half an hour after the fire opened we succeeded in driving the enemy from the break in our immediate front. The soldiers drove them slowly across the flat, or what was a gradual descent cut by small ravines and dry "washes." The Indians fought entirely on horseback, firing mostly from their animals and at long range, doing but little harm. From this point we got a good view of the camp and their herd, which was scattered along the other side of the creek for a mile or more.[5]

Apparently, the herd was now on the broad bench just to the north of the channel of Canyon Creek; and the squaws and children were pushing it as rapidly as possible toward the shelter of the previously noted gateway in the rimrock.

Up to this time, Sturgis had held Captain Frederick W. Benteen's battalion—fully half of his force—in reserve, and had kept it well to the rear. Seeing that the quarry was about to escape, the colonel ordered

that officer to make a slight detour to the left, so as to head the worst of the ravines, and thus gain what appeared to be a smooth plain, running along the base of the farther hills, and, having gained it, to charge across in front of Merrill's battalion, cross the creek, and cut off the herd before it should enter the cañon. At the same time, Major Merrill was directed to mount his troops and gallop forward so as to get beyond and in the rear of Benteen as soon as the troops of the latter should have passed, so as to protect his left flank from the fire of the Indians who had by this time occuppied the sides and mouth of the cañon in strong force.[6]

The desired result was not achieved. Merrill's battalion contained a great many green recruits and those in charge of the lead horses apparently failed to understand repeated orders to bring up the mounts of the other men. Also, the proximity of a band of Crows, who were mistaken for Nez Perce,

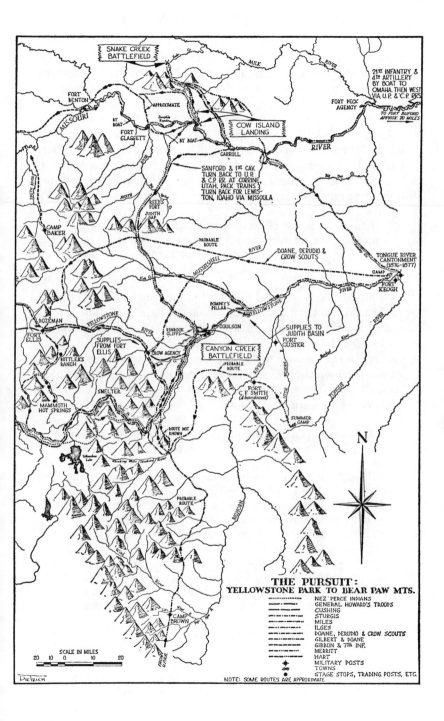

THE PURSUIT:
YELLOWSTONE PARK TO BEAR PAW MTS.

created confusion. Benteen did make a charge across Merrill's front in an attempt to head off the horse herd but—according to Fisher—what appeared to be "only one company" crossed the creek, and that soon fell back. Sturgis reported that due to this bungling of orders, "the enemy was thus enabled to bring the greater part of his herd within the cañon, although in so doing he was forced to drop some four or five hundred."

Troopers now made a futile attempt to scale the rimrock on the south side of Canyon Creek and obtain a flanking position. Finally, Otis' battery was ordered forward—this being but a single gun as the other had been lost in fording the Yellowstone—and Fisher was directed to show the lieutenant a suitable location. This effort was also unproductive.

> I tried to get this officer to take his guns [sic] up near the point where he could do some execution, but he was very much excited and insisted on running them down into the ravine, where he could not even see the bluffs on either side, so I left him in disgust.

As the Nez Perce now had their herd in the canyon where they could not be flanked, all that was necessary to insure escape was for the warriors to fight a determined rearguard action until the camp was started up the North Fork, the mouth of which was but a short distance away. Apparently, the troops managed to drive the warriors as far as the opening of this secondary canyon but here they got in among the rocks and refused to be pushed farther. The scouts skirmished with them a little longer and then withdrew. Fisher noted with disgust:

> As it was now nearly or quite sundown, we all went back to where the soldiers were camped and there learned that the Crows had stolen my pack animals, clothing, bedding, etc., as well as a number of pack and saddle animals from others. The Crows took no part in the fight, but staid in the rear and stole everything they could get their hands on. The Clark Fork scouts [Houston's men] generously divided their rations with us, we being unable to get anything from the command. The scouts were generally very much disgusted with General Sturgis' management of the fight. The firing during the day was mostly at very long range, and, as the wind was blowing nearly a gale, it was impossible to do good shooting. The ground, also, was wet and it was very seldom that we could see where our balls struck. These facts account in some measure for so few being killed or wounded on either side.[7]

In his summary of the action, Sturgis claimed:

> The loss to the enemy in this engagement was 16 and in the pursuit the next day 5, making a total of 21. The number of wounded is a matter of speculation. . . . The number of ponies lost by them in the

engagement and during the pursuit is estimated at between 900 and 1,000.

Our losses were 3 killed and 11 wounded.[8]

However, in view of the fact that the colonel failed to accomplish any substantial results during his participation in this campaign, the excuses and claims in his lengthy report probably merit critical examination.

The "3 killed and 11 wounded" may be correct although these figures do not agree exactly with the losses reported by Sutherland, FitzGerald and a scout from Montana. The latter also reported that one of the wounded died at the mouth of the Big Horn as they were being taken down the river in boats to the Tongue River Cantonment.

Most reports give five as the number of Indian casualties resulting from the skirmish the following day, but Sturgis' figure of sixteen killed on September 13th is undoubtedly considerably inflated. Sutherland's dispatch to the San Francisco *Chronicle* stated that "six Nez Perce bodies were found and about 100 of their horses driven off. [The next day] . . . several Indians being killed, and about 600 horses captured." On the 25th of September, Sheridan sent a telegram to Crook's adjutant in which he stated that Sturgis' men "killed five or six Indians . . . and captured about nine hundred ponies."[9] The Crow Agent reported that the Absaroka brought in about four scalps—while Fisher wrote later that his Bannocks could find no bodies to scalp. FitzGerald, who had a slight previous acquaintance with some of the enemy, wrote to his wife that, "Many ponies were captured and it is said that 6 or 8 Indians were killed. I have seen only two, and I made some effort to see all of them."[10] Perhaps the surgeon's comments are the most trustworthy of all.

The number of Indian ponies that were captured is equally elusive. Sutherland's figure of 100 captured the first day agrees with the number reported by the Crow Agent as being brought to the Agency—and the Crows probably took most, if not all, of the ponies captured. In the running skirmish on the following day, the Crows may have captured another 400 head. Of this action, Howard reported, on September 16th, that Sturgis had informed him: "We . . . [compelled] them to drop over 300 more of their horses, making 600 in three days." Apparently, the figure of "between 900 and 1,000" is far too high.

Fisher was not the only one to criticize Sturgis' handling of the fight. Scouts who returned to Lewiston, Idaho, told Editor Leland that they thought the colonel was timid, and that when one of his officers urged him to attack he reminded them of the disaster Custer had suffered during the preceding year—an affair in which his own son was killed. And Benteen, a crusty but staunch veteran, wrote later in a garrulous letter that the colonel "wanted me to make a 'hullabaloo' of a report; but I couldn't."

On the following day, Sturgis' command started at dawn to try to catch the Indians, and shortly afterward it was joined by a considerable number of gaudily dressed Crows eager to acquire more ponies. As the ponies of the latter were fresh, they were sent ahead while the cavalrymen pushed their mounts to the limit. During the day, the Absaroka and Bannocks hung around the flanks of the Nez Perce—allegedly killing five and cutting off about 400 horses.[11] And a free-lance reporter at the Crow Agency reported that the hostiles captured a young buck named The-Boy-that-Grabs. They put him on a broken-down horse, quirted him over the head, and told him that "the Crows were old women who would not fight and were only fit to stay at home." Having thus disgraced him, they scornfully sent him back to their fickle friends.

By evening, the cavalry had traveled about thirty-seven miles and was scattered for an estimated ten miles with a third of the men on foot. When Captain Bendire's detachment got in late that night, every man was leading his horse. Camp was made beside a small creek—but there were no rations. There were, however, worn-out Indian ponies and, according to one cavalryman, "we thought we had never tasted sweeter meat."

While here, a courier arrived from Howard—who had pushed on to the battlefield with a small force—bringing a message directing Sanford and Bendire to return to the Yellowstone. The next morning, in a pouring rain, these cavalrymen and the remnant of Fisher's scouts started back while the Seventh Cavalry resumed the futile pursuit. The colonel sent a dispatch with them in which he stated expansively that "I propose to push them until they drop their whole herd, or we drop and I think they will abandon nearly their last horse today."[12] Night found Sturgis' men on the banks of the Musselshell River, their horses completely used up, and nothing to eat but horsemeat. Here the Seventh Cavalry was forced to halt and await Howard's coming, as well as the arrival of supplies being forwarded from the new post on the Big Horn River—Post No. 2, later called Fort Custer.

Near evening, two days later, the balance of Howard's men joined their comrades at a camp near the burned stage station. Fisher and his "dozen" scouts left the following morning as their term of enlistment had expired. Lieutenant Fletcher, who had administrative control of all the scouts, gave Fisher a flattering letter of commendation, and the scout wrote in his journal that "I certainly would have staid with him had there been any prospect of his overtaking the enemy, for I must say that I was never treated better in my life than I have been by General Howard and his officers."[13]

As this group left, the "Yellowstone scouts" received some new recruits. One was Joseph Cochran, whose logging operations had been interrupted, and the other was a colorful character known as Liver-eating Johnson.

When Sturgis had left Howard's troops near the mouth of Clark Fork Canyon, the latter moved on down the valley expecting to meet Cushing bringing supplies. However, before these arrived news came of the skirmish at Canyon Creek and the general, taking 50 cavalrymen and 500 pounds of fresh beef on pack mules, set out on an all-night march for the battle-field—which he reached about five hours after Sturgis had resumed pursuit. Dispatching a courier with the information that he was at the field hospital and would follow if he could be helpful, Howard halted to rest his weary men. On this same day, Lieutenant Adams—and, presumably Captain Cushing also—met the column and all marched to the Yellow-stone. After fording the river, the column camped near the burned stage station until Sanford, Bendire and their men came in on the evening of September 16th. It was probably at this halt that the wounded were loaded into a mackinaw boat and sent down the Yellowstone to Miles' post.

Howard resumed his march on the morning of the 17th, going down the left side of the Yellowstone as far as "Baker's battlefield"—probably a few miles farther to the vicinity of Pompey's Pillar—where he turned sharply back toward the northwest and headed for the Musselshell, presumably on a trail laid out five years before by a Northern Pacific Railroad surveying party. Four days later he rejoined Sturgis near the mouth of a creek known both as Fish and Elk Creek. The combined force now started again on the trail of the Indians which was pointed straight for the ten-mile doorway between the Little Belt and the Big Snowy Mountains which provides access to the Judith Basin.

In the meantime, on the 20th, a courier arrived with a dispatch from Colonel Miles:

Headquarters District of the Yellowstone
Cantonment at Tongue River, Montana, September 17, 1877

DEAR GENERAL:

Acting on the supposition that the Nez Perce will continue their movement north, I will take what available force I have, and strike across by the head of Big Dry, Musselshell and Crooked Creek and Carroll, if I do not get any information before. I fear your information reaches me too late to intercept them, but I will do the best I can. Please send me information of the movement and course of the Indians.

Very respectfully, your obedient servant,
NELSON A. MILES,
Colonel Fifth Infantry, Brevet Major General
United States Army, Commanding

GEN. O. O. HOWARD
Commanding Department of Columbia, in the Field

I have asked to have abundant supplies of rations and grain sent up the Missouri. I would respectfully request that the movement of my command be kept as secret as possible, so that it may not become known to the Crows or other friends of the enemy.

In another dispatch of the same date, Miles added that he would try to prevent the feared junction between the Nez Perce and the hostile Sioux; and that "I expect to be six or seven days to the Musselshell, and two more to the Missouri river, near Carroll. If you get any information that shall change my course, please send me word."[14]

In order to allow Miles to get into position, Howard now deliberately slowed his march; and the Indians—keeping watch on their pursuers—also slowed down, traveling just fast enough to maintain a safe lead. After the campaign was over, Miles, who seemed determined to garner every possible crumb of glory for himself, scoffed at Howard's statement that this sly maneuver was important and expressed doubt that it actually took place. Proof that the colonel's contention was without support is contained in a dispatch which Sutherland wrote at the time, and which was published in the San Francisco *Chronicle* two days before the Nez Perce finally surrendered:[15]

Camp Sturgis (Fish Creek, Montana) September 22 (to Bozeman by courier via Helena, October 2.)—. The Indians camped at Judith Gap (now in sight) two days ago. *We do not push them much, hoping to give General Miles a chance to get ahead of them on the Missouri river*: then to attack them simultaneously. This must happen within ten days. When the expedition breaks up, the infantry and artillery going to Omaha, via the Missouri river, and the cavalry, via [Fort] Ellis, to Corrine [Utah]. (Italics are the author's)

Although there is no proof of the whereabouts of *all* the hostiles after Sturgis was halted on the Musselshell, some of the young men—now in country with which they were intimately familiar—may have raided in the country to the west of the line of march of the main camp. On the 19th, Indians were seen near the forks of the Musselshell where eight or ten bucks chased two men who were hauling wood and made off with their team. Elsewhere in the vicinity, about thirty horses were stolen. Three days later, near White Sulphur Springs in the valley of Smith River, a half dozen farms and ranches were raided and an estimated thirty head of horses run off. Captain Clifford and Sergeant Wright from nearby Camp Baker—now considerably undermanned—organized a party of about twenty civilians and scouted the surrounding country. All that was found was a trail leading through Moore's Pass to the Judith Basin. And a pioneer stated years later that when the Nez Perce went through the Judith Basin they killed one of his sheepherders—an Irish priest who was tortured by the memory of a murder he had committed.

Howard's force, with Sturgis attached and still short of rations owing to the failure of the supply train to arrive from Post No. 2, now followed the trail through the Judith Gap and into the Judith Basin. Scout J. W. Redington wrote years afterward that he found, in the vicinity of Reed's Fort (near present-day Lewiston), the remains of a hunting camp of some River Crows led by a chief named Dumb Bull. The Nez Perce, smarting over the participation of their erstwhile friends in the campaign, had destroyed the camp and killed several of the Absaroka. Although there appears to be no mention of this affair by anyone with the troops, the *Fort Benton Record*, on September 21st, noted that four Crows had come into a trading post along the Missouri and reported that, "We had a big fight with the Nez Perce in the Judith Basin."

As there appeared to be little hope that the Nez Perce could be forced to stand and fight, and as cold weather could be expected soon, Howard made plans to disband his forces. When in the central part of the Judith Basin, at the junction of Beaver Creek and the freighting road from Carroll to Helena, he replaced Sanford's battalion of First Cavalry with the six companies of the Seventh and trimmed his command of the pack animals and civilians acquired in the Lewiston, Idaho, area. On the 27th, Sanford and most of the cavalry started back down the trail for Fort Ellis, and thence via Virginia City for the railroad station at Corrine, Utah. Here they would take a train to the vicinity of their stations in northern Nevada and eastern Oregon. One company of cavalry, the packers and what was left of the mule trains, and Captain Spurgeon's "skillets" were sent home by way of Helena, Missoula and the Mullan Road via Coeur d'Alene, Idaho. On October 11th, the Helena *Daily Herald* noted that Dick Closter, in charge of 260 pack animals, had passed through town; and early in November the Lewiston *Teller* made note of the arrival of Scott Thomas and three others who had come in on October 30th with the news that 170 animals and about 50 men would soon arrive at Lewiston and Fort Lapwai.

Major Mason's diarylike letters provide an intimate picture of these days. On September 24th he wrote that they had marched 1,282 miles since leaving Kamiah, and that they had plodded over 500 miles in Idaho before starting over the Lolo Trail. On the day before Sanford departed, he penned this description:

> Today we have had a most disagreeable march of about 18 miles. A high, cold northwest wind has made it most unpleasant. * * * These great rolling plains are destitute of timber, so it's only here and there

that we may camp. We are now obliged to send one wagon miles away to the mountains to get wood enough to cook with. Our supply train [from Post No. 2?] is still behind us, and the separation has thus been delayed, but tonight we expect the wagons up, and tomorrow the cavalry under Sanford start home. * * * We will press the pursuit . . . and hope to drive him [Joseph] into the British possessions within 10 days, or if that takes too long, will let Miles finish the job while we go down the Missouri in a steamboat and home via Omaha. We must make short work of it, for the season is rapidly advancing. . . .

In subsequent letters, he noted:

[September 28th] Soon after leaving camp yesterday a courier came to us with the information that the Indians had crossed the Missouri at Cow Island. . . . This information settled the question in regard to following the Indian trail as of course that was no longer necessary. [Learning that there were steamboats at Carroll—a trading post and trans-shipment point for freight—a courier was sent to engage one for their use.] We are now within two days of Carroll. Whether we start home immediately depends on the information we receive from General Miles. . . . * * * We struck a fine herd of buffalo just as we were coming into camp. We have buffalo, deer and antelope in sight all day long and. . . . We let the men hunt freely, so they have plenty of fresh meat.

[September 30th] We marched 15 miles yesterday in a cold september rain and went into camp at 3 pm beside a water hole with no wood and consequently no fire. At 8 pm we had something to eat. I went to bed as the place to be dry and warm. This morning the blessed sun is out again. . . . We will make a short march this afternoon and go in tomorrow. Yesterday I received a note * * * that there are three boats above Carroll, The Benton, Fontenelle, and Silver City.

[Oct. 2nd] We made a short march Sunday afternoon and yesterday marched into Carroll where we found that Lieut Earnest had engaged the Steamer Benton for us. It is not quite so large as the Silver City but is a very nice boat and ample for our purpose. We put the troops into camp at Carroll [with Sturgis in charge], and then taking 100 men from the artillery and infantry battalions we started up the river [on the *Benton*] for Cow Island where we hope to communicate with General Miles.[16]

The end of the campaign was very, very near.

23

Skirmish at Cow Island Landing

>>>>>>><<<<<<<< Records pertaining to the services of couriers are fragmentary at best. And, typically, but little is known about the efforts of Howard to communicate with the forces to the north of him after the Indians headed for the Judith Gap. However, on the 21st of September, the *Fort Benton Record* noted that Cyprien Matt—the official interpreter for the Gros Ventre Indians—had "reached town at an early hour today with a message from Mr. James Wells, of Fort Claggett. The latter asks for help to protect the fort against the approaching Nez Perce."

Fort Claggett was a trading post below Fort Benton at the mouth of the Judith River on the site of Camp Cooke, a dreary, rat-infested post the Army had abandoned seven years before. Four Crows had arrived, claiming to have come from Lieutenant "Doane's command" with dispatches for Major Guido Ilges who, with "F" Company of the Seventh Infantry, was stationed at Fort Benton. They explained that they had lost the dispatches "but we were sent to warn all of you people." From this garbled story it appeared that they had been at Canyon Creek and with Sturgis on his subsequent pursuit. While en route, they had stopped at the hunting camp of the River Crows, which had been roughly handled by the Nez Perce and—perhaps—had lost their dispatches in that melee.

Ilges and his men were stationed at Fort Benton where they were expected to curb the bootlegging propensities (whiskey and ammunition) of the local residents, and to chase Indian horse thieves. The major spent no time in questioning the accuracy of Wells' intelligence. By 2 o'clock in the afternoon, Lieutenant Edward E. Hardin, thirteen enlisted men, two civilian volunteers and a mountain howitzer were on board a mackinaw boat and headed down the Missouri; and by 7 P.M. the major, one enlisted man and twenty-four (possibly thirty) mounted citizens—many of whom were "old prairie men"—were on their way overland to Fort Claggett. As there were only twenty-one enlisted men in "F" Company before the battle of the Big Hole, where two were killed and seven wounded, it is probable that Ilges took every man available. Hardin arrived at Fort Claggett the next forenoon and the mounted detachment, having made a forced march, rode in at 5:30 the following afternoon.

As Ilges found no new intelligence here, he sent out two scouts. The next day was uneventful except for the arrival of six more volunteers from Fort Benton, but about 2 o'clock the following morning the scouts returned. They had found the *sign* of an encampment of about 75 lodges, together with the tracks of over 1,000 horses, some forty miles to the south at the mouth of Big Spring Creek; and they had followed the trail far enough to determine that it was headed for Dog Creek and, probably, the crossing on the Missouri near Cow Island. The major started his detail for Cow Island at daybreak, and by pushing hard all day arrived at dusk. Hardin and the boat arrived soon afterward, bringing with him other soldiers from a guard at Dauphins Rapids, and all went into camp together.[1]

Fort Benton was an extremely important river port, and at its wharves were unloaded the major part of all the goods used in western Montana and the adjacent part of Canada. (The balance was freighted up from Corrine, Utah, and some specialty goods were packed in over the mountains from Wallula on the Columbia River.) However, Fort Benton had one very serious disadvantage—when the water in the river dropped during the summer and fall, steamboats were unable to reach it. When this condition existed, freight was unloaded on a piece of bottomland on the left-hand bank of the river opposite Cow Island. Here it was picked up by freighters and hauled the rest of the way in bull trains. Also, any passengers going to or coming from "the States" made connections with the steamboats at this "low water" port. There were, however, no permanent buildings here—only tents used by guards for government stores and an agent for the merchants and the freighting company.

Throughout most of the area between Fort Benton and Fort Peck it was extremely difficult for wheeled vehicles to reach the banks of the Missouri. In the general vicinity of Cow Island, the stream was 700 to 800 feet below the general level of the surrounding country, and it was bordered on either side by a belt of intricately eroded breaks and badlands that varied from six to twelve miles in width. Access to this landing was by way of a trail that came down Cow Creek Canyon from the north-northwest for a distance of thirteen or fourteen miles—*as a crow flies*—and which crossed the twisting channel of the "creek" thirty-two times between the landing and the open plains to the north. Carroll, to which Howard marched his troops, was some thirty air-line miles below Cow Island, and on the right bank of the Missouri. Goods for Helena and points farther south were sometimes unloaded at this trading post and freighted out by way of the Carroll Road—a trail which ran west into the Judith Basin, south through the Judith Gap, and thence westward.

Two days before Trader Wells' messenger had alerted Ilges, a bull train had arrived at the Cow Island Landing. This consisted of fifteen wagons, and probably seven *teams*—a team being the number of yoke of oxen necessary to pull a unit of two or three wagons coupled together in trail. These wagons and "bulls"—owned by O. G. Cooper, Farmer and Fred Barker and referred to as the train of Cooper & Farmer—were under contract to E. G. Mackay & Co. (the "Diamond R" outfit), which held the government contract for freighting to Army posts. At the time of the arrival of this train, the steamboat *Peneniah* had just unloaded a cargo of freight on the bank.

About ten days later, Cooper related his story to the editor of the *Fort Benton Record:*

> We arrived at Cow Island on the 19th instant. As the steamer Fontenelle had not yet arrived, there was not enough Diamond R freight to load our trains, and Col. Clendennin [sic] gave us some of Power's [T. C. Powers & Bros.—one of the two largest merchants in Montana] freight so that we could load up and get away without waiting for the Steamer. On the morning of the 21st I pulled out [with six wagons], leaving Farmer and Barker to await the arrival of the steamer, but on reaching a point about four miles up the canyon I heard the Fontenelle's whistle and returned on horseback to assist Farmer in loading. The day following Farmer and Barker pulled up to where my trains were camped, and the same afternoon . . . ˙[a party of passengers] arrived and camped with us.[2]

This party consisted of people who had arrived on the Fontenelle—four ladies in a "light wagon," Dr. Brown an army surgeon, Captain Frechett of the Northwest Mounted Police, and five enlisted men—with the men, presumably, mounted on horses. Fortunately, this group left early the next morning and proceeded on their way to Fort Benton.

Dauphins Rapids, some 18 miles above Cow Island and about 19 miles below the mouth of the Judith, had long presented a problem to steamboat captains. This year a party of engineers had been sent from "the States" to remove obstructions from the channel. To guard this work party, Captain T. S. Kirtland and "B" Company of the Seventh Infantry had been detailed from Fort Shaw. As the work neared completion, the chief engineer had sent all surplus supplies down the river; and as he miscalculated the amount of work remaining, it became necessary to send a detail to Cow Island for additional rations. First Sergeant William Moelchert, wishing to see the landing, requested permission to take the detail down.

Years later, Moelchert recalled that he took three privates and, as he was leaving, the captain warned him that he had been informed that the Nez Perce were headed that way. The sergeant and two soldiers went down in a boat borrowed from some woodhawks; and the other soldier, whose name was Person or Pearce, followed along the shore riding the captain's horse—the animal being necessary to tow the boat back upstream. As the boat arrived before the horse, Moelchert sorted out the necessary supplies and made ready for the return trip.

While the sergeant and his two men were visiting with the small detail on guard at the government dump, someone saw a file of mounted Indians on a ridge on the opposite side of the river. While the Indians went upstream a short distance to find a ford, Moelchert stationed his men and prepared for trouble. This little force consisted of two sergeants, one corporal, nine privates and four civilian workmen—"Col." Clendenin having gone downstream to see if another steamboat was nearby.

When the Nez Perce approached, a "chief" and about twenty men rode up to the dump which the little party was guarding. Moelchert motioned for them to keep their distance and, leaving his rifle behind, went out and shook hands with them. Then the Indians wanted to shake hands with everyone but the sergeant refused to be trapped. Next, two who spoke good English asked him to give them some of the freight. Moelchert refused and walked away. The pair came back a second time and offered to pay for the supplies, "showing me a handfull of gold and silver money under my nose." Again the sergeant refused, but when they returned a third time and pleaded for food, he went to the pile and got a side of bacon and half a sack of hardtack. Whereupon "they very kindly thanked me for the same." Sometime later a shot was heard across the river "and I told the boys I bet that is Private Person killed and sure enough it was. We found his body next day and buried him right there."

It was now near evening:

> Having previously distributed the ammunition and given each man his place, we were standing around and taking our supper as I jokingly remarked to the men that this might be their last sow belly and hard tack when without further warning they commenced to fire from the hills, the balls going in every direction between us but luckily nobody was hurt. This was sun down and from that time on till day break we were fighting for our lives. Of course the freight we could not save as it was piled right up against the bluff. The agent had a hospital tent there for his quarters with 500 sacks of bacon piled against it which they set on fire [and] that lit up the country for miles. We saw them in the tent and fired at them and no doubt some got hurt but of course we don't know how many.[3]

Several times during the night the Indians charged through the willows —Moelchert recalled three charges and contemporary accounts state seven —but it was "impossible to see anyone." Also, it was reported that when the freight piles were looted the Indians found whiskey and some got drunk.

About 10 o'clock the next morning the Indians moved off up Cow Creek Canyon. What casualties, if any, they had suffered was never known. The defenders had two civilians wounded, neither seriously. After the Indians had left, the Irish factotum of "Col." Clendenin is alleged to have sent a facetious note to his boss:

> *Rifle Pit at Cow Island*
> *September 24, 1877—10 a.m*

COL:

> Chief Joseph is here, and says he will surrender for two hundred bags of sugar. I told him to surrender without the sugar. He took the sugar and will not surrender. What shall I do.

> MICHAEL FOLEY

Ilges and his party camped across the river that night and ferried over in the mackinaw boat shortly after daybreak the next day. They found that "thirty tons of government freight and twenty tons of private freight had been burned by the hostiles. Sugar, coffee, hams and other groceries; calicos, stationery and other dry goods, were strewn over the surrounding hills and through the gulches [sic—up Cow Creek] for miles."[4]

The following February, George Clendenin filed a deposition at Helena in which he stated that all he recovered of one merchant's goods was one sack of sugar.[5] How much more damage the arrival of Ilges' party may have prevented is problematical. The *Benton* and *Silver City* arrived not long afterward with—reportedly—160 tons of freight. Probably the Indians would not have tarried even had they known of the whereabouts of these two steamboats.

While Moelchert and his comrades were spending a harrowing night, the train of Cooper and Farmer, together with the passengers from the *Fontenelle*, were camped several miles up the creek, unaware of what was happening. The train started early the next morning, and the travelers moved on ahead at their own pace. As the going was difficult, the bull train made only three or four miles by noon, at which time eight Indians overtook the rear wagons and continued along until all stopped for dinner.

As Cooper told the story six days later:

We strung out the teams, but before we could unhitch, the main body of the Indians came up. They offered us no violence, but remained around the wagons, some mounted and some on foot, allowing their horses to graze around. It was at least an hour from the time the first part of the main body came in sight until the whole had arrived, and the lead then began to move up the road, and all finally went into camp about a mile and a half from the wagons. But before they had moved off, five well-mounted warriors came riding in at full speed, their horses wet with sweat. * * * I asked one of the Indians who was standing near me, who they were and what the . . . [leader] had said. He replied that they were scouts and had brought the news that 300 Sioux had passed on the other side of the mountains.

While the Indians were around the wagons I tried to count them, but of course could not do so accurately. As near as I could make out there were between seven and eight hundred * * * I noticed that the young sprightly bucks had but few cartridges in their belts, while the old fellows and middle aged seemed better supplied: but I think they were all short of ammunition, as they were very anxious to buy from us. * * * They were armed with all sorts of guns, and many had cavalry carbines. * * * Their animals were very poor, and many had sore backs and feet, but they had some fine horses with them, and I think one—a fine sorrel covered with a blanket—was a race horse. I saw at least a dozen differently branded horses. * * * There were also a number of Gov. mules and horses. About twenty of their horses, crippled and dead were left along Cow Creek.

After the main body of the Indians had gone into camp, a number of stragglers remained around the wagons. They examined everything in the wagons, even to the mess-kits, but took away nothing except one pair of blankets, which we afterward missed. They all wanted food, and one young buck who staid around the wagons asked us repeatedly, in good english, when we were going to have dinner. I told him the men were afraid to go after wood as they thought the Indians would kill them. He replied, "Oh hell they wont touch them." * * *

[Later] One good-natured looking Indian, a man about forty-five years of age, whom I took to be Looking Glass [sic—Poker Joe?], spoke to us in good English and asked where the soldiers were and where there was any good grass. He said that the Indians were going to hunt buffalo. He spoke very kindly and told us we had better go off and leave the train as the Sioux were around and would kill us that night and steal our horses.[6]

The Indians left the train late in the afternoon and did not molest the bullwhackers during the night—Cooper wrote in a letter two days later that "we lay in the hills that night." After breakfast the next morning, Cooper and Farmer went after their cattle which were grazing on the other side of the Indian camp, while Barker and a man named Sinclair followed some distance behind. The first two rounded up their oxen and were about to return when

> we heard one of the chiefs haranguing the camp in a loud voice and saw some of the warriors . . . about to mount their horses. . . . so concluded to go around and reach the wagons from the other side. We had accomplished about half the distance . . . when we saw about ten Indians leave the main party and go around as if to get in the rear of us. At the same time we heard three shots in camp. . . . We paid no attention to the ten Indians, at first, but a few minutes later we saw those of the main camp tearing off the [wagon] sheets and setting fire to the wagons. We knew then that war was declared, and without stopping for further information, we jumped down a cut bank and made for the hills; where we soon found all the other [four] trainsmen, except Barker and a man named Sinclair.[7]

The missing pair had approached the camp but feared to ride through it. Sinclair escaped to relate that as they rode along, three Indians came up beside them. While two conversed in a friendly manner, the third dropped behind and shot Barker in the back, Sinclair immediately jumped his horse down a cutbank, got into some willows and escaped.

At the landing, Ilges and his volunteers stopped long enough to eat a hasty meal and make a quick survey of conditions. Then, about the middle of the forenoon, he set out up Cow Creek—with the plainsmen definitely apprehensive of "its narrow bottom, its high and precipitous sides, shutting off the traveler from the outside world." After proceeding about "ten miles" (or less), one of the scouts came back and reported that the camp was not far ahead. The major immediately halted his force and, climbing a nearby knoll, surveyed the situation with a pair of glasses. He could see the wagon train in the midst of the warriors and soon noted about seventy-five mounted men approaching "as if on a charge."

He hastily prepared for a fight by stationing his men as advantageously as the nature of the ground would admit.* * *

At 12 m. the fight was opened by the Indians firing a light volley down the valley from above. Everyone was soon in his assigned position, and the rattle of rifle shots continued until about 2 p.m. The Indians had taken the high bluffs on the right and from these points kept up an incessant fire upon the exposed men below. [Edmund] Bradley was killed by one of the sharpshooters stationed behind a high rock. Our men soon got the proper range of their guns and prevented the Indians from doing more mischief. . . . Most of the men had close calls . . . during those two long hours. Judge [John W.] Tatam was [dazed by a bullet that] struck his belt plate and some of the men had their hats and clothing perforated by bullets.

Early in the fight, Ilges sent Private Thomas Bundy hurrying back with instructions to Lieutenant Hardin to bring up his detachment and the howitzer. However, before the lieutenant arrived, the Indians ceased firing and the major, suspecting a trick, withdrew back down the creek. Hardin met them about three miles from the landing, and all retired to the rifle pits at the river. Ilges was relieved to get safely out of the tight spot. He reported four weeks later: "The citizens . . . behaved very well during the fight, with a few exceptions, but they are not very desirable material under disadvantageous circumstances."[8] After his return to the landing, the major wrote a dispatch stating the whereabouts and probable direction of travel of the Nez Perce. Then on September 28th, he gave it to Charles Buckmann, one of the volunteers, and sent him to find Colonel Miles.

The next day a party returned to the scene of the trouble and buried Barker and Bradley. During the following night Cooper and Farmer came into camp, experiencing a narrow escape when an alert picket fired at them. The bullwhackers rejoined the others the next forenoon. Although the three horses had been stolen, all of the cattle were rounded up except four which had been killed. The wagon train and its thirty-five tons of freight was a total loss; Cooper valued his six wagons, two oxen and (probably) one horse at about $2,000. The official estimate of the government supplies which were destroyed was $7,738.75—probably the civilian goods were, at least, equally valuable. Perhaps those who grieved most over the loss were the passengers whose personal baggage was lost when the wagons were burned.

As the Nez Perce moved up Cow Creek, they attacked another wagon boss, a Mr. Nottingham, who was en route to the landing. However, he managed to escape and take his train back safely to Fort Benton. And Indians—who may have been Nez Perce—killed a man identified as "R. Steele" who was apparently trying to escape "homeward" from the Bear Paw Mountains. Ilges' party found and buried the body beside the trail three days later as they returned to Fort Benton.[9]

There is no definite explanation for the behavior of the Indians while at the landing or in the proximity of the wagon train. However, it would appear that Ilges' party approached the train at an inopportune moment. Apparently, the attack on the freighters started when the Nez Perce became aware of the approach of the major and his volunteers. They then fired the train and a small party rode back and stalled this new threat—the two-hour sniping duel taking place at, reportedly, about 1,000 yards, which was beyond the accurate range of the rifles used. During this two-hour interval, the camp packed up and moved out. When it was safely underway, the fighting men withdrew.

The Indians were wasting precious time. They had only traveled a short half-day on the 24th when they caught up with the train, and they did not start until midday on the following day. The loss of a day could easily have resulted in an additional twenty-five miles behind them. And this distance may well have represented the difference between success and a bitter defeat.

24

Fresh Troops Join the Chase

>>>>>>><<<<<<< It was near evening when Private Sullivan, with some 160 miles behind him, rode along the top of the clay bluffs which rise sharply from the north bank of the Yellowstone near the mouth of Tongue River. On the other side of the stream, the commanding officer of the Fifth Infantry watched his approach—first as a dark object in the distance and, finally, as a cavalryman who requested that the little ferry be sent to carry him over to the Tongue River Cantonment. Colonel Miles recalled that

> he rode up to me, dismounted and saluted, and then I recognized him as one of the cavalrymen from General Sturgis' command. * * * On opening the envelope which he handed me I found a [five days old] report from Colonel Sturgis and General Howard, stating that the Nez Perce had left them hopelessly in the rear, and wishing I would take some action to intercept them.[1]

Sheridan had ordered Terry[2] to cooperate in defeating the Nez Perce but the latter, who disliked Howard, had complied with tongue in cheek.

Although he had approved the assignment of Sturgis' troops, he had attempted to put a subtle restriction on Miles—just as he had attempted to do with Custer just before that fatal Sunday in June of the preceding year. He informed the colonel that he might use his own judgment but that *he thought* his troops were needed "at both ends of the line."[3] However, Miles, although less impetuous than Custer, was a very aggressive officer— and something of a glory hunter. He wasted no time for, in fact, there was none to waste.

Perhaps the best record of this part of the campaign is contained in the brief, occasionally cryptic entries in the personal diary of Captain Simon Snyder, a solid, trustworthy individual who was the senior line officer of the Fifth Infantry. The entry for this day reads:

Monday September 17

At dark this evening word arrived from Genl. Howard that the Nez Pierces had gotten around Sturgis and crossed the Yellowstone at Clarks Fork as [sic—and?] also a request that Genl M cooperate and accordingly orders were at once issued for the Mounted Batn & Co "K" 5th Infy and a Co 7th Cavy to move across the river at once with view to starting to head off the hostiles in the Musselshell country in the morning   All was commotion from the time the order was recd. and no sleep for anyone   I wrote to mother.[4]

"*No sleep for anyone.*" When Sullivan arrived, all was quiet at the Cantonment, but an hour later everyone was busy. By 10 A.M. the following morning, Miles' command was across the Yellowstone and on the march. In the interval, rations for twenty days were drawn from warehouses, packed on mules and in wagons, and ferried across the river during the night; soldiers readied their arms and gear; and Miles and his staff tried to anticipate possible needs. To cushion the supply problem, a dispatch was given to a courier to carry to Fort Buford. This requested that 60,000 rations be sent up the Missouri to the mouth of the Musselshell.[5] (However, Major Orlando H. Moore did not have that many to spare so he loaded 17,000 rations, some forage and what officers' stores could be spared on the steamboat *General Meade*. Then he forwarded Miles' requisition to the officer at Fort Peck, on the nearby Indian reservation, with the request that he contribute 15,000 rations and sufficient forage (grain) to complete the shipment, and that he also send one company of his command to guard the boat and the supply dump.)

In addition, couriers were readied—if not, dispatched—to carry orders to personnel not at the post. One of these was to find Luther S. "Yellowstone" Kelly, Miles' chief of scouts, at Carroll and order him to the mouth of the Musselshell. Another was sent to overtake a detachment of cavalry which was on its way to Fort Benton, where it was to meet a party consisting of General Terry, several officers and a number of officials, and escort them to the Canadian line. This was the Sitting Bull Commission—an official party which hoped to persuade the Sioux chief and his followers to surrender and return to the United States. The troops which were ordered to delay their march comprised a battalion of the Second Cavalry—Companies "F," "G" and "H" commanded, respectively, by Captain George L. Tyler and Lieutenants Edward J. McClernand and Lovell H. Jerome—and Company "K" of the Seventh Cavalry under Captain Owen Hale.

Alice Baldwin, wife of Miles' adjutant, who confused the leave-taking of these troops with that of the colonel's column two days later, has left this poignant picture of that occasion:

> We had all gathered in our little log drawing room to say goodby. I had in my keeping a piano, waiting for its owner to arrive later. We played and sang . . . good old hymns of long ago. . . . Capt. Owen Hale, bold, dashing, dauntless trooper that he was, * * * was ever of a gay and cheerful temperment; but on this particular evening he seemed quiet and depressed. His last words to me, as he shook my hand and bade me and the others goodby, were, "Pray for me, for I am never coming back!"[6]

Years afterward Miles, in writing of the charge which opened the last battle, stated that "the tramp of at least six hundred horses over the prairie fairly shook the ground" but this is a gross exaggeration. In reporting the fight to General Terry on October 17th, he wrote, "My fighting strength at the battle of the Bear Paw was only 350 men and a steel gun."[7] These were divided into three battalions and a guard for the supply train that consisted of two trains of pack mules and forty wagons. The white scouts—a varied lot—and thirty Indian scouts were under Lieutenant Marion P. Maus. One battalion consisted of the three companies of the Second Cavalry, and another was made up of Companies "A," "D" and "K" of the Seventh Cavalry under Captains Myles Moylan, Edward S. Godfrey and Owen Hale, respectively, with the latter in command. The former consisted of about 125 men, and the latter, 108 (115 according to Moylan's report). Troops drawn from the Fifth Infantry consisted of Company "K" (40 men without mounts) under Captain David H. Brotherton, which was assigned to guard the supply train, a crew under Sergeant John McHugh to operate a breech-loading Hotchkiss gun, and a battalion consisting of four mounted companies which numbered 90 men.[8]

This mounted battalion was an unusual outfit. On the 14th of May, after the capture of Lame Deer's village, Miles had ordered that "Companies 'B,' 'F,' 'G,' and 'I' 5th Infantry will be equipped as mounted Infantry, using the Indian ponies recently captured and such horses as may be procured." This was done under the direction of Captain Snyder; and, of course, the ponies greatly increased the mobility of the "walk-a-heaps." Years later, the son of one of the company commanders recalled that the colors of the horses in the various companies were matched, as far as possible, making a very colorful outfit. "B" Company was commanded by Captain Andrew S. Bennett, "G" by Lieutenant Henry Romeyn (Captain Samuel Ovenshine being in Chicago on riot duty), "I" by Lieutenant Mason Carter, and "F" by Captain Snyder.

Snyder wrote of the first day's march:

> *Tuesday, Sept. 18*
> My Co got over river about 4 A M and occupied its old camp. Command got away about 10 A.M. marching about 20 miles up sunday Creek and camping at dark.

With the column was Major—and Surgeon—Henry Remsen Tilton of the Seventh Cavalry, who had an eye for other things beyond routine command responsibilities. He made a record of these in an article published soon after the campaign was over;[9] and this admirably complements Snyder's businesslike entries. Under the pen name of Remsen, he wrote of the first day:

> We crossed the swift Yellowstone on the 18th of September, passed up a ravine, where two of Custer's men were killed by Indians in 1873,[10] over a high plateau which gives commanding views in every direction, cast one long lingering look at the fair forms and waving handkerchiefs on the other side of the river, and our march began.
> We soon reached the valley of Sunday Creek, and passed through a camp of Cheyennes and Sioux, our enemies of last year, but now firm friends. They surrendered last March. . . . [and] Their main camp is near the post. * * * This camp has just started out for a hunt, and greet us with hearty "Hows," as we march by them. A ride of seventeen miles through dust, and our first camp was made.
> Sunday Creek varies from a roaring torrent after heavy rains, to an insignificant thread of alkali water. . . . As progress is made toward the head of the Creek, the water is found in pools.

Of the following day, the captain's diary states:

> *Wed. Sept 19*
> Left camp at 5 A.M. marching in a west & North West directions

and camping in a branch of Sunday Creek about 1 P.M. Wagons reaching camp about two hours later. Water bad and no wood. * * * Distance about 17 miles.

And of the next:

> *Thursday Sept 20*
> Left camp at 5 A.M. marching N. West and camping on tributary of Dry River about 23 miles from this mornings camp. Command reached camp at 3 P.M. but wagons did not get up until after dark. No wood. Roads not good today. Cheyenne Indians joined at dark.

Remsen described the Indians and their arrival:

> Just at dark we heard the war song of thirty Cheyennes and Sioux as they came riding into camp. * * * Each warrior has one or two extra ponies, which are not ridden until in the immediate vicinity of the enemy. The loose ponies trot along in front, nipping the grass now and then. They don't present to the eye any indication of the fire within; but when the time arrives for action, sooner than I can tell it, the warrior strips for the fight, catches up his favorite war pony, and, ye gods! what a change comes over rider and horse. The small snaky eyes of the former no longer look sleepy; they are flashing fire, while his pony picks up his ears, dilates his nostrils, and darts off with the speed of the wind.

Among these scouts, the leaders were Hump, White Bull and Brave Wolf. Hump was the principal chief of a band of Minneconjou Sioux; White Bull, sometimes called Ice, was a noted Cheyenne medicine man and the first to enlist seven months previously in Miles' detachment of Indian scouts; and Brave Wolf was a highly respected Cheyenne leader who was noted for his modesty and his fearlessness. James Finerty, the fighting reporter of the Chicago *Times*, who fought for his life against them in the Battle of the Rosebud in 1876 and rode with them against Sitting Bull's Sioux in 1879, wrote:

> The Cheyennes are as proud as Lucifer, and rarely beg. They fight like lions, and are, taken altogether, Indians of the dime-novel type. Some of them are amazingly intelligent, and . . . of gentlemanly deportment.[11]

Snyder made these entries for the next two days:

> *Friday, September 21*
> Left camp at 5:10 A.M. marching north west on good roads &

reaching Big Dry Fork at 12 M Wagons getting in about 2 hours later   Distance almost 21 miles   Antelope very plenty upon today's line of march. Overhauled the 2nd cavy [Cavalry] at noon.

Saturday, Sept 22
   37½ miles advancement
   Left camp at 4.20 A.M. reaching camp on small tributary of Mussel-shell [sic—Squaw Creek] at 4 P.M. after hard march of about 38 miles. Wagons did not get in until after 10 P.M. * * * 2nd Cavy joined us at today camp.

And on Friday, Remsen noted that "Antelope are around us in great numbers. * * * A great many were secured, and everybody had antelope for his supper." Of Saturday, he wrote:

> We see plenty of buffalo, but orders have been issued to prevent firing. The lumbering fellows act as though they had received a copy of the order. They cross our trail, running between the advance guard and the next battalion.

Although the availability of water determined the location of each camp site, Snyder's diary makes it clear that Miles was pushing his men hard. The command, having marched in a northwesterly direction up (South?) Sunday Creek and across the heads of Little Dry and Big Dry creeks, was now in the upper part of the valley of Squaw Creek—a small stream which empties into the Missouri River just below the mouth of the Musselshell. Ahead of them lay the breaks and badlands of the Missouri which Remsen called a "God-forsaken country . . . [without] enough grass to sustain a donkey."
   On Sunday, Snyder noted that:

> Command left camp on Squaw Creek which the stream has proved to be, at 5.15 A.M. reaching camp about 5 miles above its mouth at 11 A.M. where we camped. Train got in at 5. P.M. distance 15 miles Couriers from T. [ongue] River with news of fight with Nez Pierces by 7 Cavy [at Canyon Creek]. 2nd Cavy left us to cross Missouri enrout to Benton   Scout [George] Johnson drowned in Missouri in attempt-ing to cross at mouth of Squaw Creek.

The couriers noted by the captain brought Miles his first intelligence since the arrival of Private Sullivan; and the colonel now decided to divide his force. The battalion assigned to escort the Sitting Bull Commission was to be put across the Missouri to follow, generally, up the left bank of that stream while the remainder of the troops were to cross the Musselshell and scout the country between that stream and the Missouri.

Fortune now smiled on Miles. As no one was certain of exactly where they were, Lieutenant Maus[12] was sent down the valley to determine whether the Musselshell or the Missouri lay before them; and, if the latter, he was to camp there and stop any boat which might happen to come along. When this officer reached the river, he rode out on a sandbar and there, not a thousand yards away, coming downstream was the *Fontenelle*, which had unloaded at Cow Island just before the Nez Perce reached that point. A hail stopped the boat and, although the captain had no intelligence about the hostiles, he complied with the request to make his boat available for Miles' use.

The next day the wagons moved down to the river and the tedious work of ferrying men and supplies began. The Second Cavalry, together with a pack train loaded with fifteen days' rations, was deposited on the opposite bank of the Missouri; and the artillery was taken up to a little flat just above the mouth of the Musselshell. The mounted battalion of infantry then rode across the badlands to this point while the wagon train was left parked with Brotherton's company for a guard. Now Lady Luck smiled again, this time in no uncertain fashion!

Snyder's diary provides this cryptic summary:

Tuesday, Sept 25
(Total march today 6 miles)
Moved down to the mouth of Musselshell this A.M. reaching the Mo about 7 oclock—2 miles   just as we crossed the river word was recd from above that the Nez Pierces had crossed at Cow Island on the 23rd. The steamer which was still in sight was signalled to return and the entire comd transferred to the North side of the river when we encamped and the work in crossing the train began & continued all night   We take wagons from here . . . [*General Mead?*] arrived about 2 A.M. from Peck with additional supplies and . . . [cav pulled out?] soon after dark.

What happened was that, just as the infantrymen were eating breakfast, a rowboat containing two men came down the Missouri—who may have been the two civilians wounded in the Cow Island skirmish and who may have been en route to either Fort Peck or Fort Buford. They provided Miles with fresh intelligence. In the meantime, the *Fontenelle* had dropped down the river about a mile to a woodyard to take on fuel. The colonel ordered the Napoleon gun loaded, and the gunner was instructed to drop the shell near enough to the boat to attract attention. This was done and the signal was understood—thanks, no doubt, to the fact that Miles' adjutant was on board, having been sent back by the surgeon. Thus, for a second time, the vital services of a steamboat were secured at a crucial moment.

Remsen described the activity which ensued:

> It is evening. One battalion [2nd Cavalry] marches out of the valley, over the hills, the men singing as they go. With the camp fires, the scattered animals, the rumble of the moving train, the crack of the drivers' whips, the occasional scream of the steamer's whistle, and the song of the cavalrymen as they march off, the scene is intensely interesting, and it is difficult to realize that we are in the wilderness.

Leaving the wagon train to find a way out of the breaks along the river, Miles pushed his troops up onto the edge of the vast prairie which bordered them on the northern side. And, as the column was now in a country where they could be seen from a great distance, he pointed it toward the opposite—eastern and northern—side of the Little Rockies which were some forty miles away. Snyder wrote:

> *Wednesday, Sept 26*
> The work of transferring the wagon train not having been completed Gen M with my Battalion left the camp at 9.30 A.M. and after considerable delay in getting our wagons out of the Mo River bottom we reach camp a dry one, at 3.30 P.M. 15 miles from the river marching in the direction of the Little Rocky Mountains.

> *Thursday, Sept 27*
> Started at 5 A.M. march with Bat 7 Cavy having joined during night & [made?] about 8 miles to Furschell [sic—Fourchette] Creek where we found the Bat 2nd Cavy in camp 7.30 A.M. Remained here until 4 P.M. when we started with 8 days rations on pack mules. Made camp 9 P.M. on Dry Fork of Milk River [Beaver Creek?] Distance about 18 or 20 miles   Total today 28 to 30 miles.

Remsen gave this explanation for the midday halt:

> We make a noon halt to allow the wagon train to close up. Buffalo come among the mules and ponies, and quietly feed, looking up occasionally to see what their strange neighbors are doing. We march in the afternoon with the pack train, leaving the wagon train to follow more leisurely.
>
> The Judith Mountains are to the southwest [some 70 miles away], while the Little Rockies are to the west and in front of us. Buffalo are on either side; one herd ran across the train just in front of the column.

On the following day, in "clouds and rain," the command skirted the northern slopes of the Little Rockies, traveling about twenty-nine miles through what Remsen called a "hunter's paradise." At evening, camp was made in a deep ravine which would hide the campfires. The next day,

Saturday, Sept 29
Left camp at 5 A M reaching camp near Bears Paw Mountains about 1 P.M. 26 miles   Disagreeable day with rain at intervals. Slept under Reomeys [sic—Romeyn's] Tent as I did not have poles for my own. Couer from Gen Howard.

Again fortune favored Miles. Captain Godfrey was to note later that as the troops crossed the broad, open saddle between the Little Rockies and the Bearpaw Mountains "the cloud drifted very low and thus shielded us from observation."

Year afterward, Miles recalled that the courier who reached him this day had been dispatched on the day Major Sanford's battalion had left Howard's column, and that the message "made it clear that whatever encounters we might now have with the Nez Perces we were entirely beyond support." However, when the chips were down, he *did* send an urgent dispatch requesting that assistance come "with caution and rapidity" and reinforcements lost no time in complying with that request.

Remsen described this camp as being "in a valley near a pond filled with ducks. Two great hills tower above us. It soon begins to rain in the valley, while snow falls in the mountains. Our scouts report the Indian trail not far away."

Although neither Snyder nor the surgeon made note of the fact, Charles Buckmann—Major Ilges' courier—also arrived. Apparently, the troops were camped at the foot of a pair of steep, conical buttes—now called Miles and Iron Buttes—which are part of a small cluster of elevations at the extreme eastern edge of the Bearpaw Mountains. From this general area the slopes sweep northward in long stretches which are broken only occasionally by a ridge or steep-sided drainageway carved in the priarie.

About twelve miles north-northwest was another camp. This one was on a low bench on the east side of a small stream known as Eagle or Snake Creek. Here, at some time in the geologic past, the stream had meandered against the gently sloping prairie which lay to the east; and as the channel had deepened, about eight or nine acres had been left above overflow. This bit of terrace, or "high bottom," was a kidney-shaped area about a quarter of a mile long from north to south, and from ninety to one hundred and fifty yards wide. It was enclosed on the north, east and south by old cutbanks some thirty to forty feet in height which had now been rounded to form very steep slopes (called "bluffs" by some). The channel of the creek ran along the western edge, and to the northwest, west and southwest a gently rolling prairie stretched away for miles.

There were openings in the encircling cutbank wall at the northeastern and southeastern corners of the terrace. These were the mouths of small coulees or ravines which ran back across the prairie toward the southeast; and, over the years, water carried by these drainageways had cut four winding gullies across the terrace. These ranged from about four to seven or eight feet in depth, were V-shaped in cross section and, at this time, were fringed with enough sagebrush in places to provide some cover for a man's head and shoulders. Other than this, the only vegetation on the campsite was a carpet of buffalo grass.

On this little bench, over seven hundred and seventy men, women and children sought shelter from the cold rain in makeshift lodges. Scattered over the prairie to the west was what remained of a great pony herd that observers had estimated at well over 2,000 head—now either about 1,200 or 1,800 animals. The remainder—dead, crippled, abandoned, or in the hands of the Crows—were scattered along the thousand or more miles of trail that stretched back to Tolo Lake.[13]

In the morning, the Indians expected to break camp and continue on their way northward. The U.S.-Canadian border—that invisible line that spelled safety—was only forty-two miles away. Success of a sort was almost within their grasp.

25

Six Grim Days

≫≫≫≫≫≫≪≪≪≪≪≪ For Miles' troops, six grim days began about two hours after midnight on Sunday, September 30th.

> Reveille at 2 o'clock A.M. The moon and stars shine in a clear sky, the air is chilly. We march as soon as we can see to move. A wolf serenades us at our first halt by the side of a stream. We soon come upon the broad Indian trail. Our Cheyennes and Sioux undergo a sudden transformation: they are painted, stripped for a fight, on their favorite chargers, and are a study for an artist. The picture lasts but a moment; they are bounding over the plain on either side of the column, which is now in rapid motion. To be astride a good horse, on the open prairie, rifle in hand . . . [as] one of four hundred horsemen, galloping on a hot trail, sends a thrill through the body which is seldom experienced.[1]

But when night came, the thrill of those few moments was gone. The entry in Captain Snyder's diary is terse and grim:

Off early this morning. Ground frozen and ice upon streams. After
marching five or six miles discovered Indians to front and left. Soon
after struck heavy trail and soon after the Indian scouts reported Nez
Percie village 4 or 5 miles ahead and the entire command moved
forward at charge. 7th Cav charged Indians in front losing heavily
2nd Cavy swept around to left and rear of village capturing Ind &c
[sic—ponies]. 5th Inf holding hill above village for some time when
F & I Cos charged but did not accomplish much [other] than to seek
shelter. A . . . [punishing?] fight was kept up until night Our loss
today Capt Hale & Lt Biddle & 23 enld [enlisted] men killed and 4
Officers & 40 men wounded. Indians still hold their position.

In the first half hour of action, Miles lost—in killed and wounded—
twenty percent of his force.[2] Such a loss might be tolerated if it purchased
a victory, but this one had not. Apparently, the enemy was as formidable as
ever.

As the troops moved out in the morning, Lieutenant Maus, "Yellowstone" Kelly and a few white and Indian scouts probed the eastern edge of
the Bearpaw Mountains. Here they found the Nez Perce trail—apparently
about two days old—and they flushed a couple of Nez Perce scouts who
were watching for anyone following the trail of the village. These were
chased into the mountains. As this bit of action was taking place in the
distance, the officers of the Seventh Cavalry gathered to chat and "While
we were talking Captain Hale said, appropros of nothing in particular, 'My
God! Have I got to be killed this cold morning.' When he began his
remark he was trying to be facetious but when he ended he was serious and
his remark was received in silence."[3]

While a messenger was coming to Miles from Maus, the command also
found the trail and immediately turned north on it in pursuit. A few miles
farther on "information was received from the Cheyenne scouts that the
Nez Perce village was located on a creek about seven miles in front."[4]
According to a Cheyenne who heard Brave Wolf tell of the incident,

He was sent out with another on . . . [a scout] and contacted the
Nez Perces band and they were invited into the chief's lodge and they
explained their mission and the chiefs became very hostile to them and
they were threatened to be put to death. Of course the conversation
was carried on in sign language and he boldly told them that he would
rather fight to death than surrender his arms. And while the chiefs were
deciding what to do with them next, there was a great commotion took
place outside . . . [as] a herd of buffalo was passing near the camp
and the men took to their ponies and gave chase to the buffalo and
likewise the chiefs in the lodge did the same thing and the two
prisoners were left alone and they made their escape with the pack

mule following them and when they got too far out distance the mule would give a bray and they would slow up so it would caught up.[5]

Obviously, Brave Wolf and his companion were scouting at some distance from the main command. As there were considerable numbers of Assiniboins and Gros Ventres in the area, Brave Wolf's apparently rash entering of the hostile camp and the ease with which he escaped are not difficult to understand. If this incident happened—and it probably did, for Brave Wolf was a trustworthy individual—it may account, at least in part, for three significant things—that part of the camp was packed and ready to move when the troops reached it; that at least half of the warriors turned up in Canada after the surrender; and, perhaps, for the murderous fire which the Indians delivered when the initial charge was made.

The positions of the units in the column (with the exception of the supply train) rotated from day to day; and the order of march this morning was "5th Infantry, 2nd Cavalry, 7th Cavalry, and the pack train in the rear with a guard of two men from each company." However, in crossing a deep coulee, the battalions got out of order. Captain Godfrey recalled:

> At 9:15 word was received that the Nez Perce village was located on Snake creek bottom and the command was ordered to march at the trot. The Cheyenne scouts were ahead. The 2nd Cavalry battalion . . . was ordered to take the advance after the scouts and charge through the village. The 7th Cavalry battalion was ordered to follow the 2nd Cavalry as support and charge through the village. The 5th Infantry battalion (mounted) with mountain howitzer and pack train was ordered to follow as reserve. Colonel Miles rode with the 7th Cav. during our advance. After getting into the valley of Snake creek and when two or three miles from the village, we were ordered to gallop.[6]

When the order for the charge was given, the troops were almost due south of the camp and nearing the foot of a six-mile-long slope that stretched practically unbroken back to the vicinity of the conical peaks behind them. Most of the camp was hidden by the old cutbanks but the ponies grazing on the prairie to the west, and the men hurrying to secure them, were in plain sight. Miles now sent Lieutenant George W. Baird, regimental adjutant of the Fifth Infantry and his official courier, with orders for Captain Tyler to incline to the left, follow the Indian scouts who had headed for the herd, and attempt to capture the horses of the hostiles.

From his vantage point in the trailing echelon, Lieutenant Romeyn's first impression of the camp was that a portion of the lodges had been struck and about one hundred ponies packed for the day's march. These, guided by women and children and accompanied by fifty or sixty warriors, were at once rushed out and started northward. An attempt was made to cut off their retreat, Lieutenant McClernand in command of G Troop, 2nd Cavalry, being sent in pursuit. The Indians halted for a fight after going about five miles from the main body, and, finding a large portion of their pursuers encumbered by the care of the ponies they had . . . [captured], boldly assumed the offensive and forced the soldiers back toward the main body, although they failed in their attempt to retake the stock.[7]

Thus Tyler's men, sweeping to the west and northwest of the camp, scooped up most of the balance of the pony herd, variously estimated at 600 to 800 head. Joseph related about two years later that the captain's dash cut "our camp in two, and [captured] nearly all our horses. About seventy men, myself among them, were cut off. My little daughter, twelve years of age [sic—probably fourteen or sixteen] was with me. I gave her a rope, and told her to catch a horse and join the others who were cut off from camp. I have not seen her since, but I have learned that she is alive and well."[8]

Tyler's movement to the left opened the way for the three companies of the Seventh Cavalry to strike the south end of the village; and Miles now ordered them to charge "with pistols." All set to cut the camp to pieces, this battalion thundered down with Moylan's men on the left, Godfrey's in the center, and Company "K," under Captain Hale and Lieutenant Biddle, on the right. The warriors, hidden just below the crest of the cutbank and along the mouth of the coulee at the southeastern corner of the campsite, coolly waited until the troopers were within about two hundred yards. Then they rose up and delivered a murderous fire.

The inertia of the charge carried Troops "A" and "D" to the cutbank on the south side of the campsite—but no farther. The slope before them was too steep to ride down in a column of fours. Hale, seeing the broken area along the coulee, led "K" Troop well to the right, and Moylan directed Godfrey to go in the same direction and join him. The latter recalled later that

just after we started to the right I saw an Indian taking aim to me. I was not more than 50 to 75 yards from him to my left. I was riding an iron gray horse and my men were mounted on black horses. This, of course, made me a conspicuous mark and I was quite a bit nearer to this Indian . . . [trying to find a way] to get down in column of fours. His rifle cracked and down went my horse, dead. [As "we were galloping"] the momentum threw me forward; and I lit on my head

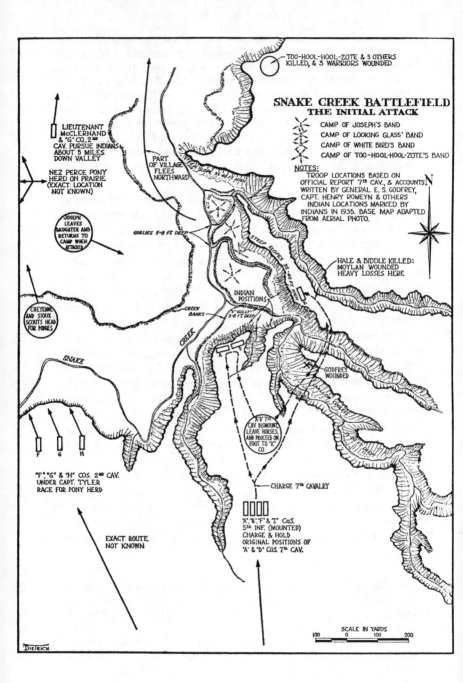

TOO-HOOL-HOOL-ZOTE & 5 OTHERS
KILLED, & 3 WARRIORS WOUNDED

SNAKE CREEK BATTLEFIELD
THE INITIAL ATTACK

CAMP OF JOSEPH'S BAND

CAMP OF LOOKING GLASS' BAND

CAMP OF WHITE BIRD'S BAND

CAMP OF TOO-HOOL-HOOL-ZOTE'S BAND

NOTES:
TROOP LOCATIONS BASED ON
OFFICIAL REPORT 7ᵀᴴ CAV., & ACCOUNTS
WRITTEN BY GENERAL E. S. GODFREY,
CAPT. HENRY ROMEYN & OTHERS
INDIAN LOCATIONS MARKED BY
INDIANS IN 1935. BASE MAP ADAPTED
FROM AERIAL PHOTO.

N

LIEUTENANT
McCLERNAND
& "G" CO. 2ᴺᴰ
CAV. PURSUE INDIANS
ABOUT 5 MILES
DOWN VALLEY

NEZ PERCE PONY
HERD ON PRAIRIE
(EXACT LOCATION
NOT KNOWN)

PART OF
VILLAGE
FLEES
NORTHWARD

SLOPE

JOSEPH LEAVES
DAUGHTER AND
RETURNS TO
CAMP WHEN
ATTACKED

GULLIES 5-8 FT DEEP

STEEP SLOPES 5-40 FT HIGH

HALE & BIDDLE KILLED:
MOYLAN WOUNDED
HEAVY LOSSES HERE

CHEYENNE
AND SIOUX
SCOUTS HEAD
FOR PONIES

INDIAN
POSITIONS

CREEK
BANKS

"V" GULLY
5-8 FT DEEP

STEEP SLOPES

SNAKE

CREEK

GODFREY
WOUNDED

F   G   H

"A","D"
CAV. DISMOUNT,
LEAVE HORSES,
AND PROCEED ON
FOOT TO "K"
CO.

"F", "G" & "H" COS. 2ᴺᴰ CAV.
UNDER CAPT. TYLER
RACE FOR PONY HERD

CHARGE 7ᵀᴴ CAVALRY

EXACT ROUTE
NOT KNOWN

"A","B","F" & "I" CoS.
5ᵀᴴ INF. (MOUNTED)
CHARGE & HOLD
ORIGINAL POSITIONS OF
"A" & "D" COS. 7ᵀᴴ CAV.

SCALE IN YARDS
100   0   100   200

DIETRICH

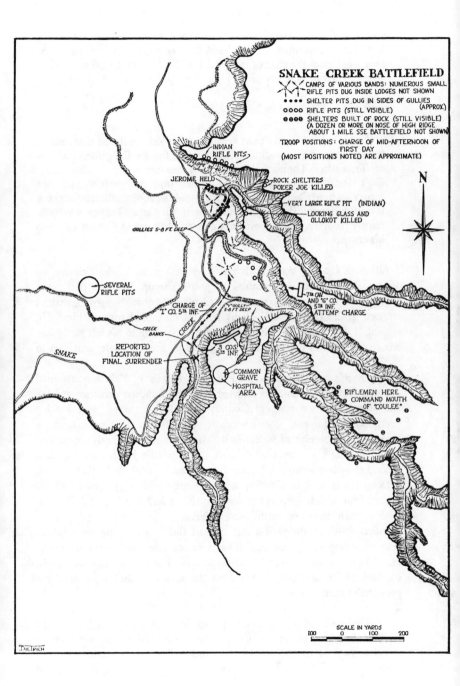

SNAKE CREEK BATTLEFIELD

CAMPS OF VARIOUS BANDS: NUMEROUS SMALL RIFLE PITS DUG INSIDE LODGES NOT SHOWN
SHELTER PITS DUG IN SIDES OF GULLIES
RIFLE PITS (STILL VISIBLE) (APPROX.)
SHELTERS BUILT OF ROCK (STILL VISIBLE) (A DOZEN OR MORE ON NOSE OF HIGH RIDGE ABOUT 1 MILE SSE BATTLEFIELD NOT SHOWN)

TROOP POSITIONS: CHARGE OF MID-AFTERNOON OF FIRST DAY
(MOST POSITIONS NOTED ARE APPROXIMATE)

N

INDIAN RIFLE PITS

JEROME HELD

ROCK SHELTERS POKER JOE KILLED

VERY LARGE RIFLE PIT (INDIAN)

LOOKING GLASS AND OLLOKOT KILLED

GULLIES 5-8 FT DEEP

SEVERAL RIFLE PITS

7TH CAV AND "G" CO. 5TH INF. ATTEMPT CHARGE

CHARGE OF "I" CO. 5TH INF.

"GULLY" 5-8 FT DEEP

CREEK BANKS

CREEK

3 COS. 5TH INF.

SNAKE

REPORTED LOCATION OF FINAL SURRENDER

COMMON GRAVE HOSPITAL AREA

RIFLEMEN HERE COMMAND MOUTH OF "COULEE"

DIETRICH

SCALE IN YARDS
100   0   100   200

and shoulder . . . but I turned a complete summersault and lit on my feet. I had a revolver in my hand and as soon as I had recovered somewhat from the daze of my stun, I thot I'd try to defend myself but when I tried to raise my pistol found my right arm was disabled. . . .[9]

According to Captain Moylan:

> Capt. Godfrey would most certainly have lost his life at this time as the Indians were advancing in his direction but for the gallant conduct of Trumpeter Thomas Herwood [a green recruit] . . . who seeing Capt Godfrey's danger, separated himself from his company and rode between where Capt Godfrey was lying and the Indians thereby drawing the attention of the Indians to himself till Capt Godfrey was sufficiently recovered from the effects of his fall to get to his feet and join his company.[10]

Although Godfrey was too dazed to remember the incident clearly, he did recall that as he was running to join his troop "Howard [sic] came along mounted and said to me, 'Well, Captain, I got it.' Supposing that he referred to the Indian who got my horse, I said, 'Did you kill him?' He replied, 'I don't know; but he shot me here,' pointing to his left side [sic— left chest]."[11] And the captain, noting that he was very pale, sent him to the surgeon.

While this was happening, Lieutenant Edwin P. Eckerson assumed command of "D" Company and led it several hundred yards toward the rear—much to the concern of Godfrey, who though things "were looking pretty squally for me." Moylan finally succeeded in stopping this movement and, on receipt of orders from Miles, dismounted both companies. Then, leaving the horses with holders, he led the balance of the men toward the place where "K" Company was hotly engaged. As they started, a trooper was sent to Godfrey with a horse—a blood-spattered, excited mount from which Sergeant James M. Alberts had just been fatally shot. The captain mounted with some difficulty; and the two troop commanders—both mounted—set out to lead their men to the place where they were desperately needed. This was not easy, as most of the men were encumbered by overcoats which they had not had an opportunity to take off, and also because they had to cross the uneven ground adjacent to the previously noted coulee.

> [Godfrey] had just "jumped" a corporal whom I saw "ducking" and I thought trying to stop in a ravine when I looked up and saw, not 50 yards away partly concealed by the bank an Indian drop to his knee and squint over his rifle. I . . . turned my horse toward the right . . . at

the same time the Indian fired and I felt a shock as if hit by a stone or club on my left side.

I was just congratulating my good fortune in having turned enough to have the bullet strike my cartridge belt and glance off . . . [when] I felt my body swaying forward and a stinging pain in my side and body. I was powerless to prevent going over my horse's neck. My horse stopped, stood perfectly quiet and, then as if knowing the situation, partly lowered his head and I slid to mother earth!

I now looked at my antagonist; he had started in my direction a few steps, stopped and seemed satisfied with his job . . . and evidently began shooting at others; then he soon ran under the bank and disappeared—evidently to join his comrades, now hotly engaged by the whole battalion. I thought it singular, if I was wounded, that I didn't bleed. . . . In order to investigate I loosened my belt and the instant I did I felt the warm blood running down my body. So I "cinched" up again as quick as I could.[12]

Holding to the saddle with one hand and guiding his horse with the other, Godfrey started back toward the place where his troop had first been engaged, a position now occupied by the battalion of Fifth Infantry. Here he was helped on his horse and started for the sheltered spot which became the site of the hospital. However, he soon fell off again and had to be assisted to where the surgeons were at work. All told, this little journey was perhaps about a quarter of a mile. The captain had not been at the hospital long before Moylan came riding up with a bright red streak down his right leg.

Hale, who had inclined toward the right when he saw the broken ground ahead, crossed the coulee which terminated at the southeastern corner of the campsite and rode up on the flat prairie adjacent to the eastern side of the camp. Moylan reported:

when opposite the village he changed front and advanced toward the village, the Indians opened fire from the top of the bluff and Captain Hale could see that he could not charge thru so he dismounted to fight on foot and advanced to near the edge [of the cutbank], but the Indians pushed up the ravines on his flanks and had the troop surrounded and rushed at his horse holders and led horses. The conflict then became hand to hand. By this time A & D were approaching [led by Moylan and Godfrey "at the double time"] and the Indians withdrew to take position along the bluff to cover the village.

Capt Hale reformed his line but some distance back from the bluffs. When the hand to hand struggle commenced several were wounded and the dead were left on the line occupied near the edge of the bluff. Such wounded as could help themselves got back, but several who could not help themselves, among them Lt. J. W. Biddle, were subsequently killed. They were in the line of fire from both sides and their bodies had many shot wounds that were made after death. Capt Moylan had just dismounted to report [to the battalion commander] when a bullet struck him in the . . . [right] thigh and sent him spinning around. Fortunately the bullet passed between the artery and the bone, making a flesh wound. A few minutes after Moylan left for the hospital, Captain Hale, who was kneeling behind the firing line . . . reloading his revolver was shot, the bullet entering just under his "Adams apple" and passing through his neck killing him instantly.[13]

With each side confronting the other at close range, the battle had now become a slugging match.

Lieutenant Baird—writing "he" instead of "I"—recalled that when he was sent with an order to Captain Hale, he "rode to the position of Hale's battalion, all of whom, seeking such slight cover as inequalities of the surface afforded, were hotly engaged, gave the customary salute to its commander, who was lying among his men, and began the familiar formlua—'The General's complements and he directs'—when observing no response was given he looked more intently and saw that he was saluting the dead. Near Hale lay his adjutant, Lieutenant J.[onathan] W. Biddle. . . ."[14]

Not only were the Indians fighting desperately, but they had been picking their targets carefully. In the three companies of Seventh Cavalry, the only officer left on the line was Lieutenant Eckerson, and every first sergeant had been killed!

Soon after Troops "A" and "D" joined "K," Captain Snyder led the battalion of Fifth Infantry up to the edge of the cutbank where Moylan and Godfey had been turned back in the initial charge, and ordered his troops to execute a "left front into line." The men

threw themselves upon the ground, holding the lariats of their ponies in their left hands, and opened a deadly fire with their long range rifles upon the enemy with telling effect. The tactics were somewhat in Indian fashion and most effective, as they presented a small target . . . and their [Indian] ponies [accustomed to the confusion of battle] . . . stood quietly behind their riders, many of them putting their heads down to nibble the grass upon which they were standing.[15]

With the soldiers holding the top of the cutbank which overlooked the camp from the south, the areas which had provided excellent protection for the Indians at the opening of the fight were no longer tenable. The warriors now sought cover in the crooked gullies in the campsite, in holes dug within the fifty or sixty lodges which were still standing, and in rifle pits scooped out on the crest of the cutbank on the northern and northeastern sides of the camp. The conflict now developed into a deadly sniping duel.

Not being able to overrun the camp, Miles had the Hotchkiss gun brought up and an attempt was made to shell it; but the range was too short and the muzzle could not be depressed sufficiently for it to be effective. Furthermore, the Indians' fire soon forced the gunners to abandon their efforts. Next, the colonel turned his attention to trying to secure a foothold in the southern end of the village—the cluster of lodges on an isolated bit of the area being those belonging to Joseph and his followers. The plan decided upon was for Lieutenant Romeyn and his company, "G" of the Fifth Infantry, to move to the southeastern side of the camp. Here he was to take command of the two companies of Seventh Cavalry which had no officers. Then he was to push his troops up to the crest of the cutbank and, in conjunction with the troops to the south of the camp, direct their fire against the Indians in the gullies below. Meanwhile, Lieutenant Mason Carter was to take his company—said to have been 13 men of "I," 4 of "F," and 2 of "B" Companies, Fifth Infantry[16]—and dash down the cutbank at the southwestern corner of the flat, get into the bed of the creek, and then try to take the above-noted part of the camp. Allegedly, this maneuver was designed to cut the Indians off from water— just how is far from obvious.

It was midafternoon when Romeyn

was to give the signal for the movement, by swinging his hat when the three companies on the high ground were ready. Crawling back to his command the order was passed along the line, and then rising to his feet he swung the hat. The troops started with a cheer, some reaching the rifle pits only to fall dead on their edge, while a shot through the lungs put their commanding officer out of the fight [nearly killing him]. Company "I" succeeded in getting among the "tepees". . . .[17] Here they were met by Joseph and some of his men. The chief stated later that "ten or twelve soldiers charged into our camp and got possession of two lodges, killing three Nez Perces and losing three of their men, who fell inside our lines. I called my men to drive them back. We fought at close range, not more than twenty steps apart, and drove the soldiers back upon their main line, leaving their dead in our hands. We secured their arms and ammunition."[18] In this bit of action, Carter had one third of his force placed *hors de combat*.

Miles was staggered by the effects of the deadly fire of the Indians who picked off officers, key noncommissioned officers and almost everyone within range who exposed himself. On several occasions, officers found men who failed to move were dead; and a trumpeter, who was asked to sound a call, replied, "I can't blow, sir. I'm shot." Romeyn noted that one officer—who was probably himself—"had one shot through his belt, another carried away his field glass, while a third took off his hunting knife and cut the skin from an ear." Surgeon Tilton, who eventually received a Medal of Honor for fearlessly exposing himself while ministering to the wounded, wrote of the action:

> The bullets hum all the notes of the gamut, fit music for the dance of death; zip, zip, zip, thud, thud; the dirt is thrown up here and there, while others go singing overhead; riderless horses are galloping over the hills; others are stretched lifeless upon the field; men are being struck on every side, and some so full of life a few moments before have no need of the surgeon's aid. *The explosive balls are not all on our side.* [Italics are the author's.] One officer [Lieut. Baird] as he rides down the line is struck by a bullet which explodes, shatters the bone, tears a fearful hole in his [left] arm and carries off a good portion of his ear. Our gallant commander, on a splendid steed, is here, there, everywhere. When the first horse is blown a fresh one is mounted, and off again. Three horses are ridden down during the day; their rider never appears to tire.[19]

Although Miles was not satisfied with the way the charges had been carried out, he now recognized the formidable aspects of the situation. On the first attempt to talk with the Indians, the defiant reply had been, "Come and take our hair."[20] The colonel dared not order his men to try again. However, the Nez Perce—without ponies—could not escape without abandoning the wounded and many of the women and children. There was nothing either side could do but await further developments.

The "hospital" was in a depression less than a hundred yards back of the crest of the cutbank on the south side of the camp. Here the wounded were gathered—safe from enemy fire but with nothing between them and the sky but a blanket. There were no fires, for the nearest fuel, other than the wet *bois de vache* which lay on the prairie, was five miles away. Some of the wounded undoubtedly died from exposure; and two who were said to have revived after being considered as good as dead were Trumpeter Herwood and Lieutenant Romeyn. Stories about the wounded who had to be abandoned in Joseph's camp were told for years. When darkness came, some were given water and one, it is said, had a blanket placed under his head with the comment, "Poor boy, you're too young to go to war. I no kill you." While going through the pockets of another, the Indian assured him, "Me no kill you. You can't kill us. Me no want to kill a man who can't shoot." And what may be another version of the same incident states that while an Indian was searching one soldier, his hair "stood up" in terror. Noting this, the Indian said, "O! bother your scalp—I don't want that; fork over your ammunition."[21] Presumably, these wounded were retrieved the following day.

Indian casualties were also heavy—probably most of the seventeen dead and forty wounded which were reported later. According to Indian accounts, Too-hool-hool-zote and five others were killed and three wounded near a rocky point about a quarter of a mile north of the camp, where the Second Cavalry cornered them. Looking Glass and Ollokot were killed near a large rifle pit which the Indians dug on the extreme northern end of the cutbank bordering the east side of the camp. Pile of Clouds was also dead. If Poker Joe had not been killed by this time, he probably was soon afterward. Only two chiefs of major stature remained—Joseph and White Bird. But these two did not give up hope. Under the cover of darkness, they sent messengers to find Sitting Bull and ask the Teton Sioux to send help. It is likely that these met some Assiniboins and were foully murdered —lest their Agent accuse them of aiding the enemy.

Whether the Sioux would have responded had these runners reached them is problematical. They did become very excited when news came that a battle was in progress; and Northwest Mounted Police, who were in Sitting Bull's camp at the time, felt it was necessary to remain and exert a strong restraining hand. Furthermore, the Police, who were edgy over the powder-keg situation which had existed all summer, had previously warned the Sioux that if they did not stay north of the border, they would be denied the sanctuary of Canadian soil.

Although Miles knew that he had part of the Indians cornered, he was fearful and jittery. The three companies of Seventh Cavalry had lost 53 killed and wounded out of 115 (or 108) officers and men,[22] "I" Company of the Fifth Infantry had lost over one third of its number, and there were over forty wounded with almost no facilities for their care. In addition to these problems, he was considerably worried about the threat posed by the Sioux—a danger he had been watching for several months. At 5:30 that evening he sent a courier to find "General Howard, General Sturgis, or Major Brotherton" and deliver this message:

I have this day suprised the hostile Nez Perces in their camp, and have had a sharp fight. I have several officers and men wounded (about 30). About 25 [sic] Indians are still in their camp, which is well protected.

P.S.—We captured most of their herd, but I may have trouble in moving on account of my wounded. Please move forward with caution and rapidity.[23]

Perhaps this was as near as the proud colonel could come to saying that he had hold of a bear by the tail, and did not know what to do with it.

Surgeon Tilton wrote that "A dreary night succeeds an exciting day," and Romeyn recalled that "As soon as darkness closed in the troops were posted around the valley to prevent, as far as possible, the escape of any of . . . [the camp's] defenders. The line was necessarily a thin one and despite all precautions a few . . . succeeded in escaping. . . . * * * If to the men on duty that night was one of watchfulness; to the wounded it was one of ceaseless agony."[24]

The second day was as quiet as the preceding day had been action-packed. To Remsen, it contained much of unusual interest.

> Oct. 1—A cheerless morning, with clouds and winds and mist, succeeded by rain and, finally, snow. Early in the day we discovered in our rear two long lines of cavalry marching toward us on either flank. Were these Gen. Sturgis' troops, or the warriors of Sitting Bull? Many anxious moments were spent before we determined that they were buffalo marching in single file, with all the regularity and precision of soldiers.
>
> The Indians were again hailed. They came out with a flag of truce, and we see Joseph face to face. He is a man of splendid physique, dignified bearing and handsome features. His usual expression was serious, but occasionally a smile would light up his face, which impressed us very favorably. Several chiefs had been killed the day before, Looking Glass and Joseph's brother among them. Joseph appeared very sad; *he was inclined to surrender, but did not have control of the entire camp.* [Italics are the author's] Joseph remained with us that night, while Lt. Jerome, Second Cavalry, remained in the Indian village. Our wagon train arrived in the afternoon, bringing a twelve-pounder brass piece, which was of great service to us, as the Indians had been industriously digging rifle pits and holes for protection, which sheltered them from small arms [fire] very effectively.
>
> When the firing began that evening there was great anxiety in regard to the fate of Lt. Jerome; but we learned the next morning that the Indians had put him in a safe place, and said that no harm would come to him if Joseph was returned safely to them.[25]

Remsen's record is of unusual interest for, at the council held in May, Joseph was one of the foremost figures. However, from that time until this Monday morning, he had not appeared in a single meeting as a leader. In fact, his absence from the parleys in Lolo Canyon had started considerable speculation in that quarter as to his whereabouts even though he undoubtedly was present but in the background. Substantial evidence indicates that when Joseph wanted to surrender at Kamiah, he was outvoted in the tribal council and thus relegated to a subordinate spot—although it is doubtful if this was as "menial" as ex-Trooper Irwin reportedly told Sutherland it was. Here he had remained until Looking Glass, Too-hool-hool-zote, Ollokot and, probably, Poker Joe had been killed. White Bird, for reasons soon to be obvious, wanted no part of any council which might result in his personal freedom being compromised. Thus Joseph—by a process of elimination—again came into the position of prominence as the mouthpiece for the Non-Treaty Nez Perce. However, the Council still remained the supreme authority even though it was now reduced to but two major members.

Thus, on October 1, 1877, the legend that Joseph was *the* great chief of this faction, *the* mighty leader in battle, and *the* clever strategist seems to have been born. Unquestionably, Joseph was a towering figure; and had he possessed the degree of authority the *Joseph legend* has ascribed to him this futile flight would probably have ended at Kamiah on the morning of July 16th. Unfortunately, the governing body was a tribal council dominated by Looking Glass, White Bird and Too-hool-hool-zote.

Snyder's diary is explicit about a matter which has long been concealed except in Indian accounts:

Monday, October 1
Entire command upon the lines last night. No shots fired today, the time being consumed in negotiations looking to the surrender of the Indians, Chief Joseph being in council with Genl M. All looked well but later in the day signs were not so promising *Joseph was kept prisoner by Gen M* [Italics are author's] & Lt. Jerome through his own folly remaining in the hands of the Indians. My Battalion took up new position in front of village after dark. Wagon train arrived about 4 P.M.

There can be no question about the correctness of Snyder's entry, for even Miles wrote two days later, in a letter to his wife—"I had Chief Joseph in my camp one night . . . but unfortunately Lieutenant Jerome got detained in their camp, . . . and Joseph had to be exchanged for Jerome."[26]

Apparently, what happened was that Joseph came out under a flag of truce to discuss possible surrender terms; and negotiations, after starting favorably, reached a sort of stalemate, for reasons no longer clear. Jerome, who "is well known in army circles as a brave soldier, and withal a perfect dare-devil,"[27] went into the camp to see what was being done with the arms and/or to spy on their "fortifications." Then, Miles decided to hold Joseph, and the Indians—becoming alarmed about the absence of their chief—seized Lieutenant Jerome as a hostage. Snyder's diary indicates that

Jerome bungled something, and Jerome is alleged to have stated a few days later that "Miles evidently wanted to keep Joseph, but wanted me to escape." In what may be a truthful statement, Yellow Wolf told years later that Joseph was "hobbled hands and feet" by rolling him in a blanket, "like you roll papoose on cradle board."

None of the four accounts are in close agreement.[28] Jerome told the story twice, once ten days later and again when he was eighty years old. Unfortunately, the account related soon afterward bears evidence of a ready tongue stimulated by whiskey. However, both accounts do agree that the Indians responsible for his custody were friendly—and watchful. They treated him with courtesy, visited with him, and even allowed him to retain his side arms. He was allowed to walk about the camp—undoubtedly the extreme northern end—where there were many shelters and rifle pits; and he spent the night, comfortably, under a buffalo robe in a deep shelter pit with several guards. Here he was safe from the sporadic firing that started at dusk. Years later, Tom Hill, a Deleware-Nez Perce breed who claimed to have been one of the guards, stated that they had to watch carefully lest some hot-headed warrior attempt to shoot him.

According to the New York *Herald* reporter with the Sitting Bull Commission, Jerome stated that when Colonel Miles decided to surrender Joseph

> he was brought down under cover of a white flag to a space half way between the Nez Perces' position and our own. The General himself went with Joseph and was accompanied by one of his staff officers. There were three Indians along with me. I suppose that was an interesting position. With the suspicion of treachery on both sides, thirteen of our men lay in their trenches scarcely forty rods off, with their rifles held at a dead rest on Joseph and my three Indian guards. More than twenty Indians had an equally sure sight over their Winchesters and Henrys straight at General Miles and me. I have since learned that Miles' staff officer held a cocked revolver in his busom ready to fix Joseph if I should be harmed. The transfer passed without trouble, and I was restored to the command of my company.

On his return the lieutenant was able to report that "there are at least 100 warriors in camp and about 250 people altogether."[29]

Apparently, the Nez Perce relaxed their vigilance after leaving Howard well in the rear in the pursuit beyond Canyon Creek. At least there is no evidence that they fortified this camp as they had others. However, when the attack started, they began to dig in, and by the time Jerome was detained, they had a formidable position. They dug rifle pits inside the lodges which were still standing on the flat, piling their belongings around the edges and banking these with earth; and they literally honeycombed the sides of the two gullies at the northern end of the camp with shelter pits that were both large and deep. Seven rifle pits along the top of the cutbank across the northern side of the camp, and a very large, rock-rimmed pit on the northeastern corner of the cutbank wall, commanded all the approaches to the camp area which, by now, had shrunk to an area less than 250 yards square. And the handful of horses which remained were undoubtedly hidden in the steep-sided coulee at the northeastern corner of the camp where they were directly below the snipers in the pits on the cutbank wall.

Although the Indian strongpoints can still be easily located, the positions occupied by the troops are less clearly defined—except for the long, oblong depression in the hospital area where the dead were buried. About the only evidence remaining in uncultivated areas are piles of rocks placed in strategic positions—mainly to the southeast of the camp area. The location of these indicate that after the first day Miles did not station troops any closer to this hornets' nest than was necessary for surveillance. And completely unexplained is a string of rock shelters, sufficient to provide cover for twenty or thirty men, which is on the tip of a high ridge about a mile southeast of the battleground area. These suggest that a picket force may have been stationed here to watch for any Sioux who might approach from the north.

The arrival of the wagon train brought some relief for the wounded in the form of tents. However, when these were erected in the gathering darkness some were pitched beyond the protection of the depression. As soon as lights appeared in them, they drew fire from the Indians and, according to Romeyn, at least one man was wounded. Also, the arrival of the Napoleon gun was greeted with anticipation by the soldiers as it was a somewhat more versatile piece than the Hotchkiss gun. However, there was but very little ammunition for it.

Discomfort caused by the rain, snow and cold now became more acute. Snyder wrote:

Tuesday Oct 2

Negotiations are still going on today. Joseph & Lt. Jerome exchanged for each other but no new signs of surrender. Last night & today very disagreeable. Snow & rain and no covering. We all suffered. I think last night the most disagreeable I ever spent.

Whatever chances Miles had for an early surrender, he had muffed by seizing Joseph. Now it was a question of how long it would take to starve them out—provided the Sioux did not come.

It was on this day that Howard's troops marched into Carroll and went into camp. Here the general learned that the Indians had crossed at Cow Island Landing; also of Miles' whereabouts. Leaving Sturgis with the responsibility of the camp, Howard loaded the artillery and a battalion of infantry under Captain Miller, some scouts, and his staff on the steamboat *Benton* and started up the river for the landing. That evening, after he was well under way, Miles' courier arrived at Carroll with the dispatch for "General Howard, General Sturgis or Major Brotherton." Sturgis immediately requisitioned the services of the only boat available—probably the *Silver City*—and started to ferry the balance of the column across the river. However, "the night being very dark and the landing very bad, but little progress was made that night, and all the cavalry did not get over until the next evening." And the colonel also noted with regret that this course of action did not shorten the distance the troops had to march, and actually wasted the greater part of a day.

About 9 o'clock Wednesday morning, the *Benton* reached the landing where Howard found the courier that Miles had dispatched when he was marching along the Little Rockies. Revising his plans, the general sent Major Mason and the boat back down the river to Carroll while he started up Cow Creek on the trail of the Indians. With him went an escort of fifteen men, some scouts and the two Nez Perce herders, George and Captain John, his aides, Guy Howard and C. E. S. Wood, and—probably—Thomas Sutherland. Mason reached Carroll just as Sturgis was completing his crossing. Picking up the remainder of the foot troops and a few pack animals, he returned to the landing—by Thursday or early Friday morning—where he regretfully took leave of the comforts of the boat "to go out and sleep on the ground again and live on bacon and hardtack." Again the weary chase was resumed, with the column in two detachments, but with the knowledge that the quarry had been brought to bay at last.

Meanwhile the battle took on the aspects of a siege while the weather became worse. Snyder's record reads:

Wednesday Oct 3

The Indians not coming to terms offered opened fire on them about noon which was kept up all day but with little apparent effect. They replied by but a few shots. They are either short of ammunition or else we are too well entrenched for them to waste ammunition upon us. All hope of their surrender is gone & I suppose we will have to starve them out   To charge them would be madness.

And Remsen noted that, "the camp is moved to a better position. Firing begins with both field piece and small arms. We are in a snow storm."

Rifle fire had only a nuisance value, and the Napoleon gun did not afford anything much better. The gunners dug the trail of the gun in, thus elevating the muzzle and making a sort of howitzer out of the piece. This enabled them to lob shells into the camp but accurate fire was probably impossible. As the supply of ammunition was very limited, and the Indians were well protected, a negligible amount of damage was done. There was some sniping on this and the following day, the Cheyennes attempting to draw the fire of the Nez Perce by using decoys, but nothing of particular note happened.

Snyder's entry for Thursday reads:

> Firing along the lines again this morning and during the day. Several attempts were made to talk with the Indians but to no purpose. Genl. Howard and staff came in from below at dark. My Co relieved from the skirmish . . . [?] line this A.M. by Co "K" 5th Infy we having been continuously on duty since the morning of the 30 ult.

And the Surgeon wrote that it was "a disagreeable, raw, chilly, cloudy day; firing all day long. General Howard, with two aids and a small escort, arrive in the evening."

Howard had experienced no particular difficulty in locating Miles but the short march had been unpleasant. At the first camp after leaving the landing, they had used water from a pool of alkali water and this had a very disagreeable purgative effect on the party. The next day they met couriers who had just delivered messages to Sturgis, and these guided them to Miles' camp. As firing was still going on when they arrived, Howard's first thought was that pickets were shooting at him, but the colonel soon came out and escorted them to his camp which "was so sheltered in a ravine that we could not even see the lights of the small camp-fires until very near."

That night, as the two commanders discussed the situation, Miles was cool and reserved at first. However, when Howard explained that he "had no desire to assume immediate command of the field," he became friendly and the two made plans for joining their forces if the siege dragged out or the Sioux threat materialized. Then Howard mentioned that he had two old Nez Perce with him who had daughters in the hostile camp, and suggested that they might be of assistance in persuading the Indians to surrender.[30]

The situation was a touchy one. Howard was the ranking officer and he could have assumed command, just as he did with Sturgis, had he so desired. Although considerable unpleasantness was to arise over this matter in succeeding weeks, Howard's mandate was clear-cut and definite. None other than the General of the Army had given him a *carte blanche* to follow these Indians wherever they went—outside of Canada. And Sheridan, next in rank to Sherman, had given Terry definite orders to supply such assistance as was available in the Department of Dakota.

About 11 o'clock the next morning, Captain John and George were sent into the camp as intermediaries under a flag of truce. During the next few hours there was "much parleying and running to and fro between the camps" as various points were considered. Finally, at 2:20 P.M., the surrender terms were arranged with Joseph, and "White Bird concurred, saying, 'What Joseph does is all right; I have nothing to say.' "[31]

Snyder made two entries for this day, the second obviously written later:

Friday, October 5

Terms of surrender agreed upon & Joseph and his men or a number of them turned in their arms.

October 5

Severe firing along the lines this A.M. About 8 A.M. all firing [ceased?] and some Indians with Genl. H. went into the Hostiles camp and after a long delay returned and then went back to the Indian camp & the result at dark was that the Indians or a good portion of them surrendered at dark. Joseph and his outfit came in but White Bird & Co have lit out.

The entry for Saturday provides some supplementary information:

Surrender completed today But during last night a number of the disaffected ones left for parts unknown taking with them all the unfound arms in camp. My Co relieved Baldwins this A M   Officer of the day.

Neither Miles nor Howard have seen fit to reveal just what the surrender terms actually were. There is evidence to indicate that the Nez Perce were promised that they would be returned to their Idaho homeland, and that they would be permitted to keep their camp equipage, saddles, bridles and other horse gear, together with a part of the horse herd which had survived.[32] Now nothing remained but the actual surrender. It is regrettable that the record of this dramatic moment should be clouded by conflicting stories; and it is doubly unfortunate that one of Howard's aides has seen fit to write two widely divergent accounts, of which only one bears the earmarks of truth.[33] Equally unfortunate are various stories which state that Joseph was openly hostile to Howard at the actual surrender, for which there is no hint of supporting evidence.[34]

At the termination of the negotiations, the two Nez Perce herders brought out Joseph's final message. In Howard's official report is this record of that communication and the actual surrender:

> This reply of Joseph was taken verbatum on the spot by Lieutenant Wood, Twenty-first Infantry, my acting aide-de-camp and acting adjutant general, and is the only report that was ever made of Joseph's reply:
>
> "Tell General Howard I know his heart. What he told me before I have in my heart. I am tired of fighting. Looking Glass is dead. Too-hul-hul-sote is dead. The old men are all dead. It is the young men who say yes or no. He who led on the young men is dead. It is cold and we have no blankets. The little children are freezing to death. My people, some of them, have run away to the hills, and have no blankets, no food; no one knows where they are—perhaps freezing to death. I want to have time to look for my children and see how many of them I can find. Maybe I shall find them among the dead. Hear me, my chiefs. I am tired; my heart is sick and sad. From where the sun now stands I will fight no more forever."
>
> In accordance with this pledge, Joseph himself, accompanied by four or five of his warriors, came inside our lines, and Joseph set the example by offering me his rifle; but as the surrender was being made to Colonel Miles, I so instructed Joseph, and then they all delivered up their weapons to that officer. From this time, about 4 p.m., until after dark a straggling line of captives flowed into Miles's camp.[35]

According to popular legend—legend for which Lieutenant C. E. S. Wood is partially, perhaps wholly to blame—Joseph made the above-noted surrender speech *when he surrendered his rifle*. Unfortunately for this legend—and Lieutenant Wood—the original pencil draft of Howard's report still exists. It is in the handwriting of two persons, apparently Howard and Wood; and the portion quoted above is in *Wood's* handwriting. Joseph's reply does not appear in this draft. Instead, written in the margin at this point, are these words—"Here insert Joseph's reply to the demand for surrender."[36] The story that Joseph surrendered his rifle with this touching little speech, while Wood stood by "with a pencil and a paper pad" to record it, does not have a word of truth in it.

The formal surrender took place near evening; and the spot as identified years later is not far from the place where the hospital was established. Snow covered much of the surrounding countryside and the air was chilly and raw. Only Howard, Miles and a small group were present to receive the surrender. Correspondent Sutherland has described the scene:

As the sun was dropping to the level of the prairie and tinging the tawny and white land with waves of ruddy lights, Joseph came slowly riding up the hill ["on a black pony with a Mexican saddle, dressed in a woolen shirt of dark slate color, with a blanket of red, yellow and blue stripes around his hips, and a pair of beadless moccasins. His front hair was tied straight back from his forehead with a small strip of otter skin, making a . . . "top-knot," and the hair at the sides was braided and held back, with the waving loose locks behind, by longer pieces of the same fur."] Five of his followers walked beside him; he, the only one on horseback, in the center of the group. His hands were crossed on the pommel of the saddle, his head bowed upon his breast. His warriors talked in eager murmurs, he listening and making no reply. The Indian camp lay in the lengthing shadows and as the little group came up from the darkening valley into the higher light which showed their wrechedness, Joseph ["rode up to General Howard, whom he immediately recognized"], lifted his head, and with an impulsive gesture, straightened his arm toward General Howard, offering his rifle, as if with it he cast away all ambition, hope and manly endeavors leaving his heart and his future down with his people in the dark valley where the shadows were knitting about them a dusky shroud. * * *

Howard motioned Joseph to Miles and the latter received his rifle—the token of submission. ["Joseph had scarcely turned his gun over to Miles, when Indians were seen in every direction coming into our camp. Among those to surrender were many blind old men and women and lame and wounded young men, and the thought naturally arose, How could Joseph have traveled so rapidly with such maimed followers?"] * * * The only chiefs to surrender with Joseph, were White Bird, Black Tail and Hush-hush-kute, but the former regretted the step almost as quickly as made, and ["At dusk, . . . with his two squaws, and accompanied by about 14 warriors"[37]] escaped with those who had been cut off in the first day's fight.[38]

The only connected account of what happened after the surrender is that set down by Lieutenant Wood. However, in this case there is positive evidence which supports this version. The aide recalled that after the surrender Miles showed Howard what was apparently a dispatch. The general read it, and returned it—apparently pleased with its contents. Miles and one of his officers then walked to a courier who, with his horse, was waiting nearby. Here there was an appreciable delay before the rider left. Wood believed that the message which Howard read acknowledged the fact that he was present and assisted in negotiating the surrender, whereas the message which was carried to General Terry in Fort Benton read:

Department of Dakota
General A. H. Terry, Commanding Department of Dakota

DEAR GENERAL,

We have had our usual success. We made a very direct and rapid march across the country and after a severe engagement and being kept under fire for three (3) days the hostile camp of Nez Perces under Chief Joseph surrendered at two oclock today. I intend to start the Second Cavalry toward Benton on the seventh inst. Cannot supplies be sent out on the Benton Road to meet them and return with the remainder of the command to the Yellowstone. I hear that there is trouble between the Sioux and the Canadian authorities. I remain, General, your very truly

NELSON A. MILES
Col. Bvt. Maj Gen. USA
Commanding

Headquarters District of the Yellowstone
Camp on Eagle Creek, M.T. Oct 5, 1877[39]

Wood believed that Miles substituted this message which gave to him all the glory associated with the final surrender.[40] In a letter which the colonel wrote to his wife that evening, he merely acknowledged the presence of Howard—"General Howard arrived last night."

Outwardly, Miles apparently tried to create the impression that he was grateful for Howard's assistance, and also for the courtesy of being allowed to receive Joseph's surrender. Sutherland wrote five days later:

This courtesy on the part of General Howard was not lost on Colonel Miles, who took occasion several times during his stay there to show the General how keenly he appreciated his services in the victory. . . . [which would be of assistance to him in securing the desired promotion to Brigadier General].[41]

26

Aftermath

➤➤➤➤➤➤➤◄◄◄◄◄◄◄ According to Miles' report dated the day after the surrender, the price of the victory was two officers, seven sergeants, one corporal and thirteen privates—a total of twenty-three—killed. The wounded numbered forty-five and included four officers, five sergeants, two corporals and two scouts, Hump the Sioux chief and White Wolf, a Cheyenne. Some of the wounded—both Indian and white—did not survive the journey to the Cantonment. As for the Nez Perce, "The Indians admit a loss of Chiefs Looking Glass, Too-hool-hool-sote, Ollicut, a brother of Joseph and two (2) other of their principal men and twenty-five (25) killed and forty-six (46) wounded."[1]

Exactly how many Indians were in the camp at the time of the surrender is not known with certainty. Remsen noted that they began the return march with 405. In a communication dated November 24th, Sheridan stated that the prisoners totaled 431, which included 79 men, 178 women and 174 children. On December 4th, General John Pope acknowledged the receipt of 418 at Fort Leavenworth, Kansas—87 men, 184 women and 147 children. The discrepancies represent difficulties in separating children from adults, and losses due to death.

When a controversy arose the next year over the property which the Nez Perce claimed was to have been returned to them, the number of horses captured became an important item in the discussion. A fragment of a memorandum, obviously prepared by Miles, states:

> . . . or captured by the troops and Indian scouts of my command to have been 800 accounted for as follows viz:
>
> | | |
> |---|---|
> | Captured and given to Cheyennes | 150 |
> | Killed in battle | 120 |
> | Died enrout plain Bear Paw to Tongue River | 105 |
> | Arrived at Tongue River | 425 |
>
> Many of those that survived the journey were broken down & worn out and subsequently died.
>
> The saddles etc mentioned in enclosures were carefully stored but were burned with a considerable amt of public property in a warehouse burned at Cantonment mouth of Tongue River.[2]

Ad Chapman, the Idaho scout who accompanied the Nez Perce as an interpreter, informed the Commissioner of Indian Affairs a little over a year later that the total number was 1,531. Of these, 300 had been given to the Cheyennes "leaving 1231 as counted by me, with which the command left Bear Paw Mountain," and "about 500" were lost, killed or stolen while en route to the Cantonment. He also stated:

> There were 300 saddles of which 60 were good Spanish saddles. . . .
> * * * . . . the Saddles, Bridles, Ropes, Robes, Blankets and Camp Equipage, &c were packed and stowed away at Ft Keogh to be returned to the Nez Perces on their return in the Spring, enrout to Idaho. The horses about 700 in number were left at Ft Keogh by order of Gen Miles with the distinct understanding that together with the Camp Equipage, &c they should be returned to the Nez Perce in the spring.[3]

If Chapman actually counted the ponies, he should have known how many were captured.

Among the scouts and soldiers were some who were curious about the weapons possessed by the Nez Perce. There were stories that an Indian did some remarkable shooting at the battle of the Big Hole from a distance of about 800 yards; and it was reported that four soldiers were killed at Canyon Creek by a marksman located 1,300 "measured" yards away. Scout "Muggins" Taylor searched the camp for unusual arms but found nothing. It is not improbable that such a rifle, or rifles, did exist and were hidden or taken to Canada by escapees. Two weeks later, Miles commented on their arms in a letter addressed to General Terry:

> [The Nez Perce] are the best marksmen I have ever met and understand the use of improved sights and the measurement of distances. They were armed principally with Sharps, Springfield and Henry rifles and used explosive bullets. I have quite a quantity now in my possession and shall forward samples.[4]

Explosive bullets were used to some extent in hunting, principally for big game in foreign lands but their use in warfare was frowned upon. Although both Union and Confederate forces had used such bullets in the Civil War, there is no firm evidence that any .45–70 ammunition of this sort was issued to troops.[5] However, such ammunition was not difficult to fabricate for anyone skilled in reloading cartridges.

While no unusual wounds were reported in the battle of the Clearwater, Captain Charles A. Coolidge, wounded at the Big Hole fight, told a reporter of the Chicago *Times:* "Some of the Nez Perces fired percussion bullets, which, striking trees or rocks, exploded with a loud report." This observation is supported by another statement made by a soldier years later; and there is a report of questionable accuracy that such bullets were used at Camas Meadows.[6] However, Surgeon Tilton made a significant comment when he wrote, "The explosive balls are not all on our side," indicating that he was aware of their use against the Nez Perce. Perhaps it was he who led the search of the Indian camp for such ammunition. What was found was a quantity of .35 caliber cartridges, probably of English manufacture, that were so unusual that Miles reported the find to Terry.

Two and a half years later, Major Tilton set down his recollections of the matter:

> . . . during the siege . . . I was disposed to doubt that the Nez Perces had any explosive balls, although several men insisted that they had been struck by them, as they distinctly heard the explosion. * * * I was curious to know how the Indians had obtained these explosive balls, and heard upon enquiry that in passing through Idaho they had made a raid upon a "ranch" of an Englishman who had hunted in all parts of the world, and who was well supplied with rifles and ammunition, and the Nez Perces had captured his outfit although he escaped. * * * My attention having been drawn to the subject, I found that a citizen employe with the 7th Cavalry had explosive balls for use in hunting. The Winchester rifle ball [.44 ?] was cast with a cavity of proper size to receive .22 calibre cartridge at its apex. . . .[7]

Obviously, the ammunition was secured when the Indians looted the ranch of Mr. Croaesdale, the ex-British officer who had settled near Mount Idaho. And if they had any unusual rifles, they undoubtedly came from the same source.

As noted, the charge of the Second Cavalry cut off a portion of the Indians from the camp. Probably some of these remained in the vicinity while the battle was in progress, for scouts going to and coming from Fort Benton reported seeing small groups of stragglers, presumed to be Nez Perce. The last to join these was White Bird, his two squaws and about fourteen warriors who escaped after Joseph surrendered. Except for the few who were treacherously murdered by Assiniboins camped a few miles away along Milk River, and a few who were picked up by scouting details, most of these probably managed to reach Sitting Bull's camp.

When *moccasin telegraph* brought the news that the Nez Perce were headed for Canada with U.S. troops in pursuit, tension among the Teton Sioux began to mount. Inspector James M. Walsh, in command of the Northwest Mounted Police at Fort Walsh—about 100 miles north of the Bearpaw Mountains—took a few men and went to their camp, where he established a twenty-four-hour vigil. Finally, the Sioux quieted down. Then, on October 8th, excitement flared again when news came that a mounted party was approaching. Walsh and about 200 warriors rode out to investigate. According to one historian, they met a party of fugitives arriving in "pitiable condition" with many wounded. One woman had been "shot in the breast and the ball had turned upward passing through the side of her head. Despite her condition she valiantly rode a small pony with a child strapped on her back." There were "98 Nez Perce men, 50 women including Chief Joseph's daughter, and about as many children and 300 horses."[8]

On October 22nd, Walsh returned to the camp and held a council with the Sioux and Nez Perce, but this was an unsatisfactory meeting owing to the lack of a good interpreter. He reported four days later that "as far as I can learn there are 90 men and 200 women and children in the Teton camp. One party of 30 and another of 10 persons arrived there two or three days ago after my leaving the camp."[9] Apparently, slightly over half of the abled-bodied men succeeded in reaching Canada. And if Joseph was correct in stating that they numbered at least 300 fighting men at the battle of the Clearwater, then slightly over one third were numbered among the missing and dead.

White Bird's desire to escape was undoubtedly motivated by a fear of reprisal. In 1858, Colonel George Wright had, in the presence of some Nez Perce warriors, summarily hanged a Yakima chief who had been accused of murder; and in October 1873, Captain Jack and five other

Modoc leaders had been hanged at Fort Klamath for the General Canby affair. The Government had established a precedent. Although White Bird's fear was probably groundless, the three original culprits had come from his band. Miles had sensed this attitude when he first attempted to negotiate with Joseph, for he reported at that time: "I believe there are many escaped villains in the village who expect to be hung when caught."[10] On July 16th at Kamiah, Sutherland made a similar comment: "Joseph and White Bird and other chiefs were determined on not surrendering, as they would all be hanged."[11] And Howard, writing a few months later about the May council, where he was guilty of a summary action, stated:

> Looking Glass came to me and begged me to release the old man (Too-hul-hul-sote) from confinement. He said . . . he and White Bird would be responsible for his good behavior. (It was doubtless this pledge to me in memory that made Looking Glass afraid to surrender, and always say: "General Howard will surely hang us," and so affected White Bird that he crept out between the lines rather than risk meeting me; for he said we would "soon begin to kill the prisoners.")[12]

After the surrender, Howard sent couriers to stop the advance of Sturgis and Mason, who were only about twenty-five miles away; and Miles spent the next two days preparing his command for their return journey. The battalion of Second Cavalry was again dispatched to escort the Sitting Bull Commission to the Canadian line; the dead were buried; and preparations were made to transport the large number of wounded. Also, detachments were sent out to try to gather up stragglers—a task that was not completed in two days or in two months, for during the following June, Lieutenant Baird was to purchase one boy from the Assiniboins for "25# sugar, 5# tea, 3# tobacco and 25# flour."[13]

In a report dated October 22nd, Inspector Walsh recorded the adventures of one of these details—perhaps Ad Chapman and one of the Nez Perce herders with Howard:

> Two persons, a white man and a Nez Perce Indian, were sent by General Miles to the Teton camp to try to induce White Bird and his camp to go and give themselves up. They arrived in the camp on or about the 16th. Had it not been for the protection afforded them by the Tetons the Nez Perce would, I am informed, have killed them. The Nez Perce women were perfectly savage. * * * Two nights before my arrival the Nez Perce Indian escaped, and one night after the white man made his escape. * * * I believe the Tetons assisted them in making their escape.

One of the most interesting features of these post-surrender days was visits with Joseph who, apparently, was cooperative, frank and honest. Sutherland reported the substance of these in two dispatches. Under a dateline of October 13th he wrote for the Portland *Weekly Standard*:

> Gen Howard and Col. Miles had several talks with Joseph. He stated his losses and revealed his actions very freely. He reiterated that he was across the Salmon river when the war began; said he knew nothing of the murders on Camas Prairie; that the murderers were now dead; says his wife was sick [confined] at the time of the outbreak. The only child left to him is a little girl, born in White Bird [Canyon], about the time of the fight. His other child ran into the hills during this last engagement and cannot be found.[14]

And in a dispatch dated October 10th for the San Francisco *Chronicle*, he stated:

> I held a long conversation with Joseph by the aid of an interpreter, the substance of which was about as follows: Poker Joe, whom I imagined at one time to be chief, was merely camp chief, directing when and where to camp, and was killed early in the Miles fight. . . . Ollicot, Joseph's brother, and Ta-hool-hool-shute were killed in rifle-pits, and Looking Glass sent to the happy hunting ground while enjoying a smoke in his tent during the fight, having half of the top of his head shot off. "Charley," who led the band that tried to kill the Cowan party, after Joseph had permitted them to leave his camp, is among the Indians now with Miles. . . . Speaking with Joseph about the Clearwater fight he said that at this place he had fully three hundred men and expected to win the day. * * * He says he wanted to surrender at Kamiah, but he was overpowered in the council by others, especially Looking Glass, who painted the picture of the future in such rose colors that he could not resist. . . . I asked him if he bore any ill will toward James Reuben, a Nez Perce Indian who acted as a scout for us near Kamia, and he answered promptly: "No; a war is a thing where there are two sides. . . ." * * * He says that he himself committed no murders, but on the contrary tried to stop them, going so far as to spare Mrs. Cowan, her sister and brother, just after the Gibbon fight, when Indian women and children dead by far outnumbered the bucks. He is a temperate man and says that captured whiskey was usually at the bottom of all murders, the Indians getting almost crazy with it and utterly beyond his influence. He was glad to see General Howard, and he felt he would receive justice, and paid him the complement of saying that it was he that broke him in spirit and strength at Clearwater, and so effectively that he never recovered from the blow.[15]

The reporter also wrote this description of the chief:

> Physically Joseph is a splendid looking man. He is fully six feet high; in the prime of life—about 35, has a splendid face and well formed head. His forehead is high, his eyes bright yet kind, his nose finely cut, and his mouth, though determined, rather too sad looking for actual beauty.

Joseph's critique of the war was unquestionably straightforward and honest. If he did not dwell on the part played by the other chiefs, it may have been because he was not questioned about such matters. It takes skill and experience to manage an interrogation properly. Perhaps the most penetrating observation was that pertaining to the role of liquor. Whiskey —probably from a trader at White Bird—may have made the malcontents edgy at Tepahlewam. Whiskey—perhaps in wagons captured on Camas Prairie—was probably to blame for the outrages committed on the Norton party. Whiskey, looted from the stores in that vicinity, fed the fires of hatred that blazed high at White Bird for two days. And there was whiskey in the wagons captured at Birch Creek, and in the piles of freight at Cow Island Landing. All this cost the Government $931,329.02—exclusive of dead and wounded soldiers and civilians, destroyed property and stolen stock none of which was recovered by civilian owners. It was to cost the Indians everything they owned, plus an incalculable price in heartbreak and sorrow.

By noon of the second day after the surrender, Miles' command was ready to march. Lieutenant Romeyn, himself among them, recalled the ordeal of the wounded:

> The only ambulance with the command was given up to two enlisted men, one of whom had a broken thigh, and the other shot through the hips. They lived to reach the river, but the latter died as he was carried on board the steamer. Wagons, the beds of which were filled with small brush covered with grass, were utilized for the conveyance of such others as could not bear transportation on horseback. Much of the country was rough and broken in character, and, although all possible care was exercised, the suffering of many of the injured was intense. The brush and grass soon became unevenly packed down and every jolt of the wagons seemed to open up fresh wounds.[16]

To the surgeon, the scene was both interesting and colorful:

> We began our march, Oct. 7, with 405 Nez Perces, from the octogenarian to the papoose born during the siege. The country is

rolling and picturesque, with snow and pine-covered mountains in the background. Sunshine and cloud shadows add to the beauty of the scene. The Indians clad in lively colors and strung out in a long line; the pack train, the pony herd, the mounted troops, the wagons, the [Indian ?] wounded on travois, all combine to make an unusual and striking picture. Soon after camping dark clouds roll up, and lightning, thunder, wind and rain threaten to cause a stampede, but the storm soon passes over. The next morning dull clouds and rain, which finally pours down in a torrent, keep us in camp all day.[17]

And, although no mention was made of the grim fact, the bodies of Captain Hale and Lieutenant Biddle were carried along. These were transported to Bismarck, and then shipped east for burial.

Howard and his little party left as soon as Miles was ready to march, and returned to his own troops. These marched rapidly, by way of the southern side of the Little Rockies to the steamboat *Benton* which was waiting for them at the mouth of "Little Rocky Creek"—probably Rock Creek. Here all went on board and the boat then dropped down to the mouth of Squaw Creek where they awaited the arrival of Miles' troops and the prisoners.

In the meantime, the Cheyenne and Sioux scouts, jubilant over their newly acquired ponies, rode directly to their camp near the Tongue River Cantonment. Although they brought welcome news, they also created consternation among the little group of wives at the post. The Indians were able to indicate that two officers had been killed, but they could not identify the dead other than to indicate that Miles was not one of them. Lieutenant Baldwin's wife recalled that the three-day wait for the courier was an agonizing ordeal, and that its end brought something akin to an attack of hysterics. Johnny "Big Leggins" Bruguier, the Yankton Sioux half-breed who came in with the dispatches, is said to have surveyed the weeping ones—the dead officers being bachelors—and then remarked dryly, "I suppose God Almighty made them that way, but I don't know what for."[18]

It was midafternoon of the sixth day after leaving the battlefield when Miles' column reached the bank of the Missouri opposite the mouth of Squaw Creek. Here they found the *Benton* and the *Silver City*, and the next day and a half were spent in ferrying troops across and taking care of details such as the transfer of property which Howard's men did not need to Miles' quartermaster. Here, and at Snake Creek, Howard issued orders which were to raise a furor. Sturgis, who apparently had a bellyful of campaigning, prevailed on the general to write an order directing him to proceed "to his proper post, there to make arrangements for the present and prospective needs of his regiment,"[19] and his men were turned over to

Miles to insure the safe delivery of the captives to the Cantonment.[20] However, the order which was to become a major point of contention was one which Howard stated later was actually requested by Miles. This read:

> *Headquarters Department of the Columbia In the Field*
> *Battlefield of Eagle Creek, near Bear Paw Mountain M.T.*

Colonel Nelson A. Miles
* 5th Infantry*
Commanding District of Yellowstone

COLONEL:

On account of the cost of transportation of the Nez Perce prisoners to the Pacific Coast, I deem it best to retain them at some place within your district, where they can be kept under military control, until next spring. Then, unless you receive instructions from higher authority, you are hereby directed to have them sent, under proper guard, to my department, where I will take charge of them and carry out the instructions I have already received. You will treat them as prisoners of war, and provide for them accordingly, until the pleasure of the president shall be known. Should you need any special authority for the issue of necessary supplies, including clothing, it is hereby given you. Also my orders with regard to the pursuit & capture or driving the hostiles beyond the limits of the United States, are now fulfilled, I shall move the troops belonging to my department and the Military Division of the Pacific, back to their posts. General Sturgis' troops that have been under my command since we formed junction near Clark's Fork Cañon, will report to you for orders. You will certainly need them to guard against any possible movement of hostile Sioux, until you shall have crossed the Missouri. Then I hope you may see proper to return them to their post as their condition from hard service plainly requires rest and re-fitting.

Permit me to congratulate you with all my heart and give you . . . my sincere thanks for your grand success—it is the cooperation with my over-worked column which I coveted, and . . . [felt certain] that I should receive the moment I came within the scope of your operations.
* * *

I am gratified to have been present and to have contributed ever so little to facilitate the surrender and disposal of your capture.

With Great Respect,
I remain
Very Respectfully yours
O. O. HOWARD
Brigadier General
Commanding Department[21]

"Before dark" on October 15th, the *Benton* and the *Silver City* with the wounded on board—the infantrymen and the critical cases bound for Fort Buford and the cavalrymen for Fort Abraham Lincoln and Fort Rice—headed downstream. Howard's troops, about 450 in number, would go down the Missouri on the *Benton* as far as Omaha. From this point they would go by train to San Francisco and thence to their respective posts. Howard and some of his staff would leave the boat at Bismarck, D.T., for a quick visit to St. Paul and Chicago.

About three years later, after wounds had healed somewhat, Howard wrote succinctly:

> After . . . [the surrender], there arose all sorts of heart-burnings, reports filled with claims and counter claims for credit. There were necessarily diversities of statement, rivalries, criminations, and controversies. . . .
> Such jealous disputations, like the smoke on the [battle] field, often obscure for a time the results of the conflict, but have a way of correcting themselves by the lapse of time. Accomplished results are the things that, in the main, concern a general, an army, a historian, a man.
> I was sent to conduct a war without regard to department and division lines. This was done with all the energy, and help at my command, and the campaign was brought to a successful issue.[22]

At times, Howard had been roundly criticized by the public and the press. Not knowing what they asked, they had demanded results which could not possibly be achieved, and then clamored for his removal when they were not forthcoming. Most of his troops, soft from garrison life, probably were not the equal of the seasoned infantry and cavalry units commanded by Gibbon and Miles or, perhaps, even of Sturgis' Seventh Cavalry, which was still licking the wounds suffered in Custer's disaster. Also, the general made a poor situation worse by continually sending dispatches that gave the definite impression that total success was just around the next bend in the trail, by criticizing others for failing to do what he had not been able to do, and by not accurately appraising the nature of the enemy and the effect of formidable terrain on his own capabilities. And the Freedmen's Bureau difficulties undoubtedly added an additional burden.

However, for the most part, the campaign had been conducted in a satisfactory manner. Howard recognized the opportunity to block the movement eastward and tried to force the Indians back when they entered the Great Snake River Plain; he used Sturgis' troops in a creditable manner; he conceived the tactics involving the use of Miles' forces, and he delayed his march—Miles' denial to the contrary—in such a way as to give the colonel all possible opportunity to head off the hostiles. And, although some criticized his religious ways, there is no evidence that he refrained from campaigning on Sunday. Furthermore, no one worked harder than he or was more fearless in positions of danger.

And so, as the *Benton* puffed her way down the Missouri, Howard had reason to feel that he had conducted a successful campaign. According to an account which his aide, Lieutenant Wood, wrote years afterward, this feeling came to an abrupt end when the steamboat tied up for the night at a point about thirty-five miles above Bismarck. Here—as he told it— officers from Fort Abraham Lincoln came aboard bringing copies of Chicago newspapers. One of these contained Miles' dispatch written after the surrender, which Terry had forwarded to Sheridan from Fort Benton. As Howard read the "We have had our usual success" message, he realized that his part in bringing the campaign to a successful conclusion had been completely ignored. "General Howard was absolutely brokenhearted over this; he could not understand it. . . ."[23]

Unfortunately, some of the things which Wood set down cannot be accepted as the truth. However, irrespective of *how* or *when* it came about, there can be no reasonable doubt that he was correct in stating that the general was deeply hurt by this selfish glory-grabbing. Miles had been one of Howard's aides during the Civil War, and the general was said to have assisted him in securing his first command. Furthermore, only eight months before, the colonel had written to Howard requesting a favor:

> *Hd Qrs Yellowstone Command Montana Territory*
> *Feby 1st 1877*

DEAR GENERAL

I presume there may be a vacancy among the Brig Genls and some of my friends will make an effort to have my name favorably considered. If you can assist them you will do me a very great favor. . . . * * * I feel that I have earned it and should prize your endorsement very highly. * * *

On March 14th, Howard addressed this letter to Sherman:

DEAR GENERAL,

I have had some private intimation that there will be a vacancy soon, probably by resignition, in the Brigadierships.

Of course there will be many recommendations and it may be that promotion will have some regard to seniority. I wish to say that Col. Nelson A. Miles (5th Infantry) served in several battles *with* me or *under my eyes*, in the early part of the war. He, once when severely wounded in the throat, had himself brought to me, stopping the flow of blood with his fingers and thumb closing the wound, in order to point out the place where he thought reinforcement would be most effective. For gallantry, persistency & ability as an officer, few if any could exceed Miles.

I give him my cordial recommendation for his own glorious service.

Should you wish from me a detailed statement of his record I will at any time gladly furnish it.

Very Respectfully yours
O O Howard
Brig. Gen. USA[24]

And Howard, understanding that credit for the Nez Perce surrender might be helpful to the colonel in securing this promotion, had graciously stood aside when he could have taken the surrender himself.

Although Wood has stated that Howard "ordered me to get one of the steamer's boats," Major Mason noted—in a letter written several hours previously—that, as the *Benton* would not reach Bismarck that day, "our plan is to take one of the small boats and make the rest of the trip after night." And this officer indicated that he was interested in making a quick trip from Bismarck to St. Paul and then rejoining the troops after the steamboat had delivered them to Omaha. Thus when the steamboat tied up for the night, Howard—together with Major Mason and Lieutenants Wood, Fletcher and Howard, and with four privates to man the oars—embarked in a "yawl" and set out for Bismarck. This point they reached at 2:30 A.M. the next morning; and, as the train left for St. Paul at 7 o'clock, there was but little time for sleep.

A "representative" of the Bismarck *Tri-Weekly Tribune* found Guy Howard at work in the lobby of the Sheridan House shortly after 4 A.M., and the general made his appearance a scant hour later. The fruits of this brief interview filled half of the front page of the issue which appeared that afternoon (October 22nd). Among other things, this story states that Howard was on his way to Chicago to confer with Sheridan about plans for handling the prisoners during the coming winter. If Howard was bitter about anything it was not obvious, for this reporter wrote:

He hadn't heard the news or seen any report of the surrender of Joseph, the comments of the press thereon or the late general intelligence, home or abroad. * * * [He] was glad to learn that Genl Sheridan had done him justice in his interviews with the newspapers and had officially recognized his pursuit of Joseph and his share in bringing the bad Indians to grief. He keenly feels the newspaper criticisms and slurs that have been so unjustly heaped upon him.

However, *sometime* before Howard reached Chicago—on board the *Benton*, in Bismarck, or en route to Chicago—he became aware of the fact that Miles had tried to garner much of the credit for ending the campaign, and that Sheridan was praising his subordinate. According to Wood's account, when he and Howard parted just after reaching Chicago—the latter to visit his brother—he asked for and was given permission to write a "true account of the surrender." Although this aide claimed that he wrote the story which appeared promptly in the Chicago *Times*, its contents indicate that it was prepared by a reporter who had interviewed an officer who had "seen much hard service in the Indian Country"— probably, Lieutenant Wood. Regardless of who prepared it, this attempt to correct the story previously placed before the public made the inexcusable error of implying that certain opinions had Sheridan's approval— which they did not. The article read, in part:

> Gen Sheridan, while according to Miles all the glory he had honorably and rationally achieved, thinks that Howard and Sturgis should share the credit of the victory with him. He says the fact should not be overlooked that Gen. Miles pounced upon and captured a game which had been chased to death by Howard and Sturgis. The lieutenant general believes that Howard, whose campaigning has been severely criticized, has done the very best he knew how, and that the soldiers under him have suffered great privations and hardships in their unparalled march. Evidently Gen. Sherman would like to see Gens. Howard, Gibbon, Miles and Sturgis share in the credit of the campaign in proportion that is due to each one for honest service performed.[25]

Shortly after the edition carrying this story appeared, Howard and Wood called at Sheridan's office, where they found that individual furious. The meeting was a stormy one—Sheridan being notorious for having a hot temper. Later in the day, Howard sent a short note of apology:

Gen. P. H. Sheridan
  Lieut. General USA
GENERAL:
  I wish to assume the entire responsibility for the publication of the dispatch sent to you from the Missouri River. I wished the publication made with the view of placing before the public the facts of the campaign as they appeared to me and I did not dream of there being any objection from yourself in the premices and I am sorry to have compromised you in any way.

Yours respectfully.
O. O. HOWARD
Brig Gen, USA[26]

Sheridan, caught in the embarrassing position of supporting a subordinote who was trying to acquire more than his share of the glory, now tried to divert attention by waving the threat of courts-martial for making an unauthorized disclosure of information. For this he was soundly ridiculed by the San Francisco *Chronicle*,[27] and politely laughed at in a letter which Howard wrote to Sherman. Furthermore, anyone who had read the Montana newspapers over the past year knew that Miles was a persistent offender in similar situations.

This acrid exchange was only the beginning. Terry, perhaps smarting from losing an argument with Howard about a year before over their respective dates of rank, now wrote a long, peevish letter to Sheridan's adjutant in which he criticized Howard for having issued orders to Sturgis and Miles after the surrender. This was forwarded to the Adjutant General, who forwarded it to Howard with this endorsement:

> General Howard was clearly wrong in giving orders to Colonel Miles concerning the future disposition of the Nez Perce prisoners and still more so in his Special Field Order No. 69 in giving instructions to Colonel Sturgis.
>
> Copy of this paper with endorsements will be sent to General Howard who will I know be prompt to disclaim any intended discourtesy to Genl Terry.[28]

This, on top of Miles' discourtesy, was too much for Howard to stomach. In an answer which pulled no punches, he quoted seven separate communications which had directed him to do what he did, as well as extending to him the necessary authority. And he insisted that,

> From previous orders and from telegrams of the Department commanders and also from the necessity of the situation I regarded myself, as previously intimated, as actually in command of all the troops in the field operating against the Nez Perces, and endeavored to exercise the functions of such commander with all possible courtesy to the Department Commanders within whose limits I was forced to go.[29]

Sherman, whose cutting across channels of command to expedite the campaign had created this situation, now had to step in and stop the feuding. He endorsed Howard's letter on to Terry with the admonition that "it is the judgment of the General of the Army that this communication should not lead to controversy." Although this ended the major quarrel, both Gibbon and Miles later objected to some of the views Howard was alleged to have expressed to representatives of the press.

Miles' troops and the captives left the mouth of Squaw Creek late in the forenoon of October 16th and, traveling by easy marches, reached the north bank of the Yellowstone a week later. Remsen described the scene:

> After a march of over 500 miles the command arrived at the canton-ment on Tuesday October 23. A lovely day. The scene was interesting and picturesque. The approach to the Post on the north side of the Yellowstone is over a high plateau, from which the road winds down a ravine to the river bank. First came the commanding officer and his staff, accompanied by Joseph and a few of his followers; then the advance guard, followed by the Indians in picturesque groups; then the pack train and more troops, the wagon train and flanking columns, the pony herd and rear guard. As the command filed down the ravine, flags were unfurled, the band struck up, "Hail to the Chief," while the cannon thundered forth a salute of welcome.[30]

Early in September, when victory was still a month away, haggling had started over the disposition of the prisoners-to-be. Inspector Watkins, perhaps concerned that he had gone too far in pressuring some of the Nez Perce to stay neutral—"I have told them that no Indian engaged in warfare against the Government would ever be allowed to return to his country and his people"—requested the Commissioner of Indian Affairs to send them "so far away that they can never return." He did not agree with General McDowell that they should be returned to Idaho for punishment; and he did voice one objection that probably had considerable logic behind it—"Besides the white people living in the vicinity would kill any and all Indian prisoners, if set at liberty, and thus begin another war."[31] The Secretary of Interior forwarded this communication to the Secretary of War with the recommendation that the Nez Perce receive the same treatment accorded to the Modocs, namely exile to the Indian Territory. And Miles had hardly begun his homeward march before Sheridan began to object to having the prisoners kept at the post on the Yellowstone—"The War Department appropriation cannot stand the enormous expense of clothing and feeding these and other Indians at those remote places." As an alternative he proposed that they be transferred to some point on the Missouri, either Yankton or Bismarck, where the cost of supply would be less.[32]

Six days after Miles' return, a courier rode into Fort Keogh after dark with orders from General Terry "to send the Nez Perces and Cheyennes to [Fort Abraham] Lincoln and points below."[33] After a day of "great effort," the Indians were started for Bismarck on the morning of October 31st. The aged, wounded, and some of the women and children, number-ing about 200, were put in mackinaw boats and taken down the Yellow-stone and the Missouri;[34] while the balance were loaded into wagons and hauled to Fort Buford and thence to Bismarck. By the time they had reached this point, Sherman had decided against returning them to their former homes and the Secretary of War had so informed the Secretary of Interior,[35] while Sheridan had recommended that they be sent to Fort Leavenworth.

Miles, who had been involved in the surrender of some of the Cheyennes the preceding April, as well as in that of the Nez Perce, now requested that he be allowed to bring twelve or fifteen of the principal men from the two tribes to Washington "in order that they may learn the intention of the Government and be satisfied that no wrong is intended"; but this was denied. And so, although General John Pope, commander of the Department of Missouri, wanted to send them to Fort Riley where he had ample quarters available, the Nez Perce were loaded into eleven coaches—with their tepees and baggage packed in freight cars—and shipped to Fort Leavenworth. Here they were placed on a squalid campsite for the winter. In January, Joseph and six other prominent men submitted a petition that they be allowed to go back to Idaho, or, if this was denied, that they be allowed to select their own land in Indian Territory and consolidate their people; but the following summer they were moved to Indian Territory. Later, Joseph was to state bitterly, "General Miles had promised that we might return to our country with what stock we had left. * * * I believed General Miles, or *I never would have surrendered*."[36]

In the meantime, at the October term of the District Court for the First District of Idaho, thirty-one Indians had been indicted for the murders at the time of the outbreak; and S. R. Metler, a Salmon River settler who had been at the crossing of the Missouri on October 13–15th, signed an affidavit that he saw four of the indicted among the prisoners at that time. The settlers wanted their pound of flesh; and, on December 21st, the U.S. Attorney for Idaho informed the U.S. Attorney General that "the people of North Idaho are very anxious that those Indians who are known to have been engaged in the murders should be brought here and tried. . . ." This was referred to the Secretary of War, and by him to General Sherman, who returned the communication with this endorsement:

> Respectfully returned . . . doubting the wisdom of proceeding against these Nez Perce prisoners.
> I do not suppose they are exempt from prosecution by the terms of their surrender in battle, but their understanding was that they were. As a tribe they have been severely punished.[37]

In addition to the prisoners at Fort Leavenworth, twenty-three men, nine women and one child were being held at Fort Vancouver. These comprised the group which had surrendered just prior to the retreat over the Lolo Trail; and who were to have been tried before a military court headed by Captain Throckmorton. After his return to Department Headquarters, Howard wrote to Sherman asking if he should bring these prisoners to Fort Leavenworth (when he came to Washington for his trial) or keep them until spring and send them at that time. Sherman, now plagued with the cost of supporting the group in Kansas, quickly replied that he did not want them sent east—"Those you have should be taken to the Nez Perce Agency at Kamiah or Fort Lapwai to be engrafted on the tribe on the reservation."

As the attitude of the Idaho settlers was definitely hostile, it was now necessary to go through with the formality of a military court. This was set up in December but did not get under way until early the next year, by which time the Treaty Indians were accusing Monteith and Howard of bad faith in the matter. The former informed the general that,

> [The chief] James [Lawyer] says that you told James Reuben to tell the Indians if they came in and gave themselves up all would be released excepting . . . [any murderers] and told the Indians, and caused them to come in. * * * We all know, at the time James Lawyer . . . [as well as] the rest of us would have been murdered by the Citizens if there had been any effort to have had the Indians turned loose without a trial. . . .[38]

As no charges of note were presented, they were released on April 22nd to Captain Boyle to escort back to the Reservation. Howard wrote to the Agent at the time that "My only fear in regard to them is that white men may molest them. I think it is very important for places to be alloted for them near Fort Lapwai and be definitely marked so there will be no shadow of excuse for dispute of boundaries."[39]

By spring, reports began to filter into Fort Shaw that the Canadian refugees were dissatisfied and wanted to know if they could return to the United States; and it was decided to send Lieutenant George W. Baird, of the Fifth Infantry at Fort Keogh, and three Indians from Fort Leavenworth to see if a surrender could be negotiated. Yellow Bull, Bald Head and Eo-pon-yez were sent up the Missouri on a steamboat in the custody of Ben Clark, a plainsman respected by Sheridan and Crook, and probably a scout named Christopher Gilson. Baird met the party at Fort Buford and they proceeded to Canada via Fort Benton. Arriving at Fort Walsh on the 16th of June, Baird found Lieutenant Colonel A. G. Irvine and Commissioner James F. Macleod awaiting them. However, these officers discouraged his going to the Indian camp. A week later, the Canadian officers took the three Nez Perces and went to the camp, returning a week later with a delegation of eight, among whom were White Bird and No Hunter, a brother of Looking Glass. The leaders of this party stated that those who had started the report that they wished to return had not spoken for the entire group. However, they were agreeable to returning provided both they and Joseph's group were returned to Idaho. Baird stated in his report that he had no authority to make commitments.

The Canadian version of this conference indicates that after the Nez Perce refused to return, the lieutenant told them that if they persisted in consorting with the Sioux, who were considered enemies, the Nez Perce might not be sent back to Idaho—but they probably would if they would join Joseph. To this, White Bird replied that he did not wish to stay with the Sioux, but that he would join Joseph—*when he was given a reservation in Idaho.* The chief was too wary to surrender his freedom for anything which was not a *fait accompli.*[40]

There were others for whom their homeland had an irresistible attraction. These slipped away in small parties and attempted to return surreptitiously. About the time Baird's party was in Canada, a band—estimated to have been seventeen men and two or three women—started for Idaho. However, instead of trying to travel without attracting attention, they stole stock, murdered settlers, and soon had the countryside aroused.

This party headed for Cadotte's Pass north of Helena and the old trail down the valley of the Blackfoot River on the western side of the Divide. In the valley of the Dearborn River, just before leaving the plains, they killed two ranchers, A. L. Cottle and John H. Wareham. Lieutenant Francis Woodbridge—who had scouted the Lolo Trail the preceding year just before the Nez Perce came over it—found the ranch house stripped of all provisions and that the trail leading from it contained the tracks of fourteen horses (3 shod) and one large mule. Farther on, other horse tracks joined this trail.[41] After following down the Blackfoot River for a ways, the refugees crossed over to Bear Gulch and headed southwest for the eastern end of the Elk City or Old Nez Perce Trail. In Bear Gulch they killed two miners and, supposedly, stole several hundred dollars' worth of gold dust; on Willow Creek they stole a number of horses from ranchers; and farther on, along Rock Creek, they murdered Jack Hayes, Amos Elliott and William Joy (or Joyce), who were also miners. In the last attack they also wounded J. H. Jones, but he managed to escape and reach Phillipsburg where a posse quickly asembled and set out to investigate.[42]

Indian runners informed Peter Ronan, the Flathead Agent, of what was happening, and he alerted Major N. L. Chipman, the commanding officer at Fort Missoula. He sent Captain James H. Gageby to block the mouth of Lolo Canyon. Then, when the Indians were reported in the vicinity of

Corvallis, he dispatched Lieutenant Thomas S. Wallace with a detachment of fifteen men—"all I could mount with the indifferent animals at my disposal"—to investigate. Wallace went as far south as the Big Hole battlefield without finding any clues but, when returning, learned of the discovery of the trail. Apparently, the Indians had crossed the trail behind him, at which time they appropriated the animals in a pack train. A posse of fifty-five citizens turned out and the chase began.

The Indians had headed westward from the Bitterroot Valley into the rugged country between the Lolo and Elk City trails. The citizens stayed with Wallace for one day and then all but two turned back, stating—in typical volunteer fashion—that "their horses were too tired to go further." Leaving his pack animals with a guard of two men, Wallace pushed on and caught up with the Indians while they were resting at noon on what he identified as the North Fork of Clearwater but which may have been the Lochsa or North Fork of the Selway River:

> After selecting a spot to place my horses ["about 1000 yards from top of Cañon leading down to the Indians"] I opened the ball with a charge. The Indians numbered about 17 bucks and two squaws. They fought like devils but were surprised so we had a little advantage. The fight lasted two hours. Loss: Indians six killed—three wounded that we know of. Ponies and mules 23 killed—31 captured which I have with me. Two horses were wounded . . . by Indians returning to attack [three shots] about sun down.[43]

Years later Yellow Wolf, who was in this party and whose reminiscences sometimes do not agree with reliable data, stated that they abandoned 52 horses but denied emphatically that any Indians were killed.[44] However, on August 4th, Captain William Flack reported that he had Yellow Wolf in the guardhouse at Fort Lapwai and that "the remainder of the band, 13 in all, crossed the Snake River . . . doubtless making for the Umatilla Reservation."[45] If there were nineteen in the party in Montana, it would appear that five were now missing—probably dead as Wallace claimed.

This was the only party which left a trail of blood behind. Other stragglers were picked up without difficulty such as the one Lieutenant F. M. H. Kendrick found on the Blackfoot Reservation in August. They surrendered without resistance and "were in destitute condition, subsisting from berries gathered in that vicinity, their ponies in poor condition. I found in their possession two Winchester carbines and one Springfield B. L. Musket, caliber 50, but not one round of ammunition." Such stragglers were shipped to the reservation in Indian Territory. White Bull never returned. The story goes that a few years later, probably before October

1881, a fellow tribesman who believed he was using his medicine powers improperly, killed him.

The prisoners at Fort Leavenworth were transferred to the Department of Interior on July 21, 1878; and as the months passed there were signs that the Nez Perce were not meekly accepting the dictates of the Government. In October, the Commissioner of Indian Affairs addressed a statement to the Secretary of Interior which stated that it was "impossible to reconcile Joseph to the reservation which had been selected for him," and wanting to know what promises really were made to the Chief by Howard and Miles. This query was forwarded to the two officers. Howard took the stand that whatever was agreed upon was voided by White Bird's non-compliance—a poor excuse at the best. Miles took a forthright stand:

> I was informed that the Interior Dept. had ordered all Nez Perces taken to be placed on what was known as the small reservation. . . . I informed the Nez Perce [accordingly]. . . . I should have started them west immediately except for the lateness of the season.
>
> From all I can learn, the Nez Perces' trouble was caused by the rascality of their Agent, and the encroachment of the whites, and have regarded their treatment as unusually severe.

Succeeding months brought additional opportunities for the Nez Perce to air their grievances and, in April 1879, what purported to be a lengthy interview with Joseph was printed in the *North American Review*. Although nothing had happened, the claims of the Indians had been considered—and one knotty problem in particular. Then, in 1880, President Hayes appointed Miles to a commission set up to survey conditions on Indian reservations in the Indian Territory. When this work was completed, the general made an aggressive move. This step was probably conditioned by several factors—his wife's father was a senator and her uncle was W. T. Sherman; during the preceding November he had received the coveted promotion to brigadier general; and his next command was to be the Department of the Columbia, within the boundaries of which lay the Nez Perce Reservation.

On January 19, 1881, Miles addressed a letter to the President in which he again outlined the injustices visited upon these people, and pointed out that the climate in the Indian Territory constituted a serious health hazard:

> Out of 450 who were sent there, together with the children born during three years since their surrender, only 358 remain alive. One hundred and eighty deaths have occurred in this small village. Many of this number died on the military reservation at Fort Leavenworth, Kansas.[46]

The President referred this letter to Carl Schurz, Secretary of the Interior. He admitted that a quarter of the entire number had died but countered with the argument that "if they were returned private vengance would likely be visited upon them without any due process of law and that therefore their return would be apt to result in the destruction of a large portion of that tribe, and in further grave difficulties."[47] In answer to this objection, Miles pointed out that many of those indicted were already in their graves, and those remaining were "willing to meet any just accusation."

Robert Lincoln, then Secretary of War, asked General Miles to survey conditions when he assumed command of the Department. On October 24th, Miles reported that seventeen indictments still stood on the dockets of the Idaho courts, and that these were against fourteen individuals for five crimes. Of these, perhaps ten were still alive. However, the post commander at Fort Lapwai had "not the least apprehension of trouble." Lincoln informed Schurz that if any of those indicted were allowed to return they should be informed that they might be called upon to stand trial in civil courts. Nevertheless, the indictments continued to be a cause for concern. In the following February, the U. S. District Attorney at Boise City informed the Attorney General that the citizens of Idaho wanted the indictments to remain on the docket, but that it was his opinion that they should be *nolle prossed* or the Indians brought into military courts and tried there. And he also requested that the Justice, War and Interior Departments confer on the matter.

In June 1883, some of the prisoners were allowed to return. The settlers evidenced some hostility but nothing serious developed. Then in 1885, the balance were sent back to the Northwest. Of these, 188 went to the reservation in Idaho and 150 to the Colville Reservation in Washington. It has been claimed that the latter group included those against whom indictments were still standing—this move keeping them from the jurisdiction of the courts in Idaho. Another suspected cause for this division was that Monteith, and the Presbyterian mission body, objected to having those of the Dreamer faith returned to Lapwai. Yellow Wolf recalled that when the group was split "the interpreter asked us, 'Where do you want to go? Lapwai and be a Christian, or Colville and just be yourself?'"

Although the return of these prisoners brought to an end most of the injustice being inflicted upon them, the life and struggles of Chief Joseph came to epitomize the entire affair. He had been the dominant figure in the struggle to retain the Wallowa Valley and adjacent area; and, at the end, he was the leader of those who pressed the Government to honor the terms of the surrender. It mattered little that he had played a minor role in the long race for freedom, or that those who died beside Snake Creek were the leaders when battle was joined. The mantle of the legend could not have fallen on the shoulders of one more worthy, for this chief was likable, honest, brave yet modest, intelligent and forthright in pursuit of what he thought was just.

Hein-mot Too-ya-la-kekt, as his people called him, was among those who was sent to the Colville Reservation of the Spokane Indians. Only once was he allowed to visit the beloved Wallowa Valley. During June and July, 1900, Indian Inspector James McLaughlin took him on a trip to the valley, during which the former investigated the feasibility of securing a small reservation in this area for the remnant of Joseph's people. This must have been a poignant experience, and the inspector recalled that there were tears in the chief's eyes when he visited the grave of his father and found that a settler, "with a spirit too rare among his kind," had enclosed and cared for the spot.

However, McLaughlin either could not, or would not, recommend that an effort be made to relocate the Nez Perce in that area—"It is enough that the white man has turned the desert into a garden, that he should enjoy the profit of his enterprise."[48] To the Indian, the reason that he should be denied because the white man had made a "garden" of that which he had acquired by questionable means must have had but little logic. In the few years remaining, Joseph had a tendency to sit in thoughtful silence. On September 21, 1904, while seated beside the fire in his lodge, Hein-mot Too-ya-la-kekt slumped forward on his face. It was said he died of a broken heart.

Notes

>>>>>>>>><<<<<<<< In order to compress these notes to a
bulk of reasonable size, the names of the references have been shortened
and related to the Bibliography. All references to books, pamphlets, etc.,
are to the edition specifically noted, unless otherwise stated. Government
publications are identified as to date and the organization originating the
reference in question as, e.g., "Rept. of Sec. War, 1876–1877." The following abbreviations have been used: NA for National Archives; LOC for
Library of Congress; LMHS for Library of the Montana Historical Society;
and LIHS for Library of the Idaho Historical Society.

Identification of documents in the Adjutant General's File, 1877–1885
(U.S. Army) in the National Archives will be indicated as "NA Record
Group 94, No. ——." The secondary identification, "AGO 3464–77," has
been omitted. The papers of General O. O. Howard in the Bowdoin
College Library will be cited as the *Howard Papers*; the Correspondence of
Edward Settle Godfrey, 1863–1933 in the Library of Congress, as the
Godfrey Papers; the Nez Perce War Letters of Governor Mason Brayman
and the letter files of the Lapwai Indian Agency in the Library of the

Idaho Historical Society, as the *Brayman Letters* and the *Lapwai File;* the papers of Lieutenant G. C. Doane in the Library of Montana State College, as the *Doane Papers;* and the Fort Dalles Collection and the papers of ex-Lieutenant C. E. S. Wood in *The Huntington Library,* as the *Ft. Dalles Coll.* and the *Wood Papers.* The typescript copy of the letters of Major E. C. Mason provided the author by Stanley Davison has been referred to as the *Mason Letters.*

As the date of a document is often important, the letters of Captain FitzGerald and his wife will be treated individually with reference to Laufe (ed), *An Army Doctor's Wife on the Frontier* abbreviated to ADWOTF. In like manner, the dispatches of Thomas A. Sutherland—even though unidentified when published—have been cited both as to date of preparation and place of publication. The possibility of an error in identification is recognized, but has been considered insignificant.

The Nimpau—Real People [19–29]

1. McBeth, *Nez Perces Since Lewis and Clark,* 257–259.
2. Thwaites (ed), *Original Journals of the Lewis and Clark Expedition,* Vol. III, Pt. 1, 77.
3. Thwaites, *op. cit.,* 76–79; Coues (ed), *History of the Lewis and Clark Expedition,* Vol. III, 1017.
4. Coues (ed), *New Light on the Early History of the Greater Northwest,* Vol. II, 819.
5. Catlin, *North American Indians,* Vol. II, 124; Chittenden & Richardson, *Life, Letters and Travels of Father Pierre-Jean DeSmet, S.J.,* Vol. I, 22.
6. J. B. Monteith, letter to H. C. Wood, April 24, 1876, Lapwai File.
7. Kappler, *Indian Affairs—Laws and Treaties,* Vol. II, 528–529.
8. Miller, "Letters from the Upper Columbia," *Idaho Yesterdays,* Vol. IV, 18–22.
9. *Ibid.*
10. O. O. Howard, Rpt. to A.A.G., Mil. Div. Pac., May 22, 1877, NA Record Group 94, No. 3394–77 (3597–76).
11. A. J. Cain, letter to O. O. Howard, May 5, 1877, Howard Papers.
12. The father is usually referred to as Joseph or "Old Joseph," and the eldest son as Joseph or "Young Joseph." However, after the death of the father Young Joseph was usually called Joseph and, at times, the younger brother, whose name was Ollokot, was apparently called "Young Joseph." The identity of the person referred to generally depends on the date of the reference.
13. Reference is to the *first* agreement drawn up by Cain. (Copy in Howard Papers)
14. Rept. Sec. War, 1876–1877, 554.
15. Helena *Weekly Herald,* June 20, 1877.
16. Typical letters are: J. B. Monteith to H. B. Meacham, Sept. 20, 1871; to E. S. Parker, Nov. 3, 1871; to T. K. Cree, Sept. 13, 1872; to E. R. Smith, Nov. 22, 1873; to E. P. Smith, Jan. 6–June 4–July 20–Aug. 1, 1874, Lapwai File.
17. Mooney, "The Ghost Dance Religion," *14th Ann. Rpt. Bur. Ethno.,* Pt. 2, 721.
18. Rept. Sec. Interior, 1876–1877, 608.
19. J. B. Monteith, letter to E. P. Smith, June 4, 1874, Lapwai File.

The Curse of Gold [30–43]

1. Quoted in Wood, *The Status of Young Joseph and His Band of Nez Perce Indians*, 25–26.
2. Charles Hutchins, letter to B. F. Kendall, Jan. 4, 1862. Quoted in Indian Claims Docket 175–180, Vol. III, 312.
3. *Ibid.*
4. B. G. Alvord, letter to A.A.G., Hq. Dept. Pac., Nov. 4, 1862, *Official Records of the War of the Rebellion*, Series I, Vol. L, Pt. II, 206–209.
5. *Ibid.*
6. Howard "The Nez Perces Campaign of 1877.–IX" *The Advance*, April 18, 1878, 243.
7. Kappler, *Indian Affairs—Laws and Treaties*, Vol. II, 644–649.
8. Joseph, "An Indian's View of Indian Affairs," *North American Review*, April 1879. Quoted in Brady, *Northwestern Fights and Fighters*, 56.
9. J. B. Monteith, letter to H. W. Corbett, March 4, 1872; draft of Second Annual Report to Comm. Ind. Affrs., Aug. 31, 1872, Lapwai File.
10. Rept. Comm. Ind. Affrs. 1876–1877, 406.
11. Laufe (ed), *An Army Doctor's Wife on the Frontier*, 201.
12. Wood, *op. cit.*, 41.
13. J. B. Monteith, letter to F. A. Walker, Aug. 27, 1872, Lapwai File.
14. Quoted in Wood, *op. cit.*, 30–31.
15. Quoted in Wood, *op. cit.*, 31–33.
16. J. B. Monteith, letter to E. P. Smith, June 17, 1874, Lapwai File.
17. J. B. Monteith, letter to E. P. Smith, Jan. 6, 1874, Lapwai File.
18. J. B. Monteith, letter to E. P. Smith, Jan. 30, 1874, Lapwai File.
19. J. B. Monteith, letter to E. P. Smith, June 15, 1874, Lapwai File; Curtis, *North American Indian*, Vol. VIII, 13.
20. L. F. Grover, letter to Columbus Delano, July 21, 1873. Quoted in Rept. Sec. War, 1875–1876, 130.
21. O. O. Howard, "The Nez Perces Campaign of 1877.–V," *The Advance*, March 14, 1878, 162.
22. Howard, *Nez Perce Joseph*, 27.
23. Grover, *loc. cit.*, 130–131.
24. Wood, *op. cit.*, 34.
25. S. G. Whipple, letter to O. O. Howard, Aug. 28, 1875. Quoted in Rept. Sec. War, 1875–1876, 128–129.
26. Rept. Sec. War, 1875–1876, 126.

"Enterprising Settlers" [44–67]

1. Bancroft, *History of Washington, Idaho and Montana*, 455.
2. Wood, *Status of Young Joseph and His Band of Nez Perce Indians*, 24–27.
3. J. W. Poe, letter to D. P. Hancock, December 22, 1877, Lewiston *Teller*, April 13, 1878, 3.
4. Lewiston *Teller*, June 7, 1878, 2.
5. J. B. Monteith, letter to E. P. Smith, Nov. 25, 1873; letter to E. C. Kimble, Nov. 28, 1873, Lapwai File.
6. J. B. Monteith, letter to E. P. Smith, Dec. 12, 1873, Lapwai File.
7. J. B. Monteith, letter to E. P. Smith, July 20, 1874, Lapwai File.
8. J. B. Monteith, letter to J. C. Lowrie, July 12, 1873; letter to E. C. Kimble, Nov. 28, 1873, Lapwai File.
9. J. B. Monteith, letter to E. P. Smith, Feb. 28, 1877, Lewiston *Teller*, April 28, 1877, 2.

10. O. O. Howard, report to J. C. Kelton, Div. of Pac., May 18, 1877, NA Record Group No. 94, No. 3003–77 (3597–77).
11. Bancroft, *op. cit.*, 484.
12. J. B. Monteith, letter to E. P. Smith, Jan. 22, 1876, Lapwai File.
13. J. B. Monteith, letter to Comm. Ind. Affrs., June 20, 1874, Lapwai File.
14. J. B. Monteith, letter to E. P. Smith, Feb. 14, 1874, Lapwai File.
15. J. B. Monteith, letter to W. A. Connoyer, Aug. 30, 1872, Lapwai File.
16. J. B. Monteith, report to J. Q. Smith, Feb. 2, 1876, Lapwai File.
17. W. R. Parnell, "The Battle of White Bird Canyon," in Brady, *Northwestern Fights and Fighters*, 91.
18. J. B. Monteith, letters to J. Q. Smith, July 3 & 31, 1876, Lapwai File; Horner & Butterfield, "The Nez Perce-Findley Affair," *Oregon Historical Quarterly*, Vol. 40, 40–51; L. V. McWhorter, *Hear Me, My Chiefs*, 123–131; Deer Lodge *New North-West*, April 24, 1878.
19. Rept. Sec. War, 1876–1877, 579; A. G. Force, "Chief Joseph as a Leader," *Winners of the West*, Nov. 1936, No. 12, 1 & 3.
20. Emily FitzGerald, letter to Mrs. R. Owen, Sept. 16, 1876, ADWOTF 205–206.
21. Lewiston *Teller*, July 7 & 14, 1877; Portland *Daily Standard*, July 16, 1877, 3.
22. I. McDowell, report to Adj. Gen., July 20, 1877, NA Record Group No. 94, No. 4117–77.
23. McWhorter, *op. cit.*, 125–126.
24. McWhorter, *op. cit.*, 124; *Yellow Wolf*, 45–46.
25. O. O. Howard, "The Nez Perces Campaign of 1877.–XVIII," *The Advance*, July 4, 1878, 418; J. W. Poe, *loc. cit.*
26. Mrs. Sam Benedict, letter to Alonzo Leland, April 17, 1878, Lewiston *Teller*, April 26, 1878, 1.
27. O. O. Howard, report to A.A.G., Mil. Div. Pac., May 22, 1877, NA Record Group 94, No. 3394–77.
28. The status of individuals bearing military titles have been indicated as follows: The rank of Army officers will be designated without quotation marks, e.g., Major Mason. When an individual was a member of a body of civilian volunteers, and therefore elected or appointed to his position, his rank has been enclosed by quotation marks, e.g., "Major" Shearer. And, as it was customary to use the title of major when referring to an Indian agent, these titles have also been enclosed in quotation marks, e.g., "Major" Frost. See footnote No. 11 of Chapter IV for further information on fictitious (brevet) ranks within the Army.
29. O. O. Howard, letter to G. M. Shearer, July 18, 1877 Brayman Letters.
30. L. Wilmot letter to Gov. Brayman, n.d., Brayman Letters.
31. G. M. Shearer, letter to O. O. Howard, Nov. 10, 1877; J. B. Monteith, letter to O. O. Howard, Dec. 5, 1877, Howard Letters.
32. J. B. Monteith letters to A. I. Chapman, Sept. 15, 1871 & Feb. 24, 1872, Lapwai File.
33. G. C. Crook, letter to O. O. Howard, Dec. 2, 1877; O. O. Howard, letter to G. C. Crook, Dec. 11, 1877; C. E. S. Wood, letter to A. I. Chapman, Feb. 22, 1878, Howard Papers.
34. J. B. Morris, letter to O. O. Howard, Nov. 4, 1877, Howard Papers.
35. J. B. Monteith, letters to E. P. Smith, May 14 & June 4, 1874, Lapwai File.
36. Duncan McDonald, "The Inside History from Indian Sources," Deer Lodge *New North-West*, May 3, 1878.
37. Bicknell, *History of Humboldt County with a History of Iowa*, 220–224;

Andrews, *Pioneers of Polk County, Iowa and Reminiscences of Early Days*, Vol. II, 173–181; Williams (ed. by Breen), *History of Early Fort Dodge and Webster County, Iowa*, 38–41.

38. O. O. Howard, report to A.A.G., Div. of Pac., May 3, 1877, NA Record Group 94, No. 3003–77 (3597–77).

39. J. B. Monteith, letter to O. O. Howard, March 19, 1877, Howard Papers.

40. E. C. Mason, letter to Mrs. Mason, July 2, 1877, Mason Letters.

41. Sutherland, dispatch dated Aug. 23, 1877, New York *Herald*, Sept. 10, 1877, 3.

A Futile Agreement [68–87]

1. Wood, *The Status of Young Joseph and His Band of Nez-Perce Indians*, 41–42.

2. J. B. Monteith, letter to O. O. Howard, July 3, 1876; letter to J. Q. Smith, July 31, 1876, Lapwai File.

3. H. C. Wood, report to O. O. Howard, Aug. 1, 1876, NA Record Group 94, No. 3597, AGO 1876.

4. Lewiston *Teller*, Oct. 28, 1876, 2.

5. Lewiston *Teller*, Nov. 18, 1876, 2.

6. Emily FitzGerald, letter to Mrs. R. Owen, Nov. 18, 1876, ADWOTF, 219.

7. Modoc Indians murdered General Edward S. Canby while a council was in progress.

8. Emily FitzGerald, letter to Mrs. R. Owen, Nov. 15 (14?), 1876, ADWOTF, 221.

9. Rept. Sec. Interior, 1876–1877, 607.

10. Emily FitzGerald, letter to Mrs. R. Owen, Nov. 19, 1876, ADWOTF, 22.

11. During the Civil War and the Indian Wars which followed, the only award for gallantry in action was the Medal of Honor which, at that time, did not require an act of Congress for its award. It was the custom during these years to recognize meritorious service by awarding brevet ranks, and military protocol dictated that they be used except in official reports. (Such service is now recognized by a whole series of various awards.) Thus Captain Perry was addressed as "Colonel" Perry, Lieutenant W. R. Parnell (lieutenant colonel) as "Colonel" Parnell, and Lieutenant (later Captain) W. H. Boyle as "Major" Boyle, according to brevet rank or, in some cases, rank held during the Civil War. In this study, the rank given within a quote has been allowed to stand but, elsewhere, only *actual rank* as of that date has been used. There is no easy way to cope with this situation, and the only really adequate solution is to become *intimately* familiar with the records of various officers.

12. Emily FitzGerald, letter to Mrs. R. Owen, Nov. 19, 1876, ADWOTF, 223–224.

13. Rept. Sec. Interior, 1876–1877, 607–613.

14. H. C. Wood, minority report to Comm. Ind. Affrs., Dec. 1, 1876, NA Record Group 94, No. 3597, AGO 1876.

15. J. Q. Smith, letter to J. B. Monteith, Jan. 6, 1877, NA Record Group 94, No. 128, AGO 1877.

16. J. B. Monteith, letter to J. Q. Smith, Feb. 9, 1877, NA Record Group 94, No. 1363–77.

17. Samuel Breck, letter to Commander Dept. Col., March 24, 1877, NA Record Group 94, No. 1824, AGO 1877.

18. J. B. Monteith letter to J. Q. Smith, March 19, 1877, NA Record Group 94, No. 2196–77 (3597–76).
19. Rept. Sec. War, 1876–1877, 590.
20. O. O. Howard, report to J. C. Kelton, Div. of Pac., April 24, 1877, NA Record Group 94, No. 2680–77 (3597–76).
21. Sternberg, George Miller Sternberg, 54–55.
22. Except when noted otherwise, all material pertaining to this council has been taken from: O. O. Howard, report to A.A.G., Div. of Pac., May 22, 1877, NA Record Group 94, No. 3394–77 (3597–76).
23. Emily FitzGerald, letter to Mrs. R. Owen, May 4, 1877, ADWOTF, 246–247.
24. FitzGerald, op. cit., 248–249.
25. O. O. Howard, "The Nez Perces Campaign of 1877.–XI", The Advance, May 2, 1878, 275.
26. Lewiston Teller, May 19 & Sept. 22, 1877.
27. O. O. Howard, telegram to Adj. Gen., May 18, 1877, NA Record Group 94, No. 2819–77 (3597–76).

Vital Intelligence [88–97]

1. Rept. Sec. War, 1877–1878, 90.
2. I. McDowell, telegrams to W. T. Sherman, June 24 & July 3, 1877, NA Record Group 94, Nos. 3593–77 & 3778–77.
3. O. O. Howard, letters to E. D. Townsend, March 31 & April 4, 1877, Howard Papers.
4. O. O. Howard, letter to W. F. Sanders, Nov. 27, 1877, Howard Papers.
5. E. C. Mason, Letter to Mrs. Mason, July 5, 1877, Mason Letters.
6. W. R. Parnell, "The Salmon River Expedition," in Brady, Northwestern Fights and Fighters, 132.
7. Major Thomas M. Vincent, Assistant Adjutant General under General E. D. Townsend.
8. O. O. Howard, letter to W. T. Sherman, Jan. 18, 1877, Howard Papers.
9. Captain B. B. Keeler, General McDowell's aide-de-camp who was with Howard at this time.
10. Lewiston Teller, Aug. 11, 1877, 3.
11. A steamship plying the coast between Portland, Oregon and Alaska.
12. Emily FitzGerald, letter to Mrs. R. Owen, June 29, 1875, ADWOTF, 139–140.

"The Die Is Cast" [98–117]

1. E. C. Watkins, letter to Comm. Ind. Affrs., June 16, 1877, NA Record Group 94, No. 4018–77.
2. B. B. Keeler, memorandum written on a transcript of Howard's telegram to A.A.G., Div. of Pac. June 15, 1877, NA Record Group 94, No. 6724–77.
3. McDonald, "Inside History from Indian Sources," Deer Lodge New North-West, May 24, 1878.
4. Reported to be a second cousin and nephew, respectively. The latter survived the war and is said to have lived out his years on the Reservation hidden under the name of John Minton.
5. Elsensohn, Pioneer Days in Idaho County, Vol. I, 279–280.
6. Elta M. Arnold, to author in August 1961.
7. J. W. Poe, letter to D. P. Hancock, Dec. 22, 1877, Lewiston Teller, April 13, 1878.

8. Helen J. Walsh, letter to Alonzo Leland, Aug. 31, 1877, Lewiston *Teller*, Sept. 8, 1877, 2.
9. Lewiston *Teller*, June 30, 1877, 1.
10. *Ibid.*
11. Sutherland, dispatch dated July 3 [sic 5?], 1877, San Francisco *Chronicle*, July 20, 1877, 3.
12. Lewiston *Teller*, July 28, 1877, 1; Aug. 11, 1877, 4.
13. L. P. Brown, letter to Alonzo Leland, June 22, 1877, Lewiston *Teller*, June 30, 1877, 1.
14. McWhorter, *Hear Me, My Chiefs*, 196; Portland *Weekly Standard*, Nov. 9, 1877, 1; *Army and Navy Journal*, Sept. 8, 1877.
15. Lewiston *Teller*, June 30, 1877, 2.
16. *Ibid.*; D. W. Greenburgh, "Victim of Nez Perce Tells Story of Indian Atrocities," *Winners of the West*, Feb. 15, 1926, 8.
17. Sutherland, *loc. cit.*
18. Emily FitzGerald, letter to Mrs. R. Owen, July 11, 1877, ADWOTF, 272; Greenburgh, *loc. cit.*
19. Lewiston *Teller*, June 30, 1877, 2.
20. Sutherland, *loc. cit.*
21. Poe, *loc. cit.*
22. Helen J. Walsh, *loc. cit.*
23. John Wood, letter to Alonzo Leland, June 20, 1877, Lewiston *Teller*, June 30, 1877, 4.
24. C. B. Wood, letter to Mason Brayman, July 4, 1877, Brayman Letters.
25. Bailey, *River of No Return*, 257.
26. Lewiston *Teller*, July 28, 1877, 4.
27. Henry Buck, "Story of the Nez Perce Indian Campaign," ms. in LMHS.
28. Bailey, *op. cit.*, 258–260.
29. J. W. Poe, letter to Alonzo Leland, July 19, 1877, Lewiston *Teller*, July 28, 1877, 1.
30. Bailey, *op. cit.*, 258.
31. Sutherland, dispatch dated Oct. 10, 1877, San Francisco *Chronicle*, Nov. 1, 1877, 3.
32. McDonald, "Inside History from Indian Sources," Deer Lodge *New North-West*, Nov. 29, 1878.
33. Lewiston *Teller*, June 30, 1877, 1.
34. *Ibid.*
35. Sutherland, dispatch dated July 3 [sic 5?], 1877, San Francisco *Chronicle*, July 20, 1877, 3.
36. McWhorter, *op. cit.*, 216–217; Hunter, *Reminiscences of an Old Timer*, 345–346.
37. O. O. Howard, letter to A.A.G., Div. of Pac., June 26, 1877, NA Record Group 94, No. 4026–77.
38. New York *Herald*, July 6, 1877, 5.
39. C. E. S. Wood, "Chief Joseph, the Nez Perce," *Century Magazine*, Vol. VI, 136.
40. H. C. Wood, letter to *Army and Navy Journal*, Aug. 8, 1877, *Army and Navy Journal*, Sept. 8, 1877.
41. J. W. Houston, letter to Charles Devens, Dec. 21, 1877, NA Record Group 94, No. 180–78.

Prelude to Disaster [118–129]

1. Captain FitzGerald had been subpoenaed to testify in a U.S. Circuit Court in a case involving bootlegging liquor to Indians in Alaska.

2. There were two Monteiths at the agency—the Agent and his brother Charles who served as a clerk.

3. Dr. (Rev.) Roger Owen was Emily's stepfather. It was a common practice for Army wives on the frontier to have relatives in "the States" shop for them.

4. Reference is made to the failure of Congress to pass a military appropriations bill, and as a result the Army went payless for several months.

5. A son, Herbert ("Bertie") aged two, and a daughter, Elizabeth ("Bessie") aged four. (Elizabeth FitzGerald Hiestand—see Chapter XI—was a correspondent of the author.)

6. Emily FitzGerald, letter to Mrs. R. Owen, June 13-15, 1877, ADWOTF, 257-258.

7. O. O. Howard, "The Nez Perces Campaign of 1877.–XV," *The Advance*, June 13, 1878, 371.

8. *The Teller* was owned by Charles F. and Alonzo Leland, with "A. Leland and Son" as editors. Its guiding light was Alonzo Leland. In the early 1860's he had left the press rooms in Portland, Oregon, to prospect in the newly discovered Idaho gold fields. In the fall of 1876, he acquired an interest in *The Teller* and, on October 21st, began to issue a small, four-page weekly paper. At the beginning of this war, Leland stated that the policy of the paper would be to print all reports as completely as possible so that an accurate record might be preserved. As a result, most of the letters and reports he received were apparently printed verbatim. Thus, in spite of the fact that he was strongly anti-Indian, and sometimes anti-military as well, Leland must be given credit for doing a creditable job of reporting.

9. Howard, *loc. cit.*

10. W. H. Baxter, letter to O. O. Howard, Feb. 23, 1877, Howard Papers.

11. W. H. Boyle, letter to O. O. Howard, May 24, 1876, Howard Papers.

12. Loyal P. Brown, a native of New Hampshire, arrived in San Francisco flat broke in 1849. He came to Idaho in 1862 after varied experiences in California and Oregon. At Mount Idaho, he was a hotel keeper and self-appointed mouthpiece for the community.

13. O. O. Howard, "The Nez Perces Campaign of 1877.–XV," *The Advance*, June 20, 1878, 387. (Installment XVI?) The following quotes are from this issue and the one of June 27, 1878, 402.

14. Peter S. Bomus, rept. to Chief Quartermaster, Dept. of Col., Dec. 20, 1877, Ft. Dalles Coll.

15. Meaning the southern part which was *upstream* from the location of the post.

16. The reference may be to the common signal used by plains Indians to indicate the rider has a message of importance.

17. FitzGerald *op. cit.*, 258-259.

18. FitzGerald, *op. cit.*, 259-260.

19. Michael McCarthy, diary, LOC.

20. *Ibid.*

21. FitzGerald, *loc. cit.*

Rout at White Bird Canyon [130-141]

1. McDonald, "The Inside History from Indian Sources," Deer Lodge *New North-West*, Nov. 22, 1878.

2. O. O. Howard, telegram to A.A.G., Div. of Pac., June 15, 1877, NA Record Group 94, No. 3422-77 (3597-77).

3. Peter S. Bomus, rept. to Chief Quartermaster, Dept. of Col., Dec. 20, 1877, Ft. Dalles Coll.
4. David Perry, "The Battle of White Bird Canyon," in Brady, *Northwestern Fights and Fighters*, 113–114.
5. Michael McCarthy, diary, LOC.
6. Emily FitzGerald, letter to Mrs. R. Owen, July 11, 1877, ADWOTF, 271.
7. McCarthy, *op. cit.*
8. McWhorter, *Yellow Wolf*, 54–56; Floy Laird (ed), "Reminiscences of Francis M. Redfield," *Pacific Northwest Quarterly*, Vol. XXVII, 1936, 72.
9. McCarthy, *op. cit.*
10. Perry, *op. cit.*, 115.
11. McCarthy, *op. cit.*
12. W. R. Parnell, "The Battle of White Bird Canyon," in Brady, *Northwestern Fights and Fighters*, 101–103.
13. Perry, *loc. cit.*
14. *Ibid.*
15. O. O. Howard, "The Nez Perces Campaign of 1877.–XIX," *The Advance*, July 18, 1878, 451.
16. O. O. Howard, *op. cit.*, *The Advance*, Aug. 1, 1878, 483.
17. H. C. Wood, telegram to J. C. Kelton, Div. of Pac., June 18, 1877, NA Record Group 94, No. 6724–77.
18. O. O. Howard, telegram to H. C. Wood, June 20, 1877, quoted in San Francisco *Chronicle*, June 23, 1877, 3.
19. Jocelyn, *Mostly Alkali*, 225; Emily FitzGerald, letter to Mrs. R. Owen, June 19, 1877, ADWOTF, 261; Joseph, "An Indian's View of Indian Affairs," *North American Review*, April, 1879; McCarthy, *op. cit.*
20. Lewiston *Teller*, June 23, 1877, 2; Portland *Daily Standard*, June 26, 1877, 3.
21. Sternberg, *George Miller Sternberg*, 65.

The Chessmen of War [142–154]

1. H. C. Wood, telegram to J. C. Kelton, Div. of Pac., July 2, 1877, NA Record Group 94, No. 6724–77.
2. There is a voluminous file on this move and the investigation of the delay in NA Record Group 94.
3. H. C. Wood, telegram to J. C. Kelton, Div. of Pac., June 18, 1877, NA Record Group 94, No. 6724–77.
4. H. C. Wood, telegram to J. C. Kelton, Div. of Pac., June 19, 1877, NA Record Group 94, No. 6724–77.
5. Jocelyn, *Mostly Alkali*, 224.
6. Sternberg, *George Miller Sternberg*, 59.
7. H. C. Wood, telegram to J. C. Kelton, Div. of Pac., June 22, 1877, NA Record Group 94, No. 6727–77.
8. O. O. Howard, telegram to H. C. Wood, Dept. of Col., June 18 (?), 1877, NA Record Group 94, No. 6727–77.
9. J. C. Kelton, telegrams to H. C. Wood, Dept. of Col., June 23, 1877; to Comm. Officer, Dept. of Col., July 2, 1877, NA Record Group 94, No. 6727–77.
10. I. McDowell, telegram to W. T. Sherman, War Dept., June 20, 1877, NA Record Group 94, No. 3473–77.
11. B. B. Keeler, telegram to I. McDowell, Div. of Pac., July 18, 1877, NA Record Group 94, No. 4117–77.

12. E. P. Ferry, telegram to Sec. War, July 7, 1877, NA Record Group 94, No. 3805–77.
13. Mason Brayman's General Orders No. 1, NA Record Group 94, No. 3723–77.
14. I. McDowell, telegram to Sec. War, July 12, 1877; A.A.G. to I. McDowell, July 13, 1877, NA Record Group 94, No. 3938–77.
15. J. Slayden, letter to J. C. Kelton, Div. of Pac., July 19, 1877, Howard Papers.
16. P. S. Bomus, rept. to Chief Quartermaster, Dept. of Col., Dec. 20, 1877, Ft. Dalles Coll.
17. Emily FitzGerald, letter to Mrs. R. Owen, June 19–24, 1877, ADWOTF, 262–264.

A Game of Hide and Seek [155–172]

1. Rept. Sec. War, 1876–1877, 120.
2. O. O. Howard, "The Nez Perces Campaign of 1877.–XXII," *The Advance*, Aug. 15, 1878, 515.
3. J. C. Kelton, telegram to Comm. Officer, Dept. of Col., June 25, 1877, NA Record Group 94, No. 6724–77.
4. O. O. Howard, "The Nez Perces Campaign of 1877.–XXV," *The Advance*, Sept. 5, 1878, 563.
5. Rept. Sec. War, 1876–1877, *loc. cit.*
6. O. O. Howard, *loc. cit.*; C. E. S. Wood, diary, Wood Papers; Frederic Mayer, "Nez Perce War Diary–1877," *Seventeenth Biennial Report of the Board of Trustees of the Idaho State Historical Society*, 28. A number of significant errors indicate clearly that this is not a "diary" but an account written years afterward.
7. H. C. Wood, telegram to J. C. Kelton, Div. of Pac., July 29, 1877, NA Record Group 94, No. 6724–77.
8. C. E. S. Wood, *loc cit.*
9. McWhorter, *Hear Me, My Chiefs*, 260–261; Hunter, *Reminiscences of an Old Timer*, 308; Mayer, *op. cit.*; Emily FitzGerald, letter to Sallie, July 18, 1877, ADWOTF, 280.
10. Howard, *loc. cit.*
11. O. O. Howard, "The Nez Perces Campaign of 1877.–XXVI," *The Advance*, Sept. 19, 1878, 594.
12. Rept. Sec. War, 1876–1877, 120–121.
13. H. C. Wood, telegram to J. C. Kelton, Div. of Pac., July 2, 1877, NA Record Group 94, No. 6724–77.
14. Howard, *loc. cit.*
15. E. C. Watkins, letter to J. Q. Smith, July 8, 1877, NA Record Group 94, No. 4499–77.
16. Howard, *loc. cit.*
17. Ed. McConville, Report to Governor Mason Brayman, August 1877; *Fifteenth Biennial Report of Board of Trustees of the State Historical Society of Idaho*, 63.
18. Howard, *loc. cit.*
19. New York *Herald*, July 27, 1877, 2.
20. McWhorter, *op. cit.*, 264–274.
21. E. C. Mason, letter to Mrs. Mason, July 5, 1877, Mason Letters.
22. Howard, *loc. cit.*
23. A. B. Leland, letter to Alonzo Leland, July 5, 1877, Lewiston *Teller*, July 7, 1877.

24. Sutherland, dispatch dated July 3 [sic], 1877, San Francisco *Chronicle*, July 20, 1877, 3.
25. E. C. Mason, letter to Mrs. Mason, July 2 [sic-3rd ?], 1877, Mason Letters.
26. Rept. Sec. War, 1876–1877, 121.
27. W. R. Parnell, "The Salmon River Expedition," in Brady, *Northwestern Fights and Fighters*, 129.
28. Mason, *loc. cit.*
29. H. C. Brown who had a store just below the mouth of White Bird Creek.
30. Mason, *loc. cit.*
31. Sutherland, *loc. cit.*
32. L. P. Wilmot, Report to Governor Brayman, August 2, 1877, *Fifteenth Biennial Report of Board of Trustees of the State Historical Society of Idaho*, 73.
33. "Major Keeler's Account of the Campaign," San Francisco *Chronicle*, Aug. 2, 1877.

Skirmishes on Cottonwood Creek [173–183]

1. O. O. Howard, "The Nez Perces Campaign of 1877.–XXVI," *The Advance*, Sept. 19, 1878, 594.
2. Lewiston *Teller*, July 14, 1877, 4.
3. Howard, *op. cit.*, 595.
4. Frederic Mayer, "Nez Perce War Diary–1877," *Seventeenth Biennial Report of Board of Trustees of the Idaho State Historical Society*, 28–29.
5. Lewiston *Teller*, Aug. 4, 1877, 3.
6. Howard, *loc. cit.*
7. They had not been intercepted but had trouble dodging Indians. Lewiston *Teller*, July 14, 1877, 2.
8. B. B. Keeler, telegram to I. McDowell, NA Record Group 94, No. 6724–77.
9. Sutherland, dispatch dated July 3 [sic], 1877, San Francisco *Chronicle*, July 20, 1877, 3.
10. McWhorter, *Yellow Wolf*, 80–83. Part of this account is of doubtful accuracy.
11. Lewiston *Teller*, July 14, 1877, 4.
12. Lewiston *Teller*, Aug. 4, 1877, 3.
13. George Shearer, report to E. C. Mason, July 26, 1877, *Idaho Yesterdays*, Vol. II, No. I, 6–7.
14. Howard, *loc. cit.*
15. Lewiston *Teller*, July 14, 1877, 3.
16. General Orders No. 23, Dept. of Col., Nov. 30, 1877, NA Record Group 94, No. 7782–77.
17. Elizabeth FitzGerald Hiestand, letter to author, March 30, 1963.
18. Frank Wheaton, letter to O. O. Howard, Nov. 4, 1877, Howard Papers.

Clearwater—the Gettysburg of the Nez Perce [184–198]

1. W. R. Parnell, "The Salmon River Expedition," in Brady, *Northwestern Fights and Fighters*, 129–130.
2. O. O. Howard, "The Nez Perces Campaign of 1877.–XXVI," *The Advance*, Sept. 19, 1878, 594.
3. Ed. McConville, report to Gov. Brayman, August 1877, *15th Biennial Report of the Board of Trustees of the State Historical Society of Idaho*, 65–67.

4. Rept. Sec. War, 1876–1877, 124.
5. P. S. Bomus, rept. to Chief Quartermaster, Dept. of Col., Dec. 20, 1877, Ft. Dalles Coll.
6. J. G. Trimble, "The Battle of the Clearwater," in Brady, *Northwestern Fights and Fighters*, 141; Rept. of Sec. War, 1876–1877, 122; Sutherland, dispatch dated July 12, 1877, San Francisco *Chronicle*, July 15, 1877, 8.
7. McWhorter, *Yellow Wolf*, 86–87.
8. Michael McCarthy, diary, LOC.
9. Rept. of Sec. War, 1876–1877, 122.
10. Sutherland, *loc. cit.*
11. Pvt. David McNally and, probably, Sergt. James A. Workman.
12. C. E. S. Wood, diary, Wood Papers.
13. Sutherland, *loc. cit.*
14. C. E. S. Wood, "Chief Joseph, the Nez Perce," *Century Magazine*, Vol. VI, 137.
15. Sternberg, *George Miller Sternberg*, 60.
16. Rept. Sec. of War, 1876–1877, 660.
17. Emily FitzGerald, letter to Mrs. R. Owen, July 13, 1877, ADWOTF, 277.
18. O. O. Howard, dispatch to I. McDowell, July 12, 1877, NA Record Group 94, No. 3973-77.
19. Trimble, *op. cit.*, 144.
20. McCarthy, *loc. cit.*
21. Sutherland, *loc. cit.*
22. O. O. Howard, "The Nez Perce Campaign of 1877.–XXVII," *The Advance*, Sept. 26, 1878, 611.
23. Sutherland, dispatch dated July 16, 1877, San Francisco *Chronicle*, July 28, 1877, 2.
24. *Ibid.*
25. *Ibid.*
26. *Ibid.*
27. O. O. Howard, telegram to J. C. Kelton, Div. of Pac., July 28, 1877, NA Record Group 94, No. 5117-77.
28. O. O. Howard, telegram to J. C. Kelton, Div. of Pac., July 12, 1877, NA Record Group 94, No. 3973-77.
29. Rept. of Sec. War, 1876–1877, 132–133.
30. Rept. of Sec. War, 1876–1877, 124.
31. Sutherland, dispatch dated July 12, 1877, San Francisco *Chronicle*, July 12, 1877, 8.
32. Charles Carlin and John G. Hineman.
33. Sergeant James A. Workman came to Lewiston on the same boat as Sutherland, who was impressed by his familiarity with Shakespeare and the English poets. "Weighed down with troubles and bitter recollections," he exposed himself recklessly and was killed.
34. Eugene A. Bancroft, letter to his father (*Boston Globe*, Aug. 13, 1877), quoted in San Francisco *Chronicle*, Aug. 27, 1877, 4.

Moments of Indecision [199–214]

1. Sutherland dispatch dated July 16, 1877, New York *Herald*, Aug. 1, 1877, 5.
2. Sutherland, dispatch dated July 15, 1877, San Francisco *Chronicle*, July 19, 1877, 3.
3. E. C. Mason, letter to Mrs. Mason, July 15, 1877, Mason Letters.

4. O. O. Howard, telegram to H. C. Wood, July 15, 1877, NA Record Group 94, No. 6718–77.

5. Sutherland, dispatch dated July 16, 1877, San Francisco *Chronicle*, July 20, 1877, 3.

6. B. B. Keeler, telegram to I. McDowell, Div. of Pac., July 17, 1877, NA Record Group 94, No. 4109–77.

7. J. B. Monteith, letter to J. Q. Smith, July 31, 1877, NA Record Group 94, No. 5259–77.

8. Sutherland, dispatch dated July 16, 1877, New York *Herald*, Aug. 1, 1877, 5.

9. A tributary of the Clearwater River—not to be confused with a stream of the same name in Montana.

10. E. C. Mason, letter to Mrs. Mason, July 19, 1877, Mason Letters.

11. Sutherland dispatch dated July 27, 1877, Portland *Daily Standard*, Aug. 4, 1877, 2.

12. Ed McConville, Report to Gov. Brayman, August 1877, *15th Biennial Report of the Board of Trustees of the State Historical Society of Idaho*, 1935–1936, 68–69.

13. W. R. Parnell, "The Salmon River Expedition," in Brady, *Northwestern Fights and Fighters*, 134–135.

14. Sutherland, dispatch dated July 17, 1877, San Francisco *Chronicle*, July 29, 1877, 8.

15. O. O. Howard, telegram to A.A.G., Div. of Pac., July 13, 1877, NA Record Group 94, No. 6718–77.

16. B. B. Keeler, telegram to I. McDowell, July 19, 1877, NA Record Group 94, No. 4109–77.

17. E. C. Watkins, letter to J. Q. Smith, July 20, 1877, NA Record Group 94, No. 5219–77.

18. Rept. of Sec. of War, 1876–1877, 125.

19. W. T. Sherman, telegram to I. McDowell, July 29, 1877, NA Record Group 94, No. 5044–77.

20. Rept. of Sec. War, 1876–1877, 125.

21. San Francisco *Chronicle*, July 15, 1877, 8.

22. I. McDowell, telegram to O. O. Howard, July 17, 1877, NA Record Group 94, No. 6718–77.

23. This is the same movement that Howard had planned to make with his troops.

24. E. C. Mason, letter to Mrs. Mason, July 22, 1877, Mason Letters.

25. Sutherland, dispatch dated July 24, 1877, San Francisco *Chronicle*, Aug. 6, 1877, 1.

26. This is the canyon of Lawyer's Creek which joined the Clearwater River near Kamiah. The one where Blewett was killed emptied into the Salmon River.

27. Sutherland, dispatch dated July 25, 1877, Portland *Daily Standard*, Aug. 1, 1877, 2.

28. E. C. Mason, letter to Mrs. Mason, July 29, 1877, Mason Letters.

29. Sutherland, *Howard's Campaign Against the Nez Perce Indians*, 1877, 19–20.

30. E. C. Mason, *loc. cit.*

31. P. S. Bomus, rept. to Chief Quartermaster, Dept. of Col., Dec. 20, 1877, Ft. Dalles Coll.

32. Sutherland, *op. cit.*, 45.

33. J. A. FitzGerald, letter to Emily FitzGerald, July 29, 1877, ADWOTF, 285.

Fiasco at Fort Fizzle [215–237]

1. B. F. Potts, telegram to President Hayes, June 29, 1877, NA Record Group 94, No. 3721–77.
2. Deer Lodge *New North-West,* June 29, 1877.
3. Hakola (ed.), *Frontier Omnibus,* 367; Henry Buck, "The Story of the Nez Perce Indian Campaign," ms. in LMHS.
4. C. C. Rawn, report to A.A.G., Ft. Shaw, July 16, 1877, in Hakola, *Frontier Omnibus,* 387–388.
5. The Pend d'Oreille tribe shared the reservation with the Flatheads. Eagle-from-the-Light was allegedly deposed because he married a Pend d'Oreille woman—hence Michelle's interest.
6. Peter Ronan, letter to B. F. Potts, N.A., Miscellaneous Letters of the Montana Superintendency.
7. R. C. Drum, telegram to Adj. Gen. Army, July 21, 1877, NA Record Group, No. 4119–77.
8. Camp Baker, later Ft. Logan, was in the Smith River Valley about 40 miles east of Helena and 75 miles south of Fort Shaw.
9. John Gibbon, telegram to A.A.G., Div. of Mo., July 22, 1877, NA Record Group 94, No. 4392–77.
10. *The Missoulian,* Aug. 3, 1877, 2.
11. B. F. Potts, telegram to Sec. of War, July 23, 1877, NA Record Group 94, No. 4217–77.
12. I. McDowell, telegrams to Adj. Gen., and to B. F. Potts July 23, 1877; Adj. Gen., telegram to McDowell, July 24, 1877; R. C. Drum, telegram to John Gibbon, July 24, 1877. In NA Record Group 94, Nos. 4218–77, 4227–77, and 4435–77, respectively.
13. McDonald, "The Inside History from Indian Sources," Deer Lodge *New North-West,* Dec. 27, 1878. Much of this material was secured in interviews with members of White Bird's people in Canada during the summer of 1878. No doubt the fact that McDonald was a relative of Looking Glass was of considerable assistance in gathering this data. Of the series, he wrote: "while endeavoring not only to keep within the limits of strict truth but also to eliminate exaggeration, any obscurity in description of incidents must be met with some allowance of an ignorance on the part of Indians in regard to dates, and also, of civilized names of localities."
14. McDonald, *op. cit.,* Deer Lodge *New North-West,* Dec. 27, 1878.
15. McDonald, *op. cit.,* Deer Lodge *New North-West,* Jan. 17, 1879.
16. W. B. Harlan, letter to James Mills, Aug. 4, 1877, Deer Lodge *New North-West,* Aug. 10, 1877, 3.
17. C. Barbour, letter to B. F. Potts, July 31, 1877, in Hakola (ed), *Frontier Omnibus,* 375.
18. *Helena Daily Herald,* July 31, 1877, 2.
19. P. H. Sheridan, telegram to E. D. Townsend, Aug. 1, 1877, NA Record Group 94, No. 4691–77.
20. McDonald, *op. cit.,* Deer Lodge *New North-West,* Jan. 10, 1879.
21. L. P. Brown, letter to Alonzo Leland, Aug. 8, 1877, Lewiston *Teller,* Aug. 18, 1877, 1.
22. Buck, *op. cit.*
23. Sutherland, dispatch dated Aug. 18, 1877, San Francisco *Chronicle,* Aug. 27, 1877, 3.
24. Rept. of Sec. War, 1876–1877, 68.
25. McDonald, *op. cit.,* Deer Lodge *New North-West,* Jan. 17, 1877.
26. *The Missoulian,* Aug. 17, 1877.
27. Claim of Myron M. Lockwood, NA Record Group 94, No. 7312–77.

28. McDonald, *op. cit.*, Deer Lodge *New North-West*, Dec. 6, 1877.
29. Deer Lodge *New North-West*, Aug. 10, 1877, 3.
30. "Seventh Infantry," letter to Editor, Bozeman *Avant Courier*, July 31, 1877, Bozeman *Avant Courier*, Aug. 9, 1877, 2.

Tortuous Trail [238–245]

1. O. O. Howard, telegram to I. McDowell, July 25, 1877 (annotated by McD), NA Record Group 94, No. 6724-77.
2. Howard, *Nez Perce Joseph*, 176–177.
3. Sutherland, dispatch *circa* Aug. 7, 1877, San Francisco *Chronicle*, Aug. 21, 1877, 3.
4. E. C. Mason, letter to Mrs. Mason, Aug. 3, 1877, Mason Letters.
5. C. C. Rawn, dispatch to A.A.G., Dept. of Col. Hq. in Field, Aug. 1, 1877, Hakola (ed), *Frontier Omnibus*, 389.
6. Howard, *op. cit.*, 183–184.
7. Heitman, *Historical Register and Dictionary of the United States Army*, Vol. I, 451.
8. F. J. P. [Frank Parker], letter to Alonzo Leland, Aug. 9, 1877, Lewiston *Teller*, Aug. 25, 1877, 3.
9. J. C. Kelton, telegram to O. O. Howard, Aug. 9, 1877, NA Record Group 94, No. 6718-77.

Death at Dawn [246–267]

1. Except where noted otherwise, this account of Gibbon's movements and the ensuing battle has been drawn from the following: Rept. of Sec. War, 1876–1877, 501–505; Gibbon, "The Battle of the Big Hole," *Harpers Weekly*, Dec. 21 & 28, 1895, 1215–1216 & 1235–1236, resp.; Deer Lodge *New North-West*, Aug. 17, 1877, 2 & 3; "Seventh Infantry" ("G" Co. ?), dispatch dated Aug. 11, 1877, Bozeman *Avant Courier*, Aug. 23, 1877, 1; Eugent Lent, "The Big Hole Battle," *The Missoulian*, Aug. 17, 1877, 2; Helena *Weekly Herald*, Aug. 30, 1877. These agree on major points, but no one contains all the details. Perhaps the best single account is that prepared by Editor John Mills after interviewing the survivors and printed in *The New North-West*, Aug. 17, 1877.
2. J. B. Catlin, "The Battle of the Big Hole," (*circa* 1927), ms. in LMHS.
3. McDonald, "The Inside History from Indian Sources," Deer Lodge *New North-West*, Jan. 24, 1879.
4. C. A. Woodruff, letter to Mrs. Woodruff, Aug. 9, 1877, *Montana Magazine of History*, Vol. II, No. 4 (Oct. 1952), 54.
5. "Seventh Infantry" wrote, "Had about half the Indians' horses cut off on top of rear hill."
6. Catlin, *op. cit.*
7. J. A. FitzGerald, letter to Emily FitzGerald, *circa* Aug. 14, 1877, ADWOTF, 304.
8. McDonald, *loc. cit.*
9. Howard, *Nez Perce Joseph*, 204–205.
10. McDonald, *loc. cit.*
11. Howard, *op. cit.*, 199.
12. P. H. Sheridan, telegram to E.D. Townsend, Aug. 11, 1877, NA Record Group 94, No. 4928-77.
13. FitzGerald, *op. cit.*, ADWOTF, 303–304.
14. Sutherland, dispatch dated Aug. 18, 1877, San Francisco *Chronicle*, Aug. 27, 1877, 3.

15. *The Missoulian*, Aug. 3, 1877, 3.
16. McDonald, *loc. cit.*
17. Howard, *op. cit.*, 203.
18. FitzGerald, *op. cit.*, 302–303.
19. *Ibid.*
20. John Gibbon, telegram to A. H. Terry, Aug. 11, 1877, NA Record Group 94, No. 4989–77.
21. Sutherland, dispatch dated Aug. 13, 1877, New York *Herald*, Aug. 16, 1877, 3.
22. Rept. of Sec. of War, 1876–1877, 549–550.
23. Sutherland, dispatch dated Aug. 20, 1877, San Francisco *Chronicle*, Aug. 23, 1877, 2.
24. McDonald, *loc. cit.*
25. *The Missoulian*, Aug. 24, 1877, 3.
26. Deer Lodge *New North-West*, Aug. 24, 1877, 3.
27. Frank Parker, letter to Alonzo Leland, Lewiston *Teller*, Sept. 8, 1877, 1.
28. E. C. Mason, letter to Mrs. Mason, Aug. 13, 1877, Mason Letters.
29. FitzGerald, *op. cit.*, ADWOTF, 304.
30. *The Missoulian*, Sept. 21, 1877, 3.
31. *The Missoulian*, Nov. 9, 1877, 3.
32. *The Sunday Missoulian*, Aug. 7, 1921, 7.
33. Helena *Daily Herald*, Oct. 19, 1877, 2.
34. Homer Coon, "The Outbreak of Chief Joseph," ms. in Coe Coll., Yale Univ. Library.
35. Quoted in New York *Herald*, Aug. 27, 1877, 5.

Horse Prairie and Birch Creek [268–287]

1. Palladino, *Indian and White in the Northwest*, 350–351.
2. *Butte Miner*, Aug. 14, 1877, 3.
3. John Gibbon, telegram to A. H. Terry, Aug. 15, 1877, quoted in San Francisco *Chronicle*, Aug. 18, 1877, 2.
4. P. H. Sheridan, telegram to E. D. Townsend, Aug. 18, 1877; Townsend, telegram to Sheridan, Aug. 18, 1877, NA Record Group 94, No. 5164–77.
5. P. H. Sheridan, telegram to A. H. Terry, Aug. 13, 1877, NA Record Group 94, No. 5244–77.
6. P. H. Sheridan, telegram to A. H. Terry, Aug. 18, 1877, NA Record Group 94, No. 5244–77.
7. J. W. Redington, "Scouting in Montana in the 1870's," *The Frontier*, Vol. XIII (Nov. 1932), 55–68. Additional material is contained in Deer Lodge *New North-West*, Aug. 31, 1877, the Nez Perce war letters of Gov. Brayman, Howard Papers, and Sutherland's dispatches to the San Francisco *Chronicle*.
8. *Missoulian*, Dec. 9, 1911.
9. Edd Swan, letter to Mason Brayman, July 18, 1877, Brayman Letters.
10. Robert Vaughn, *Then and Now*, 220–221.
11. S. F. Dunlap, letter to editor *H.D.H.*, Aug. 13, 1877, Helena *Daily Herald*, Aug. 16, 1877, 2.
12. "T. W.," letter to editor *D.I.*, Helena *Daily Independent*, Aug. 18, 1877, 3.
13. S. F. Dunlap, letter to editor *H.D.H.*, Aug. 14, 1877, Helena *Daily Herald*, Aug. 17, 1877, 2.
14. O. O. Howard, telegram to I. McDowell, Aug. 14, 1877, NA Record Group 94, No. 6718–77.

Notes ◂ 449

15. E. C. Mason, letter to Mrs. Mason, Aug. 16, 1877, Mason Letters; Howard, *Nez Perce Joseph*, 215.
16. Rept. of Sec. War, 1876–1877, 128.
17. Deer Lodge *New North-West*, Aug. 24, 1877, 3.
18. Helena *Daily Independent*, Aug. 23, 1877, 3.
19. C. H. Jeanjaquet, letter to James Mills, Aug. 22, 1877, Deer Lodge *New North-West*, Aug. 31, 1877, 3.
20. G. L. Shoup, letter to Fred J. Keisel & Co., Aug. 27, 1877, Corrine *Record*, Sept. 1, 1877, quoted in *Fort Benton Record*, Sept. 21, 1877, 3.
21. Helena *Daily Independent*, Aug. 26 & Sept. 16, 1877; *The Missoulian*, Aug. 31, 1877, 2; Bozeman *Avant Courier*, Aug. 30, 1877, 3; Deer Lodge *New North-West*, Aug. 31, 1877, 2; Alexander Cruikshank, "The Birch Creek Massacre," ms. in LMHS; Elvin Henniger, letter to author, July 29, 1964 (transcript of part of J. D. Woods' autobiography); McDonald, "The Inside History from Indian Sources," Deer Lodge *New North-West* March 21, 1879; McWhorter, *Yellow Wolf*, 164–165; Topance, *Reminiscences of Alexander Topance*, 240; Curtis, *North American Indian*, Vol. VIII, 167; Smith, *Indian Experiences*, 259–269.

Skirmish at Camas Meadows [288–297]

1. Portland *Daily Standard*, August 18, 1877, 3.
2. San Francisco *Chronicle*, Aug. 24, 1877, 3.
3. Portland *Daily Standard*, Aug. 27, 1877, 3.
4. Rept. of Sec. War, 1876–1877, 128; New York *Herald*, Aug. 23, 1877, 7; Virginia City *Madisonian*, Sept. 1, 1877, 3.
5. Sutherland, dispatch dated Aug. 23, 1877, New York *Herald*, Sept. 10, 1877, 5.
6. Sources used: O. O. Howard, telegram to J. C. Kelton, Aug. 20, 1877, NA Record Group 94, No. 5782–77; Howard, *Nez Perce Joseph*, 224–229; Rept. of Sec. War, 1876–1877, 129–130 & 572–573; H. J. Davis, "The Battle of Camas Meadows," in Brady, *Northwestern Fights and Fighters* 191–197; Sutherland, *loc. cit.* & dispatch dated Aug. 25, 1877, Portland *Weekly Standard*, Sept. 7, 1877, 2; Virginia City *Madisonian*, Aug. 25 & Sept. 1, 1877; "Participant," undated story, Helena *Daily Herald*, Aug. 30, 1877, 3. Howard's reports are apparently biased in favor of his own troops and Norwood's is painfully brief.
7. McDonald, "Inside History from Indian Sources," Deer Lodge *New North-West*, Jan. 31, 1879.
8. Virginia City *Madisonian*, Aug. 25, 1877, 3.
9. Sutherland, dispatch dated Aug. 25, 1877, Portland *Weekly Standard*, Sept. 7, 1877, 2.
10. "Participant," *loc. cit.*
11. Sutherland, dispatch dated Aug. 24, 1877, San Francisco *Chronicle*, Sept. 3, 1877, 4.
12. Davis, *op. cit.*
13. E. C. Mason, letter to Mrs. Mason, Sept. 2, 1877, Mason Letters.
14. O. O. Howard, telegram to J. C. Kelton, Aug. 20, 1877, NA Record Group 94, No. 5287–77; Rept. of Sec. War, 1876–1877, 573.

A Pause to Refit [298–312]

1. Buck, "The Story of the Nez Perce Indian Campaign" ms. in LMHS.
2. Sutherland, dispatch dated Aug. 23, 1877, New York *Herald*, Sept. 10, 1877, 3.

3. Howard, *Nez Perce Joseph*, 231.
4. E. C. Mason, letter to Mrs. Mason, Aug. 26, 1877, Mason Letters.
5. Rept. of Sec. War, 1876–1877, 617.
6. J. A. FitzGerald letter to Emily FitzGerald, *circa* Aug. 14, 1877, ADWOTF, 305.
7. E. C. Mason, letter to Mrs. Mason, Aug. 19, 1877, Mason Letters.
8. Lewiston *Teller*, Sept. 22, 1877, 4.
9. Rept. of Sec. War, 1876–1877, 12.
10. E. C. Mason, letter to Mrs. Mason, Aug. 23, 1877, Mason Letters.
11. John Q. Adams, rept. to Chief Quartermaster, Dept. of Col., Dec. 13, 1877, Ft. Dalles Coll.
12. J. C. Kelton, telegram to O. O. Howard, Aug. 17, 1877, NA Record Group 94, No. 6718–77.
13. Sutherland, dispatch dated Aug. 25, 1877, Portland *Weekly Standard*, Sept. 7, 1877, 2.
14. G. H. Weeks, letter to O. O. Howard, Sept. 23, 1877, Howard Papers.
15. O. O. Howard, letter to J. C. Kelton, Nov. 12, 1877, Howard Papers.
16. Rept. of Sec. War, 1876–1877, 12–16.
17. Rept. of Sec. War, 1876–1877, 13.
18. *Ibid*.
19. O. O. Howard, letter to W. T. Sherman, Nov. 27, 1877, Howard Papers; Howard, *Nez Perce Joseph*, 237.
20. Mason *loc. cit*.
21. Rept. of Sec. War, 1876–1877, 616.
22. Sutherland, dispatch dated Aug. 24, 1877, San Francisco *Chronicle*, Sept. 3, 1877, 4.
23. N. A. Miles, orders to G. C. Doane, Doane Papers.
24. G. C. Doane, memorandum to A.A.G., Yellowstone Comm., Aug. 3, 1877, Doane Papers.
25. H. M. Chittenden, *The Yellowstone National Park* (1964), 148.
26. Phinney, *Jirah Isham Allen*, 95; Scott, *Some Memories of a Soldier*, 60.
27. G. W. Baird, orders to S. D. Sturgis, Aug. 11, 1877, Doane Papers.
28. S. D. Sturgis, dispatch to G. C. Doane, Aug. 17, 1877, Doane Papers.
29. Bozeman *Times*, Aug. 30, 1877, 3.
30. P. H. Sheridan, telegram to Adj. Gen., Aug. 28, 1877, NA Record Group 94, No. 5391–77.
31. P. H. Sheridan, telegram to W. T. Sherman, Aug. 29, 1877, NA Record Group, No. 5522–77.

The Yellowstone Park Tourists [313–334]

1. Deer Lodge *New North-West*, Sept. 14, 1877, 2. (Helena *Daily Independent*, Sept. 12, 1877, 3; Bozeman *Times*, Sept. 13, 1877, 3.)
2. McWhorter, *Yellow Wolf*, 172–176.
3. Except when noted otherwise, the story of the Radersburg party has been patched together from the following: Frank D. Carpenter, *The Wonders of Geyser Land* (reprinted in Guie & McWhorter, *Adventures in Geyser Land*); Helena *Daily Herald*, Sept. 1, 3 & 8, 1877; Bozeman *Times*, Aug. 30, Sept. 8 & 27, 1877; McDonald, "The Inside History from Indian Sources," Deer Lodge *New North-West*, May 3, June 7, 1878, Feb. 7, 1879; S. G. Fisher, "Journal of S. G. Fisher," *Colls. of Hist. Soc. Mont.*, Vol. II, 269–274; Mrs. George F. Cowan, "Reminiscences of Pioneer Life," *Colls. of Hist. Soc. Mont.*, vol. IV, 156–187.

4. E. C. Mason, letter to Mrs. Mason, Aug. 28 (etc.), 1877, Mason Letters.
5. Buck, "The Story of the Nez Perce Indian Campaign," ms. in LMHS.
6. Mason, *loc. cit.*
7. This account of the Helena party has been drawn from the following: Bozeman *Avant Courier*, Aug. 30, Sept. 6, 13 & 27, 1877; Bozeman *Times*, Aug. 30 & Sept. 20, 1877; Helena *Daily Herald*, Aug. 27 & 31, Sept. 3, 5 & 8, 1877; McDonald, "The Inside History from Indian Sources," Deer Lodge *New North-West*, Feb. 7, 1879; Andrew J. Weikert, "Journal of a Tour Through the Yellowstone National Park in August and September, 1877," *Colls. of Hist. Soc. Mont.*, Vol. III, 153–174.
8. Emil Kopac, letter to author, Feb. 21, 1963. Kopac heard Boney relate this acount while retracing the Nez Perce route with L. V. McWhorter and several Nez Perce warriors 43 years later.
9. Helena *Daily Independent*, Sept. 12, 1877.
10. Scott, *Some Memories of a Soldier*, 64.
11. Topping, *Chronicles of the Yellowstone*, 217–218.
12. Topping, *op. cit.*, 219; Bozeman *Avant Courier*, Sept. 6, 1877, 3.

An Unguarded Gateway [335–354]

1. S. G. Fisher, "Journal of S. G. Fisher," *Colls. of Hist. Soc. Mont.*, Vol. II, 270–276. Details in this journal make possible the accurate location of routes followed by Indians and troops.
2. Sutherland, dispatch dated Sept. 3, 1877, San Francisco *Chronicle*, Sept. 17, 1877.
3. Howard, *Nez Perce Joseph*, 243–244.
4. Buck, "The Story of the Nez Perce Indian Campaign," ms. in LMHS.
5. Fisher, *op. cit.*, 275.
6. Rept. of Sec. War, 1876–1877, 618.
7. W. T. Sherman, letter to O. O. Howard, Aug. 29, 1877, Howard Papers.
8. G. C. Doane, letter to A.A.G., Dept. of Col., Sept. 1, 1877, Doane Papers.
9. Rept. of Sec. of War, 1876–1877, 626.
10. Sutherland, dispatch dated Sept. 16, 1877, New York *Herald*, Oct. 1, 1877, 7.
11. P. H. Sheridan, telegram to Robert Williams, Aug. 29, 1877, NA Record Group 94, No. 5522–77.
12. Sheridan, telegram to Williams, Aug. 30, 1877, NA Record Group 94, No. 5541–77.
13. Seventy-eight had previously been sent out to scout for the Nez Perce.
14. New York *Herald*, Sept. 23, 1877, 6.
15. Marquis, *Memoirs of a White Crow Indian*, 128–130.
16. Rept. of Sec. War, 1876–1877, 509–510. Theodore W. Goldin, "The Seventh Cavalry at Canyon Creek," in Brady, *Northwestern Fights and Fighters*, 206–213, is equally unreliable but he does provide a few details about topography which are useful.
17. Fisher, *op. cit.*, 277.
18. *Ibid.*
19. Fee, *Chief Joseph*, 320. (The account of the surrender which Wood wrote for this book is undoubtedly and unforgivably inaccurate.)
20. Sutherland, dispatch dated Sept. 16, 1877, San Francisco *Chronicle*, Oct. 3, 1877, 3.
21. Howard, *op. cit.*, 255.
22. Bozeman *Avant Courier*, Sept. 20, 1877, 2.

Canyon Creek and the Prairies Beyond [355–368]

1. Rept. of Sec. of War, 1876–1877, 623.
2. J. A. FitzGerald, letter to Emily FitzGerald, Sept. 16, 1877, ADWOTF, 311–312.
3. This account of the raid has been compiled from: Sutherland's dispatches in San Francisco *Chronicle*, Sept. 23 & Oct. 3, 1877, and Portland *Weekly Standard*, Oct. 16, 1877; Diamond City *Rocky Mountain Husbandman*, Sept. 27 & Oct. 4, 1877; Topping, *Chronicles of the Yellowstone*, 221–222; Mrs. Brown "Life on the Yellowstone," ms. at Montana State College; J. W. Redington, "Scouting in Montana in the 1870's," *The Frontier*, Vol. XIII, 60–61; I. D. O'Donnell, Montana Monographs (interview with Joe Cochran), unpub. ms.
4. S. G. Fisher, "Journal of S. G. Fisher," *Colls. of Hist. Soc. Mont.*, Vol. II, 278.
5. *Ibid.*
6. Rept. of Sec. War, 1876–1877, 511.
7. Fisher, *op. cit.*, 280.
8. Rept. of Sec. War, 1876–1877, 512.
9. P. H. Sheridan, letter to Robert Williams, Sept. 25, 1877, NA Record Group 94, No. 6041–77.
10. FitzGerald, *op. cit.*, ADWOTF, 312.
11. Rept. of Sec. War, 1876–1877, 512.
12. P. H. Sheridan, letter to E. D. Townsend, Sept. 23, 1877, NA Record Group 94, No. 5938–77.
13. Fisher, *op. cit.*, 281–282.
14. Rept. of Sec. War, 1876–1877, 627–628.
15. Howard also described this strategy to a reporter in Bismarck, D. T., on October 22, 1877, Bismarck *Tri-Weekly Tribune*, Oct. 22, 1877, 1.
16. E. C. Mason, letters to Mrs. Mason, Sept. 24–26 & Sept. 28–Oct. 5, 1877, Mason Letters.

Skirmish at Cow Island Landing [369–377]

1. *Fort Benton Record*, Sept. 28, 1877, 3.
2. *Fort Benton Record*, Oct. 5, 1877, 3.
3. William Moelchert, letter to O. O. Mueller, May 15, 1927 & letter to David Hilger, Nov. 13, 1927, in LMHS; *Fort Benton Record*, Sept. 28, 1877.
4. *Fort Benton Record*, Sept. 28, 1877, 3.
5. George Clendenin, Jr., deposition dated Feb. 15, 1878, in LMHS.
6. *Fort Benton Record*, Oct. 5, 1877, 3. Cooper's estimate of the camp was apparently very accurate.
7. *Ibid.*
8. *Fort Benton Record*, Sept. 28, 1877; Rept. of Sec. War, 1876–1877, 557. Ilges' report in the latter document appears to be a summary of the first reference, or both may have been prepared from the same notes.
9. *Fort Benton Record*, Sept. 28 & Oct. 5, 1877; *Helena Daily Herald*, Oct. 6, 1877, 3; "Message from the President of the United States," *45th Cong.*, *2d sess*, Sen. Ex. Doc. No. 14, 10.

Fresh Troops Join the Chase [378–387]

1. Miles, *Personal Recollections of Nelson A. Miles*, 261–262.
2. O. O. Howard, letter to Adj. Gen. Army, Jan. 28, 1878, NA Record Group 94, No. 1238–78.

3. Rept. of Sec. War, 1876–1877, 513–514.
4. Simon Carter, diary.
5. P. H. Sheridan, telegram to Adj. Gen. Army, Oct. 1, 1877, NA Record Group 94, No. 6075–77.
6. Baldwin, *Memoirs of the Late Frank D. Baldwin, Major General USA,* 191–192.
7. N. A. Miles, letter to A. H. Terry, Oct. 17, 1877, Godfrey Papers.
8. Henry Romeyn, "The Capture of Chief Joseph," *Colls. of Hist. Soc. Mont.,* Vol. II, 290; Transcript of Captain Moylan's report of battle of Bearpaw Mountains, Godfrey Papers.
9. "Remsen" (Henry Remsen Tilton), "After the Nez Perces," *Forest and Stream and Rod and Gun,* Vol. 9, No. 21, Dec. 27, 1877, 403–404.
10. Veterinary surgeon John Honsinger and sutler Baliran, then with the escort of the Northern Pacific Railroad surveyors.
11. Finerty, *Warpath and Bivouac,* 344.
12. Miles recalled, probably incorrectly, that this officer was Lieutenant J. W. Biddle.
13. When carefully plotted on A.M.S. maps, scale 1:250,000, and measured with a cartometer, this route measured about 990 miles. When allowance is made for overrun which cannot be measured except on the ground, perhaps a reasonable figure is 1,000–1,200 miles. Howard (Rept. of Sec. War, 1876–1877, 638) reported that his troops traveled 1,632 miles from Lewiston, I.T., to Carroll, but no statement is made as to method of calculation. When smaller reported distances were checked against accurate maps, they were invariably found to be in excess of actual map measurements.

Six Grim Days [388–409]

1. Remsen, "After the Nez Perces," *Forest and Stream and Rod and Gun,* Vol. 9, No. 21, Dec. 27, 1877, 403–404.
2. G. W. Baird, "General Miles' Indian Campaigns," *Century Magazine,* Vol. XX (1891), 364.
3. Edward S. Godfrey, unpublished manuscript, Godfrey Papers.
4. Myles Moylan, official report of battle of Bearpaw Mountain, transcript in Godfrey Papers.
5. Rufus Wallowing, letter to author, April 1951. Although this record may have minor errors, the essential facts are probably trustworthy.
6. Godfrey, *op. cit.*
7. Henry Romeyn, "The Capture of Chief Joseph," *Colls. of Hist. Soc. Mont.,* Vol. II, 286.
8. Joseph, "An Indian's View of Indian Affairs" (*North American Review,* April, 1879), in Brady, *Northwestern Fights and Fighters,* 67.
9. Godfrey, *op. cit.*
10. Moylan, *op. cit.*
11. Herwood nearly died and eventually received a disability discharge.
12. Godfrey, *op. cit.*
13. Moylan, *op. cit.*
14. Baird, *loc. cit.*
15. Miles, *Personal Recollections of Nelson A. Miles,* 271–272.
16. Fort Benton Record, Oct. 12, 1877, 3.
17. Romeyn, *op. cit.,* 288–289.
18. Joseph, *op. cit.* (Brady), 68.
19. Remsen, *loc. cit.*
20. *Ibid.*

21. New York *Herald*, Oct. 11, 1877, 3; Romeyn, *op. cit.*, 289; Coues, *History of the Expedition Under the Command of Lewis and Clark*, Vol. III, 1027.
22. Moylan, *op. cit.*
23. Rept. of Sec. War, 1876–1877, 512.
24. Remsen, *loc. cit.*; Romeyn, *op. cit.*, 289.
25. Remsen. *loc. cit.*
26. N. A. Miles, letter to Mary Miles, Oct. 3, 1877, in Virginia Johnson, *The Unregimented General*, 203.
27. Chicago *Times*, Oct. 11, 1877.
28. Miles, *op. cit.*, 274; Robert Bruce, "Jerome's Own Story," in Fee, *Chief Joseph*, 337–340 (also in *Winners of the West*, April 30, 1935, 1); New York *Herald*, Oct. 30, 1877; Curtis, *The North American Indian*, Vol. VIII, 171–172. The story told the reporter of the *Herald*, who was with the Sitting Bull Commission, has the earmarks of an evening "bull session" with a bottle of whiskey.
29. Remsen, *loc. cit.*
30. Rept. of Sec. War, 1876–1877, 629–630.
31. *Ibid.*
32. Joseph, *op. cit.* (Brady), 70; A. I. "Ad" Chapman, letter to Commr. Ind. Affrs., Dec. 13, 1878, NA Record Group 94, No. 8978–78; N. A. Miles, letter to President Hayes, Jan. 19, 1881, NA Record Group 94, No. 1565–81; N. A. Miles, undated fragmentary note, NA Record Group 94, No. 5386–87; Bismarck *Tri-Weekly Tribune*, Nov. 23, 1877, 1.
33. C. E. S. Wood, "Chief Joseph, the Nez Perce," *Century Magazine* (1884), Vol. VI, 141–142; "The Pursuit and Capture of Chief Joseph," in Fee, *Chief Joseph*, 329–330; letter to Mr. Lyman, Jan. 17, 1939, Wood Papers. Only the account in the *Century Magazine* can be trusted.
34. Typical of these is the story John Samples told Alonzo Leland—Lewiston *Teller*, Dec. 1, 1877, 2. Samples was present at the Cow Island Landing fight, and claimed to have been present at the Bearpaw fight. Lieutenant Guy Howard specifically denied the reports of friction between Howard and Joseph on October 22, 1877—Bismarck *Tri-Weekly Tribune*, Oct. 22, 1877, 1.
35. Rept. of Sec. War, 1876–1877, 630–631.
36. Manuscript of Howard's official report on the campaign, Ft. Dalles Coll., Doc. No. 869. In perfect agreement with this draft is a report carried to Bismarck, D.T., by a member of the crew of the *Silver City*—Bismarck *Tri-Weekly Tribune*, Oct. 26, 1877, 4. Joseph's message is also given in full.
37. Rept. of Sec. War, 1876–1877, 631.
38. Except for the item covered by footnote No. 37, this story is a composite of Sutherland's dispatches in San Francisco *Chronicle*, Nov. 1, 1877, 3, and Portland *Weekly Standard*, Nov. 9, 1877, 1.
39. P. H. Sheridan, telegram to E. D. Townsend, Oct. 9, 1877, NA Record Group 94, No. 6260–77.
40. C. E. S. Wood, "The Pursuit and Capture of Chief Joseph," in Fee, *Chief Joseph*, 330–333.
41. Sutherland, dispatch dated Oct. 10, 1877, San Francisco *Chronicle*, Nov. 1, 1877, 3.

Aftermath [410–432]

1. N. A. Miles, report to A.A.G., Dept. of Dakota, Oct. 6, 1877, NA Record Group 94, No. 6646–77.

2. N. A. Miles, undated fragmentary note, NA Record Group 94, No. 5386–87.
3. A. I. Chapman, letter to Commr. Ind. Affrs., Dec. 13, 1878, NA Record Group 94, No. 8978–78.
4. N. A. Miles, letter to A. H. Terry, Oct. 17, 1877, Godfrey Papers.
5. Col. B. R. Lewis, letter to author, March 2, 1963; Col. E. G. Ovenshine, letter to author, Feb. 23, 1963; T. E. Hall, letter to author, Feb. 27, 1963.
6. Chicago *Times* quoted in Helena *Daily Herald*, Oct. 19, 1877; Homer Coon, "The Outbreak of Chief Joseph," ms. in Coe Coll., Yale Univ. Library; H. L. Davis, "The Battle of Camas Meadows," in Brady, *Northwestern Fights and Fighters*, 196.
7. Otis & Huntington, *The Medical and Surgical History of the War of the Rebellion*, Part III, Vol. II, 702.
8. Turner, *The Northwest Mounted Police*–1873–1893, Vol. I, 340–341.
9. J. M. Walsh, report dated Oct. 26, 1877, quoted in New York *Herald*, Dec. 3, 1877, 5.
10. N. A. Miles, report to A. H. Terry, Oct. 3, 1877, NA Record Group 94, No. 6214–77.
11. Sutherland, dispatch dated July 16, 1877, New York *Herald*, Aug. 1, 1877, 5.
12. O. O. Howard, "The Nez Perce Campaign of 1877.–XII," *The Advance*, May 9, 1878, 290. Howard has also been quoted as stating that had the chiefs not feared they would be hung, Joseph would have surrendered at Kamiah. Bismarck *Tri-Weekly Tribune*, Oct. 22, 1877, 1.
13. W. L. Lincoln, letter to G. W. Baird, June 24, 1878, NA Miscellaneous Letters of the Montana Superintendency.
14. Sutherland, dispatch dated Oct. 13, 1877, Portland *Weekly Standard*, Nov. 9, 1877, 1.
15. Sutherland, dispatch dated Oct. 10, 1877, San Francisco *Chronicle*, Nov. 1, 1877, 3.
16. Henry Romeyn, "The Capture of Chief Joseph," *Colls, of Hist. Soc. Mont.*, Vol. II, 291.
17. Remsen, "After the Nez Perces," *Forest and Stream and Rod and Gun*, Vol. 9, No. 21, 403–404.
18. Baldwin, *Memoirs of Frank D. Baldwin, Major General*, 193.
19. Rept. of Sec. War, 1876–1877, 513; Special Field Order No. 69, NA Record Group 94, No. 8076–77; Frederic W. Benteen, letter to T. W. Goldin, Nov. 17, 1891, quoted in W. A. Graham, *The Custer Myth*, 192. Sturgis made a brief stop at his post, and then left for his home in St. Louis.
20. Howard, *Nez Perce Joseph*, 270. Three troops were ordered to accompany Miles and the Fifth Infantry as escort. Captain Benteen and the remaining eight were left on the left bank of the Missouri, opposite the mouth of the Musselshell River, to block any possible pursuit should the Sioux attempt to follow and make trouble. Bismarck *Tri-Weekly Tribune* Nov. 5, 1877, 1.
21. O. O. Howard, letter to N. A. Miles, Oct. 7, 1877, NA Record Group 94, No. 8076–77.
22. Howard, *op. cit.*, 271.
23. C. E. S. Wood, "The Pursuit and Capture of Chief Joseph," in Fee, *Chief Joseph*, 333–334. This portion of Wood's account contains a few glaring errors; however, it is probably reasonably correct as far as basic essentials are concerned.

24. N. A. Miles letter to O. O. Howard, Feb. 1, 1877; Howard, letter to W. T. Sherman, March 14, 1877, Howard Papers.
25. Chicago Times, Oct. 25 1877.
26. O. O. Howard, letter to P. H. Sheridan, Oct. 25, 1877, NA Record Group 94, No. 7113–77.
27. San Francisco Chronicle, Nov. 2, 1877, 2.
28. A. H. Terry, letter to A. A. G., Div. of Mo., Dec. 14, 1877, NA Record Group 94, No. 8076–77.
29. O. O. Howard, letter to Adj. Gen. Army, Jan. 28, 1878, NA Record Group 94, No. 1233–78.
30. Remsen, loc. cit.
31. E. C. Watkins, letter to J. Q. Smith, Sept. 3, 1877, NA Record Group 94, No. 6170–77.
32. P. H. Sheridan, telegrams to E. D. Townsend, Oct. 10 & 17, 1877, NA Record Group 94, No. 6267–77 & 6417–77.
33. Simon Snyder, diary, Oct. 28, 1877.
34. Fred Bond, Flatboating on the Yellowstone. Bond claimed to have piloted a mackinaw boat in this flotilla, and told a tall tale about his experiences. Parts of the account should not be trusted.
35. E. D. Townsend, telegram to P. H. Sheridan, Nov. 19, 1877, NA Record Group 94, No. 7053–77. According to the Bismarck Tri-Weekly Tribune (Nov. 23, 1877, 1) the Nez Perce made the move to Bismarck with but little "murmuring." But when Joseph was informed of the next move, his "head dropped and he murmured in his mother tongue, 'When will those white chiefs begin to tell the truth.'"
36. Joseph, "An Indian's View on Indian Affairs," (North American Review April, 1879) in Brady, Northwestern Fights and Fighters, 70.
37. J. W. Huston, letter to Charles Devens, Dec. 21, 1877, NA Record Group 94, No. 6062–77.
38. J. B. Monteith, letter to O. O. Howard, Jan. 24, 1878, Howard Papers.
39. O. O. Howard, letter to J. B. Monteith, Feb. 5, 1878, Howard Papers.
40. G. W. Baird, report to N. A. Miles, July 22, 1878, NA Record Group 94, No. 5994–78.
41. Frances Woodbridge, report to A. A. G., Ft. Shaw, July 13, 1878, NA, Miscellaneous Letters of the Montana Superintendency; Deer Lodge New North-West, "Extra," July 13, 1878.
42. Deer Lodge New North-West, "Extra," July 13, 1878; Peter Ronan, report to Commr. Ind. Affrs., July 29, 1878, NA, Miscellaneous Letters of the Montana Superintendency; J. H. Jones, "The Rock Creek Massacre," ms. in LMHS.
43. N. L. Chipman, letter to Peter Ronan, July 25, 1878, NA, Miscellaneous Letters of the Montana Superintendency.
44. McWhorter, Yellow Wolf, 260–270.
45. Rept. of Sec. War, 1877–1878, 182.
46. N. A. Miles, letter to R. B. Hayes, Jan. 19, 1881, NA Record Group 94, No. 1565–81.
47. Carl Shurz, letter to R. B. Hayes, Feb. 21, 1881, NA Record Group 94, No. 1565–81.
48. McLaughlin, My Friend, the Indian, 344–346, 366.

Bibliography

>>>>>>>><<<<<<<< To a great extent, the materials used in this *Estimate of the Situation* have been limited to original documents, and dispatches printed in contemporary newspapers. Articles, books and manuscripts written some time afterward by participants and knowledgeable persons have been used sparingly, usually only when more desirable intelligence has been lacking. However, many other accounts were read during the preparation of this study. Many of these have not been noted here, primarily because no valid reason exists for listing them when the basic sources have been noted. And this is particularly true when a certain piece of literature is considered biased, inaccurate and/or incomplete.

Unpublished Sources

Adjutant General's File, 1877–1885 (U.S. Army). Consolidated Correspondence File comprising Record Group No. 94 (3464–77). U.S. National Archives, Washington, D.C.

Brayman, Mason. Nez Perce War letters of Governor Brayman. Library of the Idaho Historical Society, Boise, Idaho.

Buck, Henry. "The Story of the Nez Perce Indian Campaign During the Summer of 1877." Manuscript in Montana Historical Society Library, Helena, Montana.

Catlin, John B. "The Battle of the Big Hole." Manuscript in Montana Historical Society Library, Helena, Montana.

Clendenin, George Jr. Declaration of Damage at Cow Island Landing. Document in Montana Historical Society Library, Helena, Montana.

Comba, (Captain) Richard. Report of participation of Co. D, 7th Infantry in the Big Hole Battle. Transcript of report dated September 16, 1877 in Montana Historical Society Library, Helena, Montana.

Coon, Homer. "The Outbreak of Chief Joseph." Manuscript in William Robertson Coe Collection in Yale University Library, New Haven, Connecticut.

Cruickshank, Alexander. "The Birch Creek Massacre." Manuscript in Montana Historical Society Library, Helena, Montana.

Doane, (Lieut.) Gustavius C. Doane Papers. Library of Montana State College, Bozeman, Montana.

Fort Dalles Collection. Documents involving the Headquarters of the Department of the Columbia. The Huntington Library, San Marino, California.

Godfrey, (General) Edward Settle. Correspondence of Edward Settle Godfrey, 1863–1933. Library of Congress, Washington, D.C.

Howard, (General) Oliver Otis. Howard Papers. Bowdoin College Library, Brunswick, Maine.

Indian Claims Commission. "An Evaluation Study of the Mineral Resources in the Lands Ceded to the United States by the Nez Perce Tribe of Indians on April 17, 1867" etc. Docket 175–180. Copy in Idaho Historical Society Library, Boise, Idaho.

——— "An Evaluation of Gold Mined Before April 17, 1865 from the Nez Perce Indian Reservation" etc. Docket 180A. Copy in Idaho Historical Society Library, Boise, Idaho.

Jones, J. H. "The Rock Creek Massacre." Manuscript in Montana Historical Society Library, Helena, Montana.

Lapwai Indian Agency. Copies of Letters Sent, 1872–1876. Idaho Historical Society Library, Boise, Idaho.

McCarthy, Michael. Diary. Library of Congress, Washington, D. C.

McDonald, Angus. "The Nez Perce Campaign." Manuscript in Montana Historical Society Library, Helena, Montana.

Metlen, George R. "Route of the Nez Perce from Big Hole to Birch Creek." Manuscript in Montana Historical Society Library, Helena, Montana.

Meyers, Andrew. "The Story of Andrew Meyers" transcribed by A. J. Noyes. Manuscript in Montana Historical Society Library, Helena, Montana.

Mason, (Major) Edwin Cooley. Letters of E. C. Mason to his wife. Being prepared for publication by Stanley Davison, Dillon, Montana.

Moelchert, William. Letters to Oscar Mueller and David Hilger, 1927. Montana Historical Society Library, Helena, Montana.

O'Donnell, I. D. Montana Monographs edited by I. D. O'Donnell. Parmly Billings Memorial Library, Billings, Montana.

Rothermich, (Captain) Albert E. "Epitome of the Nez Perce War." Manuscript in Montana Historical Society Library, Helena, Montana.

Samples, John. Statement regarding Cow Island fight. Montana Historical Society Library, Helena, Montana.

Syder, (Captain) Simon. Diary. In library of Custer Battlefield National Monument, Crow Agency, Montana.

Wood, Charles Erskine Scott. Diary and miscellaneous papers. The Huntington Library, San Marino, California.

GOVERNMENT REPORTS AND PUBLICATIONS

Bendire, (Captain) Charles, *Life Histories of North American Birds* (Smithsonian Contributions to Knowledge No. 32). Washington, Smithsonian Institution, 1895.

Heitman, Francis B., *Historical Register and Dictionary of the United States Army*. Washington, Government Printing Office, 1903.

Hodge, Frederick Webb, *Handbook of American Indians North of Mexico* (Bureau of American Ethnology Bulletin No. 30). Washington, Government Printing Office, 1907.

Kappler, Charles J., *Indian Affairs, Laws and Treaties*. Washington, Government Printing Office, 1904.

Mooney, James, "The Ghost Dance Religion and the Sioux Outbreak of 1890," in *14th Annual Report of the Bureau of American Ethnology*. Washington, Government Printing Office, 1896.

Otis, Surgeon George A. and Surgeon D. L. Huntington (USA), *The Medical and Surgical History of the War of the Rebellion*. Washington, Government Printing Office, 1883.

Royce, Charles C., "Indian Land Cessions in the United States," in *18th Annual Report of the Bureau of American Ethnology*. Washington, Government Printing Office, 1899.

U.S. Congress: "Message from the President of the United States," in *U.S. 45th Congress, 2nd Session, Senate Executive Document, No. 14.*

——— "Report of the Commissioner of Indian Affairs, 1876–1877," in *U.S. 45th Congress, 2nd Session, House Representatives Executive Document 1, Part V.*

——— "Report of the Secretary of Interior, 1876–1877," in *U.S. 45th Congress 2nd Session, House Representatives Executive Document 1, Part V.*

——— "Report of the Secretary of War, 1875–1876," in *U.S. 45th Congress, 1st Session, House Representatives Executive Document 1, Part 2, Vol. II.*

———"Report of the Secretary of War, 1876–1877," in *U.S. 45th Congress 2nd Session, House Representatives Executive Document 1, Part 2, Vol. I.*

——— "Report of the Secretary of War, 1878," in *U.S. 45th Congress, 3rd Session, House Representatives Executive Document 1, Part 2.*

War Department: *Record of Engagements with Hostile Indians within the Military Division of the Missouri from 1868 to 1882, Lieutenant General P. H. Sheridan, Commanding*. Chicago, Headquarters Military Division of the Missouri, 1882.

——— *Official Records of the War of the Rebellion, Series I, Vol. L, Part II.*

Wood, (Major) Henry Clay, *Status of Young Joseph and His Band of Nez Perce Indians Under the Treaties Between the United States and the Nez Perce Tribe of Indians and the Indian Title to Land*. Portland, Assistant Adjutant General's Office of Headquarters of Department of Columbia, 1876.

NEWSPAPERS, PERIODICALS AND MAGAZINES

Army and Navy Journal
Bismarck Tri-Weekly Tribune

Bozeman *Avant Courier*
Bozeman *Times*
Butte *Miner*
Chicago *Times*
Deer Lodge *New North-West*
Diamond City *Rocky Mountain Husbandman*
Fort Benton Record
Helena *Daily Herald*
Helena *Weekly Herald*
Helena *Daily Independent*
Idaho Yesterdays
Lewiston *Teller*
Missoula *Missoulian*
Montana Magazine of History (*Montana, the Magazine of Western History*)
New York *Herald*
Portland *Daily Standard*
Portland *Weekly Standard*
San Francisco *Chronicle*
Virginia City *Madisonian*
Winners of the West
Baird, George W., "General Miles' Indian Campaigns." *Century Magazine*, XX (1891), 351–370.
Cave, William, "The Battle of the Big Hole." *The Sunday Missoulian*, Aug. 7, 1921.
Gibbon, John, "The Battle of the Big Hole." *Harpers Weekly*, XXXIX (December 21 & 28, 1895), 1215–1216 & 1235–1236.
Harlan, W. B., "The Fiasco at Fort Fizzle." *Daily Missoulian*, March 18, 1917.
Horner, J. H. and Grace Butterfield, "The Nez Perce-Findley Affair." *Oregon Historical Quarterly*, XL (March 1939), 40–51.
Howard, Oliver Otis, "The Nez Perces Campaign of 1877." *The Advance*, Jan. 3–Oct. 3, 1878.
Joseph, Chief, "An Indian's View of Indian Affairs." *North American Review*, April 1879.
Laird, Floy (ed.), "Reminiscences of Francis Redfield." *Pacific Northwest Quarterly*, XXVII (January 1936), 66–77.
McClernand, Edward J., "With the Indians and Buffalo in Montana." *Cavalry Journal*, XXXVI (April 1927), 191–207.
——— "The Second Regiment of Cavalry." *Journal of the Military Service Institution*, XIII (1892), 629–642.
McDonald, Duncan; "The Nez Perces, the History of Their Trouble and the Campaign of 1877" (or "The Inside Story from Indian Sources"). *New North-West*, April 26, 1878–March 28, 1879.
Redington, J. W., "Scouting in Montana in the 1870's." *The Frontier*, XIII (November 1932), 55–68.
Remsen (Henry Remsen Tilton), "After the Nez Perces." *Forest and Stream and Rod and Gun*, IX (No. 21, December 27, 1877), 403–404.
Sutherland, Thomas A., Dispatches dated May–October 1877. Portland *Standard*, San Francisco *Chronicle* and New York *Herald*, June–November 1877.
Wood, Charles Erskine Scott, "Chief Joseph, the Nez Perce." *Century Magazine*, VI (1884), 135–142.

BOOKS AND PAMPHLETS

Andrews, L. F., *Pioneers of Polk County Iowa and Reminiscences of Early Days*. Des Moines: Baker Trisler Co., 1908.

Bailey, Robert G., *River of No Return*. Lewiston: Bailey-Blake Printing Co., 1947.

Baldwin, Alice Blackwood, *Memoirs of the Late Frank D. Baldwin, Major General, U.S.A.* Los Angeles: Wetzel Publishing Co., 1929.

Bancroft, Hubert Howe, *History of Washington, Idaho and Montana, 1845–1889*. San Francisco: The History Co., 1890.

Banks, Eleanor, *Wandersong*. Caldwell: Caxton Printers, 1950.

Beyer, W. F. and O. F. Keydel, *Deeds of Valor*. Detroit: Perrin-Keydel Co., 1903.

Bicknell, Anson Dodge, *The History of Humboldt County with a History of Iowa*. Cedar Rapids: Historical Publishing Co., 1901.

Bond, Fred G., *Floatboating on the Yellowstone*. New York: American Library Association, 1925.

Brady, Cyrus Townsend, *Northwestern Fights and Fighters*. Garden City: Doubleday, Doran and Co., 1928.

Brummitt, Stella W., *Brother Van*. New York: Missionary Education Movement of U.S. and Canada, 1919.

Burlingame, Merrill G., *The Military-Indian Frontier in Montana, 1860–1890*. Iowa City: University of Iowa Press, 1938.

Catlin, George, *North American Indians*. Edinburgh: John Grant, 1926.

Carpenter, John A., *Sword and Olive Branch*. Pittsburgh: University of Pittsburgh Press, 1964.

Chaffee, Eugene B. (ed), "Nez Perce War Letters to Governor Mason Brayman." *Fifteenth Biennial Report of the Idaho State Historical Society*, 1936.

Chittenden, Hiram Martin, *The Yellowstone National Park*. Cincinnati: Robert Clark Co. 1904 & Norman: University of Oklahoma Press, 1964.

Chittenden, Hiram Martin and Alfred Talbot Richardson, *Life, Letters and Travels of Father Pierre-Jean DeSmet, S.J.* New York: Francis P. Harper, 1905.

Clark, William Philo, *The Indian Sign Language*. Philadelphia: L. R. Hamersly & Co., 1885.

Coggins, Jack, *Arms and Equipment of the Civil War*. New York: Doubleday & Co., 1962.

Curtis, Edward S., *The North American Indian* (Vol. VIII). Norwood: Edward S. Curtis, 1911.

Coues, Elliott (ed), *History of the Expedition under Command of Lewis and Clark*. New York: Francis P. Harper, 1893.

——— *New Light on the Early History of the Greater Northwest*. New York: Francis P. Harper, 1897.

Dictionary of American Biography. New York: Charles Scribner's Sons, 1932. (Vol. IX).

Elsensohn, M. Alfreda, O.S.B., *Pioneer Days in Idaho County*. Caldwell: Caxton Printers, 1951.

Fee, Chester Anders, *Chief Joseph*. New York: Wilson-Erickson, Inc., 1936.

Ferris, W. A., *Life in the Rocky Mountains*. Denver: Old West Publishing Co., 1940.

Finerty, John F., *Warpath and Bivouac*. Chicago: Donohue & Henneberry, 1890.

Guie, Heister Dean and Lucullus Virgil McWhorter (ed), *Adventures in Geyser Land*. Caldwell: Caxton Printers, 1935.

Graham, William A., *The Custer Myth*. Harrisburg: Stackpole Co., 1953.

Haines, Francis, *The Nez Percés*. Norman: University of Oklahoma Press, 1955.

Hakola, John W. (ed), *Frontier Omnibus*. Missoula: Montana State University Press, 1962.

Howard, Oliver Otis, *Nez Perce Joseph*. Boston: Lee & Shepard, 1881.

Hunter, George, *Reminiscences of an Old Timer*. San Francisco: H. S. Crocker & Co., 1887.

Jackson, W. Torrentine, *Wagon Roads West*. Berkeley: University of California Press, 1952.

Jacobs, Bruce, *Heroes of the Army*. New York: W. W. Norton & Co., 1956.

Jocelyn, Stephen Perry, *Mostly Alkali*. Caldwell: Caxton Printers, Ltd., 1953.

Johnson, Virginia Weisel, *The Unregimented General*. Boston: Houghton Mifflin Co., 1962.

Kelly, Luther S., *"Yellowstone Kelly," Memoirs of Luther S. Kelly*. New Haven: Yale University Press, 1926.

Kephart, Horace (ed), *Hunting in the Yellowstone* (by the Earl of Dunraven). New York: Outing Publishing Co., 1917.

Knight, Oliver, *Following the Indian Wars*. Norman: University of Oklahoma Press, 1960.

Laufe, Abe (ed), *An Army Doctor's Wife on the Frontier*. Pittsburgh: University of Pittsburgh Press, 1962.

Leeson, Michael A., *A History of Montana*. Chicago: Warner, Beers & Co., 1885.

Luce, Edward S., *Keogh, Comanche, and Custer*. Privately printed, 1939.

Macbeth, R. G., *Policing the Plains*. Toronto: Hodder & Stoughton, Ltd., 1921.

McBeth, Kate, *Nez Perces Since Lewis and Clark*. New York: Fleming H. Revell Co., 1908.

McLaughlin, James, *My Friend, the Indian*. Boston: Houghton Mifflin Co., 1910.

McWhorter, Lucullus Virgil, *Hear Me, My Chiefs!* Caldwell: Caxton Printers, 1952.

———— *Yellow Wolf, His Own Story*. Caldwell: Caxton Printers, 1940.

Marquis, Thomas B., *Memoirs of a White Crow Indian*. New York: Century Co., 1928.

Mayer, Frederic, "The Nez Perce War Diary of Frederic Mayer," *Seventeenth Biennial Report of the Idaho State Historical Society*, 1940.

Merk, Frederic, *Fur Trade and Empire*. Cambridge: Harvard University Press, 1931.

Miles, Nelson Appleton, *Personal Recollections and Observations of General Nelson A. Miles*. Chicago: Werner Co., 1897.

(Montana) *Contributions to the Historical Society of Montana*. Helena: State Publishing Co.

Morton, John Elrod, *Following Old Trails*. Missoula: Missoulian Publishing Co., 1913.

Mulford, Ami Frank, *Fighting Indians in the Seventh Cavalry*. Corning: Paul Lindsley Mulford, n.d.

Noyes, Alva J., *In the Land of Chinook*. Helena: State Publishing Co., 1917.

———— *The Land of Ajax*. Helena: State Publishing Co., 1914.

Palladino, Lawrence Benedict, S.J., *Indian and White in the Northwest*. Baltimore: John Murphy & Co., 1894.

Parsons, John E., *The First Winchester*. New York: William Morrow & Co., 1955.

Phinney, Mary Allen, *Jirah Isham Allen*. Rutland: Tuttle Publishing Co., n.d.

Price, George F., *Across the Continent With the Fifth Cavalry*. New York: Antiquarian Press, Ltd., 1959.

Progressive Men of the State of Montana. Chicago: A. W. Bowen & Co., n.d.

Prucha, Francis Paul, *Guide to the Military Posts of the United States, 1878–1895*. Madison: State Historical Society of Wisconsin, 1964.

Ross, Alexander, *The Fur Hunters of the Far West*. Norman: University of Oklahoma Press, 1956.

Russell, Osborne, *Journal of a Trapper*. Portland: Champoeg Press, 1955.

Scott, Hugh Lenox, *Some Memories of a Soldier*. New York: Century Co., 1928.

Shields, George O., *Battle of the Big Hole*. New York: Rand, McNally & Co., 1889.

Sternberg, Martha L., *George Miller Sternberg*. Chicago: American Medical Association, 1920.

Smith, De Cost, *Indian Experiences*. Caldwell: Caxton Printers, Ltd., 1943.

Sutherland, Thomas A., *Howard's Campaign Against the Nez Perce Indians, 1877*. Portland: A. G. Watling Co., 1878.

Thwaites, Reuben Gold (ed), *Original Journals of the Lewis and Clark Expedition, 1804–1806*. New York: Dodd, Mead & Co., 1905.

Topance, Alexander, *Reminiscences of Alexander Topance, Pioneer*. Salt Lake City: Century Printing Co., 1923.

Topping, E. S., *The Chronicles of the Yellowstone*. St. Paul: Pioneer Press Co., 1883.

Turner, John Peter, *The Northwest Mounted Police, 1873–1893*. Ottawa: Edmond Cloutier, 1950.

Vaughn, Robert, *Then and Now, or Thirty-six Years in the Rockies*. Minneapolis: Tribune Publishing Co., 1900.

Weisel, George F., *Men and Trade on the Northwest Frontier*. Missoula: Montana State University Press, 1955.

Wheeler, Homer W., *Buffalo Days*. Indianapolis: Bobbs Merrill Co., 1923.

———— *The Frontier Trail*. Los Angeles: Times-Mirror Press, 1923.

Wheeler, Olin D., *The Trail of Lewis and Clark*. New York: G. P. Putnam's Sons, 1904.

Williams, William, *History of Early Fort Dodge and Webster County, Iowa*. Fort Dodge: Waterick Printing Co., 1962.

Acknowledgments

>>>>>>>><<<<<<<< In order to bring this *Estimate of the Situation* to an acceptable degree of accuracy, solve the various problems which have been ignored or overlooked, and put the legends in their proper place, it has been necessary to enlist the assistance of a considerable number of individuals having diverse interests and backgrounds. Among the following, the names of professors and librarians are mingled with those of ornithologists, forest rangers, cartridge collectors and housewives, all of whom—even though they had no specific interest in this subject, *per se*—contributed valuable bits of data.

Among these, the author recognizes an unusual debt to Stanley Davison of the Western Montana College of Education at Dillon, Montana. Even though Dr. Davison was preparing the private letters of Major Edwin C. Mason for publication, he provided a transcript of this important collection and generously permitted quotations to be taken from them. Not only was this a very useful collection but it also provided leads that were most helpful. Don Rickey, Jr., of the National Park Service, Merrill G. Burlingame of Montana State College, Bozeman, Montana, and William R. Felton of Sioux City, Iowa, directed the author's attention to noteworthy "new" material. Dorothy Briggs of Ralston, Wyoming, Elvin W. Henninger of Dubois, Idaho, and Aubrey L. Haines, Jack R. Williams and "Scotty" Chapman of the National Park Service assisted in solving various problems involving geography. Mr. Haines, together with Merrill J. Mattes, also of the National Park Service, provided material that was of considerable assistance. Harriet Howard of Simsbury, Connecticut, and Susan B. Well of Woodstock, Vermont, offered suggestions in the futile search for a journal which their grandfather, General Howard, once mentioned—and which the writer is now convinced never existed in the form implied. Elizabeth FitzGerald Hiestand supplied specific information from certain letters of her mother which were not published. Eugene T. Flaherty and Erwin Sias of Sioux City, Iowa, and Paul I. Wellman of Los Angeles, California, made constructive comments about subject matter and organization. And Alfred G. Dietrich, Plattsmouth, Nebraska, wrestled with the cartographic problems posed by the maps.

As most of the material on which any thoroughgoing study of this struggle must rest is in libraries scattered from Maine to California, the author is deeply indebted to those who provided copies of several thousand pages of vital documents and/or searched for hitherto unnoted material. Foremost among these are: the personnel of the National Archives, Washington, D.C.; Richard Harwell of the Bowdoin College Library, Brunswick, Maine; Mary K. Dempsey and Harriet Meloy of the library of the Montana Historical Society, Helena, Montana, and also Director Michael S. Kennedy; Merle W. Wells of the Idaho Historical Society Library, Boise, Idaho; David C. Mearns, Chief of the Manuscript Division, Library of Congress, Washington, D.C.; Haydée Noya of The Huntington Library, San Marino, California; Archibald Hanna and David R. Watkins of Yale University Library, New Haven, Connecticut; and Martin Winch of the Oregon Historical Society, and Ellen L. Brynes and Elizabeth Anne Johnson of the Library Association of Portland, Oregon.

In addition to those noted above, the following were also helpful: (Alabama) Raymond Estep of the Air University Library, U.S.A.F.; (California) California State Library; (Colorado) State Historical Society of Colorado, and (Mrs.) Alys Freese of the Denver Public Library; (Illinois) Colton Storm of the Newberry Library; (Iowa) Frank Paluka of the State University of Iowa Library, Lida L. Greene of Iowa State Department of History and Archives, Iowa State University Library, Buena Vista College Library, and Inez Young of the Storm Lake Public Library; (Kansas) Kansas State Historical Society; (Maryland) Frieda C. Thies of the John Hopkins University Library; (Massachusetts) W. H. Bond of the Harvard University Library; (Montana) Parmly Billings Memorial Library, and W. J. Petty of Custer Battlefield National Monument; (New Mexico) Michael Mathes of University of New Mexico Library; (New York) New York Public Library, and the library of the U.S. Military Academy; (Tennessee) Wayne C. Temple of Lincoln Memorial University; (Utah)

John James, Jr. of Utah State Historical Society; (Washington) Mary Avery of Washington State University Library; and (Wyoming) Gene M. Gressley of University of Wyoming Library.

From the following individuals came assistance of a widely varying nature: Elta M. Arnold, Grangeville, Idaho; Merrill D. Beale, Pocatello, Idaho; Floyd C. Bridge, Storm Lake, Iowa; Fred E. Buck, Helena, Montana; John A. Carpenter, Washington, Pennsylvania; Harry L. Crockett, Phoenix, Arizona; Clifford M. Drury, San Rafael, California; Alfred Duman, Cottonwood, Idaho; Joe DeYong, Hollywood, California; Genie Philbrick Fulmer, Rosebud, Montana; J. H. Gipson, Caldwell, Idaho; John S. Gray, Wilmette, Illinois; Dwight L. Haight, Great Falls, Montana; T. E. Hall, New Haven, Connecticut; George M. Herman, Silver Gate, Montana; George Hoyt, Cherokee, Iowa; Harvey M. Jopling, Bellevue, Nebraska; Fred C. Krieg, Billings, Montana; Emil Kopac, Oshkosh, Nebraska; Marlin and Lois Kurtz, Cody, Wyoming; Maurice Leonard, Storm Lake, Iowa; Herschel Logan, Salina, Kansas; (Col.) B. R. Lewis, Vista, California: Anne McDonnell, Helena, Montana; Ruby Miller, Cherokee, Iowa; James Moore, Cody, Wyoming; Oscar O. Mueller, Lewiston, Montana; Robert A. Murray, Fort Laramie, Wyoming; (Col.) E. G. Ovenshine, Washington, D.C.; Harold L. Peterson, Washington, D.C.; Charles E. Piersall, Casper, Wyoming; Wayne Repogle, Yellowstone Park, Wyoming; J. E. Reynolds, Van Nuys, California; Jack Richards, Cody, Wyoming; Arlen Rounds, Cody, Wyoming; "Tommie" A. Saldin, Missoula, Montana; George A. Schneider, Old Bridge, New Jersey; John Shellsted, Chinook, Montana; Ralph S. Space, Orofino, Idaho; H. A. Streed, Whitefish, Montana; John W. Vaughn, Windsor, Colorado; Rufus Wallowing, Lame Deer, Montana; and Frank Wheeler, Osborne, Kansas.

Material taken from the papers of General O. O. Howard has been reproduced with the permission of the Bowdoin College Library, Brunswick, Maine; that from the Lapwai Agency file, Governor Brayman's papers and the reports of the Idaho Historical Society by permission of the Idaho Historical Society Library, Boise, Idaho; and quotations from the papers of C. E. S. Wood and the Fort Dalles Collection with the permission of *The Huntington Library*, San Marino, California. As noted, Stanley Davison granted permission to quote from the letters of Major E. C. Mason; and materials from manuscripts in the library of the Montana Historical Society has been used with the permission of the Director. Permission to quote from *An Army Doctor's Wife on the Frontier*, Abe Laufe (ed), was given by the University of Pittsburgh Press, and from *George Miller Sternberg*, Martha Sternberg, by the American Medical Association. Montana State College released material from the Doane papers; and the National Park Service approved the use of parts of Captain Simon Carter's diary. These courtesies have been most helpful in preparing the text.

Last, but not least, the writer acknowledges the patience of his wife,

Alice, who permitted him to strew papers over a considerable part of the house for many, many months during the past four years. Without space to spread out notes, transcripts, and various papers, the tedious task of collation of these hundreds of small bits of data would have been next to impossible.

—MARK H. BROWN

Trails End Farm
Alta, Iowa

Index